# EFFECTIVE BUSINESS COMMUNICATIONS

# Effective Business Communications

Herta A. Murphy
*Professor of Business Administration*
*University of Washington*


Charles E. Peck
*Professor of Business Administration*
*University of Washington*

**McGraw-Hill Book Company**
*New York    St. Louis    San Francisco    Düsseldorf*
*Johannesburg    Kuala Lumpur    London    Mexico*
*Montreal    New Delhi    Panama    Rio de Janeiro*
*Singapore    Sydney    Toronto*

This book was set in Baskerville by Monotype Composition Company, Inc., and printed and bound by Kingsport Press, Inc. The designer was Merrill Haber; the drawings were done by John Cordes, J. & R. Technical Services, Inc. The editors were Richard F. Dojny, Cynthia Newby, and James R. Belser. Peter D. Guilmette supervised production.

# Contents

*Preface*                                                                      xiii


# Part One:  Background for Writing


*1*  IMPORTANCE OF EFFECTIVE WRITTEN
COMMUNICATION IN BUSINESS                                                        2

    Well-Written Business Communication "Pays Off"                        3
    Language of Business                                                  6
    Volume and Cost of Written Business Communication in the United States  7
    The Challenge in Writing for Business                                 8


*2*  THINK BEFORE YOU WRITE                                                     11

    Five Thinking Steps                                                  12
        Know the Purpose 12;  Visualize Your Reader 14;  Choose the Ideas 16;
        Get all the Facts 18; Organize Your Ideas 18
    Basic Organizational Patterns                                        19
        Good-News Messages 19;  Bad-News Messages 20;  Direct Requests 21;
        Persuasive Requests 23
    Openings and Closings                                                24
        Openings 24;  Closings 29
    Application to a Given Situation                                     31
    Exercises                                                            34


*3*  BUSINESS WRITING PRINCIPLES I                                              41

    Correctness                                                          43
        Levels of Language 43;  Accurate Facts, Words, and Figures 49;
        Acceptable Writing Mechanics 50

**Conciseness**     53
Omit Trite Expressions 55;   Avoid Unnecessary Repetition 57;   Prune Obviously Wordy Expressions 58; Include Only Relevant Facts 60
**Clarity**     62
Short, Familiar, Conversational Words 63;   Effective, Well-Constructed Sentences 66;   Well-Organized Paragraphs and Messages 72; Examples, Illustrations and Visual Aids 74
**Exercises**     74

*4*  **BUSINESS WRITING PRINCIPLES II**     83

**Completeness**     84
Answer All Questions Asked 84;   Give Something Extra 87;   Check for the 5 W's and Any Other Essentials 89
**Concreteness**     93
Use Specific Facts and Figures 93;   Put Action in Your Verbs 94; Choose Vivid, Image-Building Words 96
**Consideration**     98
Focus on "You" Instead of "I" and "We" 99;   Show Reader Benefit or Interest in Reader 101; Apply Integrity in Your Decisions 102; Emphasize the Positive, Pleasant Facts 104
**Courtesy**     106
Be Sincerely Tactful, Thoughtful, and Appreciative 106; Omit Expressions that Irritate, Hurt, or Belittle 110;   Answer Your Mail Promptly 113;   Grant and Apologize Good-naturedly 114
**Summary of Business Writing Principles**     117
**Exercises**     118

*5*  **PARTS AND LAYOUT OF BUSINESS LETTERS AND MEMORANDA**     **129**

**The Business Letter**     130
Stationery 130;   Parts of the Letter 131;   Letter Layout 141;   Envelopes 143
**The Memorandum**     152
Stationery 152;   Parts of the Memorandum 154;   Layout of the Memorandum Body 157;   Envelopes 158
**Exercises**     158

# PART TWO: MAJOR LETTER PATTERNS

*6*  **DIRECT REQUESTS**     **162**

**Organizational Plan**     163
**Inquiries**     163
Wording and Arrangement of Questions 164;   Inquiries about Persons 165; Inquiries about Products or Services 170

**Claims (Complaints) and Requests for Adjustments**     174
Characteristics of Well-Written Claims 174; Organization and Content of the Simple Direct Claim 175
**Requests for Action Related to Routine Business Procedures**     179
Requests to Persons outside Your Organization 179; Requests to Persons within the Organization 182
**Invitations, Orders, Reservations**     184
Invitations 184; Orders and Reservations 186
**Requests Pertaining to Civic Causes or Public Officials**     186
**Capsule Checklists**     188
**Exercises**     190

## 7   GOOD-NEWS AND NEUTRAL MESSAGES     205

**Organizational Plan**     206
**Favorable Replies**     208
Answering Inquiries for Information Related to Sales 208; Answering Inquiries for Information Unrelated to Sales 213; Granting Requests for Adjustment 218; Approving Credit 229; Favorably Acknowledging Orders 233; Granting Favors 237
**Unsolicited Favorable Messages**     238
Announcements 239; Transmittals 244
**Capsule Checklists**     248
**Exercises**     246

## 8   BAD-NEWS MESSAGES     268

**The Right Attitude**     269
**Plans for Bad-News Messages**     270
Indirect Plan 270; Direct Plan 273
**Unfavorable Replies to Requests**     274
Answering Sales-Related Inquiries When the Information Is Undesirable 274; Answering Nonsales Inquiries When the Information is Undesirable 276; Refusing Adjustment on Claims and Complaints 279; Refusing Credit 287; Acknowledging Orders You Can't Fill Now or at All 293; Declining Requests for Favors and Invitations 301; Turning Down Contract or Work Offers 306
**Unfavorable Unsolicited Messages**     308
Announcing Bad News about Prices and/or Services 308; Requiring Minimum Orders and/or Deposits 312; Penalizing for Nonconformity with Rules or Procedures 313; Conveying other Bad News 314.
**Capsule Checklists**     316
**Exercises**     325

## 9   PERSUASIVE REQUESTS     345

**Organizational Plan**     346
**Persuasive Requests for Favors**     349

Getting Attention for Favor Requests 349;   Arousing Interest and
Creating Desire to Do the Favor 351;   Asking for Action 354;   Asking
Favors That Require Time, Knowledge, or Effort 354; Asking Donations
for Money or Other Valuables 357;   Urging Cooperation on Goals and
Projects 360

**Other Persuasive Nonroutine Requests**                                362
Adapting the AIDA Plan 362;   Requesting Nonroutine Adjustments
362;   Persuasively Requesting Credit 366;   Persuasively Requesting
Changes in Policy or Performance 368

**Unsolicited Sales Letters**                                           371
Steps before Writing the Unsolicited Sales Letter 371; Suggestions for
Writing the Unsolicited Sales Letter 377;   Examples of Unsolicited
Sales Letters 390

**Exercises**                                                          402
**Capsule Checklists**                                                 404

# Part Three: Specialized Messages

## 10 THE WRITTEN JOB PRESENTATION 420

**Desirable General Qualifications**                                    421
Proper Attitude toward Employment 421;  Evidence of Intelligence and
Education 424;   Evidence of Social Development 426;   Work Experi-
ence 427;   Physical Fitness 428;   Appearance and Manners 428;   Other
Desirable Personal Traits 429

**Information Sources for Specific Types of Jobs**                      431
**Employers' Likes and Dislikes in the Written Job Presentation**       433
Businesslike versus Clever Approach 433;  Specific Information versus
Generalities 434;   Individuality versus Canned Letters 435;   Enclosures
435;   Mechanics 436

**Résumé**                                                             437
Opening Section 437;  Education 444;  Work Experience 446;  Extracurricular Activities 447;   Other Relevant Facts 448;   References 450

**Letter of Application**                                              451
Opening 451;   Creation of Desire 453;   Last Paragraph 457

**Examples of the Written Job Presentation**                           458
**Exercises**                                                          473

## 11 OTHER JOB APPLICATION MESSAGES 479

**Follow-Up Messages from Applicant to Employer**                       480
The Initial Follow-Up 481;   Other Follow-up Messages from Applicant to Employer 485

**Follow-Up Messages Written by Employer to Applicant**                 490
Invitation to Interview 490;   Notification of Impending Visit on Campus 491;   Request for Further Information 492;   Offer of a Job 493;

Granting an Extension of Time to Accept Offer 494; Reply to Applicant's Acceptance 494; Refusal of Job 494

**Situation**     496
**Exercises**     500

*12*   **COLLECTION MESSAGES—WRITTEN AND ORAL**     **508**

**Right Attitude for Effective Collections**     510
**Collection Series**     514
Collection Appeals 515; Collection Stages 515; Length of Collection Series 522
**Telephone Collection Procedure**     529
**Exercises**     533

*13*   **GOODWILL MESSAGES**     **549**

**Congratulating or Giving Deserved Praise**     551
Congratulatory Messages 551; Messages with Deserved Praise 555
**Expressing Appreciation**     556
Appreciation for Favors Extended over a Period of Time 556; Thanks for One-time Favors and Kindnesses 560
**Extending Seasonal Greetings**     563
**Conveying Sympathy**     566
**Welcoming and/or Offering Favors**     568
**Showing Continuing Special Concern**     571
**Exercises**     575

**PART FOUR: REPORTS**

*14*   **THE WHAT AND HOW OF BUSINESS REPORTS**     **582**

**Meaning of a Business Report**     583
Differences among Letters, Memos, and Reports 583; Types of Reports 584; Classification of Reports 584
**Parts of the Body of a Report**     585
Introduction 586; Text 588; Terminal Section 591
**Organizational Plans for the Body of a Report**     592
**Application to a Situation**     593
Heading 595; Introduction 595; Text 596; Terminal Section 598
**Exercises**     601

*15*   **SHORT REPORTS**     **614**

**Think Before You Write**     615
**Guiding the Reader through the Report**     616
Use Transition to Tie Your Writing Together 621; Avoid the Sub-

junctive as much as Possible 624; Talk in Present Tense Whenever Possible 625; Use Mostly Active—Not Passive—Verbs 625

Types of Short Reports ................................................ 626
Memorandum Report 626; Printed Form Report, 639; Letter Report 646

Exercises ............................................................... 656

## 16 THE FORMAL REPORT .......................................... 682

Usefulness of the Prefatory and Supplemental Parts ............... 683
Business Report versus Term Paper ................................. 684
Preliminary Investigation ........................................... 686
Other Research Steps before Writing ............................... 687
Writing the First Draft ............................................. 689
Revising the Draft .................................................. 690
Typing the Body of the Report ...................................... 693
Double Spacing versus Single Spacing 694; Proper Margins 694; Set-up of Footnotes 694; Numbering the Pages 694; Favorable Impression Throughout 695

Prefatory and Supplemental Parts ................................... 695
Cover 696; Title Fly 697; Title Page 697; Letter of Transmittal 697; Table of Contents 699; Table of Tables 699; Abstract 700; Appendix 702; Bibliography 702

Example of a Discussion Report ..................................... 703
Example of a Statistical Report ..................................... 714
Exercises ............................................................... 717

# PART FIVE: NONWRITTEN COMMUNICATIONS

## 17 SPEAKING, LISTENING, AND INTERVIEWING ................... 720

The Art of Speaking ................................................ 721
Similarities of Oral versus Written Presentation 721; Differences between Oral and Written Presentation 721; Preparing the Oral Presentation 722; The Presentation 726

The Art of Listening ................................................ 729
Need for Listening 729; Responsibilities of the Listener 730; Responsibilities of the Speaker 731; Results of Good Listening 732

The Art of Interviewing ............................................. 732
Interviewer's Role and Responsibilities 734; Interviewee's Role and Responsibilities 741

# Appendixes

A Legal Aspects of Your Business Communications ................. 751
Defamation 751; Invasion of Privacy 754; Fraud 756; Other Areas of Caution in Business Writing 757

**B Mechanics and Style**     759
Check Points When You Edit Writing for Business 759; Dangling Participles 761; Dictation 763; Numbers as Figures or Words 763; Punctuation Makes Sense 766; Syllabication 772; Trite Words (Cliches, Hackneyed Words) 772
**C Suggestions for Cutting Correspondence Costs**     775
**D Symbols Used in Marking Letters, Memos, and Reports**     777

*Index*     779

# Preface

This text covers both written and oral communications, but it stresses the important role that the *reader* of business communications plays in written letters, memos, and reports. It is a people-oriented book on communications for business.

## Need for a Writing Course for Business

A course in writing is an important preparation for business. Far too many individuals do not write well because they don't realize the importance of directing a message with a specific purpose to a specific audience for a desired reaction. Instead they think that mechanics—such as grammar and format—make up the bulk of such a message. Yet the best grammatical writing, with the best appearance on the page, will be a failure if the content and presentation of the message aren't geared to the specific reader(s), to the purpose, and to the use, of the message. Because this statement is particularly true in the business world, a course in written communications for business is not only helpful but essential.

## Purpose of Text

Anyone who is preparing for the business world, or is already dealing with people, will find this book a useful guide. Our purpose is to help you compose business messages which the receiver can easily understand and to which he will react favorably. The text presents sound principles in writing and dealing with human beings and enough application of these principles so that you can tackle with confidence the written and oral assignments you'll encounter on the job. For example, you learn that our language is ever changing and so are the rules that govern it. You realize that a businessman's time is an extremely important commodity and he appreciates—even demands—concise writing. You make favorable impressions with big ideas—not with big words. You find out that a word is merely a symbol and carries its meaning in the mind of the reader—not in the word itself. And most important of all, you are impressed time and time again in this book that you're dealing with people just like yourself who react individually to a given situation.

Here's a book for the student and the businessman who want to communicate more effectively with others. It practices what it preaches by talking conversationally and directly to you. It definitely is not a camouflaged grammar or secretarial book. Instead it applies known communication theory, psychology of language, and human relations to messages that favorably motivate the reader. It stresses simplicity in language, in choice of words, and in organizing a piece of writing. The occasional humorous examples not only put across important points, but also hopefully give you a smile.

## Plan of Presentation

The 17-chapter text begins with five background-for-writing chapters, the first of which shows the importance and challenge of effective writing. Then come the five thinking steps necessary before writing or dictating—steps that are the foundation for all effective business messages. The remaining chapters in this section discuss the seven principles of good writing for business and parts and layout of letters and memoranda.

Following the five background chapters are four chapters that present in depth the four major organizational patterns—routine request, good news, bad news, and persuasive request. The illustrations include letters and memos that inform, grant, refuse, persuade, and announce. They are based on actual business situations involving inquiries, orders, credit, references, recommendations, complaints, adjustments, favors, sales, and various other responsibilities. A unique helpful feature is the marginal notes analyzing significant parts of every example that illustrates a well-written message. Also unique is the discussion of both the deductive and inductive patterns usable for bad-news messages—depending on the type of reader involved. Capsule summaries after all four chapters provide handy organizational checklists for the many types of messages covered. These summaries, however, are to be used only as reminders and guides, because each message requires careful planning and wording so it is adapted effectively to the particular circumstances and problem.

In addition to the chapters on major letter patterns are four chapters on specialized types of letters—job application messages, collections, and goodwill messages. The job application chapters begin with general qualifications that employers look for in a college graduate and then cover both the résumé and the application letter which together comprise the initial written job application. Also included are examples of letter-résumé pairs written by individuals who apply for work in accounting, the construction industry, management, and secondary teaching. The second job application chapter discusses the use, content, and presentation of many other types of messages that both applicants and employers write. The collections chapter discusses appeals, stages, and series. Goodwill messages include congratulations, appreciation, sympathy, seasonal greetings, and others.

The report chapters give a thorough treatment in the preparation of all types of reports used in the business world. The initial chapter—what and why of business reports—defines a report and explains in detail the makeup of the three parts of the body of any report—introduction, text, and terminal section—and then develops a complete memo report from a given situation. The two remaining report chapters present, illustrate, and develop in detail the three main types of short reports—memo, printed form, and letter report —and the formal report. The chapter on the formal report is unique because the material is developed exactly as a writer develops a formal report.

The final chapter is included to show that business communication requires not only effective written messages and reports but also nonwritten communications. Coverage includes speaking, listening, and interviewing and relates the similarities in preparing and presenting an oral and written presentation.

Throughout the text are many examples of letters, memos, and reports to illustrate what to say and how to say it effectively. Also at the end of the chapters are challenging exercises and problems. The Appendix includes a brief discussion on legal aspects of written communication, plus tips on troublesome mechanics, style, cost cutting, and dictation. The list of symbols used in checking papers is a timesaver for both students and instructors.

## Acknowledgments

We extend our sincere thanks to the management executives who have contributed hundreds of illustrative materials from business, industry, and professional offices; to the leaders and our colleagues in the American Business Communication Association whose preferences and ideas through the years have enriched our knowledge and influenced the scope of this book; and to former students who have brought numerous messages from their organizational and employment experiences. Special thanks go to L. R. Goldberg, J. D., instructor in business law at Shoreline Community College, Seattle, Washington, for reviewing the summary on legal aspects and making helpful suggestions; and to Pete and Pam Hanenberger for developing several problems found in the text. Also, to the authors and companies that have given permission to quote from their writing and whose names are mentioned throughout the text in footnotes, we owe grateful thanks.

In appreciation of the thousands of students who not only tackled the assignments found in this text but also acted as a reliable feedback regarding the interest and challenge involved, we, as authors, dedicate this book to today's serious, intelligent college and university students who want to improve their ability to communicate with others.

*Herta A. Murphy*
*Charles E. Peck*

# Background for Writing

● Chapter 1: Importance of Effective Written Communication in Business
● Chapter 2: Think Before You Write
● Chapter 3: Business Writing Principles I
● Chapter 4: Business Writing Principles II
● Chapter 5: Parts and Layout of Business Letters and Memoranda

# Importance of Effective Written Communication in Business

- Well-written Business Communication "Pays Off"
- Language of Business
- Volume and Cost of Written Business Communication in the United States
- The Challenge in Writing for Business

Executives of American business, industry, and government have repeatedly expressed their concern regarding the need for better communication. In numerous surveys, business executives have ranked ability to communicate first among the personal factors necessary for promotion to and within management; and they have selected business writing as one of the most useful college studies in their present work. In the business world, the ability to write well is a highly valued asset.

This chapter seeks to answer the following questions relating to the importance of effective written communication in business:

How does well-written business communication "pay off"?

What is the language of business?

What is the volume and cost of written business communication in the United States?

How can you meet the challenge of writing for business?

## WELL-WRITTEN BUSINESS COMMUNICATION "PAYS OFF"

In college and business you concentrate on ideas, attitudes, facts, and figures that help prepare you for the type of work you may be doing until you retire. But you can take full advantage of the knowledge so acquired only if you can effectively communicate your thoughts, ideas, and proposals to prospective and existing customers, business associates, and others who need or should get them. Even after you have communicated orally on an important matter, you are often asked to "put it in writing." Your message then becomes a permanent record, which the recipient can reread anytime. Also, if geographical distance separates you and the person with whom you are communicating, or if the material is complex, technical, or lengthy, writing is often the only effective means of communication.

A well-written message can make almost any business function easier. Next to face-to-face conversation, letters and memos are the most powerful means of communication in business; and in countless business, professional, and government offices, the written business report is a necessity for executive decision making.

How do these facts affect you? That is, how can the ability to write effective business communications benefit you? Subscribers to *Harvard Business Review* have rated "ability to communicate" as the prime requisite of a promotable executive.[1] In other words, among the qualities that characterize promotable executives, the ability to communicate is probably the most important, or "the top rung of the ladder," as illustrated in Figure 1-1. *What you say and how you say it* are inseparable; content and presentation go hand-

[1] C. Wilson Randle, "How to Identify Promotable Executives," *Harvard Business Review,* May–June, 1956, p. 122.

in-hand in business writing. (This statement is true not only of written communications, but also of face-to-face and telephone conversations, which are
essential to the top executive.) Often your job, status, and reputation depend
on the success or failure of your efforts to communicate.

As a management trainee on a new job, you have opportunities to submit reports—and sometimes letters—that are tests of your ability to communi-

Figure 1-1

cate clearly and quickly. These reports can reveal how well you are doing your job, and they help management to evaluate your fitness for a substantial promotion. For example, imagine that you are one of several highly trained employees in an organization that requires everyone to submit frequent reports to clients or company personnel. If there is an opening for promotion and you each rate about the same except that you alone can write effective reports, then clearly you have the advantage. The others will be held back because of their weakness in this one area.

Effective writing in business also pays off in dealing with customers. The right letter can win back a disgruntled customer, create a desire in the reader's mind for your firm's product or service, help an inquirer who is a potential customer, and in general create goodwill. A letter that communicates fully to the receiver saves additional correspondence, which can mean substantial savings on expenses, since each dictated letter now costs, on the average, more than $3 (for instance, $3.19 in 1971.)[1] Also, when you send a letter on company letterhead to someone, you "are" the company. You can create in the reader's mind a favorable or unfavorable attitude toward your entire organization.

Various surveys have borne out the idea that effective communication is crucial in business. For example, in a 1960 survey, 80 percent of 133 United States businessmen who were questioned put "skill in letter writing" at the top of their list of essential business skills.[2] Included were company presidents; plant, production, and personnel managers; controllers and treasurers; sales and merchandising chiefs; engineers; heads of methods and production control. They represented various fields, including manufacturing, merchandising, and financing.

Furthermore, at least eight universities conducted surveys among their business graduates who had been in business or industry for periods ranging from 5 to 25 years.[3] In answer to the question: What has been the most valu-

---

[1] The cost of the business letter has been increasing every year. Before 1950, the cost was less than $1; in 1953 it was $1.17; in 1967, it was up to $2.49; and in 1970, $3.05. According to Dartnell Corporation in Chicago, the 1971 figure of $3.19 broke down as follows: dictator's time ($.98), secretarial cost ($1.00), fixed charges ($.81), materials cost ($.09), mailing cost ($.17), and filing cost ($.14).

[2] Rollin H. Simonds, "Skills Businessmen Use Most," *Nation's Business,* November 1960, p. 88.

[3] The eight schools are State University of Iowa, Loyola University of the South, two surveys at Michigan State University, Louisiana State University, University of Washington, Xavier University, and University of Texas. Sources to consult for details of these surveys are:

William Arthur Allec, *A Study of the Graduates of the College of Commerce, State University of Iowa, 1921–1951,* Ph.D. dissertation, State University of Iowa, Iowa City, Iowa, 1951.
William P. Carr, "An Evaluation of Accounting Curriculum Subjects," *Collegiate News and Views,* Loyola University of the South, New Orleans, October, 1952, pp. 5–10.
J. M. Hunter, Anthony Koo, and R. F. Voertman, "What Happens to Our Economics Majors," *Collegiate News and Views,* Michigan State University, East Lansing, Mich., March, 1954, pp. 11–13.
Raymond V. Lesikar, *A Summary of Needs of Education for Small Business Based on a 1959 Survey of Louisiana Businessmen,* Louisiana State University Press, Baton Rouge, 1959.
Charles E. Peck, "Survey of Curriculum Opinions of Business Administration," *University of Washington Business Review,* Office of Business Administration Faculty Publications, University of Washington, Seattle, 1958.
Rollin H. Simonds, "Skills Businessmen Use the Most," *Nation's Business,* November, 1960.
Steinbruegee, Hailstones, and Roberts, "Personnel Managers Evaluate a College Business Program," *Collegiate News and Views,* Xavier University, New Orleans, May, 1955, pp. 7–11.
Stella Trawaek, *An Opinion Report of the College of Business Administration, The University of Texas, 1917–1954,* Bureau of Business Research, University of Texas, Austin, Texas, 1954.

able subject you studied in college? written business communication was always listed among the top three.

Effective writing also helps you to better accomplish certain aims as an individual in society. In addition to your business or professional work, you will often need to write letters and reports in other capacities—as committee chairman, club officer, or as plain "Joe Doakes" citizen. In these various roles you might write to public officials, or to business firms, suppliers, and club members. Your purposes might include petitioning, complaining, ordering, congratulating, persuading, or refusing. The same skills that aid you in writing effective business communications will also help you accomplish these purposes more effectively.

## LANGUAGE OF BUSINESS

Business language should be informal, up-to-date, and unaffected; it must get the message across clearly to gain a favorable reaction. There isn't—or shouldn't be—a specific "business English." The language of business should be the language an educated individual uses when he communicates—whether it is with someone in a business or in a nontechnical role.

Business language depends more on an appropriate attitude than on hard-and-fast rules of composition. This attitude relates to the critical awareness of who the reader(s) will be, how the message is to be used, and the reader's feelings about "correctness." Because the first two of these three areas are so closely related, they are discussed together below.

Anyone working in the business world is a busy individual. His work keeps him well-occupied—handling day-to-day assignments, catching up with back work, or planning for the future. Thus, any businessman—whether he is a banker or broker, wholesaler or retailer—wants to read written communications as fast as he can and still retain as much of the thought as possible. He cannot afford to waste his valuable time searching for the purpose or wondering about the meaning of a technical or unknown word or expression.

The language of business has two bases: (1) what is to be communicated and (2) who will be reading the communication. A letter, memo, or report must be oriented so that the reader can absorb the details. However, this approach—called "pointing up the purpose of the message"—must not cause the reader to react negatively. For example, in a message that conveys good news, or one that grants or asks a simple request, the writer should state the purpose at the beginning. But a refusal, or a request that must be persuasive, usually requires a "psychological" approach—that is, explaining first (in a refusal) or creating desire (in a persuasive request).

No one likes difficult reading; the words in a written communication should never force the reader to the dictionary or to a specialist for meaning, thus causing a break in thought. Each sentence should flow smoothly and be short enough to permit clear understanding without rereading. Not once should the reader wonder where he is, or feel that he is lost or bewildered. He should not be distracted or irritated by misspellings, strikeovers, light ribbon, or dirty keys, or slowed down by heavy words, complicated sentence structure, or involved organization. Then, at the end of the message, the reader will subconsciously be grateful for a simple, understandable, and perhaps even enjoyable, communication. When you get such a reaction from a reader, then you're beginning to communicate. Of course, you will need to consider many other facets of writing—such as tone, credibility, and accuracy of facts—before you turn out a really effective piece of writing, but at least you have made a beginning.

Business writing differs greatly from other types of writing you are familiar with. For example, although you may think that college "term papers" should be similar to business reports, most such papers differ considerably from the type of communications businessmen will tolerate. First of all, the student's goal is a grade, and if the professor grades "by the pound," the writer will throw in everything possible. Secondly, professors often mark on the basis of the content, or ideas included; they don't usually give much weight to the method of presentation. In contrast, the business writer must save the reader's time, and he realizes that *how* you say something is often just as important as *what* you say. The language of business is functional; it is a tool, which should accomplish the task it is designed to perform.

Of course, business writers must also respect their readers' attitudes toward correctness. Businessmen expect correct use of the mechanics of language, and misspellings and sloppy grammar can be extremely irritating. With 13 to 16 years of education behind you, you should be able to spell correctly—at least the words you choose to use in a letter or a report.[1] You should also write a grammatically acceptable sentence and use punctuation that clarifies rather than confuses. Remember that businessmen *expect* you to use these mechanics correctly. Finally, you should strive for neatness, since the first impression is extremely important.

## VOLUME AND COST OF WRITTEN BUSINESS COMMUNICATION IN THE UNITED STATES

No one knows just how many billions of dollars United States industry spends on written communications, but the amount is enormous. The following discussion is intended to give merely an estimate of the volume and costs of written communications in American business.

[1] A good dictionary is an essential tool for the writer. If in doubt about any spelling, always use the dictionary.

Americans mail about 60 billion[1] business messages a year. By a conservative estimate, about one-third of these are individually dictated messages; that is 20 billion messages a year, or about 77 million a day (if we assume 260 working days a year). These figures exclude, of course, the millions of memoranda and reports that are exchanged between departments and individuals within organizations.

It has been estimated that an aircraft could not get off the ground if it were loaded with the reports and papers necessary for its construction. If the quality-control and inspection reports on rockets and spacecraft were stretched end to end, they would easily reach from Cape Kennedy to the moon.[2]

In writing about the paperwork of top executives, Robert A. Shiff[3] estimated that 750,000 *words*—in reports, letters, memos, etc.—are piled on a typical corporation president's desk *every month,* and that the president spends at least five hours daily just reading these messages. In terms of cost, about half of every corporation president's salary goes for his reading of this written material. And in many companies, lesser administrators are even more burdened with daily reading and writing.

To get some idea of the estimated total cost of individually dictated, mailed business messages, multiply the 20 billion given above by the estimated individual letter costs. For instance, in 1971, with a $3.19 individual cost estimate, the result was a staggering $63.8 billion annually! Now suppose these business correspondence costs were cut 10 percent because of improvements in the written messages. Management could save $6,380,000,000, which could be used to benefit employees, customers, and perhaps the public in general.

## THE CHALLENGE IN WRITING FOR BUSINESS

Some letters are so important to a firm that they can win thousands or even millions of dollars in business or goodwill. If you were writing such a message, you'd pour every ounce of thought and imagination into it that you could. But what about the other letters—especially the run-of-the-mill kind that you will be writing daily? They may not be individually worth a million dollars, but every one is an opportunity to promote a favorable response toward you and your company. Furthermore, such letters might lead to major business transactions and, collectively, the overall effect of thousands of routine letters is enormous.

Because letters and reports play such an important role in the operation of

---

[1] This figure is based on the Postmaster General's statement that Americans produce 80 billion pieces of mail in a fiscal year and that 75 percent of this volume consists of business mail. From UP International Press, January 15, 1965.

[2] Emmett J. Leahy and Christopher A. Cameron, *Modern Records Management,* McGraw-Hill Book Company, 1965, pp. 3–4.

[3] Robert A. Shiff, "Presidents and Paperwork," *Dun's Review and Modern Industry,* April, 1959, pp. 45ff.

a firm, and in possible promotion for the individual, writing for business should be a challenge—not a tedious, dull chore. If you approach such writing as a necessary evil, or a task beneath your position or dignity, you'll probably turn out inferior correspondence. But if you realize that through your letters and reports you are talking to customers and managers who need your advice, assistance, and individual consideration, and appreciate sincerity, you should feel differently. Writing for the business world is really part of the art of human relations. The emphasis shouldn't be on mechanics of English or secretarial practice, but on the reader—how you can help him, how you can communicate with him on paper, how you can save his time and energy.

The following discussion is an example of why writing for business should and can be a challenge:[1]

Letter writing is a boring job. It's also exciting and invigorating. Sounds like a paradox, doesn't it? But that's just the way 2 correspondents described their work to us recently. Both of them write letters for the same department of an insurance company. Yet one found his job as dull as last week's newspaper, while the other thought it interesting and challenging. Why such contradictory reactions? Could the identical job be both dull and exciting at the same time? And why? We thought we knew the answer. But to prove it to ourselves and to the correspondents, we tried a little experiment.

We gave each writer the same letter to answer as an exercise. It was a case of a policy owner who had asked what to do about his lost insurance policy.

First, here's the response of the correspondent who said he was bored with his job:

Dear Sir:

With regard to lost policy #23456, we are enclosing a lost policy form. Kindly complete this form and send it to us as soon as possible.

Upon receipt of the above requirement, this company will consider the issuance of a replacement policy.

Very truly yours,

Now let's see what the other correspondent wrote:

Dear Mr. Robinson:

Your lost policy can be easily replaced. Please don't let it worry you. I've enclosed a form that will help us replace it for you.

All you need do is fill in the requested information and send it back to us. We'll see to it that you get your policy within 3 days after this form reaches us.

Sincerely yours,

---

[1] From the November–December 1962 issue of *Effective Letters*, a bulletin published by the New York Life Insurance Company.

The first writer let a routine situation lull him into a routine attitude which made his response mechanical and impersonal. He didn't realize it, but he was boring—himself and his readers—with his own routine-sounding messages.

The second correspondent, on the other hand, had a different outlook. He viewed the routine question as a challenge to make his answer less routine. After all, though lost policy cases were familiar to him, they certainly weren't to the reader. This approach gave him incentive to put more effort into his work. And he had the satisfaction of writing a message that was warm, personal, and not the least bit boring for either the reader or himself.

Moral? While some of the work in business correspondence may not be terribly exciting, it need never be boring. If you catch yourself writing stale, repetitive messages, it may mean that it's time to try a new—and in many cases a more personal—approach. Like any other job, letter writing is only as interesting or as dull as the individual makes it.

You will have numerous opportunities in the following chapters to analyze typical business situations that involve writing, solve problems, and organize messages according to acceptable contemporary procedures and central principles which are the basis for effective business writing. In so doing, you should gain a better understanding of people, learn how to win favorable responses from them, and make friends for your company. The background provided should give you the confidence to tackle just about any task you might face in writing letters, memos, or reports.

As was emphasized above, the effectively written letter, memo, or report for business pays off. If you thoroughly understand the basics of business writing and then diligently apply these basics with a liberal dose of common sense, you'll continue to improve your ability to communicate effectively with others on paper. With that kind of goal in mind, you should find a challenge in every message you tackle.

# CHAPTER 2

# Think Before You Write

- Five Thinking Steps
- Basic Organizational Patterns
- Openings and Closings
- Application to a Given Situation
- Exercises

You know the value of preparing yourself for various activities during your business day. For example, before giving a speech to a group or presenting an idea before a meeting, you get ready for the occasion by thinking through what you're going to say. No doubt you even jot down what you intend to say.

When you communicate through letters and reports, you must think before you write, type, or dictate. This chapter discusses the mental (thinking) steps, the basic organizational patterns, and letter openings and closings—all essential to good business communication. Then a situation is discussed to show how you can apply this information and write a satisfactory message.

## FIVE THINKING STEPS

To turn out the most effective writing, you should go through the following five preliminary thinking steps before you write or dictate one word:

1. Know the purpose of the message.
2. Visualize your reader.
3. Choose the ideas to include in the message.
4. Get all the facts to back up these ideas.
5. Organize your ideas in the most effective order.

### Know the Purpose

When you pick up a letter, what runs through your mind—even before you begin to read? Usually you're wondering what the writer wants or why he's writing. In other words, you're looking for the purpose. In fact, it's rather difficult for you to grasp all the various ideas of a particular message until you *do* know the purpose.

Below is a form letter that is baffling because its purpose is obscure. As you read the message, try to figure out why the writer sent it. Notice how frustrating it is not to be able to orient yourself, or figure out what purpose the various facts are supposed to support.

Friends:

Since the new administration took over in January, I have personally visited the majority of our customers throughout the major cities of the 11 western states. In January, as agreed by all, we were suffering from a downturn in our economy. Generally this has been apparent through January and February of this new year. However, as we approach spring—March and April—there appears to be a return of confidence and optimism for the balance of 1971. I am happy to report that this change has been reflected by a heavy increase in orders both for immediate delivery and for fall. I share the feeling that 1971 will again end in a banner year of prosperity.

As I move from city to city, I cannot help but feel what a great privilege it is to be in America. Yes––we have our problems. But let me remind you that as our nation matures we are overcoming them. Segregation is with us, but will happily be erased just as religious intolerance has slowly disappeared. If there is anything wrong in America, it is probably complacency! Let us not forget that many of the loudly heralded "rights" we enjoy are not rights at all––but rather privileges conferred upon us by citizenship in this great democratic republic.

Just because we are not affected we must not sit idly by when a fellow American––individual or group––is in trouble. Work stoppages of all kinds are, in the end, disadvantageous to us and we foot the bills. There must be a better way of correcting labor disputes. But we will continue to be plagued by strikes and lock-outs at our expense until you and I––along with our fellow Americans––insist on a change. I ask you––is there authority in our Constitution or elsewhere for organizations to bring about conditions within our country to our disadvantage?

I am told that we may be threatened by a nation-wide trucking strike soon. How disastrous will this be to your business and mine? Shall we do something now to keep this from happening or are we going to wait until we are in trouble and then moan?

My business, of course, is to sell hosiery, underwear, and knit goods. Please think of me when you have need for these products and let us not forget our obligation to every other fellow American.

Sincerely yours[1]

Do you know what the writer of that letter had in mind? Is it a newsy bit of chit-chat that he sends to his customers to keep his name fresh before them? If so, why didn't he say so? At the beginning he could have said, "Here is another newsy message to keep you posted on the crucial domestic happenings of our times," and you would have known why the message was being sent. At least you wouldn't be in a quandary as you read the rest of the letter.

*In all reports and in most letters you should clearly state the purpose at or near the beginning of the message:*

1. In all reports, state the purpose in the introduction.
2. In the first paragraph of a letter of application, make clear you are applying for a specific job or field.
3. In a good-news message (for example, when you write a favorable reply to a request for credit, adjustment, or a favor), grant the request in the opening.
4. In a simple inquiry, make your request in or near the first paragraph.

---

[1] To save space, letters in this text from now on will show no complimentary close unless needed for clarity.

**5.** In most claims (complaints), indicate your unhappiness with the product or service in the opening.

**6.** In an order, tell what you want in the first paragraph.

Only in bad-news letters or persuasive requests should you not state the purpose at the beginning. In these messages you open with a buffer, or with an attention-getting device.

The purpose of your writing should be your blueprint. Are you going to grant or refuse a request? Announce good news? Ask a favor or make a routine request? When you know the purpose, you can begin to chart your course. For example, in a refusal or a collection letter, the purpose should be twofold— not only to refuse or ask for money, but also to keep the customer or at least his goodwill. The purpose of any bad-news message is never merely to "answer the letter," or "to apologize." True, you will answer and might apologize, but the purpose is bigger—to keep the customer or at least not anger him to the point where he'll want to tear you or your company down to others whenever the opportunity presents itself.

## Visualize Your Reader

Not only do you need to know the purpose of your writing, but you should also consider the reader. If you have met the reader at least once—or better yet if you are well acquainted with him—you can actually visualize the individual as you write, and fit your words and shades of meaning to the particular person who will receive your message.

The bulk of your writing, however, will probably be directed to people you've never met. If you are sending a message to one person, you should try to classify him or her the best way you can—man or woman; businessman or housewife; young married woman or widow; superior (boss), colleague or subordinate; new or long-time customer; and on and on. If you are addressing a form message to many people, you should try to discover characteristics common to all of them and then imagine you're talking to one individual within that group.

Whether you do or do not know your reader personally, you need to realize that he is a human being. He appreciates sincere praise if he has genuinely earned it, but he can detect a "phony" statement just as quickly as you can. It's perfectly correct for you to use your industry's technical terms when you're writing to someone in your field. But to a layman you need to define these terms or use synonyms he understands. Most individuals dislike wordiness —writers who take a paragraph to say what could be said in a sentence. And they don't want to be shouted at, preached at, offended, or ordered around. That's why you should ask yourself if you would like to receive the letter you are sending. If your answer is negative, than you should revise.

You must be sensitive to the feelings of your readers, as the following three examples illustrate.

**1.** A Chamber of Commerce president had this sentence in his reply to a woman who had inquired about accommodations in and near his resort town:

You can wear anything you choose and wearing nothing is approximated so closely at times that I think you could get by with that if you were so inclined.

The woman who received this reply was a business woman in her fifties who was anything but a "swinger." She definitely forgot about staying at that place.

**2.** Then there was the university professor who received from the chairman of the board of a leading corporation a stockholder's letter that explained the company's pension program. Because the letter seemed so complicated, the professor wrote the chairman and suggested the need for simplifying communications to the average stockholder. Here's part of the chairman's reply:

Yours is the first criticism we have had from the many thousands of stockholders who have already sent in the proxies saying that the purpose of the meeting was not understandable to them. I do not see how I can state the facts any more clearly and simply than was done in my letter of January 18.

No doubt the professor is still feeling the mental slap in the face and smarting from the implication that he must be stupid. Not only did the chairman insult the professor but his reply was unclear itself. The wording gives the reader the impression that the *proxies* said "the purpose of the meeting was not understandable."

**3.** Finally, there's the man who reacted angrily by letter to a mail order house that sent him a collection letter. But this fellow forgot that the person receiving his message was entirely innocent of everything relating to the mixup and misunderstanding:

I just mailed to you bunch of idiots a check in the amount of $42.00 this morning from Hayward Cal, I received this piece of paper similar to the pile of junk I received yesterday from the same source. I am getting plenty tired of all this bolony you knotheads are pulling off because I have cancelled checks from away back in 1939, I also have a copy of the last contract and my payments are not due til the 25th of the month. I have typed a copy of that contract and along with other proof I am mailing the whole package to Chicago to see if I can't talk them into tying the can to about half of you numbskulls.

This disgruntled individual should have realized he was insulting innocent people who, in turn, had to act upon his message! Being called an idiot, knothead, and numbskull hardly makes a person willing to go all out to help someone.

When you are visualizing your reader, you should remember that different groups of people have different backgrounds and special interests; for example:

1. In upward communications (to your superior), tact is important. Also, you should support factual statements with detail (but not to the degree that the boss becomes impatient), curb personal opinion, and give only conclusions unless you're requested to include recommendations.[1]
2. In downward communications (to your subordinate), diplomacy is important. You need to clarify in your own mind what you want to accomplish before you give instructions to the subordinate; otherwise you'll probably give confused or vague instructions. Be sure you supply all information he needs, clearly explain all points which could be confusing, and explain the reason(s) for giving the order. In addition, you should point out (if you can) how your order benefits those it affects.[1]
3. To a colleague, emphasize presenting and interpreting facts.
4. A successful retailer knows his business well. You'd insult him if you talked down to him by saying, for example, that the right markup and an adequate turnover of merchandise will give him a profit.
5. A businessman dislikes obvious flattery about himself in a request he receives. Be sure you do not include such offensive "buttering up."
6. If you write to a stranger for information, you must tell him how you intend to use it, particularly if the information is confidential or tends to be confidential.
7. An older person is especially interested in security, while a young person looks more toward the future.
8. A woman is sometimes more sensitive to tone (cutting words, negative words, and curtness) than a man.
9. To a customer who is not familiar with the business world, you need to choose layman's language.

In short, when you write you must visualize your reader as best you can, and write with the individual in mind.


## Choose the Ideas

After you have decided on the purpose and visualized the reader, you can begin to choose the ideas that go into the message. And if you let only the purpose and reader govern what is included in your letter or report, you're more likely to avoid irrelevant ideas and overall wordiness.

In simple messages that discuss one or two points, you can make mental notes of the subjects you want to include. In more complex messages, you'll probably want to underline key words in the letter to be answered or jot down suggestions in the margin or on a memo pad. In a complicated letter or report, you might need a full-blown outline of the major headings and subheadings. How you proceed is not important—as long as you get into the message the information that fulfills your purpose.

[1] From John Fielden's article, "What Do You Mean I Can't Write?" *Harvard Business Review*, May–June, 1964, pp. 149–150.

Naturally the ideas that you will include in your communication depend upon the type of message you're considering. For example, take a welcome letter that a savings and loan association sends to a new customer. What is the purpose of this kind of letter? If you say the only purpose is to welcome the customer, the following message should suffice:

It is a pleasure to welcome your account; we will regard it as a responsibility deserving fine service at all times.

The directors, management, and staff thank you for selecting State Federal Savings Association for the investment of your savings funds.

But *is* the purpose of this message only to welcome? A little reflection should give you your answer. When an individual comes to your association to open an account, you explain to him this, that, and the other thing about the account, your services, and on and on. By the time the customer gets back home, all you've said has probably merged into one big, hazy blur. Unless you gave him a booklet that covers what you told him verbally, he'll probably be wondering if he heard you correctly about the hours you're open, parking facilities, amount of insurance coverage on accounts, and other pertinent points.

With this in mind, just what should be the purpose of your welcome letter to this customer? Isn't the purpose to help him clearly know your policy concerning savings accounts, the overall services available to him, and your eagerness to make him realize that your association is his association and his financial headquarters? If that is so, then the following ideas should be included in your "welcome" letter. (List the ideas as they come to you; you can rearrange them in an appropriate order after you choose the right organizational pattern.)

1. Welcome him and thank him for opening an account.
2. Enclose a compact booklet that clearly tells him all the services available to him.
3. Stress one of these services; for example, let him know you have a drive-in window.
4. Tell him the hours you're open to serve him.
5. Mention percent of interest he is earning and the amount his account is insured for.
6. Assure him that you're ready to help him with his problems, suggestions, or wishes.

Once you have decided on these ideas and completed the other thinking elements discussed in this chapter, you can turn out a welcome letter that serves your purpose—like the following:

Dear Mr. Jones

*Best
news*

Thank you for recently opening a savings account with us. It is a pleasure to welcome you as a new depositor in State Federal's Savings Department.

*Explanation*

Your funds are fully protected by the soundness of our investments, conservative local management, and the supervision of the Federal Home Loan Bank. You not only earn 5% compounded daily, but your savings are insured up to $20,000 for each account by a permanent agency of the United States Government.

*Education*

All the association's services, described in the enclosed pamphlet, are designed with savings and loan customers in mind and are available to you. We welcome an opportunity to discuss any of them with you or answer any questions you might have.

*Education*

Our drive-in window is open during office hours: 9:30 a.m. to 3:00 p.m. weekdays except for Friday when the window and doors remain open until 6:00 p.m. Free parking facilities just south of the building are available to you whenever you visit us.

*Action
suggestion*

You are most welcome to come in whenever we can assist you. Please consider this association your financial headquarters for your savings and borrowing needs.

## Get All the Facts

After you have decided on what ideas to include in the message, you want to ask yourself if you need to include any specific figures, facts, or quotations that you don't have at the tip of your tongue. Perhaps you need to check with your boss, colleague, subordinates, or the files for an exact percentage, name of an individual, date, address, figure, or statement. Also, in reports that include tables or other illustrations, you should have these visual aids finished (or at least in rough draft form) at this stage. When you write, you want to write rapidly and smoothly. If you must stop in the midst of your writing to prepare a table, then you're "cold" when you begin writing again.

Actually this thinking step encourages you to pause before you start dictating or writing and ask yourself if you have the necessary facts and figures to send to your reader. By doing so, you can save additional correspondence, avoid confusion, and even create goodwill in many instances. You'll find further discussion on this thinking step in Chapter 4 on completeness.

## Organize Your Ideas

The last thinking step before writing is to arrange your ideas in the most effective order. Keep in mind that the order of ideas is usually just as important as the ideas themselves. Organization gives you direction and results in conciseness, clarity, and the best psychological presentation. The following section discusses and illustrates each of the four basic organizational patterns.

## BASIC ORGANIZATIONAL PATTERNS

Any letter falls in one of four organizational patterns or plans—good news (including neutral messages), bad news, direct requests, and persuasive requests.

### Good-News Messages

You can use the good-news pattern whenever it is psychologically sound for you to begin with a direct approach—that is, to begin with the highlight or crux of the message. Examples of this pattern include messages that grant requests, announce favorable information, or exchange routine information between companies. (Actually, direct requests also follow this pattern, but are discussed elsewhere for purposes of simplifying classification.) In short, you use the direct approach when the content of the message does not affect unfavorably the relationship between writer and reader.

In a good-news letter, you:

1. State the best news or the main idea.
2. Explain whatever is necessary and desirable.
   a. All needed pertinent information or details, as circumstances require.
   b. Resale material, if appropriate—to resell reader on your company, service, products, or the related ideas (if you think he is beginning to lose confidence in your service, company, products; if he hasn't made up his mind; or if he doesn't know the services available to him).
   c. Educational information—when you need to educate the reader on the use of an article or service or suggest additional services he might find useful.
   d. Sales promotion—when appropriate.
3. End with a positive, friendly paragraph.
   a. Appreciation.
   b. Clear statement of action desired and motivation to action.
   c. Willingness to help further upon request.

Now that you have a suggested pattern for a good-news letter, study the following example and ask yourself if you agree with the resulting reply to the customer.

*Situation*
You sell plumbing supplies. Last week you mailed to Henry Bottomly, a plumber, a second notice for $100 he owes you. This morning (April 1) you receive his reply. He explains he hasn't worked for the last two weeks because of illness. But he promises to pay something on the account in two weeks and hopes to pay up completely within a month. Although he doesn't have any financial reserves to fall back on, he is a hard and competent worker. Answer his letter.

*Decision*

Naturally you must first decide on whether you will grant his request, refuse it, or compromise. Because you can't get blood out of a turnip and because he is conscientious about this bill, you will give him an extension of time. You're not delighted to do so; yet you don't want to destroy the goodwill you're building through the extension by showing your reluctance in granting it.

*Good-news reply*

```
Dear Mr. Bottomly

As you requested, you are receiving a 30-day extension of time
to settle your account with us.

Your suggested manner of payment is quite agreeable with us.
Paying $50 by April 15 and the $50 balance by April 30 will
keep your credit in good standing.

Thank you for taking the time to explain your situation to us.
```

Notice in the reply that the message begins with a "yes" opening, then explains the terms, and ends with an expression of appreciation. In general, a good-news letter is rather easy to write because you're giving the reader what he wants or likes or needs.

## Bad-News Messages

One of the most difficult letters to write is a refusal, because you are sending the reader information he will consider unfavorable. Thus, you need to take a little longer to say no, watch the tone (which influences the reader's reaction to the message), and still try to help the reader in any way you can.

In most bad-news messages, you:

1. Get in step with the reader by means of a buffer—an opening that softens the bad news to come.
2. Explain in a positive, helpful way.
3. Refuse either by implying or expressing your decision.
4. Offer additional help whenever you can.
5. End on a friendly, positive note.

Using the five-step outline just suggested for a bad-news message, study the example below of a retailer who has requested credit from you (a wholesaler), and who must be refused credit. The suggested refusal is one satisfactory way of saying "no" clearly and tactfully, and ending on a friendly, positive note.

```
Dear Mr. Morgan

Thank you for promptly forwarding the credit information we
requested on February 19.  The statements provided by trade
references are essential to our evaluation of each request
for an open account.
```

*Buffer*

*Explanation*
> Without exception, the reports we've received strongly attest to your excellent character and integrity. Information regarding the operations of the hardware store, however, has been somewhat less encouraging. The intense local competition which you face apparently has had an adverse impact on your profit position.

*Implied refusal*
> Understandably, meeting existing obligations as they fall due has been no easy task. I'm confident that these difficulties are only temporary, but any additional credit purchases at this time would increase your obligations to an unhealthy level. Of course, we want to do everything possible to help you regain the competitive position that will allow us to arrange an open account.

*Offer of additional help*
> I've requested that our area representative, Mr. A. B. Jones, visit your store and discuss with you the programs you can use to increase your volume of business. Our experience with hardware outlets has enabled us to assist many customers with their merchandising problems. For instance, we've found that the effective promotion of leader items can quickly expand store traffic, increase the turnover rate of general merchandise, and help dispose of excess inventory.

*Offer of additional help*
> In the meantime you'll need to maintain your stock of necessary merchandise. By reducing your present order by about one-half, you should be able to obtain the essential items your store requires. Of course, you will be entitled to the 2% discount that applies to all cash purchases. Just use the enclosed order form and mail it in the envelope provided.

*Friendly, positive ending*
> Your shipment will be on its way within a few hours after we received your instructions.

One good test for any letter is what your reaction to it would have been if you had received it. Would you feel offended if you were the retailer? Would you buy from the wholesaler? True, you're not getting credit, but the writer seems sincere and interested in you.

## Direct Requests

The direct request requires no persuasion. The writer needs only to make his request clear, expanding where necessary. Such a message follows the outline below:

> 1. Begin with the main idea.
>    a. Introduce your request, major statement, or question.
>    b. State reason(s), if desirable, to justify the request.

2. Explain whatever is necessary and desirable.
   a. Include needed details to help the reader fill your request correctly.
   b. Consider numbering your questions (if more than one) for easy reading **or** answering.
3. End courteously with motivation to action.
   a. State clearly what action you want the reader to take—and when.
   b. Make action easy, if appropriate, by including a reply envelop, your telephone number, office hours, or any other helpful information.
   c. Express appreciation and, if appropriate, include a goodwill statement.

The following letter clearly presents a direct request from the personnel officer in a hospital to the chief pharmacist in a large prescription pharmacy.

Dear Mr. Kast

*Reason and request*

Mr. Peter Hanenberger, who worked in your pharmacy from January 1969 until July 1971, has applied to us for a position as Chief Pharmacist.  Because we are opening a new 320-bed teaching and research hospital on May 1, 1972, and in the latter part of this year plan to bring in a Chief Pharmacist to join a young and aggressive organization, will you please give us your evaluation of this man.

*Details*

As the personal qualifications and technical skill of this individual are requisite to such a responsible job, we certainly will appreciate a written evaluation of Mr. Hanenberger based on his performance on the job while with you.

We're especially interested in knowing:

*Details*

1.  This man's ability or potential to organize from scratch a pharmacy in a modern and well-equipped 320-bed hospital devoted to teaching and research.  We're interested in making this hospital one of the leaders in the country.

*Details*

2.  Your frank opinion of him as a worker.  What is the sustained quality of his work?  This job will demand a tremendous amount of initiative and working capacity.

*Details*

3.  His ability to work with others.  If he later should have people working under his direction, can he organize them into a tightly knit and happy working group?  Is he liked and respected by subordinates, associates, and supervisors?

*Details*

4.  The duties he performed.  In turn, we can determine whether his experience will fit our needs.

*Appreciation*

We will appreciate your candid reply to these four areas and any other comments that will permit a valid appraisal of Mr. Hanenberger as a candidate for Chief Pharmacist with us.

## Persuasive Requests

The persuasive request requires the writer to create in the reader interest and desire in achieving the writer's goal. Such a message should follow the attention-interest-desire-action (AIDA) outline:

1. Catch reader's *A*ttention.
2. Get the reader's *I*nterest.
3. Create *D*esire—by description and factual explanation (how the service or product benefits reader or user).
4. Ask for *A*ction.

The letter below follows the AIDA pattern. This message is from an office supply company to parents of graduating high school seniors who have pursued a college entrance program. You can assume the sender is mailing two letters—one to parents of a son, and one to parents of a daughter.)

Dear Mr. and Mrs. Greiner

*Attention*
With high school graduation just four weeks away, you may be searching for an appropriate present for your son. The Butler portable typewriter is a practical gift for the college-bound student, one which will provide him with continuous benefits throughout his college years.

*Interest*
Your son will find that a typewriter, like paper and pen, is a necessary part of his college equipment. Nowadays, instructors usually demand that written assignments be typewritten. Typed reports are neat and legible, and they accurately reflect student effort. Furthermore, a typewriter can work to reduce the time pressure students experience by enabling them to complete notes and outlines more rapidly than they could by hand. And, of course, a portable typewriter is especially well-suited for campus use simply because it's portable.

*Desire*
Unlike other machines, the Butler portable combines the quality features of an office typewriter with the storage and transportation convenience of a portable. Your son will find that the Butler copy-set dial will allow him to make up to 10 clear carbons; that the extra large carriage will enable him to type on oversize paper; and that changeable type bars will permit him to include a variety of technical signs and symbols in his typing. You'll find these and many additional Butler features fully described in the booklet enclosed.

*Desire*
The Butler portable is a value in price as well as features, for it costs just $100. And, if you like, we'll be glad to arrange the payment plan that best suits your budget.

*Action*

> For your convenience our offices will remain open to nine each week night from now until May 28. Ample parking is available on the west side of the building. We would enjoy meeting both of you and showing you why more people choose a Butler portable than any other make—and why it is a most useful and timely gift for your son.

This letter does an effective job in stimulating the readers (parents) to visit the store to consider the portable typewriter as a graduation gift. Notice how the different paragraphs do their job in presenting the AIDA pattern:

*1st paragraph:* Catches the attention of the parents by talking about their son (or daughter) graduating from high school and mentioning the gift that is both appropriate for the occasion and useful at college.

*2d paragraph:* Gets the readers' interest by showing need for the product (a portable typewriter) before trying to create desire for the particular brand.

*3d paragraph:* Creates desire of brand by description but mainly by explanation—how *that* brand portable will help the son.

*4th paragraph:* Also creates desire by telling parents how easy it is to purchase the portable.

*5th paragraph:* Asks action by inviting parents to come to the showroom, and mentions free parking and hours the store is open.

## OPENINGS AND CLOSINGS

Actually you determine what you'll say in the first and last paragraphs of a letter when you consider the five thinking steps and organize your message. But openings and closings are discussed separately here because of their importance and the advantage of studying them all in one place.

Openings and closings occupy two of the most strategic locations in a message. Many times the opening determines whether the reader continues reading, puts the message aside for later study, or discards it. You might look at the opening as that section especially for the reader, since it gives him his first impression of you, and the ending as especially for the writer, since it leaves with the reader the final idea(s) you want to get across.

### Openings

Openings too often sound as if the writer wasn't prepared to begin, and is going through a "winding-up" period by rambling out loud. For example, "Answering your inquiry of October 6, I wish to inform you . . ." sounds as if the writer wasn't really ready to start; he hadn't first thought what he was going to say. Or perhaps he has criticized the reader unfavorably in the first paragraph—clearly a case of not stopping to think of the reader's viewpoint.

Your opening should catch the interest of the reader and make a favorable first impression when you: (1) get in step with the reader; (2) say something important and/or interesting to him; and (3) orient him to the subject and purpose of the letter. The following are some concrete suggestions for good openings.

*1. Get the reader into the picture;* don't emphasize the writer. Although an acceptable opening can begin with "I" or "we," try starting with "you."

*Poor:* We pay 5 percent interest on savings here at Fourth National.
*Good:* You earn 5 percent interest on your savings here at Fourth National.

*Poor:* We have your letter of June 10 and we have referred it to our legal department and they tell us we . . .
*Good:* Good news! The legal department agrees with your decision on . . .

*Poor:* We are pleased to announce our new bank-by-mail service.
*Good:* Now you can enjoy the convenience of banking by mail.

*2. Begin directly with the subject* when doing so does not unfavorably affect the relationship between reader and writer. This type of opening is especially effective in a good-news message or a direct request. A good rule is to tell good news right away, but take longer to refuse a request or give other bad news.

In a routine request (or a routine claim), include the request at the beginning. Then the necessary details will follow naturally.

*Granting:*    We are pleased to let you know that your recent application for open credit has been approved.

*Granting:*    It is a pleasure to offer you whatever assistant you need regarding several of our employment and personnel procedures.

*Good news:* As you suggested, we plan to install the "right turn only" sign to improve the parking lot exit. Thank you for your interest in making a practical way to improve our operation.

*Request:*    So that the account of Mr. A. B. Smith, deceased, can be transferred to your name as Executor, will you please return to us the following:

*Request:*    Will you please give us the confidential information requested on the attached sheet.

*3. Use a buffer paragraph when you must refuse the reader.* Don't spread gloom with your first words. Smile first, or at least get in step.

*Poor:* I am sorry but we do not make contributions to everyone who asks us for money.
*Good:* I am glad to reply to your request for money and explain our policy on contributions.

*Poor:* We regret your loan application did not meet our regulations and board policies for approving a loan.

*Good:* Your application for a FHA loan has received our careful attention. It is evident you are doing your best to provide a comfortable home for your family.

*Poor:* Thank you for your order for $100 worth of Roselyn china by Lenox. But I'm sorry we cannot fulfill your order because we don't sell direct.

*Good:* Your choice of the Lenox "Roselyn" pattern indicates your fine taste for timeless elegance and lasting service in formal china.

*4. In a persuasive request* (sales letter), *get the reader's attention* by saying something that will make him want to read further. Remember that the average person dislikes a "sales letter" and will throw it away on the least provocation.

*Good:* A college education today is worth more than ever before—but it costs more too! The lifetime expected income for a man without a college education is $875,000; with four years of college a man is expected to earn $1,125,000. This is an income advantage of $250,000, or a return of $62,500 for each year of college. (To a customer who has children.)

*Good:* Like most conscientious dog owners, you know that proper food is just as important to a dog as it is to a human being. And you know, too, that if you are trying to make up a scientifically balanced diet for your dog, it involves more time and effort than you can spare. And that's where Muskies can help! (Naturally, to a dog owner.)

*5. Be positive.* Talk about the pleasant—not the unpleasant. Say what you can do—not what you cannot do. And avoid mentioning anything that you do not want the reader to think about.

If you must apologize, you should generally put the apology in an inconspicuous place; for example, in the explanation. Occasionally, however, an apology in the opening may best satisfy your reader. Writers apologize too often in messages. If a person inquires about a service you don't have—and you know there is no reason for you to have it—don't apologize. But if you have done something that is definitely your fault, perhaps you need to apologize.

*Negative:* We regret to learn from your letter of September 18 of your unpleasant experience upon opening a can of La Casa spinach. This is very disturbing to us because of the particular care taken in the preparation of all La Casa products.

*Positive:* Thank you for taking the time to tell us about your experience when opening a can of La Casa spinach.

*Negative:* We are sorry that, having closed your savings account, your name will be missing from our long list of satisfied customers. We found our relationship a most pleasant one. We sincerely hope, that, despite the best efforts of our fine staff, there was no occasion on which you felt we failed to serve you properly.

*Positive:* We noticed that you recently closed your savings account with us. It was our pleasure to serve you, and we want you to know that your account was very much appreciated.

**6. Keep the first sentence and the first paragraph relatively short.** The first sentence should not exceed 20 or 25 words. And by all means never throw a blockbuster sentence (say 50 words or more) at the reader—especially at the beginning of the message.

The first paragraph should be short enough—five to seven typewritten lines or less—to entice the reader to start reading. You want to introduce the good news, get in step, orient the reader—not get involved in details. A 23-line first paragraph, for example, would definitely bring a negative reaction.

Examples of over-long opening sentences are:

  a. As doing so may be of possible service to you, I take sending the enclosed on-press tear sheet of your sketch as a convenient opportunity to recall to you that the privilege—

  as a biographee who has cooperated with our compilers by supplying and checking data published in it—

  which you now still have to an advance of publication subscription discount of 25 percent from the regular retail price of the shortly-to-issue new edition of *Who's What in the United States*

  will soon expire on the formal announcement of the actual date of publication, for thereafter the standard price at retail must, as a matter of inflexible trade usage, invariably apply.   (113 words)

  b. I realize that it is the responsibility of the underwriter in the department office to determine when an insured shall be blacklisted, but Mr. A. B. Jones has expressed the opinion that we are not doing enough of this, and certainly if we do not file a report on a man like Mr. P. P. Peterson after the trouble he has caused us, then we are making a farce of the whole reporting program, a thought with which I am sure you in the Claim Department are in full accord.   (90 words)

**7. Use a peg opening** (if desirable). As in a newspaper article, tell the highlights of the story in a nutshell. The other paragraphs will then merely expand this "peg" beginning. Occasionally include the five W's (who, what, when, where, and why) in the opening.

  *Good:* As one of the fastest growing electronic manufacturers in the Northwest, Liddy Corporation offers something very exciting to a new graduate—opportunity and challenge. Please consider me for the position of Personnel Coordinator in your Industrial Relations Department. My qualifications include a B.A. degree, several years' experience in the personnel field, and a desire to work with people.

  *Good:* You and your family (who) are invited to a machinery demonstration (what) next Saturday from 10 A.M. until noon (when) in the ballroom of the Statler Hotel (where). The purpose of this demonstration is to show and explain to management the operation of the latest data processing equipment (why).

**8. Avoid beginnings that merely tell the reader what he told you.**

  a. Your letter of June 13, 197_, requested comments and suggestions regarding proposed working papers for the second Technical Panel, 6023.

**b.** I have your letter of the 21st, in which you informed me that Mr. John Smith called on you for the first time a few weeks ago and that he appealed to you as a capable and intelligent young man.

*9. Avoid trite beginnings.* Don't "date" yourself by using wornout expressions. Use conversational words—as if you were talking to the reader.

*Poor:* *Attached herewith please find* sketches for control panels.
*Good:* Attached are sketches for the control panels.

*Poor:* *We are in receipt of* your memorandum stating that the *above insured* is now in military service.
*Good:* Thank you for informing us that Mr. Jones is now in military service.

*Poor:* *Please be advised that* we have written the *above-captioned* policy for this *party*.
*Good:* You'll be glad to know that effective March 15 Mrs. Mary Ryan's fire and theft policy is in force.

*10. Avoid an irritating opening,* or one that might anger the reader.

*Poor:* I have your letter of (date) and I can't understand why you had difficulty in seeing that our action was correct.
*Good:* Thank you for your courtesy in letting us know your candid feelings regarding action on your claim.

*Poor:* Have you emptied your safe deposit box? If you have, please sign the enclosed cancellation form and return it with the keys to the box.
*Good:* This is just a reminder the rent on your safe deposit box has expired. If you wish to use the box another year, please send in your . . .

*11. Include the date of the letter you're answering* if the date is *beneficial* to either the reader or writer—*but don't stress the date.* The first five or ten words in your opening should begin to unfold the most important idea(s).

*Poor:* Replying to your letter of September 16, I wish to thank you for your approval for me to use your name as a satisfied user of X product.
*Good:* Thank you for your approval to use your name as a satisfied user of X product.

*Poor:* As per your letter of October 10, we have shipped your order today by Railway Express.
*Good:* The five dozen conform hats you ordered October 10 were shipped to you today by Railway Express.

*Poor:* I have your letter . . .
(Obviously you have the letter because you're answering it.)

*12. Make sure that the opening sentence is complete.* Examples of incomplete openings:

**a.** Reference your letter of September 4, 1971, to Mr. Yokohoma of Japan Air Lines Company, Ltd.
**b.** Received your letter of September 26, 1971, concerning Mr. Peter M. Smith's application for Associate Membership in the Society of Real Estate Appraisers.

## Closings

The closing plays an important role in a letter because it rounds out the letter plan and contains the idea(s) you will leave with your reader. Here you have the opportunity to bring final focus on the desired action and leave a sense of your courtesy with the reader. What you say in the closing depends upon the purpose of the letter and the ideas in previous paragraphs. The following points give suggestions for various letter situations.

*1. If you want your reader to do something, clearly ask for action*—don't hint—*and*, if possible, *show how he will benefit* by complying. Use specific dates when you want him to answer by a certain time. Say tomorrow, next week, next month, on January 17, rather than at your convenience, promptly, immediately, soon, in the near future. In sales letters you can offer a special inducement to action by offering a special price until a certain date, for example, or by emphasizing that the supply is limited.

*Poor:*    I would appreciate an interview to discuss my qualifications with
*(hinting)*    you in greater detail.
*Better:*    May I have an interview to discuss my qualifications with you in greater detail?

*Poor:*    Please take care of this matter at your earliest convenience.
*(indefinite)*
*Better:*    So that you can bring your account up to date before the first of the month, please send us your check for $102.20 today in the enclosed envelope.

*Good:*    Whichever way you prefer, you can notify us by filling in and returning to us the enclosed card. It is important that you receive the kind of service you expect at Pacific National Bank.

*2. Make action easy*—especially to someone who is likely not to reply. Include an addressed card or envelop if the occasion warrants it, and perhaps put a stamp on it. Be sure the reader has your phone number and knows your office hours if you are asking him to phone you.

*3. End on a positive note.* Include your apologies before the last paragraph. Negative endings weaken your presentation, and may give your reader the choice of two decisions (one of which can work against you). Beware especially of four words that can be negative—if, hope, trust, and may.

*Negative:* I regret we cannot be more helpful in the study you are making.
*Positive:* The best of success with your term paper. You have an interesting topic to research.

*Negative:* We do hope this has not caused you any inconvenience.
*Positive:* Thank you for taking the time to explain . . .

*Negative:* We sincerely apologize for this mishap. Under separate cover we are sending you an assortment of La Casa fruits and vegetables which we hope you will thoroughly enjoy and which we trust will restore your confidence in our La Casa products.

*Positive:* Today we're sending to you an assortment of La Casa fruits and vegetables for your enjoyment. Please accept them with our compliments.

**4. Be friendly.** Offer to help the reader further or again if that is appropriate. Remember this is the last thought you're leaving with the reader. An abrupt, demanding, commanding, or angry remark causes unfavorable reaction.

*Good:* Should you have further questions concerning this procedure, Max, please write or call me. My number is 555-4422.

*Poor:* Send us your check today.
*Good:* To keep your credit in good standing, please send us your check for $123.94 today.

*Poor:* I am sorry you had to write two letters, but of course you realize this action wouldn't have been necessary if you had supplied all the necessary information the first time.
*Good:* Thank you for giving us the opportunity to explain . . .

**5. Show appreciation.** Everyone likes sincere praise when he has earned it, but don't thank in advance. As a rule, it is presumptuous to ask a person to do something and then thank him for doing it before he agrees to do so.

*Poor:* I thank you in advance for your cooperation in informing your employees of these tours.
*Good:* I will appreciate your cooperation in informing your employees of these tours.

**6. Avoid trite expressions.** (In the examples below, the trite expressions are italicized.)

*Poor:* Thank you for your cooperation *in this matter.*
*Good:* Thank you for helping us establish a satisfactory system of compensation for the newly hired salesmen.

*Poor:* *Enclosed you will find a self-addressed* stamped envelope *for your convenience.* (It's okay to mention the envelope in the body of the letter, but tie the envelope in with a more important idea.)
*Good:* Please fill out this form and return it in the enclosed envelope by (date).

*Poor:* If we can be of service to you in the future, please *do not hesitate* to contact us as *we stand ready* to serve you.
*Good:* Whenever we can assist you again, please let us know.

**7. When appropriate, include a final "punch" line** (which is usually the last sentence of the paragraph) to remind your reader of benefit to him or other people involved.

a. So that Roger can drive to Portland for you by July 19, please let me have your approval for repairing the car and installing two Goodyear polyglass tires. Then you can be certain his car will be in good condition when he makes the trip.

**b.** When you are ready to make your reservation, please call (number) and give me the date and flight of your preference. Then you can be sure you'll leave on the plane and day of your choice.

*8. Occasionally you might wish to add a personal note*—unrelated to the subject discussed in the message—to round out the letter. Such a note is appropriate as a last paragraph or preferably as a handwritten postscript.

**a.** You're fortunate to be at Estes Park this month. The thermometer registered 103 at 3 P.M. here yesterday.
**b.** We wish you and Rudolph a wonderful wedding on June 13 and an exciting life together.
**c.** Congratulations on the excellent paper you presented to our group last week. I thoroughly enjoyed what you said about . . .

*9. Avoid incomplete endings* (statements)—especially those that begin with an "ing" participle and end with "we are" or "I remain." These endings went out with Prince Albert and Queen Victoria.

*Poor:* Trusting this information will prove helpful, I remain
*Good:* Please let us know if you need additional information.

*Poor:* Hoping to hear from you in the affirmative, I remain (or I am)
*Good:* Please sign and return the enclosed form. Then you can soon begin to enjoy the comfort of . . .

*10. Avoid a long final paragraph.* Complete your discussion beforehand. Then you can confine your ending to five or fewer lines.

*11. Stop when you have finished.* Don't tack on a worthless "hoping to hear from you soon, I remain . . ." or a statement already mentioned in the message.

*Poor:* With kindest regards, we are (or I remain)

*Poor:* Again, we thank you for your inquiry.
*Good:* Please let us know when we can help you again.

*Poor:* Thank you for your assistance, John, and best regards.

Sincerely
("Best regards" and "sincerely" result in a double complimentary close.)

To summarize, although the closing is "especially for the writer," he must continue to consider the reader's point of view, to make any desired reader action clear and easy, and to emphasize benefit to the reader whenever possible.

## APPLICATION TO A GIVEN SITUATION

You should now be ready to use the suggestions in this chapter to develop an effective letter. Take the following situation:

Assume you are manager of Blank Oyster Co. in Seattle, Washington. You have received the letter below from an Arizona housewife who tells you she found two ugly specimens in her favorite brand of canned oysters that you pack, and you must answer the letter.

Dear Sir:

I found the enclosed "specimens" in the can of your oysters (see inside label) last nite and it almost made me ill.

My husband and daughter like the oyster stew from this brand very much so I don't think you would want this stuff in the cans.

Yours truly,

P.S. I paid 85 cents for this can and then dumped it after seeing that black wire or stick or whatever it is.

Before you begin to dictate a message to this woman, you first need to perform the thinking steps, decide on the organizational pattern, and then plan your opening and closing.

1. *Determine the purpose.* You certainly want to do more than apologize, or simply "answer her letter." Isn't the purpose to keep her as a customer?

2. *Visualize the reader.* She is a housewife who has a husband and daughter. They all like your oysters for stew. Though her letter is tactful, you should realize she is at least annoyed and may be angry.

3. *Choose the ideas to include in your message.* The determining factors here are the purpose and the reader. Without thinking about any particular order, you should jot down mentally or on paper the following:
   a. Explain.
   b. Resell her on your oysters.
   c. Send her several cans of oysters.
   d. Apologize.
   e. Thank her for writing.
   f. End on a friendly, positive note that continues the feeling of goodwill and business.

4. *Get all the facts.* You need to find out what this foreign substance is. As manager, you should already know thoroughly the canning process. If you mentioned in your reply to her that "your guess is as good as mine what that foreign stuff is," you'll probably lose her as a customer.

5. *Choose the letter type and organization for the message.* Is it good news, bad news, or an inquiry? It certainly doesn't convey bad news or make an inquiry. Isn't it really a good-news message to her? Aren't you answering her inquiry? Thus your organizational pattern is as follows:
   a. Pleasant opening: tell her you're glad to answer her inquiry.
   b. Explain: but don't get mired in the negative. Because you are at fault, you are justified in apologizing.
   c. Resell: because she's disappointed or unhappy with your product.
   d. End on a positive, friendly note.

With these five steps clearly in mind, you should concentrate a little longer on the opening and closing. Specifically, what do you plan to include in the opening? Of course you're going to thank her for giving you the opportunity to reply. But that sentence standing alone might only convey abruptness. So you decide to add a second sentence to the first paragraph, showing your appreciation that she has taken the time to write you.

Now, about the closing! What specifically will you say? You'll give her several cans of oysters and add a punch line about wanting to please her.

At this point you are ready to begin and will probably produce an above-average letter like the one below.

Dear Mrs. Jones

*Pleasant opening*  Thank you for giving us the opportunity to reply to your experience with Blank Brand oysters. We appreciate your thoughtfulness in writing.

*Explanation*  Your enclosure turned out to be small pieces of the root section of a common seaweed which grows on the oysterbeds in great abundance. We are stumped how this substance

*Resale*  could stick to an oyster through three successive washings and inspections in the canning process and still escape

*Apology*  detection by our packers. But it did, and we are sorry that it happened.

*More resale*  It is of little help to explain that this harmless vegetable substance became totally sterile when the oysters were cooked in the can. You did exactly the right thing when you wrote about the incident.

*Positive, friendly ending*  Today we are sending you by parcel post two cans of Blank Brand oysters with our compliments. You are the discriminating consumer we want to please.

Of course, the effectiveness of the message to Mrs. Jones is shown by whether she'll continue buying your oysters. Perhaps no letter can keep her as a customer; but it's better to try and fail (in this instance, at least) than not to try at all. Effectiveness depends upon the overall reaction of the reader— not primarily upon the purity of English, rules of grammar, or placement on the page.

## Summary

Before writing any message, you must consider carefully the five thinking steps because they furnish the blueprint for the message, the ideas to include, and the organizational pattern. They direct your attention to the recipient of your message, and they allow you to write without unnecessary interruptions.

As a result, your message should be complete, read smoothly, and also sound friendly. When choosing your ideas, pay particular attention to the opening and closing paragraphs because of their strategic positions. The opening is especially for the reader, and the closing is especially for the writer. Using the thinking steps, and the suggestions for openings and closings, you are equipped with guidelines for producing an effective message.

## EXERCISES

1. What is your reaction to each of the openings below: Is it good, fair, or poor? Why? If there is more than one opening to consider (indicated by *versus*), which do you prefer? Why?

   **a.** I have your letter of the 21st, in which you inform me that our new representative, Mr. John Smith, called on you for the first time a few weeks ago and that he appealed to you as a capable and intelligent young man.

   **b.** John Doe, about whom you inquired in your letter of July 6, has kept an account with us since August 13, 1955.

   **c.** Just received your memo of January 13 regarding the above subject.

   **d.** As requested in your letter of June 3, we are very pleased to enclose herewith three copies of our latest administrative directory.

   *versus*

   Enclosed are three copies of our latest administrative directory that you requested in your letter of June 3.

   *versus*

   It is a pleasure to comply with you request and enclose three copies of our latest administrative directory.

   **e.** We are in receipt of your letter of recent date for . . .

   *versus*

   Thank you for your interest in . . .

   **f.** Pursuant to the association's policy, the first payment will begin on or before 150 days from date of loan closing.

   **g.** In reply to your letter, please find enclosed our check in the amount of $132.94. This check represents the sum total of the two dividends earned for June 30 and December 31.

   **h.** Our concern about your mortgage payment is not altogether selfish—we see too many people who practice paying late suddenly having to face unexpected bills, and then before they realize it, they are two months past due. Many never fully recover and eventually lose their home.

   *versus*

   You have failed to correct the existing delinquency on the above-captioned loan, and furthermore you have made no arrangements for repayment.

   *versus*

   No reply has been received to our letter of November 8, and your above-numbered loan is in default since October.

i. We are in receipt of your memo regarding the four (4) No. 1111 Cragston wheels which you say are defective.

j. Good news! After reviewing the facts again, we are issuing the desired policy.

*versus*

This is in reply to your letter of March 19 requesting us to review the application which was previously declined.

k. We will be pleased to consider issuing the desired policy provided you submit a new application by November 15.

*versus*

A new application must be submitted by November 15; otherwise we cannot consider issuing the desired policy.

l. Congratulations on making the final payment on your home improvement loan No. 4-5555. We are sure that you had a real happy feeling of satisfaction when you could finally say to yourself, "Well, that debt is paid in full."

*versus*

Our records show that the balance on the loan account above has been paid off.

m. Thank you for your letter of November 14.

n. This is in reply to your request for information regarding our various savings plans.

2. What is your reaction to each of the closings below? Is it good, average, or poor? Why?

a. Thank you for coming to see us. We are sorry we could not be of service.

b. We hope to have the opportunity of serving you.

c. When it is convenient, please let me know your decision.

*versus*

I trust you will avail yourself of the opportunity of making either of these changes and when your decision is reached, notify me at your earliest convenience. I await the pleasure of your reply.

d. With kindest regards, we are

e. You are never too young or too old to begin savings for a comfortable financially worry-free retirement. Start today by opening a Check-A-Month Retirement Income savings account at State Federal and let us help you reach a sound retirement goal.

f. A business reply card is provided for your convenience.

g. We are sorry that we are unable to be of service to you and hope that we can help you at some time in the future.

h. Please let us know when we can help you again.

i. As soon as you sign and return this contract in the enclosed envelope, we can process this loan and mail the payment book to you.

j. When you opened an account here, this became your bank. Please let us serve you in any way which will add to your convenience.

**k.** Thanks for your help, John.

**l.** We appreciate your interest and will keep you informed of all developments.

**m.** Hoping to hear from you, I remain

**n.** So that you can receive your payment book as quickly as possible, please sign and return this contract soon.

versus

So that you can receive your payment book as quickly as possible, please sign and return this contract today.

**o.** I hope this rambling may be of some little assistance to you.

**p.** If you will send in your payment today, I will appreciate it.

**q.** We thank you in advance for your cooperation in this matter.

**r.** Fill out this form and return to me.

**s.** Trust that this will answer your question.

**t.** We regret that we are unable to be of further assistance to you.

**u.** As soon as you return the four completed proposals, I'll airmail one to Chicago for prompt rating. In this way you will receive the renewal as quickly as possible.

**v.** Again let me repeat how sorry I am to have not answered sooner.

**w.** Upon receipt of this information, I will advise.

**3.** Below is a message for you to evaluate. In your discussion:

    **a.** First decide on the purpose of the message.
    **b.** Then visualize the reader. Assume you have never met or had any previous communication with him.
    **c.** Now determine whether the organization of the body should follow the pattern for good news, bad news, or a request (either direct or persuasive).
    **d.** Jot down—word for word—the best opening and closing paragraph you can think of.

The president of the Port Commission of West Coast City sends this message to local firms that have business activities in the Far East.

```
Gentlemen

Recognizing the importance of vigorous efforts toward regaining
our city's prewar position in regard to trade with the Orient
and Far East, the Port of (City) is sending two of its people
to these areas in a few weeks.  Their primary job will be
traffic solicitation, promotion and public relations for the
Port of (City) and the (City) waterfront.

The two men who are going are Col. Dwight A. Henderson, man-
aging director of the port of (City), and Henry O. Aldrich, our
director of public relations.  Col. Henderson was chairman of
the executive committee of the Japanese Trade Fair in (City),
```

and Mr. Aldrich was managing director of the Fair.  The Japanese Trade Fair was a strong promotional effort on the part of this area, and these two men will follow up its effects while they are on this trip.  They will leave (City) on 3 February (year), and will spend about five weeks in Japan and one week in the Philippine Islands.  In addition, they will make calls in Formosa and Hong Kong, and possibly will visit other economically strategic spots.

Since your Business Activities touch the above areas in whole or in part, it is thought that possibly you will wish to provide Col. Henderson and Mr. Aldrich with the names of people it would be of value for them to contact.  You might, in some instances, wish to provide them with letters of introduction.  They will make every effort to contact people you suggest, for we are vitally interested in doing all we can to promote trade through this Port by promoting trade for the people doing business through our gateway.

4. A college administrator refused to answer the following inquiry from Mr. Lukas, whose letterhead stationery states "Law Offices, Irving A. Lukas." Try to figure out the missing information that caused the receiver not to reply.

Dear Sir:

Will you please be good enough to advise me of the following, either by separate letter, or, for your convenience, by inserting answers in the spaces allotted for same alongside or below my questions.

1. Does your curriculum contain a separate and distinct course solely devoted to:  chain store-(retail) operation, organization and administration.

2. Is this course given to undergraduates; postgraduates; advanced students.

3. Is this course also given: in the evening_____; summer extension_____.
4. What is the duration of this course:
5. May this course be taken without any other course:
6. What are the requirements for an applicant to qualify for this course?

7. What are the names of the professors or instructors in charge of, or teaching this course?

The above data will be greatly appreciated.  Please respond to my residence listed below my signature.

5. On the following page is the original of the letter previously shown on page 22. Study both letters and explain why the revised message is easier to read.

Dear Sir:

Mr. Peter Hanenberger, who worked in your pharmacy from January 1969 until July 1971, has applied to us for a position as Chief Pharmacist. We are opening a new 320-bed teaching and research hospital on May 1, 1972, and in the latter part of this year we hope to bring in a Chief Pharmacist to join a young and aggressive organization interested in making this hospital one of the leaders in the country.

As the personal qualifications and technical skill of this individual are requisite to such a responsible job, we certainly will appreciate it if you could give us a written evaluation of Mr. Hanenberger based on his performance on the job while with you. We would like to know if your records show, or if you know from personal contact, that Mr. Hanenberger has the ability or potential to organize a pharmacy in a modern and well-equipped 320-bed hospital devoted to teaching and research from scratch.

Since this job will demand a tremendous amount of initiative and working capacity, we would like your frank evaluation of Mr. Hanenberger as a worker. What would you say is the sustained quality of his work?

Should he later on have people working under his direction, would he have the ability to organize them into a tightly knit and happy working group? We would especially like to know if he is liked and respected by subordinates, associates, and supervisors.

If you can indicate some of the duties he performed, we would be able to determine whether his experience will fit our needs.

Any comments you can add to help us make a valid appraisal of Mr. Hanenberger as a candidate for this position will be appreciated. We enclose a stamped, self-addressed envelope for your convenience.

6. Below is a message from an insurance broker to a customer. Is the letter good, poor, or just average? Why? Defend your decision with logical reasons.

Dear Mr. Jacobsen

I am pleased to enclose your renewal automobile policy No. AU123456789 written by the Federal Insurance Company.

This policy provides liability and physical damage coverage for your 1971 Ford Thunderbird. The annual premium charge for this coverage is $187.00. Our invoice No. 98765 for $74.00 represents the first installment premium payment for this renewal coverage. A certificate copy of this policy has been sent to the Rainier Branch of the City National Bank.

Please contact me if you have any questions, and thank you for letting us represent you.

**7.** Collect five one-page business letters—each preferably 100 words or more. If possible, try to get messages that are individually typed—not processed form letters. Study the body of each message for the following:

  **a.** Purpose—is it crystal clear?
  **b.** Which organizational pattern should the message follow?
  **c.** Is the opening paragraph appropriate?
  **d.** Does the closing paragraph carry its load?
  **e.** Notice the length of the paragraphs. The first and last should not exceed five to seven typewritten lines. The maximum length for all other paragraphs should not be much more than 10 typewritten lines each.
  **f.** Did the writer try to visualize (consider) the reader?

Be sure to keep these letters after this assignment because you'll be using them again and again for other purposes. For example, you'll check them for trite expressions, clarity, correctness, and other areas as you study these particular topics.

**8.** The following set of letters consists of an inquiry from a church to a bank and a reply to the inquiry.

  **a.** Determine what the purpose of the reply should be. *reject*
  **b.** Evaluate the opening and closing of the reply. *A.* *B. good*
  **c.** Determine if the reply includes the ideas necessary to fulfill the purpose and whether these ideas are organized effectively. *yes)*

*Inquiry*

    Gentlemen

    We would like to request your permission to post a church directional sign (Seventh Day Adventist Church) with directional arrow at the edge of your property-parking lot on First Avenue, near Central.

    This is an attractive small sign on a neatly painted post. This is very important to our church because of the fact that Central Street is probably the shortest street in (city). The size of the sign is about 15" x 15".

    The exact location of the sign will be specified to us as soon as we bring written permission from you from our office to Mr. Smith at City Hall. He will then advise us as to how and where to place the sign so that it will give a good appearance and not interfere with either traffic or your business operations.

    Please indicate your permission hereon and return your reply to this office as soon as possible.

    We appreciate your cooperation.

*Reply*

My dear Reverend Glouster

Thank you for your recent letter requesting permission to post
a church directional sign in the corner of our parking lot on
First Avenue near Central.

Unauthorized parking in the lot during our business hours has
been a continuous problem for our bank.  The parking lot
already has several signs posted for different purposes.  An
additional sign in this corner of the parking lot could cause
the public confusion regarding the use of the parking area.
We, therefore, find it necessary to decline your request.

Your parishioners are welcome to continue to use this parking
lot on Saturdays and at other times that you have church
services which do not conflict with the business hours of the
bank.  We appreciate and wish to continue the cordial relationship with you and members of your church.

# CHAPTER 3

# Business Writing Principles I

- Correctness
- Conciseness
- Clarity
- Exercises

After you have considered the five thinking steps discussed in the previous chapter, you are ready to communicate with your reader. But just what is communication? It is certainly more than simply asking or telling other people to do something, or informing them. It is a two-way channel for transmitting and sharing ideas, facts, plans, commands, policies, suggestions, and reports. It is two-way because you transmit your message with the hope of getting the desired reaction and response from your listener or reader. Some examples of particular messages, with the desired response to each one, are shown below:

| *Message* | *Desired response* |
|---|---|
| request | have request granted |
| collection | get money or at least have the debtor explain |
| sales | eventually sell article or product |
| application for job | receive request for interview |
| complaint | receive a fair adjustment |
| adjustment | keep goodwill of customer |
| refusal | say no and still keep goodwill of the individual |
| directive | get employee acceptance of a company policy |

Not only must you keep in mind that communication is a two-way process, you must also remember that people—and hence the receivers of your message—tend to react according to their attitude toward a set of facts rather than the facts themselves. Good examples of attitudes that can influence people's reaction toward messages directed to them are their feelings about war, generation gap, hippies, civil rights, women's liberation, and other controversial subjects. People also tend to react more according to their attitude toward the *source* of the facts than to the facts themselves. A staunch Democrat will more likely accept a fellow Democrat's idea than he will the same idea presented by a Republican. Similarly, employees and customers will react more favorably to a manager's communications when they respect him, have confidence in his integrity, and believe he is aware of their needs. In fact, all of us are conditioned in our reactions by feelings—regardless of how hard we try to be objective.

Hence communication is a human relations process—you deal with human beings with feelings when you communicate. Effective communication depends not so much on writing skills as on insights into human nature and the force of reactions among people. At the root of good communication is understanding and respect for the other person's feelings and attitudes. Only that understanding and respect will form a basis for good communication.

Remember that your communications reflect your personality, and it is always desirable for you to show the following in your messages:

Intelligence and sound judgment in the choice of ideas and facts

Good humor and understanding—even in dealing with the unjustly insulting reader

Integrity, backed up by a sound code of ethics

Reasonable facility with the English language

In business, words are working tools. If they're direct, forceful, clear, simple, concise, and considerate, they will do the job. But if the words used are dull, sluggish, confused, wordy, and inconsiderate, they fail—or at least don't perform the job as effectively as they should. People do not read what they find hard or dull.

To choose the words you use in letters and reports, you need to consider, after the thinking steps, certain specific writing principles, called the seven C's in this text: correctness, conciseness, clarity, courtesy, consideration, completeness, and concreteness. Used properly, these principles will aid you greatly in writing effective messages. This chapter covers the first three C's—correctness, conciseness, and clarity—and Chapter 4 discusses the remaining four C's.

## CORRECTNESS

The discussion begins with correctness because so many people have a distorted concept of this principle. They think that proper grammar, punctuation, and spelling comprise "correctness." The truth is that you can be correct grammatically and mechanically in every respect, and still insult or lose a customer.

In its broadest sense, the term "correctness," as applied to a business letter or report, means:

1. Using the correct level of language
2. Including only accurate facts, words, and figures
3. Using acceptable writing mechanics
4. Applying correctly all other pertinent C qualities

### Levels of Language

How correct should your English be when you dictate or write a letter or report? The following discussion on the levels of language attempts to answer this question. As Figure 3-1 shows, there are three overlapping levels.[1]

---

[1] These levels overlap because of our ever-changing language. Some words once considered substandard have moved into the informal level, and some once informal words are now acceptable on a formal level.

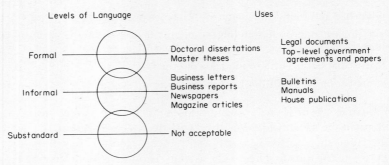

Figure 3-1

The first two—formal and informal language—are both correct; but they are quite different from one another, have different uses, and should not be interchanged.

The formal level of language is used for writing a scholarly dissertation, a legal document, or other material for which formality is expected. The phrases used are often long, unconversational, and impersonal—just what the term "formal" implies. In contrast, the informal level refers to the language of business—the language of letters, reports, newspapers, and other business communications. Such language is alive and ever-changing. Instead of the long words found on the formal level, you will use short, well-known, and conversational words, as the following list illustrates:

| *Formal* | *Informal* |
|---|---|
| terminate | end |
| domicile | home |
| deem | think (or believe) |
| transpire | happen |
| conflagration | fire |
| edifice | building |
| endeavor | try |
| obtain, procure | get |
| peruse | read or study |
| remunerate | pay |
| utilize | use |
| subsequent | next or following |
| ascertain | find out |
| contingent upon | depending on |
| anticipate | expect |
| interrogate | ask |

Obviously, if you were talking to someone, you would be more likely to use the words in the informal column. Similarly, in business writing, the words in the informal column are much more appropriate then those in the formal column. As Mr. Eddie Miller so appropriately said, "Write for your readers, not for posterity. The reports you do will not be engraved on bronze plates for future generations. They will be sent to somebody to read."[1]

Given below are comparisons of stiff, cold, wordy writing with friendlier, conversational, informal usage.

| *Formal* | *Informal* |
|---|---|
| Will attain the age of 18 years. | Will be 18 years old. |
| Render us more detail (sounds like lard). | Send us more information. |
| We will institute a mail search. | We will ask the post office to send out a tracer. |
| We thank you in anticipation of this courtesy and assure you that it will be a pleasure to serve you in a similar manner. | I'll appreciate your helping us. Let me know when I can return the favor. |
| Inform me of your intentions as to the liquidation of this balance. | Let me know when you can settle this account. |
| Should the supply of stickers sent you not be sufficient to meet your requirements, application should be made to this office for additional copies. | Pete, if you need more stickers, ask for them. |
| In order to substantiate our desire to accommodate our guests, we would appreciate your cooperation to anticipate your credit requirements before departure. | Please let us know in advance if you want us to cash a check as you leave. |
| Give consideration to a plan. | Consider a plan. |
| This plan will effect a savings of $10,000. | This plan will save $10,000. |
| To effect certain modifications in a procedure contingent upon the concurrence of management. | To make certain changes if management agrees. |
| The conclusions ascertained from a perusal of the pertinent data is that a lucrative market exists for the product in this vicinity. | The data studied show that the product is in good demand in this area. |

The following poem by Enid C. Stickel provides a humorous example of how people try to put on airs.

[1] Eddie Miller (Director, Speakers Service Department of the American Medical Association), "Quotables," *Civil Service Journal*, October–December, 1970, p. 23.

*Readability Gap*

Colleges aren't schools,
They are learning institutions;
Problems don't have answers,
They have viable solutions.
People don't spend money,
They re-allocate resources.
Newsmen don't use tipsters,
They rely on informed sources.

Speakers don't make speeches,
They give oral presentations.
Bosses don't see quotas,
They just indicate objectives.
Workers don't take orders,
Though they implement directives.

Machinery can't break down,
But components can malfunction.
A court does not command
It just issues an injunction.
Programs don't have failures,
They have qualified successes.
And jargon doesn't hurt you—
It just constantly distresses!

The formal and informal levels of language also differ in several other ways. On the formal level you don't dare end a sentence with a preposition or use contractions, but on the informal level you may do either or both. And if anyone questions you, quote Winston Churchill, who said, "This is the sort of damned pedantic nonsense up with which I will not put." Also, on the formal level, you wouldn't say "to accurately check" because you'd be splitting (putting one or more words between) the infinitive "to check." But on the informal level you can split infinitives if so doing will give your reader a better sense of what you're trying to convey. For example, take the following two expressions: "*to check* accurately" and "*to* accurately *check*." If you think you're communicating more meaningfully with the latter, use it. Say, "Joe, the boss wants you to accurately check these figures before the meeting."

Like most things in life, English is alive and ever-changing. Even the dictionaries can't keep up with its fast pace. In school you probably learned the difference between "farther," meaning actual distance, and "further," meaning abstract relationships of degree or quality. Now there is little distinction between these two words, according to Perrin's *Writer's Guide and Index to English*, one leading grammar book which has changed with the times. Listed below are other changes that are acceptable, as well as expressions that are often confused in usage.[1]

---

[1] Adapted from WRITER'S GUIDE AND INDEX TO ENGLISH by Porter G. Perrin. Copyright 1965 by Scott, Foresman and Company. Reprinted by permission.

| | |
|---|---|
| a, an | Use *a* before a word that begins with the consonant sound or long "u." Use *an* before a word that begins with a silent "h" or a vowel sound. |
| all ready, already | *All ready* means entirely ready; *already,* previously. |
| agree to, agree with | You *agree to* a plan and *agree with* a person. One thing *agrees with* another thing. |
| all right, alright | Always use *all right.* |
| a.m., A.M. | *a.m.* is easier to type and seems less noticeable than the capital letters. Save A.M. and P.M. for headlines and tables. |
| advise, tell | You give counsel when you *advise,* and you inform without counseling when you *tell.* |
| amount, number | Whenever you count the units, use *number. Amount* refers to bulk, weight, or sums. |
| anxious, eager | *Anxious* implies worry, whereas *eager* conveys keen desire. |
| between, among | As a rule *between* involves two people or two groups; *among,* three or more. |
| claims, says | *Claim* as a verb means "to ask for what is due one": He claimed his baggage at the station. |
| continual, continuous | *Continual* means to occur frequently. *Continuous* means without stopping. |
| data | You can safely use a singular verb (data *is*) with this word when you are considering all the facts as a unit. |
| different from different than | Although both are acceptable, *different from* is preferred. |
| due to, because of | These words are interchangeable on the informal level. |
| effect, affect | Only *effect* is a noun; it means result, condition or influence. Both words are verbs—to *effect* is to bring about, to *affect* is to influence. |
| farther, further | In informal English little distinction is made between the two words. Today *further* means both physical distance as well as abstract relationships of degree or quantity. |
| fewer, less | If you can count the items, use *fewer; less* refers to amount or quantity. |
| healthful, healthy | *Healthful* means giving health; *healthy* means having good health. |
| imply, infer | *Imply* means to assume, insinuate, or suggest; *infer* means to conclude. A writer *implies,* whereas the reader *infers.* |

| | |
|---|---|
| lie, lay, lain<br>lay, laid, laid | A man or a rug *lies* on the floor, but a man *lays* the book on the table or *lays* himself on the floor. If you can substitute "place(s)," use the proper tense of *lay*. |
| like, as | Used as conjunctions, they are interchangeable. |
| loan, lend | Although these words are interchangeable as verbs, some people prefer to use lend as a verb and loan as a noun. |
| off, off of | *Of* is a wasted word—omit it after "off." |
| party, customer | A *customer* is an individual or person. *Party* is a legal term for an individual or a group of people. |
| please, kindly | As a rule, use *please*. *Kindly* means "in a kind manner." If you say, kindly tell me, you are really asking someone to tell you something in a kind way. |
| principal, principle | *Principal* means "chief" or "main." Whenever you can substitute rule, use princip*le*. In all other instances, use princip*al*. |
| provided, providing | *Provided* means "if"; otherwise use *providing*. |
| proved, proven | Either is correct. He has *proved* his point; he has *proven* his point. |
| shall, will | Because few people know the difference between these two words, *will* is gradually replacing *shall*. Also some people think "shall" sounds pompous or formal. |
| toward, towards | Identical in meaning. *Toward* is used more frequently in the United States, whereas *towards* is the British spelling. |
| we, I | *We* means the organization; *I* refers to the individual. |
| which, that, who | *That* refers to persons or things; *who* to people; *which* only to things. |

The third level of language—substandard—is the one you want to avoid, because people generally don't accept it. If you use words on this level in writing (or in speaking), your reader(s) will begin to question your overall ability to use good English. Here are a few examples:

| *Substandard* | *Acceptable* |
|---|---|
| ain't | isn't, aren't |
| hadn't ought | shouldn't |
| irregardless | regardless |
| should of | should have |
| nohow | anyway |
| in regards to | regarding |
| can't hardly | can hardly |
| between you and I | between you and me |
| where . . . at | where . . . |
| haven't got | don't have |

The following sentences illustrate the three levels of language discussed above—formal, informal and substandard:

*Formal:*      Although Item 21 is enumerated in the report, the writer has ascertained that it is currently not in the organization's inventory or in the writer's possession.

*Informal:*     Although Item 21 is listed in the report, it's not in our stock now and I don't have it either.

*Substandard:* Irregardless of the report that item ain't on our shelves now, and I haven't got it either.

## Accurate Facts, Words, and Figures

Doubtless you already know how important absolute accuracy is for written messages. One erroneous digit (for example, $65,000 instead of $75,000) can make a difference of thousands of dollars. Even small errors of a few cents can be annoying to customers and undermine goodwill, as various examples in this text will show. And a wrong figure in an account number muddles up records and leads to untold problems.

Perhaps you recall reading about a telephone directory error involving two firms in a city of over a half million persons. The directory mixed up the phone number of one firm with that of a competitor. To make matters worse, each of these firms happened to have a department head with the same name. You can imagine the confusion that telephone-listing error caused! It was also costly for the telephone company because the firms rightly demanded that the company individually inform all customers and potential customers of the correct numbers—at its own expense.

Or take the following letter that a college student wrote to the registrar of a large university. No doubt the unfortunate use of incorrect words in the last sentence gave the receiving office a good laugh—but at the expense of the sender:

```
Dear Sir;

I would appreciate your sending me a catalog in the field
of Business Administration or a General Catalog for the
current year.  I must know all the requirements for out-of-
state students to enroll and any other derogatory information
that may be pertinent to my perspective enrollment in
January of 1971.
```

To be sure of the accuracy of your facts, you should verify all statements before writing and again before you sign or approve the message. Of course, you also need to be up-to-date on laws that affect your organization. Guessing or assuming that you are right can be costly. Just because a certain fact was true about a customer last year—or even last month—does not assure it is true now, as the following case illustrates:

> Mr. Henry Simson sent in a claim for medical benefits to his insurance company. In turn, the correspondent handling the case wrote back to Mr. Simson, saying, "We are pleased to enclose a check for $277.54 for benefits due you because of your confinement at the Mountain View Hospital." Unfortunately this correspondent shouldn't have sent the check because that hospital was not certified as a full "general" hospital, a requirement under the terms of Mr. Simson's policy. Innocently, Mr. Simson cashed the check.
>
> A month later the mistake was discovered and a notation made on Simson's file to the effect that no future payments were to be made because of confinement to the Mountain View Hospital.
>
> Two months afterwards Mr. Simson again sent a claim for medical benefits because he once again had been a patient in that same hospital. The man who handled the claim this time consulted Simson's file, found the notation, and wrote a letter refusing the claim.
>
> However, this refusal was wrong because between Simson's two admissions the Mountain View Hospital had been certified as a full "general" hospital. Had the correspondents at the insurance company checked all the facts, such a mix-up would not have happened.

The good business writer must be continually alert to accuracy because of changing rates, regulations, laws, and conditions both locally and nationally.

### Acceptable Writing Mechanics

This principle of correctness includes effective use of the parts of the letter and report (covered in detail in Chapter 5) and acceptable spelling, sentence structure, punctuation, capitalization, and appearance. Businessmen expect you to use acceptable writing mechanics—and *misuse* of these mechanics is a "pet peeve" of many people in the business world.

This book does not attempt to teach you grammar and the numerous other components of mechanical correctness. Years of training in English throughout grade school, high school, and college should have taught you to write grammatically acceptable sentences and paragraphs. Therefore, this text begins where a grammar usually ends. But if you need review on the dangling participle, numbers as words or figures, punctuation, and other details that seem to plague writers, you'll find helpful suggestions in the Appendix. And if you need help on the parts of speech and sentence structure, be sure to consult an excellent grammar like Perrin's *Writer's Guide and Index to English*.[1]

---

[1] Porter G. Perrin, *Writer's Guide and Index to English*, 4th ed., Scott, Foresman and Company, Glenview, Ill., 1965.

One of the most common weaknesses in writing mechanics is inability to spell correctly many everyday words—such as convenience, questionnaire, receive, accommodation, stationery, and dessert. Businessmen and customers expect you to spell correctly and may begin to question your overall ability if you misspell—especially such simple words. Don't embarrass yourself the way one graduate did when he stated in his application letter that he had a Batchelor of Arts degree. The receiver encircled the misspelled word with a red pencil and pinned the letter on the company bulletin board for every passer-by to see.

The following letter is an example of a communication that might lead the receiver (Lt. Bowser) to question the overall ability of the sender (a motel manager) and even assume that carelessness is the reason for many mistakes that occur in the motel office.

```
Dear Lt. Booser

I'am writing this letter telling you how sorry I'am about the
mistake this office and myself made concerning our business
tranaction on May 30th and the letter wich was send to you.

Please accept my apology for the mistake made to you.  Your
bill was paid in full, but the two checks tranaction were
mis-led.  My nite cashier remember very clearly that you paid
the bill, but my nite man did not sign the bill paid, which
was place on the bookkepper's deck.

Again I'am sorry about this situation, and will you please come
in the next time you are this way, and wish to thank you
personally about the whole deal.
```

If you are one of the many educated men and women who are better able to solve complicated business problems than spell correctly, you can take two precautions: refer to a dictionary often, and hire a topnotch secretary who's a whiz at spelling! English spelling does have many inconsistencies, as the following anonymous poem entitled "Pluralistics" highlights:

*Pluralistics*

We'll begin with a box and the plural is boxes,
But the plural of ox should be oxen not oxes.
Then one fowl is a goose but two are called geese,
Yet the plural of mouse should never be meese.
You may find a lone mouse or a whole set of mice,
But the plural of house is houses not hice.
If the plural of man is always called men,
Shouldn't the plural of pan be called pen?
If I speak of a foot and you show me your feet,
And I give you a boot would a pair be called beet?

If one is a tooth and whole set are teeth,
Why should not the plural of booth be called beeth?
Then one may be that and three would be those,
Yet hat in that plural wouldn't be hose.
And the plural of cat is cats and not cose.
We speak of a brother and also of brethren,
But though we say Mother we never say Methren,
Then the masculine pronouns are he, his, and him,
But imagine the feminine, she, shis, and shim.
So English I fancy, you all will agree,
Is the funniest language you ever did see.

Correctness in writing is important because it influences the reader in various ways. In the first place, he *expects* you to write correctly, and you create a bad impression when you abuse the language. In the second place, a poorly constructed sentence, a misspelled word (especially a customer's name!!), incorrect punctuation, and faulty diction distract the reader's attention. When he opens your letter, you want him to concentrate on the message—not on the blunders. Finally, incorrectness frequently results in ambiguity, misleading statements, or misunderstandings, as illustrated below:

Mr. Jones visited the school yesterday and lectured on "Destructive Pests." A large number were present.

From a newspaper column on advice to teen-agers: "Keep jewelry to a very minimum—and leave errings to your older sisters."

Sign in a New York Drugstore: We Dispense with Accuracy.

Pierce Eugene Puckett, B.A., M.A.—Assistant Professor and Aching Head, Department of Education.

Two suburbs of a certain city, believe it or not, are named Manly and Fertile. This led to a famous headline on the society page: Manly youth weds Fertile girl.

This sum will be paid you in a single amount at the time of your death, which we understand is what you prefer.

Enclosed are your contracts and Gary Greenwood in triplicate.

Your Memorial Day speech will be followed by the firing squad.

We have been authorized to make monthly advances to Miss Smith.

You should always watch for the little things in writing—for correctness in grammar and mechanics—as well as for the big things. And never leave the mechanical principles of correctness solely to your secretary. Once you sign your name or initials to the message, you assume the responsibility for everything on the page—including correctness.

## CONCISENESS

Many businessmen believe that conciseness is the most important writing principle, because a wordy message requires more time (and money) to type and to read. A businessman's time is precious. He wants to scan quickly the contents of the letters and reports he receives and at the same time retain as much of the content as possible on first reading. In addition, if a message rambles on to two pages when one would be adequate, it occupies more space in the already scarce and expensive filing cabinets and other storage areas.

Conciseness is saying what you have to say in the fewest possible words without sacrificing completeness and courtesy. If completeness and courtesy are omitted, the result is abruptness—not conciseness—as the following examples illustrate.

*Abrupt letter*

Dear Mr. Greiner:

Have you emptied your safe deposit box? If you have, sign the enclosed cancellation form and return it with the keys to the box.

If you are using the box, send us your check for $6 to pay the rent from September 15, 1971, to September 15, 1972.

*Concise letter*

Dear Mr. Greiner:

This is just a reminder that the rent on your safe deposit box has expired.

If you wish to use the box another year, please send in your check for $6. You'll then be paid up until September 15, 1972. If you have no further use for the box at this time, just sign and return the enclosed form with the keys.

Whenever we can help you with any of our other customer services, please let me know.

It is true that the concise letter just given requires more words than the abrupt message. But the end result is what counts—how the reader reacts. A reader might respond to the first sentence of the abrupt letter mentally by saying it's none of your business. He would not respond that way to the other message. Also, the "please" in the revision helps keep the reader from feeling that he is being ordered to do something.

Now consider the following contrast between a wordy and a concise version of the same resolution:[1]

*Wordy* (60 words)
Resolved, that appropriate steps be taken by the American Medical Association to encourage recruitment into the health professions of health-oriented personnel released from the armed services, that the cooperation of allied health professions and vocations be sought in this effort, and that such action be referred to the Board of Trustees and its Council on Health Manpower for implementation.[1]

*Concise* (21 words)
Resolved, that the Council on Health Manpower work with other health organizations to attract former military medical corpsmen into health careers.

Always keep in mind that the reader doesn't want to read any more than necessary. Yet he expects you to give him sufficient facts and to treat him with courtesy. Frequently you can shorten a message by including an enclosure; for example, you can hold a sales letter or a job application letter to one page by enclosing a brochure or resume, respectively. And in a report you can often put facts, tables, and other information in the appendix.

The busy executive has so many letters, memos, and reports demanding his concentration and action that he cannot tolerate wordiness. Many businessmen have an understanding with their staff that every report they read must be kept to one page; and if it is longer, the writer must place at the beginning of the report a one-page abstract or summary that highlights or condenses the entire report. Otherwise, time would not permit the busy executive to read the many pieces of data or information requiring his attention.

On the other hand, if you go to the other extreme—abruptness—you may have to write a follow-up letter (which costs another $3.19 if individually dictated). The right approach—the happy medium—is to say courteously and completely what you have to say in the fewest possible words. To achieve conciseness—the opposite of wordiness—try to observe the following suggestions:

1. Omit trite expressions.
2. Avoid unnecessary repetition.
3. Prune obviously wordy expressions.
4. Include only relevant facts.
5. Organize effectively.

This section on conciseness discusses the first four points. Succeeding chapters cover organization.

[1] Eddie Miller, "Quotables," *Civil Service Journal*, October–December, 1970, p. 23.

## Omit Trite Expressions

Trite expressions (also called hackneyed words, clichés, stereotyped expressions, deadwood, whiskered words) are usually longer than necessary, and have become stiff, formal, and relatively meaningless because of overuse. They still exist in business because correspondents think they are acceptable or refuse to exert the extra energy to replace them with more up-to-date terms.

How or why does one begin using trite expressions? If you had to write a letter at work and didn't have the training you are acquiring now, you'd probably begin by studying the wording of messages in existing files—and probably the writers of those old letters used the same language, full of colorless, worn-out expressions.

The left column below lists some ancient barnacles that have attached themselves to the language of letters and reports; the expressions in the right-hand column are generally shorter and certainly more conversational.

| *Not this* | *But this* |
|---|---|
| advise (unless you mean to counsel) | tell, inform |
| above-captioned loan | this loan, Mr. Smith's loan |
| as per your request | as you requested |
| enclosed herewith | enclosed |
| enclosed you will find | enclosed is |
| it has come to my attention | I have just learned (or) Mr. Jones has just told me |
| kindly (for please) | please |
| Our Mr. Smith | Mr. Smith, our credit manager |
| please be advised that | (4 wasted words) |
| please don't hesitate to call upon us | please write us |
| please feel free to write | please write |
| prior to | before |
| pursuant to your inquiry | as you requested |
| the undersigned (the writer) | I (or me) |
| this is to advise you | (5 wasted words) |
| under separate cover | by June 1, tomorrow, separately, by parcel post, by Railway Express |

"Cy" Frailey, one of the pro's in the writing-for-business field, wrote the following little gem of a poem chock-full of such worn-out expressions:[1]

We beg to advise and wish to state
That yours has arrived of recent date.
We have it before us, its contents noted;
Herewith enclosed are the prices we quoted.
Attached please find, as per your request,

---

[1] Actually he wrote these words for "The Whisker Song" to the tune of "Believe Me, If All Those Endearing Young Charms"—to call attention to the "Gay Nineties" style of writing business letters.

The data you wanted; and let us suggest
Your order be sent, and not held unduly,
We beg to remain, yours most truly.

The expressions above are only a few examples of the many clichés to avoid. On pages 58–59 and in the Appendix are others which should not be used in effective business writing. Don't try to memorize these words; read them carefully once or twice at one sitting and then again at the end of 30 or 60 days. Then perhaps you will remember to exclude these worn-out expressions from your writing.

You should eliminate these trite expressions from your writing for at least four reasons:

1. They usually result in a wordy message—sometimes twice as long as it ought to be. This wordiness steals the time of both the writer and the reader.

2. A letter loaded with trite expressions can give the reader the wrong impression of the sender. An individual might be young and friendly—but his writing might depict him as old and crabby; for example, the letter opening below doesn't give the reader a favorable reaction to the sender or his bank:

    In accordance with your request of recent date, we are enclosing herewith our cashier's check in the amount of $103.60, representing a withdrawal of said savings account No. 12345.

    *Improved revision:* It's a pleasure to fulfill your request of July 19 by enclosing our cashier's check for $103.60. This amount represents a withdrawal from your savings in Account 12345.

3. Certain trite expressions are quite irritating to some people. Using them is comparable to waving a red cloth in front of a bull.

4. Some of these expressions actually don't make sense. For example, what does the following sentence mean to you: "Thank you for your letter of *20th inst.*"? (The last abbreviation stands for "instant," or present month; *ult.* represents "ultimo," or last month. Isn't it much better to write, "April 20" and "March" if these are the months you're referring to?)

How do you break the habit of using worn-out expressions? Please do not try to eliminate all of them instantly. One good approach is for you to type 10 of them on a small piece of paper and place the list in a conspicuous place on your desk. Every time you write a message, look at these words—and make sure you don't use them. Once you have eliminated these ten from your vocabulary, try another 10 and then another—until you are satisfied you have rid yourself of all the offending clichés.

Not all such expressions undermine business writing to the same degree. Far from it! Some expressions *do* weaken writing whenever they appear

—such as *beg to state, contents noted, hoping to hear from you I am, pursuant to your request, the undersigned,* and *valued letter.* On the other hand, some expression—for example, *for your convenience, per,* and *for your information*—can be trite in some situations and acceptable in others, as shown below.

| *Trite* | *Acceptable* |
|---|---|
| Enclosed is an envelop *for your convenience.* | During December we're open Monday through Friday until 9 p.m. *for your convenience* in late afternoon and evening shopping. |
| As *per* your request, I am glad to tell you . . . | This car was speeding 80 miles *per* hour at the time of impact. |
| *For your information,* I wish to state that . . . | This material is *for your information* only. There is no need for you to consider any action. |

## Avoid Unnecessary Repetition

Sometimes repetition is necessary for emphasis. But when the same thing is said two or three times without reason, the letter becomes wordy. The following letter from a businessman to a firm from which he had bought for five years shows unnecessary repetition at its worst:

Dear Mr. Reymore:

Will you ship us sometime, any time during the month of October, or even November if you are rushed, for November would suit us just as well, in fact a little bit better, 300 of the regular 3" by 15" blue felt armbands with white sewn letters in the center.

Thanking you to send these along to us by parcel post, and not express, as express is too stiff in price, when parcel post will be much cheaper, we are

The writer took 81 words to say what is said in 25 below:

Please ship parcel post, by the end of November, 300 regular 3" by 15" blue felt armbands with white sewn letters in the center.

Some expressions are repetitious because they include useless words that in no way improve the meaning. Examples of such expressions, with suggested improvements, are given below.

| Repetitious | Concise |
|---|---|
| a long period of time | a long time |
| censensus of opinion | censensus |
| continue on | continue |
| continuous and uninterrupted | continuous (or uninterrupted) |
| cooperate together | cooperate |
| during the year of 1971 | during 1971 |
| each and every | each (or every) |
| endorse on the back of this check | endorse this check |
| exactly identical | identical |
| finish up | finish |
| for a price of $200 | for $200 |
| for two hundred dollars ($200) | for $200 |
| free gratis | free (or gratis) |
| grateful and appreciative | grateful (or appreciative) |
| immediately and at once | immediately (or at once) |
| in (for) the amount of $200 | for $200 |
| in the city of Chicago | in Chicago |
| refuse and decline | refuse (or decline) |
| refer back | refer |
| repeat again | repeat |
| sincere and earnest | sincere (or earnest) |

Here are two additional ways to eliminate unnecessary repetition:

1. Use pronouns rather than repeating nouns: Instead of "The East Coast Fire Insurance Company, Inc.," again and again, use "it" or "they."
2. Use a shorter name after you have mentioned the long one once: Instead of "The Inter-Allied Johnson Manufacturing Company," use "the Johnson Company."

## Prune Obviously Wordy Expressions

In addition to worn-out and repetitive expressions, other words contribute nothing to understanding. Included in this category are "gobbledygook'" expressions, and pompous, excessively long phrases. "Gobbledygook" language refers to words that waste the reader's time by requiring him to read several words when one word would be satisfactory, as the list below shows:

| Wordy | Concise |
|---|---|
| according to our records | we find |
| along the line of (salary) | about (salary) |
| at this time | now |
| due to the fact that | because |
| during the time that | while |
| for the purpose of | for, to |
| for the reason that | since (or because) |
| from the point of view of | as |

| | |
|---|---|
| have need for | need |
| in accordance with your request | as you requested |
| in all cases | always |
| inasmuch as | since (or because) |
| in case | if |
| in connection with | by, in, for |
| in due course | soon |
| in many cases | often, frequently |
| in most cases | usually |
| in order to | to |
| in other cases | sometimes |
| in regard to | regarding |
| in some cases | sometimes |
| in spite of the fact that | even though, although |
| in such a manner that | so |
| in the event that | if |
| in the matter of | about |
| in the neighborhood of | about |
| in view of the fact that | because |
| is in the process of | is |
| it should be pointed out that | please notice that |
| make inquiry regarding | inquire |
| on the basis of | by |
| on the grounds that | because |
| under date of | dated |
| with reference to | on, about |
| with regard to | on, about |
| with respect to | about |
| with the result that | so that |

Conciseness contributes to emphasis. By eliminating unnecessary words, you help make important ideas stand out, as in the following sentences. [Notice that the concise sentence eliminates from half to two-thirds of the unnecessary words in the wordy sentence. (Figures in parentheses are the number of words.)]

*Wordy:* I am writing you at this time to enclose the postage paid appointment card for the purpose of arranging a convenient time when we might get together for a conference. (30)

*Concise:* Will you please return the enclosed card and name a convenient time for an interview? (15)

*Wordy:* The picture which is enclosed will give[1] you an idea of the appearance of this home. (16)

*Concise:* The enclosed picture illustrates[1] this home. (6)

*Wordy:* We hereby wish to let you know that we fully appreciate the confidence you have reposed in us. (18)

*Concise:* We appreciate your confidence in us. (6)

[1] Whenever possible, talk in the present tense.

Sometimes you can save words by eliminating unneeded articles, prepositions, and conjunctions.

| | |
|---|---|
| *The* evidence we have . . . | Evidence we have . . . |
| He said *that* he agreed. | He said he agreed. |
| The date *of the* policy | The policy date |
| *and* | Omit "and" and use a punctuation mark—; or . |

## Include Only Relevant Facts

A fourth way to be concise is to include only those ideas that develop the purpose of the letter or report. How long should a message be? Just long enough to do the job effectively. The relatively short letter to Mr. Reymore about armbands was quite wordy. Yet a two- or three-page letter can be concisely written. Keep in mind that no one wants to read any more than he has to, but at the same time, the writer must get the message across.

Given below are two extremes. The first message[1] (illustrated on page 61) shows how a writer can be so concise that he becomes absurd. The second is an example of excessive wordiness.

### Example 1

Once upon a time, a fish dealer was planning a new sign for his store. It was to read *Fresh Fish for Sale Here Today*. A critical friend, however, had some suggestions:

"You don't need the word 'here,'" he said. "People can see where the store is. And you don't need 'for sale' either. They know you're not giving things away."

The friend continued: "And how about 'fresh fish' and 'today'? Do you want customers to think this is the only day you have fresh fish? That you sell old fish on other days? Take out 'fresh.' And while you're at it, take out 'today.' People know you wouldn't be open if you weren't selling something today."

"You might as well drop 'fish' too. Anyone within half a mile can smell what you're selling."

The moral of our fish story? Write concisely but don't destroy your message.

### Example 2
The extremely wordy letter below is from a man who graduated from a university the previous year. It seems he has had difficulty since graduation in finding a satisfactory place in the business world. As you read his letter to the Placement Office in the School of Business Administration, try to figure out why he's having so much trouble.

[1] From *Effective Letters Bulletin*, New York Life Insurance Company, Spring, 1967, p. 1.

Dear Mrs. Martin:

The university Placement Office has sent me at periodic
intervals a form inquiring as to my current employment status.
As you may recall from our discussion last spring I was most
desirous of making a favorable change in vocational locale.
After following up several recommendations made by your office
(Goodwin, etc.) I was unable to negotiate an immediate change,
and upon receiving suave assurances of rapid promotion from
my superiors promptly regressed into the torpid complacency
which characterized my thinking upon graduation.  However my
present intention to move is more than a harbinger of that most
fragrant of seasons but rather stems from a feeling of dis-
illusionment and inadequacy with my vocational environment.

May I once again prevail upon you to assist me in this
undertaking by informing me at your convenience of any job
opportunity for which you think I would be well suited.  As
indicated in my last reply to your office, I no longer look to
accounting as my forte but instead am seeking a selling
situation which is both challenging and remunerative.

Thank you for your patience and understanding in this matter.
You may reach me at EM 5-1234 during the day or at EM 4-4321 in
the evening.

Few employers would risk hiring this man because he might talk and write
to customers in the same way he did in this letter. The reader or listener

reacts negatively toward him because he uses pompous words. His writing doesn't create the right image.

In contrast to this unfavorably pretentious message, the message could be informal and at the same time save his reader's time if it read as follows:

Dear Mrs. Martin

Will you please tell me about any sales opening which is both challenging and remunerative? I am no longer interested in an accounting job.

You can reach me at EM 5-1234 during the day or at EM 4-4321 in the evening. I shall appreciate your suggestions.

The major causes of irrelevancy include:

1. Not sticking to the purpose of the message.
2. Including information obvious to the reader—such as regurgitating at length what the reader told you.
3. Using big words to make an impression.
4. Beating around the bush—not coming to the point.
5. Using excessive adjectives (good writing uses concrete nouns, and verbs that show action, but avoids excessive numbers of adjectives and adverbs).
6. Being excessively polite.
7. Writing long, involved introductions.
8. Not limiting the scope of the material.
9. Including too much explanation.
10. Not revising the first draft of a long, complicated message.
11. Including unnecessary background information.

In summary, conciseness is a writing principle that the businessman considers especially important. It saves him time, and time is—or should be—scarce to anyone who spends a large part of his day dictating and reading letters, memos, and reports.

## CLARITY

Clarity involves most of the other principles of business writing—especially correctness, conciseness, completeness, and concreteness. Clarity means getting across your message to the reader so he will not misunderstand what you are trying to convey.

You want your reader to interpret your words with the same shades of meaning that you have in mind. And accomplishing that goal is difficult because individual experiences are never identical, and words have different meanings to different persons. The meaning of a word is in the person using it. "Criticize" to one person may mean to evaluate the good and the bad features; and to another, to consider only the bad. "Cheap" means the same as inexpensive to some; to others, it means inferior quality. The interpretations of "freedom of speech" range from saying anything, anywhere, any time to much more conservative and conventional views. Other words—among many—that have different meanings to people include capitalism, poverty, foreigner, communism, air pollution, and Vietnam.

Words have two different types of meanings: denotative and connotative. The denotative meaning is that which all individuals will probably agree on; the connotative meaning refers to the unique reaction that each individual will have to a particular word. Thus, the more you are aware of, careful about, and allow for individual, connotative interpretations, the more likely you will be able to communicate clearly.

Clarity involves formulating a clear purpose of the message and following a good organizational pattern. It also involves well-organized paragraphs, each with a good topic sentence; concrete words the reader understands; coherent, unified sentences; and correct mechanics. Mechanics is an important element by itself because it includes punctuation, spelling, listing of items (when listing helps the reader), tabulation of many figures into a table or other kinds of visual aid, and proper sentence structure.

Here are some specific ways to help make your writing clear:

1. Choose words that are short, familiar, conversational.
2. Construct effective sentences.
3. Point up the purpose of paragraphs and messages.
4. Include examples, illustrations, and other visual aids when desirable.

## Short, Familiar, Conversational Words

The section on conciseness has already emphasized that good writing eliminates trite and wordy expressions.[1] Omitting these expressions usually helps not only conciseness but also clarity. Furthermore, when you have a choice between a long word and a short one, use the short word, since you can be more sure that your reader will understand it.

Winston Churchill was a masterful writer who knew the secret and effectiveness of using simple words. After the disaster in Dunkirk in 1940, he (as Prime Minister of England) reported to Parliament in a message heard around the world. Below is a small part of what he said:

> We shall defend our island, whatever the cost may be. We shall fight on the beaches. We shall fight on the landing grounds. We shall fight in the fields and in the streets. We shall fight in the hills. We shall never surrender.[2]

He said what he meant and his message came across loud and clear to millions of people. But what if he had used language like the following?

[1] See Chapter 3, pp. 53 ff., and Appendix B, page 760.
[2] Eddie Miller, "Quotables," *Civil Service Journal*, October December, 1970, p. 23.

We shall oppose the aggressors through the optimal mobilization and implementation of all existing defense-oriented modalities.[1]

Certainly, those words would be long forgotten.

Besides being short, the words you use should be familiar to your reader. Remember that your reader is a busy man, and doesn't have time to run to the dictionary for meaning. Instead, he'll guess what you mean (sometimes incorrectly), or will disregard some or all the message.

Here is a story that involves clarity. A plumber wrote the National Bureau of Standards to tell them hydrochloric acid is good for cleaning out clogged drains. (Before you go any further into the story, visualize the plumber. Assume you don't know him or have never exchanged correspondence. It is a pretty good guess he isn't a college graduate—maybe he didn't finish high school. But he probably is a good plumber—at least conscientious—because he's writing to the Bureau to tell them something he thinks will help them.)

In reply to the plumber's message, a technical specialist of the Bureau wrote:

> The efficacy of hydrochloric acid is indisputable, but the corrosive residue is incompatible with metallic permanence.

The plumber then wrote to thank the Bureau for agreeing with him—when, of course, the Bureau was actually disagreeing with him. Sensing the plumber didn't understand, another member tried to set the man straight by writing:

> We cannot assume responsibility for the production of toxic and noxious residue with hydrochloric acid and suggest you use an alternative procedure.

Again the plumber thanked the Bureau. Then in desperation the head of the department wrote:

> Don't use hydrochloric acid. It eats hell out of the pipes.

The moral of this story is to write on—not above or below[2]—the level of the reader's understanding.

Avoid professional jargon. Your professional vocabulary contains words you've been accumulating since you began your business career, and these words are quite clear to you. Furthermore, your colleagues easily understand you when you use technical terms; and it's perfectly okay to use them when

---

[1] Eddie Miller, "Quotables," *Civil Service Journal*, October–December, 1970, p. 23.

[2] It is also possible to write so many noticeably short, short sentences and idiotic tiny words that the reader feels you are talking down to him. If you scan a page or two in a second-grade school reading book, you realize the length of sentence and choice of words are for beginners. Letters and reports for the business world have no place for "I see Jane. Tom sees Jane. Jane sees Tom and me."

talking or writing to people who also use them. But avoid this professional jargon when you talk or write to a man or woman not acquainted with such words. Notice that the sentences below (with the technical words in italics) are much clearer in the revision.

1. The *conversion privilege* of this term policy *terminates* June 5, 1972.
   *versus*
   Your right to change this policy to permanent insurance ends June 5, 1972.

2. *Days of grace* under this policy *expire* May 15, 1972.
   *versus*
   The extra 31 days allowed you to pay your premium without interest end May 15, 1972.

3. To *reinstate* your policy will require *proof of insurability*, etc.
   *versus*
   To get your policy back in good standing, you must (1) pass a satisfactory physical examination, (2) etc.

4. The policy provides that your insurance shall be *nonassignable.*
   *versus*
   The policy provides that your insurance shall not be transferable.

You are writing well when your reader can read the message fast and understand the contents the first time without having to ponder the meaning of a word, expression, or sentence.

How would you like to unscramble the following doubletalk?

It is necessary, for technical reasons, that these warheads should be stored upside down. That is, with the top at the bottom, and the bottom at the top. In order that there may be no doubt as to which is the bottom, and which is the top, for storage purposes it will be seen that the bottom of each warhead has been labeled with the word "TOP."

If you must use technical words that the reader may not understand, define them briefly and clearly. If you don't, you'll confuse, embarrass, or irritate the reader, and perhaps be forced to explain later. Here are a few technical words and the synonyms that a layman is more likely to understand:

| *Technical jargon* | *Expressions familiar to the layman* |
| --- | --- |
| abstract | history of the property |
| accrued interest | unpaid interest |
| annual premium | annual payment |
| arrears | behind, delinquent, unpaid |
| assessed valuation | value of property for tax purposes |
| charge to your principal | increase the balance of your loan |
| compound dividends | dividends earned on your deposits and added to your account, which then earns more dividends on the dividends and deposits |

| *Technical jargon* | *Expressions familiar to the layman* |
|---|---|
| conveying title | signing and recording a deed |
| easement for ingress and egress | agreement allowing passage in and out |
| escrow account | reserve account for taxes and insurance |
| hazard insurance | fire and windstorm insurance protection |
| interest compounded quarterly | interest added to your account every three months |
| maturity date | final payment date |
| net worth statement | statement of assets and liabilities |
| overdraft | overdrawn account |
| per diem | daily |

A politician—using "big, unfamiliar words to fool little people"—helped defeat his opponent by telling his audience:

> Are you aware that this candidate is known all over Washington as a shameless extrovert? Not only that, but this man is reliably reported to have practiced nepotism with his sister-in-law and he has a sister who was once a thespian in wicked New York. He matriculated with co-eds at the University, and it is an established fact that before his marriage he habitually practiced celibacy.

In addition to using short, familiar, nontechnical words to make your business writing clear, you should also use conversational words, as discussed above. When you're trying to decide whether certain words will be familiar and conversational for your reader, you can usually gain an idea from the language the reader uses in his letter to you. However, even this method can backfire— if your reader happens to be the type who changes personality when he switches from face-to-face conversation to writing.

Has the following ever happened to you? Say you meet a business acquaintance on the street, and he stops to chat and seems to bubble over with friendliness. In the conversation the two of you start talking about a business subject and he says he'll send you a memo (or letter) on his final decision. Then a day or two later you receive his message, which begins: "In compliance with our previous conversation concerning . . . , I wish to advise that . . ." What a contrast the written message is to the friendly face-to-face conversation! When you answer his letter, just be sure not to fall into his writing rut. Use modern, conversational, familiar words.

## Effective, Well-constructed Sentences

To write clearly and effectively, you should arrange your words in well-constructed sentences, aiming for unity, coherence, and emphasis. In addition, you must vary your sentence structure enough to avoid monotony; instead of using only simple sentences, sprinkle your writing with compound and complex sentences.

Unity in a sentence means that you have one main idea, and any other ideas in the sentence must be closely related to it. This fact is true for both complex and compound sentences. And be sure that the two independent clauses in each compound sentence are closely related in thought. "I like you" and "George Washington died in 1799" don't belong together. Also, in a complex sentence, the main idea belongs in the main (independent) clause.

The structure of the sentence, as well as the chosen words, should make the meaning clear. Don't fall into the trap that the poor fellow mentioned below did when he placed a classified ad in the newspaper:

> For sale: R. D. Smith has one sewing machine for sale. Phone 543-1111. Call after 7 p.m. and ask Mrs. Kelly who lives with him, cheap.

Naturally, the paper was more than willing to clear things up. Next day's retraction read:

> We regret having erred in R. D. Smith's ad yesterday. It should read: For sale, R. D. Smith, one sewing machine for sale. Cheap. Phone 543-1111 and ask for Mrs. Kelly who lives with him after 7 p.m.

Still trying gamely, the paper printed another clarification:

> R. D. Smith has informed us he has received several annoying phone calls because of an error we made in his classified ad yesterday. His ad stands corrected: For sale, R. D. Smith has one sewing machine for sale. Cheap. Phone 543-1111 after 7 p.m. and ask for Mrs. Kelly who loves with him.

Final version:

> I, R. D. Smith, have no sewing machine. I smashed it. Don't call 543-1111; the phone has been taken out. I have not been carrying on with Mrs. Kelly. Until yesterday, she was my housekeeper.

The following sentence from an insurance letter is confusing and unclear primarily because the main point is not emphasized effectively.

> We have been advised that the allotment for the above-numbered policy was filed effective April, 1972, but inasmuch as the premium due March 1, 1972, of $1.91 has not been remitted and inasmuch as allotment payments are not applicable to premiums due and payable in advance of the effective date of allotment, we hereby request that you contact the insured directly and request payment of this premium due.

Don't you agree the following revision is clearer to understand?

> Allotment payments can be applied only to premiums falling due after the effective date of allotment. Since the allotment did not become effective on this

policy until April, 1972, it cannot pay the March, 1972, premium of $1.91. May we ask you to collect it?

**Coherence** in a sentence means that the sentence hangs together in such a way that the intended meaning is clear. It involves showing the reader the relationships within a sentence, as well as pointing the way from one sentence to another. Place every modifier as close as possible to the word it is supposed to modify; otherwise, the meaning may be unclear.[1] In the following examples the modifier relates to the wrong word; reorganizing clarifies the meaning.

> *Unclear:* Being a certified public accountant, I am sure you can help us.
> *Clear:* Being a certified public accountant, you can surely help us.
> *or*
> As you are a certified public accountant, I am sure you . . . .

> *Unclear:* Depositing money with us, our bank can pay you higher dividends.
> *Clear:* Depositing money with us, you earn higher dividends.
> *or*
> When you deposit money with Union National Bank, you earn . . . .

> *Unclear:* He wanted a policy for his house that would cost $100 every year.
> *Clear:* For his house he wanted a policy that would cost $100 every year.

Also, you should beware of the habit of using "this" when not followed by a noun because the reader might connect its meaning to the wrong antecedent. The two illustrations below cloud the meaning because "this" isn't clear:

1. You have changed my little boy to a girl. Will this make a difference?
2. In answer to your letter, I have given birth to a boy weighing 10 pounds. I hope this is satisfactory.

As a rule, identify "this" by adding a noun after the word so there cannot be any misunderstanding.

**Emphasis** is the quality that gives force to important parts of your sentence. You can emphasize by position, space, and repetition. For instance, important ideas deserve the most important position in the sentence—at the beginning or at the end—they should not be buried in the middle. You can also emphasize important ideas by giving them extra space or by repeating significant words or phrases. Too much repetition, however, can result in a wordy sentence; too little repetition or the use of indefinite words such as "it" and "there is" can result in an unclear sentence.

> *Unclear:* Our association recommends Mr. Johnson's article on credit, but *it* says that in *it* he makes *it* seem easier that *it* is.
> *Clear:* Our association recommends Mr. Johnson's article on credit, but says that in the article he makes credit seem easier than it is.

[1] See also the section on dangling modifiers in Appendix B, pages 761–762.

*Unclear:* (In a letter promoting a laundry's special dry cleaning process that practically eliminated ironing by the customer) When your clothing is returned *there is* very little left to iron . . . . We don't mangle your clothes by machinery; we do *it* carefully by hand.

Besides aiming for the qualities of unity, coherence, and emphasis, you should make your average sentence length about 17 to 20 words. Of course, a pleasing variety of length is desirable, and you can use a range of, say, from 1 to 40 words. But when a sentence exceeds 40 or 45 words, ask yourself how you can rewrite it into more than one sentence.

Among several guides that measure readability is Robert Gunning's well-known Fog Index,[1] which is based upon both word and sentence length. By using his Fog Index, you can determine the educational level of your writing—whether it is for a reader who has an equivalent of a ninth-grade education (freshman in high school), twelfth-grade (senior in high school), thirteenth-grade (freshman in college), and so on.

To find the Fog Index of a passage, you take the following three simple steps:

1. *Determine average sentence length*
   Use a passage of words (beginning preferably with the first word of a paragraph) in consecutive sentences which end nearest the 100-word level. Divide the total number of words in this passage by the number of complete thoughts. (A simple or complex sentence has one complete thought; a compound sentence contains two complete thoughts.) Your quotient gives the average sentence length.

2. *Figure the percent of "hard" words*
   Count the number of words of three syllables or more in the passage, but don't count words:

   a. That are capitalized.
   b. That are combinations of short, easy words (like bookkeeper, butterfly)
   c. That are verb forms made three syllables by adding *ed* or *es* (like *created* or *trespasses*)

   Divide the number of these polysyllabic words by the total number of words in the passage and move decimal point two places to the right.

3. *Combine the sentence length with the percentage of hard words and multiply by .4.*

This readability formula is especially useful when you want to determine if Mr. or Mrs. Average American will clearly understand what you are writing to him or her. Who is this person? He's the cross section of all the people in the United States. He has finished the eleventh grade—maybe even graduated

[1] *The Technique of Clear Writing*, Robert Gunning, McGraw-Hill Book Company, Revised Edition, 1968, p. 38. Used with written permission of author, copyright owner.

from high school—but he hasn't gone any further in school. He is probably a typical customer. Therefore, your level of writing to him should be no higher than the twelfth grade—perhaps even lower because no one wants to read a piece of writing that is more difficult than it needs to be. Whether highly educated or not, everyone appreciates easy reading. If your level of writing to this average person is on the thirteenth level or higher, your message runs the danger of being ignored or misunderstood by him.

As you read the following inquiry to a savings association, ask yourself on what level your reply should be.

Gentlemen

We have just sold our home here at Warm Valley and now have a new address in the same city at 1000 55th Avenue, Apartment 4. We would like to deposit about $3,000 in savings with you there in your city as that is where we plan to retire. We have a loan with you on property at 1111 West Laneroad. We wish to leave that as it is. We would like some advice from you as to what method of saving we would profit most by and how to go about it.

We plan to be here at Warm Valley about three more years as this will increase our retirement. We were very lucky in selling our home here at a $11,000 profit. We have invested quite a bit with the credit unions here at Warm Valley as they carry a $2,000 life insurance policy on my wife who is 51 and $1,000 on me as I am 62. Would appreciate an answer.

Given below is a good reply—good because it answers all the questions, because the reader can clearly understand what the message says, and because it has a friendly, helpful tone. As you read this letter, try to guess what level it is written on (the underlined words are three or more syllables).

Dear Mr. Smith

Thank you for your nice letter of March 1, 197_. Since you will be moving back to Pomona in the future, we look forward to meeting you then. To answer your questions <u>regarding</u> a savings plan, we have two types for your <u>consideration.</u>

1.  <u>Regular</u> passbook savings yield 4 3/4 percent <u>dividends,</u> compounded <u>quarterly.</u> You can make <u>deposits</u> and <u>with-drawals</u> by mail, with postage paid by us both ways.

2.  Our Savings Certificates yield 5 1/4 percent <u>dividends.</u> <u>Minimum</u> amount for <u>opening</u> this type account is $5,000 and then upward in amounts of $1,000. They can be opened for six months or twelve months and are <u>automatically</u> <u>renewable</u> unless you advise us to the <u>contrary.</u> (109 words)
    Your <u>dividend</u> check on <u>certificates</u> would be mailed to you.

We will be glad to open an account for you for either of the types described above. All you need do is sign and forward the enclosed <u>signature</u> card along with your check. As soon as they reach us, we can open your account right away. The <u>certificates</u> are an <u>excellent</u> savings <u>investment</u> for someone who will not need to withdraw for the six- or twelve-month period. Even with the <u>certificate,</u> however, you can withdraw at any time; but, of course, you won't receive as much in <u>dividends</u> as if you wait until <u>maturity</u> date. (105 words)

If you have any further questions, please let us know. We shall be glad to help you in any way that best serves your needs.

You may be surprised to learn that the first half of this letter (109 words) has a Fog Index of only 10.2 (meaning tenth-grade level). And the Fog Index for the next passage of 105 words is comparable—9.80. Here is the proof. If you begin with the first word of the body, and count to the end of a sentence that comes closest to 100 words, you stop on the 109th word—which is "contrary." Within this 109-word passage are 8 complete thoughts. By dividing 8 into 109, you find that the average sentence length is 13.6 words. Now you count the words of three syllables or more that you must count as difficult. In the entire passage are 13—regarding, consideration, regular, interest, quarterly, deposits, withdrawals, dividend, minimum, opening, automatically, renewable, and contrary. By dividing 109 into 13, you find you have 11.9 percent hard words. Adding 13.6 and 11.9 gives 25.5, and 25.5 times .4 equals 10.2. If you perform the same steps for the second half of the letter, you have the following:

| *First half of letter* | | *Remaining half of letter* |
|---|---|---|
| 109 | words | 105 |
| 8 | complete thoughts | 7 |
| 13.6 | average sentence length | 15.0 |
| 11.9 | percent of hard words | 9.5 |
| 25.5 | | 24.5 |
| .4 | multiplier | .4 |
| 10.2 | 10th grade level          9th grade level | 9.80 |

Now, in contrast to the clear letter given above, read the following from a letter to certificate depositors. As you read the material, ask yourself if you think it has a higher or lower Fog Index than that of the previous letter.

RESOLVED, That in <u>accordance</u> with the <u>provisions</u> of Section 545.3-1 of the rules and <u>regulations</u> of the Federal Savings and Loan System, and the charter and by-laws of this Association, there be and hereby is <u>established</u> this date a separate class of savings accounts <u>evidenced</u> by Separate Certificate <u>desig-</u>

nated as Class "C" which accounts shall be in a <u>minimum</u> amount
of $10,000 and in <u>additional</u> <u>multiples</u> of $1,000.  Said Class
"C" accounts shall have earnings for the <u>period</u> <u>beginning</u>
October 1, 1967 and ending December 31, 1967 and maintained for
a <u>continuous</u> period of at least six months, declared <u>payable</u> at
the rate of 5¼% per annum.  (107 words)

| | |
|---|---|
| 107 | words |
| 2 | complete thoughts |
| 53.5 | average length of sentences |
| 14.0 | percent of difficult words |
| 67.5 | |
| .4 | |
| 27.0 | 27th level |

In other words, the letter is on the 27th level—15 school years beyond a high school graduate.

Mr. Gunning considers his Fog Index a "simple warning system"—not a cure-all for any writing problem. He wants you to use this formula "to check to see if your writing is in step with that which has proved easy to read and understand."[1]

By now you've noticed that the readability formula given above stresses only two factors—length of sentence and number of difficult words. If you keep the average length of sentence to 17 to 20 words and use simple (conversational) words, you should be on your way to effective readable writing.

However, this readability guide has weaknesses. In the first place, some long words really aren't as difficult as some two-syllable words (for example, employee versus avid). Also, you must count the same word as many times as it appears in the passage. Finally, you can scramble all the words into a non-sensical order and still figure the Fog Index. Used carefully, however, the formula will serve the purpose of *guide*—guide to readability of letters, reports, books, magazine articles, or any other business writing.

## Well-organized Paragraphs and Messages

How well you organize and point up your paragraphs and the entire message also has an important effect on clarity. The first step to clear paragraph and message writing is clear thinking. This point cannot be stressed too often. Understand completely what you have to say, and say it clearly and concisely. Read the letters and reports you send as if they were addressed to you. Would you understand them without your background knowledge?

[1] Robert Gunning, "The Fog Index after Twenty Years," *Journal of Business Communication*, vol. 6, no. 2, Winter, 1968, p. 3.

Below is a letter in which incidental details obscure the meaning. The entire message needs reorganization so the reader can easily grasp what the writer wants to get across.

Dear Mrs. Smith:

Regarding Form 100-2 recently requested and properly completed and received from you with a view to our considering the continuation of waiver of premium benefits under your policies, I am glad to write you.

You state that it is your expectation to resume work within a month or two. As you are undoubtedly aware, we have already waived payment of the annual premiums due July 15, 1970, and July 15, 1971, on above-numbered policy 11 222 333 and those as of November 12, 1970, and November 12, 1971, under above-numbered policy 11 222 333.

Inasmuch as you are anticipating a termination of total disability within a month or so it follows, of course, that premiums hereinafter due and payable will be payable in accordance with the terms of your policy. May we assure you that you have no immediate cause for concern in this respect for the reason that the first premiums subject to payment will be due and payable on July 15, 1972, and November 12, 1972, respectively.

It has been a pleasure to be of service during your period of total disability.

In contrast, the revision below doesn't bury the facts under an avalanche of details, but at the same time it contains all the important facts of the original letter:

Dear Mrs. Smith:

Thank you for sending in the form we requested in connection with your claim for disability benefits. We are pleased to learn of your improvement, and that you plan to return to work within a month or two.

As you know, we have waived four payments of annual premiums. The only ones payable, according to the terms of your policy, are those for July and November of 1972. I'm sure this arrangement will help you at this time.

It was a pleasure to be of service to you; and if there is anything further we can do, please get in touch with us.

## Examples, Illustrations, and Visual Aids

When you have a complicated and/or lengthy explanation to make in a letter or a report, you'll often find that you can improve the clarity of your message by giving your reader an example, an analogy, or an illustration. Furthermore, visual aids—such as headings, tabulations, itemizations, pictures, charts—are definite aids to clarity and easy reading. Whenever you have more than one set of figures, you'll make them much clearer to your reader if you itemize, tabulate, or set them off in some attractive way. Throughout this text—especially the section on reports—are examples of writing that uses illustrations and visual aids to help clarify the material for the reader.

In summary, make your writing clear by using words that are familiar to your reader. Watch the quality and length of your sentences. Organize paragraphs and your entire message so that the purpose is clear. Itemize and tabulate figures to make them stand out clearly. And give your reader helpful examples with appropriate easy-to-read headings whenever you need to explain complicated material.

### EXERCISES

1. Below is a wordy memo from the auditor of disbursements in Seattle to his colleague, who is the auditor of disbursements in Los Angeles. Both men work for the same organization. A *rear support* is a metal holder for a large ledger or dictionary you usually find only in libraries. Your job is to revise this monstrosity. The revision should be no longer than three or four sentences.

   We previously sent you copies of our correspondence with the Albert M. Hunter, Inc., relative to the Hunter Wage Charts. Particular attention is directed to our comments relative to the rear supports 4½ inches in length, which in our opinion were too long, in our letter dated April 8. As a result of our comments, Albert M. Hunter, Inc. developed rear supports 2½ inches in length which they furnished us to replace supports 4½ inches in length.

   On July 19 we sent you by express 26 sets of the rear supports 2½ inches in length. We are of the opinion that the rear supports 2½ inches in length are a considerable improvement over the rear supports 4½ inches in length and have accordingly replaced the rear supports 4½ inches in length on the Hunter Wage Charts in use by us with rear supports 2½ inches in length.

   We assume that you will also wish to replace the rear supports 4½ inches in length on the Hunter Wage Charts in use by you with the rear supports 2½ inches in length. If you make the replacement, please return the rear supports 4½ inches in length to us in order that we can return them to Albert M. Hunter, Inc., in accordance with their request.

   For your information, the rear supports 2½ inches in length to replace the rear supports 4½ inches in length were furnished by Albert M. Hunter, Inc. free of charge with the understanding that the rear supports 4½ inches in length would be returned to them.

If you prefer to continue using the rear supports 4½ inches in length, please return the rear supports 2½ inches in length to us in order that we can return them to Albert M. Hunter, Inc.

2. Revise the following sentences so that the reader can grasp the meaning clearly and quickly. If necessary, use more than one sentence.

   a. Thank you for your letter concerning the 10 steers that we received by airmail this morning.

   b. Also enclosed in our letter are two well-known customers of ours. (Writer meant names of two well-known customers.)

   c. (Salesman to receptionist): Good morning! I represent the Wooley Wool Corporation. Would you be interested in a couple of course yarns?

   d. (From the mayor of a city to the county engineer):
   I have reviewed the plans of Metro, their ability to finance, and in some areas, realizing a great number of years may elapse, because of financial conditions and the build-up of areas, before construction is warranted of sanitary trunk lines for sewers, I think it is very appropriate at this time that the county enter into a study and possibly use their ability given to them under the County Services Act of operating lagoons and serving areas that can develop only if sanitary sewers are constructed.

   e. (From a report of one of the country's largest foundations):
   Although the elimination of the liquidity deficiency is of pressing importance, the restoration of a permanently sound financial structure at the University requires the establishment of a stronger income base, which can be maintained, matched by a rational and continuing close supervision of expenditures.

   f. (From one insurance company to another insurance company):
   Frankly, the information we have while it may disclose some contributory negligence on our assured's part which, of course, is questionable, we still feel that your assured had he not been driving at the high rate of speed that he was could have swerved to his right and avoided our assured's vehicle but due to the fact he was coming down a hill at such a tremendous rate of speed with no control over his car and struck our assured, there was enough room to the right of your assured to have turned slightly and, therefore, avoided the accident.

   g. Claims against financial institutions or financial intermediaries (the two terms will henceforth be used synonymously) those business units whose principal economic activity is the purchase and sale of financial assets, have been termed secondary securities.

   h. (To a retail store from a customer):
   On December 26 I returned these pajamas to the same store and after I was unable to find the correct size which I wanted in the same style, I requested a cash refund from the clerk who told me that the store didn't give cash refunds but that I could have a credit slip to apply to a later purchase.

3. Check the readability of three pieces of business writing that the average person reads (use examples from the following list); then ask yourself whether the Fog Index (level of understanding) is just about right for the reader.

    **a.** Letter from a company to a customer
    **b.** Annual report
    **c.** Magazine read by the masses
    **d.** *Wall Street Journal*
    **e.** Article on front page of your daily newspaper

**4.** Choose a passage from a report or textbook that you consider difficult reading. Check the readability (Fog Index) on this passage; then tell the class (or your instructor) whether you think that the reason you consider this passage difficult is that its readability level is too high.

**5.** Assume you are writing to Mr. Average Citizen. What synonyms for the following words would he better understand?

    contingent
    rescind
    accelerate
    aggregating
    accrue
    validity
    default
    concur
    discrepancy
    allegation
    rider (in an insurance policy)

**6.** What is your reaction to the following message in the form of a typewritten speed memo from a savings association to a real estate corporation? Why?

```
Gentlemen:

In rgard to your letter of the fifteenth, let me explain our
policy on our Certificates of deposit.  Your certificate comes
due on November 9, 197_.  At this time the interest check will
be dispersed as you indicated at the time of your initial
deposit and the certificate will be automaticly renewed unless
you give us instructions to the contrary.

In your letter you asked that the certificate be "rolled over
for another 30 days."  As I have explained our certificates
have a life of 6 months, if you want the certificate renewed it
will automaticly be done.  If you wish the certificate to be
dispersed please contackt us prior to the experation date.
```

**7.** Assume the following words appear in the letters and reports that your secretary has typed for your signature. Without the help of any source, determine which words are misspelled and which words are spelled correctly. Then check the dictionary for the correct feedback.

1. accomodation
2. aquainted
3. assistance
4. attatched
5. attornies
6. batchelor's degree
7. benefited
8. brosure
9. compliment (meaning supplement)
10. catalog
11. childrens'
12. colledge
13. consede
14. concensus
15. corps
16. congradulate
17. convience
18. correspondant
19. defendent
20. descendant
21. desert (meaning cake)
22. develop
23. dissadvantage
24. disatisfaction
25. envelop
26. excellant
27. existance
28. Febuary
29. heighth
30. incessent
31. insistance
32. interupt
33. it's (possessive)
34. knowlege
35. labled
36. manageing
37. mispelled
38. occured
39. oppurtunity
40. payed
41. paralel
42. personnel
43. pertinent
44. preceed
45. prefered
46. proceedure
47. proceed
48. questionaire
49. recieve
50. referance
51. referred
52. recind
53. reccomodation
54. resistence
55. salesbility
56. seperate
57. sargeant
58. servicable
59. stationary (paper)
60. writting

**8.** Revise the following wordy sentences.

**a.** You will note when you study the cost of stationery that the expenditure of stationery has gradually and steadily increased for 1968, 1969, 1970, and 1971.

**b.** I have your letter of October 14 and wish to say that we'll be glad to give you a refund for the blouse you bought here last week.

**c.** Accountants, in studying business procedures and methods of accounting, have been able to classify the businesses for purposes of their study. They have classified these concerns on the basis of the differences and similarities in the accounting functions.

**d.** The mechanization of office records is not a particularly new innovation in the business world.

**e.** Permit me to take this opportunity to call your attention to the fact that we have brought your account up to date.

**f.** For your information we are attaching hereto a carbon copy of the letter sent to Mr. Ava Knocash under date of April 25.

**g.** Please find enclosed herewith a copy of the report which is 15 pages in length.

**h.** I wish to take this opportunity to sincerely acknowledge receipt of your order for one bushel of Washington Red Delicious apples and thank you for placing it with our company.

**i.** Please be assured that we are now rechecking and reviewing all of our specifications as it is our earnest and most sincere desire to be certain and for sure that this machine gives you satisfaction and good service in every possible way in the future.

**j.** In addition, will you please permit me to state in this letter that we will welcome any suggestions or comments that you may have at any time if you think of any methods for the improvement of our service to our customers.

**9.** *Exercises on choice of words:* Choose the word or words that should be used in each sentence listed below. (For choice of words in some sentences you might need to consult a dictionary or grammar book in addition to the rules for word usage in this chapter.)

1. While attending school, (a, an) university student might run (a, an) one-man business and still be (a, an) honor student.

2. This act will not (effect, affect) my confidence in him.

3. My suit is different (than, from) yours.

4. I am (anxious, eager) to (tell, advise) you that tomorrow will be a beautiful day for the departmental picnic.

5. Make your customer feel (its, it's) a pleasure to do as he suggests.

6. This (party, customer) is (well known, well-known) in his town.

7. I (shall, will) be glad to handle the order (providing, provided) the firm is willing.

8. We have a large (quantity, amount, number) of suits on hand.

9. It will be (all right, alright) if you come later.

10. Let me know (whether, if) I (can, may) come.

11. He (claims, says) he has paid the bill.

12. The dissension (between, among) the five departments has been settled.

13. The man (who, which, that) was crossing the street was struck by a car (who, which, that) Mr. Smith was driving.

14. These (kind, kinds) of hose wear (well, good).

15. Tell him to (contact, write) the factory.

16. Will you please see that (the undersigned, the writer, I) (is, am) notified of any changes in prices.

17. The firm ordered three of its salesmen to report on Saturday, but (neither, none) of them came in.

18. He is (further, farther) away from his source of supply than is any other dealer.

19. We sold (fewer, less) fans last month.

20. We had (already, all ready) received the dress when your letter arrived. I am (already, all ready) to write this customer.

21. (Please, kindly) send us the article number.

22. Your rug should (lie, lay) (smooth, smoothly) on the floor. Please (lay, lie) the files on my desk.

23. We (are in receipt of, have received) your papers.

24. The (principal, principle) officer of this company is Mr. Jones. The (principal, principle) of honesty should be evident in our letters. Now that you've been paying on your house for three years, how much (principle, principal) have you accumulated? The (principle, principal) of the school criticized the boy because be didn't know the (principal, principle) river in the United States is the Mississippi.

25. This machine has (proven, proved) its worth.

26. It would be (real, really) interesting.

27. The difference (among, between) the two figures was easily explained.

28. Of the two plans, the second is (least, less) expensive.

29. We want (to carefully examine, to examine carefully) any papers that you have received.

30. The coat is finished and we will ship (it, same) tomorrow.

31. I am (anxious, eager) to see that show.

32. Of the two players, John is (better, best).

33. This time we will sell (better, more) than a thousand.

34. (Continuous, Continual) rains are spoiling the crop.

35. You can always (depend on, count on) Bill.

36. He succeeded (due to, because of) his persistence.

37. He was not (enthused, enthusiastic) about the promotion.

38. Sun rays help to keep (humans, human beings) (healthy, healthful).

39. Demand a payment (regardless, irregardless) of his importance.

40. He didn't master the work (as, like) I did.

41. John made a (real, very) good speech.

42. The cake tastes (deliciously, delicious).

43. Please (refer back, refer) to your copy of the order sheet.

44. (In regards to, In regard to) the second sale, here are the facts.

45. I see in tonight's *Journal* (where, that) your boy has been elected captain.

46. We (seldom, seldom ever) sell that product.

47. Are you sure the supply is (enough, sufficient) to last until the end of the year?

48. (This, These) data (has, have) (proved, proven) that we are dependable.

49. Thank you for the (very complete, complete) report.

50. We cannot (wait on, wait for) your check any longer.

51. For a moment, I didn't know (where I was at, where I was).

52. We understand (you, your) wanting to be a salesman.

53. Do you know (who, whom) the manager promoted yesterday?

54. The credit for this sale goes to (you, yourself).

55. The chief engineer and (myself, I) inspected the factory.

56. I never knew anyone could be so slow in answering when a person wrote to (them, him).

57. If one can possibly spare the money, (he, you) should lay in a large supply.

58. Your order can be shipped March (1, 1st).

59. Take the pan (off, off of) the stove.

60. She is much taller than (I, me).

61. Be courteous to (whomever, whoever) comes to your desk.

62. I will (advise, tell, notify) you when the order is ready for shipment.

63. Enclosed (please find, is) my check for ($100.00, $100).

64. He agreed (with, to) that offer.

65. He (implied, inferred) that the other person hit him.

66. We (imply, infer) from their actions that they (aren't, are not) satisfied.

67. The accident happened at (6 a.m., 6 A.M.).

68. A large number of bills (is, are) outstanding.

69. The large number of employees (prevent, prevents) us from adhering to this suggestion.

70. This man earns $250 (a, per) week.

71. He worked in the (east, East) (prior to, before) coming here.

72. We shall (try to, try and) give you our answer by tomorrow.

**10.** Encircle the correct choice of "a" or "an" before each entry in the following list.

| | | |
|---|---|---|
| (a) | an | hotel |
| a | (an) | honorary degree |
| (a) | an | unit |
| (a) | an | historical event |
| a | (an) | honest opinion |
| (a) | an | unique method |
| (a) | an | hilarious parade |
| a | (an) | heroic effort |
| a | (an) | hour |
| a | (an) | heir |
| (a) | an | union |
| (a) | an | unanimous decision |
| (a) | an | humble opinion |
| (a) | an | hysterical action |
| a | (an) | herb |
| (a) | an | eulogy |
| (a) | an | hundred tons |
| (a) | an | habitual thing |
| (a) | an | humorous tale |
| (a) | an | oneness |
| (a) | an | uniform |
| (a) | an | one-day period |

11. Revise the following letters. Message 1 needs the purpose at or near the beginning with the details following. Message 2 already has the purpose stated at the beginning, but the writer rambles and seems artificially friendly. Apply the principles of correctness, conciseness, and clarity when you rewrite both letters.

*Message 1: To the president of Purple Shield, an honorary group on campus, from Mrs. Gertrude Buffington, a stranger to the president.*

Dear Henry

    I got your name from the office in the Student Union Building the other day as being President of the Society of the Purple Shield.

    I am at present, president of the Inter-Fraternity Mothers Conference and at a recent luncheon we had an honoured guest, Mrs. James P. Manson, whose husband sparked the founding of I F. M C in 1933. We had a most pleasant visit and during the conversation she mentioned she had also actively supported and was interested in Purple Shield and that many years ago there was a Mothers Club or some such organization of this group. She was once the treasurer and she said she has a small amount of money which she would like to turn over to some sponsored groupof Purple Shield—In other words, she was the treasurer or custodian of this money for the P.S. Mothers club which apparently is non-existent nor do I hold much hopes for its reincarnation.—But I think if the matter were presented correctly to her, she would give this group these funds or if

necessary perhaps a group of Mothers of Purple Shield could
meet together once a year or something.  I think this money is
over $300--more around $350 I believe--well, anyway, if you
need the money or a small scholarship could be made in the name
of James P. Manson or something of a memorial--Perhaps Dr.
Fish, your faculty advisor could suggest what you should do.
It seems a shame to have the money just sitting uselessly in
the bank when there is a need for it or it could be working for
the good of someone.  You may use my name when and if you
discuss this matter with Mrs. Manson------Mrs. James P. Manson
                                          5240 20th Avenue N. E.
                                          La 2-6666

                         Good luck!

*Message 2: To a small manufacturer from a college book store.*

Dear Mr. Cowell:

Once again with your kind permission, will you please make for
us four armbands, blue felt, white sewn letters and white chain
stitching as per the attached layout, and if you please Mr.
Cowell, we have marked on the layout for the operator to kindly
make these up just as we show them, and not change them.
What we mean by that, in a most friendly way, this is a little
order which you made up for us a few days ago, and the
operator, thinking it would be perfectly all right, transposed
the position of some of the lettering, so that they were not
uniform all the way, and too, inadvertently on one or two of
them left one or two of the letters out, and we are not complaining about that at all, all we want to say sincerely is
that we are grateful for your taking care of these little
things for us, and we are not registering any complaint at all,
for we are using them for samples and do not expect you for one
moment to do this again without your regular charge, for you
make nothing on it, and you are just like us, we know, doing
this to satisfy a customer, we being a customer, for other
things, and if we weren't we would not have the nerve to ask
you to make these, so therefore, if you please, this is for a
bunch of women and they are a little bit more particular then
men, and if the operator will just follow what we have laid out
everything will be fine.

Thanking you so much, and with best wishes and kindest regards,
we are
                         Cordially yours

12. Assume that the following letter is a reply to a customer who asked for a copy of
the free booklet the company had advertised on television a month ago. Is this
reply concise or abrupt? Improve it in every way you can.

This is to inform you we cannot comply with your request regarding booklets.
We're out of stock and in the process of revising same.

# Chapter 4

# Business Writing Principles II

- Completeness
- Concreteness
- Consideration
- Courtesy
- Summary of Business Writing Principles
- Exercises

The preceding chapter discussed three of the seven business writing principles: correctness, conciseness, and clarity. To give your writing content, force, and friendliness, you should also apply the remaining C principles: completeness, concreteness, consideration, and courtesy.

## COMPLETENESS

Your business message is "complete" when it contains everything the reader needs for the reaction you desire. Completeness is necessary for several reasons. First, complete messages are more likely to bring the desired results without the expense of additional messages. Second, they do a better job of building goodwill. (Incomplete messages can lead to ill will, lost customers, and hence decreased sales income and profit.) Third, complete messages can help avert costly lawsuits which may result if important information is missing. Finally, papers that seem inconsequential can be surprisingly important if the information they contain is complete and effective. In high-level conferences, in courtrooms, and in governmental hearings, the battle often centers around an ordinary-looking message that becomes important because of the complete information it contains.

As you strive for completeness, keep the following guidelines in mind:

1. Answer all questions asked.
2. Give something extra, when desirable.
3. Check for the 5 W's and any other essentials.

### Answer All Questions Asked

Whenever you reply to an inquiry containing one or more questions, answer all questions—stated and implied. A prospective customer's reaction to an incomplete reply is likely to be unfavorable. He may think the respondent is careless or that he is purposely trying to conceal a weak spot. In general, "omissions cast suspicions," whether you are answering an inquiry about your product or recommending a former employee for a new job. If you have no information on a particular question, you must say so clearly, instead of omitting an answer. If you have unfavorable information in answer to one or more questions, handle your reply with both tact and honesty.

The next three "situations" illustrate various messages in which the writers failed to answer all the questions.

In situation 1 the respondent, a distributor, answered only three out of the seven questions contained in the inquiry. Although it is not hard to see how the distributor might have overlooked some of the questions, the extra effort required to answer completely would probably have paid off. Because of his incomplete, unfriendly answer, he lost the goodwill of a potential customer.

***Situation 1:*** *The following inquiry was from a St. Louis customer to a distributor of model trains.*

Dear Mr. Smythson:

I am the owner of a set of Mankin HO gauge model trains which
I purchased while in Germany in 1963.  Also I purchased another
locomotive in 1969.  All this equipment operates on a three-
rail AC current system, and I would like to convert to a
two-rail DC current system, as the rest of my engines are all
American two-rail.  A friend here told me there is a method by
which this can be accomplished.  He suggested writing you,
since as Mankin distributor, you can probably tell me whether
this can be done.

I do not want to do the conversion work myself, as I am not
experienced enough.  I will be willing to pay any reasonable
price to have this work done, however.  My three Mankin AC
locomotives are:

    1 ⎫ (This section contained the name, model number, and
    2 ⎬  present condition of each engine, and the date each was
    3 ⎭  bought.)

In addition to converting to DC two-rail operation, I would
like all three locomotives completely gone over and returned
mechanically to brand new condition.  Also, if a set of maintenance instructions could be enclosed with each engine so I can
continue to take care of these models in proper manner, I
would appreciate it very much.

In addition to the above information, could you send me (C.O.D.
if there is a cost) the current Mankin catalog for their two-
rail equipment?  (I was told it was marketed under the brand
name "Helo," and was first introduced about 1970).  Also,
could you give me the name of the Mankin retail outlet here in
St. Louis, or the closest retailer to St. Louis (Chicago?) that
handles the Mankin line?  Are there any repair shops in St.
Louis you recommend to do work on Mankin models?  Thank you
very much for your consideration of these requests.  I hope to
be corresponding with you again soon.

The distributor's response was the following note (scribbled almost illegibly),
with an ad (see next page) enclosed. Certainly his reply was not in keeping with
his ad promising prompt "sales & service."

Dear (no name here)

Sorry we do no conversion work on engins.  The Mankin .50¢ cat
has some D.C. engins in it that you don't have to convert —

                        J. O. Smythson

"SEND FOR OUR NEW CATALOGS.
1971 Mankin catalog, . . . .50
New DC HO ENGINES designed by
Mankin. Complete in above
catalog 50¢.

AUTHORIZED SALES & SERVICE
ALL ORDERS SHIPPED OUT
SAME DAY AS RECEIVED."

JAMES SMYTHSON (address)

Sometimes, in answering an inquiry, you need certain specific information from the inquirer. It is then a good idea to list the needed details on a reply form which the inquirer can fill out and return to you. In this way both your answer and that of your respondent will be complete. In situation 2, had the bank supplied a form, the desired sale could have been completed with four, instead of eight, messages: the first inquiry; the bank's reply with an enclosed form to be filled out; the owner's authorization (on the form); and the bank's final liquidation notice and check.

*Situation 2: On August 8 the owner of mutual-fund stock wrote to a New York bank's investment department that he wanted to sell his shares. He asked, "Just how does your bank want me to authorize this sale?" and he received the following reply.*

Dear Mr. Brown:          Account #9999

If you wish to terminate the above referenced account and
liquidate the shares held by this bank, we need a letter of
instructions signed by both you and your wife just as the
account is registered.  Please be sure to give us the name of
your fund, your account number, and to whom proceeds is to be
mailed.

This letter brought from the customer a second letter, signed by both himself and his wife. They included the fund name and account number, and ended with this statement, "Please sell our 37 shares effective this date (August 23, 1970) and send proceeds to us." On August 28 they received the following telegram:

RE MLF FUND A/C 9999 UNABLE ACCEPT INSTRUCTIONS TO
LIQUIDATE ON A SPECIFIC DATE FORWARD NEW SIGNED
INSTRUCTIONS

After asking for interpretation from a local broker, the Browns wrote essentially the same letter as their second; however, this time they omitted the words "effective this date." A week later they received from the bank another request—this time to include in their reply both the name *and address* to which the proceeds were to be mailed! (The bank had not *asked* specifically for the address, and the customers assumed the proceeds would be mailed to their home address.) The next day they wrote their fourth letter.

Finally—On October 8, two months after their original question—the Browns received a formal notice of liquidation with an attached check for the proceeds. However, during the delay, the price of the stock had fallen considerably and the Browns lost money on their sale.

The replies in situations 1 and 2 were incomplete because the respondent omitted the answer to one or more questions or omitted important information in an explanation that answered a question. The next situation is an example of an incomplete response that *entirely* ignores the writer's real request. Be sure to avoid such gross carelessness in answering inquiries.

*Situation 3: An insurance policyholder had read and studied his policy but could not understand the meaning of a particular paragraph. He inquired about its meaning and in doing so quoted the entire paragraph in his communication. In response to his letter he received one from the company informing him that if he would refer to paragraph 4, page 3, of the policy (the one he quoted!), he would find a complete explanation. (The correspondent added that the paragraph was clear and unambiguous.)*

## Give Something Extra

In writing letters you must sometimes do more than answer the customer's specific questions. He may not really know what he needs, or his questions may be inadequate.

For example, suppose you are president of the regional businessmen's league for your industry and receive the following inquiry from an out-of-town member:

I think I'd like to attend my first meeting of the League, even though I'm not acquainted in your city. Will you please tell me where the next meeting will be held?

If you answered only his one question, your letter would be incomplete. Realizing that your reader is a newcomer to your city and to your League's meetings, you should include in your reply a welcome plus such needed details as directions for reaching the building; parking facilities; day, date, and time of meeting; and perhaps also the program for the next meeting. Your message will then have that "something extra" that a reader really needs and appreciates.

The two letters that follow illustrate an incomplete and a complete reply.

*Letter 1: Incomplete letter to a new savings depositor.*

Dear Mrs. Eilson:

Thank you for the confidence you have shown us by the account you recently opened.

All our facilities are at your disposal, and any time we can be of service please feel free to call upon us.  Our appreciation is best expressed by our being of service to you.

The last paragraph of letter 1 contains a meaningless invitation—unless the writer is sure the customer previously received information about the association's services. (What "facilities" are at Mrs. Eilson's disposal?) Letter 2, in contrast, clearly lists the services offered and thereby makes the invitation in the last paragraph more meaningful. (The writer could also have "high-lighted" the services and referred to an enclosed booklet for details.)

*Letter 2: Revised, complete letter to the new savings depositor.*

Dear Mrs. Eilson:

Thank you for the confidence you have shown in First Federal by the savings account you recently opened.  Our goal is to make all our services to you both pleasant and helpful.

Among the conveniences and services available to you at First Federal, you may be especially interested in these:

10—DAY GRACE PERIOD each month on your deposits means that your savings earn 5% interest from the 1st day of any month if they are deposited by the 10th day of that month.

SAVE—BY—MAIL POSTAGE—PAID SERVICE helps you to add to or withdraw from your account entirely by mail.

FREE CUSTOMER PARKING is provided in the lot north of our office.  The teller stamps your parking check, entitling you to 30 minutes free parking while doing business here.

SPECIAL PURPOSE ACCOUNTS such as Christmas and Vacation Clubs enable you to save for a special purpose.

MORTGAGE LOANS help you to buy, build, or refinance a home or to borrow for property repairs and improvements.

We invite you to take full advantage of all the facilities of this specialized thrift and home financing institution.

## Check for the 5 W's and Any Other Essentials

Another way to help make your writing complete is to be sure you have answered the "5 W" questions—*who, what, where, when, why*—and any other essentials, such as *how*. This method is especially useful when you write requests, announcements, or other informative messages. For instance, when you order (request) merchandise, you should make clear *what* you want, *when* you need it, to *whom* and *where* it is to be sent, and *how* payment will be made. When you reserve a hotel banquet room, you should specify type of accommodations needed (*what*), location (*where*), sponsoring organization (*who*), date and time (*when*), function or event (*why*), and other necessary details (*how*).

For some letters—especially those that bring bad news or make an unusual request—answering the question "Why?" may be particularly important. In situation 1, below, the customer would probably not have become so angry if the sales director's first letter had contained the information given in his second letter. This situation illustrates two fundamental principles of communication, in addition to the importance of completeness:

1. The meaning a person assigns to a message is often influenced by his past experience, needs, and attitudes.
2. A message that answers the question "Why?" is more likely to motivate the receiver to take the desired action than one that does not explain why.

*Situation 1: A seemingly harmless, but incomplete, letter from a sales director infuriates a utility company customer.*

Dear Mr. Bronson:

When our wiring inspectors visited your home recently they discovered that a water heater had been incorrectly wired ahead of your meter so that current used by it did not register.

I understand that this condition has now been corrected and am asking our Billing Department to add $15 plus tax to your next electric service account, to cover a conservative estimate for unmetered energy for the period of approximately fifteen months that the water heater was used.

The customer's reaction was expressed in an angry two-page letter addressed to the sales director:

Dear Mr. Manning:

Having been out of town for a few days, I received your letter of July 12th only today.

I have been a resident of (City) since 1949 and I have often wondered why the company had such poor public relations.

Their top officials on the whole seem of a high calibre, but on the lower levels there seems to be a dreadful lack of tact and a preponderance of boorishness. Perhaps I should elucidate.

A year ago my sister, Mrs. M. Beckinridge, purchased an electric stove and an electric water heater. I personally went to your representative here in (City) and asked were there any requirements. I was told that there were none. There had been an electric stove in this house previously and the basic wiring was in. We then hired a reputable electrician to make the necessary contacts. That is all I can tell you about the business.

About a month ago two of your men came to the door, identified themselves, and asked could they inspect our wiring and meter. Of course I let them in immediately and they came to me later with the story that the wiring was such that the water heater wiring was not going through the meter. I told them then and I can repeat to you that I know as much about electric wiring as I think you do about winning friends and influencing people for your company.

The next thing I know I get a letter (why, I don't know because I didn't apply for any service from your company, nor do I lease the house) in which you display all the old world charm of the legendary sergeant major. Without any consultation, without warning of any kind you have the effrontery to announce in heavy-handed style that you have arbitrarily imposed a $15 tag on our electricity bill (with tax, God help us) and this will show on our next bill. If you will consult a copy of the letter you sent me you will note that in the first paragraph the inference to me at least is that the wiring that by-passed the meter was some dark plot conjured up by someone, possibly me, and that your men had uncovered it in the nick of time and thus rescued your company from financial despair.

Don't tell me your company approves of methods such as yours. Decent, intelligent people deserve something better than this, old boy. It would have been easy to ask either my sister or me to come in and talk the matter over. If the company feels that some financial adjustment should be made it is something that should be agreed upon, and not something high-handedly decided by yourself.

As I said at the beginning of this letter, the public relations of the (name of company) is poor, and always has been. Perhaps the reason can be found in the actions of the lower brass.

The sales director replied as follows, explaining *why* the charge was assessed. (Notice he also suggests actions that Mr. Bronson and his sister should take, and he makes the action easy.)

Dear Mr. Bronson:

My earlier letter to you, dated July 12, did not explain
that we called at your residence several times over a five-
week period in connection with your electric wiring without
finding anyone home, before resorting to correspondence in
order to settle the matter.

We did not intend to infer that you were personally responsible for the incorrect wiring, but the fact remains that
kilowatt-hours consumed by the water heater during some fifteen
months did not register on the meter, through no fault of ours.
And our charge of $15, plus tax, is considerably less than the
average cost of operating such an appliance for this period of
months.  If you or your sister wish to come to 1040 Hanson
Street or telephone Valley 2-3171, I would be glad to discuss
the matter with you.

Incidentally, we have called at your home twice since the
electrician reported the wiring changed but have been unable
to get in to make a final check.  We would appreciate your
setting a time when it would be convenient for us to make a
further inspection.  Please call me (VA 2-3171, Extension 351)
any day this next week between 9 and 5 p.m.

Situation 2, below, shows the embarrassment and needless expense that
can result when an omitted essential fact makes the action request incomplete.

*Situation 2: A costly sales campaign fails because of incompleteness.*
The sales department of a retail company decided to sponsor a direct-mail campaign to 100,000 prospects. The sales letter was to be personalized with a typed
inside address and personal salutation. A special price offer was to be good for a
limited time only. The letter ended with this request:

So that you can enjoy the advantages of (product) at this
special price, send your order--but no money--today.  Just
take these two easy steps--

     Write your initials in the upper right-hand corner
        of this letter.
     Then mail it back to us in the addressed, stamped
        envelope that is enclosed.

However, to save the expense of having typists insert the 100,000 inside addresses
and personal salutations, a budget-minded official requested that the entire message be printed and that all inside addresses be omitted. And the salutation was
changed to the general, printed, "Dear Customer." The result was that the company received over 11,000 of the letters back, but no one had the slightest idea
to whom the 11,000 initials in the upper right-hand corners belonged! Because
all inside addresses had been omitted, the letters were incomplete for the action
requested; they failed to answer the questions *who* and *how*.

An attempt to find out from whom the orders had come would have necessitated the expense of a second letter to the same 100,000 people and the embarrassment of admitting the serious slipup. Instead, the decision was made to abandon the entire campaign. No one knows the resulting disappointment and perhaps ill will caused among the 11,000 prospects who received neither a reply nor the product they had ordered. In addition, the company wasted the cost of the first 100,000 letters and lost the profits from 11,000 orders.

The following list offers further suggestions concerning the five W's (and the H, *how*) to make your *action request* complete:

1. *What and who?: Clear statement of the action you desire your reader (or some-one else) to take.*
   Should he: Phone your office for an appointment? Sign a card or a document? return it? to whom? Come to your office in person? Send you certain details? (Be sure you get respondent's name and address too.)
   What questions should he (or someone else) answer?

2. *How and where?: Easy action.*
   Include your phone number (and area code) and extension if you want the reader to phone you. If you are often away from your desk or office, you might mention the best times the reader can reach you.
   Enclose a form (card, order blank, questionnaire, document) and an addressed reply envelope (perhaps with postage paid) if you want him to furnish information or sign and mail something.
   Give complete instructions regarding *where* and *how* if you don't include a form and/or an envelope.
   Enclose an envelope large enough to hold and protect the contents whenever you want him to return something bulky, confidential, and/or valuable (a document, a check). Have your secretary address the envelope and, if desirable and possible, affix the necessary postage.
   State your office hours and location if you want him to come to you in person. When, if at all, is your office open evenings? Do you have a free parking lot? Where?

3. *When?: Dated action.*
   Name the date (and the time, if pertinent) whenever you need the reply by a certain time. Tell him tactfully the reason you need it then. (Perhaps you need to meet a printer's deadline, or the reader's opinions are necessary for a speech you are giving at a certain meeting.)

4. *Why?: Special inducement to act by a specified time.*
   When appropriate, mention some benefit(s) the reader will gain by prompt action. A reader-benefit plug in the ending paragraph(s) is a stimulus to action.[1]

---

[1] See pages 29 to 31 for further suggestions regarding closing paragraphs.

# CONCRETENESS

Writing concretely means being vivid, specific, and definite, rather than vague, general, and abstract. The following guidelines should help you write concretely:

1. Use specific facts and figures.
2. Put action in your verbs.
3. Choose vivid, image-building words.

## Use Specific Facts and Figures

Whenever you can substitute an exact fact or a figure for a general word, do so:

| *Vague, general, indefinite* | *Concrete* |
|---|---|
| These *brakes* stop *a car* within a *short* distance. | These *Goodson power brakes* stop a *2-ton car* traveling *60 miles an hour,* within *240 feet.* |
| Please send your check for the *full amount soon.* | Please send your check for *$753.50 on or before June 5.* |
| A *quick* shave. | A *3-minute* shave. |
| Our product has won *several* prizes. | (Name) product has won *first prize* in *four national contests within the past three years.* |
| Your savings earn *high compound* interest. | Your savings earn *5 percent* compound interest (*added to your account every three months*). |
| After traveling an *enormous distance,* the lunar module landed *almost on time.* | After traveling *240,000 miles* and circling the moon *18 times,* the lunar module landed *within 1 minute 17 seconds* from the preplanned time. |
| This computer reproduces sales *campaign letters fast.* | This computer types *1,000 personalized 150-word campaign* letters *in one hour.* |

Often vague, general words are "opinion" words, which may have different meanings to the sender and the receiver. For instance, how fast is fast? A bicycle rider and a racing car driver will have different meanings for this word. How large is large? A person reared in a village of 150 people may consider a population of 15,000 large; yet to a native of a city with 10 million inhabitants, 15,000 is very small. The list which follows gives words which can lead to uncertainty, misunderstanding, or confusion.

| | | |
|---|---|---|
| a few | more | slow |
| a small number | most | small |
| high | nice | soon |
| large | quick | tall |
| low | several | very[1] |
| many | short | |

Using plenty of examples, prefixed by phrases like "for instance," "for example," "such as," also helps make your writing concrete as well as clear. (You will notice that this book uses that technique often.)

It is, of course, permissible—and even desirable—to use general expressions in certain cases. Sometimes it is not possible to be specific, for you may not have definite facts or figures. A second exception to the "facts and figures" rule occurs when you want to be diplomatic. Thus, instead of writing, "We have sent you *five* notices of your overdue payment," you may be more tactful (to a usually prompt-pay customer) and write, "We have sent you *several* reminders of this overdue payment." Also, when refusing credit to a potential consumer (and customer) you may feel that it is more diplomatic to give a vague rather than a specific reason. Still a third exception occurs when you want to allow the reader to form his own opinion, or when exact figures are unimportant, as in: "*Many* of our employees attended the meeting Saturday."

## Put Action in Your Verbs

Strong verbs can activate other words in your sentence. To write strong sentences, you should (1) use active rather than passive verbs and (2) put action in your verbs instead of in nouns or infinitives.

*Active versus passive voice.* You are using a verb with active voice when your subject does the acting. In the sentence, "The computer was repaired yesterday by Mr. Jones," the verb "was repaired" is passive, not active. The subject (computer) doesn't do the acting (repaired). With an active verb, the sentence becomes: "Mr. Jones repaired the computer yesterday." The subject (Mr. Jones) does the repairing.

A passive verb has three characteristics: (1) the subject doesn't do the acting; (2) the verb consists of *two or more* words, one of which is some form of "to be" (is, is being, am, are, was, were, will be, has or have been, had been, or will have been); and (3) the word "by" is expressed or implied ("by whom" or "by what"). The examples below show the difference between passive and active voice.

---

[1] Use "very" sparingly. One respected newspaper editor told all reporters to substitute the word "damn" whenever they wanted to use "very." Then, because "swear" words were forbidden in the press, the editor deleted every "damn" (and thus every intended "very").

| *Passive* | *Active* |
|---|---|
| Tests *were made* by us. | We *made* tests. (OR: Tests *showed* that . . .) |
| A full report *will be sent to* you by the supervisor. | You *will receive* a full report from the supervisor. (OR: The supervisor *will send* . . .) |
| An account *was opened by* Mrs. Simms. | Mrs. Simms *opened* an account. |
| It *is suggested* that . . . | We *suggest* . . . |
| It *is contemplated* by the committee . . . | The committee *thinks* . . . |
| Your figures *are checked by* the research department. | The research department *checks* your figures. |

Use of the passive voice should generally be avoided because:

1. Passive verbs can be vague. "A decision has been made" is less explicit than "The Board of Directors has decided."
2. They can be impersonal. "It will be noted" is impersonal, but "You will note" is both personal and specific.
3. The passive voice requires more words and thus slows both the writing and the reading. Compare "It has been shown by figures" with "Figures show."
4. Such verbs dull action. Compare "A mile was run by the boy" with "The boy ran a mile."

Occasionally, however, the passive voice may be preferred to the active, as in the following situations:

1. When you want to avoid personal blunt accusations or commands. "The July check was not included" is more tactful than "You failed to include. . . ." "Attendance at the meeting is required" is less harsh than "You must attend. . . ."
2. When you want to stress the object of the action. In "Your savings account is insured up to $15,000 through the Federal Savings and Loan Insurance Corporation" you have intentionally stressed "your account"—not the organization that does the insuring.
3. When the doer isn't important in the sentence. In "Three announcements were made before the meeting started," the emphasis is on the announcements, not on who gave them.

*Action in verbs, not in nouns.* Seven verbs—*be, give, have, hold, make, put,* and *take*—might be designated as "deadly" because the action they introduce is hidden in a "quiet noun." The examples below show how these "deadly" verbs can be changed to action verbs which shorten the sentences.

| *Action hiding in a "quiet noun"* | *Action in the verb* |
|---|---|
| We would like to *be* of *assistance* to you. | We would like to *assist* you. |
| The function of this office *is* the *collection* of accounts and the *compilation* of statements. | This office *collects* accounts and *compiles* statements. |
| Mr. Jones will *give consideration* to the report tomorrow. | Mr. Jones will *consider* the report tomorrow. |
| I *had* a *discussion* with Mrs. Brown about your claim. | I *discussed* your claim with Mrs. Brown. |
| The contract *has a requirement* that . . . | The contract *requires* that . . . |
| They *held* the *meeting* in the office. | They *met* in the office. |
| He *made* his first installment *payment*. | He *paid* his first installment. |
| The chairman *puts* his *trust* in each committee member. | The chairman *trusts* each committee member. |
| We will *take a look* at your record. | We will *look* at your record. |

*Action in verbs, not in infinitives.* Action can also be concealed by infinitives. Notice, in the following example, that both main verbs in the left-hand sentence belong to some form of "to be," which is a verb that doesn't convey much action or meaning.

| *Action hiding in infinitive* | *Action in the verb* |
|---|---|
| The duty of a stenographer is *to check* all incoming mail and *to record* it. In addition, it is her responsibility *to keep* the assignment book up to date. | A stenographer *checks* and *records* all incoming mail and *keeps* the assignment book up to date. |

## Choose Vivid, Image-building Words

Among the devices you can use to make your messages forceful, vivid, and specific are comparisons, figurative language, concrete instead of abstract nouns, and well-chosen adjectives and adverbs.

*Comparisons.* Sometimes adding a comparison helps your reader to build a meaningful picture. Consider the vague "sense" images you get from the sentences in the left-hand column below as contrasted with the vivid impressions gained from those at the right.

| *Abstract* | *Vivid* |
|---|---|
| There are a great many solder joints in the spacecraft, and each must have just the right amount of solder. | The spacecraft has 2½ million solder joints. If an extra drop of solder had been left on these joints, the excess weight would have been equivalent to the payload of the vehicle. |

This is pure clover honey, made by honeybees.

Honeybees have gathered nectar from approximately 4½ million clusters of clover and traveled about 150,000 miles—or equal to six times around the world—to deliver this package of Bradshaw honey to you.

**Figurative language.** Figures of speech often express an idea more vividly than literal language.

| Literal (and dull) | Figurative |
|---|---|
| He is usually the one who gets things started in the organization. | *Jim Jones* is the *sparkplug* of the organization. |
| It's wrong to omit the zip code number on an envelope; also the omission slows up delivery. | *Unzipped mail* is *improper. Your* correctly *zipped* messages *travel faster.* |
| X product helps you lose your double chin in four weeks, if you use X as directed. | If *two chins quarrel constantly for a place on your collar,* X product *helps settle the argument. Only one chin remains* after you use X just four weeks as directed. |

In employing figurative language, however, beware of mixed and inconsistent figures of speech, for they may confuse the reader, or seem foolish and corny:

At the meeting, our president's remarks *hit the bull's eye right on the nose.*
You deserve a *nice bow* for *sticking to your guns right down the line.*

You must also be careful not to use figurative speech which can be interpreted literally or negatively, or which sounds inappropriate:

As you enter our new lobby, your *eye* will first be *struck* by the bright stainless steel lighting fixtures. (Does this make you think, "Ouch"? Better: Your *eyes* will first *notice.* . . .)
Good roasts are tough to get, but we have them.
If you want new dollar bills for Christmas gifts, come to us. We have as many as a dog has fleas.

**Concrete instead of abstract nouns.** Still another way to enliven your writing and help make your message clear is to use concrete nouns instead of abstract nouns, especially as subjects of your sentences. Concrete nouns represent subjects your reader can touch, see, smell, feel, hear, or taste.

| Abstract | Concrete |
|---|---|
| *Consideration* was given to the fact that . . . . | The *committee* considered . . . . |
| *Termination* of the insurance contract will be in June. | The insurance *contract* ends in June. |
| *Analysis* of the situation suggests that Mr. Smith is right. | *I* think Mr. Smith is right. |
| The *impression* your living room carpet gives is one of elegance. | The *Worthman carpet* adds elegance to your living room. |

Be exact in your titles, subjects, and references. Don't force your reader to guess.

One more caution: If you are referring to an inanimate object, avoid using the neutral word "thing" whenever possible. Use a more specific word that is related to the "thing"—such as event, element, fact, idea, condition, method, plan, purpose, principle.

**Adjectives and adverbs.** You can often build a more realistic and interesting word picture by adding well-chosen adjectives and adverbs. In the list below, adjectives are in italics; adverbs, in small capitals.

| Colorless | Realistic, vivid, interesting |
|---|---|
| The camera has a system that gives you *good* pictures. | The *Poney* camera has an UNCANNILY *precise through-the-lens metering* system that assures you PROPERLY *exposed, true-color* pictures. |
| Notice the *smooth* finish and the *grained* leather. | Feel the *satin-smooth chrome* finish and the RICHLY *grained* leather. |
| This cookware is guaranteed to withstand changes in temperature. | Because *Creston* cookware can withstand *extreme* changes in heat and cold, the guarantee assures you that you can SAFELY move any piece from your freezer to your *microwave* oven. |

In your search for vivid picture-building words, be careful not to go to extremes with either adjectives or superlatives. Choose forceful, specific words and use sparingly such statements as "the most," "the largest," "the greatest," and "the best." Good writing includes concrete nouns, action verbs, and a minimum of adjectives and adverbs.

## CONSIDERATION

You'll recall that the second thinking step you should take before you start to write any business message is to visualize the reader. Consideration—also called "you attitude," empathy, the human touch, and understanding of human nature—means that you write every message with the recipient in mind. Try to visualize your reader—his desires, problems, circumstances, emotions, and probable reaction to your request. Then handle the matter from *his* point of view. In a broad but true sense, consideration underlies the other six C's of good business writing. To make your message correct, concise, clear, complete, concrete, and courteous, you adapt your language and message content to your reader's needs. However, in four specific ways you can show that you are being considerate of your reader:

1. Focus on "you" instead of "I" and "we."
2. Show reader benefit or interest in reader.
3. Apply integrity in your decisions.
4. Emphasize the positive, pleasant facts.

## Focus on "You" instead of "I" and "We"

Your reader is usually more concerned about himself than about you or the company you represent. He appreciates seeing his name instead of merely "Dear Sir" in the salutation of your letter, and he likes seeing his name again in the body of a long letter. Also, he is more likely to read your message when he sees the pronoun "you" rather than "I, we, us." Remember that the word b-u-s-i-n-e-s-s contains both U and I, but the U comes before the I. This is a good sequence for you to remember.

When you write your next letter, try to get your reader in the first paragraph; if possible, begin with "you" or "your."[1] And keep your reader in the message until you finish.

The opposite of the "you attitude" is the "we attitude," in which the writer views every matter from his own (or his organization's) standpoint rather than from the reader's:

| *"We attitude"* | *"You attitude"* |
|---|---|
| We allow 2 percent discount for cash payments. | You earn 2 percent discount when you pay cash. |
| I want to send my congratulations . . . . | Congratulations to you on your . . . . |
| We have enclosed a reply envelope. | Just mail your check in the enclosed envelope. |

The department store letter below contains 20 "we-our-us-I-my" pronouns and only three "you's" and "your's" (underlined).

---

[1] Though a good letter may begin with "we," "I," or "our," you still need to get the reader into the first paragraph whenever possible.

### Letter 1

May I take this opportunity to express my thanks for the
account you recently opened with our store. We are pleased to
furnish a wide variety of products for the home or individual.

We want you to take full advantage of our store services, for
we have the largest stock in the city. Also we make deliveries
of our customers' purchases free of charge within thirty miles
of our store.

We always like to receive visits from our customers, but we
also fill orders by phone. Our Customer Service Department
aims to fill every order within the same day we receive it.

When shopping at our store downtown, customers are invited to
use the free customer parking privilege provided just across
the street from us.

We welcome you to Bekinson's. If we can be of additional
service in any manner, please call on us.

In contrast, Letter 2—rewritten for more "you attitude"—contains 18
"you's" and "your's" (underlined) and only two "we-our-us" pronouns (underlined):

### Letter 2

Thank you for the account you recently opened at Bekinson's.
Serving you with your needs for clothing and home furnishings
is a pleasure.

You will find 32 departments at Bekinson's stocked with a
variety of quality items. And courteous sales clerks are here
to assist you in selecting the merchandise that best meets
your requirements.

If you prefer to shop within the comfort of your home, instead
of coming to the store, you need only to telephone MA 2-5555
and ask for "Personal Shopping Service." A Personal Shopper
will gladly take your order for any number of items, answer
your questions about brands and sizes available, and see that
the goods you order reach you by store delivery within a few
days.

When you shop at our store downtown, you are invited to use the
free customer parking privilege provided just across the
street.

You are always welcome at Bekinson's. Please call on us whenever you need additional service.

As the foregoing examples illustrate, a letter is likely to have better "you attitude" when it contains more you's than I's. But there are two situations when it is advisable not to use "you."

1. When the reader has made a mistake:

   *Poor:*   Your contract tells you plainly that . . . .
   *Better:* I am glad to explain more fully about the contract terms.

   *Poor:*   You failed to enclose your check in the envelope.
   *Better:* The envelope we received did not have your check in it.

2. When the reader has expressed an opinion different from your own:

   *Poor:*   You are entirely wrong in your attitude.
   *Better:* The proposed plan shows you have analyzed the matter from two view-points. There are still three aspects which are extremely important and which we need to explain now.

## Show Reader Benefit or Interest in Reader

Keep in mind that the "*you attitude*" focuses on the reader—*and*, when-ever possible, shows the reader how he will benefit from doing as the message asks.

Even a simple request gets better response when a reader-benefit plug accompanies it. For example, an insurance company that wanted to up-date its address files sent to one-half of its policyholders a double postcard with this message:

> Since we haven't written you in some time, please help us bring our records up-to-date by filling in and returning the other half of this card.

Only 3 percent of these cards came back. To the remaining half of its policy-holders the firm sent the same request—reworded to show reader benefit:

> So that dividend checks, premium notices, and other messages of importance may reach you promptly, please fill out and return the other half of this card.

This request brought 90 percent of the cards back in a few days!

When you try to see a situation from your reader's point of view, you will find it easier to show him you are aware of and are doing something about his needs and interests. This concern for your reader should be in every letter—whether you are writing to one person or to large numbers.

**Try to personalize the reader benefits** instead of stating them in a general way. For example, assume you are a manufacturer of fine china and have to refuse an order from a bride-to-be because you sell only through retail stores. Which of the following explanations do you think is more effective—and more considerate?

To make the purchase of Menon China as easy as possible, we sell only through selected dealers. In this way, customers can save considerable time buying directly from the local stores that handle Menon China. Also, most of these stores have a bridal registry. By using the registry, friends and relatives can buy pieces of chinaware for special occasions without writing to the company. Also a gift is usually given to the bride-to-be when she registers her chinaware.

*versus*

In order that you and other buyers may have the most convenience and service possible, Menon China is sold only through selected dealers. There you may see not only regular place settings in all patterns, but also the extra pieces that match your pattern. You can confidently coordinate your china with complementing crystal, silver, and linens because all are available for your selection. The bridal registry will not only offer information to your friends who wish to know your preferences, but will provide the services of an experienced bridal consultant to help you with any ideas or advice you may wish. When you register your Menon pattern, you will receive as a memento a miniature swan made of the same fine china as your table settings.

You no doubt preferred the second paragraph—for good reasons! That paragraph contains 14 you's-your's and personalizes the benefits to the customer. The first paragraph doesn't refer to the bride-to-be directly at any time.

You can use reader-benefit appeals to help bring back checks on your collection notices and to soften the blow in a turndown letter by pointing out your company's concern for the reader and his long-term advantages. In addition, reader-benefit appeals are helpful in sales letters, requests for favors, and announcements to your employees and customers.

## Apply Integrity in Your Decisions

Personal honor, truthfulness, honesty—traits that mark an individual who is admired, respected, and trusted—are qualities brought to mind by the term "integrity." In our day-to-day living, in our jobs, in business transactions—in fact, in everything we do—integrity is indispensable. Without it business papers would prove worthless and our confidence in people would be shattered. Leadership demands integrity, be it leadership of a social group, of a business, of an athletic team, or of a charitable bazaar. The leader's ethical standards, naturally, reflect also on the organization he represents.

Because you are an agent of your company, always remember that your messages help build your company's image. And to make this image one of integrity requires consistently fair treatment of customers and emphasis on basic honesty instead of insincerity and bluffing.

***Consistently Fair Treatment.*** As the preceding section indicates, when you show concern for your reader, you try to let him know you are aware of and are doing something about his interests. This does *not* mean, however, that you yield to the temptation of showing favoritism or allowing deviations for one customer that you would not allow for all other customers in similar circumstances. Particularly troublesome (and tempting) is the demanding customer who threatens to withdraw his large-volume business unless he gets special privileges (which he knows are against company policy and not granted to your other customers).

High ethical standards are the basis of consistent, fair treatment and consideration for all. Employees as well as customers appreciate such consideration. And most people respect the man of integrity who has the courage and considerate attitude to stand up for what he knows is right.

A paragraph from *Fortune* magazine published long ago (November 1950)[1] is still completely true and applicable today.

> Language is not something we can disembody; it is an ethical as well as mechanical matter, inextricably bound up in ourselves, our positions, and our relations with those about us. When a businessman doubletalks, for example, it is often for reasons deeper than mishandled prose—hypersensitivity to criticism, fear of the competition, fear of getting out of line with trade-association policy, fear of a government suit, a serious split in the corporation.

**Honesty instead of Insincerity and Bluffing.** Is business bluffing ethical? This question has been widely discussed and also written up in two issues of *Harvard Business Review* (January-February and May-June 1968). Reputable business managers feel strongly on the subject of ethics. They realize too that many times there are gray areas involving fine decisions between what is the complete truth and partial falsehood. An honest business writer needs a strong conscience as well as knowledge of writing principles and company policies.

In *Business Management* (April 1964), A. W. Lindh[2] has this pertinent paragraph:

> The old values of honesty, sincerity and trust, sometimes dismissed as Sunday school sentimentality, are actually Monday morning business realism in the quest for better communications. They create the climate in which communications grow. Where they do not exist, communications will be faulty, no matter how they are fertilized with methods and techniques. A man's character seems to have more influence than his personality in improving communications.

In writing your letters, memos, and reports remember that employees, dealers, customers, stockholders have a right to expect and most DO expect honest dealings. When they get poker-game bluffing instead, they are frustrated and angry. Many people are so "fed up" with salesmen's tricks and doubletalk that they pay little attention to sales letters that sound insincere and exaggerated. In the long run, the ethical way to write a message is also the most

---

[1] "The Language of Business," *Fortune*, November 1950, page 138.
[2] "Plain Talk about Communicating in Business," by A. W. Lindh of EBS Consultants, Inc., *Business Management*, April 1964.

effective way. Buyers have the right to expect that an item of clothing will be as advertised, that food processors are trustworthy in their packaging, that autos have needed safety devices, that insurance companies figure premiums honestly on up-to-date actuarial tables, that a mouth wash contains no ingredients possibly harmful to health, that the home they buy is as represented by the seller's agent and/or in the sales letter they received.

Consideration for others involves the Golden Rule—showing to others the same fairness and honesty that we expect for ourselves. Remember that both your own integrity and that of your company is revealed in the business messages you write.

### Emphasize the Positive, Pleasant Facts

The fourth way to show consideration for your reader is to accent the positive. This means: (1) Stress what *can* be done—instead of what cannot be done. (2) Write about the pleasant rather than the unpleasant. (3) Avoid emphasizing ideas your reader may view unfavorably.

*Stress What Can Be Done.* The reader wants to know what you *can* do for him. However, by making clear what you can or will do, you also (by implication) often make clear what you cannot do, without using a single negative word.

For example, assume you want to open an account. Now, compare the following two communications:

It will be impossible to open an account for you until you send us your signature card.

versus

Just as soon as you send us your signature card, we will gladly open an account for you.

The first message conveys what the official *can not* do—instead of what he can do. The second message is far more positive and thus more effective.

***Write about the Pleasant instead of the Unpleasant.*** In the following examples the unpleasant (negative) and the pleasant (positive) words are italicized.

*Unpleasant:* To *avoid* the *loss* of your good credit rating . . . .
*Pleasant:* To *preserve* (keep, maintain) your *good* credit rating . . . .

*Unpleasant:* We *don't refund* if the returned item is *soiled and unsalable.*
*Pleasant:* We *gladly refund* when the returned item is *clean and resalable.*

*Unpleasant:* To *avoid* further *delay* and *inconvenience,* we are sending this information by air mail.
*Pleasant:* So that you will *get* this information *as soon as possible,* we are sending it air mail.

\ *Avoid Emphasizing Ideas Your Reader May View Unfavorably.* When a customer closes his account, do not begin your follow-up letter to the former customer with a negative paragraph, since such an opening emphasizes ideas you'd rather not have the reader think about. For example:

> We *regret* that, since you *closed* your account, your name will be *missing* from our long list of satisfied customers. We sincerely *hope* that, despite the best efforts of our fine staff, there was *no occasion* on which you felt we *failed* to serve you properly.

In contrast, the following letter shows appreciation for the customer's patronage and—by emphasizing ideas the reader may view favorably—it does a good job of building goodwill for the savings association.

```
It was certainly a pleasure to have had you as a member of
Federal Savings.

We noticed recently that you closed your account with us.
Perhaps you reached that particular goal for which you were
saving, or it may be that an emergency arose which called for a
large outlay of cash.  Whatever the reason, we are happy to
have played some small part in your financial program.

Our sincerest thanks to you for having given us the opportunity
to be of service.  We extend our cordial invitation to use
such other of our profitable, time-saving services as occasion
may require.

As in the case of so many others, the time may come when you
too will want to resume your savings account.  Our experience
has shown that saving is one habit which has the happy faculty
of persisting.

If time or distance is a problem to you, why not take advantage
of our convenient postage-free save-by-mail plan, which enables
you to transact your business with us using a minimum of
effort.  Many of our other friends have used it to great
advantage.

Please accept our best wishes for a wonderful future, and do
call upon us with your financial problems.  We shall be happy
to help you in every way.
```

Negative thinking is a habit—a bad habit. Avoid four words in particular —hope, trust, if, and may—when they carry a negative connotation. The following list shows how these and other negative-sounding words can be changed to emphasize the positive.

| *Negative* | *Positive* |
|---|---|
| *If* we can help, *don't hesitate* to get in touch with us. | Please call on us *when* we can help. |
| I *trust (hope)* this is the information you wanted. | Should you need additional facts, *please telephone* me at LA 3-3333. |
| *May* I *request* that you fill out and return the enclosed card. | *Please fill out* and return the enclosed card. |
| Thank you for your *trouble*. | Thank you for your *help*. |
| You *won't be sorry* you did this. | You'll be *glad* you did this. |

## COURTESY

"Everyone gains where courtesy reigns" is a good slogan for written as well as oral communication. Courtesy is even more important in business writing, than it is in face-to-face conversation. When you talk with a customer and see him frown over some expression you use, you can quickly redeem yourself by a smile, a twinkle in your eyes, your tone of voice, or perhaps a correction. In a letter, however, your words are on the paper forever, and you can't be with the customer when he reads the message. Your courtesy—or discourtesy—is there in black and white, and your reader will often form his impression of you or your firm from a single message. Courteous messages help to strengthen present business friendships, as well as make new friends.

Thus, courtesy is a goodwill builder. And the value of that goodwill, or public esteem, can be recorded on the balance sheet in thousands (or even millions) of dollars. Much money is spent in advertising to attract new customers and to keep desirable old customers. While advertising may bring buyers into the front door of your firm, discourteous letters—written carelessly by employees who do not care about or understand people—can drive customers out the back door!

Here are some of the more obvious ways to achieve courtesy in your business messages:

1. Be sincerely tactful, thoughtful, and appreciative.
2. Omit expressions that irritate, hurt, or belittle.
3. Answer your mail promptly.
4. Grant and apologize good-naturedly.

### Be Sincerely Tactful, Thoughtful, and Appreciative

Courtesy stems from a sincere attitude that generates goodwill. A truly courteous person sincerely likes people, is thoughtful of their feelings, and tries honestly to help them.

One of the top copywriters in the advertising business, Walter Weir, has published a statement that is good advice for all letter writers as well as for advertising copywriters:[1]

> I believe one best prepares himself for communicating by learning to love and genuinely loving all the countless other human beings with whom he inhabits the earth. I do not believe one can be a cynic and communicate effectively.

The attitudes you have toward people influence the impression your messages will make. If you believe that most people want to pay their installments promptly, that people sometimes forget, and that most of them will try to pay when reminded, your tone should naturally be courteous. On the other hand, if you dislike people and suspect they are all out to get what they can for nothing, your writing is likely to reflect this thinking. The courteous writer is tactful, thoughtful, and appreciative.

***Tact instead of Bluntness.*** Though few people intentionally want to be abrupt or blunt, these traits are a common cause of discourtesy. Sometimes they stem from negative personal attitudes; sometimes, from a mistaken idea of conciseness. A time to be especially wary of bluntness is on those days when everything seems to go wrong. At such times, you are in danger of allowing your pent-up feelings to come through in your messages. Avoid expressions like the ones in the left-hand column below; rephase such blunt or discourteous statements as shown in the right-hand column.

| *Tactless* | *Tactful* |
|---|---|
| Your letter is not clear at all; I can't understand it. | If I understand your letter correctly, . . . |
| Obviously, if you'd read your policy carefully, you'd be able to answer these questions yourself. | Sometimes policy wording is a little hard to understand. I'm glad to clear up these questions for you. |
| Apparently you have already forgotten what I wrote you two weeks ago. | As mentioned in my May 15 letter (or memo) to you, (continue with the facts) . . . . |

Writing a letter to a customer generally requires more conscious "niceties" than writing a memo to a fellow employee. In letters to customers, you usually avoid a one-sentence body. But when you are sending a memo to someone within your organization, you can omit the public-relations pitch and the suggestion of future business. A one-sentence body is quite all right to an employee or colleague whenever it adequately covers your particular message. All you need do is present the facts clearly, completely, and pleasantly. For example, letter 1, with its single (and negative) sentence to a customer, sounds blunt; letter 2, with its courteous opening and a helpful suggestion, is cour-

[1] Walter Weir, *On the Writing of Advertising*, McGraw-Hill Book Company, New York, 1969.

teous. The memorandum, on the other hand, because it is to a fellow employee is quite satisfactory even though it has only one sentence.

> **Letter 1:** *Tactless one-sentence letter to a customer.*

Dear Mr. Jeans:

Before we can replace the safety lock on the trunk of your 1970 Oldsmobile, it will be necessary that you give us the number of it.

> **Letter 2:** *Improved revision of letter 1.*

Dear Mr. Jeans:

We will be glad to replace the safety lock on the trunk of your 1970 Oldsmobile.

So that we can know the right lock to fit your trunk, please send us the casting number. You'll find it imprinted on the side of the lock.

Within the same morning we receive your reply, a new lock will be on its way to you.

> **Memo 1:** *Courteous one sentence to a fellow employee.*

Tom,
Please call me (Ext. 312) to tell me the casting number on the side of the trunk safety lock you need for that '70 Olds.

When a reader has had sorrow, bereavement, or hardship, the writer should be especially considerate of feelings and emotions. Tactlessness may not only be blunt but also (unintentionally) cruel. For instance, when writing to a policyholder who had recently had one leg amputated, a heartless correspondent included this sentence:

> Because you have lost only one leg, your policy doesn't entitle you to the full $30,000 payment. This amount is paid only when both legs are amputated.

Tact also helps the tone of requests. Generally it is better to suggest and/or to show reader benefit with your request—rather than to command.

> *Commanding:* You ought to . . . .
> *Tactful:*      Perhaps you could . . . .
>
> *Commanding:* Please remit immediately.
> *Tactful:*      To preserve your good credit rating, please mail your check by (date).

*Commanding:* Tom, get your list to me pronto.
*Tactful:*      Tom, may I have your list by tomorrow at 10? Then I'll include it in my report at the meeting.

*Commanding:* All employees must comply with this new procedure.
*Tactful:*      We (I) will appreciate your cooperation on . . . . (*or* We (I) ask that all employees cooperate on . . . .)

*Thoughtfulness and Appreciation.* Writers who send cordial and courteous messages of deserved congratulations and appreciation (to persons both inside and outside the firm) help build good feeling and goodwill.[1]

An unpretentious, sincere courtesy note can bring the writer's company thousands of dollars of business. Remember, customers indirectly help to pay your salary, and you should let them know you appreciate their orders, their payments, and even their inquiries. For example, one small plumbing firm materially increases its repeat business from homeowners by sending a courteous letter soon after a new customer pays his first bill. The surprise letter, individually typed, thanks the patron for his prompt payment and invites him to call again whenever he needs plumbing services, no matter how small or large. The next time these customers need a plumber, they call the one that sent them the friendly thank-you, instead of searching through the yellow pages of the phone book for another plumber.

Even for routine payments a printed "Thank you" or "We appreciate your prompt payment" can be added to the flap or under the window of the company envelope in which you return to the customer your bill marked "PAID."

These principles of courtesy involving congratulations or appreciation also apply to colleagues or employees. For instance, what about the salesman who made very high selling records? Or the office girls who cheerfully worked overtime every night last month in the warehouse during a trying period? Employees do react favorably to a cordial note of thanks from "the boss."

You cannot measure courtesy by the number of "please's" and "thank-you's" or consideration by the number of "you's," as the following story indicates:

A young wife returning from her second session at a night-school business writing course, had just heard about the seven "C" principles. When she came home, her husband (who had never studied letter writing) asked her opinion of the collection letter he had "slaved over" all afternoon. He fumed, "I'm telling this guy what I think of him and I'll scare him into paying!" After his wife had read the letter, she commented: "I guess this meets six of the seven C's. It's complete, concise, clear, considerate (you have eight you's), and courteous (two please's and three thank-you's right next to the sarcasm and the threats). But I think it's not quite correct, because you've misspelled "louzy" and "bumm.""

[1] For examples of courteous goodwill messages, see Chapter 13.

## Omit Expressions That Irritate, Hurt, or Belittle

The good business writer should avoid any expressions that might offend the reader. Such expressions are discussed here in three groups: irritating, questionably humorous, and belittling statements.

*Irritating Expressions.* The following list contains irritating expressions to be avoided. (They are particularly irksome when used with "you" and "your.")

| | |
|---|---|
| contrary to your inference | we must insist |
| delinquency (delinquent) | we take issue |
| due to your questionable credit we are unable to | why have you ignored |
| | why is it always |
| failed | you are delinquent |
| failure | you are probably ignorant of the fact that |
| force | |
| I'm sure you must realize | you claim that |
| I do not agree with you | you did not tell us |
| if you care | you don't expect us |
| ignored | you failed to |
| inexcusable | you forgot to |
| irresponsible | you have to |
| it is against our office policy to do so | you leave us no choice |
| lack of response | you neglected to |
| mistaken | you overlooked sending |
| must | you say |
| neglected | you should be aware |
| obnoxious | you should know |
| obviously you overlooked | you surely don't expect |
| regrettably | your apparent disregard of our previous request leaves us no alternative |
| simply nonsense | |
| surely you don't expect | your complaint |
| we are confused | your failure to |
| we are surprised | your stubborn silence |
| we don't believe | your insinuation |
| we expect you to | your neglect |
| we find it difficult to believe that | |

As you read the following collection letter containing several of these irritating expressions, try to think of ways the language could be rewritten to be firm, yet also courteous.

Dear Mr. and Mrs. Moran:

You have _failed_ to correct the existing _delinquency_ on the above-captioned loan, and _furthermore_ you have _ignored_ our arrangements for repayment.

A Notice of Default has been filed with the Veterans Administration advising them of your _failure_ to make payments as agreed. It is not the policy of this association to carry a loan in such a _delinquent_ condition.

<u>Failure</u> to comply with your payment program will result in <u>termination</u> of this agreement <u>without</u> <u>further</u> <u>notice</u>, and State Federal Savings Association may then <u>institute</u> or <u>continue</u> <u>foreclosure</u> <u>proceedings</u>.

We <u>must</u> <u>insist</u> that you make payment <u>immediately</u>.

*Questionable Humor.* Humor is often quite effective in business writing. However, before you try to be funny, be sure your humor is good-natured and appropriate for the situation. A flippant attitude can be irritating, as the following two letters from the Correspondence Improvement Section of the Prudential Insurance Company of America illustrate.[1] Letter 1 is offensive rather than humorous; letter 2 conveys the same message informally but courteously.

*Letter 1*

Dear Mr. and Mrs. Smith:

We were mighty happy to learn about the package the stork brought you. And what a distinguished tag you put on him . . . Joshua Gerald Smith II. You tell "Josh" that as soon as he's ready his Prudential agent will be around to help him set up his insurance program.

In the meantime, I guess it's up to us to take care of the little fellow's insurance needs for a while—you know, educational funds and a little nest egg to help him start his journey through life.

I'll phone you in a couple of days to find out when it will be convenient for you to talk about insurance for your new bundle of joy. Till then, keep his powder dry!

*Letter 2*

Dear Mr. and Mrs. Smith:

Congratulations on the birth of your son, Joshua.

It may seem early to be concerned about financing his college education. But we at Prudential have seen all too many youngsters miss out on college because their parents put off the problem too long.

If it is convenient, I would like to call at seven o'clock Friday evening to show you how Prudential can help you solve this problem. I'll phone Thursday to confirm the appointment or to arrange a different time if Friday is inconvenient.

---

[1] From *Dear Sir*, vol. 3, no. 1, Correspondence Improvement Section, Public Relations Department, Prudential Insurance Company of America, 1961–1962.

Two other examples of humor in questionable taste are the following paragraph in a customer's letter to a department store and the store's reply. (The customer had received a lamp with the wrong base.)

The lamp I selected was sold to me by a highly untrained fellow in your lamp department. For some reason he was designated as salesman number 1. If it is impossible to send me the right base for my lamp, perhaps you could send me salesman number 1. That should help your sales department, I would think, as he would make a better lamp base than a salesman.

The store correspondent apparently tried to be funny too; here is his reply:

Our records show that the base you wished was sent to you on May 10. We are surprised you have not received it.

Having examined salesman number 1 from all angles, we feel rather reluctant to think he would make a good lamp base. We are gratified this didn't involve the cheese department, for you might have suggested that we put him in the showcase.

We are sending you another lamp base. If the one we originally sent should reach you in the meantime, we would appreciate your returning it to us. We might have to use it in a pinch as a salesman.

**Belittling Statements.** Talking down to or belittling a reader is another form of discourtesy that can have a profoundly unfavorable effect. The following example is a flagrant case of discourtesy of this type:

To substantiate a railroad claim, the accountant of the AMC company needed the exact charges on certain returnable drums in which the XYZ Chemical Company annually shipped thousands of dollars worth of chemicals to AMC. AMC's accountant checked with the local representative of XYZ Company for this information, but was asked by him to contact Mrs. Lancaster at Diamond, California. After writing to her, the accountant received the following reply, which he said caused "a much greater explosion within our department than could have all XYZ chemicals combined."

Gentlemen:  Attention Mr. Howard Doe, Accountant

In reply to your letter of October 10th addressed to Diamond, California, attention Mrs. Lancaster, you made two mistakes. In the 1st place we have no Mrs. Lancaster and in the 2nd place Diamond is not a place to send mail.

We make a charge of $8.50 on the Carbon Bisulphide–Carbon Tetrachloride Mixture drum to AMC Company, in your city.  That is for the drum only.  We trust is what is meant.

## Answer Your Mail Promptly

An inexcusable form of rudeness is represented by the unanswered letter or the letter that remains unanswered for days or even weeks. Every inquiry should be acknowledged within 24 to 36 hours. A person who doesn't answer a letter is just as rude as the one who doesn't acknowledge a greeting when passing a friend on the street—or the man who fails to remove his feet from the desk when a visitor enters his office. Even a prompt reply on the bottom of a customer's inquiry, or a handwritten brief note, is usually better than a late reply.

If you need time to gather certain information before you can answer a request, sending a short explanatory note like the following distinguishes you as a courteous person:

I'll gladly send you the information needed. It may take a few days to assemble the facts.
You will hear from me by . . . .

The next three examples illustrate the value of promptness.

### Example 1
A certain retailer in fine china tried an experiment in promptness. For one week he "dumped" all incoming inquiries (many inspired by his regional advertising) into two piles without sorting of any kind. One pile he answered within 24 hours; the others, in three weeks. Result? The prospects who had been answered promptly turned in almost 70 percent more orders than those who had to wait.

### Example 2
A businessman mailed his order with enclosed money order to an out-of-state nursery that had run a full-page ad in his local newspaper. After 30 days, having received neither an acknowledgment nor a package, he wrote a second letter. In ten days came an abrupt card stating the writer had been swamped with orders and that the customer would get his plants "in due time." Never again will he buy from *that* nursery, although its ads appear regularly every year, and the quality of its stock is good. A courteous form message on a post card—mailed within a day of receipt of the order—might have kept this customer "sold" and a repeat buyer year after year.

### Example 3
Customers pleased with a company's courtesy often comment on the promptness of its messages. The following paragraphs quoted from *The Better Letter Gazette*[1] of Teachers Insurance and Annuity Association illustrates well the effect that promptness had on two policyholders:

But what impressed me still more was the extraordinary speed with which TIAA handled my claim . . . . It seems that special comment is called for when one of your policyholders sends in a claim one day, the check is made out the

---

[1] *The Better Letter Gazette*, TIAA and CREF, August, 1960.

following day and he has it in his hands two days later. If this is typical of your operations, I can see why TIAA is regarded by the academic profession as a fairy godmother. So please accept my hearty congratulations along with my grateful thanks . . . .

I want you to know that I have policies with several different insurance companies. In no other instance have I received the prompt, courteous attention given me by TIAA . . . .

Sometimes promptness can be achieved by unusual methods. For example, when the owner of a retail men's store in the Dakotas asked a Chicago manufacturer to check his previously submitted order and let him know when it would arrive, the manufacturer sent the following message:

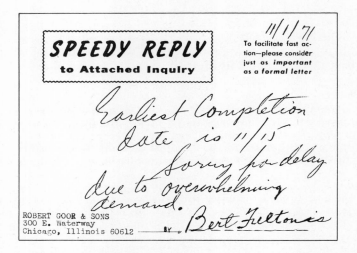

In this situation the manufacturer saved time by not dictating and sending a letter, and the retailer accepted the reply favorably. (Note that the printed explanation in the upper right-hand corner shows reader benefit.) If you are, however, writing to a new customer or if you don't know whether your customer would react favorably to such a reply, be safe and write a courteous card or letter instead!

## Grant and Apologize Good-naturedly

Whenever you have occasion to comply with a customer's request, begin your letter with the best news first and inject a courteous, ungrudging tone. Notice the difference in tone of the following two paragraphs:

*Grudging:*

Your request causes a great deal of extra paper work to change monthly payments. However, in compliance with your request we hereby reduce your monthly interest and principal payments called for in our note to $_____, plus $_____ for taxes and insurance; effective (month-day-year) your total monthly payment will be $_____.

*Good-natured:*

As you requested, we will reduce the monthly interest and principal payments called for in your note to $_____, plus $_____ for taxes and insurance. Thus, starting (month-day-year) your total monthly payment will be $_____.

If a request has caused you extra work, you may tactfully tell the customer somewhere in the letter—but not the first paragraph—to notify you by a certain time if he again wishes to change such and such.

Occasionally you may get a "nasty" letter from a customer, who is wrong in his accusations. A courteous reply can lead not only to an apology from the customer but also future staunch loyalty as a booster for your organization. How would you react to the following letter (dated September 30, 1970)?

Gentlemen

Enclosed please find Deposit book # R 000 under the name of Michael Hall in trust for our son Marvin Hall as well as a check for .30¢ to be deposited in same account.

As you will see there has never been any dividends posted on this Bank deposit book. Your failure to do so in March 1968 as well as in June 1970 when the amount of deposit was over the $10.00 minimum for dividend earnings, is quite inexcusable.

I would expect from you a proper crediting of all dividends and I am calling this discrepancy to the attention of the State Banking Department at 1000 First Street. I am sending them a copy of my letter to you.

You might also tell me how to restore a child's confidence in your institution as you have failed to indicate to him that indeed his money "grows" when placed into the hands of a banking organization.

This letter is certainly discourteous. The cutting words "failure" and "inexcusable," plus the implications in the last two paragraphs, leave an unfavorable impression. Even though you might feel like telling the customer off, refrain from doing so. Traded insults don't win friends—they only create enemies. Remember, you are speaking as an agent for your company! The letters below, show two possible ways of answering this customer—one cold and unfriendly; the other, courteous and encouraging.

***Letter 1:*** *Cold, unfriendly, cutting.*

Dear Mr. Bramhall

We are returning herewith your passbook for account # R 000 posted to date.

We regret, of course, that the account has not earned dividends up to this time.  The reason for it is that almost seven years ago, starting January 1964, the Board of Directors of the Association raised the minimum balance required to earn dividends to $50.00.  In December of 1963, a notice of this change of policy was mailed to all savings account holders; and also, at the same time, posters and counter cards bearing this information were placed and displayed in all our offices for the entire year of 1964.  In addition, in April of 1964, another mailing was made to all savings account holders whose balances were less than $50, reminding them of the change in policy. We feel, therefore, that every reasonable effort was made to convey this new information to our savings members.  We regret, of course, that for some reason you were unaware of this policy change or have forgotten it.

It has always been our practice to fully inform our savings account holders of any changes that take place.  We also want to assure you that we value very highly each one of our members and their continued loyalty to the association.  We hope that you will continue to maintain this account, and add to it in order that you may receive dividends in the future.

***Letter 2:*** *Courteous revision.*

Enclosed is your passbook for account # R 000 posted to date.

Your desire to have the account earn dividends is certainly natural and understandable.  I am glad you've given me the opportunity to explain why the account has not yet earned dividends, so that you can bring the account to the desired balance in the future.

A little over six years ago, starting January 1, 1964, the Board of Directors of the Association raised the minimum balance required to earn dividends to $50.  In the preceding month a notice of this change of policy was mailed to all savings account holders; and also posters and counter cards with this information were displayed in all our offices for the entire year of 1964.  In addition, in April of 1964, another letter was sent to all savings account holders whose balances were less than $50 reminding them of the change in policy.

You can see, therefore, that we really tried to convey this new information to our savings members.  We're sincerely sorry that

for some reason you were unaware of this policy change.  It
has always been our practice to fully inform savings account
holders of any changes that take place.

Your continued loyalty to the association is very much appreciated.  We invite you to continue adding to this account; one
of these days soon your son will see that his money does grow
when deposited with Ninth Federal Savings Association.

When someone in your organization makes a mistake, you can apologize
and correct the error perhaps even before the customer discovers it. Sometimes
a small, printed form like the following (used by a bank) is useful to admit
an error promptly and courteously.

---

Date _____ 19_____ Account No. _____

### PARDON US . . . IT WAS OUR ERROR!

An incorrect entry was made. Please return your passbook in the enclosed
envelope for the following reason:

Interest
not entered ☐                    Balance incorrect ☐

Thank you.

By _____

(Name of bank)

---

Of course, if the matter is more serious, a special letter may be more
appropriate, as you will see in later chapters.

## SUMMARY OF BUSINESS WRITING PRINCIPLES

To achieve the seven "C" qualities in your writing, try to follow these principles:

| | |
|---|---|
| *Correctness:* | Use the correct level of language |
| | Include only accurate facts, words, and figures |
| | Use acceptable writing mechanics |
| | Apply correctly all other pertinent "C" qualities |
| *Conciseness:* | Omit trite expressions |
| | Avoid unnecessary repetition |
| | Prune wordy expressions |
| | Include only relevant facts |
| | Organize effectively |

Clarity: Choose words that are short, familiar, conversational
Construct effective sentences
Point up the purpose of paragraphs and messages
Include examples, illustrations, and other visual aids when desirable

Completeness: Answer all questions asked
Give something extra, when desirable
Check for the 5 W's and any other essentials

Concreteness: Use specific facts and figures
Put action in your verbs
Choose vivid, image-building words

Consideration: Focus on "you" instead of "I" and "we"
Show reader benefit or interest in reader
Apply integrity in your decisions
Emphasize the positive, pleasant facts

Courtesy: Be sincerely tactful, thoughtful, and appreciative
Omit expressions that irritate, hurt, or belittle
Answer your mail promptly
Grant and apologize good-naturedly

## EXERCISES

1. Discuss orally what is needed to make each of the following requests complete. (Some lack other "C" qualities in addition to completeness.)

   a. The red coat you had in your window last Thursday is exactly the style I would like to have. Please send it to me on my charge account.

   b. Do you have an opening for a young man who has completed three years of college and who needs to work to pay his tuition through school?

   c. Here is my check in payment of the new yearbook you sent me recently. (To an encyclopedia publisher)

   d. I am interested in the portable TV you advertised in yesterday's newspaper. Will you please tell me more about it? (The firm advertised one television set in the city's morning paper and a different set in the evening paper.)

   e. Please reserve three seats for the opera "Turandot" on Saturday evening.

   f. My daughter and I wish to repaint two bedrooms, each of which is 10' x 12'. Please send us the right amount of paint—in pink—to do this job.

   g. The next meeting of the chapter will be held Monday at 8 p.m.

   h. Will you please send me the necessary parts to repair the general purpose steam locomotive for my Vionel model train? It refuses to run. Enclosed is my check, which I hope will cover the necessary replacement parts.

   i. Please send me C.O.D. five more shirts exactly like those I bought from you three months ago. (From a cash customer)

2. Two months before his honorable discharge from overseas military service, a college graduate wrote to a large Eastern university asking about requirements for

entrance into its law school. He said he wanted to make his home in the New England states and practice law there; therefore he preferred to take his law training in the area. Evaluate the following reply he received from that university. The letter was signed by "Director, Program for Servicemen."

Blank University does not have a law school. If you are interested in such training, you should apply to a university where such work is offered.

3. Assume that Letters A and B were written by two correspondents in your insurance company to the widowed mother of a young man who was killed in an airplane crash. Which do you like better? Why? Revise the better of the two letters to make it excellent.

### Letter A

Dear Mrs. Oaks:

The policy under which you have filed claim contains aviation restrictions which limits the Company's liability if the insured's death occurs under certain circumstances.

As the evidence received indicates the insured's death came within these restrictions, the Company's liability is for the restricted amount. Our check representing the Company's liability will be sent shortly to our South Jersey Office for delivery to you.

### Letter B

Dear Mrs. Oaks:

May I extend to you my sincere sympathy in your bereavement.

When your son applied for his insurance, he was a pilot in the RCAF. He stated he did not want to pay an extra premium for the additional aviation hazard. Thus, the policy provided for payment of a restricted amount should his death result from non-passenger travel or flight in any kind of aircraft. The restricted amount is a sum equal to the premiums paid to the Company, together with compound interest at the rate of $2\frac{1}{2}\%$ yearly.

Because the evidence received shows that your son was pilot of the plane that crashed, I am sorry to say the Company's liability is for the restricted amount.

Our check for the Company's liability will be sent shortly to our Chicago Office for delivery to you.

4. Which of the following three memorandums is best? Why? In your evaluation, be sure to consider the probable purpose of the message and whether the memo is likely to be filed.

a.

> Jack to Bob, 4-23-7__
>
> B O O K L E T   S C H E D U L E
>
> Johnson now says Saturday sure.

b.

> TO:     RJL
> FROM:   JS
> April 23, 197_
> HEALTH BOOKLET SCHEDULE
>
> I checked with Johnson and now have a definite
> promise that the 6000 Standard "Your Health"
> booklets will be delivered Saturday, April 26.
>
> This rescheduling will not affect our other pro-
> duction schedules.

c.

> TO:       Dr. Robert Lawson, Vice-President
>
> FROM:     John Spam, Managing Editor
>
> April 23, 197_
>
> RESCHEDULING OF STANDARD "YOUR HEALTH" BOOKLETS
>
> I talked with Thomas Johnson this morning in an
> effort to reschedule production of 6000 Standard
> "Your Health" booklets to permit delivery Saturday,
> April 26.
>
> He indicated at first that such a rescheduling
> would delay either the "Travel Plans" or the "Vaca-
> tion Hints" booklets, but after talking with his
> production manager he agreed to make the schedule
> change without delaying our other production.
>
> Thus we can definitely count on delivery of "Your
> Health" Saturday.

5. Choose an active verb to replace each "deadly" verb hiding in some of the following nouns.

   **a.** Make substitution

   **b.** Have intention

   **c.** Become an imposition

   **d.** Improvement in quality has been made.

   **e.** A sharp increase in profits occurred.

   **f.** Increases in sales of 10 percent were obtained in July.

   **g.** Evaporation of the liquid takes place.

   **h.** Make a decision.

   **i.** Take action.

   **j.** Over the signature of

   **k.** We will give thought to your proposal.

6. Revise the following sentences to eliminate the negative aspects.

   **a.** We are looking forward to pleasant business relations with you.

   **b.** This information is being sent to you now so that we will avoid later misunderstandings about our credit terms.

   **c.** We know you will agree that our prices are not any higher than those of competitors.

   **d.** On COD orders we require a 20 percent deposit to safeguard ourselves against loss in case of refusal of merchandise.

   **e.** We will hold shipment of this hardware until we receive your confirmation.

   **f.** Unfortunately, I will not be able to give you any definite price until you let me know the size and quantity of cartoons you need.

   **g.** We are sorry that we cannot add a car to the policy without a specific description of the vehicle.

   **h.** There will be a delay of four days in filling your order because the material for your coat has to be ordered from Chicago. We are sorry about this delay, but there is nothing we can do about it.

   **i.** Because of shortages of material, we will not be able to ship before June 10.

   **j.** I am sorry I cannot send you the booklet you requested as we have not received it from the publishers.

   **k.** Your bicycle has been repaired and we hope you will have no further trouble with it.

   **l.** We regret that we cannot extend your payment date for more than two months.

   **m.** I hope this adjustment will be satisfactory with you.

**n.** We trust this mistake will not happen again because it is our desire to serve you at all times.

**o.** If you are so inclined, please send us $67.50 today for your two-month delinquent account.

**p.** We regret to inform you that your organization cannot use the conference room tomorrow. In fact, it won't be available to you until next Monday.

**q.** Class, if you are interested, we will have a test tomorrow.

7. Rewrite the following letter, from the Service Department of Benson, a well-known automobile manufacturer; change its tone from negative to positive:

Dear Benson Owner:

Benson has determined that the carburetor fast idle cam on your 197_ Benson may crack over a period of time. If such cracking is followed by a separation of the cam from the shaft, the likelihood is that the only problem noticeable to the driver would be the absence of any fast idle on cold engine startup. However, it is also possible that a piece of the cam may become lodged in the throttle linkage which could prevent the throttle from closing. If this should occur while the vehicle is in motion, the vehicle will not slow down when the driver removes his foot from the accelerator pedal. While this is a remote possibility, if it does occur, the driver should shift the transmission into neutral and bring the vehicle to a complete stop.

To prevent the possibility of this condition occurring, you are requested to contact a Benson dealer who will install a new fast idle cam on the carburetor. This service will be performed at no charge to you.

We are sorry to cause you this inconvenience; however, we have taken this action in the interest of your safety and continued satisfaction with our product. Your cooperation is appreciated.

8. Change the following sentences so that they emphasize "you attitude" instead of "we attitude."

**a.** This is just the kind of job I am looking for, since it offers me a chance to get practical experience in personnel work.

**b.** We hope to have the pleasure of showing you what we think is the finest assortment of Italian boots in the city.

**c.** We value your patronage, for satisfied customers are the foundation of our success.

**d.** Since we have our own obligations to meet, we must ask your immediate attention to your past-due account.

**e.** We do not send receipts because of the extra work involved for us; of course, you have your canceled checks anyway.

**f.** Our pamphlet is designed to help its readers get the most out of raising beautiful roses.

**g.** These sweaters fit well around the shoulders, as our ads show.

**h.** You should send us your dry cleaning because you will be helping us increase our business.

**i.** We are pleased to announce our new bank-by-mail service.

**j.** To help us clear our records, please send us a duplicate copy of our invoice.

**9.** Rewrite the following letters to show a friendly, conversational tone and more "you attitude."

*Letter A*

Dear Sir:

This will acknowledge receipt of your order of June 16 for 12 dozen No. 109 jigsaw puzzle boxes.

Price of $1.60 quoted you last April has been advanced to $1.90. We are billing you at this price for 2 dozen which are going forward today.

We have only a limited supply of these puzzles on hand, as manufacturer is behind on orders. Therefore must backorder 10 dozen, as there are many orders to be filled ahead of yours.

Trusting you will understand this situation, we remain,

*Letter B*

Dear Madam:

We wish to acknowledge receipt of your letter of October 8 enclosing order for a brown tweed suit, Style 346, and check in the amount of $92.00.

In reply we wish to advise that same has been shipped under separate cover and should reach you without undue delay.

Permit us to take this opportunity to enclose a recent brochure which describes our new line of winter furs, and to call your attention to a special sale of fur scarves and hats to be held November 1.

*Letter C*

Dear Home—Owner:

I am writing this letter to offer the services of Inca Millwork and Construction Company in the remodeling of a home.

We are primarily in the business of kitchen and bath remodeling. We can furnish custom cabinets and any type of built—in appliance using such name brands as General Electric, Frigidaire, or Hot Point.

Our customers are given the latest selection of floor coverings and counter top materials.

We maintain our own craftsmen to do the specific job and we guarantee all of our work.

We offer customers bank financing, F.H.A. or conventional with nothing down and no monthly payments until sixty days after completion of the job.

Our company is not the largest in the home improvement field and we do very little advertising. The bulk of our business is acquired through the recommendations of satisfied customers, low prices and quality work.

Please use the self—addressed, stamped card for a free estimate or call 904—8888.

10. Underscore once all active verbs and underscore twice all passive verbs.

A passbook savings account for any amount may be opened anytime. When your first deposit is received, you will be issued a passbook with the amount credited inside. Additional sums may be deposited whenever you desire. Savings received on or before the 15th of any month earn interest from the first of the month. Savings received after the 15th earn from the first of the following month. If the 15th falls on a Saturday or Sunday, the period of earning from the first is extended to the 16th or 17th. Dividends at $4\frac{1}{2}$ percent annually will be added automatically to your passbook account at the end of each quarter, in March, June, September, and December.

Savings certificates are available for a minimum of $1,000 and may be increased in multiples of $100. Interest on these certificates is paid at the end of six months. They earn interest from the day of purchase. The interest is mailed by check to its holder every six months from the date of issue, instead of being automatically credited to the account. If you have a passbook savings account here, we will gladly credit your earnings from the certificate to the passbook account. Savings certificates are automatically renewed on maturity date for an additional six months unless we have notified you at least 30 days before a maturity date. Your certificates earn, at the current rate, $5\frac{1}{4}$ percent annually.

Your savings are insured up to $20,000. We lend our funds upon the security of carefully selected monthly reducing first mortgages on homes. Withdrawals from your savings account may be made anytime without advance notice.

11. Revise each of the following letters to improve their tone and to eliminate any other weaknesses.

> **Letter A:** *A reply from a sardine cannery in Canada to a college student who wrote that he especially liked the sardines but please improve the can.*

Dear Mr. Jones

We thank you for your letter of April 28th and might say that we have a letter before us from our broker in Seattle wishing to purchase a carload of our sardines.  After we received your letter we were a little uneasy about shipping him another car; however, on thinking the matter over if you had not liked our sardines we presume you would not have taken the trouble to write us.

We know the cans do not open right; it seems they will go alright for awhile and then we get a run of cans that everything seems to be wrong; the last thing we found out was that the grain in the tinplate had been changed without our knowledge.  We have a special dye maker chasing this trouble all the time but let me tell you it is a headache.  Don't think for a minute that you are the only one that writes in; we have good customers all over the country and when we get a run of cans that don't open right you can bet your life we get a lot of letters but we are going to keep trying and we hope in the meantime our customers will not be too hard on us.

We are going to send you a few tins from the new pack and will just pray that the dye maker has got the cans opening alright. With kindest regards.

> **Letter B:** *Reply from a motel to a man and wife who requested accommodations.*

Dear Sir and Madam

Your letter of the 23rd. inst was received on the 25th, and in reply will say, I can give you two rooms for time you desire them, and can make you very comfortable with the exception of hot water.

My wife is away on a vacation and shut off the gas water heater, but the few guests here at present find the water warm enough for a shower bath.  Sea bathing is close by, and we are in a very desirable location and very central.  You could come and stop with me for a day or so and if it meets with your approval stay for the two weeks.

The price would be $7.00 per person per day or $45.00 per week each.  Please let me know if you decide to be my guest and the time you expect to arrive. Thank you kindly.

*Letter C: Reply from an insurance company to a policyholder's note of appreciation.*

Dear Mr. Jones:

We have received your letter of August 27, and we wish to state how grateful we are for your expression of confidence in us.

Our wish has always been that we should be of service to our policy holders whenever we are called upon.

Let us say again how much we appreciate your writing to us.

12. A subscriber, Louis Klein of Right Fite Hanger, Inc., recently wrote to three television stations asking if they would like to handle his product on a commission basis. He had heard that some stations occasionally used their open time in this manner. Which of the three replies below do you think adheres best to the writing principles for business? Why? Compare your choice with the other two replies.

*Reply A*

Dear Mr. Klein

I don't know where you got your information as stated in the opening sentence of your letter, "I have been informed that your station promotes items on a commission basis.", and we don't appreciate it.  If you want to do business with us, buy; if you don't, don't write us.

*Reply B*

Dear Mr. Klein

This will acknowledge your recent letter offering your ladies' all plastic dress hanger on a commission basis.

I am quite sure that you did not run your advertisement in the Sunday newspaper supplement on a commission basis.  By the same token we will not accept business on a percentage on per inquiry basis.

For your information, I am attaching our rate card.

*Reply C*

Dear Mr. Klein

Your information must have been somewhat misleading inasmuch as NUTZ has never promoted items on a commission basis.

We would be delighted to handle the Right Fite hanger, and I
personally think it is an item of great demand.

Enclosed is our rate card so that you can choose the time,
frequency, and length of message which will promote your
product as you wish it.

As soon as your reply to these points reach us, we will be glad
to put all our resources at your disposal.

13. Rewrite the following letter so that—in spite of the Congressman's limits on the
number of free booklets he may send out—he can still retain (even build!) goodwill.

> Dear Mr. Cruher:
>
> Inasmuch as I have had so many requests for Botanical Yearbooks
> from students of your college who should look to their Con-
> gressman from the State and Congressional District in which
> they or their families are registered voters, and in order to
> give the legal residents of my District their rightful share of
> these books, I find it necessary to ask for the registered
> voting address when I do not find it listed in the Register.
>
> Because of this, may I ask you for the above information and if
> you do know the name of your Congressman I shall refer your
> request to him for fulfillment. However, if you are a con-
> stituent of mine I shall be glad to send the book.

14. For the following, refer to the five letters you collected and have been studying
for various purposes. (If you prefer, use any other five letters.) Evaluate each
message by:

   **a.** Underscoring once all trite and wordy expressions

   **b.** Underscoring twice all technical language that the reader might not understand

   **c.** Placing parentheses around all negative expressions

   **d.** Encircling all words and expressions that produce an unpleasant tone—such as
   cutting words and abruptness

   **e.** Checking for violations of mechanics—misspelled words, confusing punctuation,
   vague or incomplete sentences, number of sentences exceeding 45 words,
   "goozling" words (unnecessary big words when shorter words accomplish the
   job better), and incorrectly used words.

15. Below are two letters for you to evaluate. Is the message above-average, just average, or unmailable? Why? Be sure you are ready to support your decision before
the class.

**Letter A:** *From a hotel to a person who asked for reservations.*

Dear Mrs. Wolf:

Thank you kindly for your letter of February 18.

We are sorry that we cannot make reservation for you on the nights of June 10, 11 and 12, as Hotel Jefferson is booked to capacity at that time.

Regretting our inability to serve you at this instance, and hoping we may have the opportunity again at some future time, we are

**Letter B:** *From a hotel to a man who had registered there for two days the previous month.*

Dear Mr. Durien:

A short time ago you and Ed Taylor registered in our hotel on September 18 and stayed two days, checking out the 20th.  The rate on this room is $7.00 per day.  Our clerk, Mr. Slyface, was on duty (his first day) when you checked out and he made an error and collected for only one day.

You still owe us for that, and while Mr. Slyface wrote you he would have to stand good for the $7.00 we thot you would send it to us.  However you probably didn't give it much thot and perhaps have forgotten it.  So we will appreciate your sending this to us at once.  For we are sure you would not intentially dismiss the subject and refuse to pay.

However, if this is not paid by November 1, we are forced to turn the account over to the American Hotel Association and they would print your name in all the hotel magazines as one not paying hotel bill which would go to every hotel in the U.S.

I know you are a fine fellow and will take care of this.  For we do appreciate the visit you made us and we want you to come back the next time you are in Omaha.

P.S.  American Royal Stock Show is now on in our city.  It's a wonderful show.  Why don't you come see it?

# Chapter 5

# Parts and Layout of Business Letters and Memoranda

- The Business Letter
- The Memorandum
- Exercises

A letter is judged on its excellence in three areas: content, presentation, and physical appearance. Planning the content and presentation is your responsibility; typing the message so that it is neat, accurate, and attractive is usually your secretary's job. But when you sign your name at the bottom of the letter, you assume final responsibility for everything—mechanics, proper layout, content. If the message contains misspellings or grammatical errors, or if its appearance is poor, the reader judges you, not your secretary. Therefore, you and your secretary must work as a team to produce effective and attractive messages.

This chapter gives you information concerning the appearance of letters and memoranda—discussed from the dictator's viewpoint.

## THE BUSINESS LETTER[1]

Recipients of your business letters form their first impressions even before reading your messages. Elements of appearance that help produce favorable reactions are appropriate stationery, correct letter parts and layout, and properly addressed envelopes.[2]

### Stationery

Although your organization's stationery may be selected by your purchasing department and thus not be your concern, if you have an opportunity to make a choice or suggest a change, keep the following guidelines in mind.

*Quality and Size.* To help build an image of quality and stability, the paper you use should have at least 25 percent rag content. Good-quality paper is not only more attractive, but it permits easier and neater erasing. The difference in price is nominal: Even the best stationery (75 to 100 percent rag content) costs (retail) usually less than two cents a sheet—and that's very little considering that the average cost of a letter is over $3.

The standard size sheet is 8½ by 11 inches, but other sizes are also appropriate for various uses. Executives often prefer slightly smaller sheets—perhaps 7¼ by 10½ inches—for their top-level correspondence. Some firms use half-size stationery (5½ by 8½ inches) for any letter containing less than four sentences.

*Color and Weight.* White is the most popular color, although many firms achieve a distinctive and warm touch by using stationery and envelopes that

---

[1] See pages 154 to 157 for a discussion of the memo-letter, which is becoming popular as a speedy means of communication among middlemen.
[2] In addition to these elements, neat typing also helps make favorable impressions. Poor appearance caused by strikeovers, dirty keys, light ribbon, smears, or poor erasing reflects on you as much as on your secretary.

are pastel (buff, gray, blue, etc.). The weight of general correspondence stationery ranges from 16 to 20 pounds; and of airmail, from 13 to 15 pounds. (Each of these figures is the actual weight of four reams of standard-size paper.)

*Letterhead.* Every business, even if it is a one-man operation, should use letterhead stationery for its correspondence. Only when you are writing a business letter for yourself (that is, not as an agent or representative for any company, club, or organization) will you use paper without a letterhead.

The modern letterhead adheres to three rules—simplicity in design, moderation in size of pictures and lettering, and limitation of information. The letterhead area occupies no more than two inches at the top of the page.[1] Printed or engraved in this area are name and complete address of the firm, including ZIP Code. For some businesses the telephone number may also be essential; and if the organization operates internationally, the cable address is included. Also useful are words indicating the nature of the business and the name of the department or branch office sending the correspondence. Optional details are names of officers and directors, trademark or symbol, slogan, starting date of the firm, and an appropriate picture—perhaps of the building, product(s), familiar landmark, or person whose name the organization bears. Figure 5-1 shows some sample letterheads.

Some organizations take advantage of the usually blank space at the bottom of the sheet by adding printed information. Included are such facts as an important event in the city, listing of services, number of and/or addresses of branches, a quotation or slogan, or some of the information usually found at the top of the sheet.

The paper for pages beyond the letterhead page is of the same quality, color, and weight as the first page, but is either blank or headed simply with the organization's name and address in smaller-size print.

## Parts of the Letter[2]

Most business letters have seven standard parts: (1) heading, (2) inside address, (3) salutation, (4) body, (5) complimentary close, (6) signature area, (7) reference section.

When appropriate, any of these optional parts can be included: (1) at-

---

[1] A comparatively recent innovation, used by a relatively small number of firms, is printing the letterhead along the left margin instead of the top of the sheet. Advocates believe it is not only "different," but also easier to read when it is in the file folder (that "stands" upright in a drawer).

[2] For additional details about typing mechanics and numerous other helpful tips, consult such reference manuals as: Ruth E. Gavin and William A. Sabin, *Reference Manual for Stenographers and Typists,* Fourth Edition, 1970, Gregg Division, McGraw-Hill Book Company, New York; or Clifford House and Apollonia Koebele, *Reference Manual for Office Personnel,* Fifth Edition, 1970, South-Western Publishing Company, Cincinnati.

PRICE WATERHOUSE FOUNDATION
60 BROAD STREET
NEW YORK, N.Y. 10004

**TWA** ─── *TRANS WORLD AIRLINES,* Inc.─── 7001 WORLD WAY WEST
P. O. BOX 90909 AIRPORT STATION
LOS ANGELES, CALIFORNIA, U.S.A. 90009

Weyerhaeuser Company

Tacoma, Washington 98401
A C 206 · 383-3361

THE ***BOEING*** COMPANY

HEADQUARTERS OFFICES · P.O. BOX 3707 · SEATTLE, WASHINGTON 98124

IN REPLY REFER TO

HONOLULU   INTERNATIONAL   AIRPORT   P. O. BOX  9008   HONOLULU,  HAWAII  96820   CABLE  HAWAIR   TELEPHONE  855-911

*HAWAIIAN AIRLINES*

**ALLENITE PRODUCTS COMPANY, INC.**
801 ADDISON STREET · BERKELEY, CALIFORNIA 94710 · (415) 548-1252

| **ALUMINUM** | **STEEL** | F. W. PETER McCHESNEY |
|---|---|---|
| SCAFFOLDS | ROLLING STEPS | President |
| LADDERS | | |
| STAGING PLANKS | | |
| WORK PLATFORMS | | |
| ROLLING STEPS | | |

Fig. 5-1.   Illustrations of modern letterheads. (All the above letterheads are printed in black, except the following: TWA initials, circles, and horizontal lines, in red; Weyerhaeuser outer triangle, in dark green; Allenite, all printing in medium green.)

tention line, (2) subject line, (3) file or reference number, (4) enclosure(s), (5) carbon copy notation, (6) mailing notation, and (7) postscript.

*Heading.* To tell the reader where the letter comes from and when it was written, the heading consists of the letterhead and the date. If the letterhead is printed or engraved, only the date is typed. It is usually placed in one of two locations: (1) halfway (vertically) between the last line of the letterhead and the inside address or (2) two lines below the last line of the letterhead.[1]

When you are writing a business letter for yourself (or family) on blank paper, type both your return address and the date, but *not* your name (see Figure 5-7, page 149). This information is typed single-space, starting at least one inch from the top of the page, either at the left margin (for full-block form, Figure 5-4) or anywhere to the right of center just as long as it doesn't extend into the right margin.

*Inside Address.* The inside address (sometimes called the "introductory" address) includes the complete name and address of the person or persons and the organization to whom the letter is directed. (Whenever possible, address your letter to a person or persons rather than to an organization alone so it seems more personal.) Within the recipient's company, the inside address helps to direct the message to the right person, and it also shows whether any correction in name and address is necessary. Within the sender's organization, this address is the sender's record of to whom and where his letter was directed.

*A courtesy title* should always precede the addressee's name (full first name or two initials plus surname). If the addressee has no professional title—such as doctor, professor, superintendent, etc.—use Mr., Mrs. or Miss. If you are not sure from the name or initials whether the reader is a man or a woman, use Mr. If you don't know the marital status of a woman, use Miss or Ms.,[2] which stands for either Miss or Mrs. If your letter is addressed to two or more men, use Messrs. (plural of Mr.); if to two or more married women, use Mesdames (plural of Mrs.); and if to two or more unmarried women, use Misses (plural of Miss).

*The business or executive title* of your addressee should be included in the inside address. It is a matter of judgment (depending upon the relative length of lines) whether this title is typed (1) on the same line with the addressee's name, (2) on the second line preceding the company name, or (3) on a line or two by itself. Any of these is correct:

[1] The date sequence in American business letters is always month, day, year. The names of the months should be spelled out, and the days (in figures) following the month should not be followed by st, rd, nd, or th. The same rule applies in the body of the letter. But when the date of the day stands alone, add st, rd, nd, or th; for example, "The goods arrived on the 15th of this month."

[2] The Administrative Management Society (AMS), formerly National Office Management Association, has been recommending the abbreviation "Ms." for many years. Although Ms. has gained some degree of popularity since the beginning of the women's liberation movement, persons unfamiliar with this abbreviation are likely to consider it a misspelling.

1. Mr. William Stassen, President
   Western Construction Company
2. Miss Marietta R. Worthington
   Treasurer, Ace Credit Company
3. Mr. Harry M. Fitzsimmons
   Vice President and General Manager
      in Charge of Sales
   Building Services, Inc.

Duplication of titles should be avoided. For example, do not use two titles meaning the same thing, one before and one after the name:

*Wrong:* Dr. Herbert Moore, M.D.
*Right:* Dr. Herbert Moore *or* Herbert Moore, M.D.

**Abbreviations** are appropriate for the following titles: Mr., Mrs., Ms., Messrs. (as for a law firm of Messrs. White, Green, and Black). Other common abbreviations are: Jr., Sr., Mt. (Mount), St. (Saint), Inc. (Incorporated), Ltd. (Limited), D.C. (District of Columbia); compound directions, NW. or NW or N.W. (Northwest); and the professional degree symbols such as B.B.A., Ph.D., M.D., C.P.A. The title Dr. (Doctor) is usually abbreviated, especially when the first name or the initials are used with the surname.[1]

The following words should be spelled out whenever possible: president, superintendent, honorable, reverend, professor, building, association, department; as well as street, boulevard, avenue, east, west, north, south. City names, and generally state names, should also be spelled out. It is best to use abbreviations sparingly. A good rule is "When in doubt, spell it out." However, if you are using the new U.S. Post Office Department two-letter state abbreviations on envelopes, you may wish to abbreviate the state the same way in the inside address for consistency. (See footnote 2, page 151.)

**The order of arrangement** for the various elements of the inside address is comparable to a pyramid. On the top line you place the smallest unit (an individual's name). The remaining items progress downward to the largest unit, as the pyramid below illustrates:[2]

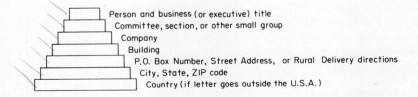

Person and business (or executive) title
Committee, section, or other small group
Company
Building
P.O. Box Number, Street Address, or Rural Delivery directions
City, State, ZIP code
Country (if letter goes outside the U.S.A.)

---

[1] Some authorities suggest abbreviating "doctor" when the first name or initials precede the surname (Dr. John Brown) but spelling it out in a salutation (Dear Doctor Brown). Business people, however, feel that applying two rules is impractical, and they abbreviate "doctor" in both situations.
[2] See also discussion of correct address layout for envelopes, pages 151–152.

The number of lines usually ranges from three to six, as the following five-line address illustrates, but sometimes more than six lines may be necessary.

Mr. James Bengstone, Manager
Southwest Title Company
1601 Tower Building
2973 Lerpson Boulevard
Somecity, Anystate 99999

**Omission of the inside address** is permissible only when you feel sure you cannot justify the extra costs of personalizing; for example, you might wish to omit the inside address in large-scale mailing campaigns or on announcements to your prospects or customers. In such cases a "faked inside address" can attractively fill the space with a reader-interest statement that is part of or leads to the first sentence, as in this letter to parents:

*Faked*    Give your college student
*inside*    a head start
*address*  toward financial security!

    Every young person needs an insurance program and there's
    no better time to plan for the future than right now . . .

*Salutation.* The salutation is the friendly greeting that precedes the body of the letter. It is typed two spaces below the inside address and even with the left-hand margin.

**The most popular salutations** in use today are:

1. Dear Mr. (Mrs., Miss) Doe—when writing to a customer, acquaintance, prospect, stockholder, supplier, or stranger.
2. Gentlemen (not Dear Gentlemen or Dear Sirs)—when writing to a company or P.O. Box, or Ladies (not Dear Ladies or Dear Mesdames)—when you're sure that all employees are women.
3. Dear John (or Mary or nickname)—when writing to an individual you'd address this way in person and when it is appropriate for you to do so in your letter on this occasion.

Such salutations as Dear Sir and Dear Madam are impersonal and should be avoided whenever possible.

The first line of the inside address determines the salutation. For example, if it contains the name of a group, committee, or company, the salutation is plural—"Gentlemen" or "Ladies." If it contains the name of an individual, the salutation is singular—"Dear Mr. Smith" or "Dear John." An intervening attention line does not change the salutation:[1]

---

[1] Some businessmen do not use this rule. If they must begin the inside address with the organization name, and must also have an attention line to an individual, they personalize the salutation, using, for instance, "Dear Mr. Jones" instead of "Gentlemen." As an alternative, if you feel strongly that you want to use Mr. Jones's name in the salutation and it's agreeable with your firm, then add his full name (first name or initials and surname) on the inside address, above the company name, and omit the attention line.

```
Midwest Office Equipment Company
(Street address)
(City), (State), ZIP
```

Attention: Mr. A. B. Jones

Gentlemen

**Two other variations** pertaining to the salutation are (1) the "salutopening" and (2) the omitted salutation in the "simplified letter."

If you feel that a salutation such as "Dear Mr. Brown" is not appropriate, because he is a stranger to you, or the "Dear" just seems unnatural, you might prefer a *salutopening*. This is typed on the salutation line, but it omits "Dear" and begins with the first few words of your opening paragraph plus your reader's name. After the name the sentence continues a double space down to the first line of the letter body, as in these examples:

*Salutation line*  What do you think, Mr. Brown,

*Body*          of the enclosed suggested arrangement for . . . ?

and

*Salutation line*  Thank you, Miss Smith,

*Body*          for writing us so promptly about your new address.

Most businessmen have not yet accepted the salutopening in their daily writing. They use the conventional salutations already discussed.

The "simplified letter," (Figure 5-5) sponsored by the Administrative Management Society (AMS), omits the salutation entirely; but it uses the reader's name near the beginning of the first sentence. For example:

*Body*          What do you think, Mr. Brown, of the enclosed
               arrangement for . . . ?

and

*Body*          Thank you, Miss Smith, for writing us so
               promptly about . . . .

**On mass mailings of form letters** it is best to have a personal salutation (and inside address) whenever possible typed to match the rest of the letter. However, if you must cut down on costs by *omitting* the personal inside address, you have three alternatives for the salutation:

1. Use an appropriate general salutation to fit the individual(s) getting your letter. Below is a partial list of words used; each is preceded by "Dear."

| | | |
|---|---|---|
| Borrower | Friends | Professor |
| (City) Attorney | Graduate | Saver |
| Credit Union Executive | Loan Customer | Savings Customer |
| Customer | Member | Shareholder |
| Educator | Newcomer | Sportsman |
| Folks | Parents | Student |
| Friend | Principal and Teachers | |

2. Omit the salutation and substitute an appealing short statement on the salutation line, like these four examples:

   A dividend for you . . .
   (Name of firm) has a special offer for you!
   Welcome to (name of city or town)!
   Good news for college graduates . . .

3. Place the first few words of the first sentence in the position of inside address (three lines) and salutation (fourth line); then double-space and begin the body of the letter.

| | |
|---|---|
| *Faked inside address* | The last time you had<br>a chance like this<br>to get World and Home News |
| *Faked salutation* | at a big savings . . . |
| *Body* | . . . business was coasting along without any serious worries, the war in Asia seemed to be cooling off, the President had . . . . |

**Body.** This book discusses in detail the content and presentation of the body; thus only general guidelines are summarized here. In the body you must try to:

1. Organize according to an appropriate plan.
2. Keep your first and last paragraphs short—preferably 5 to 7 lines or less (not more than 50 words).
3. Vary the intervening paragraph lengths, up to 10 lines maximum.
4. Make the average length of your sentences about 17 to 20 words.
5. Use a topic sentence in each paragraph.
6. Achieve the "C" qualities.

Generally all letters should be typed single-space, with double spacing between paragraphs.

When the body of the letter is two or more pages, each page beyond the first is headed by a combination of the addressee's name, the page number, and date. With these three items all pages of the message can be easily identified and kept together. This information is typed one to two inches from the top of the sheet in any of the following ways:

**Mr. John Jones**
Page 2
May 3, 197_
   *or*
Mr. John Jones               2             May 3, 197_
   *or*
Mr. John Jones—2—May 3, 197_

If the letter is addressed to a company for someone's attention, any of the formats above are acceptable, except that both the company and the person's name should appear:

General Supply Corporation       2       May 3, 1972
Attention Mr. John Jones

***Complimentary Close.*** The complimentary close should agree, with respect to formality or informality, with your salutation. Most business letters use one of three key words—"sincerely," "truly," or "cordially." The following salutations and complimentary closes are appropriate together:

| | | |
|---|---|---|
| Dear Mr. (Mrs., Miss, Ms.) Smith | *and* | Sincerely, Sincerely yours, Yours sincerely, Very truly yours, Yours very truly[1] |
| Gentlemen (Ladies) | | |
| Dear John (Mary, or a nickname) | *and* | Sincerely, Cordially, or some more familiar phrasing in good taste— such as Best regards[2] |

If you are using the AMS simplified letter, you omit the complimentary close. At other times, you may want to use a complimentary close that ties in with your message or product; for example:

| | | |
|---|---|---|
| Warmly | Yours for fashion | Yours for extra profits |
| Gratefully | Yours for cleaner air | Season's Greetings |

[But avoid inappropriate "gimmick" complimentary closes, like the following: "Gastronomically yours" (from a restaurant), "Hopefully yours" (from a collector), or "Saltily yours" (from a salt processor).]

---

[1] Businessmen's views differ widely on the use of "yours" and "very" in the complimentary close. Many writers prefer to omit both these words with "sincerely" and "cordially," because they feel that adding them makes these friendly closes sound stilted or inappropriate. On the contrary, with "truly" many prefer both "very" and "yours," for just plain "Yours truly" has fallen in disfavor because of jokes about this expression. Thus they use "Yours very truly" or "Very truly yours." Still others dislike all the "truly's." The choice is up to you.

[2] Avoid double closings, such as using both "Best regards" and "Sincerely."

**Signature Area.** You can include in the signature area four separate identifications—name of your company, your signature, your typewritten name,
and your business title.

**Your company name,** if printed on the letterhead, need not be repeated
after the complimentary close (except in legal documents and negotiable
instruments).[1] However, if you wish to include the company name (many firms
require it, for various reasons), type it in capital letters a double space under
the complimentary close.

**Your typed name** appears three to five lines under either the company
name (if included) or the complimentary close.

**Your signature** is usually written in blue or black ink—never pencil—
above the typed name.

**The typed business title** usually follows the typed name.

Very truly yours,

*Thomas L. Sutton*

Thomas L. Sutton
Manager, Plant 2

Yours sincerely

THE PRONSON COMPANY

*James P. Tracy*

James P. Tracy
Office Manager

Cordially yours,

*Roy Layton*

Roy Layton, President

If you prefer, instead of having your name typed under the complimentary close, it may be typed flush with the left margin, usually on the same
line with your title, which appears four lines under the complimentary close.
You sign above your title. (See Figure 5-3.)

If you are a man, "Mr." is omitted before and after your name, unless
your first name is used by both men and women (for example, Robin, Chris)
and you want to be sure the respondent addresses you "Mr."[2]

If you are a woman, it is better to add "Miss" or "Mrs." to your name in
the signature section. Usually parentheses enclose either title when it is included in the handwritten signature, but not when it appears with the typed
named. If no title is used, the assumption is that the woman is unmarried.
For business and professional women, the following signatures are commonly
used:

Unmarried woman:

*Sara Mae Jones*
Miss Sara Mae Jones

*(Miss) Sara Mae Jones*
Sara Mae Jones

*Sara Mae Jones*
Sara Mae Jones

[1] Even though the firm name is not typed in the signature lines, the firm is considered responsible for
the content of a message written by one of its agents about business he is *authorized* to handle.

[2] The Mr., Miss, or Mrs., when inserted, *precede* the typewritten or the handwritten name. A few men
and women, however, prefer to type or write the title in parentheses *after* their name—Marion
Moss (Mr.) and Pat Jones (Miss). This arrangement emphasizes their name rather than their
status.

Married woman or a widow: (If Sara Mae Jones married Albert B. Smith, she uses her first name and husband's surname, or she inserts for a middle name or initial her maiden surname or her middle name.)

*Sara Smith*
Mrs. Sara Smith

*(Mrs.) Sara J. Smith*
SaraJones(or J.)Smith

*Sara Mae Smith*
Mrs. Sara Mae (or M.)Smith

Divorcee: same form as for a widow unless the court has restored her maiden name, in which case she uses the style of the unmarried woman.

*Reference Section.* Your initials as dictator of the message, and those of your typist, usually appear at the left margin on the same line with the last line of the signature area (your name or title) or one or two lines below that. If your name is typed at the left margin instead of in the signature area (Figure 5-3), the typist's initials follow it. Among the common forms used are:

KLM:tr                 KLM:TR                 klm/tr
K.L.Morning:TR         KLMorning-tr

If someone other than the signer of the letter composes it, practice varies regarding reference initials. Many firms show at least on the file copy the initials of signer, writer, and typist (KLM:JC:tr); the original, to the addressee, may omit all or the writer's initials, to avoid showing that the signer did not dictate the letter.

*Attention Line.* Considered part of the inside address, the attention line directs a letter to a particular person or title or department when the letter is addressed to a company. It is useful when the writer doesn't know the name of an individual but wants his message to go to a particular title (Sales or Adjustment Director) or department (Personnel). It is also useful when the writer knows only the surname of an individual and thus cannot use the name on the first line of the inside address.

The usual placement of the attention line is between the inside address and salutation (a blank line before and after it), flush with the left margin, indented with the paragraphs, or centered. (See Figures 5-3.)

ATTENTION PURCHASING MANAGER          Attention Miss Erickson

*Subject Line.* Considered part of the body of the letter, the subject line helps to tell your reader at a glance what your letter is about. It also helps in filing. The subject line may include or omit the word "subject" or "about" but should be underscored so that it will catch the reader's eye immediately. It is usually placed either on the same line with the salutation or double-spaced below the salutation and centered. Avoid "re" or "in re"; they are outdated. (See Figures 5-5 and 5-7.)

*File or Reference Number.* To aid in filing and quick recognition for both the sender's and the reader's company, some firms require that file, loan, or account numbers be typed above the body of the letter in a conspicuous place.

*Enclosure Notation.*[1] To remind whoever prepares your envelope for mailing that something is to be enclosed, the enclosure notation is usually typed a single or double space under the reference initials. This notation also alerts the addressee's incoming mail department to check for enclosures. An enclosure is anything in the envelope other than the message itself. One enclosure is a unit that can consist of one or more pages (for example, a two-page résumé with an application letter is only one enclosure). When more than one item is enclosed, your secretary should indicate the number: "Enclosures 3" or "Enc. 3." When the enclosures are especially important (checks, legal documents, or blueprints), it is desirable to list in the enclosure notation exactly what the enclosures are.

*Copy Notation.*[1] When you want other persons to receive a copy of the letter you have written to the addressee, the names of these persons (arranged in order of importance or alphabetically) should be typed after "cc" or the like just below the reference initials or the enclosure notation (if any):

cc: Mr. Sims                           Copies to A. E. Brown and R. J. Sims

If you do not want the addressee to know that other recipients are getting a copy of the letter, your secretary can type "bcc" (blind carbon copy) and the recipients' names *on the carbon copies only.*

*Mailing Notation.*[1] Words such as "Special Delivery," "Registered," or "Certified Mail," when applicable, may be typed either below the carbon copy notation (or whatever is the last notation) or on the second line below the date.

*Postscript.*[1] To emphasize a point already in your letter or to include a personal brief message unrelated to the letter, a postscript (typed or handwritten) may be added—below everything else typed on the page. However, if you forgot to include an important idea in the letter body, it is usually better to retype the letter than to add the information in a postscript. (See Figure 5-7.)

## Letter Layout

Although the layout of the letter is primarily the typist's responsibility, it is covered briefly here to give you a basis for choosing the style(s) you prefer.

---

[1] If you have occasion to use several notations after the signature area, the initials **RECMP** indicate the proper order for arranging them vertically at the left margin: reference initials, enclosures, copy notation, mailing notation, postscript.

Many progressive companies have adopted a format that is used throughout the company, so that all their letters contribute to an attractive, uniform image—regardless of dictator, deparment, or stenographer.

*Punctuation Styles.* The two forms of punctuation most used in business letters are *open* and *mixed.* In open punctuation, no line of any of the seven standard letter parts (except the body) has any punctuation at the end unless an abbreviation requires a period. Mixed punctuation—the most popular style today—is like open except that a colon follows the salutation and a comma follows the complimentary close.

*Letter Styles.* Business letters are usually arranged in one of the letter styles described briefly below. You will find additional details discussed within the letters illustrated in Figures 5-2 to 5-7.[1]

1. *Blocked* form is currently the most popular style. All parts are blocked; there are no paragraph indentions. The date, complimentary close, and signature sections begin near the center of the page; the other parts, at the left margin. (See Figures 5-2 and 5-7.)
2. *Semiblocked* style is the same as blocked, except that the paragraphs are indented. It is also a popular style. (See Figure 5-3.)
3. *Full blocked (or extreme block)* begins every line at the left margin. (See Figure 5-4.) This is the fastest style to type, especially when used with open punctuation. To offset a lopsided appearance at the left, some firms use a letterhead with most of its printing at the right side.
4. *AMS simplified* style, adopted by the Administrative Management Society, uses full block and open punctuation; omits the salutation and complimentary close; and includes a subject line without the word "subject," typed in all capital letters a triple space after the inside address. The first paragraph contains the reader's name. (See Figure 5-5.)
5. *Hanging (or inverted) paragraph* style is unsuitable for daily correspondence, but distinctive for a sales or advertising letter in which you want to emphasize the first words of each paragraph. All lines of the letter body are indented except the first line of each paragraph. (See Figure 5-6.)

Public and government officials—as well as businessmen writing formal messages—often use what is called the *official letter style.*[2] Its general layout may be blocked or semiblocked, but the inside address—instead of being placed above the salutation—is typed at the left margin two to five lines below the last line of the signature section. Reference initials and other notations, if any, then appear after the inside address.

*Tips for Letter Placement.* The easiest way to achieve pleasing appearance for all your letters is to have a competent secretary. However, most students—and even many young businessmen—find it necessary to type some

[1] The discussion in these letters is adapted from *Reference Manual for Stenographers and Typists,* Ruth E. Gavin and William A. Sabin, Gregg Division, McGraw-Hill Book Company, New York, 1970.
[2] Some writers also use this style with informal letters that begin with a first-name salutation.

letters themselves. Though there are other good placement guides, the following table is easy to use. It assumes a fixed vertical position for the date—on about the 13th line from the top of the page. Notice that the line length of any letter is 4, 5, or 6 inches, depending on letter length.[1] Before using the guide, you should:

1. Estimate the approximate number of words in your letter.
2. Know whether your typewriter has elite (E) or pica (P) type.[2]
3. Place the typewriter paper guide at zero.

(The letters in Figures 5-2 to 5-7 are based on this guide, for elite type.)

| Letter length | Words in body | Line length in | | Margins | | Number of lines between date and inside address |
|---|---|---|---|---|---|---|
| | | Inches | Spaces | Width in inches | Machine settings* | |
| Short | Under 100 | 4 | 40 P | 2¼ | 22–62 P | 6–10 |
| | | | 50 E† | | 26–76 E | |
| Medium | 100–200 | 5 | 50 P | 1¾ | 17–67 P | 4–8 |
| | | | 60 E | | 21–81 E | |
| Long | 200–300 | 6 | 60 P | 1¼ | 12–72 P | 2–6 |
| | | | 70 E† | | 16–86 E | |
| 2-page | Over 300 | 6 | 60 P | 1¼ | 12–72 P | 2–6 |
| | | | 70 E† | | 16–86 E | |

* To allow for the ringing of the typewriter bell and to avoid frequent use of the margin release key, add five spaces to the settings for the right margin.
† Rounded off.

## Envelopes

Your organization's envelopes not only get your messages to their destination, but help, indirectly, to advertise your company. The quality of the envelope paper (preferably the same as the letter stationery) and the pictures and slogans, if any, all contribute to your organization's image. Each envelope should show the sender's return address, which is usually printed (in a format identical with that of the letterhead), or typewritten if necessary, in the upper left corner.

The inside address of the letter is the outside address on the envelope. To speed the processing of your mail at the post office, your company should keep up to date on Post-Office-recommended location and legibility of the address on the envelope, and the layout of information within each address.

---

[1] To save time and money, some firms use the same line lengths for all messages regardless of length.
[2] With pica type you get 10 characters to the horizontal inch and 85 across the 8½-inch page; with elite, 12 to the inch and 102 across the page. Both have 6 vertical lines to the inch.

LETTERHEAD

January 27, 197_

{ 3 blank lines
after date

Mr. Walter Bronson, Office Manager
Intermountain and Valley Farm
  Equipment Company, Inc.
456 Glenhaven Building
Blanktown, Anystate  99999

Dear Mr. Bronson:

The blocked form (also called modified block) is used most frequently in business.  All parts except the date, complimentary close, and signature sections begin at the left margin.

The date may be centered (horizontally) or begin anywhere to the right of center, as long as it doesn't extend into the right margin.  In this letter, for example, the date (on the 13th line from top) ends at the right margin. In the inside address an unusually long title or company name (as shown here) may occupy two lines; the part carried to the second line is indented two spaces.  For the saluation, "Dear Walt:" might be correct too (and the signature could be merely "Gene").

Because this letter uses mixed punctuation, the only end-of-line punctuation is the colon after the salutation and the comma after the complimentary close.  No punctuation is used after the date nor after any line in the inside address, except after an abbreviation; for instance, "Inc."

The complimentary close may start at the horizontal center of the page, as in this example, or to right of center so that the longest line in the signature area ends at the right margin.  Company name may be omitted. Here the signer's typed name and his business title are typed on the fourth line below the complimentary close.  The signer's title may be typed on the line below his name; or it can be split and typed on two lines.

The term "Enclosures 3" in the reference section shows that three additional items are being enclosed in the envelope.  Each different item is counted as one, regardless of the number of pages it may have.  The notation "cc" indicates that a carbon copy is being sent to Mr. Jami and Miss Brown.

Sincerely,

*Eugene A. Milton*

{ 3 blank lines
for signature

Eugene A. Milton, Director
Customer Service Department

EAM:HM
Enclosures 3
cc: Mr. Thomas Jami
    Miss Helen Brown

Fig. 5-2.  Blocked (or Modified Block) letter with mixed punctuation. Length: "long"; side margins, 1¼"; line length, 6".

LETTERHEAD

December 15, 197_

{ 4 blank lines

Accounting Department
Eastern Register Company
1969 Fourth Avenue, NE.
Sometown, Anystate  99999

Attention Mr. Johnson

Gentlemen:

The semiblocked form is like the blocked except that its
paragraphs are indented five or more spaces. The date should
be placed so it does not extend into the right margin. In this
example the date begins at the horizontal center of the page.

The attention line here is at the left margin, two lines
below the inside address, and underlined. It could also have
been centered and typed in all capital letters without underscoring. If you wanted Mr. Johnson's name in the salutation,
you would type his first name (or two initials) and his surname
above Accounting Department. Then you would omit the attention
line and use "Dear Mr. Johnson" in the salutation.

In this example the complimentary close, like the date,
begins at the center of the page. The company name is omitted,
but it could have been included. Also the signer's name--
instead of being at the left--could have been typed above the
"General Manager" and reference initials (like "MM:hm") could
then have been used at the left margin.

Very truly yours,

*Millard Morrison*   { 4 blank lines
                       for signature
General Manager

Millard Morrison:HM

Encl.--Check

Fig. 5-3.  Semiblocked letter with indented paragraphs and mixed punctuation. Length:
"medium"; side margins, 1¾"; line length, 5".

LETTERHEAD

June 22, 197_

6 blank lines }

Mr. Thomas R. Swenson
Director of Personnel
Providence Insurance Company
First and Market Streets
Somecity, Anystate 99999

Dear Mr. Swenson

In this full-blocked letter, every line begins at
the left margin. A full-blocked letter is <u>never
double spaced</u>.

Many firms prefer open punctuation with this form,
but mixed can also be used. The writer's company
name may be typed under the complimentary close,
as here, or omitted.

Other accepted forms of reference initials could,
of course, be used with this letter style. Also
the "Registered Mail" or other special service
(such as special delivery) notation could be
typed in full capitals two lines below the date
instead of under the reference initials.

Sincerely yours

WESTERN OFFICE EQUIPMENT COMPANY

*James Briggs*

3 blank lines
for signature }

James Briggs, Manager
Adjustment Department

JB/jd

Registered Mail

Fig. 5-4. Full (or Extreme) block letter with open punctuation. Length: "short"; side
margins, 2¼"; line length, 4".

LETTERHEAD

July 26, 197_

3 blank lines }

Mrs. Mary Hurlbut
P. O. Box 9152
Sometown, Anystate   66666

FORMAT FOR SIMPLIFIED LETTER

This letter form, Mrs. Hurlbut, has been recommended by the
Administrative Management Society (formerly NOMA) as an
important time-saving step when typing business letters.
This letter setup saves about 19 key strokes.  Here are its
features:

1.  It uses full block form and open punctuation.

2.  It omits the saluation and the complimentary close, but--
    to personalize--the reader's name is used at least in the
    first sentence.

3.  The subject line is in all capitals, omits "subject,"
    and has at least one blank line both before and after it.

4.  The signer's name and business title are typed in all capi-
    tals, starting at the left margin at least four blank lines
    below the last line of the letter body.

5.  The typist's initials are typed at the left margin two lines
    below the signer's name.  Enclosures are indicated below the
    initials.  Names of persons receiving carbon copies are typed
    below the initials and enclosures.

Mrs. Hurlbut, the efficiency of this Simplified Letter suggests
that it is especially desirable where output must be increased.

4 blank lines
for signature }  *Paul A. Mullins*

PAUL A. MULLINS - RESEARCH DIRECTOR

hm
Enc 4
Messrs. Ronald Scharf, Mike Luberts, Erich Wittor

Fig. 5-5.  Simplified letter style with Full Block and open punctuation. Length: "medium";
side margins, 1¾"; line length, 5".

LETTERHEAD

September 17, 19--

} 5 blank
  lines

For Those Who Need to Display
A Special Sales or Advertising Letter
So It Looks Special

Dear Mr. Salesmanager:

The hanging-indented form is commonly used in sales and advertising
    letters or letters containing a number of different topics that
    should be set off from one another.

The key words are "hanging" in the left margin at the start of each
    paragraph, with other lines indented. Sometimes the key words are
    typed in all capitals for even more emphasis.

This letter style is designed solely for sales promotion; it is too cum-
    bersome for daily correspondence. The main reason for this display
    is to feature the paragraph starters. Thus the letter must be pre-
    pared to fit this arrangement.

The typist, after typing the inside address, salutation, and first line
    of the letter, sets a stop some appropriate number of spaces to
    the right of the margin. She then indents all lines except the
    first one in each paragraph. An alternate way to type this letter
    is to move the left margin stop to govern all lines of paragraphs
    except the first lines. The typist then sets a tab stop at the
    desired starting point for the first line of paragraphs, and uses
    the margin-release key when returning the carriage. When she de-
    presses the tabular key, the carriage moves to the correct position
    for starting the first line of each paragraph.

The company name may be typed (in all capital letters) two lines under
    the complimentary close, or it may be omitted. The signer's name
    may be typed three or four lines under the last typed line or even
    with the left margin, as in Fig. 5-3. Reference data are placed
    even with the left margin.

Cordially yours,

SPECIAL LETTERS, INC.

*Otmar Moonson*

Otmar Moonson, Vice President

} 3 blank
  lines

om/jm

Fig. 5-6.   Hanging paragraph (or Inverted Paragraph) style with open punctuation. Length:
    "long"; side margins, 1¼"; line length, 6".

1½" from top

4524  17th Avenue
Seattle, Washington 98102
October 4, 197_

3 blank lines

Mr. Joseph M. Albrecht
Manager, Jupiter and Jones, Ltd.
815 Fourth Avenue
Vancouver, B. C.
Canada

Dear Mr. Albrecht:

Subject:  Letters with Quotations and Tabulations

The subject line (if given) is typed on the second line below the salutation.  It may be at the left margin, indented the same as paragraphs, or
centered--as in this example.  It may be typed either in all-capital
letters or in capital and small letters that are underscored. The word
"Subject" often precedes the actual subject.

When you have quoted matter, numbered paragraphs, tabulations, or other
material that you want to emphasize in the body of your letter, your
secretary should always double space before and after such material.  For
instance, here is a quotation from an article in a handbook:

        When a quotation occupies more than three lines,
        give it special display (use a shorter line length
        than that used for the remainder of the material) and
        type it single spaced, instead of using quotation marks.

When you want to set off listed items or tabulated material, your secretary should indent the left and right margins equally and single space
such material.

|  | 1971 | 1972 |
|---|---|---|
| Gross income | $550,972 | $588,974 |
| Expense and taxes | 390,004 | 392,593 |
| Net income | $160,968 | $196,381 |

To bring out points more forcibly, the items may be indented an equal
number of spaces from the left and right margins and numbered.  These
methods help to bring material to the reader's attention quickly and
artistically.

        1.  Your profit will increase 10 percent.
        2.  Your savings are insured up to $20,000.

1½" from
bottom

Fig. 5-7.  Personal Business Letter, Blocked with mixed punctuation. First page of a 2-page
letter typed on blank paper (with no letterhead) . Side margins: 1¼"; line length, 6".

1" from top

Mr. Joseph M. Albrecht
Page 2
October 4, 197_

2 blank lines }

Letters over 300 words in length usually require two pages, particularly when typed on a pica-type machine. The right, left, and bottom margins on the first page should be balanced. The second-page heading begins at least six line spaces (1 inch) from the top and consists of the name of the addressee, "Page 2," and the date. The letter continues on the second or third line below the heading—with at least two or more lines of the body.

Tabulations, quoted material, and enumerations in the body of any letter affect the working out of the letter-placement rules. It is often necessary to adjust the marginal stops for a longer line of writing and very often to raise the letter on the page.

A postscript is typed at least two spaces below the reference initials or enclosure notation. The "P. S." may be omitted.

Sincerely,

*Franklin G. Worthington*

Franklin G. Worthington

4 blank lines for signature }

FGW:re
Enclosure--Insurance Policy #95991

P. S. The signer of this letter has no title. He is writing on blank paper, not on a company letterhead.

Fig. 5-7.   (continued) Second page of a 2-page letter. Length: "2-page"; side margins, 1¼"; line length, 6".

***Recommended Address Location and Legibility.*** If you are in a city where the Optical Character Reader (OCR) has been installed in the post office, you can obtain maximum benefits from this program by following suggested guidelines.[1] (Even if your city's post office does not yet have the OCR, a gradual adjustment to machine-compatible addressing may be desirable.)

Because the OCR is programmed to scan a specific area on all envelopes, the address must be located completely in what is known as the read zone. In general a safe location is in the *lower right quarter section* of the envelope so that the last line is more than one-half inch from the bottom (see Figure 5-8). The OCR can read envelopes ranging in size from a minimum of 3 by $4\frac{1}{4}$ inches to a maximum of $5\frac{3}{4}$ by $11\frac{1}{2}$ inches.

To be read by the OCR, the envelope address should be clearly imprinted with dark print (or typewriter type) on a light background. The address should be parallel (within five degrees) with the bottom edge of the envelope; slanted or crooked lines can confuse OCR recognition.

***Recommended Address Layout.*** To be processed quickly and accurately by OCR, the envelope address should meet these requirements:

1. **The format** must be single-space and blocked, not indented.

*Good*

Mr. John Smith
6 Vale Street
Worcester, MA[2] 01604

*Poor*

Mr. John Smith
6 Vale Street
    Worcester, MA 01604

---

[1] Most information in this section is adapted from *Addressing for the Optical Character Reader,* United States Postal Service, Publication 114, January 1971.

[2] Although you can use any of the traditional spellings and abbreviations for states, the Post Office also permits use of the following new abbreviations—two capitals without periods or spaces—as listed in *Address Abbreviations,* United States Postal Service, Publication 59, August 1970:

| Old | New | Old | New | Old | New |
|-----|-----|-----|-----|-----|-----|
| Ala. | AL | Ky. | KY | N.Dak. | ND |
| Alaska | AK | La. | LA | Ohio | OH |
| Ariz. | AZ | Maine | ME | Okla. | OK |
| Ark. | AR | Md. | MD | Oreg. | OR |
| Calif. | CA | Mass. | MA | Pa. | PA |
| Colo. | CO | Mich. | MI | P.R. | PR |
| Conn. | CT | Minn. | MN | R.I. | RI |
| Del. | DE | Miss. | MS | S.C. | SC |
| D.C. | DC | Mo. | MO | S.Dak. | SD |
| Fla. | FL | Mont. | MT | Tenn. | TN |
| Ga. | GA | Nebr. | NE | Tex. | TX |
| Hawaii | HI | Nev. | NV | Utah | UT |
| Idaho | ID | N.H. | NH | Vt. | VT |
| Ill. | IL | N.J. | NJ | Va. | VA |
| Ind. | IN | N.Mex. | NM | Wash. | WA |
| Iowa | IA | N.Y. | NY | W.Va. | WV |
| Kans. | KS | N.C. | NC | Wis. | WI |
|  |  |  |  | Wyo. | WY |

2. **City, state, and ZIP Code,** in that sequence, must all be on the bottom line.[1]

| *Good* | *Poor* | *Poor* |
|---|---|---|
| Sellmore Co. | Sellmore Co. | Sellmore Co. |
| 1000 Main Street | 1000 Main Street | 1000 Main Street |
| Detroit, MI 48217 [2] | Detroit, MI | Detroit, MI |
| | 48217 |        48217 |

3. **Street name—correctly spelled—or box number** should be on the line immediately above the city, state, and ZIP Code.

| *Good* | *Good* |
|---|---|
| Mr. Bob Brown | Mr. Joe Gray |
| 12 Hurd St. | Box 2 |
| Duluth, MN 55808 | Duluth, MN 55803 |

4. **Number of an apartment, room, suite, or other unit of multiunit unnamed** building should appear immediately after the street address on the same line—never above, below, nor in front of the street address.

| *Good* | *Poor* | *Poor* | *Poor* |
|---|---|---|---|
| Miss Sue Smith | Miss Sue Smith | Miss Sue Smith | Miss Sue Smith |
| 2605 Cole St. Apt. 12 | 2605 Cole St. | Apt. 12 | Apt. 12 2605 Cole |
| Dallas, TX 75204 | Apt. 12 | 2605 Cole St. | Dallas, TX 75204 |
| | Dallas, TX 75204 | Dallas, TX 75204 | |

5. **On-arrival instructions** such as "Confidential," "Attention Mr. Drake," "Please forward," and account numbers should be typed either (a) outside the read zone (as shown in Figure 5-8 for the account number) or (b) inside the read zone on any line above the second line from the bottom of the address (as shown in Figure 5-8 for the attention line).

## THE MEMORANDUM

In contrast to the letter, which is directed outside your organization, the memorandum goes to someone within your organization. The stationery, parts, layout, and envelopes of the memo are somewhat different from those of the letters described in the preceding section. (The memo-letter, which is directed outside the organization, is illustrated in this section because it is more similar to a memo than to a letter.)

### Stationery

Memorandum stationery often differs from letter stationery in quality, color, size, and printing.

---

[1] Placing the ZIP Code alone on the bottom line relegates the city and state to the *second* line from the bottom, where the Optical Character Reader is programmed to look for the street address or box number when sorting incoming mail.

[2] Some items are boxed merely to draw your attention to them. They are not to be boxed on the envelope.

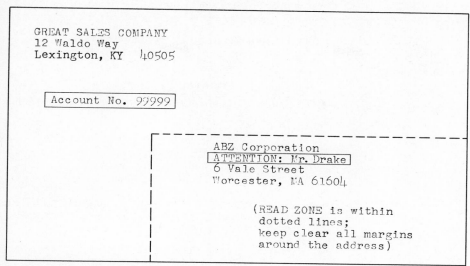

GREAT SALES COMPANY
12 Waldo Way
Lexington, KY  40505

Account No. 99999

ABZ Corporation
ATTENTION: Mr. Drake
6 Vale Street
Worcester, MA 61604

(READ ZONE is within
dotted lines;
keep clear all margins
around the address)

**Fig. 5-8. Sample envelope.**

*Quality, Color, Size.* When the message goes to employees within the firm, consideration of public relations is not necessary. Memo stationery is usually of a much less expensive quality paper than that for regular letters; instead of rag, it is generally made of wood pulp. Instead of white, memo paper is often in pastel colors—yellow, cream, pink, blue—for easy identification. Sometimes each color indicates the department to which a particular copy should go. Sizes of sheets range from the standard 8½ by 11 inches to small slips 4 by 5 inches.

*Printing.* At the top of the full-page memorandum are usually printed such words as OFFICE MEMORANDUM and the company's name (but not address). Along the left margin (or in various other locations) are printed: TO, FROM, SUBJECT, DATE—and sometimes also MESSAGE. In some memos FROM is omitted and the writer signs at the end—as on a letter. Some memos also include such printed words as File number; Telephone; For your: approval, information, comment (see Figure 5-9). Printed lines to write on are useful for employees who are likely to communicate in handwriting. Often when a person has only a few sentences to convey, it is quicker to write than to call a secretary. Printing at the bottom sometimes includes various instructions and reminds employees of the risks of oral messages (Figure 5-9).

The combination *message-and-reply memorandum* form is an especially good time (and expense) saver for both sender and recipient. A packet of three or more sheets of paper (white and colored), plus carbons (unless special "carbonless" paper is used), makes up a message-reply packet. Printed instructions at the top or bottom tell the sender and the reader how to use the

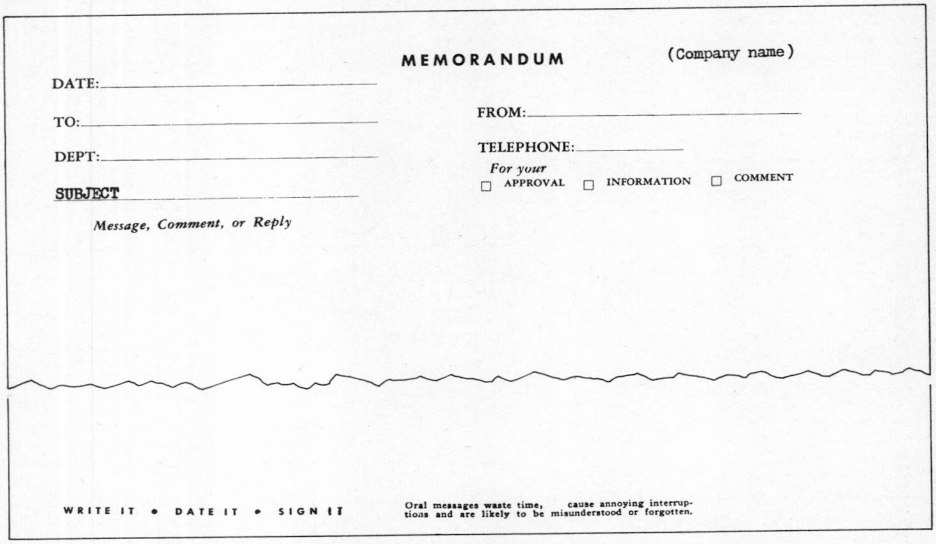

MEMORANDUM (Company name)

DATE:

TO:

DEPT:

SUBJECT

*Message, Comment, or Reply*

FROM:

TELEPHONE:

*For your*

☐ APPROVAL ☐ INFORMATION ☐ COMMENT

WRITE IT • DATE IT • SIGN IT

Oral messages waste time, cause annoying interruptions and are likely to be misunderstood or forgotten.

Fig. 5-9. Office Memorandum. (Jagged line indicates a portion of actual sheet removed here only to save space.)

sheets. Each packet is perforated near the top for easy removal of sheets, and each sheet is divided into two sections—one labeled MESSAGE, for the sender, and one marked REPLY, for the recipient. These two sections may be side by side or one above the other. (See Figure 5-10.)

In the interest of speed and lower costs, many firms (especially wholesalers and manufacturers) use a similar combination reply-message or memo-letter form for routine short messages directed *outside* their organization. Compare the reply message memo-letter packet in Figure 5-11 with the interoffice memorandum shown in Figure 5-10. The main differences are that in the memo-letter: (1) after the FROM, the full name and address (perhaps also phone number) of the sender's company are printed (sometimes in the same format as for the firm's regular letterhead); and (2) after the TO, a larger space is provided so that the typist can insert the full name and address of the recipient, because he is outside the sender's firm. Some firms have the words "memo-letter" printed near the top of the sheet.

## Parts of the Memorandum

The standard parts of the memorandum are: to, from, subject, date, and body. Optional are such items as reference initials, enclosure(s), file number, routing information, and department and telephone number of sender. Most of these parts are printed on the memo stationery, as illustrated in Figures

**INTEROFFICE COMMUNICATION**

| TO | | PLANT/DEPARTMENT | |
| --- | --- | --- | --- |
| FROM | | PLANT/DEPARTMENT | |
| SUBJECT | | | DATE |

**M E S S A G E**

SIGNED

**R E P L Y**

| DATE | SIGNED |
| --- | --- |

PERSON RECEIVING COMMUNICATION - RETAIN THIS COPY FOR YOUR RECORD  (1st page:  white)

**ORIGINATOR:** DETACH THIS COPY. SEND REMAINING SET, CARBON INTACT, FOR USE OF REPLIER.  (2d page: yellow)

(3d page: pink)

RETURN THIS COPY TO SENDER

Fig. 5-10. Inter-Office Memorandum packet containing carbons under sheets of paper (white, yellow, pink) with sections for both the Message and the Reply.

5-9 and 5-10. Unlike the letter, the memo requires no inside address, salutation, complimentary close, or full signature. The combination message-reply forms do, however, provide lines for both the writer's and the reader's signature. (See Figures 5-10 and 5-11.)

What you write after the TO, FROM, and DATE will vary with the situation and your organization's practices. A courtesy title—Mr., Mrs., Miss—before your reader's name (after TO) may be used or omitted, depending upon your relationship with the reader (superior or subordinate) and the degree of informality within your organization. You omit the title before your name. Also, if the memo is a temporary message, not to be filed, and if you and the writer work together regularly, you may merely use initials, first name, or nickname after TO-FROM, and all figures or abbreviations for the date:

Fig. 5-11. "Memo-letter" stationery for routine short messages. (Jagged lines indicate a portion of actual sheet removed here only to save space.)

| TO: | J. E. H. | | TO: | Jack |
|-----|----------|-----|------|------|
| FROM: | T. R. M. | *or* | FROM: | Ted |
| DATE: | 2/10/7_ | | DATE: | Feb. 10, 197_ |

However, if the memo will be filed, these parts should be spelled out:

TO:    Mr. (optional) James E. Hill, Personnel Manager
FROM: Theodore R. Murdock, Accounting Department
DATE: February 10, 197_

If you are sending the same message to several persons, their names and/ or titles should be typed after TO. If you write to the same persons often, you might have a form prepared with their names printed (or dittoed or mimeographed) after the TO. When you have only one copy of a document, book, or other important papers that you want everyone in a certain group to read and comment on, circulate a covering memo—the single original, with no copies for readers to keep—among those on your list. Brief instructions (printed or typed) tell the readers what to do:

DATE:      May 2, 197_

TO:        Tom Brown _____     Please initial and pass on; last reader
            James Person _____   please return memo and attachment to
            Anita Jones _____     sender.
            Searl Lichen _____
            Harry Green _____

FROM:   Kermit Hobson, Personnel

SUBJECT: Your suggestions on attached Procedures Manual

For form memos that you are sending to a large number of persons within a group, it is both impossible and undesirable to list all names. In these cases the TO is followed by such words as "All Employees" or "Management Personnel." If such memos are duplicated (perhaps dittoed) on plain paper, the parts which are usually printed are typewritten.

The body of the memo, as for the letter, is its most important part because it contains your message. In general, you can use the same guidelines and organizational plans for the memo as for the letter; the few differences are pointed out in succeeding chapters.

## Layout of the Memorandum Body

The memo body, unlike that of a letter, is not centered on the page. The first line usually begins a double or triple space under the subject line regardless of the length of the message. Left margins are usually lined up evenly below the TO, but there are exceptions. (Notice, for example, that in Figure 5-11 the left margin of the message is lined up neither with the TO nor the M in MESSAGE, and also that margins for the reply are different from those in the message. Speed and convenience are of primary importance when message-reply or memo-letters are used.)

The heading at the top of memo pages beyond the first are the same as those for the business letter, namely, reader's name, page number, and date. Reference initials are typed a few spaces below the body, at the left margin. If only your title appears in the FROM line, or if the FROM line is omitted, you should sign your name a few spaces below the body of the memo. If your typewritten name follows FROM above the body, you may place your handwritten initials above or to the right of your name, to indicate that you have read the memo.

### Envelopes

How your memo is routed to the addressee depends partly upon where you and the reader are located. If you are in the same building, the memo might be inserted into the reader's mailbox, put on his desk by a messenger, or routed through compressed-air tubes. If you are in different buildings, your memo may be mailed in a manila or regular company envelope. The envelope address contains your name and department in the upper left corner, and the reader's name, department, and address according to your organization's procedures. The memo-letter is mailed in the same kind of envelope as a regular business letter.

## EXERCISES

1. *Parts and layout of business letters and memoranda.* Each of the following parts of a letter has one or more faults. Treat each part as an independent unit. Correct errors and change all obsolete forms.

*In the heading* (that doesn't have a letterhead):

a. 3 April 197__
   15,447 E. 5th. St.,
   Seattle,  Wn.  98155

b. Mr. John F. Slyfield
   15 Mt. Vernon Ave.
   New Orleans, La. 52345
   Jan. 5th, 197__

*In the inside address:*

c. Mr. John E. Henning, Esq.
   4317-18 Avenue N. E.
   Chicago
   Illinois

d. Professor Lee Stephenson, Ph. D.
   School of Business Administration
   University of California
   BERKELEY    94900

e. Campbell and Morris Furniture Co.,
   1,496 Westlake Ave.
   City

*In the signature and annotation:*

**f.** (open punctuation)

D.E.S./A.R.F.
INCLOSURE

**g.** (mixed punctuation)
Richard E. Scroggs:ab

**h.** (mixed punctuation)

RAJ:AF
cc: Thomas Brown

Very Truly Yours,
State Federal Savings Assn.,
Mr. Donald E. Smith
President

Sincerely Yours,
Credit Manager

Cordially yours
MEURER & HOHANNES, INC.
Raymond Jensen
Prod. Mgr

*In the inside address, salutation, and complimentary close* (assume mixed punctuation for parts i through n):

**i.** Veterans Adm.
Detroit, Mich.   23456

Attention: Dr. Chester Allen Powers

Dear Dr. Chester Powers

Respectively yours,

**j.** Dr. William Knapp, M.D.
618 Wrigley Bldg.
Chicago 14, Ill.   34567

Dear Carl,

Sincerely yours

**k.** Byron Renshaw
17,672 3rd St., N.E.,
New York City   11111

Dear Sir:—

Yours

**l.** Gladyne Lucchesini
644a Liberty Bldg.
Des Moines, Ia.   22222

Dear Miss Gladyne Luchesini

Yours truly

**m.** Northwest Company, Inc.
Accounting Department
Phila, Penna.   33333

Dear Miss Swanson

Your faithful friend

Pasco & Co.

Incl.                                 Clifford D. Bergerson
al;cdb:TR                             Personnell Mgr.

**n.** HAVDAHL MANUFACTURING COMPANY
Attention: Miss Helen Burgess
Eleven South Fifteenth St.
Kansas C'y, Mo.    76543

Dear Sirs:                   RE: February Sale

2. Visit a firm of your choice and ask for the specified materials or answer the following questions.
   a. Bring to class a sample of a firm's letterhead stationery and envelopes and be prepared to evaluate them orally. If the firm has several sizes, qualities, and colors of stationery, evaluate them all and discuss briefly the uses of each.
   b. Bring to class a sample of memorandum stationery and any intracompany envelopes used for memos. Be prepared to evaluate them orally. Can you suggest improvements—perhaps time-saving additions or changes?
   c. Which of the standard styles of letter layout does the firm use? If the firm has not adopted a uniform style for all letters, try to collect—from various secretaries—as many different styles and layouts as you can. Be prepared to:
      (1) Illustrate those you like best and tell why.
      (2) Discuss those you like least and tell why.
      (3) If possible, find out why the secretaries and/or their bosses prefer the style they use.
   d. Find out from two or three secretaries in the firm what their pet peeves are concerning their bosses' use of letter parts or manner of dictating these parts.
   e. What is your reaction to slogans on envelopes? What are the slogans used on the firm's envelopes?
   f. Does the firm require all typists to follow the Post Office suggestions for machine-recognizable typed addresses? If not, in what ways do the firm's envelope addresses differ from the suggestions—and why?
   g. Be prepared to discuss the following aspects of memos in the firm you visited:
      (1) How frequently are memos used rather than telephone conversations?
      (2) Who writes memos? Only department heads? Nontitled employees? Others?
      (3) To whom do employees write memos?
      (4) Are memos usually routed through a superior? If so, through whom?
      (5) What is the average length of memos?
      (6) What standard and optional parts do the firm's memos contain?

3. Evaluate (in writing or orally, as your instructor assigns) the following, using the five letters that you have already collected and been studying:
   a. Regular parts of each letter
   b. Optional parts
   c. Appearance—layout on page, strikeovers, type alignment, ribbon lightness
   d. Spelling accuracy

# Major Letter Patterns

- Chapter 6 Direct Requests
- Chapter 7 Good-news and Neutral Messages
- Chapter 8 Bad-news Messages
- Chapter 9 Persuasive Requests

CHAPTER 6

# Direct Requests

- Organizational Plan
- Inquiries
- Claims (Complaints) and Requests for Adjustments
- Requests for Action Related to Routine Business Procedures
- Invitations, Orders, Reservations
- Requests Pertaining to Civic Causes or Public Officials
- Capsule Checklists
- Exercises

When the main purpose of your message is to ask the reader to do something, you are writing a *request* letter or memo. Whether you organize your message according to the direct- or the persuasive-request pattern depends upon the nature of the request and, most of all, upon how you think the reader will react to that request. Generally when you make a simple inquiry or a routine request, you will *not* have to persuade your reader to do what you ask. You can usually handle the following types of messages with the direct-request plan:

Inquiries
Claims (Complaints) and requests for adjustments
Requests for action related to routine business procedures
Invitations, orders, reservations
Requests pertaining to civic causes or public officials
Early-stage collection messages

This chapter presents the direct-request organizational plan, discusses the first five types of requests; then compares them briefly in capsule checklists. Chapter 12, Collections, discusses early-stage collection messages.

## ORGANIZATIONAL PLAN

For a routine inquiry or request you assume that the reader will do as you request once he understands what you want and why you want it. Thus you use the direct approach—introduce your main idea in the first paragraph. The direct-request plan has three basic parts:

1. Main idea
   a. Introduce your request, major statement, or question.
   b. State reason(s), if desirable, justifying the request.
2. Explanation
   a. Include details necessary to help the reader respond to your request correctly.
   b. Consider numbering your questions (if more than one) for easy reading and answering.
3. Courteous close with motivation to action
   a. State clearly what action you want the reader to take—and when.
   b. Make action easy, if appropriate, by including a reply envelope, your telephone number, office hours, or any other appropriate helpful information.
   c. Express appreciation and, if appropriate, include a statement of goodwill or reader benefit.

## INQUIRIES

To get facts that you need and cannot conveniently or economically obtain yourself, you write inquiries requesting information. Because the questions asked are important in all inquiries, this section begins with suggestions about phrasing and arranging questions. Then follows a discussion of direct-request messages that seek information about persons and messages that ask about products, services, and other matters requiring no persuasion.

### Wording and Arrangement of Questions[1]

So that you can get exactly the information wanted, you must be especially careful when planning the questions to be included in your inquiries. The following suggestions apply to all kinds of direct-request inquiries:

1. **Make your questions specific.** If the product about which you inquire is technical, include specific physical dimensions, technical specifications, exact intended use of the item, architectural drawings, or whatever else will help the respondent. A single general question such as "Will you give us any information you can on this applicant (or product)?" will probably bring an inadequate reply or one so general that it will be almost useless.

   The more penetrating your questions, the more likely you are to get the information you need. Most respondents who would not *volunteer* unfavorable facts (especially about a person) will, however, be frank when asked specific questions provided you promise confidential treatment.

2. **Use a separate paragraph for each main question if the questions require explanation.**

3. **If you have more than one question, consider numbering them.** If you have only two or three questions, you may place them in the body of your letter, but it is generally better to list your questions on the same sheet below the body. Then the respondent can answer directly in the spaces provided and need not write a separate letter.

4. **When you have more questions than space at the bottom of your letter page,** or when your questions require lengthy answers, place them on a separate sheet and be sure to allow enough space for adequate answers.

5. **Keep your questions to a minimum and make them clear.** A long or vague questionnaire decreases the number of returns.

6. **Word your questions to get more than "yes" or "no" answers if you need a detailed opinion or description.** For example, a yes or no answer to: "Did the applicant have duties that required responsibility?" would probably be inadequate. To obtain a more helpful answer, you might ask: "What kinds of duties requiring responsibility did the applicant perform especially well?" In contrast, a yes or no answer would be adequate for such a question as: "Does the applicant have an account with you?"

7. **If you wish the respondent to "rate" a person, product, or service, it may be better to define each category on your rating scale.** For instance, the following example shows one of eight questions on an employer's questionnaire about an applicant for employment. Notice how both the squares and the definitions make responses easy. The best choices may be at the right (as in the example) or at the left, but consistent placement of best choices is more convenient for both the reference and you—especially if you must compare many replies.

[1] See also Stanley L. Payne, *The Art of Asking Questions* (especially Chapter 14, which lists 100 considerations), Princeton University Press, Princeton, N.J., 1951; and Lyndon O. Brown, *Market Research and Analysis*, Ronald Press Company, New York, 1969.

ABILITY TO GET ALONG WITH OTHERS:
   Is the applicant a likeable, friendly, and tactful individual, or is he egotistical, unpleasant, or thoughtless of others? Will he draw to him the men with whom he deals, or keep them at a distance? Is he well-poised in normal social situations? (Check One)

| ☐ | ☐ | ☐ | ☐ | ☐ |
|---|---|---|---|---|
| Egotistical, unfriendly or tactless | Somewhat neutral, does not easily attract friends | Approachable | Likeable, friendly and tactful | Exceedingly pleasant and agreeable; will draw others to him |

8. Carefully arrange your questions—generally with the easiest to answer first.
9. Consider sending to your reader two copies of the questionnaire if you think he might need one for his records.

## Inquiries about Persons

When you need information about a person, you usually direct your request to a reference—a responsible source of information. The person about whom you ask the reference to give information may be an applicant for a job, a loan, credit, membership in an organization, an award, or for some kind of special training or insurance protection.

Inquiries to a reference may be written by the applicant himself or, more frequently, by the person who seeks information about the applicant.

*Applicant's Request to a Reference.* Sometimes an applicant asks a reference if he will send a recommendation direct to someone who needs confidential information about that applicant. For instance, suppose you are seeking admission into a graduate school that requires at least four confidential recommendations. Perhaps you can approach some of your selected references in person or by telephone. To others, however (if they are out of town or if you have a questionnaire they need to fill out), you will have to write a letter.

Because your request to a reference is asking a favor, it is best to state courteously in the first paragraph why you are writing to this person and what the recommendation is for. If you haven't been in touch with the reference for some time, you may need to refresh his memory about who you are.

The explanation section of your request should include a brief summary of pertinent facts about yourself. Consider carefully the reference's relationship to you and decide what facts he will need to grant the favor you are asking and to give a fair, helpful recommendation. (Sometimes an attached data sheet is useful to him.) If, for example, the reference is a former professor, you might include the following information:

1. The course you studied under him—when, where, and your grade.
2. Your major, and your grade-point average (GPA) in the major.
3. Your overall GPA in college, and your high school GPA if it is good. If the professor will or might recall that you made poor grades, include perhaps an honest brief explanation as to why your college GPA wasn't higher (for instance, number of hours each week you worked to provide finances; a bad first year or first two years, but higher GPA the last year; or whatever is pertinent).

4. Difficult courses you studied (if grades are good), from whom you took the courses and the grades you received.
5. Test scores—graduate record exam, law school admission test, admission test for graduate study in business or medical school, or any other pertinent scores.
6. Honors, honor societies (Phi Beta Kappa, Beta Gamma Sigma, etc.), studies in any special honors programs.
7. Scholarships awarded.
8. Leadership qualities; for example, offices held in living group, on campus, in political groups, etc.
9. Activities—College Bowl, tutoring, United Nations Model Congress, etc.
10. Guidelines, if possible, for the recommendation. Enclose, if you can, a form or letter from the graduate school stating what information it seeks from the reference about you—distinguishing intellectual traits or abilities, leadership capacity, quality of work done, character, integrity, or other personal traits.

Your closing paragraph should state to whom the letter or form is to be sent; be sure to state the full name and address, unless this information is printed on the form. And, of course, include a statement of appreciation.

If it is necessary for you to obtain recommendations about your work in specific courses or jobs in which your work was just mediocre, be sure to provide an explanation regarding the quality of your work, if possible. In Inquiry 1 the applicant shows consideration for his reader by his courteous tone, by the facts he includes about courses he studied, by mention of factors that influenced the quality of his chemistry studies, and by the reasonable time he allows for action.

*Inquiry 1: An applicant's well-written request to a former professor.*

Dear Professor Brown:

*Introduction of request and reason*

This letter is to reintroduce myself to you and to ask a favor of you. The University of Montana's Dental School has asked for a recommendation from my Organic Chemistry professor.

*Explanation, details about past relationship*

Almost four years ago—in Winter and Spring Quarters of (year)—you were my chemistry professor here at the University of Montana. The courses I took from you were Chemistry 241 and Chemistry 242, both of which met at 3 p.m. daily. The grades I received were C's, but I believe I could have done better if circumstances had been a little different that year. Besides the lapse of two years between my inorganic and organic studies, there was also my part-time job in the Applied Physics Laboratory until 3 p.m. four days a week. Because this work caused me to come to your class about 15 minutes late, I sometimes missed important laboratory work, a fact which necessarily affected my grade. In our several conferences, however, you often commented very favorably on my work.

*More*
*details,*
*leading to*
*reason*
*for this*
*request*
Currently I am a senior, graduating this quarter with a grade point average of 3.02 (out of 4.0) in Business Administration. I am applying for admission to the Dental School at the University of Montana. To this date I have completed successfully all the pre-dental requirements, and would like to begin dental studies next fall.

*Easy*
*and*
*dated*
*action*
The enclosed form is one the Dental School requires regarding my studies in organic chemistry. Professor Brown, will you please fill out and return this form in the enclosed envelope to the Admissions Officer? I will appreciate very much your mailing this information within the next two weeks—before the admissions deadline, March 1.

***Inquirer's Request to a Reference.*** The most frequent requests to references are those written by persons who need confidential information about the applicant. Suppose, for example, that you are the employer, lender, creditor, insurance underwriter, or officer of any organization that is considering an applicant for a special reason. The letter of inquiry you write to each reference the applicant has listed can be organized according to the direct-request pattern.

Your opening paragraph usually includes the full name of the applicant you are considering, why you are considering him, and why you are writing to the reader.

The explanatory section should include:

1. Sufficient details about the requirements of the job, loan, credit, scholarship, or membership for which the applicant is being considered. Such facts help the reference to visualize whether the applicant can meet the requirements.
2. If appropriate, a few pertinent facts the applicant has already told you about himself—such as length of time he says he worked for the reference, his job title, achievements, etc. This way you can check on the applicant's accuracy and honesty.
3. Clearly stated questions (preferably numbered) asking exactly what you want to know about the applicant.

The ending paragraph usually includes appreciation, promise of confidential treatment of the reply, and (if appropriate) provisions for easy action[1] and an offer to reciprocate.

Obviously, the content and processing of your inquiry to a reference will depend upon your purpose and your reader. If, for example, you are writing to references about an applicant for a unique position, you will no doubt compose a special message with special questions. Not only will your letter be

---

[1] When you write to a businessman at his business address, you can usually omit the enclosed reply envelope because many businessmen prefer to use their own firm's stationery. However, when you write to a reference at his home (for instance to a personal reference whose business address is unknown to you), or to someone who may be in a one-man office or in a nonprofit organization, it is appropriate to enclose a stamped reply envelope.

individually typed, but also you will usually expect a letter reply from the reference. The letter below (Inquiry 2) from a hardware store manager to a department store manager, is an example of such an inquiry.

*Inquiry 2: Personalized request listing numbered questions in the letter.*

Dear Mr. Mueller:

*Name, why* Mr. Morton L. Dryer, one of your former employees, has
*being con-* applied here as assistant manager of our electrical sup—
*sidered, and* plies department.  He states that he was in charge of your
*a few facts* electrical appliances section for about a year, and he has
*he has told* given your name as a reference.

*Request* We need a qualified person who can, in about two years, become department manager.  I will appreciate your frank answers to the following questions and any other pertinent facts you can include.

*Questions*
1.  How long was he in your employ and why did he leave?
2.  How satisfactory were his services as a section head in your store?
3.  Do you know of any personal habits or characteristics that might hinder or help his success in a position of responsibility?

*A promise* Your statements will, of course, be kept entirely con— fidential.

Inquiry 3 below is an exceptionally thorough individually typed inquiry which interweaves explanation and unnumbered questions for each qualification.[1] It is reproduced here as an example of the care that a reputable firm takes in placing an outstanding candidate.

*Inquiry 3: Personalized request interweaving explanations with questions in the letter.*

Dear Mr. Arthur:

*Full name;* We are seriously considering Barbara Rankin for a position
*reason for* in our Research Department here.  She has given your name
*request* as a reference.

*Details—* As you may know, Barbara has been working in a clerical
*applicant's* position for us part—time for about a year in our branch
*work* office in your city.  Now she has expressed interest in getting into more professional work and pursuing her career in writing for our head office.

---

[1] For another example of a good direct-request inquiry that interweaves questions with detailed explanation, you might reread the letter from a hospital personnel officer to a chief pharmacist, page 22.

*Details; specific request and explanation*

Because of Barbara's outstanding record at school, to say nothing of the fine work she has done for us, we are making every effort to find, or create, a position for her here. And for that reason I am asking for help in finding out as much as possible about her relative strengths and weaknesses. In this way we can do a better job of fitting her talents to our needs and in assigning her work which is not either beyond her present capacity or out of line with her interests and skills.

*Two implied questions*

I understand that Barbara worked about two years part-time in your advertising office, and I will welcome information about how effectively and concisely Barbara writes, particularly how readily she can compose business letters to advertisers.

*More questions with details*

In addition, we would like to have your impressions of the attitudes and skills which Barbara can carry over from school to the business world––her ability to organize her work, her originality, initiative, reliability, and ability to work smoothly with others while under pressure. Under what degree of supervision and guidance is she likely to do her best work? Any and all comments you may care to make will be a great help and, of course, entirely confidential.

*A promise*

*Easy action (phone)*

Your schedule is probably particularly heavy at this time of year––and I hesitate to call you when you may be busy. Perhaps it would be simplest for you to telephone me collect (area code and phone number) when convenient for you. I am usually at my desk between 9 and 11:30 Monday through Friday.

If you (for example, as personnel manager) need references on hundreds of new applicants, sheer volume will force you to plan a duplicated form that you can use again and again. For instance, Inquiry 4, used by a national business machines firm, is printed with lines for typewritten fill-ins, including name and city of the applicant, in the opening. The questions on the lower half of the same sheet ask the reference to evaluate the applicant—from superior to unsatisfactory—on various personal qualities; also there's a small space for comments. (If you prefer to define each rating category, use a form with questions similar to that illustrated in suggestion 7, page 165.) As is customary and desirable, the last question gives the respondent additional space for "other comments." The information obtained from such open-ended questions can be extremely important and helpful.

*Inquiry 4: Printed inquiry adaptable for any reference about any prospective applicant; evaluation form on same page below the request.*

*Name and reason*     M_____(name)_____of_____(city)_____states that he was employed by you as_(type of work)_ from_(date)_ to___(date)___. He has listed your name as a reference.

*Type of work*     We are making a careful study of the qualifications of this applicant to determine whether it would be in his best interests to consider a position as Sales Representative in our business of furnishing a complete line of (type of machines are named here).

*Request and easy action*     Will you please give us your answers and comments on the following points and any other comments which you feel will be helpful to the applicant in choosing a life's work? Just mail your reply in the enclosed stamped return envelope as soon as possible.

| | Superior | Good | Average | Below average | Unsatisfactory | Comments |
|---|---|---|---|---|---|---|
| Potential ability to sell a quality product (your estimate)_____ | | | | | | |
| Personality_____ | | | | | | |
| Industry—determination_____ | | | | | | |
| Aptness in learning_____ | | | | | | |
| Creative ability—resourcefulness_____ | | | | | | |
| Dependability—Co-operation_____ | | | | | | |
| Disposition—balance_____ | | | | | | |

For what type of work do you think applicant is best fitted?_____

Would you strongly recommend that applicant enter sales work?_____

Other comments (you may also use reverse side) :

 

(Signed)_____

Date_____     (Title)_____

## Inquiries about Products or Services

Both as a consumer and as a business or professional man, you will have many occasions to seek information from the seller of products and services or from customers, employees, and others.

*Direct Request to the Seller.* When your inquiry goes to a seller—whether he is a manufacturer, retailer, investment broker, or hotel clerk—the addressee's self-interest should make him glad to comply with your wishes. Perhaps you want a free catalog, price list, or booklet about products, deliveries, or payment plans. At such times your complete direct request need be only one sentence, such as:

Please send me your latest sporting equipment catalog and the descriptive folder you advertised in the April issue of *Sportsman Illustrated.*

If, however, you have a unique individual problem, you may need to ask questions for which the recipient does not have prepared answers. Following the direct-request plan, present your main idea (request and/or reason) in the first paragraph. Deciding whether to place your reason or request first depends upon your request and reader. In most inquiries to a seller concerning his product or service, it is entirely optional whether to present request or reason first. But if you think your request is somewhat unusual or will be time-consuming for the reader to answer, state the reason first. After the opening paragraph, include all needed explanation and/or questions. The final paragraph contains the action request.

Inquiry 5 is written by a purchasing manager requesting information from a manufacturer about a product he is considering buying. Notice that his letter begins with the major request; but if you prefer to begin with the reason, you might interchange paragraphs 1 (request) and 3 (reason).

*Inquiry 5: Inquiry about an advertised product; numbered questions within the letter.*

Gentlemen:

*Major request*

Your ads in <u>Good</u> <u>Business</u> magazine have attracted our attention, and we will appreciate your answers to the following questions:

*Specific numbered questions*

1. What is the price of each Quiktyper?
2. How long does it take an average typist to learn to operate this machine?
3. To what extent can your experts estimate about how much money a company can save in a year with Quiktyper, if it uses--for instance--25 different one-page form letters and mails a total of 270,000 letters a year?
4. What guarantee do you offer?

*Reason for request*

Before deciding whether our firm should invest in one or more automatic typewriters, we should like as much information as possible about leading brands.

*Suggested action*

If you have a factory agent in this area, we welcome a demonstration any time within the next two weeks, preferably after receipt of your written reply to these four questions.

**Direct Requests to Customers, Employees, and Others.** As the seller of products or services, you can often use inquiries to win back "missed" customers who have not bought from your firm for some time, or to obtain information about your firm's products or services.

"Miss you" messages can be either simple requests (as discussed below) or persuasive requests (see Chapter 9). Many firms have revived hundreds of unused accounts by mailing a series of direct requests—ranging from colorful postcards to form letters on specially designed stationery. Such messages concentrate on telling the reader that he is missed, appreciated, and important, and asking him to come back. Specially designed letterheads and colors often aid in making visual the word pictures expressed in miss-you messages.

Inquiry 6, from a firm of auto service specialists, includes a touch of humor on a descriptive letterhead that introduces the theme of the message.

*Inquiry 6: A "miss you" request designed mainly to get the customer to come back. A picture at the top shows a home hallway, a lighted lamp, a clock with hands at 2:15, and a man entering the front door cautiously on tiptoe while carrying his shoes. A voice from upstairs calls:*

*"WHERE HAVE YOU BEEN?"*

Mr. Hildirch . . .

*Main idea*

We've missed you too!  And we've been asking about you, because it's the repeat appearances of good customers like you that play the leading part in our business.

*Reason*

In fact, customers like you are the balance-wheel, the spark plugs, the drive shaft that keep us going.  With us, customers are about the whole works.

*Suggested action*

That's why we've been wondering about you.  Remember that our door is always open for you--from 8 a.m. to 6 p.m. Mondays through Fridays.  You won't have to tiptoe in. Every appearance you make in our shop is sincerely appreciated.  DRIVE IN SOON, won't you?  WE'LL DO OUR BEST TO PLEASE YOU.

Inquiry 6 is designed simply to get the customer to come back with his business. Other types of miss-you letters go one step further, and ask what is wrong. Then, if the customer has a complaint, he feels he can express it; if he has none, he will probably say so and perhaps place another order. Either way, the silence has been broken and a dead account may be revived. Also, your firm may have gained useful information about its products or services.

When you ask your customer what is wrong, you have several ways to make replying easy. Some messages, like Inquiry 7, merely ask the reader to jot down his reason on the margin or back of the letter. Others invite him to phone, and still others list a few possible reasons for the reader to check off. (The list may include also some humorous unlikely reasons.) A later sentence then asks for another chance to serve the customer soon.

*Inquiry 7: A "miss you" inquiry aiming mainly to get a reply that answers "What is wrong?"*

Attention:  Purchasing Agent

Gentlemen

*Main idea*
Perhaps you have the answer to a question that has worried us. For a long time we have received no order or mail from you; and as we do not know why, we are concerned.

*Explanation*
We have missed the privilege of serving you--a good business friend. Often we have asked ourselves, "What did we do or say to offend this good customer?" What causes his absence? We've checked all the orders and correspondence from you plus our shipment schedules and prices to you--and everything looks OK.

*Suggested reasons*
But something must be wrong, to keep you from us so long. Please tell me about it frankly. If in any way our merchandise or service did not come up to your expectations, let us make amends. There may be some other reason why we have not heard from you; and if so, will you please tell us?

*Easy action*
Just write your note on the margin or back of this letter and mail it in the prepaid envelope addressed to me. I'll very much appreciate your reply.

**Other inquiries about your firm's products or services can also be in the form of direct requests.** Besides asking lost customers what is wrong, you can ask steady or new customers for their comments about your products which they have bought or returned. Then not only will you obtain valuable information, but you will also help build customer confidence in your genuine desire to maintain good service. (For examples of messages showing continuing concern see Chapter 13, Goodwill, pages 549 to 580.)

Often you will need information from employees, colleagues, or other persons *within* your organization. Inquiry 8, launching an employee survey, can be adapted so that it is suitable for other types of readers—inside or outside your organization—whenever your questions are easy to answer and no persuasion is necessary.

*Inquiry 8: A memo seeking employee needs and preferences about parking on company premises; questionnaire attached.*

TO:       All employees

FROM:     Parking Division, Personnel Department

SUBJECT:  <u>Your</u> <u>preferences</u> <u>about</u> <u>parking</u> <u>permits</u>

<table>
<tr><td>*Reader-<br>benefit<br>reason*</td><td>In an effort to improve the parking situation for all<br>employees, your Parking Division is conducting a survey of<br>your needs and preferences.</td></tr>
<tr><td>*Request<br>and<br>dated<br>action*</td><td>Will you please fill out the attached questionnaire and<br>return it, unsigned, to your supervisor by Friday, May 1,<br>at 5 p.m.  Then you will be sure that your feelings are<br>included in the survey.  The results of employee opinions<br>and suggestions will be tabulated and announced at the next<br>employee meeting, May 15.</td></tr>
</table>

## CLAIMS (COMPLAINTS) AND REQUESTS FOR ADJUSTMENTS

Whenever you are dissatisfied with a product, service, or policy, it is to your advantage—and the company's—to communicate with the right person promptly about the desired correction. Oral complaints to salesmen or clerks often do not bring results; a much better procedure is to write an effective letter to the proper company official who does care when a problem exists and who can and will do something to correct it.

When you state your complaint, you usually make a claim or request for some kind of adjustment. All such requests are grouped together in this section and labeled *claim letters*. Claim letters should be organized by the direct-request pattern whenever they involve a routine matter that is covered by a guarantee or by established procedures for customer relations. Typical situations for direct-request claims about merchandise involve defective materials or workmanship, malfunctioning parts, soiled or shopworn items, or products not as represented. Claims about services include delivery mixups, broken promises, discourtesy, carelessness, clerical or bookkeeping errors, and minor inconveniences relating to violation of published company policies. (For those claims that involve controversial issues, substantially large sums of money, repeated errors, and other serious matters you will need to write a persuasive request, as discussed in Chapter 9.)

### Characteristics of Well-written Claims

To be fair to the seller, to the product or service, and to yourself—write promptly. Also, be sure your letter has all the "C" qualities. Show by your attitude and wording that *you have confidence in the reader's fairness*—confidence that he will make the adjustment after he gets the facts. Omit any statements that sound like appeals or threats.

When you complain about the poor condition of a product, for instance, state all the pertinent facts logically, courteously, and impersonally, without exaggeration or irrelevant material. Guesses and opinions about who may be to blame for an error are unwise and unhelpful. Let the reader determine causes; you present facts as you see them. And when your purpose is to call attention to an employee's poor service, make clear you are doing so because you think his behavior is not representative of the firm's usually good customer relations policies.

Anger and name-calling are, of course, taboo. Remember that the reader is not the person who made the mistake. The purpose of your claim letter is to get as satisfactory an adjustment as possible. A writer who antagonizes the recipient merely lowers his chances of satisfactory adjustment—or at least of being considered a reasonable individual. One extra caution: When you write as an agent for your employer or business, you must be even more careful to avoid tactless, intemperate accusations. Such outbursts not only reflect unfavorably upon you *and* your company, but they also may place you in danger of a libel suit.[1]

It is often a good idea to state both sides of the case—for example, you might comment on something you *like* about the firm's products or service. Such a statement can be in the opening paragraph or in the explanation. Even humor (not sarcasm) is appropriate when the matter is relatively small.

## Organization and Content of the Simple Direct Claim

Begin your direct claim with the main idea—namely, the need for an adjustment or correction of an error. Do not waste the reader's time by giving lengthy details or background information in the first paragraph.

In the explanatory paragraph(s) of your letter, include all facts the reader will need to understand your claim clearly. For instance, if you wish free repairs on an item that is malfunctioning within the guarantee period, present evidence of the date of your purchase, make clear that you followed carefully the operating instructions (if you did), and state clearly what is wrong.

In your action paragraph, ask for what you want or leave the decision to your reader. Depending on circumstances, you will usually request one or more of the following. (The numbers in parentheses after each request refer to the claim-letter examples illustrated in this section.)

1. Free replacement of the defective part(s), the whole item, or the whole shipment. (2)
2. Free repairs. (3)
3. Refund—for all or part of purchase price. (1)
4. Credit to your account (or a credit slip). (4)
5. Reduction in the price (because of a product or service defect). (3)
6. Free inspection, leading to redecorating, complete overhaul, etc.
7. Explanation and/or change in policy or procedure. (4)
8. A new shipment with the correct item(s) ordered. (1)
9. Cancellation of an order or part of an order.

[1] See Appendix A, pages 751 to 758, about legal aspects of letters.

If you need the adjustment by a certain time, state why, as in the last paragraph of the following claim. You should also consider (and perhaps ask) whether the defective or incorrect product should be returned to the seller. Although the claimant in the letter below returned the wrong-size item without asking, often it is better not to return goods until you have the seller's instructions.

*Claim 1: A courteous Claim (dated June 9) to a men's sportswear department manager from an out-of-town cash customer who needs an exchange or a refund.*

Gentlemen

*Main idea —request*
Enclosed is the sweater which Nelson's delivery truck left yesterday and which I wish to exchange for the correct size or a refund.

*Explanatory details*
When I selected and purchased this Hudson sweater in your department last week (for $20.38 cash), I asked that a size "L" be sent to my home. The size I received is only an "S", and of course I can't wear it. My sales check is #7902, dated June 4, written by salesclerk #801.

*Specific request*

*Dated action*
Will you please send me the correct size "L" in exactly this same style and color or, if this is not available now, a cash refund of $20.38. As I am leaving on a one-month trip June 17, it is necessary that I receive the sweater or the check before that date.

Sometimes you may have to present your direct-request claim a second time. A second request usually goes to a higher official and your letter will probably have a dual purpose—to obtain the desired action and to complain about the lack of response (or incorrect response). For example, suppose that instead of receiving the sweater or cash refund you requested by letter in Claim 1, you received only a credit slip which you don't want. Or suppose that instead of writing your first claim, you returned the sweater in person to the sportswear department, and there both the salesman and the department manager rudely insisted that you accept a credit slip. If you know the refusal is contrary to the store's published policy, you will justly feel that a higher official should know about the situation.

For such a dual-purpose direct-request letter, you might begin with a paragraph like one of the following:

The purpose of my letter is to ask you for a cash refund which I am unable to obtain through normal channels. Also I'm sure you will want to know about the discrepancy between the treatment I received in your men's sportswear department and your advertised company policy of customer satisfaction or a full refund.

*or*

You will be interested, I think, in the experience I had with a wrong-size sweater I received from your store June 8. I believe I am entitled to a cash refund, though two of your employees refused to give it to me.

Your explanatory paragraph should tactfully present all pertinent facts about your purchase and the department employees' statements; you should also enclose a copy of the credit slip or its date and number. The ending paragraph will be a forthright request for the refund.

The next two examples are written by businessmen for claims concerning their companies. Claim 2 concerns faulty products; Claim 3, faulty service. Notice that in both letters the writers present all needed facts without anger and with good "you attitude."

*Claim 2: A considerate complaint from a gift store owner to a wholesaler, about faulty merchandise.*

Dear Mr. Onorgard:

*Main idea; request*
Our shipment of Swedish tumblers was checked in yesterday and put on sale, then hurriedly withdrawn when the stock room reported it to be a completely defective shipment. We are asking you for an adjustment on these tumblers.

*Details*
The news about this shipment was especially disappointing to me because we had already advertised that the sale was to begin today. I personally washed and examined a dozen glasses of each size, four each (and not necessarily the worst) of which we are sending you by express for your examination and comment.

There is no regularity in the mars, scratches, and abrasions, or whatever the defects should be termed, to indicate faulty moulds. In fact, I've never seen anything in domestic or imported glass to equal the variety of imperfections apparently present in some degree in every glass of this shipment.

*You attitude*
I realize fully that you had no opportunity to check this merchandise and that it is only through your customers that you learn of its condition and can in turn seek an adjustment from the factory.

*Action*
We are withholding sale of the glasses and payment of the bill until we hear from you.

*Claim 3: A considerate complaint (May 18) from a restaurant manager to a laundry, about faulty service.*

Dear Mr. Ragen:

*Main idea—*
*something*
*is wrong;*
*compliment*
*too*

What has happened to Spic's starching and mending service?
You may recall my April 19 letter complimenting you on the
neat appearance of the uniforms Spic sent then.  But the
last three shipments have contained both torn and incorrectly starched garments.

*Details*

On May 10, nine of our twenty waitresses' uniforms came
back as limp as though they had not been starched at all.
Though our girls were disappointed, we decided that
"accidents will happen" and surely next week they'd be as
good as ever.  But on May 14, all 20 uniforms came back
again limp--in collars and cuffs.  Also four had unmended
rips on the pockets.  That morning on our outgoing laundry
bag I pinned a note for the driver asking if the laundry
would please again observe the following request, which
had been overlooked the previous week:

EXTRA HEAVY STARCH ON ALL COLLARS AND CUFFS

*More*
*details*

Today--same thing happened.  All collars and cuffs were
limp as though they had no starch!  BUT this time five of
the cotton slacks of our men waiters had extra heavy
starch in them.  They were so stiff they stood up alone!

*Good-natured*
*attitude*

It took a bit of persuading to get the men to wear them;
we had a good laugh each time.

*More "you*
*attitude"*

Yet all this mixup hurts the image of our restaurant.  We
like our employees to look neat.  As you know, I'd much
rather compliment than complain.  But the change has been
so abrupt that I'm sure you want to know.  I ask that you
please:

*Specific*
*request*

Reduce your charges for the 49 unstarched uniforms and
    the overstarched five pairs of slacks, and
Make free repairs on the four torn uniforms, which we
    will return to your driver on his next call.

In the future, can we count on the usual good mending as
well as starching service?

The last example of a direct-request claim (Claim 4) is a customer's somewhat humorous, but effective, complaint to a loan company.

**Claim 4:** *Humorous complaint about a premium computation error; directed to a
computer, not a person.*

Dear Computer #      :

*Main idea*

It seems you're trying to take my bank account and home
away from me, and you haven't even told me your number yet.
You have my number--Social Security #99-81-9999.

On 12-1-70 (I'm using figures as you do, Mr. Computer) I
obtained mortgage loan #999,9999 from the company you run.
On 2-2-71, I received notice that because of real estate
*Detailed*      property tax rate increases, my monthly mortgage payments
*explanation* were increasing.   You asked whether I wanted to continue my
$164.20 monthly payments and pay an annual sum to the
escrow account of $108.12, or add 1/12 of the tax amount to
each monthly payment.   My choice was #2.

On 3-1-71 you billed me for a monthly payment of $17,321.
Now obviously, computer, since I didn't have enough money
to make the lump sum payment to the escrow account, I don't
have enough to make a monthly payment of $17,321.   My old-
fashioned arithmetic makes $164.20 + $9.01 = $173.21.   Per-
haps the remainder, $17,321 - $173.21, is interest?   In my
opinion, such an interest charge is excessive, even though
computers may be exempt from usury laws.   Since you are the
only one from your department who ever writes me, I suspect
there are no human workers in your employ who could help
me.

Anyhow, I'm enclosing my check for $173.21, which I think
should be credited as a full monthly payment on my loan.
*Action*        If you can't accept it, please ask your president to ex-
*request*     plain the company policy to me.   And please do not bend,
fold, mutilate or punch all your little holes in this
letter until he has a chance to read it.

In this pleasantly witty letter, the customer reveals not only what he considers a premium computation error, but also his woes in getting computerized replies to his inquiries.

## REQUESTS FOR ACTION RELATED TO ROUTINE BUSINESS PROCEDURES

The messages in this section include business or professional people's requests
that are directly related to routine business procedures within their firm. The
discussions and examples are grouped in two categories—according to
whether the requests go to persons outside or within the organization.

### Requests to Persons outside Your Organization

As a business or professional person you may need to ask your customer,
supplier, transportation company, or others to sign an enclosed signature card
or form or document. Or you may need missing answers on a customer's
credit application, or the return of his budget payment book, or his correction of an irregularity in a check he sent your firm. These and numerous
other routine matters can be handled by direct-request messages.

You can use form letters, either processed or individually typed, but it is often a good idea to personalize the letter by individual typing as in Request 1 below. However, even obviously processed form messages—like Requests 3 and 4—are satisfactory when the messages are clearly the same for all members (customers) in a group.

Notice that all the following letters except Request 2 are concise, clear, and courteous. And they all begin with the reason or the request (or a major statement that leads to the request) in either the first paragraph or at the beginning of the second.

*Request 1: A bank's trust department asks the executor of an estate to return an affidavit, signature card, and passbook; individually typed message.*

Dear Mr. Romane:

*Reason and request*
So that we can transfer the account of Mr. R. S. Roe, deceased, to your name as Executor, will you please do the following:

*Numbered specific requests*
   1. Sign the enclosed affidavit.
   2. Fill out the enclosed card and sign it.
   3. Return to us the signed affidavit, card, and your passbook No. 222-222.

*Reader benefit and easy action*
The same day these important materials reach us, we will transfer the funds to a new account with no loss of earnings. Please use the enclosed air mail envelope to speed your reply.

In contrast to the foregoing message—which contains the clear request, reason, necessary details, and provision for easy action—Request 2 has several weaknesses. (How many can you find? Does it have good qualities? After you have read the letter, compare your evaluation with the comments that follow.)

*Request 2: Unclear request from a mortgage loan company to a borrower regarding increased loan payments; processed form letter signed by the company's president.*

Dear Homeowner:

We wish to inform you that the Homeowner's Mortgage Protector Plan Certificate which you recently received is to be read carefully and then filed with your other valuable papers. The benefits provided by the Plan are very valuable.

The protection will become effective on the date indicated on the Certificate after the premium has been paid. The premium which is shown on the enclosed Certificate should be added to your future monthly payments.

If your mortgage payment has already been made for the
month the protection is to become effective, the premium
should be sent now so that you will be fully protected for
the month. Next month, combine the payments.

We are pleased you have secured this protection for yourself and family. The acceptance of this Plan by so many of
our customers indicates to me that it is certainly a
valuable and worthwhile program.

Obviously, the purpose of this message needs to be emphasized. The serious
faults are incorrect organization, vague statement of the action requests, and
overuse of (nine) passive verbs. As the letter is organized, the main request
seems to be that the Certificate should be "read carefully and then filed . . . ."
However, the second and third paragraphs mention adding something to future
monthly payments—and sending the premium "now." These requests are
important; yet they are vague and buried. Further, the writer does not state
what the exact future monthly payments are; he leaves the adding entirely up
to the borrower: "Next month combine the payments." This request is risky,
since it is quite likely that some of the homeowners to whom the request is
addressed will add incorrectly, or misinterpret or overlook the instruction.

Request 3 eliminates the faults of Request 2 and retains its good qualities—the emphasis on reader benefit in the opening and closing sentences. The request to pay the insurance premium is introduced in the first
paragraph. The explanatory details include the exact amounts for both the
insurance premium and the new combined payment amount. The suggestion
to file the Certificate with other valuable papers comes in the last, not the first,
paragraph.

*Request 3: Improved revision of Request 2.*

Dear Mr. and Mrs. Jeans:

*Main
idea*

The valuable benefits your Homeowner's Mortgage Protector
Plan provides become effective on the date the Certificate
indicates--if you have paid the insurance premium for the
plan.

*Request
with
specific
payment
amounts*

In case you have already mailed your mortgage installment
for the month in which your protection is to become effective, please send the premium--$    --to us now so that you
will be fully protected for the month.

Next month and for all future payments please be sure to
combine your mortgage and insurance payments into one
check for $    .

*Reader benefit*
We are pleased you have secured this protection for yourself and family.  Many of our customers have found this is
a very valuable and worthwhile program.  After you have
read the Certificate carefully, please file it with your
other valuable papers.

Whenever common errors—for instance in checks, order forms, registration, etc.—occur frequently among your customers, a well-worded form request
is a time-saver. Request 4 illustrates a simple, concise form.

**Request 4:** *Multipurpose printed form (7" x 3½") to inform customers of needed
check correction.*

*Request*
Your check is being returned with the request that you
please make the correction(s) as indicated below.  This
check . . .

*Details
(what
should be
done
instead
of what's
wrong)*
__ Should be signed by maker.
__ Should be properly endorsed.
__ Needs an individual endorsement.
__ Must have the written amount agree with the figure.
__ Should be made payable to us.
__ Needs the correct date.

*Action;
reader
benefit*
As soon as you have made the correction(s), please return
this check or a new check, and we will be glad to credit
your account.

## Requests to Persons within the Organization

Included here are straightforward requests exchanged between employees,
colleagues, supervisors and subordinates, and others, such as stockholders, who
are part of an organization. (Although letters of authorization for special
studies and reports also fall in this direct-request group, they are discussed
in Chapter 16, Reports.)

The next two examples illustrate well-written requests to persons within
the writer's organization. As you read Request 5, notice its good features—the
six numbered details for easy reading and the definite, courteous instructions
about the desired action. Enclosed with the letter was a two-page sample report with detailed discussion of each of the six headings.

**Request 5:** *A division manager's memo asking field representatives to send monthly
reports.*

TO:  Jim Inkley      Emmett Koontz
     Ron Lindquist   Dick Dubuque
     Tom Sedlock

FROM:   James Pearson

SUBJECT:   <u>Monthly</u> <u>Reports</u>        DATE:   September 10, 197_

*Request*   Starting October 1, will each of you please submit to this
office on the 21st of the month a monthly report including:

1.   Major orders received during the month.
2.   Anticipated major orders for the following month.
*Numbered*   3.   New business activity.
*details*   4.   Lost orders.
5.   Industrial trends.
6.   General comments.

*Helpful*
*sample*   A copy of the form I would like you to use is attached.

*Clear*   By no later than the 21st of every month, please mail your
*statement*   monthly report to me, with copies to the following:
*of where*
*and when*   1.   Each of the salesmen other than yourself
*report*   2.   Gary Rankin, Sales Manager
*should*
*be sent*   I will appreciate your cooperation.


Request 6, to stockholders, includes both a reader-benefit reason and two
suggestions for easy action.

*Request 6: A corporation secretary's second request to stockholders for a proxy;*
*printed message.*


Second Request
For Proxy For
Annual Meeting of Stockholders May 9, 197_

*Main*   At the close of business on April 25, we had not received a
*idea*   proxy from you for the Annual Stockholders Meeting to be
held May 9.

Perhaps you have already mailed that proxy.  If so, we
thank you and ask that you disregard this request.

*Request;*   If you have not yet returned your proxy, however,—or are
*easy*   doubtful whether you did so—will you please fill out
*action*   either the enclosed proxy form or the one we sent to you
April 8 along with the meeting notice and invitation.

*Reader-*
*benefit;*   So that you will be represented at the meeting, please mail
*easy action*   your proxy today in the enclosed reply envelope.

## INVITATIONS, ORDERS, RESERVATIONS

Though quite different from each other, invitations, orders, and reservations are similar in that the reader is asked for his own presence (or participation), merchandise, or facilities.

### Invitations

Invitations that require no persuasion can be both good-news announcements and simple requests. Regardless of how you classify them, they are organized according to the same three-part plan: main idea, explanation, action.

The main idea in the first paragraph is the invitation request, and you should try to include in it as many of the 5 W's as you can. The following sample openings are representative of different kinds of invitations you may need to send in business.

1. *To all management personnel, from the Public Relations Department:* The purpose of this memo is to invite you to attend the Business and Education Conference to be held at the Chamber of Commerce Building Georgian Room on Saturday, February 4. You will personally gain from exchanging views with other businessmen and college educators in this community.

2. *To all employees, from the company's house-organ editor:* Do you have an item of news or a suggestion you would like to share with other employees in our company? If so, you are invited to submit it for inclusion in our Semi-Annual Company House Organ before March 1.

3. *To all customers, from an administrative officer:* You are cordially invited to attend the Open House of our Topname Airplane Company . . .
   Sunday, June 10, from 2 to 5 p.m.
   in Plants 2 and 3.

In the explanation paragraph of your direct-request invitation, include all details that your reader(s) will appreciate and need. The ending paragraph clearly states the desired reader action and makes the action easy. If you need a reply by a certain date, be sure to say so.

The first letter below invites businessmen to a luncheon meeting; the second invites customers to attend a grand opening.

*Invitation 1: From a program chairman of a businessmen's club, to members.*

Dear ALTRUA member:

*Request*    The next meeting of ALTRUA is one you are especially invited to attend.  As your yearbook shows, this is the

| | |
|---|---|
| *What* | FORUM LUNCHEON, sponsored jointly by |
| *Who* | the Chamber of Commerce and our club |

to be held

| | |
|---|---|
| *Where* | at Lake City Community Hall, (address) |
| *When* | on Thursday, April 21, 197_, |
| | 12:15 p.m. |

*A detail*
*about the*
*program*

A highlight of the program is the panel discussion on the topic, "Problems of the Small Businessman in K County." You will find the discussion timely, challenging, and thought-provoking.

*Easy*
*action*

To make your reservation, please call either Tom Norden (KE 3-7777) or Mike Browne (At 9-9999), Springfield, before Tuesday, April 19, 5 p.m. How about phoning right now while you think of it?

*Reader*
*benefit*

We look forward to seeing you April 21 at the luncheon. For your convenience, free parking is available on the north side of the Hall.

**Invitation 2:** *From a savings association president, to customers.*

Dear Customer:

*Request*
*(invita-*
*tion);*
*who,*
*what,*
*where,*
*when*

I personally invite you and your family to be our special guests at the grand opening of Bronson's new quarters at 217 East Third Street, Mount Vernon, Thursday, Friday and Saturday, September 8, 9, and 10.

On Thursday and Friday, we will be open from 9:00 a.m. until 5:00 p.m. and on Saturday from 9:00 a.m. until 1:00 p.m.

*Details*

There will be handsome gifts for the ladies and gentlemen, special door prizes with drawings every two hours, and balloons and refreshments for all. Also each current passbook holder will receive a special present.

*Details*

Our new building is handsomely and graciously furnished in the hospitable Georgian style. The furnishings include a number of authentic period antiques which we are eager to show you.

*Easy*
*action*

Enclosed is your SPECIAL GUEST name tag which entitles you to your gift.

## Orders and Reservations

When you are ordering supplies or equipment and do not have an order blank or purchase form of the company with which you are placing the order, you can accomplish your purpose by writing a letter according to the direct-request plan. The same is true when you wish to reserve hotel accommodations, a meeting room, parking facilities for a conference, or any other premises.

Order letters include three kinds of facts: details about what you are ordering or reserving, directions for shipment, and manner of payment. In both order and reservation messages, the main idea in the first paragraph is that you are ordering or reserving something. Your explanatory paragraphs give whatever details the order or reservation requires—about quantity, color, style, size, price, payment, location, shipment date, place—plus any special instructions your reader might need. The last paragraph invites prompt shipment and dated action, if desired.

The following letter illustrates the organization and content of a complete order letter, with items tabulated for easy reading. You can use a similar organization plan for reservations.

*Order Letter: For office supplies.*

Gentlemen:

*Request* Please ship the following supplies to reach our main office at 9251 Grand Avenue (City, State, Zip) by Wednesday, June 3:

| Quantity | Description (and or Catalog number) | Unit Price | Total |
|----------|-------------------------------------|------------|-------|
*Details*

Total      $___

*Payment* These items are to be charged to our account on the usual 2/10, net/30 terms.

*Shipment* As we plan to distribute the ball-point pens for customer
*Courtesy* gifts on the opening day of our new branch, June 5, it is imperative that this shipment arrive on time. We count on your company's usual promptness in filling orders.

## REQUESTS PERTAINING TO CIVIC CAUSES OR PUBLIC OFFICIALS

Public officials need and appreciate suggestions from enlightened business and professional men and concerned citizens. Often, when an important issue is up for debate, they welcome direct communications that are not part of an organized drive.

Whenever you have a request, plan, or information that you sincerely believe is in the best interests of the community—or at least of your business or industry—remember the power of a good letter to the proper officials. As former President Kennedy said, "Everyone's vote counts in America, but those who write letters to express their opinions make their vote count more often."

Messages regarding civic causes or to public officials can involve any of the previously discussed four types of common situations—inquiries, complaints, requests for action related to routine business procedures, or invitations. But because of their special nature, they are grouped together separately in this section. Letters of this type are generally best handled by the direct-request plan. The busy official receiving your letter will welcome the message that states the purpose in the first paragraph. The following opening paragraphs about various issues should give you ideas on how to begin your request with the main idea:

1. *From a businessman to a Senator in Washington, D.C.:* The proposal to increase the truck weight and sizes on the interstate highway system deserves your serious consideration. I believe such an increase would be extremely unwise and wish to join the many others who ask that you oppose such a measure.

2. *From a store owner to the City's District Engineer:* This letter protests the proposed underpass at 60th Street and Highway 409. This change would cause an undue hardship on small businessmen who have invested their savings to build businesses convenient to the community in this area.

3. *From a citizen to a county highway commission:* The newspapers have stated that your department is installing numerous directional signs, in an attempt to help people (especially strangers) find their way around (city name). This action is a tremendous and useful job. My suggestion concerns how to help the many people who miss the right exits and need to get back to the freeway again.

4. *From a serviceman in the U.S. Army to his state senator:* This letter respectfully requests your assistance for my early release to accept employment because of family hardship.

5. *From a citizen's committee favoring a certain bond issue:* To help keep public education in this area on a sound footing, we urge your support of Special Levy 102.

As with all other direct requests, after you have introduced your main idea (request and reason), continue with adequate explanation. You may also find it desirable to enclose drawings, printed summaries with documentation, or any other visual material pertinent to your explanation. End with a forthright request such as, "we will appreciate whatever you can do to urge that Congress will legalize . . . during the current session."

The capsule checklists on pages 188 and 189 provide a quick summary of each type of direct request discussed in this chapter—inquiries, complaints,

| I | II | | III |
|---|---|---|---|
| | *Inquiries about persons* | | |
| *Direct-request general plan* | *To reference by applicant* | *To reference by person interested in applicant* | *Inquiries about products or services* |
| 1. MAIN IDEA<br>  a. Request, main statement, or question<br>  b. Reason(s) if desirable | 1. Main idea<br>  a. Reason for writing to this person<br>  b. Introduction of request<br>  c. Memory refresher | 1. Main idea<br>  a. Applicant's full name<br>  b. Why you are considering him<br>  c. Why you are writing to this reader | 1. Main idea<br>  a. Major request and/or<br>  b. Reason(s) for interest in product or service |
| 2. EXPLANATION<br>  a. All necessary and desirable details<br>  b. Numbered questions, if helpful<br>  c. Easy-reading devices | 2. Explanation<br>  a. Summary of pertinent facts about yourself: courses, major, GPA, outside work, tests, scores, honors, scholarships, leadership<br>  b. Guidelines for the recommendation: kinds of information the inquirer needs<br>  c. Enclosure of form(s), if helpful | 2. Explanation<br>  a. Requirements for job, loan, credit, scholarship, membership<br>  b. A few pertinent facts applicant told you about himself<br>  c. Specific questions:<br>    (1) More than "yes, no" answers<br>    (2) Explanations if necessary<br>    (3) Itemization—in body, underneath, or on separate questionnaire | 2. Explanation<br>  a. Specific questions<br>    (1) More than "yes, no" answers<br>    (2) Explanation whenever necessary<br>    (3) Itemization if more than one and desirable for clarity and/or ease of response<br>  b. Promise of anonymity, if desirable |
| 3. COURTEOUS CLOSE, WITH MOTIVATION TO ACTION<br>  a. CSAD[1]<br>  b. EA[2]<br>  c. DA[3]<br>  d. Appreciation and goodwill | 3. Courteous close<br>  a. CSAD;[1] to whom recommendation should be sent<br>  b. EA[2]<br>  c. DA[3]<br>  d. Appreciation | 3. Courteous close<br>  a. Appreciation<br>  b. Promise of confidential treatment<br>  c. EA[2]<br>  d. DA[3]<br>  e. Offer to reciprocate (if appropriate) | 3. Courteous close<br>  a. Suggested or specific action desired<br>  b. DA[3]<br>  c. EA when appropriate[2]<br>  d. Appreciation and courtesy |

[1]CSAD = clear statement of action desired
[2]EA = easy action
[3]DA = dated action, if desirable

| *IV*<br><br>*Complaints, claims, requests for adjustment* | *V*<br>*Requests for action related to routine business procedures* | *VI*<br><br>*Invitations* | *VII*<br><br>*Orders and reservations* |
|---|---|---|---|
| 1. Main idea<br>  a. Purpose(s) (need for adjustment or correction of error or procedure) | 1. Main idea<br>  a. Reason and<br>  b. Request (interchangeable) | 1. Main idea<br>  a. Invitation request with all pertinent 5 W's—who, what, when (day, date), where, why | 1. Main idea<br>  a. Statement of order or reservation |
| 2. Explanation<br>  a. Something good about reader or product or service, if true<br>  b. All relevant facts pertinent to the claim<br>  c. Omission of anger, threats, sarcasm, exaggeration, persuasion<br>  d. Desirable qualities: promptness, faith in reader's fairness; good humor (when appropriate) | 2. Explanation<br>  a. Desired details and, if helpful, instructions<br>  b. Itemization preferably when more than two items are requested<br>  c. Reader benefit, if any | 2. Explanation<br>  a. All necessary details—if to a function: program, time, apparel, costs, refreshments, location, directions, parking; if to submit material: length, method, format, etc.<br>  b. Set-up and enclosures as needed for easy reading | 2. Explanation<br>  a. Details about:<br>   (1) Needed items or facilities—quantity, size, color, style, catalog number, price (or rate)*<br>   (2) Payment—method, time, deposit (if any)<br>   (3) Shipment—date and place<br>   (4) Special instructions, if any<br>   *If reservation: function, number in expected attendance, requirements |
| 3. Courteous close<br>  a. CSAD:[1] Free replacement, free repairs, refund, credit, price reduction, inspection, explanation, apology or change, new shipment, or adjustment left up to reader<br>  b. EA[2]<br>  c. DA[3]<br>  d. Appreciation and courtesy | 3. Courteous close<br>  a CSAD[1]<br>  b. EA[2]<br>  c. DA[3]<br>  d. Courtesy | 3. Courteous close<br>  a. CSAD[1]<br>  b. EA[2]<br>  c. DA[3]<br>  d. Courtesy | 3. Courteous close<br>  a. CSAD[1]<br>  b. EA[2]<br>  c. DA[3]<br>  d. Courtesy |

[1]CSAD = clear statement of action desired
[2]EA = easy action
[3]DA = dated action, if desirable

requests for action related to routine business procedures, orders, and invitations that require no persuasion.[1] As you study these direct-request plan lists, notice that you introduce your main idea at or near the beginning, include whatever details your reader needs, and end courteously with easy and dated action, if appropriate.

## EXERCISES

### *Inquiries about Persons, Products, Services*

1. Comment orally on the good and poor qualities of the following inquiries about persons (sent to references). Which ones do you think will best accomplish their purpose? Why?

   **a.** From a national oil company:

   Dear Mr. Morrill,

   We are considering Mr. Larry R. Terrill, for a position with this Company and he has given your name as a personal reference.

   May we have your frank comment both as to his ability and personal qualities? Do you know of any reason for our not giving him full confidence? We shall appreciate any additional comments which will help us in reaching a correct decision, and also in adapting him to our organization in the event of our employing him.

   Since this matter is very active at present, we shall appreciate a prompt reply, and are enclosing a stamped and self-addressed envelope for this purpose.

   **b.** From the Big Brother volunteer service organization of a city:

   Dear Mr. Willman:

   About:  _Robert Zurbach_

   The above-named gentleman has applied to us to serve as a Big Brother. He has given your name as a reference.

   We feel you, in your contacts with him, would be able to advise us as to his stability and moral character. As a Big Brother, he will be working with a young, fatherless boy, establishing a friendship and offering moral and character guidance to the boys.

---

[1] For every direct request pertaining to a civic cause or public officials, follow the checklist on whatever type of situation best applies. If you prefer, merely follow the "direct-request general plan" in the first column and use your good judgment about what details to include.

We would like your frank appraisal, which will be held in strict confidence. Since your evaluation is necessary to complete the application, we will appreciate hearing from you soon.

**c.** Day letter telegram from an agency of the United States Government: PATRICIA M. MONELL DATE OF BIRTH 5/18/48 BEING CONSIDERED FOR EMPLOYMENT AS VETERAN'S CLAIMS EXAMINER QUASILEGAL POSITION HAS GIVEN YOUR NAME AS REFERENCE. REQUEST EVALUATION BY RETURN NIGHT LETTER COLLECT WITH APPLICANT'S DEMONSTRATED POTENTIAL TO PERFORM SUCH DUTIES, AND PERSONAL CHARACTERISTICS EXHIBITED DURING EMPLOYMENT WITH YOU. DO YOU HAVE ANY ADVERSE INFORMATION? WOULD YOU RECOMMEND FOR FEDERAL EMPLOYMENT?

**2.** Messages a and b are forms used by two law schools to get information about the many applicants who seek admission. Compare them for completeness, clarity of questions, information sought, and ease of action.

**a.** The above named person has applied for admission into (school name) Law School. Because your name was listed as a reference, we will appreciate a letter of recommendation from you.

No special form is required. Letters should be detailed and frank appraisals of the applicant as to (1) qualities of intellect, (2) communication skills, (3) character, (4) maturity and (5) personality. Comparisons of the applicant with other students known by the writer to have been admitted to the Law School are helpful.

**b.** Mr.
Mrs. _____
Miss        (LAST NAME)        (FIRST NAME)        (MIDDLE NAME)
is an applicant for admission to the (school name) Law School. Each year the number of applicants to the School far exceeds the number that can be accepted. You will greatly assist this applicant and the School by providing specific and candid answers to this inquiry. The information you provide will be treated as confidential. Prompt completion of this form will be appreciated by both the applicant and the School, for the application cannot be acted on until this form is received from you. Thank you for your cooperation.
1. How well do you know the applicant? _____
2. Has he conducted himself in an honorable and trustworthy manner in academic work and social relationships? _____
3. Has he been the subject of disciplinary action or proceedings (for misconduct) or of academic censure (for deficient scholarship)? _____
If so, please explain. (Please use the reverse side if this space is insufficient.)
_____
_____
4. Has he any physical handicap or any illness, physical or mental, that in your opinion bears on his ability to do law school work? _____
If so, please explain. _____
_____
5. In classes with you, how have you graded his academic performance (percentile, if possible)? _____

6. What is his approximate rank for all work taken in your college? _____

7. To what degree did the applicant's scholastic achievement measure up to his capacity?

☐ Fully realized his capacity.
☐ Performed reasonably in view of capacity.

☐ Had capacity to do considerably better.
☐ No basis for judgment.

Remarks: _____

_____
_____

8. Please furnish any other information that will be of assistance to a consideration of the applicant's transcript and his college record as a whole. Helpful remarks can relate to, but need not be limited to, unusual time-consuming extracurricular activities, leadership performance, motivation, capacity for interpersonal relations and significant participation in outside employment. We will also appreciate your estimate of the applicant's grades, courses taken and major field as a reliable measure of his academic capacity. (Please use the reverse side if this space is insufficient.) _____

_____
_____

9. Do you recommend the applicant for admission to the (name) Law School?

☐ I recommend with enthusiasm.
☐ I recommend.

☐ I recommend with reservation.
☐ I do not recommend.

Signature _____

Name (please type or print) _____

Title _____

Date _____ Address _____

3. Prepare to discuss orally the strengths and weaknesses of the following letters designed to get information. Comment particularly on organization, clarity, completeness of explanations, and motivation for action.

a. To subscribers of a magazine:

Dear <u>Journal</u> Reader:

You're right.  Another questionnaire.

But we feel it's an important one, and the short time required to complete it should be well spent, for it will help shape the course YOUR magazine, the <u>Journal</u>, will take in the important years ahead.

We say YOUR magazine because it's written and edited with readers like you in mind.  That's why the editors would like to take stock of what you like and dislike about the <u>Journal</u>. What parts are good?  What needs improvement?  What might be cut down or eliminated?  What might be added?

Your answers will help the <u>Journal</u> keep step with the rapidly changing field of (name of field).

You will note that we have not provided a space for your
signature.  This is by design.  We believe that anonymity will
produce more straight-from-the-shoulder opinion and constructive criticism.  Thank you for your help.

**b.** From a firm of research counselors in New York to an addressee in a state
2,500 miles away. Addressee is an employee of a city light company (letter is
an obvious form):

Dear Sir:

May we ask a favor that takes only a minute of your time?

We are conducting a special study to help determine how
familiar men in industry are with one of our clients.

We would appreciate it very much if you would answer the
questions on the attached sheet and return the questionnaire to
us in the enclosed, stamped envelope.  Your reply will be
confidential, of course, and the results of the study will be
shown in statistical form only.

**c.** To a real estate agent:

Dear Mr. Kramer:

I have clients who are very much interested in the Sand
& Surf in (town name).

They are prepared to make an offer of $110,000.00.  This
seems to be in line for a restaurant that grosses between
$115,000.00 and $118,000.00 a year.

My clients have a background in this type of business,
restaurant and lounge.  They have been wanting to locate this
side of the mountains and preferably in (town name) area.

**4.** You are director of employee education in a large industrial organization. One of
your jobs is to secure up-to-date pertinent training films. In a professional magazine advertising products related to your industry (assume one related to your
major), you have read about a new film on "Comparative . . ." (select your title).
The ad mentions only one rate: "Rental fee as low as $8." Before ordering the
film, you need to know if the rental charge is $8 for each showing or on a time
basis. If on a time basis, you wonder how long you may keep the film; you'd like
to show it at all three of your production plants to about 100 employees at a
time; you have 2,000 employees altogether. Other matters to inquire about include: length of film; need for special screen, amplifier, or projector; age group
or educational level for which film is produced. Write to the film producer, Top
Grade Films, Inc., Chicago.

**5.** As manager of the Hudson Real Estate Development, Inc., you need to replace three electric typewriters that are beginning to show their age. They have been good machines, but lately they have been breaking down frequently.

Already you have asked for and received bids on four makes. Each of the four distributors has quoted you practically the same price on the three new electric machines and offered you just about the same allowance on your three old typewriters. Thus, you don't favor one distributor over another because of price.

Since you don't know much about typewriters, you decide to write to a college chum who now heads the business education department at a distant university. He teaches typing and his classroom should contain a good representation of all leading makes. He certainly should know the good and bad points in the latest models he has available for his students. His name is Dr. Robert Gribbs, Professor of Business Education, College of Arts and Science, University of (state), (city, state ZIP).

Write a letter to Dr. Gribbs explaining your problem and asking which of the four brands you should select. Be specific. So that he can help you, you must explain what you expect from these machines. You can do so by asking specific questions and/or explaining what the machines will be used for. If you use questions, decide where they should go—in the body of the letter, at the bottom of the sheet the message is on, or on a separate enclosure?

**6.** As a management trainee of an exporting firm, you have become interested in preparing yourself for work in one of the company's South American offices. To qualify you need to learn Spanish. The local community college and the university both offer courses in Spanish, but you wonder if a correspondence course might serve your needs better, provided you have enough time for study. You want to learn how to read and write the language fluently enough for business use.

Write to Verlits Schools of Languages in New York City, asking for all the facts you need. Today is August 1 and the new position you'd like to fill opens September 1 next year. You want to know how long it would take by correspondence to get the equivalent of a year's university Spanish course. You also wonder whether Verlits Spanish instructors are natives of Spanish-speaking countries, and/or former Verlits students, and/or former university students? Also you wonder about costs, examinations, certificates, home study assignments, and tempo of the work.

**7.** Assume that a 45-year-old friend or relative of yours has developed a painful, incurable illness. His doctor has decreed that a certain operation—majory surgery —would help alleviate the pain but could not be guaranteed. The patient might have only 80 percent mobility afterwards. He has endured the pain for two years, but it is getting worse. The surgery would involve placing a steel ball at the top of the patient's femur bone (upper leg bone) and a shank inside. Your friend or relative worries about whether the probable results will be worth the great expense (three weeks in the hospital) and long recuperation period. Also he wonders whether he would be more or less able to walk after the operation. His doctor has given him the names and addresses of five patients on whom he has performed similar operations. Compose a form letter that you can send to these references. Consider whether you should include a questionnaire on a separate sheet. Carefully word the questions you will include. Will you address your letter personally to each reference?

8. You are personnel director in charge of training for Security Stores, Inc., a chain of department stores with headquarters in Los Angeles, and with branches in Arizona and Oregon. Yesterday you interviewed Thomas Brainston (24), who seeks to join your management training program. His application form indicates he graduated from the University of Ohio three years ago and that he served in the Coast Guard for the next two years. He says he worked "for a while" at the Midwest Appliance Company in Cincinnati. He thought he wanted to work up to top management with that firm, but finally decided he'd rather live on the Pacific Coast, because he enjoys the ocean and water sports. He seemed to be very enthusiastic about working up into a branch-store management position with your firm.

   His application letter—and his comments during the interview—indicated that he also worked part-time as a salesman in a men's clothing store two months, while attending the university; one-half year in a service station, part time; and "also in several other places."

   His scholastic record—with a major in marketing—is excellent (he says), although you don't have the transcript of his work. You are more concerned right now about his disposition to stick with a two-year training program. Your company's usual procedure is to place young trainees in the smaller towns, most of which are inland. (Some are over a hundred miles from the ocean.) You wonder if Brainston would stick with the company during the years (perhaps up to six or seven) that he would be situated inland. Also, as you talked with him you noticed that he interrupted you several times to tell you about his views, and he knocked two of his former employers, including Midwest. One of the references to whom you will write today is Mr. Bronson Quist at Midwest Appliance Company. Try to find out whether his experience with Brainston indicates that he has the qualifications to do effective work—first as a management trainee and later as a branch store manager. He'd also be in the Customer Service and Adjustment Departments for a while.

9. You are planning to enroll for graduate work at the American Institute of Foreign Trade, Phoenix, Arizona. It will be necessary for you to earn part of your expenses while attending there.

   Write to the registrar to get the necessary information. You need to know how much money must be paid in advance of attendance, what kind of lodgings are available for families, and whether any part-time jobs are obtainable. Also you'd like to know if the placement office at the Institute places the school's graduates in domestic or foreign opportunities, whichever the graduate may prefer.

10. You are assistant credit manager in the mortgage loan department of a savings and loan association. You need information from credit references that an applicant has given you on his application for a mortgage loan. Write to the Topcraft Department Store's credit manager asking about the applicant's credit record with that store. You need to know how long he has been a customer there, how well he has paid his account balances, what the terms of sale have been, any credit limit imposed on him, etc.

## Claims (Complaints) and Requests for Adjustment

1. Evaluate the following opening paragraphs of claim letters, and tell how to improve the poor ones. Which one(s) do you consider effective? Why?

a. In the past year I have ordered nearly $200 in goods from your store, by mail. Two weeks ago I came there in person and bought a gray overcoat. As I was heavily loaded with packages I asked the clerk to send the garment to me by store delivery. When the overcoat arrived, I was busy and so I didn't open the package until two days ago.

b. Never in my life have I been treated so rudely as I was the other day in your store, by two jerks you call employees. I tell you, the way I was insulted gave me a good indication of what kind of people you're hiring these days. I'm so mad I will never go back to your store again.

c. You should be interested in an experience I had in your store recently.

d. To the adjustment-department manager:
   In line with your policy on consumer satisfaction published in your recent catalog, I am requesting a cash refund of $35.38 for a toaster I purchased two weeks ago for cash. The reason I have directed this request to your office is that your department manager indicated that such a refund would not be possible.

e. From a gift-shop manager to a newspaper about a desk lamp advertised:
   Please stop the presses for a second to take a quick look at the Bramhall classified ad in your September 4 issue of the (city) *Times*. Its form is excellent, but it is in the wrong pew "sitting" under the "for rent" caption. Will you set it straight, please, by rerunning it without charge?

2. Comment on the following claim letters. Consider tone, organization, clarity, accuracy, and probable effectiveness in getting the desired result. What changes, if any, do you recommend? Please be specific. Try to determine first what each writer really wants.

a. From a landlord to apartment tenants:

```
Dear Mr. & Mrs. Jaeger:

It seems some of your typing late at night disturbs some
tenants.  Perhaps when all is quiet it is easier to hear.

I was wondering if you type on the nook table--as that is bad
because the table is fastened to the building.  A felt pad will
help if you do not already have one.  The University Book
store has them just for that purpose.

I know your typing is important to your school work, however
I would like to keep everyone happy.
```

b. From a disgruntled branch-bank customer to an officer of that bank's main office. (The customer's bank account was at the main office, but he forgetfully wrote a check drawn on one of its 95 branches.):

```
Friend James.

     Enclosed please find check I had to chase uptown to pick
up because your northlake branch uptown did not have the
courtesy to try to locate this account.  I overlooked changing
the check to indicate it was main branch, but common courtesy
```

at least could have been used.  They do not have so many checks like this come in but what they can make an effort to locate the account in your various branches instead of subjecting a person to the embarrassment of having a check bounce back and make me feel small.

    I only changed my account from a bank that suited me because of your courtesy to me while you were at the Northlake Branch.  I deal a lot with Flint and Morris stock brokers, and as I told you a while back I would possibly deal with your Bank's stock dept.  I carry a large bal. with this Firm and can at any time get a large order honored over the phone.

    But since your bank branch is so unwilling to cooperate after all the efforts your bank makes to attract accounts through your advertising medium, I shall close my account on the last day of this month and be glad I did not change my stock broker account, also.  Shall also give up my safety box.

    I do not feel unkindly to you and shall do anything in my power for you personally in your Dept.  But I am like the city of Boston.  Had Enough.

**c.** From a public stenographer to a typewriter company:

Gentlemen:

    Can you on an adjustment decide,
    And thus an answer to my problem provide?
    That typewriter sirs—
    Of which the purchase occurred
    On February 25 last,
    Was extremely effective
    For six days—and then alas,
    Suddenly became most defective.

    The shift key won't lock;
    Nor the ribbon reverse;
    And the space bar only responds to a sock,
    Now I hate to be terse,
    But if worse comes to worse;
    My typing won't even sell on the block.

    A local repairman
    Whose quite well adapted
    To fixing this thing and that;
    Has quoted quite thrifty,
    The price of $16.50,
    To remedy the troubles I've got.

    Thus, I'm sending to you
    This little review

```
          To find out what you can do;
          In order to give me
          The most from your fine guaranty.

          So, Gentlemen--please help me,
          I am desperately in need,
          Of a typewriter you readily can see,
          Which will do the work required of me.
```

**d.** From a college student in a small town to a discount house in another state:

```
To whom it may concern:

     I don't know who packs your boxes but they sure blew this
order.   (A) I ordered ice bucket 86103NF gld w/blk trim, &
received ice bucket 86-118NF Tahitan Holiday pattern w/ivory
trim.   (B) I ordered a trip nip bottle tote 416VT & get a
Deluxe Carry-all Diaper bag 516HR.

     Now listen I'll keep the ice bucket OK.   But the diaper
bag has got to go.  I'm a senior in college & single.  I don't
even have a pregnant girl friend let alone a wife or baby.

     Please send me my trip nip bottle tote & advise me on what
to do with the diaper bag.  Come on give me a break; this is a
small campus what are you trying to do--start rumors?
```

**3.** Last Saturday you took an interesting tour with a group of 15 other businessmen —through the Ace Lumber Mills. All of you had attended a conference and the tour was scheduled as part of the conference. After walking from one building to another, you happened to be the target for a glob of tar that dripped from a roof of one of the mills as you entered. It fell on your left shoulder, on your new suit. One of the employees suggested that after the suit is cleaned you should send the bill to this lumber mill. Now you have had the suit cleaned and you want reimbursement. Write a courteous letter to get the desired refund.

**4.** The following is a copy of a handwritten letter dated 2/17 in the current year. It was received by the manager of a used-car sales agency in your town. The car is 12 years old. Identify all errors, and then rewrite the complaint so it will produce the desired results.

```
Mister Manager,

You people sold me a car last week which was a 196_ brown
Palomar 4 door sedan.  with a rod nocking in the engin.  the
transmittion and engin blew up on me yesterday morning on my
way to work near (a town 60 miles from you).

Eather refund my $75.00 payed for cash to me. or rebuild the
engin and transmition of said auto.  If I dont get a letter
from you personally by Friday noon of this week I shall com-
pelled to write a letter to Washington D.C. and have your
Company investigated for fraudulent activities.
```

Ford Motor Co. gives a one year warrenty on used automobiles in
(your town name). Why cant you? Ive already seen three
businesses out of business already for fraudulent transations.
Would you like me to run your business out of town. If you
dont think I have power to do so then refuse to write me a
letter so I can get it befor noon Friday of this week. Nobody
has ever made a fool out of me yet. If you think Im some kind
of a Goverment undercover agent, Im not Im just an ordinary
ex G.I. law abiding citizen, who hates to be cheated out of his
rightful hard earned money. Im a disabled veteran of the
Vietnam fight. I earned my pention fighting unamerican like
unconstitutional like activities.

NOT: All I want is my $75.00 cash back and Ill sell whats left
of my car to the junk yard for $40.00 unless your co wants to
rebuilt the engin and the transmition for me. Do I make myself
clear. nobody is going to trick me and get away with it see.

5. The newsboy who delivers your daily newspaper folds the paper and hurls it at
your home as he speeds past on his bicycle. Last summer you had to replace the
wire on the screen door because of the repeated impacts. You spoke to the boy
about the damage, and he promised to be more careful. Now, on January 18, you
find that he has broken a pane of glass in one of your living-room windows.
Write to the North End News Agency and endeavor to have the situation righted.
You cannot speak to the boy directly because you are away from home at the
time he delivers the paper.

6. You are purchasing agent for a large company that has its own employee
lounge and library. Recently you bought, by mail order, five copies of a certain
book ($12 each) related to your industry, and placed them in the company library.
One of your employees has just discovered some serious page discrepancies in
one of these books. In checking all five books you find that two of the five have
the same inaccuracies:

On the back of page 92 is page 121
On the back of page 94 is page 129
Pages 120, 252, 255, 341, and 395 are missing entirely.

Write to the Hall Book Company, New York City, to get the needed adjustment.

7. Assume you bought a new convertible automobile last month. You garage it during the week because you live in a big city and want the car mainly on weekends.
But whenever you planned a trip and got the car out on Saturday morning, the
valves have stuck. The service garage each time refused to fix them until the following Monday or Tuesday. Four weekends in succession have been ruined this
way. Last Saturday morning (the fifth week) you planned to drive your son to
summer camp. You loaded the car with camp equipment, got into the driver's
seat—and the valves stuck again. You finally had to rent a car. Send your claim
letter by registered mail to the vice-president of the auto company factory, with
a copy to the head of the company's sales division. The service garage to which
you have taken your car is an authorized dealer for the auto company. You want
the valves replaced without charge, reimbursement for the car-rental expense, and
some kind of assurance of better service in the future.

**8.** Assume that today is April 2. A 60-year-old friend (or relative) of yours has asked you to help in writing a letter about a dental problem, which he relates to you as follows:

"Last year, in March I think it was, I had all my teeth pulled out; and on April 21 my dentist fitted me with upper and lower plates. He charged me $600, which included also 2 reline jobs on the upper plates and 2 on the lower plates within the next year. Well, so far Johnny—(that's my dentist)—I call him by his first name 'cause he has been my dentist for the past 40 years and he's a good friend of mine—has given me one reline on the upper plate and two relines on the lower plate. So I have one upper coming free. I guess by now I really need to get them both relined again. (Just then both uppers and lowers rattled noticeably.)

"Well, last February I phoned his office for an appointment, but to my surprise a new feminine voice told me that Doc Tallman has retired and is living with his wife at a resort on Fun Island, Anystate. Dr. Weasel has taken over his practice. I talked to this Dr. Weasel too. When I explained my problem to him, he said he'd talk the matter over with Dr. Tallman and ask him to phone me the next time he came to the office—probably in two weeks. He said he was sure Dr. Tallman would make a satisfactory adjustment. He also offered to send us right away a printed announcement card about his (Weasel's) new practice and office.

"Three weeks passed and no phone call; also no announcement came. My wife phoned his office again, only to find that the office girl knew nothing about the matter and that Dr. Tallman had been in the office just 'yesterday.' She said she'd make a note of my wishes and ask Dr. Tallman to phone me. She thought he'd be back in the office in another two weeks or so. Well, another three weeks passed and no phone call. This time my wife went to the office in person. The office girl, without any apology, admitted in a rather bored tone that she had plumb forgotten to tell Dr. Tallman, but she would do it next time he came in. That would probably be in about two weeks. Now another three weeks have gone by and I have heard nothing from them. When I phoned yesterday the girl said in a rather abrupt tone, 'I think it would perhaps be better if you write to Dr. Tallman yourself.'

"One thing I'm sure of now—I wouldn't have that Weasel do any work on me! And so long as Johnny has retired and is out of town, I've found me another good dentist. He says he charges $40 for relining upper plates. But I don't think I should have to pay that $40 again, do you? I want Johnny to refund what I have coming to me. Then I'll get both upper and lower plates relined. 'Course I expect to pay for the reline job on the lower plate because Johnny already gave me two."

Write the claim letter to Dr. Tallman for the signature of the patient. Supply any essential missing details, and of course omit all unessentials. Watch your tone! Assume that Dr. Tallman is quite well off financially. Your friend (or relative) is a former successful business executive, but because of poor health he has been unable to work for two years. He and his family have been living on his small sick-pay income. His wife tells you that her husband has refused to go anywhere until his rattling plates are anchored. She hopes he can get both uppers and lowers relined within the next three weeks, so he will be able to attend an important function to which they've been invited.

9. Today is November 23. On November 19 a businessmen's fraternal organization of which you are a member held its annual Thanksgiving dance. As is customary, most members decided to have dinner before the function. Thinking very highly of a certain restaurant (the El Tropicana), which enjoys a fine reputation in your city, you recommended that a group dine there. Unfortunately, their experience was such that none of the men or their wives will ever want to patronize it again. Though the food was good, the service was disappointing in several ways. When your waiter brought in the glassware, he grabbed each glass by the top when he placed it in front of the diner. Once he bumped a lady's shoulder, but said nothing. After dinner, you received the bills and placed payment on the trays provided. As a courtesy to the cashier, one of the men in your group placed the exact amount of change on the tray. The waiter snarled a sarcastic "Is that all?" Later, at one time, because you were enjoying yourself, you smiled at the waiter. However, he snapped: "Is something funny, sir?" For the $15 a couple paid for the dinner, you feel that both good food and good service should have been provided. Despite the poor service, the group did leave a $14 tip, which they felt was more than adequate. Although you too are extremely disappointed with the waiter's service, you now wonder if you shouldn't give the manager an opportunity to restore your faith (and that of your friends) in this restaurant. Write an appropriate letter to him. Consider carefully just what you want of this manager. What will restore the faith of your members? Will you ask outright for a cash allowance or another meal, or leave the adjustment up to the manager?

10. Assume that while visiting a friend in Fairbanks, Alaska, after your graduation from college, you were asked one day (April 20) to write an important letter for neighbors—Mr. and Mrs. Leonard Nolittle. This middle-aged couple, extremely worried and entirely uninformed about business procedures, told you their problem and offered to pay you for your help. Here is their "story":

We have a contract with Americana Encyclopedia Company to purchase their 30-volume set for $399.50. The contract was made out on the 20th of December last year and the terms read $15 a month until paid for. They informed us we were to make these payments to the Fairname Credit Corporation, Seattle, by the 7th of every month, starting with February of this year.

We are buying a house here in Fairbanks and by mistake we began sending our monthly house payments to the Fairname Credit Corp. The person we are buying the house from told us that an agency in Seattle would be collecting our monthly payments and that this agency would be sending a booklet, etc., to use for further correspondence. We received the Fairname Credit Corporation booklet and mailing address January 15, and since there was no mention of the Americana Encyclopedia, we took this to be the house-payment book. When we did hear from Americana we thought it only a coincidence that the same Seattle agency was collecting for house and books—since the party we are buying the house from lives in Seattle—so we continued to make house payments and our encyclopedia payments to the Fairname Credit Corporation.

As of now we have sent Fairname $417.33 in house payments and $45.50 in Encyclopedia payments. This makes a total of $462.83. If our house payments are being applied to the Encyclopedia, this means then that we have overpaid Fairname $63.33 over the total cost of the Encyclopedia. Nothing has been mentioned about this so far; in fact we have never received a receipt from Fairname and we wrote them about the last payment last month (March 28). It seems odd to us that no one in their office wondered why we would send two separate checks—one for $15.00 and the other for about $140.00 per month—when the Encyclopedia contract calls for $15.00 per month.

We want our house-payment money back as soon as possible before May 1. We have made three monthly house payments to Fairname. Our check No. 493 on February 1 amounted to $140.25; check no. 498 on February 25 was for $138.00; and on March 28 we sent another check, no. 524 for $139.08. That is a total of $417.33. If we don't pay Mrs. Bronson as promised in our house contract to her, she takes the house back. If we don't pay Americana Corporation, they will demand the books back. So we hope you will urge the Fairname Credit Corporation to send our money back and in the future to send receipts for money they receive.

Following principles stressed in this course, write an effective letter to the Fairname Credit Corporation for the signature of Mr. Nolittle. Assume, of course, that your letter will be typewritten. Indicate in the correct way that copies are being sent to all parties concerned.

11. Assume you ordered two venetian blinds for your bedroom windows from a reputable department store in your area. The store clerk said that delivery would take one month because she had to order them from the manufacturer in another city. The manufacturer would send them directly to you, and you would pay the department store.

    Two weeks after you placed your order, an employee of the store called and said the girl who took your order had forgotten to specify color and the manufacturer had asked the store for that information. The caller told you the store would put a rush on the order to try to get the blinds to you within two weeks. However, four weeks later (six weeks from date of order), the blinds had not arrived. When you phoned the store, no one could provide an explanation. Two weeks later, *one* venetian blind arrived. When you complained, the adjustment department head said the manufacturer's representative was in the store and promised to wire his company to get the blinds to you right away. The second blind arrived two weeks later (*ten* weeks from date of order), but you found that the blind was missing an important end cap. Although you would have preferred to do without the end cap (you didn't want to return the blind because you were afraid you wouldn't get it back for another two months), you found that it was essential. Without the end cap the blind will not stay in the bracket above the window; it crashes to the floor completely disassembled every time you try to close the blinds.

    Your assignment is to write the manufacturer and ask for the cap you need. You do not want to send the blind back, and you want them to send you the part at no cost so that you can install it yourself. Needless to say you are not particularly pleased with the company's service.

## Miscellaneous Requests, Orders, Invitations

1. The following letters deal with routine business situations. Analyze each situation and then decide whether the message is adequate. Suggest improvements.

   a. A printed form letter from the president of a savings association to customers; it has no salutation, but the customer's name and address are inserted at the top.

————Please sign the enclosed withdrawal slip and return to us.

————Would you please send us your signature card. ————————.

————Would you please send us your social security (reporting) number.

————We need your *original* hazard (fire) insurance policy (with extended coverage) in at least the amount of $————.

————An error was made on your last transaction which has already been corrected on our records (we'll correct your passbook the next time we have it).

————We are returning your check because ————————————.

————Your construction interest payment starts ————————, 19——. in the amount of $————; thereafter, interest payments will be $———————— until regular payments ($————————) start ————————, 19——. YOU MAY MAKE FULL PAYMENTS AT ANY TIME AND RECEIVE CREDITS TOWARD FUTURE PAYMENTS.

Thank you.

**b.** Memo inserted in each employee's pay envelope; from the personnel department.

```
Hereafter, coffee breaks will be limited
to the original 10 minutes.
```

**c.** Memo from the departmental social director to all employees in his department.

```
Subject:  Christmas gifts for our departmental secretaries

With Christmas just around the corner, it's time for me to
raise my ugly head above ground once again to remind you it's
time to consider our departmental secretaries.

If you wish to contribute toward a gift for each gal, please
leave your donation in my box by December 10.  Fifty cents from
each of you will be adequate.
```

**d.** From an auto insurance representative to prospects; a mimeographed letter with personalized typed insertions for address and salutation.

```
Dear Mr. Clark,

        If you are under age 25 and object to paying high auto
insurance premiums, why don't you check with me?

        I can write liability coverage for qualified drivers
under age 25 for less than $100.00 per year.

        Give me a call if you want more information.  Or, if
you would like me to contact you, return the enclosed card.
```

2. You are area coordinator for your company's blood bank. Last year, through the cooperation of various departments, your blood bank had ample credits to provide the 289 withdrawal units requested by employees. Now the annual drive is approaching again. On March 3 your company's employees are to participate in this worthwhile cause from 10 a.m. to 4 p.m. (You decide on the place and on other necessary details.) You want donors to sign up for the time most convenient for them. Provide sign-up sheets in convenient places, and write a memo to all employees, attaching a folder about the blood bank and on donor qualifications.

3. Assume you are the new assistant manager of Apex Life Insurance Company's office in your city. Your company will be holding interviews on a nearby college campus January 30 for winter and spring quarter graduates. You want to send a concise personalized form letter to graduating seniors inviting them to sign up for an interview (wherever you specify) or to call you for further information. You will also grant off-campus interviews. You believe your company has jobs that graduates should be interested in. They can build a business career with no capital investment, they can get comprehensive training to develop their talents, and a monthly life income after 20 years of qualified service. Is there anything else you should include?

# Chapter 7

# Good-news and Neutral Messages

- Organizational Plan
- Favorable Replies
- Unsolicited Favorable Messages
- Capsule Checklists
- Exercises

A message that conveys good news is usually easy to write, because you are giving or telling your reader something that pleases him. A neutral-reaction letter is also relatively easy to write, because the message is about something that the reader considers neither good nor bad news—just information that may be useful to him.

You can adapt the good-news plan to a variety of situations. Use it whenever you answer a request or when you initiate an unsolicited message yourself—if the news will be favorable or at least not unfavorable to your reader. Among the many kinds of letters and memoranda you can organize with the good-news plan are the following:

*Favorable replies*

Answering inquiries for information related to sales
Answering inquiries for information unrelated to sales
Granting adjustments on claims and complaints
Approving credit
Acknowledging orders
Granting favors
Accepting invitations
Granting any other requests—pertaining to business, government, and organizational procedures or individual needs
Accepting job offers, franchises, and other negotiations

*Unsolicited messages favorable*

Announcements about
    Sales and events
    Procedures, policies, and responsibilities
    Honors and activities of people
Transmittals
Congratulations, appreciation, and other expressions of goodwill

This chapter discusses the good-news organizational plan, the first six types of favorable replies listed above, and all the listed favorable unsolicited messages except the last entry (Congratulations, etc.) Additional illustrations of messages adaptable to the good-news pattern are included in Chapter 11, Other Job Application Messages, and Chapter 13, Goodwill Messages.

## ORGANIZATIONAL PLAN

The direct approach—putting the best news or the main idea (if it is favorable or at least not unfavorable) in the opening paragraph—is the most effective plan to use for good-news and neutral messages. As with direct requests, the organizational structure of these messages has three parts. Hereafter this good-news and neutral pattern is called simply the "good-news plan":

---

1. Best news or the main idea
2. Explanation, which includes one or more of the following, when desirable:
   a. All necessary details
   b. Educational information
   c. Resale material
   d. Sales promotion
3. Positive, friendly ending
   a. Appreciation
   b. Clear statement of action desired and motivation to action
   c. Willingness to help further

---

Because the items in the explanation section form the basic core of your message, you must use good judgment in deciding which items to include. The following discussion highlights the content and uses of these four items:

a. *All necessary details:* Include whatever facts, terms, reasons, and other explanations pertain directly to the best news or the main idea. Consider, for instance, whether the reader needs specific details on the why, what, when, who, where, and how of the news or main idea.

b. *Educational information:* Include instructions for use and other educational facts about a product or service the customer has bought if such information is necessary to help the customer get the utmost benefit from his purchase or his relationship with your firm. If you enclose an instruction booklet, a short paragraph within the letter may call special attention to certain pages in that booklet.

c. *Resale material:* Include appropriate favorable information about a product or service the reader has already bought or is planning to buy, or about your organization. Such material usually answers the question "What will this do for me?" and strengthens the reader's confidence in your product, service, or organization. Write concisely and with restraint. Avoid exaggeration and superlatives (such as "sensational," "perfect," "out-of-this-world value," and so on), because most readers react negatively toward them. Good resale keeps the customer "sold" on the product and company and helps to encourage repeat orders.

d. *Sales promotion:* Include suggestions about other products or services related to those the customer has bought or is considering buying—whenever doing so indicates your desire to be of further service to the customer or whenever it seems appropriate. This material should be presented without sales pressure; the emphasis should be on what the customer may need or appreciate and not on a desire to get more business. Also you need to consider the reader's probable mood before you decide to include or omit sales promotion. For instance, near the end of a good-news message—when you are fairly sure the customer will be in a receptive frame of mind—sales promotion may be quite appropriate.

# FAVORABLE REPLIES

To help build goodwill, any progressive organization replies to all reasonable requests courteously, helpfully, and promptly (within two days, if possible). If you know there will be a delay, a brief acknowledgment should state why and then tell the inquirer approximately when he can expect a complete answer. Even in such a message you can begin with the best news first—with information that is useful to the reader or shows you are doing something for him. Don't start with such negative statements as: "We are sorry we cannot answer your request here. . . ." Emphasize the positive; for example:

> Your request for information about solenoids has been forwarded to our Chief Systems Analyst, Mr. Richard Hacket, in our Chicago offices.
>
> You can expect to receive his helpful comments regarding your special needs soon after he returns from Alaska next week.

In every good-news reply your compliance with the reader's request is more important to him than any expression of gratitude or pleasure. Depending upon circumstances, you can begin by saying that you have done it (the preferred beginning), that you are doing it, or that you will do it. Thereafter the material you select for the explanation and ending varies significantly with the circumstances.

The discussion in this section includes guidelines and examples of favorable replies to requests for information, adjustment, credit, orders, and favors, and provides a basis for deciding how to answer all other types of good-news replies.

## Answering Inquiries for Information Related to Sales

Requests for information about services or products you sell are inquiries related to sales. Included are questions about catalogs, prices, terms, discounts, deliveries, products, manufacturing methods, types of accounts available, sources of supply, and similar information.

Replies to many of these inquiries are actually sales letters, and are often called *solicited,* or *invited,* sales messages.[1] The inquirer is often already your customer, or a potential buyer. He may become a steady, satisfied customer *if* you send him a reply that impresses him favorably. This section discusses content of the three good-news parts and suggestions for handling inquiries prompted by advertising.

*Positive Opening Paragraphs.* The best way to begin these letters is by courteously doing one of the following:

---

[1] For a discussion of unsolicited sales messages see Chapter 9, Persuasive Requests.

1. *Sending the requested material*
   Enclosed are three samples of the nylon materials you asked about. We are glad to send these to you with our compliments.
2. *Answering favorably one of the inquirer's questions*
   a. Yes, Mr. Jones,
      You can use Latex Enamel paint in your bathroom with complete assurance that it is washable.
   b. You're right! Model XL2, about which you inquired, can easily become an exceptionally good profit-maker for you. Our dealers have reported it to be their most popular do-it-yourself maintenance kit.
3. *Introducing the main idea(s) that your letter will cover*
   a. Thank you for giving us the opportunity to tell you about the two insured savings plans available for you at First Federal.
   b. I am glad to explain to you the differences in the three Portable Vibration Monitors we manufacture. Thank you for your letter of January 5 concerning your interest in these recorders.

**Answers to All Questions.**[1] In your explanation section, you should answer all questions—direct or implied. In many cases, you will also provide educational, resale, or sales promotion information. Arrange your answers so that the favorable responses are at the beginning and end of your explanation section, to accent the positive and "imbed" the negative aspects. Maintain a "you attitude"; keep the reader in every paragraph if possible.

Imbedding the negative does not mean that you should omit or twist the truth. It means that you can emphasize what something *is* rather than what it is *not*. Like a good salesman, you try to determine what the customer really needs. Sometimes this need enables you to handle favorably an answer that seems to you at first to be negative. Contrast, for instance, the negative and the positive answers to the following four questions:

1. *Question:* Is the raincoat sprayed with ABC liquid so that it will be waterproof?

   *Negative reply:* No, I'm sorry to say the raincoat is not sprayed with ABC liquid. However, the material itself is made of durable vinyl which is completely waterproof.

   *Positive reply:* The material in this raincoat is made of a durable vinyl which is permanently and completely waterproof. Thus you need never bother with any spray even after the garment is cleaned many times.

2. *Question:* Do you carry the Bronson tape recorder? If so, how long would it take for you to send one to my office if I should decide to order it? (Inquirer lives 500 miles from seller, and only 100 miles from the factory. Seller is out of the item today, but notice that the inquirer has not yet ordered it.)

   *Negative reply:* We are temporarily out of stock of the Bronson, and so we couldn't send you one right away. If we reorder especially for you, it will take ten days after after we receive your request.

[1] See also the section on answering all questions asked, pages 84–87.

*Positive reply:* Yes, we do carry the Bronson tape recorder, and we can usually send it to you within one day after we receive your order. As it is an extremely popular model, we sometimes run out of it temporarily. In such a case, we will gladly reorder immediately so you can expect delivery within ten days. Occasionally, for a rush order, we could have the item sent to you direct from the factory within two days after your request reaches us.

3. *Question:* Do you send these washing machines c.o.d.?

*Negative reply:* No, we don't send c.o.d.
*Positive, helpful reply:* Instead of c.o.d., which would require you to pay the full amount upon delivery of the machine, you have a choice of several payment plans. With every purchase the required down payment is 10 percent sent at the time of the order; the balance is payable in convenient monthly installments which you can arrange with our representative, Mr. Jepson.

4. *Question:* Will you refund our money if we buy these draperies by mail and then find they don't blend with our other room colors?

*Negative reply:* No, we don't refund all your money; you must pay for shipping charges.
*Positive reply:* If you should wish to return the draperies within two weeks from the invoice date, you will get a full refund less shipping charges.

When quoting prices, be sure to use the same positive psychology by considering your reader's needs and circumstances. Unless the price of a particular product is a bargain, mention it only *after* you have stated most selling points and reader benefits. (For additional suggestions on methods of handling price quotations honestly as well as effectively, see Persuasive Requests, pages 345 to 418.)

*Effective Action-getting Paragraphs Leading to Sales.* To get the desired action from your invited-sales reply, remember to make action clear, easy, dated if necessary, and beneficial to the reader when possible.[1] Sometimes itemizing the steps that the reader should take is effective, as in the following example:

To start either account, you need take only three easy steps:

*Action, clear and easy*
1.  Complete the enclosed application card.  Be sure to check which plan you prefer, indicate which name or names should appear on your account and what address we should send your mail to, add your social security number, and sign your name at the bottom of the card.
2.  Enclose--in the prepaid envelope provided--both this application card and your money order or check that you wish to deposit.
3.  Drop the sealed envelope into the nearest mailbox.

*Reader benefit*
As soon as your application card and deposit reach us, we will open an account which will begin earning 5% or 5½% dividend immediately for you.

[1] To refresh your memory about other suggestions for all good closings, you might wish to reread pages 29–31 and 92.

   Letter 1 below is a helpful reply to an inquiry related to sales. A potential customer who planned to cover both her kitchen and concrete basement floor with linoleum wrote to a manufacturer of nationally known flooring products asking for "any booklet that will help us choose the right linoleum." She also asked, "Please tell us how much the product you recommend for us would cost per square yard." The reply, from the supervisor of the customer information bureau, not only sends the requested booklet but also answers each implied and direct question in a positive reader-benefit way. Instead of stating that the customer's choice of linoleum for her basement is poor, the writer emphasizes that, while linoleum is an excellent flooring for some areas of the home, other kinds of flooring are more suitable for use in basements. Also, instead of stating that he can't quote prices in one letter, the respondent suggests how a nearby resilient flooring retailer can help the inquirer.

*Letter 1:* *A well-written reply that answers questions tactfully, encloses a booklet containing decorating ideas, and suggests where to go for additional help.*[1]

Dear Mrs. Sumer:

*Best news first and reader benefit*

We appreciate the interest you have shown in Armstrong's products and are sending you a copy of our latest decorating booklet showing how resilient flooring can be used to make your home more attractive, more comfortable, and easier to care for.

*Educational information*

In your letter, you mention plans for a basement family room and ask about linoleum for this purpose. It's important here to make a distinction between linoleum and other types of flooring, such as vinyl. Even though linoleum is an excellent flooring for kitchens and some other areas of the home, it should not be used in basements or in any room where it would be installed on concrete that is in direct contact with the ground.

Several other kinds of Armstrong flooring are highly recommended for use in basements. Many homemakers prefer one of the vinyl floors that come in sheet form, because these can be installed with virtually no seams in a typical room. If you're planning a do-it-yourself installation, though, you should consider Excelon Tile, a vinyl-asbestos flooring that is much easier for the home handyman to install.

*Further help available*

An Armstrong flooring retailer near you will be happy to discuss your ideas with you when you call on him. He is familiar with conditions in your locality, and he can help you choose the flooring that will give you the most satisfaction. Also, he can show you the styles and colors that are available and can provide you with price information.

[1] Courtesy of Armstrong Cork Company, Lancaster, Pennsylvania.

Suggested
action

For a list of Armstrong retailers near you, please consult
the Yellow Pages of your telephone directory, under "Floor
Materials." Visit one of these stores soon to see what's
new in flooring. Again, thanks for writing. We wish you
every success with your new family room.

**Suggestions for Handling Inquiries Prompted by Advertising.** Whenever
a firm advertises, it should be prepared in advance for various kinds of inquiries. To save time and expense, you can compose pertinent form paragraphs, and even entire messages, as guides for answering the most-often-asked
questions. Some messages should look personalized and individually typewritten
(as Letter 1), even though the body may be essentially the same for other inquirers who asked the same questions.[1]

On the other hand, many favorable replies do not need to be personalized
—especially in routine situations when you are sure your reader will not
object to a processed form. Most readers would rather receive promptly a
high-quality courteous form that is complete than a poor personalized letter
that is late, incomplete, or perhaps even inaccurately—and hurriedly—typewritten. Letter 2 is typical of the well-written processed sales-oriented replies
that accompany booklets or samples or other free information sent in response
to a coupon or inquiry.

*Letter 2: Processed sales promotion reply (without inside address) with easy action
order form.*

Good news
with
courtesy;
no salu-
tation

Here is your  . . .

Foremost Radio catalog to aid you in your selections.
Thank you for requesting information on Foremost communication receivers.

Resale

You will find much useful data in the section on "precision
construction and advance design." Other sections show you
why Foremost sets are the world's finest receivers. In war
they met the most severe military requirements and in peace
they are the choice of radio amateurs, short—wave

Reader
benefit

listeners, industrial and scientific users. A Foremost
set places the whole world at your fingertips.

Reader
benefits

All communication receivers listed in your catalog are in
stock now for prompt shipment at the prices shown. You can
get liberal trade—in allowances on standard communications
receivers (Hallicrafters, National, Apex, and Howell). If
you prefer a time—payment plan, the attached sheet gives
you details.

[1] The cost of personalized messages can be decreased considerably by using automatic typewriters or
computers.

*Easy action*

To assure delivery within 10 days, just enter your order on the enclosed order form and mail it now in the postage-free envelope. Your order may be accompanied by a deposit as low as 10%, with shipment to be made c.o.d. for the balance due, or you may include full remittance if you prefer.

*Reader benefit*

You can begin to enjoy the unusual reception of a famous Foremost set by placing your order now.

## Answering Inquiries for Information Unrelated to Sales

Among the most frequent nonsales inquiries you might need to answer are requests for information about personnel and credit applicants. Other inquiries may be from students, researchers, educators, and the general public—about a variety of subjects. The following section focuses on recommendation letters (about personnel and credit applicants), but also briefly discusses other replies to nonsales inquiries.

*Letters of Recommendation.* When you furnish pertinent information about an applicant's qualifications, character, and/or general conduct, you are writing a recommendation. It should preferably be addressed to the specific person interested, instead of "To whom it may concern."[1] You have a three-fold responsibility when you write a recommendation. You must be fair—(1) to the applicant, so he can get what he is best qualified for, (2) to the inquirer (prospective employer, creditor, landlord, or whoever he may be), for he is depending upon your frank comments, and (3) to your own conscience and reputation for integrity.

Basically, a recommendation is a confidential report.[2] Recommendation letters are included in this section, however, because they are important good-news or neutral replies to non-sales inquiries. Discussed below are the expanded good-news outline, recommendation letters on outstanding candidates, and recommendations on candidates with shortcomings.

The following expanded good-news outline serves as a basis for a recommendation letter.

1. Main idea
   a. State the applicant's full name and what his relationship was to you—employee, customer, friend, tenant, club member. Mention dates, length of time, and type of job, credit, tenancy, or whatever is pertinent that he held under you. Use facts; don't guess.
   b. Work in an expression of pleasure, if sincere, combined with your statement of purpose for writing the letter. (A subject line can cover part of

[1] A to-whom-it-may-concern letter is sometimes given to a satisfactory employee before he leaves the company; but because it must necessarily be general and not confidential, it carries much less weight than the confidential specific recommendation.
[2] See Chapter 15, Short Reports, for additional discussion on letter reports.

item b with such words as "Confidential report by request on Thomas W. Jones as a prospective field representative.")

2. **Explanation**
   a. Answer all questions—direct or implied. (Omissions cast suspicions.)
   b. Arrange answers in the best psychological order, depending upon facts.
   c. Back up your statements of evaluation (excellent, outstanding, etc.) with specific facts about performance. For a job applicant:
      (1) Tell specific job duties that applicant performed.
      (2) If the inquiry states requirements of the job for which the applicant is being considered, talk about those duties that will be significant.
      (3) When desirable, tell work habits that show personality characteristics.
   d. Be honest and fair with negative material.
      (1) Include it only if pertinent to the inquiry and likely to affect the applicant's success.
      (2) Imbed and subordinate it through amount of space and word choice.
      (3) Know the legal aspects of recommendations (pages 751 to 756, Appendix A).

3. **Ending**
   Include if possible a candid statement of your personal opinion about applicant's probable fitness for the position (or whatever he is being considered for —lease, credit, membership) and your recommendation, qualified or unqualified.

**Recommendation letters for outstanding candidates** are easy to write, because everything you want to say is favorable, as in Letters 1 and 2 below.

*Letter 1: A Marine Corps Commanding Officer writes a good solicited recommendation to the Regional Manager of a nationally known business firm about a Corporal seeking a management trainee position.*

*Pleasure,* Dear Mr. Bronson:
*purpose,*
*name, job,* I am glad to answer your inquiry about Wayne S. Prochas.
*length* Because Wayne has worked with me nearly two years as a
*of time* correspondence clerk, I know him well.

*Answers* During this time he has demonstrated outstanding abilities
*to* in both general office and management work. In twenty
*questions* years of military service I have only once before made such
a high recommendation, and presently I have over 800
*Duties* officers and men in my command. With speed and efficiency
*performed* Wayne has attended to the administrative correspondence of
more than 800 men attached to this command, and he has
never once complained of the work load or poor conditions
under which he has had to work.

I recognize in this man a great potential because he is
intelligent, industrious, and so well liked by all who come
in contact with him. Corporal Prochas does his work with
*Personality* no supervision and can be relied upon to deliver a finished
product at all times. Also I get the very definite impression that he could, if placed in a position to do so,
*and* generate ideas as well as process those of others.

*character* As to conduct, personal habits, and ability to handle himself properly this man has no faults, to my knowledge. He doesn't appear to have to work at being a gentleman. It seems to come natural to him. His loyalty is unques- tionable and by his practices he has influenced others to a great extent.

*Unqualified recommen- dation* I have two regrets: first, I can not take this man to my next command and, secondly, I do not possess the word power necessary to describe this man. But I do say this; my information is accurate and I am sincere. He will make a real contribution to any organization which he may choose to join. I recommend him very highly without any reservation.

Though the statement following "secondly" in the last paragraph above seems overdone (and could be revised), this commanding officer is to be com- mended for his sincerity and for including more than mere glowing adjectives to describe a man he considers outstanding.

*Letter 2: A retailer courteously answers an inquiry about a credit applicant.*

Gentlemen:

*Name and relationship* Mr. George L. Wardman, about whom you inquired in your May 2 letter, has been a customer of ours for the past eight years.

*Answers to questions* He has used our credit facilities with a limit of $400. His orders have been placed, on the average, about twice a month. I am pleased to report that he has always paid his bills promptly according to invoice terms.

*Candid opinion* We consider Mr. Wardman one of our preferred customers, thoroughly responsible with his financial obligations.

Notice that in Letter 2 the reference correctly refrains from making un- warranted statements about the applicant's probable ability to shoulder any other debt. He merely reports on Mr. Wardman's past credit record with his (the reference's) firm; he does not (and cannot) promise future payments elsewhere.

Sometimes an inquiry will contain a question which you can't answer— either because you don't know or because you can't reveal the information. In either case be sure to tell the reader why, instead of ignoring the question.

**In recommendations for candidates with shortcomings** you must decide whether to include or omit negative material. If the candidate has the needed good qualities, you may be able to give him a qualified or even an unqualified recommendation. In any case, you should mention the weakness only if it meets these conditions:

1. You are sure it is true (not hearsay, or the result of personal prejudice or jealousy).
2. It occurred often enough to be worth mentioning.
3. It is pertinent to the job (or credit, etc.) for which applicant is being considered.
4. *It is sufficiently serious* to affect applicant's probable success.

For instance, an applicant who was discharged because he was caught twice stealing from the petty cash drawer should probably not be employed in a job that will require him to handle company funds. Likewise, such serious shortcomings as the following should usually be mentioned tactfully: habitually disagreeable temperament, excessive drinking or drug use, poor health causing frequent absences, unwillingness to cooperate or to obey laws, dishonesty, extreme emotional instability. If you prefer not to present them in writing, you can write a short letter acknowledging the request and inviting the reader to call you. To protect yourself whenever you must make negative statements, you should know the legal aspects of recommendations.

If you are writing a recommendation letter about a candidate who has one serious shortcoming, but who was otherwise satisfactory (or excellent), organize your letter so that you establish the applicant's more favorable characteristics before you mention his defect. In Letter 3, for example, the negative information is imbedded and the former employer ends his message with a candid qualified recommendation.

*Letter 3: A department manager comments on a former employee who had a serious shortcoming.*[1]

Dear Mr. Dirkes:

|  |  |
|---|---|
| *Full name and brief summary* | Confidential Appraisal by Request on Morton L. Dryer |
|  | Mr. Dryer worked hard for us as a salesman in the electrical appliances section for about a year. He was such a dependable salesman that when the section manager resigned to go to the East, we placed Mort in charge and found him |
| *Answer to part of question 1* | well qualified for the job. He was with us 22 months—until last November. |
|  | As section manager, Mort had much responsibility. Besides ordering all merchandise for the section, he was also in charge of the eight salesmen working under him. He was exceptionally well liked by both subordinates and customers. |
| *Answer to question 2* | He had a knack of being genuinely tactful and thoughtful with every customer. Because of his personality and his knowledge of the stock, he pleased a good many steady patrons and increased the total sales within his section by over 15 percent in his first half-year as manager. |

[1] Letter 3 answers Inquiry 2, page 168.

*Favorable comment before and after the negative answer to part of questions 3 and 1.* Mort's work at the store was entirely commendable for about 18 months. Then he developed a drinking problem, which gradually affected his disposition and his attendance. When I talked with him about the change, he mentioned home problems and serious worries. He tried hard to stop drinking and did so for several weeks. But after he had missed a day's work every week for two months, I regretfully had to let him go. Often I have wished I had kept him, for he was such a good worker and a pleasant friend.

*More about question 3* Mort's other personal habits are good. His pleasant personality, honesty, and fine physical appearance are an asset to any company. He takes an active part in outdoor sports and, except for the problem I mentioned, is in fine health. It is quite probable that his move to your town will be a definite advantage to his family and himself.

*Qualified recommendation* Mort is intelligent and well educated (a marketing graduate of Broadway College). Because he knows the electrical appliance business well and has so many other fine qualities, I would definitely give him another chance to lick his problem, if I had the opportunity. He can be a top-notch department or section manager especially in the electrical field.

**Other Replies to Nonsales Inquiries.** Answering the nonsales inquiries that businessmen receive from various people often takes a good deal of time. Nevertheless, to build goodwill and give genuine service, helpful replies like Letter 4 are desirable.

*Letter 4: A collection manager replies with a personalized letter to a college student who requested information.*

Dear Mike:

*Courtesy and best news* It is a pleasure to return to you the completed form as requested in your letter of April 12.

*Comments* I was very favorably impressed with the sample collection series you enclosed. As a whole, the letters are courteous and also appropriately firm. Achieving the right tone in this type of letter is very important, and I believe you have done so.

*Offer of further help* Any further information you may need from us will be gladly forwarded.

*Interest in survey* The recap you offered to send showing your survey results should be interesting. I will appreciate receiving a copy.

If your firm in its advertising offers free information pamphlets not related to sales, you can handle replies with processed form messages, which cut costs substantially.

## Granting Requests for Adjustment

An adjustment letter is the reply to a complaint (called a claim letter). In general, the best attitude is to give the customer the benefit of any doubt. Most persons are honest in their claims, and it is usually better to make the desired adjustment than to risk losing a customer.

Even though your firm's adjustment policy may be generous, the ultimate success of your good-news adjustment letter depends not only upon what you say but also upon how you say it. The discussion in this section concerns (1) the tone of adjustment-granting messages, (2) organization and content when the seller is at fault, (3) variations when the buyer or a third party is at fault, and (4) organization when the fault is not yet determined and will be investigated.

*Tone of Adjustment-granting Messages.* Consideration and courtesy are exceptionally important when you grant an adjustment. Because your reader has been inconvenienced, irritated, and perhaps angered, he is especially sensitive to the tone of your message. Even when the letter grants a request, it can lose a friend and destroy good will if its tone is poor. Compare, for example, the following "poor" sentences (in which the antagonizing expressions are italicized) with the suggested "better" versions:

> Poor: We are *amazed* that you are *dissatisfied* with the range you ordered from us. (Amazed is overdone; dissatisfied is negative.)
> Better: You have every right to expect top quality performance from the range you ordered from us, and we will see that you get it.
> Poor: Nevertheless, *so that we can keep you as a satisfied customer,* we are *willing to allow you to* exchange these toys. (The motive sounds selfish; "willing to" and "allow you" sound condescending and grudging; the sentence lacks "you attitude.")
> Better: Because we want you to be completely pleased, we will gladly exchange the toys for you.

Saying "I'm sorry," "We apologize," or even "Please forgive us" is quite disarming. You are more likely to lose face by *not* apologizing than by doing so. One apology (preferably in the explanation section) is enough, however, for most situations.

*Organization and Content When Seller Is at Fault.* When your company is at fault, you should, of course, always grant the adjustment. In general, the best organization is:

Begin with the best news—what is being done about the claim.

Include whatever explanation and details are desirable concerning cause of the mistake; resale on the product, service, or your firm; sales promotion and/or educational material.

End courteously, showing a desire to cooperate, please, and assist.

The following discussion aims to help you avoid common pitfalls and plan carefully. After reading about various parts and paragraphs of adjustment grants, you will see examples of complete letters.

**In the opening paragraph,** try to begin with whatever you think the reader will consider best news. Your choice depends upon the customer's request and sometimes upon his attitude. If he asked for something specific— like a refund, exchange, credit memo, or speedier service—you should grant or promise immediately. However, if the nature of the customer's request or attitude makes a "granting" opening inadvisable, you will try to get in step with him in some other appropriate way. For example, if a customer has found a bug in a jar of oysters and vows never to buy your products again, you can't very well *begin* by saying you're sending him another jar of oysters to replace the faulty one! Instead, you might express appreciation for his thoughtfulness in writing and/or agree with him on a comment he made in his complaint.[1] In the following examples, the first three grant immediately, and the last three open with various statements to get in step with the reader.

| *Customer's request or complaint* | *Suggested opening* |
|---|---|
| **1.** That you refund his money. | I agree with you that you are certainly entitled to get back the $6.80 you paid to telephone us—and here's the check. |
| **2.** That you "eliminate the delays" in your merchandise shipments or risk losing his business. | You will be glad to hear that we have found a new way to speed deliveries of fresh vegetables to you. From now on your produce can reach you within two hours after we receive your order. |
| **3.** That you replace immediately ten defective copies of a book he needs by a certain date. | Today ten copies of (book title) were sent to you by air mail, shipping charges prepaid. You should receive them three days before May 15. |
| **4.** That you refund to his friend the $30.50 he had to pay because of your firm's "inexcusable error." (Your customer bought a wedding gift for his friend. Instead of charging it to your customer's account, your store incorrectly sent the "gift" to the friend c.o.d. That was two months ago; the friend does not yet know about the mixup.) | (To the customer's friend) You have had the unusual experience of paying for your own wedding gift—much to the embarrassment of our mutual friend, James L. Lamson. The mixup is due entirely to our inexcusable error, for which we extend to you our sincere apologies. (Note: In this case the refund check is mentioned only after the explanation.) |

[1] Later in the letter, after appropriate explanation and resale, you can tell the customer you are sending a gift replacement. See, for example, Letter 3, page 224.

| *Customer's request or complaint* | *Suggested opening* |
|---|---|
| 5. That two special toys he ordered four weeks ago did not arrive in time for Christmas. | We have disappointed you and your children at what is usually the happiest time of year, and we are truly sorry! Now I want to do everything possible to make amends. |
| 6. That the service of a certain waiter in your restaurant was disappointing and he will never bring his friends there again. | You are perfectly right to feel that you should receive prompt and courteous service from our waiters. That is exactly our goal for every guest, and we thank you for taking time to write us. |

**Explaining what caused the mistake** requires tact and judgment. When your firm is at fault, admit it frankly without blaming "a new employee" or the enormous volume of your business. (If you're so big, maybe you should improve your methods.) How much explanation to include depends upon the kind of mistake and the customer's probable interest, but generally it is desirable to include at least *some* explanation. (See, for example, Letters 3 and 5, pages 224 and 225, which include careful explanation plus resale.) Paragraphs such as the following—from three different adjustment grants—help the reader understand how the error occurred:

> You guessed correctly. Apparently all the shipping papers, including the original ones that should have been kept for our use, were sent to you. As a result, we have no record of the ordered paint. We are certainly sorry that you were inconvenienced by our slip-up. We always try to be careful in processing every customer request accurately and promptly.

> I am distressed to learn that you have not received our shipment of Volumes 3 through 20 and that your previous correspondence received no reply. During the past few months, we have been converting our accounts to computer; and you should have been sent a letter informing you of the delay in processing our files and asking your cooperation. I cannot explain why our announcement missed you.

> Sometimes we find that a package miscarries in the mails. This occasionally happens because of a stenographic error in addressing the label, or damage to the label in the mail, obliterating the address. Apparently that's what happened with your parcel.

Avoid the following pitfalls in your explanations:

1. Don't blame an inexperienced clerk. Your firm should have trained him adequately; thus it is better that the company (we) assumes the mistake rather than the individual.
2. Don't suggest that your employees are careless or inefficient. Describe your normal businesslike methods to indicate that this error was an exception.
3. Don't say "mistakes are bound to happen" or that because of the size of your firm there will naturally be frequent errors.

**4.** Don't promise the error will never happen again. If it *does* happen again, the situation will be doubly embarrassing. Better show the care you are taking to assure correct service in the future.

Sometimes an explanation isn't necessary, for example, when the mistake merely involves a small routine clerical error between two business firms. Also, if the matter is complicated (or perhaps even confidential), or if for no good reason someone just "goofed" several times, no explanation at all is sometimes better than a lengthy discussion which may sound like an alibi or which will be filled with negatives.

Resale is necessary if the person complaining seems to be losing faith in your firm. If possible, include concrete evidence of your efficient service, safe and correct shipments, and/or your care in producing or selecting high-quality products. If certain steps have been or will be taken to prevent recurrence of whatever the customer is complaining about, mention them. Sometimes you can honestly state that a new procedure is developed "on the basis of helpful comments like yours" (see Letter 4, page 225).

When you grant a customer's request to exchange unsatisfactory goods, you can strengthen his confidence in the replacement you have sent by including a resale paragraph similar to these (from a nursery and a hardware store, respectively):

This new flowering quince is a choice plant from our sturdy Penbrook stock. It is hardy enough to withstand zero temperatures and requires little care. You will be delighted with its deep-pink blossoms twice each year—at Christmas and in midsummer. In size it fits beautifully with the other trees you selected last month.

You can use this (name) cleaning solvent safely and successfully on cloth materials, painted surfaces, and even on your varnished furniture. The easy-to-follow directions on the box label help you to remove any spot confidently without rubbing.

Sometimes it is desirable to resell the customer on keeping both the replacement you are sending *and* the original slightly defective shipment. (You save return-shipping charges and the bother of processing the damaged merchandise.) A consumer may be glad to keep slightly damaged articles if you substantially reduce their price. Likewise, a dealer customer may be willing to accept a below-average shipment on which he can have a special sale and quick profits if you give him sufficient inducement—price reduction, consignment terms, or perhaps longer payment time.

Sales promotion material is usually helpful in adjustment grants, but there are exceptions, depending partly upon the type of product or services involved and partly upon the type of adjustment granted. If, for instance, a retailer sells only one type of costly product (like furnaces, home insulation, or roofing), which the average consumer buys only once in a great while, sales promotion material would be out of place. On the other hand, if the seller carries a variety of often-replaced items, sales promotion may be desirable. Without sounding greedy, you want to encourage the customer to continue to buy other goods from you.

Also, if the customer returned the original shipment and is receiving credit or a refund, he really needs a different replacement. Sales promotion material is then appropriate, as in the following paragraphs from different firms:

> Your nephew Tommy may be happier with toys designed especially for his age group. Tillman's carries many toys just right for four-year-olds, as the enclosed folder illustrates—on pages 12–14. Tommy may enjoy our heavy steel rocket (#R-6322), which is sturdy, entertaining, and educational. Other toys he will like are the plastic set of modern cars (M-8909), the metal boat kit (B-6222) that can be assembled easily, and the Commando uniform with self-defense equipment. All these and others shown are educational toys to help Tommy learn as he plays with his friends.

> For your customers who want to do their own wallpapering, you'll find the ready-pasted product an especially good seller. Walton Cedar Closet Wallpaper containing DDT insecticide is not only an effective protection for all homes in your area, but also easy and convenient to apply.

With a genuine desire to serve the customer well—and *not* mainly to make a sale—you can sometimes also include informal, no-pressure sales talk regarding products useful with goods you have just sent him. This information focuses the customer's attention on your thoughtfulness and gives him a feeling of a pleasant future relationship.

The ending paragraph of the adjustment grant should bring the message to a logical, pleasant close. It may tie in suggested action with sales promotional material; it may comment on the pleasure the reader will gain from the high-quality new article you have sent; it may express your appreciation that the reader took time to write; it may issue a cordial invitation that he continue to come to your firm for top service. Be sure not to include any negative thoughts, such as an apology or a reminder of the inconvenience the mistake caused him. Don't suggest future trouble or imply that the customer may be so displeased with your firm that he will stop buying there.

Now that you have read about the parts of adjustment grants when the seller is at fault, you are ready to analyze and compare complete messages.

In Letter 1 a manufacturer agrees to accept defective merchandise for exchange, but the reader does not learn until almost the end of the last paragraph that his request for exchange has been granted. A better opening would have been: "You can expect to receive a prompt exchange for the coats you purchased from us recently." Also, in the third paragraph the negative statement "we don't believe you will have this problem" should be replaced by a positive resale statement like "We are sure you will like the material and expert tailoring of these Worthington coats." (A specific detail or two about the merchandise inspires confidence.)

*Letter 1: An incorrectly organized good-news message from a manufacturer to a con-
sumer.*

Dear Mr. Hansard:

Thank you for telling us of the problem you have had with the coats you purchased.

Sometime ago, a batch of material having bad formulation escaped detection by our quality control people. The line inspectors caught most of the finished coats before they were invoiced. However, some were shipped. Apparently your order was among them.

The situation has since been corrected and we don't believe you will have this problem with a replacement. Accordingly, a special shipping label is enclosed for returning your defective merchandise to us. It will be promptly exchanged upon receipt. Please let us know if we may be of further service.

Letters 2 and 3 both concern situations in which the seller is at fault in a canned food product that the disappointed customer has stated he will probably never buy again. However, Letter 2 is blunt and completely lacking in explanation, resale, and sales promotion. Letter 3, on the contrary, contains an exceptionally detailed explanation, which helps to resell the customer on the firm's care in canning. Though both letters offer a replacement, Letter 2 gives the impression that such errors are routine occurrences which the writer doesn't care much about. In contrast, the writer of Letter 3 sounds sincerely concerned about keeping the customer's goodwill—and he is more likely to do so. Notice also that in this message the writer does not begin by "granting" or even giving the free assortment; instead he wisely chose as his main idea a statement of appreciation and resale. The assumption is that only after reading the explanation—and more resale—will the customer be a in mood to accept the replacement. The last paragraph effectively ties in a gift with a hint of sales promotion.

*Letter 2: A poor adjustment-granting letter from the Poultry Operations Manager of
a national food chain store to a customer in another state.*

Dear Mrs. Garviss:

We are sorry to learn that you found a piece of bone in a Manson Chicken Pie which you recently purchased.

Will you please present this letter to the Rightside Store
Manager, who will be happy to give you three (3) Manson Chicken
Pies free of charge.

**Letter 3:** *A good adjustment-granting letter from the Assistant Manager of Quality*
*Control Department of a national Packing corporation to a customer in*
*another state who found a fly in the can.*

Dear Mr. Dennis:

*Main*
*idea:*
*thanks*
*and*
*resale*

Thank you for writing us of your experience upon opening a
can of DeMona Spinach. We are very concerned about this
because of the particular care taken in the preparation of
all DeMona Products to assure you of receiving a wholesome
and high-quality food item.

*Explanation*
*with*
*resale*

Upon arrival at the packing plant, the spinach is run
through a large perforated cylinder where it is tumbled and
shaken apart to eliminate particles of soil, etc. From
there, it is transferred to wide traveling belts where
women inspectors remove all imperfect leaves and any other
defects present. The spinach then goes into the washers in
which a series of paddle wheels keeps it in a state of
constant agitation while high pressure jets of water wash,
rewash and rewash again. After that, it is subjected to a
further careful inspection as it is placed in the cans;
therefore, you can see we do everything possible to produce
a clean, wholesome product.

*Easy*
*action*
*and*
*apology*

To further investigate this incident, we will appreciate
your sending us the code mark which was embossed on the
lid of the can in question. This will enable us to refer
the matter directly to the plant where the spinach was
packed. If you made a note of it, please send it to us
on the enclosed reply card. We appreciate your bringing
this situation to our attention and offer you our sincere
apology.

*Gift to*
*regain*
*goodwill*
*and promote*
*sales*

Within a few days you will receive an assortment of DeMona
Fruits and Vegetables. We want you to enjoy them so
thoroughly that you will continue to be a regular DeMona
satisfied customer.

Letter 4 brings good news to a customer who is irritated because there is
no "right turn only" sign in a bank's parking lot. No resale is necessary in
this reply because the customer isn't losing faith in anything relating to the
bank. Sales promotion also is unnecessary here.

*Letter 4: A banker courteously grants an irritated customer's request for a parking-lot sign.*

Dear Mr. Alberts:

*Best news first*  Because of your excellent suggestion, we plan to install the "right turn only" sign to improve the parking lot exit at Emmett Street. Thank you for your interest in suggesting a practical way to help traffic move smoothly.

*Explanation (details)*  We have been concerned with the traffic flow problem caused by the congestion on Emmett Street. This exit problem has interested us from a long-range point of view, as well. As you probably know, we acquired holdings to enlarge the parking lot and provide both an entrance and exit on Ravenna Avenue. Our new parking and traffic plan should be in operation in about one year's time.

*Friendly close*  We invite you to make further suggestions which will help First National maintain the finest banking service in the Ravenna District.

In Letter 5 a customer service manager answers the complaint of an old customer who had to wait too long at a sales counter. His main purpose is to regain her confidence in the store's desire to serve promptly. Thus he begins with the idea that he thinks will most please this reader—a sincere indirect compliment and appreciation, which suggest that her request is being granted. Resale follows his explanation and apology. The last paragraph, with its cordial forward look to "seeing and serving" Mrs. Larson again soon, is adequate implied sales promotion for such a longtime customer.

*Letter 5: A tactful reply to a department store customer's complaint about not being waited on in turn.*

Dear Mrs. Larson:

*Compliment implying granted request*  You were thoughtful to write us about the service you have received in our store. Your letter helps us in our constant effort to improve and make Gill's a place where you and others can enjoy shopping.

*Explanation*  Your friendship and goodwill mean a lot to us and we have thoroughly investigated the incident about which you write. Miss Simkins feels her error keenly, Mrs. Larson, because she has always assisted our customers to the utmost of her ability. In all sincerity, she said she did not know you were ahead of the other customer at her hosiery counter. Miss Simkins will be most appreciative if you permit her to see and talk with you, for she feels a personal apology is the least she can offer you.

*Sincere apology and resale*

Though an apology will not take the place of the good service you should have received, we do want you to know that we are sorry the incident happened.  Prompt and courteous service is Gill's pledge--a pledge every sales person in the organization must follow.

*Courtesy and forward look to service*

My office is on the third floor, Mrs. Larson, to the left of the elevator.  On your next trip to Gill's, won't you stop in just for a minute or two.  Your interest in Gill's is highly valued, and we look forward with pleasure to seeing and serving you again soon.

*Variations When the Buyer or a Third Party Is at Fault.* A few differences may be desirable in the organization and content when someone other than the seller is at fault. In many cases you may, of course, be justified in refusing—instead of granting—the request. Nevertheless, firms will occasionally grant a buyer's claim even though he or a third party is at fault.

When the buyer is at fault and you decide to grant his adjustment claim, you have two choices for letter organization. You can begin with the best news (granting the claim) and continue with the usual pattern (as shown on pages 218–219), or you can begin with a statement that gets in step with the reader, then explain the mistake, and after that grant the claim. The reason for the latter alternative is that sometimes the psychological effect on the reader is better if you allow his claim *after* you have shown tactfully that he, not your firm, is at fault. The next two letters handle the same situation in these two different ways: Letter 6 begins with the refund, and Letter 7 begins with a buffer and explanation.

*Letter 6: A sales manager grants a refund on a blouse that faded because someone washed it incorrectly; best news first.*

Dear Mrs. Hamilton:

*Best news, refund*

We were very concerned to hear of your experience with the "Lady Marlow" blouse you purchased recently at our downtown store.  As a result, you are receiving the enclosed cash refund for the original purchase price, plus sales tax, totaling $11.50.

*Resale with tactful (impersonal) explanation of necessary washing care*

The "Lady Marlow" is one of the finest lines of ladies blouses made.  The synthetic fibers and the special dyes which make possible the beautiful colors in these blouses do, however, require special care.  Whenever these blouses are laundered, washing in a solution of very mild detergent and lukewarm water gives the best results.  As the instruction tag on every blouse states, these garments are very sensitive to heat and should therefore always be dried at room temperature, never in an automatic dryer.  Furthermore, any staining substance which comes in contact with the material must be loosened in cold water, because hot water often causes a chemical change that loosens the dye and results in fading.

*Resale and additional emphasis on care; educational enclosure*

Although the "Lady Marlow" line does require special care, I'm sure you will agree that its beauty and elegant fashion lines outweigh the special care required by the fine fabric. Because of the many new materials on the market, I think you will find the enclosed booklet on the laundering of all types of synthetics both interesting and educational.

*Sales promotion with implied action and courtesy*

As you are one of our regular customers, we invite you to our upcoming June sale. A complete line of summer fashions, including new pastel and print blouses, will be waiting for your inspection. The sale begins June 12, but the general public will receive an announcement on June 14.

It's been a pleasure to help you.

**Letter 7:** *An alternate for Letter 6; explanation before the best news.*

Dear Mrs. Hamilton:

*Resale on the firm*

As a regular customer of Finestein's, you know that we are proud to guarantee the quality of each of our garments. In light of this, we were very concerned when we received your "Lady Marlow" blouse in the mail.

*Resale on the blouse, and explanation*

(Resale and explanation paragraph may be similar to paragraph 2 in letter 6, but the resale portion usually goes after the explanation and granting.)

*Tactful statements showing seller not at fault*
*Best news— refund, with sales promotion*

Since our laboratory tests show that the fading in the trim of the blouse is not due to defective dye, the stripes have apparently come in contact with some other chemical agent, or water that is hotter than lukewarm, or with excessive heat. Although we cannot assume responsibility for the fading in this blouse, we are glad to give you the opportunity to replace it. Enclosed is a check for $11.50, covering the purchase price plus sales tax.

*Sales promotion and invited action*

We invite you to visit the blouse department again soon to select your choice from any of the newest arrivals. Besides the popular "Lady Marlow" you will find also several other famous-name brands. And of course you may also be interested in the new summer fashions in dresses and coats.

**If a third party (say the transportation company) is at fault, many firms accept responsibility for adjusting claims and seek reimbursement from the**

third party. This method is customary with wholesalers shipping to small dealers or retailers sending to individual customers who are unfamiliar with claim-filing procedure. You can state the best news before or after the explanation. Letter 8 is an excellent example of a good-news letter in which the seller plans to file a claim with the transportation firm for the customer.

*Letter 8: A gift-shop owner replaces a lamp damaged in shipment.*

Dear Mrs. Luberts:

*Best news—replacement* — A new Brighton lamp should reach you in a few days to replace the one you received in damaged condition. We sent it today by prepaid express.

*Explanation showing seller not at fault* — As the (name) Railroad gave us a receipt acknowledging that they received the original lamp perfectly crated, the porcelain base must have been cracked in transit. We are sorry this happened, for we know how much you want this beautiful gift for your cousin's wedding anniversary. Although our responsibility ended when the railroad accepted the package, we·are glad to make this replacement for you.

*Suggested action to help claim with carrier* — Will you please give the damaged lamp to the expressman when he delivers the second lamp. We will enter a claim with the railroad, so that you will not be inconvenienced further.

*Courtesy and resale* — Thank you for writing promptly. Our main concern is that you receive the lamp in time for the anniversary and in perfect condition.

**Organization When the Fault Is Not Yet Determined.** Sometimes the final adjustment decision cannot be made until the seller determines who is responsible for the mistake. In such cases, let the buyer know promptly that you want to investigate the claim. Your letter should have a neutral effect on the reader, for you are neither granting nor refusing his request. The best organization is: express interest in his problem, assure him you are looking into the matter, include brief resale if desirable, and courteously state you will give him the facts as soon as they are available.

*Letter 9: A hatchery manager promises to investigate.*

Dear Mr. King:

*Interest in problem* — Thanks very much for your report on the N&H "Nick Chick" Leghorn pullets delivered to you on March 29. I sympathize with you, for pullets you buy from Nerving's should meet the high standards of previous lots. We want to do everything possible to cooperate with you.

*Possible causes of problem; promise of investigation*

Tints, egg size, broodiness are characteristics both genetic and environmental. That fancy phrase simply means pullets can be influenced by both breeding and rearing, management, etc. Because there are so many factors involved in the conditions you describe, we are asking our Oregon fieldman, Mr. Vern Jackson, to call on you within the next few days. You will find him cooperative and helpful.

*Resale*

Most hatcheries would be satisfied if 90% of their stock was good 90% of the time. Not Nerving's. We are aiming for 100% on both counts and won't rest until we reach that goal. Of course, when you are dealing with "life" there are numerous variables making this difficult. But, we keep trying. That's why letters such as yours help in pointing out where improvements can be made.

*Courtesy*

We want you to be a satisfied customer, Mr. King. If we are at fault in any way, you are assured we'll do our level best to make amends. Thanks again for writing; you help us take steps to make things right.

## Approving Credit

The message telling the customer he has been granted credit often includes all parts of the basic good-news plan—best news first, then terms,[1] resale, sales promotion, and appreciation.

***Decision or Shipment in First Paragraph.*** If the customer has not yet ordered any merchandise on credit, begin with the credit-grant decision and a cordial welcome. If he sent an order with his request for credit, begin with the date and method by which his goods are being shipped (thereby implying the credit grant). Make clear the purchase details (name and quantity of goods sent, item prices, freight, and total charge); for more than two or three items, attach an invoice copy. Mention cordially that the shipment has been added to the customer's new account.

***Explanation of Credit Terms.*** In your explanation section, mention briefly the basis on which credit was earned, and clarify the terms. If, for instance, an applicant's references all speak highly of his prompt-pay habits, it is psychologically a good idea to tell him so. He is then encouraged to continue to live up to his good reputation in his dealings with you.

Your explanation of the credit terms must be clear and concrete to help reduce collection problems later. Suppose, for example, your wholesale firm's terms are 2/10, net/30. You must be sure that every new credit customer

---

[1] You can place the terms either before or after the resale and sales promotion. If before, you're more certain the reader will notice them because you're emphasizing the terms; if after, you seem to be stressing the other person and not "what's in it for me."

(dealer) knows whether your terms are based on invoice date, shipping date, delivery date, or from the end of the month (e.o.m.). Misunderstanding on this important detail can cause a customer's payments to be as much as a month off. Compare these vague and clear statements regarding credit terms:

> *Vague:*  Our credit terms are the usual 2/10, net 30.
> *Vague:*  Under our credit terms of 2/10, net 30, you earn a 2 percent discount if your payment is made in 10 days. (10 days after what?)
> *Clear:*  Our credit terms are the usual 2/10 net 30, based on invoice date.

To an inexperienced businessman, or one whose payment record has been shaky, you might write:

> Under our credit terms of 2/10, net 30, you earn a 2 percent discount if your payment is postmarked within 10 days of invoice date; the full amount is payable in 30 days. On the enclosed March 28 invoice you save $5.40 by mailing your check on or before April 7—a saving to you almost equivalent to the cost of two shirts.

Of course, if all wholesalers within your industry abide by the same standard interpretation and your new customer is an experienced businessman in this industry, you need merely state your terms.

Besides stating terms clearly, you need also to use positive wording about a credit limit, if any, as these examples show:

> *Negative:*  We are limiting you to $500 maximum credit each month (each credit period).
> *Positive:*  In any credit period you are welcome to (you may) purchase up to $500 of merchandise on your new account.

If you are in a retail firm, you must likewise make your billing and payment obligations clear to the consumer. Are you opening for him a monthly charge account,[1] a budget account,[2] or a revolving credit account[3]? Do all statements (bills) from your firm go out on the same day each month or do you have cycle billing[1]? Be tactful in telling the customer when payments are

---

[1] With a monthly charge account the customer may charge his purchases during any month and he is required to pay for them in full usually upon receipt of a statement (or within 10 days of its receipt) the month following the date of charge. Some retailers mail all statements the same day each month. Others use *cycle billing*, which helps to level out the billing department's load over a 30-day period. For example, customers whose names begin with A–C may be billed for 30-day purchases through the 5th of a month and statements may be mailed on the 10th; those whose names begin with D–F may be billed through the 8th and statements mailed on the 14th; and so on through the alphabet.

[2] With a budget account (a time-payment plan) the customer makes a down payment (usually 10 percent) on the purchase and agrees to make monthly repayments on the unpaid balance. Purchases on home furnishings, appliances, and electronic equipment usually must be paid within 18 months; apparel and other "soft" items, within 12 months.

[3] With revolving credit the customer and the store agree on a maximum amount of credit, and then the customer agrees to pay a certain monthly amount according to the store's established terms

due. Compare, for example, the poor tone in "We expect you to pay" or "You are expected to pay" with the improved tone in "Payments are due within 10 days after the billing date" or "Please send your payment within 10 days."

***Resale and Sales Promotion.*** The credit-granting message should include customer-benefit resale information on the firm's services. Also, it is sometimes desirable to include sales promotion material (in the next-to-last or last paragraph) about such news as a forthcoming sale, new seasonal merchandise, or products allied to those ordered (if any). Such news encourages the customer to use his credit.

To keep your letter short, you can enclose a leaflet describing departments and services such as the following:

*For the consumer*

Free parking, mail and telephone shopping, personalized services for men, home-planning bureau, bridal consultants, tearoom and other restaurants, child-care services, gift wrapping, free and frequent deliveries, special discount or purchase privileges

*For the middleman (retailer or wholesaler)*

Nearby warehouses, factory representatives, quantity discounts, free window or counter displays, national advertising, cuts and mats for newspaper and other advertising, repair services, manuals, factory guarantees, prompt, speedy deliveries, research department.

***Future-service Ending.*** Close your credit grant with statements which indicate your desire to serve the customer well in the future, or which specify particular services. Inviting the reader to a special sale, for example, helps to get him to use his account. The tone must in no way sound greedy for orders, and you must observe the usual suggestions for easy action and courtesy.

Each of the following two letters establishes a pleasant and clear relationship with the new credit customer—Letter 1 to a consumer and Letter 2 to a wholesaler.

***Letter 1:*** *A retailer uses a processed form letter to grant credit to a consumer; applicant's name and address are typed in the inside address and salutation.*

*Best news: welcome and new account*
We welcome you as a Bon and Nelson credit account customer. Your new charge plate is enclosed and we invite you to use it often. This plate will identify you at all Bon and Nelson stores; so please sign it in ink before putting it into your wallet or purse.

*Credit terms*
You will receive your statement soon after the first of each month, showing purchases up to the 23d of the preceding month. Bills are payable by the 10th of each month.

(ranging from $10 to $25, usually, on account balances from $100 to $150). The customer usually pays an interest and service charge on the unpaid balance. He may make additional purchases any time, provided they do not raise his total balance beyond the agreed limit.

*Resale
on store
services*

As one of our regular charge customers, you will receive announcements of all our sales before they are advertised for the public.  If you should wish sometimes to shop in the comfort of your own home without a trip to town, you can do so conveniently by phone.  Just ask for "Personal Shopping Services," tell your needs to the shopping assistant, and then just say "Charge it to my account."

*Invitation
to future
use of
account*

The enclosed leaflet explains the numerous Bon and Nelson services available for your convenience.  Do use them often to save yourself both time and money.  We look forward to giving you friendly courteous service in any of our colorful stores...for many years to come.

**Letter 2:** *A wholesaler grants credit (and ships merchandise) to an established hardware store owner; the letter is personal and individually typed.*

Dear Mr. Bower:

*Best news:
shipping
goods;
new
account*

The Topskill tools you ordered April 3 are on their way to your store today by B&L Motor Freight.  You can count on having them for your gardening customers by Saturday.  This merchandise, as itemized on the enclosed invoice, has been added to your newly opened account.

*Explanation
of terms*

We are pleased to extend to you our most favorable terms of 2/10, net 30 (based on invoice date).  The information we received about you is completely complimentary to you personally and as a businessman.  We appreciate your choosing

*Resale on
products*

us to supply you with our nationally advertised hardware and gardening products.

*Resale on
wholesaler's
services*

Packed with your order is our latest assortment of window display materials with full directions for making them attractive.  Our representative, Mr. Carl Webber, will call on you about twice a month and gladly assist you in answering any questions you may have about Topskill.  If you would like free envelope stuffers to mail to your customers and mats for your newspaper advertising, indicate your wishes on the enclosed illustrated check list.

*Resale on
product*

You will notice the enthusiasm men express for your new line of tools.  Their durability and precision is appreciated by both the craftsman and the amateur do-it-yourselfer.

*Easy action
for orders*

To place your future orders, just use the easy-mail order forms at the back of your catalog.  You can expect deliveries within three days after we receive your orders.  You may be assured of our cooperation at all times.

## Acknowledging Orders

An order acknowledgment performs several important functions. It lets the buyer know that his order has been received, is appreciated, and is given attention. It helps to build goodwill. Furthermore—and very important—by identifying and accepting the order, the acknowledgment completes a valid contract between buyer and seller. For these reasons the acknowledgment must be definite and complete, in keeping with the situation.

Orders that your firm can fill immediately fall into two types—first orders and repeat orders. Although the acknowledgment for both types should identify the shipment and show appreciation, the message contents will be quite different.

*Acknowledgment of First Order.* The new customer needs to know that his order is being filled promptly and correctly, that it is appreciated, and that—because of your products and services—his dealings with your firm will be pleasant and profitable.

Sending the ordered items on their way is usually the best beginning for your first-order acknowledgment to the new customer. State what, when, and how you shipped, and if possible state approximately when the shipment should reach him. Express appreciation for both the order and remittance (if you received it).

Then take care of any needed details about shipping charges and payments. If you opened a new credit account for this customer, you will of course explain the credit terms.

Here are a few overworked expressions to avoid in first-order acknowledgments; they are followed by comments and or suggested revisions:

*Vague, trite, and a little inaccurate:* "We have shipped your order . . . ."
Comment: The order is really a piece of paper on which the customer authorizes you to send requested items; your firm fills the order and ships merchandise, groceries, livestock, or whatever he ordered.

*Better:* "The bedspread (No. 204) and the electric blanket (No. B43) which you ordered September 4 were sent to you today by parcel post. You can expect them in a few days. Thank you for your order and your enclosed $50.20 check in full payment."

*Trite:* "Welcome to our long list (or family) of satisfied customers."
Comment: Omit such statements and show elsewhere in your letter by actions —prompt service, reader-centered resale, sincere thoughtfulness—instead of by empty words that you appreciate his order and want to please him.

*Trite:* "Thank you for your order, which we are glad to have."
Comment: He's more interested in when you're sending the goods than in your thanks; also, the "glad to have" may seem a bit greedy to some customers.

**Specific resale material** should be adapted to the purchaser. Resale on company services (as listed on page 231) is appropriate for both the consumer and the middleman. Resale on the products ordered is usually more desirable for the consumer than for the middleman. Before ordering, the businessman who will resell your products has usually studied their merits carefully— through sales literature, catalogs, and perhaps information from your sales representative—and you generally need not repeat what he has already read. However, he may appreciate a few additional facts and any special product features he can emphasize to his customers.

To a consumer, resale material from the "home office" is sometimes extremely helpful. After placing his first order with a firm (either by mail or through a house-to-house salesman), the consumer may wonder if he did the right thing—especially when the item he bought is, for him, a luxury. For example, suppose that you bought a 20-volume deluxe encyclopedia for $400 and gave the traveling salesman a $20 down payment. Afterward you have "buyer's remorse," and feel that you can't really afford such a purchase. Now, suppose you receive from the publisher a three-paragraph order acknowledgment devoted entirely to your payment obligations. Such a letter would hardly be reassuring!

On the other hand, suppose that instead of the letter just described, you received one like Letter 1 below. Notice that eight of its nine paragraphs contain reader-benefit and resale material and only one mentions payments. Don't you agree that such a letter would help reinforce your confidence in your purchase? Depending upon circumstances, adequate resale may range from one sentence to several paragraphs.

***Letter 1:*** *Resale in a completely processed acknowledgment to a consumer purchaser of an encyclopedia (and perhaps other educational materials).[1]*

Dear (NAME OF ENCYCLOPEDIA) Purchaser:

*Contract acceptance; thanks; resale*
With sincere thanks we accept your contract covering the items listed on the enclosed Summary of Purchase. By placing your order with us, you have joined hundreds of thousands of parents, teachers, and children to whom these outstanding educational materials have become an important part of daily living.

*Resale*
In addition to these fine products that you will soon receive, there are several important and exclusive supplemental benefits and services that we want to tell you about:

*Summary of purchase; payment details*
Your Summary of Purchase lists all of the items that you ordered on your contract and the total price of the order less the amount of your down payment. If you have chosen our budget plan, it also states the payment terms of the contract. If you paid for your order in full, this Summary will serve as your paid-in-full receipt.

[1] Courtesy of Field Enterprises Educational Corporation, Chicago, Illinois.

*Reader-
benefit
suggestions;
resale*

Also included on your Summary of Purchase is your Account Number. This number is our primary means of identifying your account. If you should have occasion to write to us, we would appreciate it if you would use your account number. It will help us quickly identify your account and give your inquiry prompt handling. So that your account number is always handy, we suggest you record it on your Quality Guarantee (enclosed with your order shipment) and keep it with one of your sets.

*Reader
benefits;
resale and
sales
promotion*

The enclosed Exchange Certificate offers you the opportunity to purchase at a discount, another set of World Book under the conditions specified. In addition, you can choose other learning and teaching aids prepared for children and adults.

*Reader-
benefit
suggestion*

Be certain to look at these enclosures very carefully, and then put them in a safe place. They are most valuable and important to you, and will be helpful if it is necessary to answer questions about your account.

*Reader
benefits*

As a World Book purchaser you will be able to keep your set up to date with The World Book Year Book, an annual supplement which reviews the important events of the preceding calendar year. You will also find our Science Year Annual very helpful and informative. You'll receive an announcement regarding these supplements before they are published each year.

*Resale*

We congratulate you on your decision to purchase this marvelous encyclopedia which has been serving American education for more than five decades. The present World Book is the result of years of planning under the supervision of an editorial advisory board of specialists and was produced by more than 1400 noted scholars and authorities. It includes all the features on which the World Book has built its reputation.

*A confi-
dence-
building
close*

A year from now, I feel certain, you will agree that this purchase has proved one of the most satisfactory investments you have ever made. It will serve you well for many years to come.

**Looking forward to future orders and reader satisfaction** is usually the best way to end the first-order acknowledgment. You can tie your suggested action in with resale or sales promotion; be sure your reader has order blanks or whatever else he needs for easy action. If you wish, you may invite the cash customer to fill out and return a credit application form; but avoid suggesting that credit will be automatic.

Letter 2 on page 232 is typical of a good first-order acknowledgment to a dealer buying on credit. With a few changes, that letter could be adapted for a dealer who sent a check with his first order. Letter 2 below, to a cash customer, includes a credit application form.

*Letter 2: Personalized acknowledgment of a first cash order from a dealer.*

Dear Mr. Morehouse:

*Restatement of order*
You can expect to receive the two dozen Topskill lawn edgers, #L592, and the five manual mowers, M 687, in time for your garden sale Monday, May 15. They were shipped by prepaid express this afternoon.

*Appreciation and check acknowledgment*
Thank you for your order and for your $425.50 check, which exactly covered the items as priced in your new dealer catalog. As you know, the suggested markup on these items is 30 percent.

*Resale on services for dealer and customer benefit*
Your customers will be pleased with these highly popular Topskill tools. Currently they are advertised in 1/2-page two-color ads in <u>House and Home</u> and <u>Western Garden</u> magazines, April through July. You can assure your customers that every Topskill is factory guaranteed according to the contract that accompanies each tool. A special feature of the Topskill edger is its ability to trim neatly within one inch of flower beds and rockeries. On the mower, a simple twist of the Dial knob adjusts both wheels and roller for precise cutting height and ease of operation.

*Services to dealer*
Illustrations of counter and window displays and other free sales helps are sent with this letter. Just let us know your needs on the enclosed check list.

*Suggestion for credit*
You may be interested in our regular credit terms of 2/10, net 30 on future orders. If so, just fill in and return the enclosed form; we will gladly consider your credit application. Also, if you have any questions with which we might be able to help, just write us. We'll do our best to
*Courtesy*
serve you promptly.

**Acknowledging Repeat Orders.** Most orders come from repeat customers who know and like a firm's products and services, and who don't expect a typewritten letter acknowledgment. Usually the goods can be sent as quickly as an acknowledgment can be mailed. In some cases standard purchase order forms give complete instructions about terms and delivery date, and they stipulate that the buyer will be notified only if the order cannot be filled as requested. In others, an adequate good-news order acknowledgment is an inexpensive (perhaps printed) form, a carbon copy of the shipping invoice, or a postcard as illustrated on page 237. Various rubber stamps enable clerks to insert pertinent comments, such as the one shown referring to the will-call.

**HERE'S A NOTE,
to let you know**

about our order No. *M664*

your order No. _____

Job Name _____

*1— Remco NX-25*

THIS ORDER IS IN WILL-CALL AND
READY TO BE PICKED UP.

**TOPCO LIGHTING FIXTURE CO.**
222 - 2nd Avenue  - - - Pittsburgh, Pa. 15215

Cordially, _____
Shipping Department

Though most repeat orders are filled without letter acknowledgments, an unusually large order may occasionally warrant a personalized letter. This message may include appreciation, a statement of how the order is being handled, and perhaps a few cordial comments about your past relationship and future plans to supply the customer's needs.

## Granting Favors

Whenever you decide to grant a favor, you have a comparatively easy letter to write. Whether the favor is serving on a committee, speaking without pay at a convention, donating money, or lending your firm's equipment without charge, the good-news plan is the best to use. Usually all you need is the acceptance first, pertinent comments or explanation, and a cordial ending, as in Letters 1 and 2 below.

*Letter 1: A businessman accepts an appointment.*

Dear Dr. Keithley:

*Acceptance*  I will be glad to serve as a panel member on the program of the National (name) Association's 197_ regional convention in Chicago.

*Comments*  The date—March 25—has already been circled on my calendar. Also, my employer warmly approves of this participation. Arrangements have been made so that I can be away from the office three days.

*Comments on the assignment and participation*  The topic you suggest is one I've been interested in for some time. If they will work in, I might bring several charts which our company has been using this past year with some success. With four members on the panel, however, and one hour allotted to us I know I should limit my comments to no more than 12 minutes, as you suggest. Then we'll have time for questions and answers.

*Courtesy*  I'm looking forward to working with you and the other panel members toward putting on a stimulating panel discussion.

**Letter 2:** *The general manager of a seafood restaurant corporation good-naturedly grants a favor—sending to a businessman speaker rare booklets from his company's files.*

Mr. Browne . . .

*Grant of favor; courtesy*  You're certainly most welcome to use the enclosed booklets in any way you wish. I'm glad your members have asked to see them.

*Comments*  These pamphlets are rather humorous "fishcal statements" that we prepared for two reasons—to entertain and to enlighten our stockholders and gourmet friends. As they are all now out of print, I've sent you the last copies we have left of our mailing supply.

*Courteous good wishes*  Best of success to you on your talk. The next time you're in our city, give me a call. Perhaps you can spare time to let me treat you to one of our famous seafood specialties.

By following the good-news plan plus the suggestions and cautions discussed in this section, you can also write effectively favorable replies to all other kinds of requests—from customers, employers, employees, friends, government officials, or anyone else.

## UNSOLICITED FAVORABLE MESSAGES

The previous section considered messages that are written because someone inquired. This section discusses *unsolicited* favorable and neutral-reaction messages—specifically announcements and transmittals. Good-news unsolicited messages that congratulate, thank, welcome, and show continuing concern are covered in Chapter 13, Goodwill Messages.

## Announcements

Like all other good-news messages, favorable announcements should follow the good-news plan—best news or main idea first; then adequate explanation, resale, or educational material; and, finally, the appropriate ending.

Though some announcements are written for one person only, most are intended for members of various groups. If the same processed (printed, mimeographed, dittoed) letter goes to each member of a group, the salutation is usually general—such as "Dear depositor" or "Dear (company name) customer." Those announcements that are directed to persons within your organization usually have memo format with "All employees" (or members) after the TO.

Included in this section are group and personal announcements about sales and events; procedures, policies, and responsibilities; and honors and activities of people.

*Announcing Sales and Events.* Whenever you wish to announce a sale or an event (luncheon, conference, celebration, meeting, or other function) about which you need merely to inform your readers, you can use the good-news plan. The opening paragraph usually includes as many of the 5 W's as possible.

An excellent way to build and strengthen goodwill with regular customers is to let them know—by various special announcements—that you appreciate them. For example, Message 1 announces a sale before newspaper publication.

*Message 1: A store's preannouncement to charge customers about a forthcoming sale; processed form without insertions.*

Dear Customer

*Reason and best news; 5 W's*

Because you are a regular (store name) customer, we are glad to announce to you a special sale of an unusual collection of winter coat values...in one of the Designer Room's greatest coat events. This announcement comes to you now so that you can make your selection during a three-day period before newspaper ads appear.

*Displayed items for emphasis*

PRE-ANNOUNCEMENT SELLING
Wednesday, Thursday and Friday
November 6, 7, and 8
NEW WINTER COATS BY OUR FOREMOST MAKERS
all priced far below regular
$69        $109        $149

*Details*

FINE COATS FROM OUR BEST MAKERS...IN MISSES' AND PETITE SIZES. Coats such as you'll see at much higher prices after this great selling. Every one a new, just-arrived 197_ fashion!

EXCITING FASHIONS AND COLORS including shiny black coats, neutrals and bright colors, fur trimmed coats, town tweeds, dressy and casual styles, almond shapes, coats that wrap or button.

LUXURY FABRICS by Forstmann and Stroock. Silken fleeces, plush textures, imported and domestic tweeds.

*Easy
action*

TAKE ADVANTAGE OF THIS OPPORTUNITY FOR FIRST CHOICE! For three days...November 6, 7 and 8, you may come in and choose your coat in advance of newspaper announcement. We consider this one of our most outstanding coat events of the year. Come in early...prices will return to regular immediately after this event.

Whether you call your message an announcement (as in the above example) or an invitation (as in Invitations 1 and 2, pages 184–185, you use the same three-part organizational structure.

*Announcing Procedures, Policies, and Responsibilities.* You will have numerous occasions to announce procedures or policies and to explain reader responsibilities to customers, employees, and others. Though some of these announcements may be good news, many may simply contain neutral information. Whenever you do have good news to announce, it is desirable to begin with a statement of pleasure or reader benefit (the "why" of the 5 W's). Contrast, for example, the following openings. Notice that in the first, the reader is likely to wonder if the news is good or bad, especially because of the negative words "discontinue" and "restrictions." The overuse of passives ("are received" and "will be paid") and the absence of any "you's" keep the paragraph impersonal. In contrast, the second opening presents the good news clearly and effectively.

*Blunt, negative opening:*

Starting Tuesday, October 1, 197__, this Association will discontinue the policy of paying earnings from the 1st of the month when funds are received on or before the 10th of the month. Also, restrictions will not be imposed as to minimum time period nor minimum balance.

*Pleasant, positive good-news opening:*

We are pleased to announce to you that effective Tuesday, October 1, 197__, your passbook savings accounts will earn interest on daily balances—from the date you deposit savings to the date you withdraw them. Also, you can now deposit any amount for any length of time because the minimum time period for earnings and minimum balance restrictions have been removed.

Throughout the message try to get and keep the reader in each paragraph, if possible and desirable. Use resale and show reader benefits whenever possible, as in the following announcement to customers of a savings and loan association:

*Message 2: Announcement about converting bookkeeping system to on-the-line computer method; processed form without insertion of the reader's name.*

### IMPORTANT ANNOUNCEMENT

Dear State Federal Customer:

*Main idea; why, when, who, what*
To give you the best and newest service available, we are pleased to announce that on or after March 1 (year), your State Federal Savings Association will convert its bookkeeping system to an On-Line computer method.

*Explanation with customer benefits*
This conversion will enable us to give you up-to-date information on your account at any time in any of our four offices. You will be served faster, more efficiently, and with neat, accurate passbooks. Each teller will have complete access to all savings records at all times. Of course, this information will remain confidential.

*Resale*

*More resale*
In taking this giant step forward, State Federal becomes the first association in the Northern (state) area to place its accounts on the On-Line System. This move demonstrates the efforts of the officers and directors to keep your association in the forefront of these changing times, even as our adoption of the Daily Dividend way of computing dividends has led the area in that field.

*Action*
We will continue to use the same passbook which you are now using. To make the transition easier, please send in your passbook to be posted to date.

Many announcements about procedures, policies, and responsibilities can be processed form messages. Others—like Message 3—must be individually typed with a personal salutation.

*Message 3: A lending officer's message to a new loan customer, telling about his payment responsibilities; individually typed.*

Dear Mr. and Mrs. Mooney:

*Congratulation and main idea*
Several days ago it was our pleasure to congratulate you on your plans to improve your home. Now we are pleased to give you details concerning the loan you received from Central Loan Association to provide the funds you need.

Here is the important data pertaining to your Home Improvement Loan:

*Details*
*tabulated*
*for easy*
*reading*

```
Date of Loan . . . . .  June 15, 197_
Amount of Loan . . . .  $1,349.88
Number of Payments . .  60
Monthly installment. .  $25.40
First Payment Begins .  July 1, 197_
```

*Offer of*
*further help*

Should you have any questions or inquiries as to any of our
services, please come in, or just give us a ring at
222-2222.  We are always glad to help you.

Though the preceding message is individually typed, it can be based on a
guide form, since all paragraphs except the figures and dates in paragraph 2
will be the same for every borrower.

Message 4 tells all employees of a firm about insurance privileges available to them.

*Message 4: Announcement to all employees about enrollment for company insurance*
*plans.*

TO:          All Kenmore employees    DATE: November 22, 197_

FROM:        John K. Wood, Retirement and Insurance Officer[1]

SUBJECT:     Open Enrollment Period for Company Insurance
             Plans

*Why, when,*
*for whom,*
*where, what*
*(itemized)*

The annual open enrollment period for employee insurance
plans will be between December 4 and 27 at the Retirement
and Insurance Office.  During that time, you may
1.  Enroll in medical, life, salary continuation or
    accident insurance plans for the first time
2.  Transfer from one basic medical plan to another, or
3.  Add previously uninsured dependents to medical in-
    surance plans.

*Effective*
*date*

Changes and additions made during the open enrollment
period will take effect next January 1, 197_.

*Enclosure*
*and*
*instructions*

Please refer to the attached individual "Insurance Program
Summary" which shows the premiums, company contributions
and payroll deductions for the plans in which you are presently enrolled.  Then refer to the rest of the attached
material which explains just what to do if you wish to make
changes in your coverage.

*Offer of*
*more help*

Brochures describing the plans and individual counseling
services are available at the Retirement and Insurance
Office, 4th floor; or phone extension 3-9876 if you wish
one mailed to you.

[1] Some officers omit the FROM line and sign above their typed signature and title at the bottom.

*Announcing Honors and Activities of People.* To inform customers and employees about promotions, awards, new appointments, and other activities of various persons, it is thoughtful to send announcements.

Announcement of a promotion can be similar to Message 5, which informs employees of a colleague's promotion to managership. Similar announcements can be sent when a new officer has joined the staff or when one or more employees have been shifted to new departments, been elected to noteworthy offices, or won any other honors deserving of recognition.

*Message 5: Announcement of an employee's promotion to an office.*

|  |  |
|---|---|
| Memo to: | All employees |
| Copy to:[1] | E. B. Wells<br>Richard W. Bram<br>W. M. Glass |
| From: | James T. Camp |
| Date: | February 15, 197_ |
| Subject: | Mr. Remo S. Galston, new St. Paul Manager |

*Best news first*

We are very pleased to announce that Mr. Remo S. Galston has been promoted to the position of St. Paul Manager. He will be responsible for all aspects of the St. Paul–Minneapolis Warehousing and Trucking operations.

*Details about the new officer*

A native of St. Paul, Mr. Galston was graduated from the University of (name) in (year) with a BA Degree in Business Administration, emphasizing transportation. He has had extensive experience in all phases of transportation and in all phases of our own company's operations. Also he is a Captain in the United States Army Reserve and a member of the National Guard Association.

*Suggested action*

We know you will all join us in congratulating Mr. Galston on his promotion and in wishing him success in his new position.

A letter of introduction announcing a new field representative who will be calling on customers is often printed on the company's letterhead or on a special card. Another use for this type of letter (individually typewritten, usually) is to introduce a friend or acquaintance to a businessman you know in the city to which the friend is moving, or in which he will visit. Message 6

---

[1] Though the usual position for copy notations is at the end of the message (a double space under the reference initials), some firms have a standard procedure to indicate the copy routing in the memo heading, especially if the persons receiving copies are officers.

is typical of an introduction to a business acquaintance. (If you were writing to a friend, you would of course use his first name in the salutation and be more informal throughout the letter.)

*Message 6: Letter of introduction from a businessman to a business acquaintance.*

Dear Mr. McAlpine:

*Full name*   This note is to introduce to you Rudolph M. Parker, the son
*and why*   of a dear friend and customer of ours.  Rudy is doing a
*being*   survey among business firms in your city.  His interest
*introduced*   concerns problems of the small businessman.

           He has just finished college and is expecting to enter the
           Graduate School of Business at the University of (name in
*Explanation*   another state) next fall.  In the meantime, Rudy is
           donating his summer to this voluntary study.

           I would consider it a great favor if you would give this
           young man a few minutes of your time and open the door for
*Request and*   him to meet other businessmen in your community.  You'll
*courtesy*   find him appreciative and bright.  Both his father and I
           will be grateful to you for any courtesy you show to Rudy.
           I really think you'll find him quite interesting.

*Courtesy*   The next time you get to our city, give me a call.  I'd be
           delighted to have you as my guest for lunch or dinner.

## Transmittals

Transmittals differ from announcements in several ways. Announcements always include an explanation whose main purpose is to convey information. Transmittals may or may not include explanation; their main purpose is to transmit something, which is usually mentioned in the first paragraph. This section discusses two types of transmittals—those without discussion and those with discussion.

**Transmittals without Discussion.** Many times you will need to mail something—such as a check, document, form, passbook, booklet, map, or other item—to a consumer or a business house. If your action is routine, you can transmit the item without explanation. Such transmittals don't even have to be individually typewritten, or even in the format of a letter. They can merely be in the form of a cordial, short note. Given below is an example of an acceptable printed transmittal, to which a typist adds the missing usual parts.

*Transmittal 1: Document transmittal letter.*

      Dear

Subject:

*Main idea:* We are enclosing the following instruments for your file
*transmittal* regarding the above property:
*and reason*

           ( )  Owner's Policy
*List for*      ( )  Warranty Deed conveying property to your name
*easy*       ( )  Cancelled Note and Deed of Trust, Loan #_____
*checking*           Payable to _____ .
           ( )  Copies of Closing Papers
           ( )

*Courtesy*   Thank you for allowing us to be of service to you.

### Transmittals with Discussion.[1]

When you include discussion in a transmittal, your message may be quite similar to favorable replies to requests. The main difference is that in the transmittal the writer is sending the enclosure of his own volition, not because the reader asked for it. These messages may be personally typewritten or processed, depending upon the circumstances. Transmittal 2 is individually typed; Transmittal 3 is processed.

*Transmittal 2: Individually typewritten transmittal of savings certificate's first dividend.*

      Dear Mr. and Mrs. Briggs

*Best news:*  Six months have gone by and your Savings Certificate has
*transmittal* earned its first dividend.  Enclosed is a check for the
amount earned.

*Explanation* As agreed, your certificate will be renewed automatically
*and news of* for another six-month period.  At the same time, we are
*increased* glad to announce that as of January 1, 197_, dividends on
*earnings* Savings Certificates will be computed at the rate of 6%
instead of 5½%.  Because each account is now insured up to
$20,000, you might want to increase your account.

*Easy*   If you wish to purchase another certificate—and saving by
*action* mail is more convenient for you—just state your wishes on
*and* the enclosed signature card and mail it with your check in
*thanks* the postage-paid envelope. Thank you for saving here at
State Federal.

---

[1] See also the discussion of transmittal letters with reports, Chapter 16.

***Transmittal 3:*** *Processed form with opening words in simulated blue-ink handwriting that matches the signature (a complete form with no insertions).*

*Best news:*
*courteous*

$\mathcal{I}t\ is\ a\ pleasure$

*transmittal*      to send your new annuity to you.  A copy of your
*and reason*  annuity application is also enclosed for your records.

*Comments*        Each year you will receive a report of what your
premiums have purchased.  You will also receive an Annual
Report and a ballot for selecting Policyholder Trustees.
*Offer of*       If you do not already have the booklet, <u>Your</u> <u>Retirement</u>
*helpful*    <u>Annuity</u>, which describes the main features of annuities, we
*booklet*    shall be glad to send you a copy.

*Pleasant*         We want our lifelong annuity relationship with you to
*close*     be helpful and pleasant for you, and we will work to
deserve your confidence in us.

Whenever you answer favorably a request or announce news that will be favorable or neutral to your reader, keep in mind the three-part organizational good-news plan. The capsule checklists on pages 248 to 251 give you a review of both the basic plan and various adaptations when you answer requests for information, adjustment, credit, order filling, favors; and when you announce or transmit something.

## EXERCISES

*Favorable Replies to Inquiries for Information Related to Sales*

1. Letters A, B, and C below are all replies to routine, direct requests. Suggest improvements where needed in opening and closing paragraphs, "you-attitude," and adequacy of resale material. Which of the three do you like best? Why?

   **A.** Individually typed reply from a steam specialty company:

   Gentlemen:

   Replying to your letter of 30 Sept. 197_, please be advised that we are mailing to your attention, under separate cover, four copies of our current #57 General Catalog describing products of our manufacture, at no charge to your company.

   Appreciating your inquiry and hoping to be favored with your orders, we remain

**B.** In simulated handwriting, on a 4- by 6-inch slip without date, inside address, salutation, complimentary close:

In response to your request, it is a pleasure to send you the enclosed literature. If it does not supply all the information you need about the use of wax in your home, be sure to write me again.

**C.** Processed form reply from a clock manufacturer;[1] personalized address and salutation:

Here is the Seth Thomas booklet which you recently requested.

As you look over the wide variety of styles offered for your choice, we are sure you will find the Seth Thomas clock you have always desired--either for your own home or for that certain someone who appreciates an outstanding gift. There are distinguished Period designs, charming colonial reproductions and smart moderns for those who appreciate this mode of furnishing.

All clocks illustrated represent the finest in designing achievement and are truly the creations of experts in the craft of fine clockmaking. Their friendly presence in your home is a tribute to your appreciation of fine living.

May we suggest that you pay a visit to your local Seth Thomas dealer. Many appliance stores handle Seth Thomas self-starting electrics--while keywound and electrics are offered by better jewelry and department stores.

For gifts that will surely become treasured possessions, select Seth Thomas clocks--they are always appropriate. And, for finer--friendlier living in your own home, be sure to choose an authentic Seth Thomas--"The Finest Name in Clocks."

**2.** The following two letters are replies that motel managers in a small resort town sent to a young man who inquired about their rates and accommodations. To each he wrote that he and his wife were planning a three-week automobile trip and they expected to stay five nights in the town (Lagina) "sometime in July."

Comment orally on the good and poor qualities of each reply. How many errors can you find? (The crossed-out words in B appeared that way on the mailed letter.) Rewrite the better of these replies, so that it is accurate and contains appropriate you-attitude and resale material. Make any necessary assumptions.

**A.**

Dear Sir:

We can reserve accommodations for Mrs Roberts and yourself for five nights commencing Wenesday the 18th of July. We would appreciate a deposit of $10.00 to secure your reservations,

---

[1] Courtesy of Seth Thomas Clock Company, Thomaston, Connecticut

**CAPSULE CHECKLISTS FOR**

| *I* | *II* | *III* |
|---|---|---|
| *Good-news (and Neutral):* *General Plan* | *Answering Inquiries for* *Information Related to Sales* | *Answering Inquiries for* *Information Unrelated to Sales—* *Letter of Recommendation* |
| 1. BEST NEWS or MAIN IDEA | 1. Best news or main idea <br>   a. Positive opening with one of these: <br>     (1) Requested material <br>     (2) Favorable answer to a question <br>     (3) Introduction of main idea(s) <br>   b. Courtesy; appreciation | 1. Best news or main idea <br>   a. Applicant's full name and relationship to you; job(s) held <br>   b. Pleasure; reason for writing |
| 2. EXPLANATION <br>   a. All necessary details <br>   b. Resale material <br>   c. Educational material <br>   d. Sales promotion | 2. Explanation <br>   a. Answers to all questions—direct or implied <br>     (1) Positive, helpful tone <br>     (2) Imbedded negatives <br>     (3) Emphasis on what something *is*, what you can do or have <br>     (4) Reader benefits <br>     (5) Prices after most selling points (unless price is a bargain) <br>   b. Resale (with reader benefits) when appropriate <br>   c. Educational material on product use, if pertinent | 2. Explanation <br>   a. Answers to all questions—direct or implied <br>   b. Best psychological order for threefold responsibility to: <br>     (1) Applicant <br>     (2) Person considering applicant <br>     (3) Your conscience <br>   c. Specific facts about <br>     (1) Applicant's job, duties, conduct <br>     (2) Applicant's work or other habits <br>     (3) Personality, etc. <br>   d. Honesty and judgment about negatives <br>   e. Caution to know legal aspects; establishment of confidential nature of reply "by request" |
| 3. POSITIVE, FRIENDLY ENDING <br>   a. Appreciation <br>   b. CSAD[1] <br>   c. EA[2] and motivation <br>   d. Willingness to help further <br>   e. DA[3] <br>   f. RB[4] | 3. Courteous close <br>   a. CSAD[1] (sometimes) Itemized steps, if desirable <br>   b. EA[2] <br>   c. DA[3] <br>   d. RB[4] and courtesy; offer of further help, if appropriate | 3. Courteous close <br>   a Candid statement of your personal opinion about applicant's probable fitness for whatever he is being considered for <br>   b. Positive (not negative) attributes at end |

[1] CSAD = clear statement of action desired
[2] EA = easy action
[3] DA = dated action, if desirable
[4] RB = add a reader-benefit statement

## GOOD-NEWS MESSAGES

### IV
#### *Granting Requests for Adjustment*

| *Seller at Fault (A)* | *Buyer or Another at Fault (B)* |
|---|---|
| 1. Best news<br>  a. Whatever will please buyer most<br>  b. Courtesy | 1. Best news or buffer<br>  a. Same as IV, A, 1a<br>    or<br>  b. Get-in-step-with-reader, courteous comment and concern |
| 2. Explanation<br>  a. Brief resale with tactful explanation of error (if desirable)<br>  b. Instructions for buyer action if needed<br>  c. Concrete resale on firm, services, or goods if desirable<br>  d. Cautions<br>  e. Sales promotion on replacement of returned item(s) or on allied goods | 2. Explanation<br>  a. Brief resale with tactful explanation of error, showing seller not at fault<br>  b. (If use of 1,b above, Best news after explanation)<br>  c. Concrete resale (Same as IV, A, 2c)<br>  d. Cautions<br>  e. Sales promotion (same as IV, A, 2, e) |
| 3. Courteous close<br>  a. Suggested action and forward look to future pleasant use of goods and services<br>  b. EA[2]<br>  c. Positive idea; help<br>  d. RB[4] | 3. Courteous close<br>  a. Same as IV A, 3, a-d |

CAPSULE CHECKLISTS FOR

| V<br>*Approving Credit* | VI<br>*Acknowledging First Orders* | VII<br>*Granting Favors* |
|---|---|---|
| 1. Best news<br>  a. Credit grant (if no purchase)<br>  b. Shipment (if goods ordered)<br>    (1) Description<br>    (2) Quantity<br>    (3) Prices, costs<br>    (4) Method, charges<br>  c. Courtesy | 1. Best news<br>  a. Shipment details Same as V, 1, b (1) through (4)<br>  b. Thanks for remittance and/or order | 1. Best news<br>  a. Acceptance of favor, request<br>  b. Courtesy |
| 2. Explanation<br>  a. Basis for credit; compliment<br>  b. Concrete, positive statements of credit terms; payments, dates, discounts, limits<br>  c. Resale on services—<br>    (1) Consumer: parking, shopping services, departments, conveniences, deliveries, price benefits<br>    (2) Middleman: warehouses, discounts, selling aids, advertising, factory guarantees, repairs, deliveries<br>  d. Resale on product choices<br>  e. Sales promotion sometimes—allied goods | 2. Explanation<br>  a. For credit customer: same as V, 2, a and b<br>  b. For cash or credit: Resale on services same as V, 2, c<br>  c. For cash or credit: Resale on products ordered; highlights on special features— adapted to buyer<br>  d. For cash customer: Perhaps credit application form enclosed, with invitation to return it for consideration | 2. Explanation<br>  a. Pertinent comments and details regarding favor—what is being or will be done, etc.<br>  b. Questions, if necessary, pertaining to favor |
| 3. Courteous close<br>  a. Forward look to pleasant service and orders (no greedy tone)<br>  b. Suggested action<br>  c. EA[2]<br>  d. RB[4]<br>  e. Courtesy; suggestion of further help, if pertinent | 3. Courteous close<br>  a. Forward look to pleasant service and orders (no greedy tone)<br>  b. Suggested action<br>  c. EA[2]<br>  d. RB[4]<br>  e. Courtesy; suggestion of further help, if pertinent | 3. Courteous close<br>  a. Cordial, pertinent comment; perhaps a forward look, a good wish, a compliment, or a request |

[1] CSAD = clear statement of action desired      [3] DA = dated action, if desirable
[2] EA = easy action      [4] RB = add a reader-benefit statement

## GOOD-NEWS MESSAGES (Continued)

| *VIII*<br>*Announcements* | *IX*<br>*Transmittals* |
|---|---|
| 1. Best news; main idea<br>    When appropriate:<br>    a. 5 W's (all or most);<br>       reader in first and all<br>       other paragraphs<br>    b. Statement of pleasure,<br>       compliment, con-<br>       gratulations<br>    c. Admission of error;<br>       with good news | 1. Best news; main idea<br>    a. Transmittal of<br>       specific item(s)<br>    b. A concise reason<br>    c. Courtesy |
| 2. Explanation<br>    a. Details to emphasize,<br>       reader benefits, if<br>       possible<br>    In admission of error:<br>    b. Explanation and<br>       apology; emphasis on<br>       sincere desire to serve<br>       well<br>    c. Resale on firm, prod-<br>       ucts, or services, as<br>       appropriate | 2. Explanation<br>    If needed:<br>    a. Comments<br>    b. Instructions |
| 3. Courteous close<br>    a. CSAD[1]<br>    b. EA[2]<br>    c. DA[3]<br>    d. RB and/or offer of<br>       further help[4]<br>    e. Courtesy | 3. Courteous close<br>    a. CSAD[1]<br>    b. EA[2]<br>    c. DA[3]<br>    d. Offer of further help<br>       or other items or RB<br>       about items trans-<br>       mitted[4] |

**B.**

Dear Mr. Roberts;

Thank you for your postal card regarding rates for Summer. Our rates for two are; $70.00 per week & xxxxxxxxxxxxxxxx Oceanview are $80.00 per week.

These Apartments consist of Bed Sittling room, fully equipped kitchen, bathroom and Shower and Garage.

We are located in the North section of Lagina about a mile from the main business District. The market is a block away and we are about two hundred yards from Crescent Bathing Beach.

We do not allow Pets.

On receipt of $10.00 deposit we will be pleased to reserve the accomodation you require.

Thanking you for your courtesy, I am,

**3.** Evaluate orally the reply to each of the following inquiries. Does the reply answer all questions adequately? Does it inspire confidence in the respondent? Suggest specific needed improvements for each and be prepared to tell why.

*Situation A:* Regarding services of a geophysical explorations company.

*Inquiry:* Our company wishes to explore the possibilities of developing some of our wooded properties. Would your firm be able to tell us the rock layer and water strains in the land as much as 1,000 feet below the surface?

We shall appreciate any information you can give us about the extent to which your firm's services might help us.

*Reply:* (A completely processed form with no typewritten inserts; three brochures were enclosed, illustrating geographical explorations.)

Thank you for your inquiry. Your interest in our instrumentation and services is appreciated, and your inquiry received our careful attention.

We wanted to answer you as promptly as possible, so we are using this informal way of giving you the information you requested. Handling procedure for a formal letter would have taken longer.

When we can be of further service, please do not hesitate to contact us.

*Situation B:* Regarding products and services of a film service.

*Inquiry:* We would appreciate your answering the following questions:
1. Does your firm do photoengraving?
2. Do you develop film from Kodak Instamatic 300 cameras?

If so, how much do you charge and how prompt is your
service on black and white—and on color?
3.  Do you sell film cartridges for the Kodak Instamatic
300?  If so, how much are the black and white and the
Kodacolor?

*Reply:*   (Individually typed)

Dear Linda M. Snyden;

To answer your inquiry about our Vendor Film Services.

Yes, we do develop film from the Kodak Instamatic 300
camera.  Prices for developing of this film on the Vendor
Film Service Envelopes enclosed.

Time of developing and mailing for B&W or Color film
rolls, we strive to serve you with 1 to 2 day services.
Enlargements take a little longer.

No, we do not do photoengraving.

Yes, we do sell fim cartige for the Kodak Instamatic
300.  Prices;;;;; Kodacolor $1.65   Black & White::::::90¢

We sincerly hope we have your inquirys answered our
film service.s.  Also enclosed:  Order blanks for our photo
greeting cards.  We will be glad to fill your film orders
for you.

4. The inquiry in Problem 4, pages 193, has been referred to you, the Booking Department Director of Top Grade Films, Inc., Chicago, Illinois. Write the reply, to
James Jepson, National Products Corp., (assume address), giving specific answers to
all questions, plus any other information you consider desirable. Your firm sends
films to any state in the United States for a rental of $8 for three days, plus
shipping charges. Transportation time is not counted in with these three days.
Usually shipping time takes about five days to adjoining states; across the continent, it may take as much as ten days. If a customer wants a film for a whole week,
the charge is $16 for the week. If he rents it for two weeks (the maximum you
allow), the charge is $24. Each customer is expected to return the rented film
promptly. If, for instance, he rents it for three days but keeps it five days, he is
charged a full $8 per day for each day over the rental period; Saturdays and Sun-
days are not counted, however. Assume any other pertinent details about the film
(related to your major). You have a complete film catalog that you can send free
of charge.

5. As correspondent for the Renton Electric Products Company, manufacturers of
electric mixers, toasters, and other kitchen appliances, you need to answer an
inquiry from Pellon Electric Company, one of your new distributors in St. Louis,
Missouri. They carry your complete line of eight products in their two stores, and
they need the free newspaper mats to use in their local advertising campaign and
also window display materials. Also they would like to see a sample of the envelope

stuffers (illustrative sales leaflets) that they might enclose with their customers' monthly statements. These leaflets are not free, although of course the one sample you're sending today is free. He'll have to pay $5.60 a thousand for these colorful leaflets, but customers get good ideas from them. This is the first inquiry you have had from this new distributor since the welcome letter you sent him ten days ago.

6. You, manager of the customer service department of your savings bank, have received the following inquiry from Robert Simmons, in a nearby town:

> As I have a six months savings certificate with you and six
> months are up, will I have to renew that or will it automat-
> ically go on? Will the interest be added to the capital or
> will it be mailed to me? Is there any way I could earn
> higher interest? Would like to hear from you.

Mr. Simmons' certificate now has a principal of $9,000. If he increases this amount by $1,000 (to $10,000), he'll be eligible to purchase a one-year certificate which earns at the rate of 5¼ percent. It's important that he recognize the difference between the certificate he has and this one-year certificate. The one-year certificate pays ¼ of 1 percent more per annum, but it does not contain the automatic renewal clause that his present certificate has. If he should desire not to make any change, his present certificate will automatically go on at the rate of 5 percent a year. The interest is mailed to him and does not add to the certificate. He should already have received the dividend check, which was mailed five days ago. If he would like his dividends to earn for him also, he can open a passbook savings account and endorse his dividend checks to your bank "For Deposit Only" to his savings account, and send them to you together with his passbook. The deposit will be made and the passbook returned to him immediately. Write your courteous reply to Mr. Simmons' inquiry.

7. Assume you work in the passenger department of United Airlines, whose planes fly in and out of your city, Tacoma, Washington. Answer the following letter from Mrs. Metilda Oldtimer, who lives in a rural area about 30 miles south of Tacoma:

> Gentlemen:
>
> For several years now I've been wanting to get up courage to
> take an airplane trip from Tacoma to Los Angeles. I have saved
> up the money and the bus to downtown Tacoma goes right by our
> house. Now I'm 78 and I guess that is supposed to be old. My
> family has been urging me to come. My favorite grandson is
> getting married in L. A. and I want to attend his wedding, and
> I want to go the safest and fastest way. How long does the
> plane take?
>
> There are a few things I want to know first. I've heard that
> lots of people get sick on airplanes. I also hear that you
> serve alcohol and I can't drink anything but milk or tea. I
> suppose, too, that nothing but cold food is served, and I have
> to have hot meals. Oh, and one more thing, would we be too
> high up to see objects on the ground?
>
> If you can clear up these points, I think I'd like to take the
> trip.

Here are facts: Fewer people get airsick than get sick in trains or autos. You don't serve cold meals. Hot meals are prepared and served individually by the stewardesses—not just lunches but full dinners. Also, there is no charge for the meals. You don't serve alcohol free in economy and tourist classes. Champagne cocktails are served free in first-class travel, but for those who don't want champagne, there's tomato or fruit juice. Jet planes between Tacoma and Los Angeles fly at between 30,000 and 39,000 feet altitude, from which passengers can see the ground when weather is clear. One stop is made in San Francisco—the plane swoops down smoothly before it lands. Scenery is gorgeous along the way. Flying time is about two hours. Airport bus picks up passengers at Sleepeze Hotel in Tacoma and takes them to the Sea-Tac Airport in 35 minutes; the charge one way to the airport is $1.50. Give all the information Mrs. Oldtimer needs to make a reservation. Your goal is to try to encourage her to travel by air *on your line*. Skillfully combine reader-benefit sales talk with your answers to all her questions, implied and stated. Assume any other needed pertinent details.

8. As manager of the Appliance Service Department of Eastern Aluminum Company, Compton, Wisconsin, write the processed form letter which accompanies the free Electric Ovenette recipe booklet advertised by your firm and often requested. Your goal is to interest the reader in visiting the nearest local department store that carries your Ovenette (a portable 18-quart capacity oven, 14½ by 24 by 15 inches; big enough to roast a 20-pound turkey). The Ovenette is rapidly becoming a favorite of homemakers throughout the nation. It bakes or roasts foods so economically that it pays for itself in just a short time. People save up to two-thirds the electricity required by a regular range unit every time they use the Electric Ovenette. Baking time is shorter; temperature-control regulator is the same as on a modern range oven. It is graduated from 150° to 450°F. Dials are conveniently placed on the front of the Ovenette. A red pilot light glows until the Ovenette is preheated to the temperature called for in the recipe. The recipe booklet gives complete instructions on its operation. The Ovenette is helpful in dozens of ways, and is ideal for families of two to five. It bakes pies, cakes, custards, muffins, casseroles and many other wonderful treats. It roasts meats and browns them beautifully. It supplements a regular range oven when additional capacity is needed. (Be sure to include the name and address of the nearest dealer.)

### Favorable Replies to Inquiries for Information Unrelated to Sales

1. Compare the following three replies by personnel men to a college student's questionnaire inquiry about application letters the company receives from graduating seniors. Which reply do you like best? Why? What improvements can you suggest for each letter? (Each has a "Dear Mr. Smith" salutation.)

A.

Enclosed is the questionnaire which you sent us.

B.

I am pleased to return to you the completed questionnaire regarding application letters.

The importance of first impressions cannot be over-stressed in this day of keen competition for good jobs. Letters of application are the knock that open the door. Good letters allow the foot to be placed in the door.

May I supplement the questionnaire information with two
thoughts.  First, the letter of application and data sheet
should show originality in presentation.  A good "eye-
catcher" will be read, will leave a favorable impression,
and will be remembered.  Second, the applicant should be
conversant with the background and products of the company to
which he is applying.  This is especially true if he is
granted an interview.

Any further information you may need will be gladly forwarded.

C.

I have your letter of April 24th to which you attached a letter
of application and ask our reaction to this type of letter.

Have filled out the form as you have requested.  My only
suggestion is, in an application of this kind, that you make
your first letter brief and to the point and then after a
response from the firm go into detail in the second letter
giving the information the firm may desire.

Trust this is the information you are seeking.

2. Rewrite the following reply to remove the negative tone, inaccuracies, and unnecessary repetition. Also arrange the material for easier reading. Sign it as Assistant
Chief of your state's Fishery Management Division. Assume today is September 29.

Dear Mr. Fowler:

Your letter of August 21st addressed to the State Department of Fisheries was misplaced, hence we have not had an
opportunity to answer it sooner.  We regret the delay a great
deal.

Following is the information you requested.  It concerns
only plantings made in comparitively recent years.

Heather Lake was stocked in 1961 with 19,600 rainbow
trout fry.  It was stocked again in 1971 with 6,240 rainbow
fry.  Bear Lake was stocked in 1967 with 10,305 rainbow trout
fry.  It was stocked again in 1971 with 6,000 rainbow fry.
Canyon Lake or Lake Twenty-two was stocked last in 1969 with
16,170 rainbow trout fry.

We hope this information still had some value despite the
lateness with which it is reaching you.

3. As senior supervisor in the test support division of your factory, you have been
asked by the personnel department to write your recommendation on Steven J.
Barkman, Clock No. 2409. Today is August 31. Your résumé of Steven's summer
employment will become part of the permanent personnel records. A carbon copy
of your memo is to be sent to J. A. Bore and M. D. Taylor, both department
heads in your firm. Steve arrived in your department on June 15 this year and was
assigned to your most tedious job—No. 5377 (you can decide what this job is)—

which lasted two months. Steve is returning to college next month, as agreed when he was hired in June. Steve reasons well and has the ability to organize his workload. Should he apply for reemployment next summer, you would gladly welcome him into your group. Steve learns quickly and has adapted himself to your methods with minimum difficulty. His attitude, attendance, and cooperation are excellent. He is highly thought of by his lead personnel and supervisors. Write the recommendation, using correct memo format.

4. You are Assistant Manager of the Loan Department of the Merchant's National Bank, your city, and you have received a letter of inquiry from Mr. Lawrence Dirks, Public Relations Director of the National Environmental Council. He is considering Nathan Jaro for a field representative job and asks your recommendation of Jaro, who worked for your bank as a field collector of unpaid loan installments. Jaro's job was to call at debtors' homes and collect their payments which are past due. In the new job he would work with businessmen to upgrade environment conditions.

Nathan worked for your bank from June 19 to December 20 last year, and quit on impulse with one week's notice after a disagreement with his immediate supervisor. This supervisor happens to be the most strict of all your supervisors in his collection policies. He insists that every item of property should be promptly repossessed when a debtor is delinquent in his payments. Nathan Jaro, on the contrary, believed in the gentle "soft sell" method. He was pleasant, honest, and extremely patient with customers, often much more so than the supervisor wanted. With one customer in particular, Nathan and the supervisor clashed; it was finally the cause of Nathan's leaving. The customer had borrowed $5,000 to lease a fleet of trucks for an out-of-state construction job. Although he was financially able to pay the monthly installments, he was habitually late; furthermore he threatened to transfer all his business—including his checking and savings account—to a competing bank unless the collection department quit harping about his late payments. Jaro sided with the customer, arguing that as long as the customer cheerfully paid extra interest on all his late payments and because he always did pay (though late), the bank should "go easy" in its dealings with him, to save his goodwill. One day the supervisor angrily told Jaro to repossess this customer's trucks or quit; Jaro chose the latter, for he refused to compromise with what he thought was the right course of action.

When you heard about the incident, you called Nathan back to your office and tactfully told him that his record had been very satisfactory with the bank and you hoped he would reconsider and stay. Nathan's collection record for the six months he was with your bank was second to the top for your twelve collectors in the field. He was exceptionally well-liked by customers and fellow employees. Jaro thanked you for your invitation to return and said he would like to; but, because he would have to remain under the same stern supervisor, he thought it best to return full-time to his university studies and give up the job until another opening might occur the following summer.

Nathan is a sociology and English major at the university, and an ardent supporter of social justice. He spoke occasionally about his desire to do something worthwhile in the community to help improve environment and help the underprivileged. You honestly believe he will be happier in the type of work for which Mr. Dirks is considering him. Write a tactful, frank recommendation.

5. You are sales manager for the Ace Wholesale Plumbing Supplies Company, located in an old warehouse building in the south end of your city. You have just received a letter of inquiry from Mr. L. M. Rufus, Personnel Manager of the Bay

Area Designers, Inc., of Berkeley, California. The letterhead states: "West Coast's Finest Designers of Distinctive Home Furnishings." He is considering Miss Mabel Thomson for a position as secretary to the manager of the Customer Service Department. He seeks your frank comments on the following points regarding Miss Thomson:

a. Responsibility—understanding, sense of values, tolerance
b. Work techniques—independence, initiative, organizing ability, accuracy
c. Personality—emotional maturity, appearance, poise

Miss Thomson, a graduate of your state university in Secretarial Science, was your secretary for almost two years. She left three months ago in search of a position offering a better salary than your company could pay her. (She was getting $425 a month.) Frankly, you were very sorry when she left. Unfortunately, although she was an excellent stenographer, she seemed to be bored with the job. She took dictation from three men in your office and transcribed her notes promptly and accurately. She did a grand job reorganizing and improving your whole filing system which had been a mess before she took over. She was always immaculately neat in her personal appearance. The fact that she wore suits, heels, and hose while the other girls came in extremely informal clothes and sandals made Mabel sometimes appear to be "above" the others. A few plumbers thought she was a bit snobbish toward them when they called in person. Mabel, in turn, was annoyed by their somewhat rough language. Occasionally she engaged in arguments with them if they wanted certain supplies which were not in stock at the time. She showed little sense of humor. She did every task assigned to her accurately and quickly, but she resented having to do the other girls' work (who, frankly, were less efficient than she). She was a whiz at typing, stenography, and filing. Whenever you gave her any job requiring these skills, you were sure she would do it better than anyone else in the office.

The last three months of her employment with your company, she was president of an art society and you felt she received too many telephone calls at the office during company time. (Of course, she always had her work finished on time, so you never said anything to her about the matter. Her picture frequently appeared in the society section of the paper.) Write an impartial letter of recommendation about Miss Thomson, remembering that you have a threefold responsibility —to Mr. Rufus, to Miss Thomson, and to your company.

6. You are Credit Manager of Topcraft Department Store. Answer the credit inquiry in Problem 10, page 195, assuming that it requires a letter because no questionnaire was enclosed. The applicant is Mr. Thomas Mortinson, whose credit record with your store has been excellent ever since he opened the account seven years ago. He has bought an average of $90 monthly, under terms that require payment by the 10th of the month following purchase. Assume any other pertinent, necessary facts, and answer the six questions from the assistant credit manager of the savings and loan association. (You may assume a negative answer to one of the assumed questions.)

## Granting Adjustments

1. Evaluate the following adjustment letters. What do you like and dislike about each? Suggest specific improvements where needed—in the tone, organization, accuracy, and adequacy of explanation and resale.

**A.** This letter, dated January 27, from a department store, accompanied a gift box of assorted cheeses which a charge customer had bought and asked the store to send for Christmas to a friend, Mrs. Greaves, in another state.

Dear Mrs. Greaves:

   We are replacing the box of cheese which was purchased by Miss Mueller in December.  This original purchase was returned from the Post Office because the label was not legible.  Due to an error in our shipping department, the second box of cheese was not mailed.  However, this third box of cheese should reach you in a few days.

   We are sorry for the inconvenience this has caused you.

**B.** From a hotel to a businessman who had complained about an accounting mix-up; he had attended a national convention and, because of overcrowded conditions at the hotel, had been placed in a suite of two rooms with two other delegates. They had run up large bills in "room services," some of which wrongly appeared on Mr. Plebuch's bill.

Dear Mr. Plebuch:

I very much appreciated your letter of January 25th and the statement that you make relative to your account.  I assure you I deeply regret the fact that our office staff did not present you the correct statement upon your departure.

I am taking the liberty of enclosing completely itemitzed statements of all three accounts so that you will know exactly what was paid and what was charged.

I well realize the importance of our public relations, especially on such a matter as this when you were so kind to share a bath in the suite of rooms with other persons attending the National Management Association Convention.

We do want you to know, however, Mr. Plebuch, that we do appreciate your patronage and shall look forward to serving you under more favorable circumstances on your next visit to (city).

**C.** From the Chicago (head office) Service Department of a national electrical appliances firm to a customer in a city 1,000 miles away. The letter is mimeographed; the customer's name and "coffeemaster" are obvious typewritten fill-ins.

Dear Mrs. Campbell:

   We are concerned with your report about your appliance*. Our service work is guaranteed and if our service man failed to repair the appliance correctly, we want to see that the proper repairs are made without further expense.

We would suggest that you return the appliance* to us and use the enclosed shipping label on the package so that it will be connected with this correspondence when it arrives here. If we failed to make the correct repairs, we will not only take care of that for you without charge, but we will also pay the postage both ways.

*coffeemaster

2. Assume that two months ago Mrs. James Lock, one of your long-time good customers, bought a dual-control four-slice chrome-plated electric toaster from your store and asked that it be sent as a wedding anniversary gift to her out-of-state friends, Mr. and Mrs. Horace Beeson. Since then she has found no charge for the $26.50 on her monthly statements from your store; neither has she received a thank-you from the Beesons. Last weekend, as a guest at the Beeson's home, she noticed they were using the exact toaster she had sent them. To her chagrin they called it their "mystery toaster" because it had reached them c.o.d., although neither of them had ordered it. Because they needed one they kept it. Mrs. Lock then told them of her gift. She is furious with your store and wants you to make a proper adjustment immediately. This situation requires two letters—one to the Beesons and one to Mrs. Lock. Will you send her a copy of your message to the Beesons? Also, should your letter to the Beesons mention the refund in the opening paragraph? Why or why not? The salesclerk forgetfully omitted Mrs. Lock's name on the sales slip. Finding only the name and address of the Beesons (who have no account at your store), the shipping department sent the toaster to the Beesons c.o.d.

3. You are adjustment correspondent for the R. L. Buck Co., a mail-order firm with nationwide distribution. Three weeks ago today Mrs. John Norton, of your city, placed an order (in person) for one galvanized steel Tower Climber with flying trapeze (#79 FP 3077, priced $20.99, shipping weight 51 pounds). She wanted your store to send it to her grandson Donald Brown, 417 North Sixth Street, Billings, Montana. She paid you $20.99 plus 84 cents sales tax. She left emphatic instructions with your mail-order department to bill *her* for all shipping charges, because at the time the clerk who waited on her could not determine the exact charges to Billings.

Today you received the following letter from Mr. Dennis Brown, 417 North Sixth Street, Billings, Montana:

Gentlemen:

If the enclosed material exemplifies the efficiency of your operation, I'm glad I don't patronize your firm! You sent this bill to Donald Brown, our 5-year-old, who can't write you himself.

Enclosures:
Order blank
Due slip for $2.03

Across the address on the order blank is clearly written "Send due to customer Mrs. John Norton, 1439 East Spruce Street (your city)" Under the caption "shipping charges" at the bottom of the order blank is another notation: "Send due to cust." Both these notations were made at the time the clerk first took the order. Therefore, it's quite obvious that someone slipped up. Since you want to try to keep the goodwill of Dennis Brown (he may trade at your Billings store), write a letter trying to erase the bad impression he no doubt has of the efficiency with which your store seems to operate, especially regarding the $2.03 due slip.

4. You are passenger service manager of a transcontinental airline. Today (September 12) you receive a complaint letter from Mr. Melvin Dawson, assistant manager of the Fairview Distributing Company, Chicago, Illinois. He says that because your flight 222 was canceled last September 4 and he had to wait five hours for the next flight, he missed connections with the last bus that was to take him from downtown Denver to a resort hotel in Estes Park 80 miles away. He had been scheduled to preside at a regional convention banquet that same evening. As a result of missing the last connection he had to hire a taxi, which cost him $22 and he thinks you should reimburse him. On top of the expense, he was greatly inconvenienced—sitting in your air terminal five hours.

   Write a tactful adjustment letter to Mr. Dawson. You are of course disappointed to learn of Mr. Dawson's plight. That particular flight 222 was canceled because your firm's operations staff found it necessary to ensure a safe operation. (Assume any reasonable details you wish.) You do appreciate Mr. Dawson's using your airline for his travel and you don't want to lose his goodwill. He travels often, and of course he has friends who attend numerous conventions annually. You are gladly refunding his $22. Should you apologize for the inconvenience you caused him?

5. As assistant manager in the customer service department of A.B. Atlas Company, "jewelry's finest craftsmen" in Hartford, Connecticut, you need to answer today (January 2) an airmail complaint from Olaf Lampson, vice-president of Beta Gamma Sigma, business honorary, at the University of Alabama chapter. He asks what happened to the order he mailed to you almost three months ago (October 5). The chapter needs 25 crested pins for an initiation to be held two weeks from today. Your records show you received his official order and that the pins were shipped to him November 8 by first-class mail. Since the package has not been returned to you unclaimed, you can only assume it was lost in the mail. Company procedure requires that the customer complete the enclosed insurance affidavit so that you can file a claim and tracer with your insurance company. Upon receipt of the affidavit properly executed, you will immediately enter a no-charge replacement order. Write a goodwill-building adjustment (this chapter has bought jewelry from you for many years).

6. As circulation manager of the North End News Agency in your city, answer the complaint in Problem 5, page 199. Because the newsboy who broke the customer's pane of glass is one of your employees, you assume responsibility and agree to pay for replacement of the living room window pane. You've also taken the necessary steps to see that the boys understand how they should deliver papers in the future. Make clear what the customer is to do so that you can pay for the glass promptly.

7. As manager of the El Tropicana Restaurant it is your responsibility today to answer the complaint in Problem 9, page 201. (Write to Mr. Jules Verneson, 915 Tower Building, your city.) You do appreciate his writing to you and of course

he's right that your restaurant has an excellent reputation, which you certainly want to protect. You want him and all his friends to feel confident of getting not only top-quality food (featuring gourmet dishes from all parts of the globe) but also courteous, efficient, friendly service. Decide upon a reasonable adjustment (perhaps a complimentary dinner for two?) that you can offer to Mr. Verneson. Assume reasonable pertinent facts regarding the waiter (and all waiters, if desirable), include whatever explanation the situation calls for, and aim for a sincere cordial tone that will regain this customer's (and his friends') confidence.

8. You are assistant manager of the Mountain Commercial Bank, Denver, Colorado. Today (May 31) you have a touchy matter to handle by mail. A depositor (Mr. O. U. Holler, 519 West 25th Street, Lynnwood, a town 15 miles from you) has written that on May 26 he gave your teller two $10 bills, both of which were to be deposited to his account. However, his passbook shows a deposit of only $10, and he is returning it requesting that you add the other $10. After discussing the situation with your branch manager, you have decided to give Mr. Holler the extra $10 deposit, and you mail him the evidence (passbook posted). In making this deposit you do not want to imply that you have in any way found your teller was negligent in handling his transaction; nor do you find any reason or any records to indicate that your bank received more than the original $10 credited to Mr. Holler's account. However, because you believe he honestly feels he deposited $20, you are crediting the money to him. You feel it's a good idea to "educate" him a little about double-checking any time he deposits funds with your, or any other, organization, or does any business involving cash. He should do this before he leaves the area in which the transaction was handled and make sure the transaction has been handled to his satisfaction. Aim to keep Mr. Holler as a continuing customer.

### Other Favorable Replies about Credit, First Orders, Favors

1. One of your first jobs as assistant credit manager for the College Gift and Bookstore is to write a good credit-granting form letter. The manager wants it to be neatly mimeographed on Bookstore letterhead paper. A space is to be left at the top for typed insertions of date, inside address, and personalized salutation. Your store opened just two months ago in the heart of the main business district near your campus, and offers a variety of items and services. Departments include technical books, trade books, sports equipment, records, commercial supplies, leather goods, photographic supplies. Your credit department sends itemized statements every month on the first, showing all transactions up to the 27th of the preceding month. Payment should be made within ten days if customers don't want to lose their good credit standing. Your store also sells miscellaneous gift items, cosmetics, men's clothing, girls' sportswear, and art supplies. Write the cordial letter that can be used for every customer to whom credit privileges are extended. Although you'd like to send with it an illustrated folder, the decision from the controller's office and the manager is to save the cost of a folder; thus your letter must be as complete and attractive as possible without an enclosure. Each credit customer gets a charge plate. One more service: free customer parking for one hour with any purchase of $1 or more.

2. You are a correspondent in the credit department of the leading department store in a city of 100,000 population. Several weeks ago Mrs. Ima Rich wrote you, saying she just moved to town from a distant city and wants a credit account with your

store. In turn, you sent her an application form to fill out because the local credit bureau had no information available on Mrs. Rich. She filled out the form and returned it to you promptly. In turn, you checked her facts—including the references—and find she has an excellent credit reputation. The references complimented her for prompt payment throughout the years she traded with them. Your assignment is to notify her that you have granted her credit with your store. Assume your department store has the services you'd expect in a city of 100,000. In preparation for this assignment, you (or a representative from your class) might want to find out what services are available at a comparable department store, and also the type of message the store sends to an individual like Mrs. Rich.

3. You are credit manager of the National Athletic Supply, Inc., a wholesale firm in Bloomington, Illinois. Today (January 25) you approved a credit request from Mr. Robert Rainsdale, owner-manager of Bob's Sporting Goods in Muncie, Indiana. He has ordered 20 Little League baseball bats, Catalog #BB987 ($2); 30 baseballs with cork centers, BC 0711, ($1.50); and 10 Deluxe table tennis sets, #TT 8106, ($6), totaling $145 plus $4 shipping charges. This is his first order to your firm. It came to you through your field representative Tom Browne, who reports an exceptionally favorable location of Bob's Sporting Goods—within two blocks of both junior and senior high schools and in the heart of a residential shopping area catering to young families with children. Mr. Rainsdale (a college graduate six years ago, majoring in Recreation) bought the store three years ago with savings and a small inheritance. Although his capital investment is limited, he is a well-liked manager with progressive ideas. As a former captain of his college football team and as a Little League coach for four years, he is widely known and respected in the community. His character and ethical standards are above reproach. His references report that he has always paid his bills, although often payments have run past the 30-day periods. You decide to grant him credit on your usual 2/10, net 30 terms and to give him a little "education" (tactfully) on what he gains from paying within the discount period. You are setting a credit limit of $200 until you see how well he keeps his account up to date. The items he ordered were sent by Railway Express today; delivery will be within two days. The Little League bats (of white ash) are approved by the American Baseball Association; the Deluxe table tennis sets (with 5-ply basswood paddles and sure-grip vinyl handle bindings), as well as the bats, are nationally advertised in *Sports Illustrated* and *Parents* magazines. You're enclosing with the shipment some counter and window displays, plus the needed order lists and blanks and your new spring catalog.

4. Mr. and Mrs. Grayson Tilly, 924 Malaki Street, Eugene, Oregon, have applied to your savings and loan association for a $14,500 mortgage home loan. Through the local retail credit association, and other references they gave you, you have checked their credit record and found it to be excellent. Also, all other conditions regarding their home and neighborhood are fine. Thus you have decided to approve their loan application. Write the appropriate letter, telling them what they need to know. The length of the loan is 17 years. Monthly payments will be $105, plus 1/12 of the annual real estate taxes and fire insurance premium. The interest cost of the loan is 7 percent yearly. Closing costs are $250. This loan commitment by your association is good for only 30 days. It is necessary that these borrowers sign and return a form which you are enclosing. By signing it, they will formally notify you of their acceptance of the loan. If they have questions, you'll try to answer them. Of course, their reply must come within the 30 days.

5. As the new assistant manager of Eastside Branch of City National Bank, you need to write a good welcome letter to customers who have just opened a new account with your bank. Besides paying a good interest on savings accounts, your bank offers a variety of other services—including personal and business loans. In the files you find the following form that your predecessors have used. Select what you like, make necessary improvements, and write your own message.

Dear Mr. and Mrs. Doe:

I am pleased to welcome you as a depositor of the City National Bank. We appreciate your opening an account with us and are looking forward to many opportunities to serve you.

All of our Bank's services, described in the enclosed pamphlet, were designed with our customers in mind and are available at this Branch. We would welcome an opportunity to discuss any of them with you or answer any questions. Our drive-in window is open during banking hours: 10:00 a.m. to 3:00 p.m. weekdays except Friday when we remain open until 6:00 p.m. Our parking facilities are open whenever you visit our bank.

Please look to us whenever we may be of assistance. Your friendship and trust is our primary concern.

Welcome to City National Bank.

6. You are sales manager for American Wholesale Office Supplies Mart, Cincinnati, Ohio. Acknowledge a first order from Carson's Office Equipment and Supplies, 797 Second Avenue, Scranton, Pennsylvania. Mr. John Carson, owner-manager, has ordered by letter the following from you:

| | | |
|---|---|---|
| 20 cartons of standard mimeograph stencils (MS952) | @ $1.20 | $ 24.00 |
| 50 reams MP 621 mimeograph paper | @ $1.50 | 75.00 |
| 50 reams easy-erase typing paper EP 632 | @ $1.80 | 90.00 |
| | | $189.00 |

Mr. Carson enclosed his check for $200, saying he was estimating the shipping charges and would forward more if necessary. You must refund the excess paid, because shipping charges are only $7.50. These supplies are being wrapped and shipped tomorrow afternoon by motor freight, and should get to Scranton the next morning. From his order, it appears that Mr. Carson has only your paper and Duplicating Supplies Catalog. Send him your folder illustrating your new line of other office supplies, which range from letter scales and portable envelope sealers to typewriter erasers and ten different colors of pens and pencils. Can you think of anything else you should send or tell him to make this retailer's future ordering from your firm easy and profitable?

7. Assume that a retail mail-order chain store has sent you the following acknowledgment of your first order. You live about 50 miles from the store, and you have its catalog. The letter is completely processed and has neither date nor inside address. In spite of this lack of personalization, do you think the letter will accomplish its purpose? Why? Evaluate the message specifically as to organization, you attitude, resale, sales promotion, and easy action. What, if anything, is missing? Considering

the circumstances, can you justify a complete form letter like this without personalization? Why?

Dear Customer:

Thank you for your recent order. You are always welcome at Wards, and have used one of the many easy ways to shop with us—at home by mail.

Another easy way is ordering by telephone from any of our Catalogs. It is really a pleasant way to buy and, in connection with our Metropolitan Delivery Service, it is both fast and convenient.

Under this plan we handle all the details of order writing for you. If you call during the morning, in most cases your purchases will be delivered to your door within 48 hours. You'll find our delivery charges are reasonable . . . well worth the saving in time and shopping expense. Just call one of the numbers at the top of this letter.

It is our constant aim to bring you better merchandise at lower prices in our general Catalogs and Sale Books. It will therefore pay you to think first of Wards whenever you need anything, as your orders will always be filled at the lowest current price.

Our telephone shopping service brings you a complete department store, with over 100,000 items from which to choose in our various Catalogs. Our Telephone Shoppers will gladly answer any question you may have . . . help you with your selections, tell you about our Monthly Payment Plan, and take care of all the ordering details.

Whether you prefer to use credit or pay cash . . . whether you order by telephone, in person or by mail . . . Wards look forward to serving you often in the future.

8. Your company, the Hammond Musical Instrument Manufacturing Company of Chicago, Illinois, sends free to anyone who requests it a monthly booklet called the *Hammond Times*. Today you receive a letter from Marvin Hilliard, a young man who tells you how much he enjoyed the *Times* you have sent him monthly for three years—even while he was in military service. Now he gives you his new address, to which he hopes you'll mail future *Hammond Times* copies. He was married last month, has a new management trainee job, and is settling down in Tulsa, Oklahoma. He hopes some day "before too long" to be able to buy one of your electric organs because he really is "a nut" on them. Answer his letter. Grant the requested favor of address change and continue to send him the free *Times*. You have in Tulsa an excellent dealer who sells your complete line of musical instruments. Will you invite Mr. Hilliard to visit that dealer?

9. Assume that in the five years since you graduated from college you have become active in the local chapter of a national businessmen's organization relating to your

major work. (Assume a pertinent name.) Last month you were presented with the "Man of the Month" award, and a short article appeared about you in this organization's national magazine. Today you receive a complimentary letter and invitation from the president of the organization's chapter in another city (100 miles away) to be dinner guest (7 p.m.) and banquet speaker (20 minutes) on Thursday evening, one month from today. Your wife or a friend will also be a welcome guest, he says, and the organization will provide for your car expenses and hotel overnight costs. There is no fee for speaking. After thinking the matter over, you decide to accept, even though you must be back at your office at 8 a.m. the next (Friday) morning. The topic he suggested for your talk is one that's dear to your heart. Write your pleasant acceptance and make clear any details the president will need to know. Assume any additional necessary facts. He said that his chapter publicity will go to press 10 days from today; so of course he'd appreciate hearing from you soon. The earliest you can get to the banquet is 7 p.m.

## Good-news and Neutral Announcements

1. You are chairman of the Chamber of Commerce second annual spring luncheon, and you've been working hard on plans for the past two months. The Governor of your state, the Honorable Daniel J. Doe, has accepted your invitation to be principal speaker. Because you anticipate that recent events in the state capitol will generate a high level of interest, you have moved the luncheon to a larger room at the local athletic club. You have decided to permit a member to bring one nonmember guest. The purpose of these luncheons is to provide an opportunity to get reacquainted with other businessmen in your community and to hear a challenging and provocative message from a prominent public figure. The program this year should provide both. The date is Thursday, April 20, 197_. The total number you can accommodate is 175. Your cutoff date for reservations is April 17. Luncheon will begin at 12 noon. Write the letter announcing this event and make action easy for reservations. Be specific.

2. Design an eye-catching announcement memo for all your employees to take part in your company's annual blood bank drive. You are assistant personnel manager. The date is Friday, March 13, from 10 a.m. to 4 p.m. in the company's health annex, room 84-A. Your memo goes to each of 500 employees. You are providing donor sign-up sheets that will be posted on bulletin boards in 10 areas, two on each of five floors. Because of the recent flu "epidemic," donors have been light and demands for blood have been heavy. Ask your employees to give this drive their full support and to sign up by a certain date.

3. You are supervisor of your company's stores division. Your assistant has just laid the following memo on your desk for your approval before it will be dittoed and sent to all 45 store managers. Revise it completely to improve the tone and you attitude. Use memo format and supply a suitable subject line.

   From the reports being received in this office, as well as personal contact, it is evident that the employees in our store operation are not well versed on the duties and responsibilities that are expected of them.

   All indications point to the lack of knowledge, due to laxness in not reading and absorbing the contents in the Board's

Circular Book, with respect to the duties that they are compelled to abide by and comply with.

The Circular Book is for the benefit of everybody and it is,
therefore, compulsory that all employees read the Circulars
that mainly pertain to them and to their responsibilities and
perform their duties accordingly.

Indifference in attitude and laxness in ability to shoulder
required responsibilities will not be tolerated.

Ignorance and excuses as to procedures is hardly excusable
when the performance of your duties have been spelled out for
you by the Board in Circular and Bulletin form.

4. You are sales manager of a national petroleum products firm. Your advertising
department and you have just finished working out a special nonexpiring Gold
National Credit Card that you'll send to all "preferred" (good-credit-record) customers. In the past you've issued paper cards each year; the enclosed charge plate
gold card is neat and conveniently fits into wallets. (In the past, the paper cards
had to be destroyed every time a new card was issued.) The Gold Credit Card
entitles holders to travel all over the United States using the card for quality products and services that your firm sells for cars, boats, or airplanes. You have over
48,000 conveniently located dealers in 50 states; also in Canada and the United
States Virgin Islands. In addition, your firm has a touring service, which gives
out convenient map routings and other pertinent travel information. This can be
arranged through customers' neighborhood dealers who sell your products. They
can also charge tires, batteries, and accessories; and they can even use the credit for
Johnnie Howard's Motor Lodge accommodations. Write the announcement that
will accompany the new Gold Credit Card.

5. Today you (customer service manager of the Ace Department Store) received by mail a
wallet containing five cards and a charge plate bearing the name of your customer,
Mrs. Anna Inglis. An honest stranger (Miss Elsie Allbright, St. Louis, Missouri)
writes that she found the wallet without any money in it, along the roadside north
of a small town 50 miles east of St. Louis. Return the wallet to Mrs. Anglis. (Her
address did not, of course, appear on the charge plate, and that's why Miss Allbright returned it to your store. Write a good-news letter to accompany the wallet.
You notice that the date on the charge plate expired last week; thus you are
sending a new card so that Mrs. Inglis may continue to enjoy your many credit
card advantages. (She is a good customer.) In checking her account, you find that
no one else has used her credit card.

6. You are accountant for H&H Distributors. Today (February 23) you have discovered an error you made regarding freight bill #730016, dated November 11 last
year, from Howard Carloading Company, 908 Utah Avenue, Salt Lake City, Utah.
Through your oversight you have not yet paid this bill, though payment was due
last November 18! Your firm tries always to pay its bills on time. It was an honest
mistake and you want to apologize for it. You received freight bills 730016 and
72119 from Howard on the same day. Since these two freight bills were identical
except for the bill number, you had put them together assuming that one was
a copy of the other. You hope this incident will not hinder any future good relations
your firm may have with Howard Carloading. Write an appropriate letter with
which you transmit your check for the $20.98 that was due three and one-half
months ago.

# Chapter 8

# Bad-news Messages

- The Right Attitude
- Plans for Bad-News Messages
- Unfavorable Replies to Requests
- Unfavorable Unsolicited Messages
- Capsule Checklists
- Exercises

Whenever you must write a message that your reader will consider disappointing or unfavorable in some way, the situation requires special planning and careful choice of words. A competent letter writer can actually win or keep a friend for his company even when he is refusing an inquirer's request or transmitting other unfavorable facts.

Most of the bad-news letters and memorandums you may have to write can be grouped under the following unfavorable replies and unfavorable unsolicited messages:

*Unfavorable replies*

Answering sales-related inquiries when the information is undesirable
Answering nonsales inquiries when the information is undesirable
Refusing adjustments on claims and complaints
Refusing credit
Acknowledging orders you can't fill now or at all
Declining requests for favors and invitations
Turning down contract or work offers

*Unfavorable unsolicited messages*

Announcing bad news about prices and/or services
Requiring minimum orders and/or deposits
Penalizing for nonconformity with rules and procedures
Conveying other bad news

This chapter discusses the right attitude for transmitting bad news, suggests plans for bad-news messages, presents various examples of unfavorable replies and unsolicited messages, and provides capsule checklists. Additional illustrations of bad-news messages are in Chapter 11, Other Job Application Messages, and Chapter 12, Collection Letters.

## THE RIGHT ATTITUDE

Everything you learned in preceding chapters about consideration and courtesy toward your reader[1] applies to bad-news messages. In such messages it is especially important that the *tone* of your letter be appropriate. Because the right attitude toward your recipient will improve the tone and thus the effectiveness of your letters, keep the following additional suggestions in mind when you write bad-news letters:

1. *Remember that every letter you write can be considered a sales letter.* With bad-news letters, you are trying to sell your customer on the idea that your decision, though contrary to his request or action, is fair and reasonable— and possibly even to his advantage in the long run.

2. *Try honestly to see things from the other person's point of view.* Show him *why* your suggested plan or requirement is needed and/or to his advantage.

[1] See especially pages 98–117, which cover consideration and courtesy in depth.

A statement such as "It will be advantageous to you if you work it out this way . . . ." is much more effective than the selfish "It would be inconvenient for us (or against our policy) to do as you ask."

3. *Avoid leaning on company rules or policy;* it seldom soothes your reader. Include, if possible, the *customer-benefit reasons* that are behind your rules and procedures.

4. *Look for the best in the other person.* Although a customer may be mistaken, try to have confidence that he honestly wants to do the right thing. The following expressions show faith in the reader:

We are confident that you . . . .
You are probably wondering how you can . . . .
You will agree, I believe, that . . . .
You will want to . . . .

5. *When praising a man, single him out; when criticizing him, put him in a group.*

Single out:  You certainly made the right decision, Mr. Brown.
As a group: Sometimes customers, unknowingly, make the wrong decision.

6. *Shield the reader's pride.*

Tactless: If you had read the instructions I gave you, you would have noticed that they specifically state you had to sign the acceptance form within 30 days.
Tactful: Our commitment was good for 30 days. In the instructions that you received with the . . ., you will find. . . .

7. *Talk with the reader, not down to him.*

Condescending: We are willing to look into this matter for you.
Agreeable:    Thank you for taking the time to tell us about . . . . We always appreciate . . . .

## PLANS FOR BAD-NEWS MESSAGES

The underlying purpose of every bad-news message is to present the unpleasant facts with *you* attitude—in such a way that the reader will consider you fair and reasonable and will preferably remain a friend of the organization you represent. Your choice of message plan is influenced by the circumstances —your purpose, your relationship to the reader, and the particular facts in each case. You have two choices of plans: the indirect or the direct.

### Indirect Plan

Before you read the suggested indirect pattern for stating bad news, try an experiment on yourself. Suppose you as a customer have been waiting for a reply to your request for something you want very much from a business firm—a refund or perhaps a loan. How would you react if the reply began with a negative statement similar to these:

We regret (are sorry, wish to state) that we are unable to refund the $300 down payment you made on the car.

or

Your application for a loan (refund) has been denied (refused, rejected).

Wouldn't you feel more receptive toward the firm and its bad news if the reply had opened with at least a brief agreeable statement—like the following—and then presented an explanation *before* the bad news?

We appreciate your letter telling us how you feel about the 197_ hard-top Mercury you purchased from us three months ago.

Thank you for giving us the opportunity to consider your loan application for financing your proposed home purchase.

Most people appreciate hearing at least some explanation before the bad-news decision, especially if it seriously affects them. Usually a good rule to consider is "Be quick to give good news, but take longer to tell the bad news." Thus, whereas the good-news message uses a direct approach, the bad-news message usually follows the indirect approach. Using this approach, the bad-news plan has the following five-part suggested organizational structure:

---

1. Buffer
2. Explanation and analysis of circumstances
3. Decision—either implied or expressed
4. Resale and/or constructive suggestions
5. Friendly, positive close

---

Under each part of this bad-news basic pattern you have several alternatives, as shown in the expanded list below.

1. *Buffer.* If possible, fill your first paragraph with mainly reader-interest material—to get in step with your reader. However, your buffer must begin close to the general subject of your letter; avoid irrelevant material. Also, avoid statements that might mislead the reader into thinking you are granting his request; such statements merely build him up for a sad letdown! Apologies are unwarranted if your firm is not at fault. One or more of the following buffers can help put your reader in a more receptive attitude:

a. *Agreement.* Agree with him on something, if possible (perhaps a matter-of-fact comment on which there is general agreement—business conditions, costs, or any other pertinent item).

b. *Appreciation.* Thank him (for his check, information, application, request, inquiry, cooperation, or whatever applies).

c. *Assurance.* Assure him of careful consideration and explanation of all available facts about the problem.

d. *Compliment.* Try to compliment him on something good about his past record or his request (his sincerity, careful listing of all facts as he sees them, etc.).

e. *Cooperation*. Show a sincere desire to be as helpful as possible.

f. *Good news*. If you can grant any part of a request and you think your reader will be pleased, begin with that good news.

g. *Neutral courtesy*. Keep your opening paragraph noncommittal. For instance, if you must announce an unfavorable price increase or service decrease, use neutral words such as "needed change."

h. *Resale*. Begin with brief, appropriate resale (on your merchandise, services, or organization).

i. *Sympathy*. Express sympathy—if the matter is very serious and likely to be greatly disappointing to him.

j. *Understanding*. Show understanding of his needs and problem (his desire to have a dependable product, to pay at least a partial amount due, etc.).

2. *Explanation and Analysis.* Include honest, convincing reasons why under the circumstances the matter must be different from the way the reader wants it. In two types of situations, however, stating a reason is unnecessary: (1) when the matter is routine and obvious (clerical error) and (2) when you'd get mired in negative or confidential material if you tried to explain. When you decide to include an explanation, place it *before* the decision and remember these suggestions:

a. Try to convince the reader that you are acting in his best interests in the long run, or at least according to a law that is enforced equally for all. Avoid the insincere: "Much as I would like to...however...." Also avoid reasons that suggest benefit only to your firm.

b. Explain courteously all pertinent facts behind your decision. Mention first the favorable factors, then the less favorable ones.

c. Don't dodge with such statements as "our policy prevents...." State, if possible, specific reasons (especially customer-benefit reasons) for your policy.

d. If the reason is confidential or too complicated to explain, then show—as a substitute—that the reader's request has been carefully and sincerely considered (for his benefit as well as your company's).

3. *Decision.* Either express or imply your decision, but make it clear, positive, concise—and imbed it in favorable material. You have these alternatives:

a. If the reasons are so sound that your reader will conclude you *must* refuse his request, payment, etc., you can omit the negative entirely and make the bad-news decision clear by implication. For example, if you are already scheduled as luncheon speaker in Chicago May 6, omit saying, "Therefore, I cannot attend your luncheon in St. Louis that same day."

b. If an implied decision might be misunderstood, express your decision briefly and clearly, near the end of the explanation. Be careful never to mislead your reader or cause him to be uncertain about your decision. The best place for a negative decision is in the middle—not the beginning—of a paragraph, and never in a paragraph by itself. Sometimes you can add a short favorable statement—perhaps a long-term customer benefit or another positive idea—after the refusal. Avoid "must refuse," "cannot grant," and similar negatives.

c. If you say "yes" to something else (see item 4 below), imply your decision by emphasizing what *can* be done and thereby make clear what cannot be done, without actually saying "no" at all. For instance, if you must refuse requested credit, you can offer the layaway plan; instead of a requested personal interview, you can enclose a helpful booklet to answer questions.

d. If a compromise is desirable, suggest what your firm can do and what the customer can do.

4. *Resale and/or Constructive Suggestion.* This section is optional because many times you don't need to resell and you can't help the reader. Whenever you can and want to help him, try one or more of these suggestions:

a. Offer a constructive suggestion, substitute, counterproposal, or alternative course of action. (This might be part of 3c or 3d.) Thus, though you cannot help him in one way, you try to do something else for him. The material here must definitely relate to the subject discussed in the letter.

b. Give your reader something positive to think about (perhaps a ray of hope for the future).

c. Resell him on your firm's services and/or practices and policies.

5. *Friendly Positive Close.* End on a positive note, with one or more of these ideas:

a. Assure the reader he is appreciated as a customer (or as an interested inquirer and possible future customer).

b. Invite his future patronage, cooperation, suggestions, and/or compliance with the decision. Include mild, no-pressure sales promotional material if you think your reader is in the right mood for it. (See page 207.)

c. If you are awaiting his approval, or he should take some action, make clear exactly what he is to do, when he should do it, and how he can do it easily. (See page 92.)

d. Express continued interest, service, and reader benefit.

Genuine sincerity must underlie whatever words you use to express your message. The writer who has a true feeling of goodwill toward every customer will find it easier to convey his bad-news messages effectively, and at the same time protect the interests of his company.

## Direct Plan

Though you can use the indirect bad-news plan for most unfavorable messages, there are situations that may warrant the direct approach. Again, the choice depends upon the particular circumstances. You may decide to begin directly with the bad news if you have:

A routine or small matter on which your reader is likely not to be seriously disappointed or personally emotionally involved—especially a message between employees of two business firms or within the same firm (and perhaps also to a person who is known to prefer reading the bad news in the first paragraph!).

*or*

An urgent message that should be called to the reader's attention forcefully—as in the late stages of a collection procedure.

If you use the direct approach, the pattern is essentially the same as the direct good-news plan, except that the opening contains bad instead of good news:

---

1. Bad-news decision (with or without a brief buffer)
2. Explanation
3. Appropriate courteous ending

---

Most of the bad-news replies and unsolicited messages in this chapter are organized by the indirect approach (hereafter referred to as the bad-news plan), but you will also find examples of messages organized by the direct plan.

## UNFAVORABLE REPLIES TO REQUESTS[1]

This section focuses on unfavorable replies to requests for information (sales-related and nonsales subjects), adjustment, credit, orders, favors, and some kinds of contract offers.

### Answering Sales-related Inquiries When the Information Is Undesirable

If you have no honest favorable answer to your reader's direct question(s) regarding catalogs, prices, terms, products, and similar sales-related information, your reply should be organized by the bad-news plan. In some situations all five parts of such a message may be expressed adequately in four or five sentences. For example, in Letter 1 below, the district manager of a national tire manufacturing firm answers a rancher's two-page letter about his world-famous pet lion. The lion had outgrown pet-store rubber dog bones, and the rancher asked if the rubber company could make a 12- to 14-inch heavy rubber toy with a hidden bell inside.

*Letter 1: A concise, helpful bad-news reply about a product the writer's firm does not manufacture.[2]*

Dear Mr. Westbeau:

*Buffer:* Thank you very much for your interesting letter
*thanks*  concerning Little Tyke.

---

[1] To imbed negative material in replies that are chiefly good news, see pages 209–210 and 214–217.
[2] Adapted from a letter by Goodyear Tire and Rubber Co., Akron, Ohio.

*Explanation; implied decision*

Goodyear does not make rubber sundry items such as balls, toys, etc., and we have no molds with which to make up the item you need for Little Tyke.

*Helpful suggestion*

Some rubber company specializing in rubber drug sundries may be able to help you. You might try the Miller Rubber Company, Division of Goodrich, in Akron, Ohio.

*Pleasant close (good wishes)*

The best of success to you in finding just what you need for your famous pet.

When the inquiry is about a complex or more serious matter, much more detail may be necessary, especially in the explanation and resale portions. The next example—from the president of a wholesale cement firm to a contractor who had asked why the firm's prices were so high—illustrates how tact and specific details can help to retain a reader's goodwill despite bad news.

*Letter 2: A goodwill-retaining bad-news reply to an inquiry about high prices.*

Dear Mr. Gerald:

*Buffer: thanks for inquiry and business*

Thank you for your inquiry and concern over the amount we charged you for your concrete. Because your business is very much appreciated and valued highly, it is important to me as well as to you that you understand why we billed you $525.08 instead of $463.13.

*Explanation*

*Decision*

*Fairness to all and reader benefit*

Due to the $1.44 hourly employee wage increase, the increase in the price of cement, and overall increases in direct and indirect operating expenses it was necessary to increase the price of our concrete. For the past 11 months our prices for 5 sacks of our concrete have been $17.90 to individuals and $17.40 to all contractors. If we lower the price to one contractor, all others would rightly expect equal treatment. By maintaining our price, we treat everyone equally and can assure you that you are getting the quality of material you order and expect.

*Resale*

I realize that you were able to buy concrete at a lower price in the past, but the company that you bought the concrete from is no longer in business just because their price was not sufficient to cover their direct costs and expenses. Neither you nor we would want this condition to happen to us. We are proud of our reputation for quality products and service and want to be of service to you in the future.

*Pleasant close (thanks; further service)*

Thank you for your inquiry. If I can be of any service to you in the future, please call me between 7:30 a.m. and 5:30 p.m. at 999-3333, or call evenings at 666-6666.

## Answering Nonsales Inquiries When the Information Is Undesirable

Occasionally you may have to write bad-news answers to non-sales inquiries. Whenever you send bad news to anyone outside your firm—even though your bad-news information is not directly related to your company's sales or products—it is usually better to follow the bad-news plan. Contrast, for example, Letter 3 (which opens with the refusal and stresses the negative throughout) with Letter 4 (which has an assuring buffer plus a positive, helpful tone).

*Letter 3: Wordy, negative, I-centered answer to an inquiry; refusal opening.*

> Dear Mr. James:
>
> I am sorry to say that, unfortunately, our editors did not find anything in our plan files that would apply to your problem regarding pension plan digests for trade association staff employees.
>
> We have also not yet found any plan elsewhere that would fall into the class you discussed.
>
> I wonder if, when you looked through the Reports, you did not notice that there is a pension plan for the Employee Association League of New York state?  I found this plan on pages 106–12.  I am not certain whether this is the type of plan you are interested in.

*Letter 4: Rewritten, improved version of Letter 3.*

> Dear Mr. James:

*Buffer:*
*assurance*
*of help*

> We are trying to assist you in your endeavor to find pension plan digests for trade association staff employees.

*Explana-*
*tion; positive*
*view on*
*alternate*
*search*

> In our own files our editors have been able to find no plans up to now that apply to your particular problem. However, other sources that we are contacting may have some plan that does fall into the class you discussed.  As soon as we have something definite, I will write you again.

*Suggestion*

> A pension plan for the Employee Association League of New York State is discussed on pages 106–12 in the Reports. This plan may give you something to go on.

*Courteous*
*close*

> If I can be of any further help, please let me know.

When you receive a request for a recommendation on a person about whom you have only unfavorable information, and whom you honestly cannot recommend, you have four alternatives:

1. Call the inquirer on the telephone to discuss the matter with him.
2. Write a brief refusal similar to the following:
   On the basis of my experience with Tom Dawson, I am sorry to inform you that I do not have sufficient favorable information to recommend him for the position (credit) for which you are considering him.
3. Omit the applicant's name throughout the reply (use "the person about whom you inquire in your letter of April 10")[1] and include whatever facts are pertinent regarding his employment, credit, or personal record.
4. Include both the applicant's name and an honest, frank report, as in Letter 5. Because of libel laws it is imperative to be cautious and scrupulously accurate. Though you can use the direct plan, similar to that discussed in Chapter 7, pages 215–217, the following letter uses the bad-news plan. Notice that the first paragraph is basically a buffer of neutral courtesy; it does not reveal the bad news. Only after stating facts does the writer state his decision.

*Letter 5: A frank nonrecommendation of an unsatisfactory former employee.*

Dear Mr. Carson:

*Full name and work*    Tom Zoe, about whom you inquire, was on our payroll five months--from April 197_ until two months ago. He was hired as a messenger and a sign painter's helper.

*Facts*    Because his job with our firm was his first since he quit high school, we tried to be more understanding about his personal problems that affected his work. I must tell you confidentially that Tom had been victimized by unfortunate home experiences which caused him to drift into careless habit patterns from the standpoint of responsibility and regularity.

*Unfavorable work*    His attendance record with us shows an average of one absence every six days. Both as a messenger and as a helper he abused rules and privileges. Because each time he promised to do better, we gave him several extra opportunities to straighten himself out. Unfortunately the pattern became worse instead of better and we finally had to replace him. Thus, on the basis of our experience with *Decision* him, I am sorry I cannot recommend him for responsible work.

*Hope for the future*    I am glad to see that he is now getting the help of your counseling service and sincerely hope he will develop right attitudes. Perhaps in time he will be able to establish himself with really worthwhile activities. You have my sincere good wishes.

---

[1] Omitting the applicant's name is acceptable if you are sure your reader knows whom you are writing about. However, such a practice could be extremely confusing and lead to mixups if the same two firms happen to correspond about two or more persons on the same day! Employers who exchange information frequently might set up a file number for each person on whom they seek information. Replies would then be about a file number (known to the employer and respondent as a specific person).

When writing unfavorable recommendations, resist the temptation to write such "humorous" responses as the following; they are smart-alecky and unbusinesslike:

> Miss Perkins was our office secretary for the month of August and, although her typing still is not rapid, her letters display imagination and originality, especially in punctuation and spelling.

> In her short stay with us, Miss Giddy devised an office filing system which is unique and so complex that only a person of the rarest gifts can master it.[1]

The best overall policy is: be honest, tactful, and aware of your threefold responsibility—to the applicant, to the addressee, and to yourself.

When you're writing to someone in your own organization about a relatively small matter with which the reader is not emotionally involved, you probably should use the direct refusal plan, as shown in the memo below.

*Letter 6 (Memo): A bad-news direct-plan memo about company equipment.*

```
TO:      Tom Brown, Purchasing              May 2, 197_
FROM:    Harry Mills, Plant 2
SUBJECT: New ventilating fans needed
```

*Bad news*
Today Jake Jones, representative of Ace Electric, told me that the noisy fans you asked about can't be repaired or adjusted again. He says they're a total loss. The only thing possible for ventilation is to buy new fans.

*Details*
Three fans, model XA22, should do the job well. They'll cost us $80 apiece installed. Jake says he can install these fans this coming Saturday.

*Action request*
If you approve, I'll go ahead and make arrangements. Jake needs two days' notice, because he'll order what we need from the factory. Will you give me a jingle by Wednesday afternoon?

If your firm is a nonprofit organization that gets large numbers of requests for free information—and if you often need to send bad-news replies—you may, to cut correspondence costs, even devise a form letter listing the most recurring negative facts, as in Letter 7.

*Letter 7: Printed form letter to handle multiple inquiries for which many answers may have to be bad news.*

*Buffer: thanks*
Thank you for your recent inquiry. In the interest of economy your request is being answered by this form letter. Check marks and the comments below indicate the action taken.

[1] Adapted from a quotation by George W. Feinstein in "How to Recommend a Deadbeat," *American Business Writing Association Bulletin*, March 1962, page 24.

1. The item or information you requested is
   (a) enclosed.
   (b) out of print.  Copies are in many libraries.
   (c) not yet available; (___ will be sent later),
       (___ related material is enclosed).
   (d) not a publication of this organization.

*Facts*
*and*
*implied*
*decisions*

2. Your request will be filled as soon as our supply is
   replenished.
3. The free supply of this report is exhausted.  Copies may
   be purchased from (name and address) for___cents a copy.
4. Your request has been referred to _____
   _____

*Suggestion*  If you write us again in regard to this request, please
*for future*  return the enclosed correspondence since we have retained
*action*      no record of it.

                      (Printed name and title of writer)

Comments:


## Refusing Adjustment on Claims and Complaints

When you refuse a request for adjustment, realize that the customer is probably disgruntled and even irritated, and be particularly tactful when "selling" him on the fairness of your refusal. Especially important material to include—besides your buffer and explanation—is resale material, constructive suggestions, and even sales promotion when appropriate.

This section discusses three kinds of unwarranted customer claims on which you may have to write a refusal: (1) when the customer is at fault regarding a product, (2) when he is mistaken in his complaint about an account or a service, and (3) when he makes an unjustified policy complaint.

*When the Customer Is at Fault regarding a Product.* Often customers who claim free replacement or repair of a "malfunctioning" product are at fault because they violated instructions for using it. Also, many customers seek a refund or credit on items simply because they have changed their mind. Or a customer might return as "new" an article which cannot be resold because of something the customer did wrong. The next three examples illustrate satisfactory adjustment refusals in such cases.

**Misuse of a product** is the basic reason for the refusal in Letter 1. Notice that the writer calls attention to the user's mistake indirectly and that he shields the reader's pride. He doesn't say, "You violated the instructions" or "You obviously failed to read the directions." Instead, the message includes a tactful logical explanation and an implied but clear refusal, followed by a constructive suggestion and easy-action reader benefit ending.

**Letter 1:** *A mail-order house refuses to replace free a broken, misused garden hose.*

Dear Mr. Sims:

*Buffer:*
*agreement*
*and*
*appreciation*

When you buy a Widgeon product, you are right to expect high quality. We appreciate your returning the hose for our inspection so that we can meet our goal--satisfying your needs.

*Resale and*
*assurance*
*about*
*honoring*
*guarantee*

To provide each of our thousands of Widgeon customers with the specific hose he needs, we carry a wide selection. Each type of garden hose described in the Widgeon catalog is guaranteed to give you the service it was designed for. We are always glad to replace a hose provided its defect lies with workmanship or materials.

*Reason for*
*Opaque hose*
*breakdown*

As stated in the catalog, the Opaque Plastic Hose you bought is recommended only for use in mild climates and also it is not to be shut off at the nozzle. Since Mount Vernon's weather ranges in temperature annually from −15 to +105°F, you can see how these extremes may have affected the splitting of the hose. Laboratory analysis indicates that the damage was caused by excessive water pressure resulting from either shutting the hose off at the nozzle or from water pressure greater than that normally found in most cities. Because Mt. Vernon has the normal water

*Implied*
*refusal*

pressure of 60 pounds per square inch, the split occurred because someone shut the hose off at the nozzle.

*Constructive*
*suggestion*

Two Widgeon hoses--the Gold-Line Plastic and the Neoprene Rubber--are especially recommended for shutting off at the nozzle. In addition, you can use the Neoprene Rubber Hose even in harsh weather. Both are described on the enclosed copy of catalog page 977.

*Easy action*
*and reader*
*benefit*

After you have decided which hose best meets your needs, fill out the enclosed postage-paid order form and mail it in the envelope with your check or money order for $6.47 or $8.58, which include shipping costs; or indicate that you wish c.o.d. shipment. Either way you can be watering your garden again just three days after we receive your order. And you can be sure of many years' dependable service.

Unsalability of the returned product is another common reason for adjustment refusals. The customer who claims he has changed his mind about a purchase may be trying to return an item that has been damaged while in his possession or kept out so long that the store can no longer resell it. Letter 2 is a retailer's refusal to a consumer; Letter 3, a wholesaler's refusal to a new dealer.

**Letter 2:** *A retail clothing store adjustment manager refuses to accept a returned evening gown for credit.*

Dear Mrs. Dodge:

*Buffer:*
*assurance*
*and thanks*

To please our customers is the foremost aim of Bon-James. Thank you for writing us explaining your wishes about the evening gown you purchased here last month.

*Reader-*
*benefit*
*facts about*
*exchange*
*policy in*
*general*

We want you and all our other customers to enjoy the confidence of knowing that any purchase from us is for merchandise of outstanding quality and style and that it is absolutely clean, fresh, and new. Wearing apparel may be returned for full credit anytime within 30 days provided the garment is in clean, resalable condition.

*Findings*
*in this case*

To maintain the high standard on the goods we sell, we carefully check returned merchandise before it is again placed for sale. This examination of the gown you mailed to us disclosed facial makeup at the neckline and several brown spots near the hemline. Because cleaning would

*Implied*
*decision*

render the garment "used" to anyone wishing to repurchase it, the gown is unacceptable for resale.

*Helpful*
*suggestions*

You can be sure that the skillful touch of our fitter will make the sleeves of your Dior evening gown just the length you like best. For this reason, we suggest that you stop in to see Miss Davis, who served you when you purchased the gown. She will hold it for you until you can come in for a fitting; or, if you want us to send it to you without any changes, she will arrange its prompt return.

*Easy action*

Please check and mail your preference on the enclosed postal card. You can depend upon us to do everything possible to help you feel pleased with the gown. You can wear it several years with confidence that it is a highly

*Resale*

fashionable evening garment. As you may recall, it was an outstanding success in the Designer Show held in New York on June 2.

**Letter 3:** *A wholesaler refuses to accept returned out-of-season clothing from a new small retail shop owner (who started in business six months before). Letter is dated December 13.*

Dear Mrs. Hope:

*Buffer:*
*courteous,*
*neutral*
*opening*

The three suits and two coats which you returned to us arrived today. We appreciate the business you have done with us and, as you are new in the apparel field, we would like to inform you again about our policy of returns.

*Explanation about wholesaler requirements; reader benefit*

Women's clothing is highly seasonable merchandise and items move very fast. No wholesale firm accepts returned clothing when it is out of season. As we explained in our first letter to you, we must ask that any retailer who may wish to return anything on open order, do so within two weeks of his purchase. Such a system of merchandising benefits you in the long run, because you are assured of top quality fashion clothing at lower prices.

*Specific facts on this case*

*Decision*

All the five garments we received from you today have been out of our house almost seven weeks. You purchased them October 23 when we were selling fall and winter goods. Now in the present time of year we in the wholesale business are going entirely into spring merchandise. Thus you will understand why we cannot accept these garments for credit and are returning them to you.

*Suggestion*

*Resale*

You will surely find appreciative customers for these suits and coats through a specially advertised sale before Christmas. As they are in popular colors and materials, your customers can get several years of good wear from them.

*Future orders and service*

When you are ready to select your spring stock, use the handy order blanks in the back of your Marco Spring Catalog. You can choose from a wide variety of leading spring fashions and expect deliveries within four days after we receive your order.

**When the Customer Is Mistaken in His Complaint about an Account or a Service.** In addition to refusing adjustments on returned merchandise, you may also have to write bad-news letters to customers who make erroneous claims resulting from a variety of intangible grievances. Among them are unwarranted claims about their account balances or payments and unjustified gripes about various aspects of your firm's service.

Unwarranted claims about account balances or payments may arise when the customer thinks you have made an error because your statements do not agree with his records. If you find your records are correct, you must give him the bad news that he owes more than he claims. In your response, be sure to explain each additional charge clearly, for your reader may have forgotten that he made a purchase or that late charges were added or that some of his past checks were returned by the bank for various reasons. A tabulation of figures, as in Letter 4, or a photostatic copy of the record may be helpful to your customer.

*Letter 4: A loan company's credit manager explains why a borrower owes more than he thought.*

Dear Mr. White:

*Buffer:*
*assurance,*
*cooperation*

As you requested, I have rechecked all your loan payments back to the first one you made after our company purchased your loan in June 1966. I'm glad to give you this summary so that it will help you reconcile your record with ours.

*Detailed*
*explanation*

Your $87 check just received was credited as follows: Interest $1.50 and principal $85.50. The amount still past due is $138.93, made up of the following:

| | | |
|---|---|---|
| 1970 | August payment missed | $82.93 |
| | October and December payments each short $2 | 4.00 |
| 1971 | February payment short | 10.00 |
| | March, April, May, June, July, August, September, October payments each short $2 | 16.00 |
| | December interest | 23.00 |
| 1972 | February payment short $3 | 3.00 |
| | Balance past due | $138.93 |

*Suggested*
*action*

To make payment of this amount easier for you, you may add $11.58 each month for the next 12 months. In this way your monthly payments of $94.51 ($82.93 and $11.58) will help you pay the overdue balance within a year.

Insurance policyholders sometimes make unwarranted requests which the claims department must refuse. In these and similar instances, if you can grant any part of a claim, be sure to begin with that good news. After a positive good-news opening, the reader will be in a better frame of mind to accept whatever refusal is necessary. For instance, compare the following two openings to a policyholder who requested both an $825 refund (which he could not have) and a $55 annual reduction in his future premiums (which he could have).

*Negative:* We are sorry to inform you that we cannot refund the $825 you have paid us in extra premiums the past 15 years. As you were rated a substandard risk because of high blood pressure, the additional premium was mandatory.

*Positive:* The good news from our medical examiner's report that you no longer have high blood pressure now makes you a standard risk in all respects. We are glad to tell you that you will no longer need to pay the $55 annual extra premium.

Even if a situation has no good news or alternative, careful organization and wording can help soften the blow. For example, notice how Letter 5 (excessively negative and organized by the direct plan) can be improved by emphasizing positive ideas and using the indirect plan, as in Letter 6.

**Letter 5:** *A poor, negative liability denial sent by a death benefits division.*

Dear Mrs. Smith:

*Bad-news decision*
Careful consideration has been given to your claim for double indemnity, and I regret to have to inform you that it is the Company's position that no liability exists for this benefit.[1]

*Negative explanation*
It cannot be found that we have been furnished with the due proof required by the policy contract that death resulted directly and independently of all other causes from bodily injury effected solely through external, violent and accidental means.  On the contrary the proof of death furnished by you indicates that death was due solely to disease.  Furthermore, the denial of the authorization for examination and autopsy has deprived the Company of one of its rights under the policy contract.

*Negative decision*
On these grounds liability for double indemnity is denied. The amount of single indemnity already paid represents the Company's entire liability.

**Letter 6:** *Improved revision of Letter 5.*

*Buffer: assurance, careful con- sideration*
Your claim for double indemnity has been given careful consideration.  Our study included the evidence you sub- mitted and information obtained by the Company through investigation.

*Explanation of policy's coverage*
The policy provides for the payment of the double indemnity benefit upon receipt of proof that the death of the insured resulted directly and independently of all other causes from bodily injury solely through external, violent, and accidental means; and, furthermore, that double indemnity shall not be payable if the insured's death resulted directly or indirectly from infirmity of mind or body, illness or disease.

*Facts in this claim*
The certificate of death you submitted in support of your claim gave the cause of death as disease.  It does not refer to any accident.  Moreover, information obtained through our investigation appears to confirm that death was due solely to natural causes.  Also, refusal to furnish authorization for an autopsy deprived the Company of sub- stantial rights under the policy.  In these circumstances, the Company denies that it has any liability for double indemnity.  I am sorry, Mrs. Smith, that our decision
*Decision*
could not be more favorable to you.

---

[1] Though the blunt bad-news opening in Letter 5 was undesirable for the policyholder, a similar direct opening *could* be used in a memo to the agent or to other employees concerned with the case.

*Positive
thoughts*
The single indemnity payment that you have already received represents the Company's entire liability under the policy. I am glad it is of some help to you, and wish you many years of continued good health.

**Unjustified gripes about company services** deserve careful and tactful explanation that establishes your company's accuracy and resells the reader on its usual high-quality service. For instance, the printer who is wrongly accused of misspelling a name on the customer's stationery may have to enclose a copy of the customer's original handwritten order showing the identical spelling.

An unusually knotty problem concerning an unjustified gripe is handled by Letter 7. A customer had told a rug cleaning company's pickup man that though she had had the rugs 12 years, they had never before been cleaned professionally. The rugs were badly worn and extremely dirty; the cleaner devoted about four times the amount of care and time given the usual carpet. Yet the first time the rugs were delivered to the customer she refused to pay for the cleaning, saying they were "not clean enough." She paid after the second cleaning, but then asked for a refund, saying she was still not satisfied.

*Letter 7: A rug cleaner refuses a request for refund.*

Dear Mrs. Schmo:

*Buffer: an
agreeable
comment*
It is often said that a carpet will more than double the comfort of a room, and a clean carpet does even more. It gives you longer service and is more attractive.

*General
educational
facts about
carpet care*
Carpet experts agree that the best care for a rug is to have it professionally cleaned about once in three years. The hardest wear and tear on a rug comes from grinding the dirt into it over a period of time. Sometimes it is hard to realize how worn and spotted a rug can become from 12 years of normal wear--especially with growing boys in the family. Some spots and dirt get ground in and just won't yield to even the best cleaning methods like ours.

*Specific
facts on
cleaning
customer's
rugs*
I well remember your carpets as they were brought in. It was determined by our experts that to give you the best job possible, we would double the time and care given the usual carpet. When your carpets were returned to us we were somewhat surprised, but nevertheless we indicated to you on the phone that we would do the second cleaning free of charge.

*More facts
about
service;
resale*
Altogether your rugs received four times the amount of time and care given the usual carpets, and we only asked that you pay for one cleaning. With experienced workmen skilled in modern cleaning and spot-removing processes, we try to

*Decision*

satisfy all our customers.  Because we have well earned the charge of $41.72 on your rugs—and in fairness to our other customers—we must charge you for an honest reasonable cleaning job.

*Sales promotion; easy action; reader benefit*

Please allow us to place your name on our customer calendar, from which we automatically send you a rug cleaning reminder every third year.  Just fill in and mail the enclosed postcard if you wish this exclusive service. We are glad to be able to give you free pickup and delivery and prompt dependable service to keep your rugs in the best of condition through the coming years.

***When the Customer Makes Unjustified Policy Complaints.*** Customers' incorrect complaints about company policies cover a wide range—from prices to employees' activities to merchandise displays. The main purpose of your reply is to explain and justify whatever policies and procedures the complainer finds undesirable, and to resell him on your company. The suggestions in this chapter should help you handle such situations effectively with the bad-news plan.

Often a "soft" answer can not only placate the customer, but even lead to an unexpected happy relationship. For instance, one new customer had the audacity to write a sarcastic complaint to a company president because a welcome letter to the customer referred to his friend, the salesman, as Mr. R. Brown instead of Ragmar Brown. Letter 8 is the president's courteous reply.

*Letter 8: A good-natured reply to a sarcastic policy complaint.*

Dear Mr. Simpson:

*Buffer: agreement and partial explanation*

I agree with you that the name R. Brown sounds rather abbreviated.  But in preparing these welcome messages to new customers, we abide by the wishes of each field representative concerned.  Mr. Brown, in asking us to welcome you, directed us to refer to him as R. Brown.

*More explanation*

Now, if I had changed R. to Ragmar because I prefer it or because I surmised you might prefer it, then Mr. Brown might have informed me he detests "Ragmar" and thus requests that we use his initial.

*A few "human" comments*

I'm sorry the abbreviation upset you.  You can be sure that "rushing off to a golf course" which you mention, is not within my day's activities.  I haven't found how to run a nationwide company and still find time to play golf at all.

*Pleasant resale*

Please don't feel too unhappy toward us.  At least we <u>tried</u> to welcome you as a new customer.  I believe you'll even like us as time goes on.

The president's courtesy paid off, as the following message from Mr. Simpson indicates:

> Dear Mr. Plumb:
>
> Please forgive my unkind remarks and accept my apology.
> You're a gentleman and I will try to be a good customer.
>
> After reading a copy of my original letter, I find it
> slightly nauseates me.  I should have dumped it into my
> circular "file."
>
> If you should ever visit my town, I would be honored to
> have you as my guest at the golf course.  I'm going to take
> up that sport and discontinue writing nasty letters.

Mr. Plumb did visit Mr. Simpson one day. The happy ending of this story is that Mr. Simpson later became an employee of the company—as field representative.

When customers write anonymous complaint letters, you usually have no way to reply. However, some businessmen receiving anonymous complaints about matters that should be cleared up for all customers run both the complaint and the reply in local newspapers, or even magazines. Among complaints adaptable to such a procedure are, for example, those about store hours ("Why aren't you open evenings and Sundays?") or service ("Why do you have a self-service policy?"). A businessman's display reply underneath such a complaint can be an effective, excellent advertisement, filled with resale, customer-benefit explanations, and sales promotional material.

## Refusing Credit

Even when you are refusing a credit application, you want to try to keep the reader's goodwill. A person's credit reputation is quite important and personal; therefore a credit man must be careful about what he writes and how he expresses his reasons.[1] Refusals of both retail and mercantile credit are organized by the bad-news plan, but since their content can differ, they are grouped separately in the following discussion.

*Retail Credit Refusals.* To an individual consumer, a refusal usually begins with a buffer that refers to the firm's appreciation or careful consideration of the reader's request for credit and/or to his interest in the store.

---

[1] Some credit departments use the telephone for all their refusals. Even if you work in such a department, you will find that you can apply many of the writing principles of this chapter to your oral refusals.

Explanation portions of retail credit refusals vary considerably, but four ways of handling the reasons for refusal are in common use:

1. Reason is omitted entirely (see Letter 1 below).
2. "Insufficient information" is the only reason given (see Letter 2).
3. Factors generally considered in evaluating credit applications are stated without indicating specifically which apply to the reader (Letter 3).
4. Specific reasons are stated (Letters 4 and 5).

The first three of these methods can be easily adapted by credit departments that find it necessary to use form letters because of a large number of applications (often over a wide geographic area)—for example, chain stores, national oil companies, travelers' card services. Because of similar names among the thousands of individual requests, mixups and errors do occur. Thus credit men for firms handling large numbers of requests find it safer to omit giving specific reasons, especially those that pertain to undesirable character and poor-pay habits. However, from the customer's standpoint the refusal which omits the reason entirely is the least helpful (although it may spare him some embarrassment). The "insufficient explanation" reason is considered by some customers to be artificial and insincere; nevertheless both methods 2 and 3 are popular and usually acceptable under certain circumstances, provided the constructive suggestion is tactful and helpful.

The fourth method—stating specific reasons—is desirable when the following conditions exist:

The situation requires an individually typed reply (as in an application for a large loan).
The reason does not involve poor (dishonest, unreliable) personal character.
The desired relationship between the credit department and the applicant is somewhat personal.
The applicant cannot come for a personal interview and is likely to be offended with anything but an individual helpful letter.

Such letters are usually longer—and harder to write—than the first three types, but when tactful and accurate they are highly appreciated by the recipient because they indicate what he must do to earn (or restore) his good credit standing.

In stating your decision, try to use positive words and, if possible, stress what can be done. Avoid such negatives as "not able," "did not approve," "unfavorable," "does not meet," "must decline." Instead of stressing what is wrong, suggest (whenever possible) how the situation can be improved. Often you can combine resale and constructive alternatives with either the decision or the ending paragraph. In line with circumstances, the applicant may be invited to take one or more of these steps:

1. Come to an office to discuss his case if he has questions or thinks an error has been made
2. Apply again later when conditions have improved
3. Contact another lender or credit agency that you name
4. Use the layaway plan or another suitable credit plan
5. Continue buying from the company on a cash or c.o.d. basis

The ending usually ties in with one of these suggestions and, if possible, includes a reader benefit. Compare the next five examples for methods of handling reasons and for application of other suggestions on credit refusals to consumers.

*Letter 1: No stated reason. A weak and unhelpful retail credit refusal.*

Dear Mr. Roe:

*Buffer:*  We sincerely appreciate your confidence in us as expressed
*appreciation* by your recent credit application.

*Decision*  After careful consideration, we find that at this time it would be better for you to continue your purchases from us on a cash basis.

*Forward*  We hope you will give us frequent opportunities to serve
*look (weak)* you from our wide selection in each of our stores.

*Letter 2: Insufficient-information reason. A popular retail credit refusal inviting a conference as well as cash purchases.*[1]

Dear Mrs. Erson:

*Buffer:*  Thank you for the preference you have shown Bon-Frederick
*thanks*  by your application for a charge account.

*Explanation:* As you know, the usual custom before opening a new account
*insufficient*  is to get information which will serve as a basis for
*information* credit.  Such information as we have thus far obtained is insufficient (or: does not permit us) to pass favorably
*Decision*  upon your request at this time.  If you feel there are other details which would favorably affect your credit, you are welcome to call on us so that we can consider all the
*Suggestions:* facts.
*conference,*
*cash buying* In the meantime, please let us supply your needs on a cash basis.  We will make every effort to serve you well with
*Resale*  high quality merchandise and friendly service.

---

[1] The last paragraph of Letter 2 refers to buying on a cash basis. Because some customers consider this suggestion obvious—maybe even offensive—you can avoid reference to cash by wording the last paragraph in a way similar to that in Letter 3.

**Letter 3:** *List of factors usually considered (general reasons). A popular retail credit refusal inviting reapplication and layaway (with no reference to cash buying).*

Dear Miss Olson:

*Buffer:*
*thanks*

Thank you . . .

for your recent inquiry regarding the status of your credit application.

*Explanation:*
*list of factors*
*considered*

A number of factors are taken into consideration when reviewing an application.  Length of time at one residence and employment are of vital importance to us as well as income, assets, age, number of dependents, and the paying record of current and past obligations.

*Implied*
*decision;*
*assurance and*
*invitation*

You are assured that all of the above available information has been carefully analyzed in your case.  Circumstances may change in the future, at which time we would be pleased to reconsider your new request for credit.

*Invitation to*
*purchase; no*
*mention of*
*cash*

In the meantime, we invite you to save on your household and clothing purchases at Ranney's regular everyday low prices and frequent sales.  Also, of course, you're welcome to use our easy layaway plan for bigger purchases.

**Letter 4:** *Specific reason—inadequate income. An individually typed loan refusal.*

Dear Mr. Lavender:

*Buffer:*
*compliment*
*and*
*consideration*

You are to be complimented on your desire to provide the best possible housing for your family.  We are pleased you have given us the opportunity to consider your loan application for your proposed home purchase.

*Favorable*
*aspects*

Both your loan application and credit report indicate that your interests are centered in your home and family, and you have maintained a steady employment record.  This is all commendable.

*Explanation:*
*reasoning*
*from general*
*to specific*

*Reader-*
*benefit*
*decision*

In mortgage lending, however, extensive studies have revealed that a certain relationship between a person's income, fixed monthly expense, and loan amount should exist to make a loan advisable.  Our maximum loan is two and one-half times the annual income, or payments may not exceed 20 percent of the monthly income.  Since your income at present meets neither of these requirements, you can understand why we feel that an additional financial burden will not serve your best interests.

*Suggestion*

If you would like to stop in my office, I will be glad to go over with you the minimum requirements for a smaller loan. This discussion might help you in setting and planning your desired goal for home ownership. As time goes on and your income increases, you will be able to improve your financial position to the point where we can help you buy a newer and larger home.

*Future help*

Feel welcome to come in any day between 9 and 5. We sincerely want to help you reach your desired goal.

A credit manager can provide helpful "education" to an applicant. For instance, when a charge-account applicant with sufficient income has a miserable poor-pay record, some credit men tactfully state the reason somewhat as follows:

Customarily we make a routine check on credit applicants according to three factors—ability to pay, character, and record of prompt payments. Since you have such a fine record on two of these factors, I know you will want to establish a good-pay reputation too. Lampson's can then gladly reconsider opening an account for you sometime in the future. In the meantime, may we continue to serve you on a cash basis?

Letter 5 is an example of a form letter used by a firm handling a large volume of applications, but which prefers to include more than general reasons for refusal.

**Letter 5:** *Both general list of reasons and specific reasons. A processed form retail credit refusal.*

Dear Customer:

*Thanks*

Thank you for your recent request for a charge account at Berry's.

*Specific reason(s)*
*Decision*

Because of the reasons checked below, we regret that we cannot open an account with you at the present time.

    _____ under age 21
    _____ age not indicated on application
    _____ short time on present job
    _____ unemployed at present time
    _____ unable to verify employment
    _____ application incomplete (returned once to be completed)
    _____ insufficient information for credit bureau to work with
    _____ inadequate response from credit references
    _____ references given are too new to rate
    _____ overextended
    _____ no banking

*Forward look*    When the checked condition is changed, please give us the opportunity to reconsider your application.

*Mercantile Credit Refusals.* Wholesale or mercantile credit is that which is extended by one business firm to another. The preferred organizational pattern for mercantile credit refusals is the bad-news plan.

For the buffer you have choices similar to those used in retail refusals—appreciation, assurance of careful consideration, brief resale on products or services. If the firm sent an order, refer to it only incidentally, because you are not filling it now and should not detract attention from the main concern —credit.

The most noticeable difference between retail and mercantile credit refusals is that the latter are generally more forthright in the reasons for refusal and of course are individually typewritten. The explanation usually states the pertinent facts—first the favorable and then the unfavorable—tactfully but completely. The decision is based on the firm's financial statement plus other credit ratings (by Dun and Bradstreet, special rating agencies, creditors, and sales agencies of the wholesaler or manufacturer considering the applicant). As with retail credit, the emphasis should be on the positive— the desirable goal—rather than on what is wrong now.

Often a refusal can be accompanied by one or more suggestions for reader benefit:

1. Reduction of apparently excessively high inventory by special means
2. Ways to build up customer's volume of sales (and working capital, if pertinent); perhaps offering assistance of your firm's sales representative
3. Advantages of modest buying, local financing, and cash discounts
4. Cash purchases—smaller, more frequent orders
5. Cash on delivery or cash with orders earning discount privilege
6. Review of the applicant's credit situation again at a future time

As always, the message should end with a cordial forward look and, so far as is possible, a promise of cooperation and top-quality service for the reader's benefit.

The following example illustrates an effective mercantile credit refusal to a long-time dealer customer. (For an example of a good refusal to a new dealer customer, see page 20.)

*Letter 6: Temporary refusal of credit to a long-time credit customer.*

Dear Mr. Sydney:

*Buffer:*
*compliment,*
*appreciation*

We value the accounts of our long-time customers highly. Yours has been one of the finest—we have done business together for over eight years. And we want to continue to serve your needs.

| | |
|---|---|
| *Analysis,* *facts* | During the past eighteen months however we have noticed that, instead of discounting your bills with us each month as had always been your policy previously, you have taken the full period and longer. In fact, the last seven payments have been 60 to 90 days late. Though we realize that many of us in the construction industry have been experiencing higher operating costs and fewer new contracts, |
| *Decision* | it is essential to keep accounts receivable current. Thus, as a temporary solution, we can supply your current needs on a cash basis only, until your past statements are paid up and your condition has improved. You will find that smaller orders and the 2% cash discount will be of real value to you in reestablishing your former excellent credit |
| *Suggestion* | standing. |
| *Action,* *resale* | Please let us——or Jim Lang——know how we can help you in any other way. You are assured that we want to cooperate with you. |

## Acknowledging Orders You Can't Fill Now or At All

Whenever you get an order which you cannot fill immediately, your acknowledgment will be at least temporarily bad news to your customer. He is expecting the goods he ordered and any intervening message from you may delay delivery and cause some inconvenience. This section discusses bad-news acknowledgments regarding: incomplete or vague orders, back orders, substitution orders, and diverted or declined orders.

Many firms handle routine and repeat orders by preprocessed forms. These are acceptable when the firm sells catalogued, small, or low-profit items and when the situation does not require much detailed explanation. One common time-saving way to indicate portions of routine orders that cannot be filled as requested is to use rubber-stamped (or typewritten) comments inserted on printed acknowledgments (like the stamped S7 comment regarding a substitution in Letter 1 on page 294).

Though processed form letters are time-savers, they are impersonal and cold. Many times the customer expects or deserves a more detailed explanation. Situations that require personal letters are discussed below.

*Incomplete or Vague Orders.* If an order that omits necessary information comes from a customer who has never before ordered the items in question, you probably have no way of guessing what he wants. It is always better to write him than to risk errors and annoyance. Your main goal is to keep the customer sold on your goods and to get from him whatever is missing so you can fill his order soon.

If the order lists some items that you are sending now, mention them first, of course. If not, begin with a buffer—usually short resale on the product about which the order is incomplete, appreciation for the order, and, if a first

**Letter 1:** *A printed order acknowledgment with stamped comment, used by a national retail mail-order firm.*

| COMPANY NAME OF SELLER | | INVOICE | | |
|---|---|---|---|---|
| Thank you for your order. It received our careful attention. Any changes necessary in filling your order, are explained by stamp impressions or by letters. | Catalog Number     Current Price<br><br>*L5021*     *3.85* | VALUE OF GOODS | | |
| | Catalog Number *L5053* Current Price *4.95* | TAX | | |
| **PLEASE DO NOT DESTROY THESE PAPERS** until you are satisfied that your order is all right in every respect. | (S7) OUR SELECTION IS THE NEAREST TO YOUR | SHIPPING CHARGES | | |
| | CHOICE THAT WE CAN FURNISH. IT IS BETTER | | | |
| **IF YOU WRITE US** about this order, please be sure to return ALL of these papers with your letter. It will help us give you prompt service. | MERCHANDISE AT NO INCREASE IN PRICE. | TOTAL AMOUNT | | |
| **IF YOU RETURN ANY PART** of this order, please glue the envelope containing these papers and your letter to the outside of the package and apply additional mailing postage for the envelope. | This is the amount charged by the Postoffice for C.O.D. service. The Delivering Postmaster also collects a fee to pay for the money order sent to us. You can save the C.O.D. fee expense by including total remittance with future orders. | ←U. S. MAIL C. O. D.—FEE | | |
| | | TOTAL AMOUNT OF C. O. D. | | |

order from a retailer, welcome. Then, before you request the missing information or payment, state a reader-benefit reason—that you want to be sure to send him exactly what he will like best. Shield the reader's pride by omitting such words as "you forgot" or "you failed to." Be sure to include explanatory facts the customer needs to complete his order, such as sizes or color choice available. Include pictures, catalog numbers, sketches, swatches, and other helpful items when appropriate. Make the action easy and clear for him, and assure him of prompt shipment (if true).

Letter 2 handles well a charge customer's special order mailed shortly after she began her three-month vacation in Alaska. She asked the clothing store to rush to her "the 3-piece Adrien cotton suit, size 12," which she had tried on before leaving for her trip. "I'm sure the salesgirl who waited on me will remember," she added. As the store had in stock two styles of Adrien suits in four colors, and as no salesperson recalled the customer's exact choice, the following letter was airmailed to her:

*Letter 2: Acknowledging an incomplete rush-order from a charge customer.*

> Dear Miss Worthington:

|  |  |
|---|---|
| *Buffer:*<br>*resale* | You have made a perfect choice in ordering the fashionable three-piece Adrien suit for your vacation. Smart styling, combined with sophisticated simplicity, gives you a suit you can wear for many activities in Alaska and elsewhere. |
| *Reader-*<br>*benefit*<br>*request*<br><br>*Facts* | So that we may send you the exact suit you have in mind, let's doublecheck on the style and color. The enclosed leaflet pictures the two models available. You may choose each of these suits in pink, aqua, light green, or white. Presently we have your size in all of them. |
| *Easy action* | To help you get your reply to us easily and quickly, we are enclosing a telegram order form addressed to me, with spaces for your choices. Just fill in the model number and color you want and wire it to us collect. Your suit will be sent air express the same day I hear from you. |
| *Prompt*<br>*delivery,*<br>*resale,*<br>*courtesy* | In less than two days you will be enjoying the use of your smart crease- and soil-resistant no-iron Adrien for your pleasure in vacationing and traveling. Thank you for giving us this opportunity to serve you. |

Often incomplete-order acknowledgments are much shorter—perhaps even postcard size. The opening might omit the resale and begin with "Thank you for your order for . . . ." The second paragraph then states the available sizes (or colors or whatever is pertinent); the last paragraph makes action easy and perhaps states a reader benefit.

**Orders for Out-of-stock Items to Be Back-ordered.** If your stock of an ordered item is temporarily depleted and you expect a new shipment within a reasonable time (one or two weeks), you can ordinarily back-order and assume that the customer would rather wait than cancel the order.

As with the incomplete-order acknowledgment, your main goal in the back-order letter is to keep the customer sold on your goods and to serve him well. Because of the necessary delay in waiting for the return of the out-of-stock item, your message should again be organized by the bad-news plan.

Your buffer can be resale on the ordered item (to reinforce the customer's confidence in his choice), appreciation, and (if appropriate) a welcome.

Your explanation should focus on the positive aspects—the date the goods will or can reach the customer. Be sure to omit such negatives as "cannot send," "out of stock," "exhausted," "Won't have any . . . until." Instead, word your idea something like this:

We will be able to ship these parts to you not later than May 15, when our reordered new shipment from the factory is expected here.

Your explanation should preferably include a reason for your being out of the item, so the customer won't think your firm is inefficient. If such reason(s) pertain to high popularity or exceptional demand, they even strengthen your resale and the customer's desire for the item. In your action-getting close, positive suggestion is again useful. The easiest way for the customer to "show" that he approves the back order is to take no action. Thus back-order acknowledgments often include the positive:

Unless you instruct us to the contrary, shipment will be made as soon as we receive the new supplies.

If the wait is likely to be unreasonably long, you should ask the customer to let you know (perhaps by an easy-action reply card) whether he approves of your shipping on the later date. Your emphasis whenever possible should be on acceptance, not cancellation. Sometimes a bit of sales promotion material on seasonal or related goods is appropriate, provided that it is included clearly for the customer's benefit—that is, as a service to him rather than just another sale for your firm.

A short message such as Letter 3 is sufficient on an order for one temporarily out-of-stock item. Letter 4 shows how to mention the same item in a combination order.

**Letter 3:** *Acknowledging an order from a charge customer on an item to be back-ordered.*

Dear Mr. Jones:

| | |
|---|---|
| *Buffer:* *thanks and acknowledgment* | Thank you for your order for one dozen Perkup 26-inch Window Fans, at $32 each. |
| *Resale and explanation* | The demand for this newest three-speed reversible fan has far exceeded our most optimistic expectations at this time of year, with the result that we have twice reordered from the factory. The manufacturer has assured us that our new supply will be delivered within ten days. |
| *Decision:* *expected delivery date* *Reader benefit* | You may plan on receiving a rush shipment of your fans before March 20. Your customers will like the way these automatic thermostatically controlled Perkups enable them to enjoy cool breezes indoors regardless of the heat outdoors. |

*Letter 4:* *Acknowledging a combination order that includes an out-of-stock item to be back-ordered for a business firm (old charge customer).*

Dear Mr. Jones:

*Items shipped*

The following items you ordered March 8 are being shipped to you today by National Motor Freight:

10 Bellam Door Chimes, walnut grain  @ $10.50
 5 Hassock Fans, four-speed, woodtone @  30.95

*Resale and explanation on out-of-stock item; expected delivery date*

Thank you for your order. You can expect to receive the one-dozen top quality Perkup 26-inch Window Fans ($32 each) before March 20. The demand for this newest three-speed reversible fan has far exceeded our most optimistic expectations at this time of year, with the result that we have twice reordered from the factory. The manufacturer has assured us that our new supply will be delivered within ten days.

*Resale*

We will rush your fans to you as soon as they reach us, so that you'll have them a good while before the usual hot weather spells in your area. You can assure your customers that these automatic thermostatically controlled Perkups will enable them to enjoy cool breezes indoors regardless of the heat outdoors.

**Orders for Out-of-stock Items on Which You Suggest a Substitute.** When you get an order for a certain model or brand that you cannot supply soon enough by back-order or that has been discontinued, you can often suggest a substitute—provided you honestly think it will meet the customer's needs.

Usually it is safer to ask permission to substitute before you ship, as in Letter 5, especially if the customer must pay a higher price for the newer line and if the items are breakable or otherwise costly to ship. (Unfortunate shippers who have sent large substitute shipments without permission have sometimes had to pay many dollars in express charges both ways for rejected merchandise returned by a displeased customer.)

*Letter 5:* *Suggesting a substitute in place of an ordered discontinued item.*

Dear Mr. Blount:

*Buffer: thanks and brand resale*

Many thanks for your order on June 27 for a Semco office storage cabinet. You can be sure that your decision to buy a Semco was a decision to buy the finest.

*Explanation for new model (substitute)*

Early this year, in line with businessmen's increasing need for better internal security, the Semco factory came out with a new model storage cabinet, the C-402. Because it has all the features our customers have been

asking for, we now stock this model exclusively.
Though it's possible that George's Supply in North

*Where*
*ordered item*
*might be obtained*

Center may still have the model C-302 you ordered, we
are sure you will want our newest after you check these
improved features of the C-402:

√...HEAVIER GAUGE STEEL than any other cabinet on the
      market assures extra heavy duty for extra safety.
    √...REINFORCED DOORS and BASE provide added
          sturdiness.

*Reader-*
*benefit*
*features of*
*substitute*

      √...A DEPENDABLE YALE LOCK makes the cabinet
            tamper-proof for stored articles.
        √...ADJUSTABLE SHELVES--six of them--allow easy
              storage for almost any size supplies.
          √...NEW COLORS blend with your office decor:
                mint green, fog grey, or walnut-grained
                brown.

For all these advantages the C-402 is inexpensively
priced[1] at only $81.95 delivered to your office.   To

*Easy action*

give me your "OK" for shipment, just call me at
EA 3-9999 any weekday between 8 and 5.  I'll have your
new Semco cabinet on its way to you the same day.

*Reader-*
*benefit*
*resale*

We'll be happy to deliver it on open account giving you
a full 30 days for payment.  You'll be glad you bought
the newest Semco 402.

Letter 5 exemplifies well the desired organization for the substitution
letter. Notice that the buffer begins with appreciation and general resale—
emphasizing the strongest point of reader appeal that the two articles have in
common, namely, the Semco brand. It omits any point of difference (model
number, in this case) between ordered and substitute items.

The explanation and bad-news decision stress what the firm *does* have
instead of what it does not carry. The new substitute—Model 402—is introduced with one of its merits before the bad news that the ordered item—
Model 302—is unavailable. One good way to do this is to state that you now
stock the substitute exclusively. (It is psychologically inadvisable to actually
use the word "substitute" in your letter because of its negative connotation.)
If the substitute is a different brand instead of merely a new model of the
same brand (as in Letter 6), do not mention the ordered item by brand name
more than once (or at all), because you want the reader to focus attention on
your product. However, don't knock your competitor's product; sell your
product on its own merits. You can mention where the ordered product may

---

[1] Instead of "is inexpensively priced at" you might write "is well worth the small additional $5," or
"is an excellent value even at $5 more than the older model," if you think your reader would
appreciate knowing the price difference.

be obtained, but subordinate your statement in a dependent clause, as in Letter 5. If the price of the substitute is higher, be sure to state adequate selling points to justify the difference. If your substitute is lower in quality but an excellent value because of price or other reasons, stress these benefits.

Your ending paragraph asks for authorization to send the substitute—or tells why you have already sent it, as in Letter 6. In the latter case, make clear that the item comes to the customer on trial or subject to his approval. Although you are safer to get approval before sending a substitute, many sellers (such as mail-order firms) substitute quite regularly in orders from repeat customers whose preferences they know. Sometimes substitution is also made in rush orders for very similar same-price inexpensive items or when the company absorbs the price difference. The writer of Letter 6 mailed the substitute because it was identical to the customer's order in every way except the print, and he felt sure this buyer would like the one sent.

*Letter 6: Sending a substitute before asking permission.*

Dear Mr. Jake:

*Buffer: thanks*

Thank you for your order of May 20 for a Hailani Hawaiian sport shirt, size 40.

*Facts about the substitute*

We are sending you today by parcel post a Hailani shirt of the same high quality, casual style, and bright colors as the one you specified. Though the printed design on the fabric is a little different from the one you described, we feel sure you'll be delighted with it as soon as you see it.

*Resale*

As you know, one of the distinctive features of Hailani Sportswear is the great variety of fascinating exotic prints, with only a few in each size. We are fortunate to have the gay "tropic garden" pattern in your size. It is

*Return privilege*

being sent to you on your account for your approval, of course, on a money-back guarantee.

*Resale*

You'll appreciate this wash-and-wear shirt, we're certain, on many carefree days this summer.

**Orders That Must Be Diverted or Declined.** Some orders you will have to divert or refuse because the customer has come through the wrong marketing channel, he does not meet your standards as to payment or other requirements, or he has ordered goods or services that you cannot supply in time for his needs.

For instance, if your firm is a manufacturer or a wholesaler and you cannot sell to an ultimate consumer, your refusal should preferably keep this consumer's goodwill. Convince him to buy your products where he should—from your authorized dealers. Your buffer thus will be basically resale, to build the customer's confidence in his choice of product or brand. Your explanation will give reader-benefit reasons for your merchandising policy—stressing how you do market your products (exclusively through authorized dealers) instead of how you don't. Make your refusal clear and combine it with a reader benefit. Among consumer benefits for local dealerships are:

> Customer's privilege to see all goods before buying
> Faster deliveries
> Lower shipping costs—or none
> Personal services

Provide for easy action, by returning any check the reader sent you and including names and addresses of nearby dealers plus a reassuring statement about them. A last reader benefit bit of resale will help keep him sold on the product and encourage him to buy it.

*Letter 7: Diverting a consumer's order from the factory to an authorized dealer.*

Yes, Mr. Janetti,

*Buffer resale*

all those nice compliments you've heard about TOWER musical instruments are true. And you're right to insist on buying a TOWER for the first--and every--guitar you own.

*Explanation for local marketing*

One of the reasons that so many musicians are enthusiastic over their TOWER instruments is the special individual care they received before selecting just the right guitar for their own particular preferences. This is why we market all TOWER instruments exclusively through authorized music stores instead of by mail from our factory.

*Easy action*

The name and address of the authorized music shop that handles all TOWER products in your city is:

> Polk Music Supply House
> 422 Broadway East

*Reader benefit*

Any of their experienced music representatives will gladly show you the different styles and sizes of TOWER guitars. They range from the slim, fast-action flat-top guitars to the mellow-sounding classic-type and electric guitars.

*Motivation to action*

So that you can select your favorite personally, we are returning your check. Do stop in at Polk's soon--to hear, feel, and buy the TOWER guitar you like best.

There are times when you must refuse an order because you have no other choice. If you cannot supply the customer's needs now but want him to return to you for future orders, you will of course include resale on your product or service. In addition you will mention where the customer can get what he urgently needs now—*if* you think such suggestion will be helpful. For instance, a hotel manager can mention to out-of-town customers other hotels (competitors) if his own hotel will be filled during a certain weekend. However, he should also include some resale on his own hotel and invite the customer to stay there on his next visit to the city. In contrast, the orchard owner in the situation handled by Letter 8 finds it both unnecessary and unfeasible to mention where his repeat customer might buy apples elsewhere. Instead, he concentrates on reselling his own apples.

*Letter 8: Refusing an order from an orchard's repeat mail-order customer.*

Dear Mrs. Christopher:

*Thanks and resale*
Thank you for your order of one crate of Wilfred Orchard's red delicious apples. We are pleased that the popularity of our fruit extends into the Eastern states to good customers like you.

*Resale and reason*
As a steady customer for five years, you understand the care we take in shipping our fruit nationwide. You may have heard that eastern Washington experienced a heavy storm during blossomtime, and an unusually cool summer. As a result, the fruit in our orchards is not up to the quality you have a right to expect. Therefore, I am

*Decision*
returning your check at this time.

*Forward look and resale*
Next year I will notify you when the apple crop is ready. Then you can order the delicious apples you and your friends have enjoyed in the past.

## Declining Requests for Favors and Invitations

Customers, noncustomers, and employees may request various privileges or favors, other than information, which you have to refuse. The bad-news plan is usually the safest to use in most favor refusals. However, in some instances you may use the direct plan, placing the refusal in the first paragraph. This section illustrates a variety of favor refusals, both business-related and personal.

*Declining Business-related Favors.* Among the numerous favors that customers ask and that you may have to refuse are: changing requirements or payment due dates, transferring from one type of account to another, seeing your firm's confidential material, getting special reduced rates, or skipping several payments on a contract (as handled by Letter 1 below).

**Letter 1:** *A loan officer refuses a customer's request to skip several loan payments.*

Dear Mr. Howe:

*Buffer:*
*thanks*

Thank you for telling us your viewpoint regarding your loan payments during the summer.

*Explanation*
*and appeal*
*to fair play*

Accommodating customers is one of our main objectives. This service involves fair treatment to every borrower with accepted business practice that also protects the invest-ments of our depositors. Exceptions granted to one cus-tomer could rightfully be expected of others too, and thus eventually disrupt the entire credit structure. Therefore, the long-established rule is that all payments not made within ten days of the due date are subject to an added "late payment" charge. When a loan becomes 90 days past due, the law requires that foreclosure action be started.

*Implied*
*refusal*

Mr. Howe, when you obtained the loan last December, you agreed to repay it in regular monthly payments. Though you were a schoolteacher then there is no indication in our file that you requested any deviation from the usual 12-month payment schedule. Because most of the high school teachers in this area get their salary each of 12 months, we assumed the same was true for you. However, even on a 9-month basis you, as a teacher, know in advance that you will receive no paychecks during the summer. Many other people have little or no advance indication when their source of income will cease.

*Reader-*
*benefit*
*suggestion*

The enclosed leaflet was prepared for persons who need to allocate earnings over a 12-month period. You will find it useful, I believe. For the present, you will save the late-payment surcharge if your check reaches us by June 10.

*Action*
*request*

If you feel that mailing your June check before that due date would impose an extreme hardship on you, please call me at CA 2-7222. At that time we can make an appointment so that we can work out your problem with you.

When your firm offers free booklets or other premiums in its advertising, you may need to write bad-news replies after the supply is exhausted (Letter 2).

**Letter 2:** *A courteous processed form refusal regarding an out-of-stock booklet offered in advertising.*

Dear Angler:

*Buffer:*
*thanks*

Thank you for writing for copies of the 197_ Shakesville fishing booklets.

*Reason* The demand for these popular booklets far exceeded our expectations and, unfortunately, exhausted what was thought to be a plentiful supply. Since many new tackle items will be introduced at the start of Shakesville's new fiscal *Implied* year, August 1, it is impractical to reprint the booklets *refusal;* at this time. However, we are pleased to enclose for you a *alternative* few helpful hints on this year's Shakesville tackle.

*Reader-* Your name will be held in a special list of anglers who *benefit* will receive "Hot-off-the-Press" booklets on the new year *suggestion* line of Shakesville tackle as soon as they are printed.

When you must refuse to lend your company's supplies or premises or other valuables, you should also use the bad-news plan (Letter 3). Remember to consider your reader's feelings and be as helpful as possible.

*Letter 3: A tactful goodwill-building refusal to lend a bank's lounge and parking facilities for a Cub Scout area meeting.*

Dear Mrs. Vogt:

*Buffer:* Your letter extending us the opportunity to contribute to *appreciation,* the activities of your Cub Scout group is warmly received. *agreement,* As a Den Mother, you surely must share our high esteem for *compliment* scouting and all it stands for.

*Reasons* On November 20, the date of your scheduled meeting, our Main Office will host a group of visiting bank managers and board members from throughout Illinois, Missouri, and Indiana. Thus, for most of that day our lounge will be *Implied* filled with businessmen. May I suggest, however, an *refusal* alternative location for your meeting.

*Suggestion* When I spoke to my friend, James Scott, building manager of the Lakeside Eagles, about your needs he said he could offer their hall November 20. The room is large enough to easily accommodate 40 to 50 scouts and chaperones, and parking space is adequate. Mr. Scott suggests that you phone him soon (AT 3-9992) weekdays between 7 a.m. and *Easy action* 4 p.m. to confirm your plans and discuss necessary details.

*Cooperation* You may be assured that we at First National are sincere in *and good* our desire to help you and your group whenever we can. *wishes* Best of success always with your group of scouts!

On somewhat routine matters between departments of the same firm it is quite permissible to begin directly with the bad-news decision, as in Letter 4:

**Letter 4 (memo):** *An acceptable first-paragraph refusal of a specification change; message between two departments of a commercial airplane manufacturer*

To:      J. R. Lander

From:    T. M. Jepson

Subject: <u>Food</u> <u>and</u> <u>Beverage</u> <u>Elevator</u>

Reference: RPD-5244-12 dated 6-15-7_

*Refusal*   As shown on page 5 of the specifications, paneling for elevator walls remains a valid requirement. Thus the referenced request to use paint instead of vinyl paneling is unacceptable.

*Explanation*   Because of the particular uses for this elevator and the expected altitudes for flights, it is necessary that all walls have the extra protection of the exact vinyl as in the specifications instead of mere coats of paint.

*Request*   Will you please, therefore, see that the paneling requirement is met, according to specifications.

**Declining Nonbusiness and Personal Favors.** Requests concerning nonbusiness activities may involve donations of your time, money, property, or other assistance. In refusing a nonbusiness favor, include an appropriate buffer, reason(s) before your decision, and (if possible) a helpful suggestion.

**Letter 5:** *A refusal to accept the office of regional director.*

Dear Jim:

*Buffer: agreement, compliment, appreciation*   XYZ Club has a great deal to offer for both businessmen and women. I've always found it worthwhile. And so I appreciate even more the compliment you expressed in nominating me for the office of Regional Director.

*Reasons*   To perform this job adequately, I realize I should travel to the three State Days this coming year and to correspond regularly each month with the 22 chapters in this region, before sending monthly reports to our national office.

*Implied refusal; emphasis on positive*   I've given your invitation a good deal of thought, in the light of my present responsibilities as executive trainee at the ABC Company here. My job requires that I devote long hours to the program daily. Often I work Saturdays too. In addition, Sally and our 3-month-old son have also been very demanding on my time. Considering everything, I'm convinced the job would be better filled by someone else for the coming year.

*Suggestion*  If you'd like a suggestion, you might find Herbert J. Smith would be interested in this type of chapter office. He's been active in XYZ for 10 years, two of them as our excellent president. He's an established accountant at the National Gadget Company and is unmarried. Herb enjoys being involved and in my opinion would be a perfect regional man. I'm enclosing a card with Herb's address in case you would like to contact him.

*Cordial wishes*  You have my best wishes, Jim, for getting the right man. You're doing a terrific job for the organization.

At times you may honestly feel that a request is extremely unreasonable and you're tempted to tell the reader so. If you must get some negative thoughts off your chest, go ahead and write the grumpy letter. But don't mail it immediately. Chances are that the next day you'll decide to soften the tone (which writer of Letter 6 didn't do but should have done, as in Letter 7).

*Letter 6: Untactful refusal from a manager of a marketing research firm to a college student.*[1]

Dear Mr. Durft:

I have your request for advice and booklets regarding the practices and experiences of this Company in consumer research and market testing. You list seven questions, each of which is so broad in scope that an adequate answer would require at least a written chapter. A comprehensive answer to all seven questions would comprise a thesis on marketing research. I would like to ask you a few questions:

1. Do students think a manufacturing company has any responsibility to contribute to their education? Do they think the company should help students prepare their thesis for the sake of building goodwill? or for securing a possible future customer?

2. If an affirmative answer is given to #1, what do students regard as a reasonable amount of cooperation?
   a. To check a few Yes or No questions?
   b. To furnish available and pertinent literature if available?
   c. To write a dissertation for them on one subject? on seven subjects?
   d. To write a thesis for them?
   e. To teach them by mail?

[1] Though Letter 6 (which was actually mailed) is untactful, its questions may deserve serious consideration by those who seek detailed information. Requests like "Please give us information about all the goods you sell" are so broad that they are impossible to fulfill.

3. Do university instructors advise their students to request commercial companies to contribute their knowledge of market research to the students? Can not your instructors answer most of the questions you ask? For example, you ask "What effect do consumers' desires and needs have on the adoption of specifications and designs for a product? Is this not in your textbook, or can it not be answered by your instructor?

4. If the answer to #3 is affirmative, how do university instructors think commercial companies would justify the time and expense involved in writing educational material for students in answer to specific but broad scope questions?

You need not answer the above questions nor reply to this letter. My questions are rhetorical and I have no intention of writing a reply to your questions. My contribution to your education is this letter and in my opinion it should be more valuable to you than an answer to your questions would be.

*Letter 7: An improved version of Letter 6.*

Dear Mr. Durft:

*Buffer: thanks*

Thank you for your interest in our practices and experiences in consumer research and market testing.

*Desire to help Decision*

We definitely want to share with you this requested information, and it's possible to do so if you limit yourself to specific questions which permit answering in a few minutes. Preferably a questionnaire form that allows us to fill in *Alternative* answers seems to be the best format. The seven questions you submitted to us are so broad in scope that each one requires a lengthy reply to cover the subject adequately.

*Suggested action and reader benefit*

Please send your one- or two-page questionnaire to Mr. Michael Leach, vice president of research in our organization. He is our authority on consumer research and market testing. Since he will not be starting on his three-week survey trip for another month, he will probably have time to fill out and mail your material to you the same day he hears from you.

## Turning Down Contract or Work Offers

Grouped in this category are the refusals you may have to write to business firms, clubs, and individuals that propose various jobs and services for a fee. Letter 1 illustrates a refusal to enter a bid on a business firm's project; Letter 2 turns down a nonprofit organization's idea for raising money. Both use the bad-news plan. Refusals by and to individual job applicants are covered in

Chapter 11, Job Applications. Letters of resignation are discussed in the section on bad-news announcements, pages 315–316.

*Letter 1: Declining to bid on a construction job.*

Dear Mr. Edgars:

*Buffer*    Thank you for the opportunity to bid on the plumbing work for the 50 homes in the Highland Park development.

*Reason*    Because of other large commitments we have lined up for the coming year, our time schedule is such that we must reluctantly pass up the opportunity to compete on your job
*Refusal*   this time.

*Suggestion*  Please keep us on your list for your next project. Best
*and cordial* wishes for your satisfactory completion of the Highland
*close*     Park plan in time for occupancy next fall.

*Letter 2: Refusing a nonprofit organization's proposal to earn funds by subcontracting services for an out-of-state management corporation. (Letter was mailed to the president of a university business honorary.)*

Dear Ed:

We appreciate very much your letter inquiring about the
*Buffer*    possibility that Milton Management Corporation might be able to subcontract some of our handwork through your chapter.

Ed, if we were to ship any of our large mailings to your city from St. Louis in order for your chapter to complete the necessary work, we would encounter many difficulties. To give you an example, an annual report mailing for Milton Funds weighs approximately 18 tons. You might also be
*Explanation* interested to know that we no longer mail our annual and semi-annual reports in envelopes because of the terrific expense involved with hand-stuffing. We now pack each report in a polyethylene bag which is electronically sealed, thus saving us a considerable amount of money each year.

I do want to assure you that your request for obtaining work from our corporation has been given very careful consideration; but because of the distance involved between
*Refusal*   our Home Office and your University, it is not feasible. You might contact some of your larger printing companies or firms that do mailings in your local area and subcontract work from them. You might also consider such fund raising
*Suggestions* projects as tuition dances, car washes or bingo games.

*Forward*   With your good leadership and your chapter's cooperation,
*look*      you will surely reach your very commendable goal.

## UNFAVORABLE UNSOLICITED MESSAGES

You may sometimes have to send unpleasant messages which are not in response to an inquiry. This section illustrates unfavorable announcements about prices and services, orders and deposits, rules and procedures, plus miscellaneous bad news. You are generally wise to use the bad-news plan whenever you think your readers will be seriously disappointed or even angered by your bad news. However, when you write to employees or other business associates on routine matters, you may use the direct plan.

### Announcing Bad News about Prices and/or Services

When your firm finds it necessary to increase prices and/or curtail services to customers, a buffer opening followed by reasons before the unhappy decision will help break the news gently, as in Letters 1 and 2.

*Letter 1: A well-written bad-news announcement about a laundry's increased prices.*

Dear TRIM customer:

*Buffer: comment*

Yes, "Times have changed!" A quarter century ago when TRIM first started lending homemakers a hand with the family laundry, you could buy good quality ladies' blouses or men's shirts for two or three dollars. Now they cost six to ten dollars.

*Reasons*

During the same period soap prices rose from 15 to 59 cents a package and wrapping paper from 6 to 27 cents a roll. Wages too have at least tripled in many instances. To continue giving our customers high quality service, we too had to increase our prices twice, the last one eight years ago. In the meantime, all these and other items—taxes and costs we cannot control—have also risen substantially.

*Reasons*

So that we can continue to assure you the same twice-a-week pickup and delivery service with the same top standards of careful laundering and cleaning of your clothing, our new prices will go into effect as listed on the enclosed card.

*Decision*

The starting date is May 1, 197_.

*Forward look; resale*

You can count on TRIM to do everything possible to continue giving you the same high quality service you have enjoyed through the years. We appreciate your confidence and your patronage.

*Letter 2:* *A clear, acceptable announcement by a wholesaler regarding limitations in services.*

TO OUR CUSTOMERS:

*Buffer:*
*neutral*
*courtesy*

In reviewing 197_ business and trying to plan for a future in which we can continue to give you good service, it has become evident that some modifications must be made.

*Reasons*

Our problems are not unlike yours or anyone else's in business today. All items of expense in business have been constantly increasing without a corresponding increase in profit margin on goods and services. Rather than increase prices in general, the following changes as an alternate plan will become effective July 1 this year:

*Decision*

(1) Free local delivery will be continued only on orders of at least $15. Orders for a lesser amount, if received by 1 p.m. can be delivered the next business day by United Parcel Service or can be sent by our regular delivery service if the customer wishes; but the actual cost of this service will be added to the invoice.

*Details*
*on the*
*decision*

(2) Out-of-town shipments will continue to be shipped as instructed by the customer, or instead of instructions, will be routed by the least expensive of Parcel Post, United Parcel Service or Auto Freight. Actual shipping costs will be added to the invoice.

(3) Collect telephone calls will be accepted only in cases where we have been in error.

*Fairness to*
*customers;*
*courteous*
*invitation*

A decision on these three changes was made after a very careful analysis of our costs in relation to service. We are sure you will agree that these changes are minimal and fair to our customers. If you have any suggestions on how we may improve our service to you, we will greatly appreciate your writing or calling us right now.

In contrast to the *buffer openings* of Letters 1 and 2 to customers, you can use *bad-news direct-approach openings* similar to the following when you announce the same decisions in memos to your employees. The first is an opening for a memo about the laundry's increased prices:

Because of increased costs of all materials and operations, TRIM now finds it necessary to increase prices of laundry services. The following new prices will go into effect for all customers May 1, 197_:

And an opening for a memo about the wholesaler's limited services might be:

So that Gray's can continue to give good service without a general increase in prices to our customers, the following restrictions in delivery and telephone services will become effective July 1 this year:

Even for employees, however, you should follow the bad-news plan and begin with a buffer when they are likely to be personally affected or seriously disappointed by your bad-news decision. Suppose, for instance, that your company management has decided to close the employee cafeteria food service mornings and evenings and to keep it open only during noon hours. To partially offset this decrease and to provide for changing employee food preferences, the snack-bar service will be increased. Letter 3 illustrates a poor way to announce these changes to employees; Letter 4, a good way. Notice the difference even in subject lines.

*Letter 3 (memo): A poor, negative, incomplete bad-news announcement to employees about decreased cafeteria service; direct plan.*

TO:       All employees of ABC          January 25, 197_

FROM:     Thomas Whitson, Food Services Director

SUBJECT:  <u>Closing of Cafeteria for Breakfasts and Suppers</u>

Starting next Monday, February 1, there will be no more break-fasts or suppers served in the cafeteria.  This facility will hereafter be closed every morning and afternoon.  Lunches will be served in the cafeteria only between 11 and 2 p.m.

However, to provide continuing service to our employees, the snack bar will be open from 8 a.m. to 5:45 p.m. and offer a wider selection of food.

*Letter 4 (memo): An improved version of the preceding bad-news announcement to employees; indirect plan.*

TO:       All employees of ABC          January 25, 197_

FROM:     Thomas Whitson, Food Services Director

SUBJECT:  <u>Changes in Company Snack Bar and Cafeteria Service</u>

*Buffer:*    To keep food prices at their present level, in spite of
*reader-benefit* rising costs, and to meet your changing needs—the snack
*noncommittal* bar and cafeteria services will be modified <u>starting</u>
*statement*    <u>Monday, February 1.</u>

*Reasons*

Changes are necessary because during the past three years
fewer employees have been eating breakfasts and suppers in
the cafeteria, and costs of operating it have steadily
increased.  So that you can continue to benefit from both

*Employee benefits*

low prices and good quality food, we are altering the
services and we believe you will like them.

*Decision: favorable changes first*

Snack Bar Services--The snack bar will be expanded to
offer a wider selection of food than ever before.  From
the semi-self-service counter and the vending machines you
can choose:

| | | |
|---|---|---|
| Packaged cereals | Fruits and Juices | Sandwiches |
| Doughnuts | Soft Drinks | Hamburgers |
| Rolls | Ice Cream | Salads |
| Coffee, Tea, Milk | Pies and Cakes | Potato chips |
| Hot Chocolate | Candy Bars | Soup |

*Decision: emphasis on the positive*

Cafeteria Service--Each day a lunch special consisting of
a hot main course, salad, dessert, and drink will be
served, as before, for less than $1.  The cafeteria will
serve only lunches.

New Hours--The new hours effective February 1 are:
Snack Bar      -      8 a.m. - 5:45 p.m.
Cafeteria      -      11 a.m. - 2:00 p.m.

*Employee benefits*

In addition, the cafeteria doors will remain open, however, between 8 a.m. and 6 p.m. for those of you wishing
a meeting place during work breaks or to enjoy food
brought from home or the snack bar.

*Forward look; employee benefits and invited action*

You are invited to use these facilities whenever you can.
They are available to you at no extra price on snacks or
lunches.  If you have any suggestions on the new cafeteria
or snack bar services, please jot them on a slip of paper
and drop them into the Suggestion Box at the cafeteria
door.

Occasionally for a relatively small matter you can put across a bad-news
decision effectively by using good-natured humor:

**Letter 5 (memo):** *Humorous announcement of a price rise.*

TO:      All employees

FROM:    Cafeteria Management

SUBJECT: An Invitation to a Funeral Service

*Sad(?) news*

On Friday, September 30, 197_, your company cafeteria will
bury a very dear servant, a veteran of 20 years whom most
of you enjoy every day.

*Details*     There will be no music, no solemn ovations, no (we hope) violent outbursts of emotion.  Instead, there will be FREE COFFEE for everyone in the cafeteria during the lunch period September 30.  We hope you will attend the last

*Decision*    rites of the seven-cent cup of coffee.  On Monday, October 3, the price will rise to ten cents.  It has been decided that coffee service should no longer be subsidized and the current cost of producing and selling a cup of coffee is more than seven cents.

*A happy*    We're sorry.  We loved that seven-cent cup of coffee too.
*thought*    But here is a cheery thought:  Your pennies still buy more when you use them in your company cafeteria!

## Requiring Minimum Orders and/or Deposits

At times you may need to tell a customer that he must either give your firm more business or lose his former privileges. For instance, a manufacturer may require his authorized distributors to sell at least a certain minimum amount or lose their franchise; a retailer may discontinue sending free catalogs if he does not receive orders; a publisher may want to cut costs by decreasing the length of his "free" mailing list; and a bank may have to announce bad news about minimum balances on dormant savings accounts. For such messages the bad-news plan is advisable. Letter 1 erroneously follows the direct plan, while Letter 2 correctly uses a buffer.

*Letter 1: A poor bad-news announcement from a large producer of fully prepared baking mixes to a wholesale firm.*

Gentlemen:

We are sorry to see that your business with us has fallen down so that it does not pay to have you on our books any more, as we can only afford to have accounts on our books who sell merchandise right along.

We appreciate the Alaskan situation where it is seasonal buying, but your business has fallen off so that now there is practically nothing.

We would appreciate a line from you as to whether you think you could build this business up, or whether it would be best for all concerned for us to discontinue your company as one of our jobbers.

Will you please advise us by return mail so we will know what to do.

**Letter 2:** *An improved version of Letter 1 (asking a wholesaler to increase his orders or drop off the list).*

Gentlemen:

*Buffer:*
*favorable*
*past*

In the past five years we have had the pleasure of filling your orders for prepared baking mixes. We have also appreciated the prompt manner in which you have always paid your account.

*Explanation:*
*minimums*
*and reasons*

When you first started trading with us, we extended jobbers' prices to you—on the condition that a minimum amount of merchandise be bought during the year. Setting our price structure on this minimum for jobbers enables us to sell at lower prices. In spite of seasonal buying from Alaskan customers, you have in the past sold the product well.

*Concern;*
*implied bad*
*news*

*Suggestions*

Because during the last year your purchases fell far short of the agreed minimum of $500, we are concerned about ways that we might help you, rather than assigning your territory to another jobber. Pasty Cake Mixes are nationally advertised to help create a demand at grocery stores, and orders should be flowing your way. Housewives use cake mixes the year 'round. Perhaps you would like to work out with our representative, Bill Hempstead, a special plan adapted to your particular situation. During the busy summer season your volume could be higher to offset the decreased size of orders during the slack winter months.

*Requested*
*action*
*and implied*
*decision*

Will you please let us know, in the enclosed envelope, within a week if you plan to continue to represent Pasty Cake Mixes. We want to have your firm distribute our products provided you meet your jobber's quota regularly.

## Penalizing for Nonconformity with Rules or Procedures

Announcements about penalties for deviating from required procedures or disregarding previous notices quite often begin with the bad news. The direct plan should be used, especially when the situation is urgent or when the writer wants the reader to be sure to read the main idea, as in Letters 1 and 2.

**Letter 1 (memo):** *Notification about service fees on checks returned by banks.*

TO:        All employees

FROM:      Comptroller

SUBJECT:   <u>Service Fee on Checks Returned to the Company</u>
           <u>by Banks</u>

*Bad news*   The Board of Directors has approved the following schedule of service charges to be assessed—starting October 1, 197_—for each check returned unpaid from banks because of insufficient funds, accounts closed, or any other error that is the fault of the maker:

*Details*

| Time of Payment | Service Charge |
|---|---|
| Within first 7 days after date of notice | $2.00 |
| Within 8 to 14 days after date of notice | $3.00 |
| Fifteen days or more after date of notice | $5.00 |

When a check is returned to the Comptroller's Office by the bank, a notice will be prepared at the appropriate department and sent to the maker of the check. The date of the notice will represent the starting point for determination of service charge.

**Letter 2:** *A reader-benefit bad-news (processed) announcement regarding an inactive savings account.*

Dear Saver

*Main idea*   It is my duty to discuss with you a federal ruling that will drastically affect the status of your inactive account #111-1111.

*Explanation*   Effective August 28 of this year, federal regulations governing our operations were revised with respect to a service charge on inactive savings accounts of less than $10. We are now permitted to charge $1 each year to maintain each account that has not been used in the last three

*Decision*   years. As you realize, this minimum charge permits an association to just about break even financially in maintaining these small inactive accounts year after year.

*Suggestion*   May I suggest that you arrange to convert your account into an active one before (date) so that you earn a high 5% dividend with complete safety of your money. By doing so, you also avoid the $1 yearly charge on an inactive account. But, if you do not wish to add to this account, then you should close it immediately to avoid this charge.

*Pleasant close*   Please come in or call me at 222-2222 if you have any question concerning your account. We are here to serve you.

## Conveying Other Bad News

You may have to write other bad-news unsolicited (and solicited) messages. As a rule, you can handle most of them well by the bad-news plan.

However, one situation that is an exception to the usual rule for customer bad-news letters is when you must announce that you made a mistake which is not in the customer's favor. In such cases it is often better to admit your error in the opening, as in the next example.

*Letter 1: Announcement of an error that unfavorably affects the reader.*

Dear Mr. Sunday:

*Tactful lead to bad news*

We always appreciate the opportunity to be of service to our customers, but I'm sorry to tell you that last month we did you—and ourselves—a disservice.

*Details*

The correct amount of your February, 197_ premium was $125.61, and we billed you for only $120.55, a difference of $5.06. We overlooked the difference in insurance premium between your former policy and the new policy which has given you additional coverage since January 1.

*Request and easy action*

May we ask you to sign the attached form and send it to us with your check for $5.06? Just slip it into the enclosed envelope and mail it.

*Goodwill*

You can be sure we'll do our best to see that you get accurate service in the future.

Another bad-news announcement you may have to write is the letter of resignation. Whether you resign from a job for which you have been paid or from an elective office, you consider your reader(s) and your relationship to them before you decide to organize by the direct or indirect plan. Your letter should include your reason for resigning (ill health, better position, etc.), appreciation and pleasant comments about the people you are leaving, perhaps a statement of regret, a definite effective date for the resignation, and a sincere cordial ending. The following two letters of resignation are both well written. In Letter 2 the writer felt that the busy board of directors would prefer reading the main idea (though it is bad news) in the first paragraph. Letter 3 gives the bad news *after* the reasons.

*Letter 2: A direct-plan letter of resignation (to a board of directors).*

Gentlemen:

*Main idea: bad news*

With much reluctance and regret I must ask to be released from my position of State Director of Civil Defense.

*Reason*

Because I have developed a heart condition, my doctors have instructed me to move on a slow bell and particularly emphasized my giving up Civil Defense. While the condition is not dangerous at present, it is of the "warning" type.

## CAPSULE CHECKLISTS FOR

### I
### Bad News

| General plan (A) (indirect) | Exception (B)† (direct) |
|---|---|
| 1. BUFFER<br>  a. Agreement<br>  b. Appreciation<br>  c. Assurance<br>  d. Compliment<br>  e. Cooperation<br>  f. Good news<br>  g. Neutral courtesy<br>  h. Resale<br>  i. Sympathy<br>  j. Understanding | 1. Main idea<br>  a. Bad-news decision, some times with a brief buffer and/or reason |
| 2. EXPLANATION<br>  a. Necessary details—general to specific<br>  b. Pertinent, tactful favorable then unfavorable facts<br>  c. RB[4] reasons<br>  d. Emphasis on desired goal | 2. Explanation<br>Same as I, A, 2, usually a and d |
| 3. DECISION—implied or expressed<br>  a. Imbedded statement of bad news—clear, tactful, positive, (what CAN do), concise; often tied to 4 (suggestion) | 3. Decision omitted (already in I, B, 1) |
| 4. RESALE AND/OR CONSTRUCTIVE SUGGESTIONS<br>  a. Helpful counterproposal, plans, alternates<br>  b. Resale<br>  c. Sales promotion | 4. Resale and suggestions often unnecessary and omitted; sometimes same as I, A, 4, a |
| 5. POSITIVE, FRIENDLY APPROPRIATE CLOSE<br>  a. Appreciation<br>  b. Invitation to future action<br>  c. CSAD[1]<br>  d. EA and motivation[2]<br>  e. DA[3]<br>  f. Willingness to help further<br>  g. RB[4]<br>  h. Good wishes<br>  i. Courtesy | 5. Positive, friendly appropriate close<br>Sometimes same as I, A, 5, a through i |

[1] CSAD = clear statement of action desired
[2] EA = easy action
[3] DA = dated action, if desirable
[4] RB = reader benefit

See also pages 29 and 92, discussing complete action requests and the five W's

## BAD-NEWS MESSAGES*

---

*II*

*Answering Inquiries When the Information Is Unfavorable*

| Sales-related (C) | Nonsales inquiries (D) |
|---|---|
| 1. Buffer<br>  a. Appreciation<br>  b. Assurance<br>  c. Resale<br>  d. Understanding | 1. Buffer<br>Same as II, C, 1, a-d, for non-sales inquiries except unfavorable recommendations; for the latter:<br>  a. Inclusion (or omission) of applicant's name, relationship to you<br>  b. Reason for writing |
| 2. Explanation<br>  a. Answers to all questions<br>  b. Pertinent facts and details<br>  c. RB reasons for company policy | 2. Explanation<br>  a. Answers to all questions<br>  b. Pertinent facts (favorable and unfavorable)—record, duties, habits<br>  c. Caution on legal aspects<br>  d. Establishment of confidential nature |
| 3. Decision<br>Same as I, A, 3, a | 3. Decision<br>  a. Frank, honest statement on nonendorsement of candidate |
| 4. Resale and/or suggestions<br>  a. Ideas for getting needed help<br>  b. Possible future changes<br>  c. Resale on firm, products, services if appropriate | 4. Constructive suggestions<br>  a. Possibility of intervening changes since you last saw applicant |
| 5. Positive, friendly close<br>  a. Good wishes<br>  b. Appreciation<br>  c. CSAD[1]<br>  d. Willingness to help further | 5. Positive, friendly close<br>  a. Ray of hope for improvement<br>  b. Willingness to help further<br>  c. Good wishes |

---

\* All lists include possible content. For any one message, choose only pertinent and appropriate items.

† For uses of direct plan, see page 273.

**CAPSULE CHECKLISTS FOR**

| *III* | *IV* |
|---|---|
| *Refusing Adjustments on Claims and Complaints* | *Declining Requests for Favors and Invitations* |

| | |
|---|---|
| 1. Buffer<br>   a. Agreement on something<br>   b. Appreciation<br>   c. Assurance<br>   d. Cooperation<br>   e. Neutral courtesy<br>   f. Understanding<br>   g. If granting part of a claim is good news, opening is on the portion granted | 1. Buffer<br>   a. Appreciation<br>   b. Compliment (to reader)<br>   c. Assurance<br>   d. Agreeable comment |
| 2. Explanation<br>   a. Tactful, logical statements of reasons<br>   b. General RB[4] procedure, policy, instructions, guarantee<br>   c. Resale interwoven<br>   d. Education on product use<br>   e. Impersonal specific facts about buyer's mistake | 2. Explanation<br>   a. Facts and (sometimes personal) reasons leading to refusal |
| 3. Decision<br>   a. Impersonal, expressed or implied, but clear refusal in positive language, perhaps tied with 4 (below)<br>   b. Clear indication if you are returning the product | 3. Decision<br>   a. Clear, tactful decision, implied or stated; emphasis on the positive aspects (desire to help, etc.) |
| 4. Resale and/or constructive suggestions<br>   a. RB,[4] constructive suggestion(s) for using rejected product or selecting another<br>   b. Resale on the product, service, and/or firm | 4. Resale and/or suggestions<br>   a. RB, suggestions—when, how you *can* help<br>   b. Alternate sources of help to reader |
| 5. Positive, friendly close<br>   a. CSAD (tactful suggestion without urging)[1]<br>   b. EA[2]<br>   c. Positive forward look<br>   d. RB and satisfaction[4]<br>   e. Courtesy | 5. Positive, friendly close<br>   a. CSAD[1]<br>   b. EA[2]<br>   c. DA[3]<br>   d. Good wishes<br>   e. RB[4]<br>   f. Courtesy |

[1] CSAD = clear statement of action desired
[2] EA = easy action
[3] DA = dated action
[4] RB = reader benefit

## BAD-NEWS MESSAGES (Continued)

*V*

*Refusing Credit*

| *Retail credit (E)* | *Mercantile credit (F)* |
|---|---|
| 1. Buffer<br>  a. Agreeable comment<br>  b. Appreciation<br>  c. Assurance<br>  d. Brief resale on product and/<br>    or firm<br>  e. Incidental reference to the<br>    order, if any | 1. Buffer<br>  a. Same as V, E, 1 a-e |
| 2. Explanation<br>  Choice of:<br>  a. No reasons<br>  b. "Insufficient-information"<br>    reason<br>  c. List of all usual reasons<br>  d. Specific reason(s); same as<br>    I, A, 2 | 2. Explanation<br>  a. Specific reasons<br>  b. Favorable, then unfavorable<br>    facts<br>  c. Emphasis on desired goal |
| 3. Decision—same as I, A, 3, a | 3. Decision—same as I, A, 3, a |
| 4. RB[4] counterproposal and sug-<br>  gestion(s)<br>  a. Conference<br>  b. Other lenders<br>  c. Future review<br>  d. Other credit plans available<br>  e. Layaway<br>  f. Cash or c.o.d. buying | 4. RB[4] counterproposal and sug-<br>  gestion(s)<br>  a. Inventory reduction<br>  b. Sales or capital increase<br>  c. Local financing<br>  d. Cash or c.o.d. buying;<br>    smaller, frequent orders<br>  e. Help of sales representative<br>  f. Future review |
| 5. Positive, friendly close<br>  a. Invitation regarding a sug-<br>    gestion; CSAD[1]<br>  b. Forward look<br>  c. Resale<br>  d. RB[4] and EA[2]<br>  e. Courtesy | 5. Positive, friendly close<br>  Same as V-E |

*VI*

*Acknowledging Orders You*

| *Incomplete or vague (G)* | *Back orders (H)* |
|---|---|
| 1. Good news, if any, and buffer<br>  a. Shipment details on items you're sending, if any<br>  b. Buffer: short resale on vague item(s)<br>  c. Brief order acknowledgment (date, item)<br>  d. Appreciation<br>  e. Welcome, if new customer | 1. Good news, if any, and buffer<br>  a. Same as VI, G, 1, a<br>  b. Buffer: specific resale on ordered depleted item; no mention of depletion<br>  c. Same as VI, G, 1c, d, and e |
| 2. Explanation<br>  a. RB[4] reason for requesting missing information<br>  b. Facts about choices available (sizes, colors, models)<br>  c. Descriptive enclosures | 2. Explanation<br>  a. Approximate date goods expected to reach buyer<br>  b. Reason unavailable now (RB?)[4]<br>  c. Resale |
| 3. Decision<br>  a. See G, 2, a above—implied decision | 3. Decision<br>  a. See H, 2, a above—implied decision |
| 4. Resale and/or constructive suggestions<br>  a. Perhaps brief resale on the item(s) in general | 4. Resale and suggestions<br>  a. Possibly mild sales promotion on allied item(s) to be shipped with back-ordered item<br>  b. Perhaps brief resale on back-ordered item |
| 5. Positive, friendly close<br>  a. CSAD[1]<br>  b. EA[2]<br>  c. DA[3]<br>  d. RB (prompt delivery?)[4]<br>  e. Courtesy | 5. Positive, friendly close<br>  a. If shipment in reasonable time: no action; assumption that back-order is OK<br>  b. If longer:<br>    CSAD[1]<br>    EA,[2] DA[3]<br>  c. RB[4] |

[1] CSAD = clear statement of action desired
[2] EA = easy action
[3] DA = dated action
[4] RB = reader benefit
* S = substitute; O = ordered item

## BAD-NEWS MESSAGES (Continued)

VI

*Can't Fill Now or At All*

| *Substitutions* (*J*) | *Diverted or rejected* (*K*) |
|---|---|
| 1. Good news, if any, and buffer<br>   a. Same as VI, G, 1, a<br>   b. Buffer: broad resale embodies both S and O\*; omits points of difference<br>   c. Same as VI, G, 1 c, d, and e | 1. Buffer<br>   a. Resale only if your products or services are to be bought elsewhere<br>   b. Brief order acknowledgment<br>   c. Appreciation |
| 2. Explanation<br>   a. One or two merits of S before revealing unavailability of O<br>   b. Sales point on why we carry O exclusively | 2. Explanation<br>   a. One or two RB's[4] for your sales policy: (selections, deliveries, shipping costs, extra services)<br>   b. Any other pertinent facts |
| 3. Decision<br>   a. Unavailability of O—in positive terms (exclusively stock S) | 3. Decision<br>   a. Positive statement of your policy to clarify what you can't and can do<br>   b. Payment return, if any |
| 4. Resale and suggestions<br>   a. Passive statement on where O may be bought<br>   b. Price and quality justification of S, with RB[4]<br>   c. Sales promotion | 4. Resale and suggestions<br>   a. Justification of price difference at local dealer<br>   b. Help on where to get what reader wants |
| 5. Positive, friendly close<br>   a. If substitute already shipped: assurance of money-back "shipment on approval"; RB[4]<br>   b. If substitute not yet shipped: CSAD[1] EA,[2] DA[3] RB[4] | 5. Positive, friendly close<br>   a. Resale<br>   b. CSAD[1]<br>   c. Future service<br>   d. RB[4] |

## CAPSULE CHECKLISTS FOR

| *VII*<br>*Turning Down Job or*<br>*Contract Offers* | *VIII*<br>*Announcing Bad News about*<br>*Prices and/or Services* |
|---|---|
| 1. Main idea or buffer<br>  a. If routine matter be-<br>    tween businesses, maybe<br>    I, B; 1<br>  b. Otherwise, I, A, 1<br>    buffer:<br>    (1) Appreciation<br>    (2) Agreeable comment<br>    (3) Compliment | 1. Main idea or buffer<br>  a. If routine (or reader<br>    not emotionally in-<br>    volved), I, B, 1<br>  b. Otherwise, I, A, 1<br>    buffer:<br>    (1) Agreeable com-<br>      ment<br>    (2) Neutral courtesy<br>    (3) Brief resale |
| 2. Explanation<br>  a. Reasons leading to turn-<br>    down (already full<br>    schedule in writer's<br>    firm; usual require-<br>    ments or qualities<br>    sought, with or without<br>    revealing reader's<br>    specific lack) | 2. Explanation<br>  a. RB[4] reasons and anal-<br>    ysis of increasing<br>    costs, etc. |
| 3. Decision<br>  a. Clear, tactful decision,<br>    implied or stated—em-<br>    phasis on positive<br>    aspects—(what your<br>    firm *is* doing about such<br>    work, etc.) | 3. Decision<br>  a. Effective date of new<br>    plan<br>  b. Clear statement and<br>    itemizing if needed<br>  c. Enclosures |
| 4. Resale and suggestions<br>  a. Invitation for possible<br>    future reapplication<br>    and review<br>  b. "Filing" for future<br>  c. Alternate employers | 4. Resale and suggestions<br>  a. Resale on your firm's<br>    products, services,<br>    prices |
| 5. Positive, friendly close<br>  a. Good wishes<br>  b. CSAD[1]<br>  c. Courtesy | 5. Positive, friendly close<br>  a. Forward look<br>  b. Resale<br>  c. Invitation to action<br>  d. CSAD[1]<br>  e. EA[2]<br>  f. RB[4]<br>  g. Courtesy |

[1] CSAD = clear statement of action desired
[2] EA = easy action
[3] DA = dated action
[4] RB = reader benefit

# BAD-NEWS MESSAGES (Continued)

| IX *Requiring Minimum Orders and/or Deposits* | X *Penalizing for Nonconformity with Rules or Procedures* | XI *Conveying Other Bad News* |
|---|---|---|
| 1. Main idea or Buffer<br>  a. If routine (or reader not emotionally involved), I, B, 1<br>  b. Otherwise, I, A, 1 buffer:<br>    (1) Agreeable comment<br>    (2) Neutral courtesy<br>    (3) Compliment on past<br>    (4) Hint of urgency or need for change | 1. Main idea or buffer<br>  a. Same as IX, 1, a<br>  b. Same as IX, 1, b | 1. Main idea or buffer<br>  a. Same as IX, 1, a<br>  b. Same as IX, 1, b |
| 2. Explanation<br>  a. Tactful review of reader's record— favorable to unfavorable<br>  b. Emphasis on desired goal and helpfulness | 2. Explanation<br>  a. Details about the requirements<br>  b. Reasons leading to the penalty | 2. Explanation<br>  a. Details on what is wrong |
| 3. Decision<br>  a. Clear tactful statement of what will happen unless reader meets requirements | 3. Decision<br>  a. Same as IX | 3. Decision<br>  a. What needs to be done |
| 4. Resale and suggestions<br>  a. Suggestions (improved advertising or merchandising; assistance of sales representative<br>  b. Enclosures; aids<br>  c. Resale | 4. Resale and suggestions<br>  a. Suggestions for eliminating penalty in future<br>  b. Forms and deadlines | 4. Suggestions<br>  a. How to do it |
| 5. Positive, friendly close<br>  a. Same as VIII, 5 | 5. Positive, friendly close<br>  a. CSAD[1]<br>  b. EA[2]<br>  c. DA[3]<br>  d. RB[4]<br>  e. Assurance<br>  f. Good wishes<br>  g. Courtesy | 5. Positive, friendly close<br>  a. CSAD[1]<br>  b. EA[2]<br>  c. Goodwill<br>  d. Courtesy |

*Pleasant*    As you may guess, this is pretty much of a blow to me, but
*comments*    it isn't smart to ignore the advice of our doctors.  During
the past four years I've greatly enjoyed working with the
many fine people of our state organization.  It is thus
difficult for me to request that you accept my resignation
*Date of*    to become effective immediately after your next month's
*resignation* board meeting.

I'm convinced of the importance of our Civil Defense cause
*Good wishes* and assure you that my good wishes will continue to go with
you and the great work you are doing.

**Letter 3.** *An indirect-plan resignation (to a college senior's employer for whom he
worked five years); dated May 1.*

Dear Mr. Owens:

*Buffer:*    Just as each business must chart its course for the future,
*agreeable* so must every individual ask himself:  Where am I going?
*statement* and Where do I want to be 15 years from now?

*Appreciation* Over the past five years I have given serious thought to
these questions.  I will always remember how much your
company has meant to me.  You have given me not only
valuable experience and a sense of perspective, but also
work and earnings that helped pay my expenses through the
University.  As both you and I realize, however, my chances
for long-run advancement necessary to satisfy my goals are
*Reason*    limited here at Ace Sign Company.

*Reason*    To make full use of my college training and in an effort to
provide better benefits to my family, I am accepting a
position in the Finance Department of the International
Products in (city).  As my reporting date will be June 11,
*Resignation* please consider this resignation to be effective June 5.
In the meantime I am willing to work any necessary over-
time, at no additional cost to you, to insure an effective
transition for my successor here.

Again, thank you for your many kindnesses during the years
*Cordial*    I have worked in your firm.  I hope that you and all my
*close*    co-workers at Ace will continue to be my personal friends
in the years ahead.

In summary, whenever you must write unfavorable news—whether you
are replying to a request or initiating an unsolicited message—you are usually
safe to follow the indirect, five-part bad-news plan. If you use the direct plan,
be sure that the type of message, the situation, and the relationship between
yourself and your reader warrant that approach. The preceding checklists review both plans (**Column I**) and adapt the indirect plan to 10 kinds of bad-
news messages.

# EXERCISES

*Answering Inquiries When the Information Is Undesirable*

1. Assume that you are manager of the Jay-Fraser Sales Corporation for an automobile manufacturer in Michigan and that your new assistant has just written
   the following reply (dated May 4) to an inquirer 2,000 miles away. What improvements can you suggest? Rewrite the reply so that it will be a goodwill
   builder even though you cannot at present give the information asked for in
   the "four points." He wants to know about the Jay convertible automobile because he is interested in owning one some day.

   Dear Mr. Stewart:

   This will acknowledge receipt of yours of April 23. At the
   time of this writing we are not in a position to give you any
   information on the four points which you mentioned in your
   letter since no information is available to us for release at
   this time.

   We are sure, however, that your local dealer will be only too
   happy to keep you informed as to when the Jay convertible will
   be made available to the public.

   We would like to thank you for your interest in our cars.

2. Letters A and B are replies from two state colleges to a university junior living
   in another part of the same state. She had inquired on June 2 about admission
   requirements for a transfer student currently majoring in Business Education and
   intending to teach in elementary or junior high schools. Compare these replies
   for opening and closing paragraphs, and for helpful explanation. Which letter
   do you like better? Why? What improvements can you suggest for each reply?

   **A.**

   Dear Miss Hopson:

   We are happy to hear of your interest in attending Central
   State College. Enclosed you will find information on admission
   requirements and application procedures for transfer students.
   At your request, an application for admission is also enclosed.

   Your particular combination of elementary education with a
   business major cannot be endorsed for teaching at Central. I
   would suggest that you give me a call at 963-4214 so that I may
   further explain our program to you.

   If I can be of further assistance, do not hesitate to contact
   me.

**B.**

Dear Miss Hopson:

In response to your letter of May 21, we are sending you the catalog for the academic year just completed.  The new catalog is in the process of preparation but will not be available until some time in July.

On page 40 of the catalog, you will find the professional education sequence of 36 credits required of all candidates for a B.A. in Education and provisional certificate.  On page 41 are listed the programs for elementary teachers and secondary teachers.  You will see that Business Education is not an approved major for elementary or junior high teachers and that Business Education majors planning to teach in the senior high must complete a minor in Economics.  Thus, if you were to transfer to Western to become an elementary teacher, you would have to develop a new 45-hour major.  You could continue with your major for teaching senior high and would then need to complete the Economics minor.  Requirements for the Business Education major are listed on page 70 in the catalog and course descriptions follow.  Descriptions of the Education courses begin on page 76.  Dr. James Palm is adviser for the Business Education program, and Dr. Stewart Van is chairman of the elementary domain.  If you have specific questions for either of these gentlemen, it would be well for you to include a copy of your college record to date so that they would be better informed to answer your questions.

An application for admission with advanced standing is enclosed for your use if you decide to make the change.

**3.** As purchasing assistant for a national life insurance company, answer Miss Linda Mond's courteous request for literature about attitudes of drivers. She needs this material for a speech she will give at a community meeting of taxpayers. Your company does not handle any other insurance except life insurance. Therefore you do not have any material which will help her. What constructive suggestion(s) can you add to aid her? Can you name two or three firms that specialize in accident or car insurance? State and local law enforcement officers may also have useful information.

**4.** Point out the negative expressions in the following form letter. Then rewrite it to emphasize the positive aspects, instead of the negative, keeping the basic facts the same. This form reply was sent from the Government Printing Office to a businessman who requested a copy of the text on the summary and conclusions of FTC *Reports on Coffee Price Investigation*. Is the direct plan usable here? Why or why not?

Thank you for your inquiry which is enclosed.  We are sorry the publication you desire is not in stock at this time.  However, we hope to have more definite information concerning the availability of this publication in a short time.  We have recorded your interest and will notify you just as soon as definite information is available. We regret that factors beyond our control make it impossible for us to be more defi- nite at this time, and hope you understand that we act merely as a distributor of Government publications and not as the author or the issuing agency. For this reason, we sometimes cannot be specific as to when or whether or not a publication will be available.

The large number of orders and letters of inquiry received each day by this Office makes it impossible for us to write you a personal letter. We hope this reply is satisfactory, and that you understand that we value your inquiry none the less highly despite the necessity of our answering in this form.

5. The following letter from a national manufacturer of party favors has several weaknesses. Rewrite it (to Jim Brown, chairman of a college football banquet) to improve it in every way you can. Assume additional pertinent facts, if neces- sary, and try to be more helpful to this banquet chairman. He wants individual souvenirs ("about 2 or 3 inches wide") to use as favors or place cards for the 250 persons expected to attend the banquet four weeks from today. Although your factory does not have any such souvenirs in stock, you do manufacture special items to order. All you need is a design and three to four weeks' time; your skilled workmen turn out really attractive novelties. Assume that your reader (the chair- man) lives 2,000 miles from your factory. Time is short. It is possible that the L. G. Baldwin Company may have football souvenirs in stock. What can you say to be helpful?

Dear Sir:

We have pleasure in acknowledging your letter of 20th September concerning your inquiry about small individual football sou- venirs for your banquet. Though we note that you had been advised by Marcus Company to approach us in this connection, we are sorry to inform you that we do not have football novelties and thus cannot supply the material which you need.

We regret we cannot be of service to you for this occasion.

### Refusing Adjustments on Claims and Complaints

1. The following goodwill-killing message is a processed form letter sent by a state- wide hospital service association to customers who hold a certain hospital insur- ance policy. Mr. Austin Grimshaw, a business executive who received this letter, was angered by it and considered it a "horrible letter." How many reasons can you find for agreeing with Mr. Grimshaw? (His wife had been rushed to the hospital in an ambulance; he had paid cash for this service, and now included his receipt, along with other hospital bills which he thought his hospital insurance policy covered.) Suggest specific ways to present the bad news tactfully in this form letter.

Dear Mr. Grinshaw:

We are returning your receipts for ambulance service.

We realize when you know you are not paying a rate for such service, you can understand our reason for rejection of this bill.

We are sorry we are unable to be of assistance to you with this charge.

2. Compare the following two letters for tone, organization, and content. Discuss specifically why the revision is better than the original. (The messages are individually typewritten from the home office of an insurance company to an insured policyholder who claims that certain illness expenses he incurred should be covered by his policy.)

*Original*

I would like to acknowledge the application for benefits and itemized bills which have been referred to us through the Vermont Office. I regret to find that we will be unable to be of service to you on your claim.

The primary purpose of your hospital expense policy, as its name implies, is to provide protection to help defray the high expenses usually resulting from those conditions which are serious enough in nature to require hospital confinement as a result of accident or sickness, emergency treatment, maternity, surgery, and polio.

As you can see, there is no benefits provided for out-patient services in a hospital incurred as a result of sickness, nor does it provide for the payment of doctor's fees in the absence of surgery.

Inasmuch as the bills you have presented indicate that no losses covered by the policy have been sustained, the Company has no alternative to disallowing your application for bene-fits. I am sorry that the circumstances do not permit giving you more favorable advice.

*Revision*

Thank you for the opportunity to explain the Company's position on the August 3 statement from the ABC Hospital.

The main point is that the primary purpose of your Hospital Expense Policy is to cover in-patient hospital charges and surgery. An in-patient is one who incurs at least one-day room and board charges. The policy also covers maternity, polio, and emergency treatment as an out-patient from accidental bodily injuries.

Your claim is for out-patient care at the ABC Hospital for treatment of a sickness. Also, the doctor's bill does not show any surgery was performed. These charges are not covered by the premium being charged, and no provision is made for them in the benefits. Therefore, we cannot approve benefits for these particular expenses.

If you should present another claim in the future, benefits will be considered in accordance with this explanation. And if you have any questions, please contact me.

3. Your firm repairs cameras and electronic equipment. One of your out-of-town customers sent you for repair a GRAPHLIX camera, Model 412, bearing the serial number 39866. He claims the camera is defective and asks for free repairs, because he has had it only six months on a one-year guarantee. Examination shows that the camera is not defective, but it has been dropped and badly misused. These repairs are needed: replace broken lens, $32; repair range finder, $4.50; repair and readjust electronic eye, $4. These repairs will put the camera in first-class shape; it cost originally $165. Write to the customer, Mr. Gene A. Murdock, letting him know why he will have to pay for these repairs. You are customer service manager.

4. As consumer service assistant manager of the Bleachex Company in Los Angeles, you have today received a complaint from Mrs. E. A. Lubbock, of Spokane, Washington. She writes that after using your Bleachex liquid to remove a stain from her new white nylon car seat belt, she found the belt turned "an ugly yellow." She wants you to pay the $5 for a new belt. However, from her description of the yellow discoloration, it appears that the nylon had been treated with a resin (for soil resistance and "body") that is not compatible with any dry or liquid chlorine bleach. Your label states that Bleachex removes fruit, vegetable, etc., stains from washable cotton, linen, nylon, and other synthetic materials. But you do not advocate Bleachex for stain removal unless the entire item can be immersed in the properly mixed solution and then rinsed well, which is important to stop the bleach action. Thus, Bleachex should not be used on a car seat belt because of the inconvenience of removing the belt and all metal trimmings before immersing the material in the right solution. Though you can't guarantee 100 percent results, she may wish to immerse the belt for a few minutes in a solution of 1 gallon water, 2 tablespoonfuls of sodium sulfite (from a drug store or photo supply shop), and ½ cup of white vinegar, and then rinse thoroughly. Although you must refuse her claim, make your reply tactful, helpful, and positive.

5. Shown below is part of a claim (complaint) letter from an irate Alaskan customer to the general manager of a large mail-order house that serves all 50 states. The complaint indicates the importance of filling orders correctly and of using good judgment in case back orders or substitutions are necessary. Discuss the type of reply that the general manager should use. Will a letter do the job? If not, why not? Why can (but not necessarily should) a customer talk so frankly to the buyer but the buyer can't talk as frankly to the customer? Consider the best way to win this customer back.

Dear Sirs—

This is a letter of complaint and I can't express it too
loudly or too clearly. We have traded with you for the past
fifteen or more years to an amount which in all probability
amounts to a minimum of $15,000.00 over this period of time.
Perhaps it is a small account for such a big company. Perhaps
you are getting so big that you have forgotten what made you
that way——small customers looking for the biggest spread for
their money. If this is the case, perhaps we should find some
other concern interested in expanding.

I used to be mildly irritated only when you would send my
wife a notice of "no longer in stock," "your order will be
delayed," "we will ship late," and so on. Last month when I
telegraphed for a spare wheel for my outboard——I sent a complete description——your store answered words to the effect that
my order could not be filled unless I specified the department.
Just what in the hell department would you expect an outboard
part to come from and how in the h——— should I know? I ordered
a part, gave you a complete description number——all pertinent
information on the engine. Why should I be required to tell
you where to buy it at your own store?

About two weeks later my wife ordered some clothing. You
said that it had been shipped, but we still have not received
it. I have never complained before but I am damn well sore
about your deteriorated attitude towards what you call "preferred customers." The letters you send when our account is
paid are beautiful. Why in the bloody hell don't you treat us
like preferred customers then when you want more of our
business after we are all paid up?

The last part of June I personally sent in a written order
for exhaust parts, sleeping bags, air mattresses, etc.——an
order amounting to only $100.00 approximately. I specifically
stated that I was depending on receiving this order complete.
I underlined this request and set a deadline for it to be
received here complete by the 19th of July. Fine. On the 13th
of July we received a speedometer cable which would not fit my
car. I made no error in ordering——this I am positive of. I
received the wrong ignition parts——they will not fit the distributor——it cost me an additional half hour of a mechanic's
time to tell me why. We did not receive either the three air
mattresses or three sleeping bags. I specifically stated that
"we are depending on receiving these items." Do I have to get
down on my hands and knees to ask you to send what is ordered?
Can't you substitute? Why in the devil can't your shipping
head use his head for something other than a bet? We needed
these items and depended on obtaining them. You did not even
send an advance shipping notice of what you did send so I sent
you a telegram asking where is this order, when will it arrive?

Did you answer me?  Hell no, you answered your office in Alaska
which had no interest in the order whatsoever and which action
gave your local office manager a bad time in trying to figure
out what had happened.  On top of this you added that you could
not trace the order unless I sent the order numbers.  Just what
am I and my family—a bunch of numbers now too?  My name and
address was on the order.  You got the order.  You mailed the
order.  I received <u>part</u> of the order and part of that part was
haywire.  If your accounting is that weak, perhaps I should not
pay any more money to you.  I'll bet sure as hell that you
would find my name in a damn big hurry then, wouldn't you?  If
I was to run your business, I would tell you all about order
numbers, catalog numbers, part numbers—ad infinitum.  But, I
am not a number and only order by your numbers listed.  If you
can't relate your numbers with my name signed to the original
order, just what kind of a clip business are you beginning to
operate? . . . .

(<u>one</u> <u>paragraph</u> <u>omitted</u>)

Since receiving these items I have talked to a number of
people—mechanics, garage owners, and they have universally
stated that they no longer trade with you because your orders
are so badly fouled up.  They have concluded that you play the
odds that the average person won't say anything or do anything.
Well, let me tell you, if this is the case you didn't get a
cherry here but hit three of them in a row.  If you . . . .

(<u>four</u> <u>more</u> <u>paragraphs</u> <u>omitted</u>)

Believe me, you better shape up your shipping department or
ship them out of shape. . . . You didn't ruin my coming vacation but you sure as hell threw a crimp in my operating cash.
I didn't want to write until I cooled off a bit and am glad
that I didn't.  If I don't get any satisfaction from you I'm
going a damn site further.  Also, advertising works two ways.
This is not a threat—it's a statement of fact.

**6.** You are the manager of a reputable appliance store in Iowa City. You sold Mrs.
Lotta Moneybags a new washing machine which was a gift for her daughter who
recently got married. Mrs. Moneybags is a very wealthy widow and Clara is her
only child. Mrs. Moneybags also is a very influential person in the town and a
very good customer of yours. She is very narrow-minded, however, when it comes
to her daughter—Clara can do no wrong. Just today you received this letter
from Mrs. Moneybags, who is currently vacationing two weeks at a resort in
another state:

Dear Mr. (your last name)

I purchased from you six months ago a brand new 197_ Jetwash
washing machine for my daughter.  You assured me that this was
the best machine on the market and that it would give years of
trouble-free service.  You even guaranteed it for 3 years.

My daughter has been using this machine and she informed me that last week it quit running. She had a repairman from your store come in and look at the machine to see what was wrong and he told her that the motor had burned out as a result of a bearing in the spin mechanism burning out. I was very upset to learn of this trouble so I talked to the repairman myself by phone. He told me that the damage to the bearing could have only resulted from improper loading of the machine, and it appeared to him that Clara grossly overloaded the machine every time she used it.

I don't believe your repairman, and it is perfectly apparent that this machine was defective and he is trying to shift the blame to my daughter. Now I know that you are a rational man, Mr. (your name), and I am sure that you agree with me that this machine is defective. Therefore, I would like your store to replace this machine at once, as it is a terrible incon- venience to my daughter not to have a washing machine in good working condition.

To be fair to both Mrs. Moneybags and to yourself, you telephoned Clara and made an appointment to go to her home to examine the washer. After observing the condition of the motor and talking with the daughter, you realized that the repairman told the truth. The machine is not defective and the breakdown was the result of improper use. The instructions for using are printed on the inside of the lid of the washer, giving all the details for loading the washer properly. Furthermore, anyone ought to be able to understand these instructions. The tub has a clearly marked red line over which you are not to load clothes. Overload- ing causes the tub to spin in an irregular manner, which in turn places undue pressure on a particular bearing located just below the tub agitator. This bearing —the one that burned out on Clara's machine—receives the full weight of the load, plus the centrifugal force when spinning. This bearing was badly burned and melted in several places. Because the lubrication around the bearing is still sealed in, the only thing which could have caused the failure was improper loading. If a burned-out bearing isn't replaced right away, the motor also burns out because of the excessive strain exerted as it tries to spin the tub agitator.

Write a letter to Mrs. Moneybags denying her request as tactfully as possible. You would like to keep her business. Also, she is very influential in your com- munity, and you do not want her hurting your market with malicious gossip. You will have to charge her $31.45 (including tax) for the needed replacement parts to put the machine in top-notch working order again. Furthermore you will have to keep the machine in your shop for three days for repair. But you will not charge her for labor that would amount to another $30, or for a $15 service call. Giving her a new machine is ridiculous.

7. Assume that you are customer service department manager of the Ketchum and Pleasam Department Store in your city. Today you get a letter from Mrs. James Gleason, 919 North 20th Street, in a small town about 20 miles from your store. Attached to her letter is a package containing three pairs of ($6.50 each) faded blue jeans that she bought from your store when she was there in person. She describes exactly from which of your basement departments she bought the jeans, and she's right. Her complaint is that they have shrunk and faded so that she will

not wear them. She wants you to send, without extra charge, three pairs of sanforized navy blue jeans that won't shrink or fade. She complains that she's surprised your store's merchandise doesn't stand washing. Here are the facts: To meet the demands of the numerous young people who insist on wearing jeans skintight, who prefer to cut them off at odd places, and who want them to look "grubby" soon, you carry a special brand that pleases these customers. On the counter at several places are signs stating: "These jeans are guaranteed to shrink and fade!" This is the counter from which Mrs. Gleason bought her jeans. Clearly she just didn't read or see the signs, and you can't be responsible for her error. From your third-floor sports department you can send her three pairs of Topco brand sanforized navy blue jeans ($6.70 each) in her size, and they're guaranteed *not* to shrink. Of course, she'll have to pay for them. If your instructor approves, you may suggest a compromise to Mrs. Gleason; perhaps you won't suffer a complete loss on the faded jeans she returned. If you make no compromise, be sure to return the unwanted jeans and add a constructive suggestion.

## Refusing Credit

1. You are an officer in the Security Loan Company. During the past week you gave loan commitments on the homes of Mr. Thompson and Mr. Simpson, who are neighbors. Upon learning that Mr. Simpson's commitment ($16,250) exceeded his by $1,000, Mr. Thompson writes you for an explanation. As far as Mr. Thompson can see, his house is just as good as his neighbor's. In checking with your appraiser, you find the reason for the difference. Of course many factors can affect the valuation of home property for mortgage loan purposes. Some items might actually be advantages in the eyes of a specific owner, but an impartial appraiser may feel they detract from the value of the property. Mr. Thompson's property has two shortcomings as to location, which seriously deflate its value: (1) a highway runs on the east side of his lot and (2) a somewhat blighted area plus a playfield are right across the street from his home. After a careful review of the appraisal report, you still feel that the $15,250 commitment offered to him is the maximum amount you can lend him on his home. Of course, if he should be able to find a buyer who will pay the same for his home as for Mr. Simpson's, you will increase your loan commitment at that time. Write the proper bad-news letter, trying to keep his goodwill—and also the opportunity to process his loan application. Mr. Thompson's home does have a neat appearance on the outside, and his carpets and drapes add to the attractiveness of his home on the inside.

2. As credit manager of a national oil company, you receive hundreds of applications for credit cards. One refusal which you must write often is to young people under legal age. Draft a goodwill-building form letter (which can be processed) to handle such refusals. If the applicant could get an adult who would be willing to guarantee his account, you'd do your best to accommodate him. Enclose a necessary form together with a second credit card application. The guarantor is to sign both forms and the applicant is to return them to you with a reference to his original application.

3. As vice-president in charge of the mortgage loan department, you receive today a written request from an old contractor friend with whom you've done business for years. He has financed all his construction loan business through your office, has sent in numerous borrowers over the years, and is generally considered "your contractor."

In his letter today he states he has "sunk his bankroll" in a piece of property at 785 Oakley Street. He has assumed you will grant him the necessary loan to build four sizable rental units. The purpose of his letter is to let you know who has the title to the property so that you can have the loan set up for him when he returns from his present business trip.

You know through personal experience that the neighborhood is subject to the first stages of blight. You have misgivings about constructing rental units in that area because the blight will be a big problem as time goes on, and thus you feel you will not be able to grant him a loan.

Write a tactful, helpful letter telling him this bad news.

4. Compare the following processed credit refusals used by three national large retail credit firms—mail-order, banking, and travelers' aid, respectively. Notice that each has the refusal in or near the opening paragraph.

   a. From the standpoint of a credit applicant, discuss your personal reaction to each of these letters. Consider the opening, adequacy of reasons, and constructive suggestions.
   b. Rewrite either letter B or C, placing the decision *after* the reasons (and revising the wording as needed).
   c. Do you like your rewrite better than the original? Why or why not?

   **A.**

   We sincerely appreciate the opportunity you gave us of considering your recent credit application but find we are unable to accommodate you on a credit basis at this time.

   We hope you will continue to shop at (name), taking advantage of our everyday low prices and grant us the privilege of serving you again.

   **B.**

   Thank you for your application for a (name) credit card. Your interest is appreciated, but we sincerely regret that we are presently unable to approve your request.

   Because of the many uses of (name) card, the requirements for obtaining a card are different than those for many other types of credit, and these requirements cover many areas of consideration. From the information given to us in your application, we are unable to issue a card at this time.

   However, if you have additional information which you believe would warrant a review of your application, or if you believe that there may be a misunderstanding, we would be pleased to have you contact us.

   **C.**

   We are genuinely sorry that we cannot comply with your request for a (name) credit card at this time.

Any one of a number of factors may be responsible for this decision. The unique nature of the (name) credit card—offering as it does virtually unlimited credit at over 150,000 service establishments throughout the world — obliges us to place unique requirements on its availability. Consequently, a large number of applications fail to qualify.

Some of the factors considered in evaluating applications are: job longevity, length of residency, number of dependents, income as reported to us, net worth, ratio of income to liabilities, nature of employment, credit references, credit history, and property ownership. As much as we regret to decline an application, we are compelled to do so if it does not meet the requirements in any one of these categories.

It has been our experience that persons who do not meet our requirements at one time may qualify later on. You are cordially invited to reapply at a later date, if you feel your circumstances have changed.

Thank you for your interest in our service.

5. Mr. John Anderson is the President of Northwest Pacemaker, Inc., manufacturer of small camper trailers. His company has been in operation for three years, and is just beginning to show a small profit after two unprofitable years. The year-end financial statement reflects a nominal net worth; however, sales have increased from $20,000 to $140,000 and the company's potential looks very favorable.

Mr. Anderson has asked for a $10,000 line of credit to "floor" (carry the inventory on the showroom floor until sold) his trailers because he does not have enough capital to carry an adequate supply to offer customers a good selection. After careful analysis you—loan officer of the Merchants' National Bank—determine that you can not make this type of loan until a longer and more stable earnings pattern has been established. You do notice, however, that Mr. Anderson indicates on his personal financial statement cash value of life insurance amounting to $6,000, and this would be adequate collateral for a $6,000 line of credit.

Mr. Anderson has not banked with you previously, but has transferred all of his business to your bank regardless of your decision on the loan (primarily because a young teller has caught his eye and he wants to be able to see her more often).

Write a letter to Mr. Anderson in which you thank him for his account, turn him down on his original request, and offer him the alternative arrangement.

6. You are the manager of a wholesale fabric business. You distribute fabrics to many stores in your state. You allow them 30 to 90 days to pay for goods and sometimes longer if necessary. Just recently you have run into a very difficult situation. You extended credit to one small fabric shop that was run by a very personable fellow, Mr. Greenfab. He has come in several times to your warehouse and ordered and picked up fabric. He seems quite at home with all the personnel in your company and everybody likes him. For these reasons when he was unable to pay his bill in 90 days you gave him an indefinite extension. He continued to

place orders and his bill has become larger and larger. It has now been a year since he has paid for anything. Of course part of the blame is yours for letting it go on as it did, but you have decided that you can no longer extend credit to this man until he starts paying his past bill. You had explained that you had to stop credit and he said he understood, but when he called up on what he termed "emergency" situations, you always said, "Well, only this time." The situation is now out of hand, and you want your money. Decide on a course of action and write an effective letter.

7. As credit manager of the Regis Department Store, you have received a credit application from Mrs. George Bann, who seems to be doing a noble job of making the family ends meet on her $450 monthly wages. She and her husband and four children rent a $90-a-month cottage. Her husband has been unable to work for three months because of illness, but he hopes to get a job within two or three more months. You honestly feel that a charge account is not what this family should have now. Unexpected emergencies in their financial position could cause them serious problems. Cash purchasing from your complete catalog, where they pay as they go, lets them know where they stand at any time. Also you have end-of-month sales regularly, with savings up to 50 percent. Send Mrs. Bann a catalog supplement with all the news about your sales. Perhaps when Mr. Bann is working you will reconsider her application for your monthly payment plan. Make your letter specific and genuinely helpful.

## Acknowledging Orders You Can't Fill Now or At All

*Incomplete Orders*

1. You are assistant research director of the united chapters of Beta Gamma, a national business honorary. Your organization publishes and mails (free) a *Quarterly Newsletter* to all members across the United States. Also you publish (for sale at cost) a few scholarly reports and booklets on various phases of business. Because your organization has no credit department, none of these published booklets can be sent unless the member sends cash with his order. You do not send c.o.d. Part of the back page of every *Quarterly Newsletter* is devoted to announcements about new publications and their cost (which includes postage for mailing to any town in the United States). There is a clear statement on this back page about the cash-in-advance policy. Nevertheless, today you received an order from Mr. John Land, Shelby, Illinois, asking that the following reports be sent c.o.d. (or that you bill him later):

   2 "Ethical Principles in Modern Industry," Memorial Study #1 ($2 each)
   1 "The Incredible Paradox of the 70's"                              ($1.50)

   You must hold up shipment of these booklets until you receive his remittance. Write a tactful acknowledgment of his order, explaining both your policy and the reason for it. Your prices on the pamphlets are at cost; the saving that your organization makes by operating without credit and collection procedure is passed on to members in lower prices.

2. As customer service representative for Lipman Department Store, Pasadena, California 91109, you have today (July 8) received an order from Mrs. Rose Fairmont, 135 Third Street, Victorville, California 92392. She writes that last Saturday eve-

ning on her way to a theater in Pasadena, she happened to pass your store windows on the west side. In the center window she saw a pantsuit that she would like you to send her in size 12: in "red, white, and blue. I think the price was $19.50; just charge it to my account. It's just the thing I'd like to take with me on a trip; we'll be leaving Tuesday, July 15. Will you please send it to reach me no later than Monday?" In checking with your window decorator, you learn that six pantsuits were displayed in the center-west window last Saturday. Worse yet, three of them were in red-white-blue prints—(1) horizontal stripes in the jacket top, with navy blue slacks, (2) vertical stripes for both the jacket and slacks, and (3) plain red jacket with navy trim on the collar, and white slacks. Which does she want? Your secretary tried four times today to phone Mrs. Fairmont, but received no answer. You must now write her a letter which goes in the 5 p.m. mail pickup and should reach her tomorrow or Thursday morning. If she will get her answer to you by no later than Friday noon, you can be sure to send the right suit to her on the store delivery truck Monday morning. Devise easy action for Mrs. Fairmont, and also make sure you will get all the information you need to fill her order immediately.

3. From Mr. Marvin Randall, assistant manager, Northwest Marine and Pool Supply, 910 Western Avenue, Seattle, Washington 98101, you receive an order for:

| | |
|---|---|
| 10 Boarding ladders, 3 steps | @ $7.50 |
| 50 ft. #6314 Marine Mat and Dock Runner, red | @ 2.00 per ft. |

These items are to be shipped freight charges collect, and billed on the firm's usual credit terms of 2/10, net/30. You can't ship any of these items, however, until you get more information. The boarding ladders come with 7-inch and 11-inch hooks—so they can clamp securely to boats, rafts, pools, or docks. Which size does he want? It is even possible that he might want five of each, but you think it is risky to guess. The ladder prices are the same for both sizes of hooks. These white vinyl-covered hooks turn a full 360 degrees for fast and easy fitting, and they fold so that the ladder is flat for convenient storage. The steps are varnished oak hardwood, 15 inches wide.

The Mat and Dock Runner #6314 is in aqua color, not red. The red is listed in your catalog (which Northwest Marine has) as #6316. Though he probably wants the red and just wrote the wrong catalog number, you want to be sure before you ship this heavy roll. (Shipping weight is 3 pounds per foot!) This is an excellent runner for deck or dock. It is made of all-weather nonslip brush-action polyester pile with heavy rubber backing, and is 36 inches wide.

Write for the needed information, make action easy, and cover all pertinent details. You are assistant sales manager for Pool and Patio Wholesale Company, San Francisco, California 94101.

## Back Orders

4. In your Wholesale Camera Supply Company (Norman, Oklahoma 73069) you have just received an order from Angel's Photo Shop, 931 Wabash Avenue, Shawnee, Oklahoma 94801, for parts to repair a Model #25 box camera. Mr. Angel stated that his customer cherishes this old camera as an heirloom and wants to get it into good working order. Facts: This model of American camera is obsolete and new parts are no longer available. If Mr. Angel's customer desires, you will try to obtain these parts on special order; however, there will be a delay from three to four weeks and the part may be used. The price also may be con-

siderably higher than current material prices on similar parts for newer models. At this moment you have no way of knowing just what the prices may be. Write to Mr. Angel to get his approval of the back order and some kind of understanding about what his customer considers the maximum he would be willing to pay for the parts. You will, of course, try to get them for the very lowest price possible and assure Mr. Angel that such an old-model camera in top working order will indeed be a possession to be proud of. Make action easy.

5. As a correspondent in the customer relations department of Publishers' Bureau, New York City 10001, it is your job to write Mr. Sydney Cline, Director of Rocky Creek Camp, Great Falls, Montana 59401, that the new printing of the book he ordered—B9551 ($4.98)—has been delayed about one month. From your catalog he ordered three copies of this book, which he says he wants for his camp counselors. He enclosed a check in full payment, including $1.10 shipping charges. As it is still early in the summer (today is June 10), you wonder if he would like you to ship the books when they come off the press. In case he needs books sooner, you do have other titles similar to the one he ordered. Enclose a new brochure from which he can select other books at the same price, any of which you can send so they'll reach him within a week. Ask Mr. Cline whether he wants you to back-order B9551 and if he'd like you to send any other books to tide him over. In case he wants to reorder instead of or in addition to waiting for B9551, enclose an order form and make clear what you'll do about his check.

6. Mr. Lawrence Meisner, a charge customer at 854 Glenwood Drive, Eugene, Oregon 97401, orders five more rolls of the #TG3772 gold color flocked raised damask wallpaper ($15.95 a roll). He writes that he just finished papering the dining room with this pattern and his family likes it so much that they now want the hall to match. Your store (Galli's Interior Design Shop, Portland, Oregon 97208) is completely out of this pattern; you sold your last roll three days ago. You are the exclusive dealer for these distinctive wallpapers in Oregon, and get them direct from the Mayberry Mills in Massachusetts. A wire from the mills yesterday promised that your special order of #TG3772 would reach your shop in 10 days. Write Mr. Meisner the appropriate letter to keep him convinced that this choice wallpaper is well worth waiting for. It is one of the most elegant you carry. Its beautiful flocked damask pattern has the lovely look and feel of velvet. Textured to simulate fine silk, all on tough vinyl, it is strong and won't tear even when wet. Also, it's prepasted and pretrimmed, and can be cleaned with soap and water. Shipping time between Portland and Eugene is one day.

*Substitution Orders*

7. From Mr. Verne Jackson, owner of Tip Top Variety Store, Macon, Georgia 31201, you (Acme Closet Accessories, Inc., wholesaler, in Hartford, Connecticut 06101) receive an order for:

| | | |
|---|---|---|
| 3 dozen #25C538 12-pocket Todd shoe bags | @ $2.20 | $79.20 |
| 2 dozen #25P862 16-garment Todd vinyl bags | @ 2.50 | 60.00 |

These are to be added to his account. You have today shipped by parcel post the shoe bags, but the particular garment bags he ordered are no longer manufactured by Todd Brothers. This item was discontinued last month. The new (#35P880) garment bag comes in three colors—sea green, sky blue and pink—of electronically quilted vinyl instead of the clear plastic formerly used. The quilted vinyl wears better, and is guaranteed to resist splitting at the seams. The zipper is 48 inches long instead of the former 40 inches, and thus makes inserting garments easier. Because this bag was not included in last year's catalog, Mr. Jackson of course did not know about it.

You are sending him the new spring catalog, just out. The bag in question is pictured on page 5. Its price is $3.00 each, but well worth the 50 cents difference over the clear plastic. A complete assortment of other color-mated closet organizers is also available. His customers will like, for instance, the matching eight-suit bag and the five-shelf file, both with zipper front, sturdy steel frames, and see-through 1-foot square windows of clear vinyl. Though you're sure Mr. Jackson will be glad to carry the new #35P880 bags—and also the other accessories—you write to ask his approval before shipping the bags. Provide order blanks and any other information he may need.

**8.** In the Broadway Pet Shop, which you manage, you receive today a handwritten letter from 10-year-old Tommy Bronson, son of a long-time good customer of yours who lives in a fashionable suburb 30 miles from you. He says that his new pedigreed dog which his uncle gave him for his birthday yesterday needs a house. (Presently he's tethered outdoors.) Tommy's parents have said he can pick any doghouse he wants. He described one which a friend of his bought from you last month—medium size, white with red roof, $34.99. He wants you to send one like it right now because the weather is getting cold. Unfortunately, you don't have that exact doghouse in the store now. The one that's most similar to it is the same size, shape, and color; but it has a painted picture window which the other doesn't have. This big 13- by 10-inch window with red trim has a see-through area of clear, tough, shatterproof glass—so Tommy's dog can keep an eye on the world outside at all times. Tommy's dad may want to know that this doghouse costs $38.50, though price isn't much worry to this family. Because Tommy wants a home for his pet immediately and because you're sure he'll like this extra-nice house, you're sending it (on approval, of course). Painted white both inside and out with two coats of exterior latex paint over sturdy $\frac{5}{16}$-inch pine sides, this house has a red swinging door and raised floor for air circulation underneath. It's strong enough for even the most active dog. Write Tommy everything that both he—and his dad—will want to know about your shipment.

**9.** Mr. Maurice Pittman, a senior at Central College in your state, writes to your Richards Men's Clothing Store (in his home town). He sends you the label from the all-weather coat he bought from you over four years ago and states he'd like another one just like it, for it has given him excellent service all this time. He says he couldn't find anything like it in the college town where he is. "Please send me this coat in tan color and just charge it to my account. I'd appreciate your rushing it to me by Saturday the 16th (that's 10 days from today), because I need something new for a special function that day." Facts: You do still carry this same Ralston brand in the same handsome all-cotton poplin material—in both black and tan. Its sharp good looks, careful tailoring, welted seams, and reasonable price have made it a perennial favorite among college men. However, the style has been changed a little during the past year. Instead of the four exposed buttons, this year's style has a "fly front" that neatly covers a convenient 30-inch zipper. Instead of the former patch pockets, these pockets are set in, with an attractive lower flap. Like the former coat, this one is treated with Scotchgard Brand Fabric Protector to resist water and oily stains. The price, $20, is about $3 more than

Mr. Pittman paid four years ago—but all prices have increased and this coat now has additional features. Decide whether you will send this coat before or after you get Mr. Pittman's approval. His college town is 400 miles from you; shipping time is normally two days.

### Diverted or Rejected Orders

10. Mrs. Jordan Alton, 9540 Riverside Drive, Chillicothe, Texas 79225, has ordered from Friedman Jewelry Store, Dallas, "three more teaspoons in Rosedale Pattern, National Sterling" and she encloses her check for $38, which she hopes is enough to cover postage too. Friedman's however, does not carry National Sterling; you have the exclusive franchise for Regis Sterling, which you think is one of America's finest. The Hancock Jewelry Store, 1971 Fifth Avenue, in Dallas, has the exclusive franchise for the National Sterling brand. So you'll return her check and build whatever goodwill you think appropriate for your store. You carry a complete line of exquisite silver hollow ware (teapots, candy dishes, trays, serving dishes), chime clocks, watches, necklaces, rings, and other jewelry that Mrs. Alton might be interested in.

11. You are a correspondent at the home office of Lenox China, makers of fine china, in Passaic, New Jersey. This morning (May 1) you receive an unusual letter—one that won't permit you to use an existing form letter. This letter comes from Suzi Braun, who lives in Salt Lake City, Utah 84101.

   She tells you she is getting married to the "most wonderful man in the world," and her mom and dad gave her $100 for a wedding present. She wants as many place settings of a particular pattern—Roselyn—as she can buy for that amount. She's writing to you because she had a basic course in marketing and learned that she can save money by circumventing the retailer. This gal must have good taste because Lenox China is world-renowned; it is one of the best in the United States and is even used in the White House. The Roselyn pattern is one of the most elegant you make; it has a beautiful delicate red rose surrounded by golden leaves in the center of a plain ivory background, and there's a gold rim around all the plates, cups, and saucers. This pattern blends gracefully with the most exquisite silver and linens.

   A five-piece place setting (dinner plate, teacup, saucer, salad-dessert plate, and butter plate) sells for $28.95, not including tax, and so she can't even get four place settings for her $100. To make matters worse, you can't sell her Lenox China direct from you to her. She has to buy from a retailer because you sell nationally only through selected dealers. In Salt Lake City there are two dealers (you decide which two) that carry a complete line of Lenox China—all patterns and extra pieces (platters, vegetable bowl, etc.). It's to her benefit to buy locally because she can purchase her pieces, take them home that same day, and use them that night. Or the store will deliver them within a day or two. The store also has a bridal registry, which permits her friends and relatives to call the store, find out her patterns (for china, silver, etc.), and surprise her with an appropriate gift without pestering her or her mother. The store knows at any moment what it has already sold for her so the inquirer won't choose a duplicate. The dealer gives free a miniature swan to every girl who registers her pattern(s). This swan is made of the same fine china as all other Lenox pieces. You don't know whether the dealer will extend credit to her, of course.

   Your job is to reply to Suzi. Write so that she'll want to go to one of the local dealers to buy her place settings. Naturally you'll return her check. This assignment requires you (the student) to "study" the Roselyn pattern, visualize the reader, and think of why she will benefit by buying from a local retailer. Organize your message effectively, and write tactfully and positively. You might assume an enclosure if it performs a useful function.

### Declining Favors, Invitations, and Miscellaneous Requests

1. Assume you receive the following letter from Mr. Harry Gaylord, chairman of the local United Good Neighbor Campaign for this year:

   Dear Mr. (or Ms.) (your name)

   As you know, our city conducts a United Good Neighbors' fund drive annually. Many people volunteer their help to coordinate the campaign. Will you be willing to serve as a captain this year?

   Captains are responsible for a particular geographic area. Yours would be a ten-block area bounded by _____ Street on the west, _____ Street on the east, _____ Street on the north, and _____ Street on the south. You would be responsible for selecting chairmen in each block, who in turn will canvass each house in their particular block.

   Needless to say, your effort will be for a most worthy cause. Will you drop me a line...soon, saying you'll accept?

   Unfortunately you must decline the request. Since the campaign is kicked off in August, and since you will be out of the state on vacation at that time, you won't be around to do your duty.

2. Mr. John Field, 425 Ninth Street, North Platte, Nebraska 69101, writes to you—loan officer of the Second Federal Loan Company, Lincoln, Nebraska 68501—requesting a favor. He would like you to let him change the due date of his loan payments from the 1st of each month to the 10th, but you have to refuse his request. Mr. Field borrowed from your company on a Government Guaranteed Loan and signed a Deed of Trust Note. The due date on such mortgage loans is determined by the date the mortgage is signed. It is written into the mortgage contract that his payments must be received within 15 days of his due date, which is the 1st of each month. His remittance must arrive by the 15th of that month to avoid a late charge. It is possible, of course, for him to use the payment date of the 10th of the month, but he would have to prepay one month in advance. You are unable to change due dates on Government Guaranteed Loans. Write the appropriate reply to Mr. Field.

3. As chief clerk of the traffic department of the Washington State Ferries, you have to answer a request you received two days ago from Miss Sally Harada, Star Route 3, Box 95C, Bremerton, Washington 98307. She asks if you would please make a special search for a pair of manicure scissors she lost on the ferry from Bremerton to Seattle, February 8. They were a gift from her boyfriend who is now in the Navy 3,000 miles away, and she will be heartsick until they are found. She was sitting by a window seat in about the middle of the ferry on the right-

hand side and she thinks these scissors dropped either on the floor or into a crack along the wall. As she doesn't mention the name of the ferry nor the exact time of her trip—and as you have four ferries on this route—you had to search on all four ferries. So far no scissors have been found. But you'll keep this a matter of permanent record and if the item is found or turned in, you will notify her immediately. Write the bad news to Miss Harada; send copies of your letter to: Information Booth, Colman Ferry Terminal; Dock Superintendent, Colman Ferry Terminal; and Agent, Bremerton—and indicate these copies on your letter to Miss Harada.

4. You are manager of the special service department of National Photographic News Service, 952 E. 45 Street, New York City 10017. Today you must refuse a request from Mr. George McVey, business manager of *The Engineer,* a magazine by and for college engineering students. (Address: 542 McKinley Building, University of Illinois, Urbana, Illinois 61801.) He asks if you would send him from time to time any news pictures which are related to the engineering field. Because his magazine has an extremely low financial budget, he asks if you will please allow the magazine substantial discounts on pictures. You can't allow any discounts to anyone. Your standard charge is $6, from which you are unable to deviate. Your news service has extremely high costs of production, as your staff covers a wide area both in types of pictures and in geographic location. If the $6 rate (for each picture) meets his budget, you suggest that he send you a list of specific subjects in which he is interested. This list will be turned over to your researchers who then will submit for his consideration all photos received which are in line with his requirements for editorial reproduction in his magazine. Pictures are sent on approval and he will be charged only for those he accepts from each shipment. All rejected photos must be returned. Write a goodwill-building letter, showing that you are interested in being of service to his magazine.

### Bad-news Announcements

1. Your company cafeteria, built 19 years ago to serve about 1,000 employees, is definitely too small for your 1,900 employees. As a remedial step you (vice-president for food services and finance), together with the board of directors, have decided upon a temporary solution. You will close the directors' lounge as a lounge facility—starting September 5, 197_—and will no longer serve just officers and guests there. The plan is to convert the directors' lounge—which is a table service dining room of very limited capacity and use—to an employee vending-machine food service room, supplemented by short-order counter service during peak demand hours. Present patrons of the directors' lounge are mainly a few officers and a few guests; the average patronage daily has been less than 30 during the three hours a day the present table service is open. Economically this is a marginal operation that cannot be justified. This lounge is conveniently located so that it can easily be used by your swing shift during evening hours without keeping the rest of the building open. This planned change will of course greatly alleviate the pressing demands for additional food service facilities for employees. But the table service will be missed by the few who enjoyed it before. To them this announcement will be bad news. Word your announcement so that every loyal officer will accept your decision with understanding, and even approval. The new plan should help decrease employee lunch-hour tardiness and improve morale. The officers still have the officers' dining room on the 12th floor. To partially offset the loss of table service from the directors' room, this officers'

dining room now has additional private seating space. The recent enclosure of the south porch has been equipped with comfortable lounge facilities in the latest decor and a modern sliding partition is usable for those officers who want a separate space for private conferences. Write your memo to all management members.

2. For many years your company has been sending free copies of a glossy magazine *Improving Your Correspondence* to anyone who requested to be on your mailing list. Seldom do you hear from your readers. The cost of this little publication is about $2 each. In an effort to try to pare unnecessary expenses, your firm's directors have suggested that the mailing list be revised to include only those persons and firms that still read and appreciate the publication. They realize that after a passage of years those who originally requested to be on the mailing list may no longer be reading the magazine. Write a pleasant, positive-sounding, processed message that will offend no one, even though it is basically bad news. Your goal is to find out out which readers wish to keep the magazine coming. They'll help you keep your mailing list up to date by taking a certain action that you request. Can you word your announcement in such a way that the readers will be dropped from your mailing list if you don't hear from them?

3. Announce to your employees in building B that all electricity will be turned off between 10 and 11 a.m. next Thursday morning, June 10. They will have to plan their work in such a way that they can get along without using any electric machines that hour; in fact they won't have any electric lighting either. However, as these are sunny days, lack of electricity for lighting should not be too much of a problem. Everyone will be responsible for getting out the amount of necessary work that day, and the electricity shutoff will not be an excuse for working over-time in the afternoon, for no extra pay will be allowed. The electricity shutoff is necessary while workmen hook up a major power cable between building B and the highway. New fluorescent lighting will be installed within the next month. In organizing your memo, consider whether you should use the direct or indirect plan—and have reasons to defend your decision.

4. Today is December 20. As head resident of MacMahon Hall, the newest dormitory on your campus, you have just discovered a foolish mistake you made. When the dormitory managers and head residents met last week, they made as many hall transfers as space allowed for next semester (or quarter). Assignments for re-quested transfers are made on the basis of number of semesters (or quarters) the applicant has lived in residence halls. Preference thus is given to upperclassmen. Hence last week you notified 50 juniors that, starting January 2, they could transfer to MacMahon Hall, which is the dorm most students prefer. Now you find that only 30, not 50, rooms are available, and therefore 20 students cannot transfer from their present halls after all. Of course you're sorry for causing them the trouble of changing plans. Send them a dittoed memo—which will be mailed to their home addresses because they have already left college for Christmas vaca-tion. Of course, sometimes spaces do open up during vacation, and sometimes during the first week of the new semester. As space becomes available, *if* it will, you promise to notify these students first to see if they would still like to move. Write as good-natured and casual a memo as you can, considering the probable mood of your readers and your relationship to them.

5. You are president of the Exchange Building Garage, Inc. Your company manages a 400-car garage used by businessmen who occupy the Exchange Building. Be-

cause of steadily increasing operating costs (mainly wages) you have found it necessary to increase the monthly parking rates to $40 a month (instead of the former $35), plus the state sales tax. This increase will become effective January 1, 197__.

For the past two years you have been absorbing the increased operating expenses, but cannot continue to do so any longer. After several conversations with Mr. J. L. Dorff, vice-president of Commercial Properties, Inc., and with Exchange Building owners who lease to the business firms in the building and from whom you lease your garage facilities, you received permission for the rate increase. Now that you have decided on the rate and date, you will write two messages:

**a.** A letter to Mr. Dorff, telling him your final decision regarding the monthly rate and the effective date. Inform him that you will notify all your parking customers before a certain date. You might restate to him briefly the reason for this increase, refer to your previous conversations, and show appreciation for his understanding. Will you organize this message by the direct or indirect plan? Why?

**b.** A letter to all customers who have been renting monthly parking space from your garage. This increase comes to them as a bad-news surprise. Give them whatever details you think they will appreciate having. Will you organize the same way as for message a? Why or why not?

6. As service manager of the Servu Wholesale Hardware Supply Company, you need to notify all your customers—hardware stores and locksmiths—of a change in policy and some suggestions about ordering. In the past, many of these hardware store and locksmith customers have sent people to you to buy retail articles that they (the stores) did not have. Sometimes these individuals (consumers) came to you with a note, some after a phone call from the retailer, and others just came in to buy. These people take a lot of your employees' time which you would rather devote to serving your wholesale customers' orders. Therefore, as of April 1, 197__, you will not sell anyone retail locks, keys, or door closures and parts. You will discontinue all service on locks and door closures. No keys will be cut or fitted, as you have no one to do labor service. Tell your wholesaler customers (the hardware stores and locksmiths) they should please not send anyone in to you for advice or retail selling of any item.

You want to give the best fast service to all orders you receive direct from your wholesale customers. You appreciate their cooperation and business of the past too. Some of these customers, however, could be more helpful in the way they fill out order blanks they send to you. When these wholesale customers forget to give stock numbers on items, their orders must be set aside until someone has time to research and look up the numbers. If they write the stock numbers right on the order, shipment can be made the same day the order is received by you. Also, different catalogs may have the same number for different articles, and each customer must be sure to state which catalog he is using. You have cross references for most catalogs. Write an appropriate message to all your wholesale customers in a way that will make them understand how they benefit from your decision and suggestions.

# CHAPTER 9

# PERSUASIVE REQUESTS

- Organizational Plan
- Persuasive Requests for Favors
- Other Persuasive Nonroutine Requests
- Unsolicited Sales Letters
- Exercises
- Capsule Checklists

Besides situations in which mere *asking* is sufficient (routine direct requests), you will face situations in which you need to *persuade*. The favor or action you ask—the reader's time, money, support, or agreement—is such that you anticipate some objection. To persuade your reader to take the requested action, you develop rational and/or emotional appeals. Analysis of and consideration[1] for your reader's circumstances, needs, and emotions are especially important for effective persuasion.

You can use the persuasive-request plan for the following kinds of messages:

> Requests for favors that—
>   Require time, knowledge, or effort
>   Ask donations of money or other valuables
>   Urge cooperation on goals and projects
> Other Nonroutine requests:
>   Adjustment
>   Credit
>   Changes in policy or performance
> Unsolicited Sales letters to—
>   Make a direct sale
>   Serve as stimulus to future sales
>   Bring back lost customers
>   Apply for a job
> Collections (discussion and late stages)

This chapter discusses the persuasive-request plan and how you can adapt it to various requests for favors, other nonroutine requests, and sales. Job applications are covered separately in Chapter 10 and collections, in Chapter 12.

## ORGANIZATIONAL PLAN

The persuasive request, like the bad-news letter, uses the indirect approach. You assume that if your request were stated directly at the beginning, it would be bad news to your reader and he would react unfavorably. Thus, before you mention the specific request, you will have to prepare him for it and, when possible, present facts to indicate that your proposal is beneficial or useful to him or others in whom he is interested. Remember, your reader is not expecting your message, and you should attract his attention and arouse interest *before* revealing what you'd like him to do.

The basic structure for persuasive letters usually has four parts, commonly known as the AIDA formula for sales presentation:

[1] For a review of general ways to show consideration, see pages 98–106.

**A**—Attract the reader's favorable *attention*.
**I**—Arouse his *interest*.
**D**—Create *desire* and convince him.
**A**—Make clear the *action* he needs to take.

Although attention, interest, and desire are listed here as distinct steps, they are usually combined or blended so smoothly in the well-written persuasive message that it is difficult—and unnecessary!—to separate them. Also, the parts do not always occur in the sequence given above; for example, it is possible to omit or deemphasize those points that have been covered in earlier letters, advertising, or personal contacts with the prospect. You-attitude content and reader benefits are most important. What you call the parts and whether you have three or four is unimportant. In fact, the persuasive-request plan is sometimes called the four P's—promise, picture, prove, and push—or discussed under *three* parts—star, chain, and hook. In the AIDA persuasive-request *general* outline below, the other names for the parts are indicated in parentheses.

### *1. Attention (promise; star)*

Attract favorable attention with a reader-interest or a reader-benefit theme. Begin with a relevant statement or a challenging question that entices the recipient to read on because he wants to know "What's in this letter for me?" Highlight a point that is close to his interests or needs, instead of talking about yourself or your organization. Avoid exaggeration, foolish questions (Do you want a steady income?), and obvious statements (Money helps you pay your bills).

Because many people throw away envelopes that look like part of bulk mailings, even the envelope plays an important part in getting favorable attention. Among the devices used with varying degrees of success on envelopes are color, handwritten addresses, contest announcements, questions, and a few enticing words from the message printed on the envelope. Some firms conceal their identity on envelopes, omitting their name and address. However, because many people resent such tactics, this practice has questionable value.

The letterhead can also be an effective, important attention getter. For favor and sales letters that are sent to numerous readers, letterheads can and do deviate from the usual simplicity suggested for other business letterheads. Some contain different pictures and colors to tie in with each favor or sales message. (Advertising agencies and stationery design specialists can help you with these needs. The discussion in this text concentrates on the written message itself.)

### *2. Interest (picture; chain)*

Build upon the theme started in the attention-getting opening. Begin to tell what your project, product, or service is and what it will do for the reader. Describe it clearly and specifically in two ways (not necessarily in this order):
  **a.** Its physical description—important features, construction, appearance, performance, beauty, functions (any or all of which may be omitted for a long-established subject well known to the reader).
  **b.** Its value or benefits to the reader (or others in whom he's interested). (Some writers call this material "psychological description.")

Of the various features and uses that the project, product, or service has, emphasize the central selling point—that point you think is most likely to make the strongest appeal to the prospect. For instance, will your proposal bring him comfort? entertainment? health? recognition? security? Show the reader how your proposal gives him one or more benefits like the following:

Appreciation (by others)
Approval (by others)
Beauty or attractiveness
Cleanliness
Comfort
Convenience
Cooperation
Customer satisfaction
Distinctiveness
Efficiency
Enjoyment
Entertainment
Extra earnings
Fair treatment
Friendships
Good reputation
Health
Improvement
Love of home, family, others
Money and other valuables
Peace of mind

Pleasure
Popularity
Position of authority
Prestige
Pride
Profits
Protection for family, business, self, or others
Provision for the future
Recognition
Reduced work
Respect
Safety and security
Satisfaction of helping others
Savings
Self-preservation
Solution to a problem
Success
Thrift habit
Usefulness

### 3. Desire and Conviction *(prove; chain)*

So that your reader will desire to do as you request and be convinced that he (or others in whom he is interested) will benefit from your proposal, you usually present proof. Give evidence that your statements are true. Include needed facts, figures, testimonials, tests, samples, guarantees, and any other proof that your proposal may call for.

A descriptive folder permits you to avoid cluttering your letter with many details. However, if you have an enclosure, mention it only after stating most of your selling points and then motivate your reader to read further details in the folder. Link your reference to the enclosure with a sales point. Don't depend on the enclosure to do your selling.

Emphasize positive aspects, but be honest about stating costs when pertinent; minimize negative aspects, and write from the reader's point of view.

### 4. Action *(push; hook)*

Clearly state what the reader should do to comply with your request and thus to gain the benefits. Make action easy—by including a reply form, envelope, phone number, office hours, location, etc. Induce him to act now or within a certain time, and end on a reader-benefit plug, which may tie in with your opening statement. (See pages 29–31 and page 92.)

# PERSUASIVE REQUESTS FOR FAVORS

As a conscientious business or professional person you probably participate actively in various committees and organizations. And you have numerous opportunities to write (as well as to answer) favor requests, that is, requests seeking the recipient's donation of something—time, knowledge, effort, money, or cooperation. The AIDA plan helps you to ask a favor effectively, as described below.

## Getting Attention for Favor Requests

To begin your favor request with something close to your reader's interest or benefit, consider what appeals are likely to be most meaningful to him. Try to introduce a direct or indirect benefit that you can develop as a central selling point more fully later in the letter. You want to get the reader's attention *before* stating your request, but you need to use good judgment in introducing benefits. Be careful that your statements don't sound like high pressure or bribes, as in this poor opening for a letter inviting a political candidate to speak: "How much would it be worth to you to influence the views of 2,000 voters?"

Effective openings you can use—with discretion—for various favor requests are: (1) a sincere compliment, (2) one or more rhetorical questions, (3) an assertion with which the reader will agree, (4) a problem that is the basis for the favor request, (5) a statement of what is being done or has been done to solve or lessen a problem, and (6) a frank admission that your message is a request for a favor. Many good letters even combine one or more of these openings, as in some of the following examples.

### *Sincere-compliment Openings*
*Request to speak, without fee, to a local chapter:*
> Ever since your stimulating speech last year to delegates at KSA national convention in Atlanta, our Tri-City chapter members here have wanted to meet you personally. We believe you could be a profound influence on our future program and growth.

*Request to accept an important chairmanship:*
> Your exceptionally fine work in People-to-People projects, as well as your present Council position, emphasizes that you deserve a place on this year's East Coast conference program of the National Personnel Association.

### *Question Openings*
*Request to participate in a six-month research project:*
> Have you ever had the fun of participating in a market research study? As you know, market research is the study of consumer reactions and attitudes to products. This research is extremely useful to manufacturers in helping them to give you and your family products to better suit your needs.

*Request to become a member of a University YWCA:*
WHAT'S THE USE?
"What's the use of getting an education?"
 "What's the use of planning ahead?"
  "What's the use of living thoughtfully?"
   "WHAT'S THE USE OF ANYTHING?"

### Agreeable-comment or Assertion Openings
*To speak to students majoring in advertising:*
Advertising is the spark plug of any business and a challenge to the creative thinker. Yet what advice can you give to the many students who cannot decide what area of advertising to enter?

*To join a campaign committee for preservation of a historic landmark:*
Pike Place Market holds colorful memories of the early days in Seattle. It's a gentle reminder of an era that will soon be almost forgotten—unless responsible citizens like you show their concern.

*To help in getting community support:*
If there is one topic in which you and I share a special interest, it is the education of our children. The success of our school levy will determine the quality of education received by Bellevue students.

### Basic-problem Openings (sometimes introduced as stories and suspense)
*To sign a pledge and contribute to a reward fund:*
The bombing of the Center Building is an act of violence which has outraged many members of this community. Its significance lies only in part in the $300,000 of physical damage and in the gross inconvenience created during reconstruction.

Certainly of greater significance for all is the fact that this incident is a blatant violation of the principle of common decency and of respect for the orderly and humane life of the university.

*To contribute to a lab fund:*
DIAGNOSTIC LABORATORY IN DANGER!
INDUSTRY STANDS TO LOSE $60,000!
Contributions for the new diagnostic lab in (town name) have stopped coming in. Unless we can immediately raise $11,000, we will lose the $60,000 appropriated by the last legislature on the condition we in the industry match it with $35,000. Only $24,000 of the necessary $35,000 has, so far, been pledged.

### "What Has Been Done about a Problem" Openings.
*To send a gift to the Fund for the Blind:*
Thousands of blind Americans wait eagerly each month for their copies of the Braille or Talking Book edition of *The Reader's Digest*. It is the only magazine of its kind they may receive in Braille or Talking Book form (long-playing records) which is exactly like the ink-print edition read by their sighted friends. This means something very special to them.
    With the help of friends like yourself, we can supply these. . . .

*To hire jobless men through the Millionair Club:*
During the past year homeless and needy men, women, and children enjoyed 123,000 warm nourishing meals at Millionair Club; 3,088 adults and children

received clothing; men received 9,321 jobs, 406 units of blood transfusion, emergency hospital treatment, and many other kindnesses.

*"Frank Admission of Favor" Openings*[1] (Disarming frankness encourages some readers to discover for themselves how they will benefit from complying.)

*To accept an honorary state appointment:*

The state needs your help!

As a prominent respected psychiatrist, you have been recommended to serve on the State Board of three to conduct oral Civil Service examinations of applicants for psychiatric work in State Rehabilitation Centers.

*To be moderator at a national convention:*

To get and keep our 197_ NRMA convention program on the beam, we shall need three top-grade people to serve as moderators. You can no doubt guess why I am making this appeal to you.

Yesterday, while our national president, Henry Gibson, visited me—I suspect mainly to see what I was doing about providing a good program—I said, "We need new faces to lead the show in New York City next December. How about Herb Murdock from ABC Company? He replied that he knew you and that we couldn't find a better NRMA dependable.

*To fill out and return a questionnaire:*

WILL YOU HELP DMAA?

—AND HELP YOURSELF, TOO?

I'd like to ask a favor of you. It concerns the gathering of important facts and information regarding postal rates. Here, in a nutshell, is the story:

## Arousing Interest and Creating Desire to Do the Favor

Once you have decided on an opening that sets the theme and encourages the recipient to read on, you can continue to build on your idea. To get both the reader's interest and desire, you need to (1) include all necessary description—physical characteristics and value of the project, (2) present facts and figures through which he can determine direct or indirect benefits he may derive, and (3) handle negatives positively. This material comprises the greater portion of your persuasive request.

*Physical characteristics and value of project.* If your reader is not a member of your organization or familiar with it, you need to give him brief, but adequate information about its purpose, scope, and members. But be sure not to *begin* your letter by talking about yourself and your organization, especially if the reader is an outsider! Place this material after a you-attitude opening.

In addition, you need to describe to all readers the problem or project to which the favor relates, and establish its values. For instance, if you are asking

[1] These frank openings are like those used in direct requests; however, the remainder of such letters contains appeals and persuasion.

for funds to send underprivileged children to summer camp, you might describe (perhaps with the use of a folder) the physical camp facilities, size and number of buildings, surroundings, recreation areas, and number of children and counselors. Then you show the value of these facilities to the children—character-building, friendships, appreciation of nature, fun, etc. Sometimes you can effectively get the reader to visualize himself in the shoes of those his funds can help, and in this way arouse his interest in your project.

*Direct and Indirect Reader Benefits.* Usually near the middle of your letter you explain how the reader is to take part in the project. So that he will desire to do as you ask, be sure to include all necessary facts and figures to convince him that his contribution will be enjoyable, easy, important, and of benefit to him (as much as is true and possible). Try to show direct and/or indirect benefits.

*Direct benefits* to a person who does a favor vary with the type of favor. For example, if a person is to speak (without a fee and perhaps even without a traveling expense allowance) at a widely publicized convention, he may gain direct benefit from the favorable publicity as well as from his personal contacts with the audience. If other prominent speakers are on the same program, say so; for this fact is an additional compliment to your reader. Both the speaker and his employer (who perhaps pays his traveling expenses) can gain directly from recognition, prestige, and popularity—plus increased future sales of products or services. However, it is better not to actually state these benefits, but rather to let the reader determine them himself from the facts. Be sure to tell him when he is to speak, where (date, day, hour), on what topic (or if he is to choose it), for how long, to whom, and to how many people.

Direct benefit may also come to the company that donates merchandise to, for instance, a charity or well-attended event. The people who see the company's name on the donated product will feel goodwill toward the donor and tend to buy its products when they need them. Again, it is better not to state such benefits specifically, but to let your reader determine them himself. Stating obvious benefits bluntly may make the favor request sound like a bribe.

If your reader is to become a member of your club or to take part in a project, describe that club or project and tell how it will (directly) benefit him. Try to keep the reader in each paragraph and write from his viewpoint.

In some favor requests the direct benefit offered may be a premium or gift or other small reward or token of appreciation. Those who participate in a questionnaire survey may gain because the results will ultimately lead to improvements that make their work easier or help them to save money.

*Indirect benefits* may come to the participant who helps the members of a group he is interested in or of which he is a member. For instance, you can use indirect-benefit appeals to get a sales manager to speak (without a fee) to your school's marketing club or an auditor to talk to an accounting club. In each case your reader's contribution may benefit him or his profession at least indirectly, because he helps a group of listeners whose interests are in a field of work he himself is interested in. Similarly, when you want to urge a busy person to accept a time-consuming office without pay, you can appeal to his sense of loyalty to the organization and the good his leadership can provide. Such indirect reader benefits are often persuaders.

In still other cases you can get a reader's cooperation by appealing to him on the basis of altruism—his selfless devotion to the welfare of other human beings (or even animals). When he contributes to a charity drive, for instance, he benefits by knowing he has helped bring happiness and hope to folks who are less fortunate than he is.

Though there may be times when you honestly cannot see or show reader benefits, try always to present every favor request from the reader's point of view.

*Positive Handling of Negatives.* With the persuasive-request plan you must not only use appeals and stress reader benefits, but you need to ask yourself, "To what will my reader probably object?" Then stress the positive aspects—what *can* be done—to minimize the negatives, as in the following examples:

| Probable Objection | Possible Points to Stress |
|---|---|
| 1. Allowance for traveling expenses and/or speaker's fee is inadequate | a. Will you gladly meet him at the airport or any other station?<br>b. Will he be guest of honor at a banquet? Maybe his spouse too?<br>c. Will a car be available for his use in your city?<br>d. Is his part on program so important that his employer will want to take care of his expenses?<br>e. Are other famous functions, exhibits, or attractions available in your city?<br>f. Can you arrange overnight accommodations?<br>g. If he lives in the same city, will someone pick him up at home or office?<br>h. If he'll drive his car, how about parking and easy access to place where he'll be speaking? |
| 2. Expected pledge or contribution is too large | a. Will you accept contributions in small installments?<br>b. May he pledge now and pay after a future date?<br>c. Can you compare the donation to amounts spent on luxuries?<br>d. Can you show the great relief his gift will bring to those who need it? |
| 3. Requested questionnaire looks long | a. Are the questions easy to answer? Why?<br>b. Is taking part in the survey fun because . . . .?<br>c. Can the entire questionnaire be finished within $x$ minutes?<br>d. Will the ultimate gain or reward be an incentive? |

## Asking for Action

Having included necessary facts, benefits, and positive aspects, you can confidently ask for the reader's acceptance. Make his action clear, easy, and dated if necessary. If you need his reply by a certain date, tie this request in with reader benefit whenever possible—prominent billing on the program, adequate time for publicity, etc. Omit such negative statements as "*If* you can donate anything, please . . . ." Better say, "To make your contribution, just return . . . ." Your last sentence often can tie in with an appeal or statement featured in the opening paragraph, as a last reader-benefit plug.

## Asking Favors That Require Time, Knowledge, or Effort

By using the persuasive-request AIDA plan, you can effectively request favors that require time, knowledge, and/or effort. You can urge a busy person to be speaker at an important banquet or conference for little or no pay—and even partly or entirely at his own (or his employer's) expense. You can encourage people to accept time-consuming chairmanships or to serve without pay on long-term committees and boards. You can obtain answers to research and questionnaires which require more than routine effort by the recipient. You can give employees or club members a pep talk about attending certain functions; and you can increase membership in a business, professional, social, or religious organization.

Of the following five examples, four are well written; only Letter 2 is poor —for reasons that will be apparent to you as you rate it on the basis of the foregoing discussion of the AIDA plan.

*Request for a Speaker.* In Letter 1, the president of an aircraft owners and pilots association invites an author (who is a member of the same nonprofit association in another city 500 miles away) to be principal speaker. The letter includes all needed details about date, time, place, audience, length and topic of talk. The underlying appeal or central selling point is the reader's ability to help in a serious crisis those with interests similar to his. Notice how paragraph 3 emphasizes the positive aspects and also makes clear that the group *can* pay transportation expenses (but is not offering a speaker's fee). If you are writing for a nonprofit organization to someone not a member, you should explain the club's purpose and nonprofit nature before you state what you *will* pay for the speaker. (For some very large functions—with an attendance of several hundred persons—even a nonprofit organization might assess each member a small amount to cover both a speaker's fee and his traveling expenses.)

*Letter 1: Inviting a speaker to address a banquet without an honorarium.*

Dear Mr. Fee:

*Attention, reader-centered; compliment*

The article you wrote in the March issue of <u>Flying</u> has been of great interest to us in the Viewmont Chapter of AOPA. We are currently involved in a battle to acquire a surplus Naval Air Station for general aviation use, and find your ideas on airport facilities just the approach we need to convince those not familiar with general aviation problems.

*Interest; the problem*

Three months ago we learned that the Highpoint Naval Air Station would be surplus in August of this year. It looked at first that general aviation would easily acquire this badly needed airport. But recently much opposition has developed. The area residents simply do not understand why another airport for "small planes" is needed. We have planned a banquet for the leaders of the community to con-

*and the request*

vince them of the genuine need for this facility and would very much like you as our dinner guest and speaker. Your views on the general crisis of airport congestion would be extremely helpful in presenting our case. Will you tell us how you put the new program into effect last year in your city?

*Reader benefit*

You will enjoy, I'm sure, the dinner and entertainment we have planned. The banquet will be held at the new Century Plaza Hotel on June 20, at 7 p.m., but the time can be changed if another hour is more convenient for you. You will, of course, be reimbursed for your traveling and over-night hotel expenses; and I personally will see that you

*Desire and conviction details*

are picked up and returned to the airport at your con-venience. We expect about 100 persons to attend. After two local speakers present their views, we would like you to speak for twenty to thirty minutes to conclude the arguments with an expert's opinion which will add much strength to our cause.

*Dated action*

A brief letter from you indicating acceptance will assure the success of this function. Also, please include your preference as to dinner hour. Because the program goes to press in three weeks, will you send your decision by

*Value of reader's talk*

May 20? The members in this area will sincerely appreciate the contribution you can make to our obtaining another urgently needed general aviation airport in this area.

Letter 2 illustrates how the preceding letter should *not* be written. (How many specific faults can you find?)

***Letter 2:*** *A poor, writer-centered, incomplete, discourteous version of Letter 1.*

Dear Mr. Fee:

I was recently appointed program chairman of a special banquet the Viewmont Chapter of AOPA is having.

The members will get together June 20 for dinner starting at 7 in the Century Plaza Hotel to discuss ways to get a surplus Naval Air Station for general aviation use. Two of our local people will speak on this subject, but as program chairman I would like to know if you will be our main speaker at this dinner.

Please let me know if you will be able to come or not so that we can make further arrangements.

***Request for Help in a Survey.*** Whether you are a student gathering firsthand information for a report, a businessman surveying your employees, or a research consultant working for numerous clients, you will get better cooperation from your readers when you write persuasively.

Letter 3, for example, stresses reader benefit throughout. This letter also illustrates one way you can save money if you have a slim budget and a long mailing list: in place of the personalized inside addresses and salutation, you can use a reader-centered attention-getting statement or question. A letter similar to the one below gained a 79 percent response.

***Letter 3:*** *A persuasive, effective request for return of a questionnaire by college teachers.*

*Attention;*
*reader*
*benefit*

Would knowing what other
college teachers are doing in their
computer programming courses
help you?

*Reader*
*benefit or*
*interest*

Perhaps you, like many others, have wondered how the content, emphasis, and assignments of your basic course compare with those in other colleges that offer courses similar to yours in credit hours, size of sections, and prerequisites. Or you may have considered changing your courses and you could use tips on what others are including.

*Interest;*
*description*
*of project*

To gather this information about this rapidly expanding field of study, we are making a nationwide survey of computer programming courses taught in schools holding membership in the American Association of Collegiate Schools of Business (AACSB). This study is planned to get specific details on the subject matter and written assignments in 1971–72 courses.

*Desire;*
*facts and*
*reader*
*benefit*

You are the only teacher in your institution receiving this letter and the enclosed form. All names of participants will remain confidential in the report of this study. By completing the questionnaire and returning it, you will be helping expand knowledge about the teaching of this vital subject matter. Also, you'll know how your courses compare with others. You will find the questions easy to answer, we believe, because most of them require only your check-mark.

*Dated,*
*easy*
*action;*
*reader*
*benefit*

To make sure that your college is included in this study, please mail the form by May 1, in the stamped envelope provided. In appreciation of your cooperation in this study, you will receive a summary of the findings, if you wish,[1] before the information appears in print.

The benefits offered to the college teachers for mailing the questionnaire enclosed with Letter 3 are mainly intangible, yet they are adequate because the readers are expected to have a keen interest in helping to improve their profession. On the other hand, when you ask information from persons who have no built-in interest in your questionnaire, you may—if your budget allows—also have to offer a tangible inducement. For instance, the director of consumer panels for a national market research firm, in a request to "Dear Homemaker," included a tangible gift (tableware), as well as intangible bene-fits (enjoyment, usefulness, safety, and anonymity). The following two para-graphs from his letter come after three paragraphs that describe this particu-lar product study and how it helps manufacturers "to give you and your family products to better suit your needs":

All we ask is that you keep a record of your purchases of these items. In addition to the fun you will have being a part of this interesting study, you will receive a place setting of International Silver Company's Rogers Cutlery Stainless Table-ware from their "Modern Living" group—for every month of diaries we receive. It will be important, however, that you return every diary for each of the six months so that you can continue on the panel.

You will never be approached by a salesman as a result of your participation in this study, nor will the purchase information you send us ever be reported as coming from your family. Your information will be strictly CONFIDENTIAL.

## Asking Donation of Money or Other Valuables

Many people are even more reluctant to part with material goods than they are to donate their time. Thus all you have learned about persuasiveness, appeals, factual presentation, and reader benefits is even more important for requests to donate valuables.

---

[1] The respondent could indicate his wish—and also protect his anonymity—by returning his name and address on an enclosed separate slip.

If you want your reader to donate money, describe the problem and tell what is being or has been done, what needs to be done, and what your organization is doing about the problem. After stating meaningful facts, tell what it will cost to do what your organization wants to do—and how the reader can help.

If the donation is for a cause from which the reader benefits directly—as in improved recreation facilities for a club of which he is a member—you can choose from appeals such as comfort, enjoyment, friendships, health, love of family, etc. However, if the donation goes to charity, your main appeal is usually altruism, as in Letter 4 from the director of a nationally famous boys' home, and Letter 5, a memo from a business executive. Notice how appealingly these messages present the problem, tell what has been done about it and how the organization is helping, and persuade the reader to help.

*Letter 4:* *A persuasive, effective request before Christmas for a donation to charity—unusually sentimental, but especially appealing to readers who have a generous spirit at Christmastime. (A colorful letterhead shows two homeless boys in the snow peering forlornly into a bright Christmas-decorated home living room in which a fire is glowing warmly in the fireplace.)[1]*

My dear Friend:

*Attention: what has been done*

HOW MUCH IS A HOMELESS BOY WORTH?  Today thousands of proud productive citizens who live in the cities and towns across the nation were, only a few years ago, homeless, destitute boys.  Many are skilled mechanics in the various trades; others are farmers, business and professional men.

*The problem*

These men came to Boys Town as young boys, of all races and religious creeds.  They all had the same qualification -- they were homeless.  They were sad, sensitive, with many heartaches because some tragedy had robbed them of their home and parents.  Some wandered along the crossroads of the nation, their only home in some empty freight car.  The shrill shrieking of the whistle as the train plowed forward was the only mother's lullaby they had ever heard.  Others, who had been in trouble, came to us with snarls on their faces, with eyes that were hard, sullen and suspicious.

HOW MUCH ARE THEIR LIVES WORTH TODAY -- TO THEMSELVES, THEIR WIVES AND CHILDREN, AND TO THE NATION?

*What our institution does*

Here at Boys Town we continue, year after year, to rebuild the lives of homeless, deserted boys.  We give them a good home, good food, and a parent's rightful attention which they have been denied.  I talk with them individually, discuss their problems, and help them solve these problems.  They are educated in our schools, and are taught a practical trade in our well-equipped trade school, on our farm

[1] Courtesy of Boys' Town, Omaha, Nebraska.

and dairy. During their spare time they engage in athletics, music, Scouting, and many hobbies. Their mental
and moral training, and our self-government system teach
them to become stalwart, wholesome citizens.

*What needs* My boys need you, and there are many more to come. As
*to be done* Christmas approaches, won't you help me provide for more
homeless boys who will come to Boys Town, and who have no
other place to go? I am enclosing your 19__ Christmas
seals. Most contributions I receive are in $2, $3 and $5
*Action* amounts, but any amount you care to send will let me serve
*request;* as your Santa Claus to my family of almost 1,000 boys.
*altruism* Because they've already had life's share of grief and hard-
*appeal* ships, won't you help them to be happy now?

*Reader* God bless you, and may your own Christmas be doubly happy
*benefit* because you have brought happiness to a homeless, helpless
boy.

      (Complimentary close and signature area)

*Reader* Your contribution is an allowable income tax deduction. We
*benefit* employ no solicitors or fund-raising organization; we pay
no commissions.

***Letter 5 (Memo):*** *An executive's persuasive request to employees to contribute gen-*
     *erously to an annual fund drive.*

  TO:   All Members of the Wigget Staff

  FROM:  Albert Jones, President

  SUBJECT: An appeal for the UGN Fund

*Attention:* All of you are aware that this year our community has a
*problem* larger number of needy, desperate, afflicted people of all
ages, creeds, and races.

You know also of the fine work that the United Good
*What is* Neighbors Fund does to provide community services through
*being done* 82 Good Neighbor agencies. Hundreds of persons volunteer
freely of their time and money to make this drive successful each year, with no thought of tangible rewards.

*Reader* Your one contribution helps in many ways, and you are
*benefit* spared from being dunned by separate agencies. I would
like to make a personal appeal this year that all of us
reassess our values of this program and make an honest
*Request* effort to give just a little bit more. All contributions
are voluntary, of course. Each of us sets the figure our
conscience dictates, but I sincerely hope you can find it
in your hearts to join me in increasing our donation this
year. Our company's goal is $52,900.

*Appeal to altruism*

We are all most fortunate in not being on the receiving end of this program, and one way to count our blessings is by helping those less fortunate, as described in the enclosed leaflet.

*Reader benefit and easy action*

The home drive commences after the contributions are collected from business employees (November 2-6). When you contribute your entire amount through your Company solicitors, the sticker you receive, placed in a window at home, tells the story that you have given and you will not be again disturbed. Remember, UGN pledge cards make it possible to make contributions in small monthly or quarterly installments, or if you choose, you may make payments by payroll deductions.

*Appeal to pride, altruism*

Let's give serious consideration to the amount we contribute this year and try to make it one of which to be proud. Your support will be received with appreciation by the many agencies within UGN.

You can adapt the foregoing suggestions and illustrations to any persuasive request for donations—whether of money or of other valuables such as food, clothing, furniture, films, housing, or parking facilities. Whatever the request, remember to choose appropriate appeals and convince your reader that your project is worthy. Then include sufficient facts so he will want to do as you ask.

## Urging Cooperation on Goals and Projects

As a committee chairman or officer you may from time to time need to get your readers to support various goals and projects that your organization considers important. Letters 6 and 7, sent to members and voters respectively, illustrate how persuasive requests can help move readers to action toward which they would otherwise be indifferent.

*Letter 6: A membership chairman appeals for help in boosting membership.*

*Attention: agreeable comment and question*

NPRA MEMBERSHIP
JUMPS 100%

Wouldn't you be delighted to see that headline in the NPRA Journal? And you can . . . for it can be done easily . . . without gimmicks or strings or expense to you.

*Reader-benefit goal*

Increased membership will strengthen our effectiveness and benefit each of us as well as the entire field of public relations. If you—each member—will find us one new NPRA member, our size can double.

*Easy-action request*

The method is simple and effective. Go over your firm's executive roster, your list of business associates. Think of everyone you know who might be interested in public- and customer-relations. Write the names and addresses on the enclosed card and drop it into the mail.

*The followup*

That's all you need to do! Our secretary, Jim Banks, will take it from there. He will check the names against our current NPRA member and prospect lists and write to those who haven't joined, or been invited before.

*Tie-in with opening*

Isn't that easy? Find one new member for NPRA . . . and look for that headline soon . . . NPRA MEMBERSHIP JUMPS 100%.

**Letter 7:** *Four citizens (one expert each in engineering, medicine, business leadership, and law) persuade citizens to vote for a bond issue.*

Dear Southside resident:

*Attention: reader-benefit comment*

Each of us has the opportunity on May 19 to leave a legacy for the future when we vote on the Forward Move bond issue--rapid transit. This program will substantially improve the quality of your environment for many years to come.

*Interest: reader benefits*

Rapid transit will reduce traffic congestion and air pollution, both of which are becoming increasingly difficult problems in the Southside area. In addition, it will be of enormous benefit to you as a resident of Southside. To you and the employees in this area rapid transit brings easy access to plants and businesses plus increased mobility from the southside to all parts of the greater (city name) community.

*More benefits*

The proposal was conceived with the environment in mind. In fact, one of the major goals of the May 19 rapid transit election is to win the fight against pollution by creating an attractive alternative to the automobile. One-third of the system will be entirely underground. The cost can be covered adequately by the 1.3 mill tax levy, which amounts

*Easy breakdown of costs*

to about $20 annually per taxpayer on a $20,000 home. This is only $1.67 a month or less than 6 cents a day for each family!

*Interest and desire; facts*

Access to the Southside area will be improved by express bus service to a new bus transfer station at East 65th Street and the Freeway. Service from the east side and north end will be vastly improved. When the electric rail network becomes operative, the Southside District will be served by two stations--25th Avenue SE and East 65th Street, and another in the vicinity of the Southside Hos-

pital. These facilities will be entirely underground.
Thus the beauty of Southside will be maintained while
convenient access is enormously improved.

*Reader-*    On the basis of the compelling need and an opportunity to
*benefit*    preserve and strengthen your area, we ask you to vote "Yes"
*request*    with us on May 19.

## OTHER PERSUASIVE NONROUTINE REQUESTS

You can also use the persuasive plan effectively when you must convince your
reader to grant your request for adjustment or credit, or for a change in
a policy or performance. This section discusses how the AIDA parts can be
adapted to these kinds of requests and then presents illustrative letters.

### Adapting the AIDA Plan

For your attention-getting opening you can use any of the suggested six kinds
discussed above for favor requests (pages 349 to 351). However, to present a
concise logical argument, it is usually best to begin with an assertion. This
statement often is a principle—a major premise on which both you and the
reader agree or about which you wish to persuade him; for example, these
two (which can also be considered agreeable-comment openings):

> No doubt you expect your authorized dealers to uphold the good name of your
> products.
>
> I am sure you want your company to have a reputation for fairness and honesty.

You will get the reader's interest and desire when you state all necessary
facts and details—interwoven with reader benefits. Include whatever description the reader needs to see that his firm is responsible (if this applies) and
that your request is factual, logical, and reasonable. Your action request
should be a logical conclusion based on the major premise and the clearly
stated facts.

### Persuasively Requesting an Adjustment

When a product or service from a reputable firm is unsatisfactory but you
know that your claim for an adjustment is outside the warranty or otherwise
unusual, your message should follow the persuasive-request instead of the
direct-request plan. You also need to be persuasive when your request is *not*
unusual but the seller disregarded your first direct request.

In Letter 1, because of unusual circumstances, the customer persuasively asks for a new camera and certain other expenses—even though the printed guarantee includes a statement that the firm will service the camera but "cannot assume responsibility for loss of film, for other expenses or inconveniences, or for consequential damages occasioned by the equipment." This is an unusually long letter, but the details included are necessary to achieve the goal. The writer did get essentially what he wanted, though in slightly different form—six free rolls of film with processing mailers (worth about $34 total) and an exchange of his camera with one owned by the manager of the local Picturetronics, Inc.

*Letter 1:* *A consumer writes persuasively to a manufacturer's adjustment manager requesting an unusual adjustment.*

Dear Sir:

*Attention: assertion of major premise*

"Let your Wessman camera preserve those precious moments for you." This appealing advertising slogan, plus your company's good reputation, helped me to choose a Wessman camera for my once-in-a-lifetime trip to South America. Because of unusual circumstances I now find it necessary to appeal to you.

*Interest; facts about purchase*

Six months ago I purchased my Wessman "Instanshot" camera from a reputable store here. That was two months before my trip so that I would have time to become thoroughly familiar with the camera before traveling in a foreign country. (I was a member of a group representing the Foundation for International Understanding, and our long-planned trip was a goodwill tour which I wanted to preserve in good pictures.)

*Conviction facts; the problem*

It soon became obvious that the electronic eye and the little black bar indicator were not functioning. The reputable dealer from whom I had bought the camera had retired a month later, sold out his business, and closed his store. Your authorized dealer—Picturetronics, Inc.— here in (city name), however, repaired these parts under your company's warranty. But the next time I used the camera the flash attachment did not work, though the batteries were new. Again Picturetronics had the camera for a week's checkup and repair. Finally, two days before my departure on the trip, they called to report that my camera was "now in excellent working order." Little did any of us guess the picture problems ahead.

*More on the problem*

Nevertheless, the camera was again a disappointment only two days later—on my first attempt to take a picture with it before leaving the airport. Twice the flash did not go off and two pictures on my film were thus wasted. Because it was Sunday morning and only a few minutes before depar-

*Reader in writer's shoes; writer's care and trust*

ture, there was of course no way to have further repairs then. Perhaps you can imagine how you would feel at this moment. I had depended upon your authorized dealer's word that my camera was in excellent condition! (Incidentally, I always handle a camera with care according to instruc- tions, for I know it is a delicate precision instrument.)

Throughout my trip there were numerous "precious moments" I wanted to preserve with my new Wessman camera. Most of these were on indoor occasions—receptions, dinners, and

*Tie-in with major premise*

other functions with people. I can buy postcards of the buildings and nature. But no one sells pictures of the precious moments with other human beings who assembled just for our group! Yet these moments are lost forever because

*Writer's losses*

the flash attachment failed numerous times. These failures also resulted in my ample supply of Wessman film being exhausted much too soon. I thus had to purchase additional film plus flash bulbs in foreign stores at much higher prices.

When my developed film was returned I found that <u>72</u> nega- tives were total blanks. In other words, 72 times that flash attachment failed: 72 precious moments are lost instead of preserved, as your slogan advertises.

*Appeal to fairness and pride*

Picturetronics, Inc. have said they can't understand what is the matter with this camera and they've done all they can. Even they suggest that my camera must be one of the very rare defective products from your usually dependable high-quality stock. Thus I am returning this camera to you

*Request*

for your inspection. But after all the heartaches it has given me—in losing instead of preserving precious moments —I ask that you please keep this camera and send me instead a new dependable Instanshot camera. Also, will you please reimburse me for the $32.92 I paid for wasted film, processing, and flashbulbs. Copies of sales slips are enclosed.

*Tie-in with major premise*

By making these fair replacements you will help to restore my faith in Wessman. Also, not only I myself but friends who share my disappointments, will again believe that Wessman does "preserve those precious moments."

Letter 2—also long—is a persuasive request written after previous direct requests had failed. Because of the seriousness of the situation, this writer (the dealer) uses some negative appeals—*loss* of reader benefits—along with the positive benefits. Mr. Lampson is production manager.

**Letter 2:** *A dealer persuasively requests better deliveries of a manufacturer's products.*

Dear Mr. Lampson:

*Attention-getting assertion*  Repetition is an accepted mechanism for achieving emphasis. Although we have stated to you before our situation with respect to Crown tools, we are writing again now to emphasize to you the probable sad consequences of your current performance and allocations.

*Interest; problem*  Because of population influx in this area and the tremendous increase in construction here, we believe you are taking a serious hazard by overlooking your competitive position in Arizona. Too many new users of electric tools and too many established Crown customers are finding it *Risk of losing benefits* necessary to turn to other brands. Come the day when you have more tools than orders, you'll be sorry, and we with you will suffer in pride and pocketbook.

*Reader benefit*  Our plea to you is certainly more deserving than most distributors you know, here or elsewhere. We sell Crown saws and no other hand saw; we sell Crown drills, not eight other kinds; your sanders, your grinders, your shear and even your good little nibbler are all we have. We have no connection nor do we seek one with any of your competitors.

*Conviction; facts that affect reader benefit*  Now, we have lots of lines, big equipment and small. We represent 84 manufacturers and we have 14 salesmen outside, 4 inside. Whether on commission or on trainee salaries, these men get paid in direct proportion to the gross profit they bring the house and they know it. Their total mass sales effort is split in direct proportion to the gross profit. Our total allocation of tools for September was $2400. Even if we had received these tools, which we didn't, each man could have had $150 worth to sell; his maximum personal gain on Crown tools, about $13. What percentage of a man's sales effort do you expect to command for a maximum monthly potential of this amount, especially *Description of problem* if he had to wait 6 to 12 months after the sale to get delivery for his by then, irate customer?

*Appeal to fairness*  From the viewpoint of management, how can we reasonably spend time training our young men in your line? Let me assure you that we do spend time and energy all out of proportion to our immediate profit. We took about 115 down payments on saws based on promises we made on your authority and in good faith. So far, we have refunded 68, you have lost 68 customers at least temporarily, and our expense of handling these and other Crown tool orders has been serious. We have, to our present sorrow, booked a

*Reader loss of benefits*　tremendous backlog on your saws.  Should we keep booking orders even on extremely indefinite delivery?  We wish you'd tell us.

*Facts on the problem*　Yesterday we checked our customer orders against our backlog with you.  It was a shock even to us.  We have 6 of your tools in stock.  Four are air saws; two are samples not to be sold.  After heavy cancellations we have remaining now firm orders for 192% of the orders we have with you.  Our backlog with you slightly exceeds 12 times your intended (unmet) September allocation.

*Reader benefit*　We mentioned 192%.  With a guaranteed promise of 60 days on saws, we could run this to 300% in signed sales orders within three days.  Every man we have has a list of customers who want to be informed of any break in the situation.  Now, a word about our customers.  We have the best quality trade.  The major industrials and their responsible contractors in Arizona comprise the bulk of our backlog in Crown tools.  They are our friends and can be yours!  We want you to help us serve them to insure their helping us when there are more tools than tool buyers.

*More risks*　In conclusion, a word about competition.  It is public information that Rall brand has made us and you look pretty foolish here.  We have heard some mechanical complaints about Rall, but the difference of say 40% in the life of a saw is not noticeable to the man who has only Rall saws.  Because of your unbalanced and locally unfavorable allocation flow here, very few fellows we know have been able to compare new Ralls with any but old Crown saws.  We cannot in honesty divert Crown saws to rental for the present, and the number we have to sell doesn't allow many chances for comparison.

*Request; reader benefit*　Therefore, please do everything you can to step up your shipments to fill the backlog of orders while you can still save this excellent market!

## Persuasively Requesting Credit

Most credit applications are direct requests, made in the routine course of business. However, sometimes you may seek a special credit privilege which on the surface you appear to be unqualified for. In such cases a persuasive request is more effective. For instance, if you are a businessman just starting your own first store and your capital, inventory, and current income are barely adequate, you will need to convince a prospective creditor that he can depend upon you to pay regularly. Or you may wish to ask for 120-day credit terms instead of the usual 30-day period. Whatever your unusual request may be, be sure to include sufficient facts and figures to show how you have planned carefully and perhaps how the reader will benefit—for example, from your expected expanding market.

Sometimes a credit applicant's first direct request is turned down and he cannot understand why. If he still wants credit with that firm, a persuasive request such as Letter 3 may help accomplish his purpose. This letter brought a prompt pleasant phone call, an apology, and the granting of a Blank's revolving credit account "gladly."

*Letter 3: A persuasive request for credit after a turndown.*

Dear Mr. Reef:

*Attention: assertion*

Your form letter of January 31 refusing my request for the Blank's Revolving Credit (BRC) account and suggesting I consider an Easy Payment Account came as a mild shock.

*Interest; applicant's work and knowledge*

Blanks, without a doubt, maintains certain policies regarding credit applications from individuals. In my occupation as a bookkeeper and assistant manager of City Paint and Hardware Company, I process many applications for credit. Therefore, I feel that when you considered my application, either sufficient information was not given or the fact that I am renting a house, rather than buying, was regarded as grounds for listing me as a person of "questionable" credit standing. In either assumption, I believe the following information will give you a clear picture of my "present circumstances."

Employment and Income
    (7 lines)

*Conviction facts*

Assets and Liabilities
    (8 lines)

References
    (11 lines)

*Reader-benefit request*

The Easy Payment Plan you suggest is an expensive way to buy merchandise. To buy on this plan partially defeats the purpose of "SHOP AT BLANKS AND SAVE!" Small easy payments do not appeal to me. Nor does dragging out payments over a long period of time. Your BRC account would be one I would use frequently. And you can be sure that you will receive prompt payments. BRC fits my present needs and my ability to pay. Your extending this privilege to me will be greatly appreciated.

## Persuasively Requesting Changes in Policy or Performance

Besides requesting nonroutine adjustment or credit, you may at times need to persuade a company to make other exceptions from its usual policy. Or you may wish to persuade individuals to change their actions, or to give employees a written pep talk hoping to improve their future performance. The basic persuasive-request pattern is again applicable here.

*Changes in Policy.* In Letter 4, an advertising consultant tries to persuade the public relations officer of ABC Company to deviate from its usual policy of not giving away or lending products. An outstanding magazine feature writer (renamed Jake Edlis in this example) had written for permission to borrow, free, ABC Company's new XX boating equipment—to use, photograph, and mention in all or some of his new series of feature stories on outdoor life. Because Jake knew ABC's usual policy, he wrote a persuasive request to both the advertising consultant and the public relations officer (Harry) presenting to them numerous facts about the magazines for which he writes and names of other large companies that regularly lend their equipment and products to him.

*Letter 4: An advertising consultant's persuasive request to deviate from the usual no-loan policy regarding equipment.*

Dear Harry:

*Attention: assertion*
Though I know it is ABC's policy not to loan or give away its products, I think sticking to it in the case of Jake Edlis would be a mistake.

*Interest and conviction*
There are very few writers in the recreation field for whom I'd take a stand on this issue. Among them are_____, _____, _____, and Jake Edlis.

*Company benefit*
First, lending your boating equipment is a relatively small expense for the publicity ABC is bound to receive in return. The space value could, conceivably, amount to tens of thousands of dollars. As you know, his writeups reach about 16 million readers each month.

*More company benefit*
Second, ABC is big league now. Big leaguers play the game by getting respected writers like Edlis to use their products (many of them carrying big price tags) and write about them.

*More company benefit*
Third, as a member of the Outdoor Writers Association of America and a well-known feature writer, Edlis is bound to talk to a lot of other "influentials" in the field. He could, intentionally or not, start word that ABC is willing

*Risk of*
*harmful*
*results if*
*change is*
*not made*

to take lots of free space, but unwilling to extend the accepted courtesy of letting legitimate feature writers try its products without charge. Ultimately, this could lead to poor press relations and a resulting drop in our publicity lineage.

*Company-*
*benefit*
*request*

In the interest of maintaining exceptionally good press relations, please reconsider your company's "no give-away" policy when someone with the stature of a Jake Edlis offers his services. I'm sure you'll be glad you did.

*Changes in Performance.* Persuasion is necessary whenever you need to convince individuals to change their performance (which may include personal appearance and habits as well as business practices) and if direct requests have been or would be unheeded.

The next two examples[1] illustrate how important the right tone and use of appeals are for getting reader cooperation. As you read Letter 5, note these faults:

1. Overemphasis on negatives—"disturbed," "horrified," "will have to be removed," "senseless," "punishing," "destroying"
2. Overuse of "we"—meaning Landlord, Inc., rather than all people (us) in the neighborhood
3. Manager's domineering, threatening, discourteous attitude, which places all parents on the defensive and seems to blame their children, although the vandals may have been outsiders
4. Total lack of reader appeals

*Letter 5: A poor, negative, unpersuasive request from a building manager to tenants.*

<u>DEVELOPMENT LANDLORD, INC., Metropolis, U.S.A.</u>

TO ALL PARENTS LIVING IN 100 OAK AVENUE AND 50 ELM AVENUE

We have become seriously disturbed because of the recent vandalism in your neighborhood. Every day now, storage room doors are being broken, tires removed from bicycles, parts of baby carriages are taken off, etc. etc., but today we were horrified to see a beautiful living tree (in front of 50 Elm Avenue) completely cut in half. Now the tree will have to be removed.

We would like all the parents to have a good talk with their children in order to stop this senseless destruction.

We will start patrolling this section very closely from now on, and if necessary, we will call in the municipal and school authorities of Metropolis, in order to start punishing children who are found destroying property.

[1] Courtesy of New York Life Insurance Company, *Effective Letters Bulletin,* Summer 1965.

In contrast, Letter 6 eliminates the main faults of Letter 5. Its tone is friendly, courteous, and positive. Equally important, this letter emphasizes community spirit, *mutual* concern, and cooperation. Letter 6 appeals to the parents' pride, love of family, health, and desire for security; and it includes the young people as citizens instead of accusing them indirectly of being vandals.

*Letter 6: An appealing, improved version of Letter 5.*

TO ALL FAMILIES IN THE ELM AVENUE SCHOOL DISTRICT:

*Attention: a mutual problem*

    I know you will be as sorry as I was to learn that the lovely old elm tree which gave our school its name was destroyed today.  Its beauty and grace are now lost to us forever, and all of us regret this tragedy.

*Interest; need for mutual effort*

    The destruction of our landmark appears to be another in a recent series of acts of vandalism in our neighbor- hood—a problem which can affect all of us unless we make a mutual effort to rid ourselves of it.

*Conviction; appeals to safety, health, security, and civic pride*

    A number of residents of our community have volun- teered to do patrol duty in their off-hours, protecting the safety of our families and our property.  Though we appre- ciate their desire to help, we need to ask ourselves if a patrol is what we really want.  Do we want our neighborhood to be a prison for our children or a place of freedom and healthful growth?

    Shall we instead face this problem frankly and con- structively?  Let us consider a few facts.  Does our community have adequate provisions for recreational activi- ties, or should we be contributing more to the creativity, growth, and culture of Metropolis?  Have we done everything possible to make this the city in which our young people will be proud to grow up?

*Request*

*Appeals to pride and cooperation*

    It has been suggested that we discuss these things both in our own homes and then together as a community. Will you meet with us next Monday evening, January 18, at 7:30 in the auditorium of Elm Avenue School so that we may plan a constructive program of progress?  Perhaps we can form a "Civic Pride Committee" comprised of both young people and adults—a committee which can investigate our needs and help us plan a calendar of events to appeal to everyone.  Our mayor and councilmen share our enthusiasm and have agreed to be present.

*Reader benefits*

    Let's make Monday evening "Family Night."  Fill the auditorium with families, ideas, and appetites for cake, coffee, and cokes,  See you at 7:30!

## UNSOLICITED SALES LETTERS

Every year millions of dollars' worth of goods and services are sold through sales letters—both solicited[1] and unsolicited[2]—to consumers, businesses, and industries. Direct mail[3] successfully urges people to buy products ranging from mail-order catalogued items to real estate. Not only large retail chains such as Montgomery Ward and Sears Roebuck, but also thousands of lesser-known big-city and small-town merchants, wholesalers, and manufacturers sell effectively by mail. (Many firms sell exclusively by mail.) Even managers of shops selling services (for home and auto repair, health, beauty, protection, and others) stimulate their businesses by sales messages.

Although you should be aware of the enormous potential income that is possible using well-written sales letters, you need also to be aware of the strong resistance that many people have toward such messages. Common criticisms from readers who look unfavorably on sales letters are these: insincerity, appeals to the wrong group, hidden gimmicks, lack of personalization, "Madison Avenue" approach, excessive length, exaggeration.

In general, your success in sales letters will depend upon three factors: the mailing list, the right appeals, and the presentation. The first two of these factors are *prewriting* steps. The remainder of this chapter discusses the steps to take before writing unsolicited sales letters, gives suggestions for writing them, and offers examples of various kinds of unsolicited sales letters.

### Steps before Writing the Unsolicited Sales Letter

Because your sales letter may go to hundreds—even thousands—of people, you need to do exceptionally careful planning before starting to write it. The five thinking steps—about purpose, reader, ideas to include, fact gathering, and organization—are especially important. You usually first gather facts on your product and your prospective buyer and then give extra thought to the purpose, appeals, and presentation of your entire sales message.

*Gathering Facts about Your Product.* Before you write a sales letter, you first analyze thoroughly the product you want to sell. (The word "product" as used here includes both tangible products and intangible services.) You gather information through reading, observing, testing, using, comparing, questioning, researching.

[1] For solicited sales letters—which are answers to inquiries about products and services—see Chapter 7, pages 208–213.
[2] Unsolicited sales letters are also known as "prospecting" and "cold turkey" letters. They are initiated by the seller for various reasons and are not direct answers to inquiries.
[3] In general, the term "direct mail" refers to any printed matter, other than periodicals, that attempts to sell or promote sales by mail. It includes—in addition to letters—postcards, manuals, brochures, order blanks, pamphlets, leaflets, gadgets, and reply forms. These items usually supplement the letter and help create a favorable seller-buyer relationship.

If yours is a tangible product, what are its physical characteristics—size, color, shape, content, composition? How is it made and where did raw materials come from? How does it operate? What is its performance record? How does it compare with and differ from competitors' products in durability, efficiency, appearance, price, terms? What are its weaknesses? Strengths?

For your future buyers, benefits (psychological description) are usually much more significant than physical description. What will the product do for each user? What human needs or desires does it fulfill? For instance, a magazine may be a certain size, with *x* number of pages, on glossy paper, with hundreds of half-page pictures. But what information and enjoyment—even profits—does it bring to the user? What good does it do him in his business, home, family, and community contacts?

A new real estate subdivision may consist of 100 six-room brick, ranch-style houses on one-quarter-acre tracts. But why should the reader purchase in this subdivision rather than elsewhere? Perhaps living here is unique because of the climate and scenic beauty which allow year-round sun, fun, and sports, plus a plentiful supply of fresh water and fertile soil? Perhaps a trend of prolonged rise in real estate values makes this property a good investment? Perhaps it is an exceptionally good place to rear children?

Your vinyl jackets may have the same "rich grain as expensive buckskin leathers" and be available in ten sizes. But of special interest to your customer are these facts about what a jacket will do for him:

> It is completely water-repellent, so he will be dry in any downpour.
> Though the jacket is fully lined, he can wear it in any weather all year round.
> It's soft and pliable and never needs costly dry cleaning.
> Dirt and stains come clean with a damp cloth and a little mild detergent.
> Its classic style won't go out of fashion.
> He saves money by buying direct from the factory, and no salesman rushes or pressures him.
> He can try the jacket on at home and wear it ten days without obligation.

Whatever your product, you must know all its physical features and its reader benefits before you can confidently and effectively sell it.

*Knowing Your Reader and Obtaining Mailing Lists.* To sell your product effectively by letter requires also a knowledge of your reader and a selective, up-to-date, accurate mailing list.[1]

Previous discussions in this text on you attitude and visualizing your reader also apply to sales letters, and they need not be repeated here. It is especially important to remember that the sales letter must be adapted to the

---

[1] You'll use the mailing list both for a test mailing and for the entire mailing of one or several sales letters. Testing means mailing the letter to a small percentage (perhaps 5 to 10%) of the names on your list to see whether the letter brings the percentage of response necessary for you to make a profit.

needs and interests of your specific group of readers. When your product has almost universal use, you may have several different, reasonably homogeneous groups of prospects. Thus if you want to sell lighting fixtures by mail, you need to know the tastes, problems, preferences, and conditions of your various prospective users—homeowners, architects, store or office managers, plant or hospital or school superintendents, etc.,—and you'll write different letters to each group.

*Selectivity* in your mailing list is important because even an excellent sales letter about the best product in the world will not sell if the message goes to the wrong readers. You would not sell office filing cabinets to outdoor laborers, or fishing boats to low-income girls in a desert area, or Cadillacs to pensioners.

You can buy, rent, or make up a mailing list that includes the best potential buyers for your product. The more similar their characteristics and circumstances, the better. You can buy names and addresses of almost any kind of specialized group of people—classified by income level, age, marital status, sex, number of children, occupation, geographic location, color of eyes, height, education. However, you need to be cautious. For instance, even if your product is for people with above-average incomes, you must take other factors into account. For example, a man with a $30,000 income and eight children may be less able to spend for luxuries than a childless man with a lower income.

If you wish to make your own list, you will find one or more of these sources useful: telephone books, directories, membership lists, vital statistics, newspaper articles, replies to your advertising, and—sometimes best of all— your own company records.[1] Your credit and sales departments can give you lists of present and former customers; other departments can furnish lists of stockholders, employees, suppliers. Any or all of these may be good for your own company-prospect list.

*Up-to-dateness and accuracy* can save a firm needless waste on costs of labor, postage, paper, and processing. Postal authorities tell us that over one-fourth of all addresses change within one year. Names and titles may change too. The mailing list must be correct in addresses, spelling of names, use of prefixes (Mr., Miss, Mrs., Dr.) and titles (vice-president or executive vice-president), etc. No matter how selective the list may be, it is good only when it is updated and correct.

*Deciding on Purpose.* The purpose of an unsolicited sales letter may be to make a direct sale, to serve as stimulus for future sales, or to win back lost customers.

---

[1] Among the many firms that have compared the pulling power of rented versus their company-prospect names is Merrill, Lynch, Pierce, Fenner and Smith. They found that 10,560 rented names brought a 7.4% response; 10,900 company-prospect names brought a 24.9% response. (*The Reporter of Direct Mail Advertising Newsletter*, November 1966)

***To make a direct sale*** is usually the purpose of a sales letter about a relatively inexpensive convenience item or a service that the prospect can buy without previously seeing or discussing it in person. Sometimes even for more expensive or complex items your purpose may be to sell with only one letter, as you will see later in this chapter. More often, however, for such products the direct-sale letter follows previous groundwork laid by former letters (in a campaign series), by demonstrations, by advertising, or by salesmen. The requested action to clinch the sale is that the prospect send for the article.[1]

***To serve as a stimulus for a sale sometime in the future*** is the long-range purpose of a variety of sales letters, many of which are known as sales promotion messages. They help to build goodwill, to supplement advertising that failed to bring desired results, to give a pep talk to distributors. Or they may serve as part of a campaign series involving complicated costly products (like factory machinery) or services (like mortgage lending) that require planning and/or individual consultation with a company representative before purchase. In these letters the purpose may be to introduce the product and then follow up with a salesman. The requested action may be that the customer should: ask for a booklet, catalog, or other information; invite a representative to call; or come to the salesroom himself.

***To win back lost customers*** is the goal of other sales letters. The purpose is to let customers who haven't bought anything for some time know you miss them, to find out why they haven't been buying from you, and to sell them on coming back. The requested action is usually that the customer return a questionnaire; often an enclosed order blank brings a direct sale. For dissatisfied customers, good followup can help bring in future sales.

***Choosing Ideas and the Main Appeal.*** After you have collected facts on your product, obtained a mailing list of likely prospects, and determined your purpose, you are ready to decide on ideas to include in your sales letter. Instead of cluttering your letter with a long list of facts about your product, you should select for emphasis a central selling point and translate it into user benefits. You stress whatever appeal is most likely to convince the prospect that he should buy your product. Often this is the feature or benefit that differentiates your product from competitors'. After you have stressed the central selling point, you can introduce other appeals about your product. (For a second letter to the same prospects, you can stress a second central selling point.)

Your central selling point is always based on what you estimate are the prospect's needs. Will the product cut his costs? protect him? make him more attractive? If your product will appeal to different groups of prospects for

---

[1] In some letters—those offering a free trial or money-back guarantee—the requested action (sending for the article) is usually only a preliminary, conditional step. The sale is really not closed until the customer has examined and perhaps used the product within a specified time limit.

different reasons, you will write a different sales letter to each group. In each letter you will feature the central selling point and appeals that you estimate are most pleasing to the readers for whom you write it. For example, to dealers who expect to resell your product, you will emphasize quick turnover and profits. To consumers you may feature comfort, pride in personal appearance, safety, or any other appropriate appeals like those listed on page 348.

Suppose, for instance, you want to sell by mail the vinyl jacket described briefly on page 372. To readers living in rainy areas you might feature year-round comfort (dry in any downpour). To readers in arid regions your major appeal may be convenience (easily cleaned and wearable the year around). For students you might focus on both attractiveness (in style) and saving money (infrequent replacements, factory prices, no dry-cleaning bills).

*Planning the Presentation.* The fifth thinking step—organization—involves much more than deciding upon the organizational plan of the letter itself. Consider your letter as part of an entire mailed sales presentation which includes the letter with all enclosures—whether it is to be a single sales effort or to be part of a campaign series. That presentation must move readers to take the desired action—and yield a satisfactory profit. The percentage of response needed for profitable returns may range from less than one percent[1] to a much higher figure, depending upon various factors. The returns the mailing brings must be sufficiently greater than its total cost—for the list, plus planning, consulting (with direct mail specialists),[2] writing, reproducing, and mailing the letter with all its enclosures.

Ultimately, though the initial cost of these steps may be high, the cost per mailing may be as low as 10 to 50 cents or as high as several dollars each—and the resulting profits many times these amounts. Plans and decisions (by you and perhaps other executives and a consultant) are essential. You need to consider enclosures and also the length, appearance, and timing of the entire sales message. Your budget and numerous other factors enter into this plan.

*The number and kinds of enclosures* that supplement your sales letter should be planned before you write it. Will the envelope contain any descriptive pamphlet, separate testimonials, pictures, samples, gimmicks, gadgets, order blank, and/or a reply envelope? Gadgets and gimmicks should be used only if they help to dramatize a point, not if they merely attract attention. (Some readers dislike them; others become absorbed in them and fail to read the letter.) The usual enclosures are leaflet, order blank, and reply envelope.

*The length of the sales letter* depends on various factors. For example, if the enclosures adequately take care of all needed details, the letter should preferably be only one page. This is especially true if its purpose is to get ac-

---

[1] For instance, the Mercedes-Benz letter mentioned on the next page (footnote 2) successfully achieved its goal, though only three-tenths of one percent of the readers purchased a car.

[2] Many firms (except those with specially trained direct mail staffs) ask outside specialists to write their sales letters and plan the enclosures.

tion other than a direct purchase. If a catalog or booklet is to be sent later upon request, or if a demonstration or salesman is to follow, these methods will help make the sale. On the contrary, if you do not have a separate enclosure—and especially if you want to make a direct sale—your letter may have to be longer than one page. Just be sure it is as concise as possible!

Many conflicting ideas exist about the desirable length of sales letters. Don Francisco, a former great in the advertising business, once gave a good answer to the question, "Why do all direct mail experts believe in long copy for their selling letters?":

> They find that it is better to have 20 people read the entire letter and be convinced than to have 100 merely see it.[1]

Direct mail experts have proved again and again that long copy works—if it catches and holds the reader's interest and is sufficiently convincing.[2]

*Appearance* of the sales letter may be coordinated with the letterhead, envelope, and enclosures in color, pictures, designs, etc. To a prospect a company is what it appears to be in its printed mailing. You need to decide (usually with the help of experts in direct mail, advertising, and/or processing) on the quality and color of paper to be used and also whether the printing will be in one or more colors. Other factors to be considered in your planning are these:

> Should special pictures, designs, handwritten "teaser" statements, or other attention-getting devices or gimmicks be used on the outside envelope and the letterhead?[3] If so, they will to some extent affect the wording of your letter . . . and your costs too.

> Should the letter be personalized with the reader's name and address? You will be well repaid for carefully comparing relative costs. If your mailing list is long, computer facsimile (preprinted) letters with computerized matching fill-ins can be effective. Or, if you want to avoid the cost of well-matched fill-ins, you may have the name and address processed in a different color from that of the letter's body. Thus you show your reader the courtesy of a personalized salutation without attempting to deceive (as with a poorly matched fill-in). Another alternative is to insert a catchy appropriate statement in place of the inside address and salutation.

---

[1] *Sam's Almanac of Direct Mail*, vol. V, no. 5, The Mail Advertising Bureau, Inc., Seattle, Washington, 1967.

[2] One of the more startling success stories is the case of the Mercedes-Benz company that sold 1,500 Model 190D Sedans for $4,068 each, one summer before Labor Day (1965)—entirely through a five-page letter which their advertising agency designed and mailed to 500,000 people. This letter's success was remarkable for another reason: these cars used diesel fuel, a hurdle because diesel fuel stations were scarce at the time. (Courtesy of Mercedes-Benz of North America, Inc., Fort Lee, New Jersey).

[3] See also paragraphs 3 and 4, page 347, regarding the attention-getting importance of envelopes and letterheads.

What about the sizes of the letterhead, envelopes, and other enclosures? Should any be oversize? Transparent? With what size and kind of type?

Should the envelopes have windows? Should part of the letter's message show through one or more windows?

Should you "dress up" the sales letter itself? You can add interesting variety and emphasis by occasional underscoring or capitalizing of important ideas, by indenting some sentences or paragraphs on both margins, by use of more short than long paragraphs, and by "inked" lines, arrows, or other marks to emphasize ideas.

The reproduction of your mailing pieces should preferably be done professionally. Using your company's duplicating machine may be all right for some small sales efforts, but professional jobs make the best impression. Also it is best not to try to disguise direct mail with "cute" attempts to fool the recipient, for most people react negatively to them. The honest, well-written factual presentation that is reader-centered and pleasing always outpulls the others.

*Timing* of the sales message also affects its success and should be carefully planned. Consider what is likely to be the best time of the week, month, season, and year to launch a certain sales campaign. The time of your mailing will naturally affect the wording of your sales letter and sometimes your choice of appeals (as for certain seasons, holidays, etc.).

Figures released by the National Association of Manufacturers show that 80 percent of orders are placed after the salesman's fifth call. Remember that a sales letter is a "salesman" too. Some firms have effectively sent the same letter (perhaps on paper of a different color) to the same prospects two or three times and received orders only after the last mailing.

## Suggestions for Writing the Unsolicited Sales Letter

After you have completed the prewriting steps—about your product, mailing list of prospects, choice of ideas and main appeals, and the planned presentation—you are ready to develop the sales letter itself. This writing (and revising) will probably take hours, even days. If time and budget permit, you may decide—with the help of a consultant—to prepare several versions of your letter to test their pulling power before mailing one to the entire mailing list.

Your basic guide is the AIDA organizational pattern discussed on pages 346–348. Although the discussion below focuses separately on each part of the AIDA plan, the parts need not always be in this sequence, nor need all parts be in every letter. Some sales letters begin with desire-creating material such as testimonials or guarantees. Some start with action-inducing statements such as special offers or free trial. Some may skip product description and uses (the interest section) and devote most of the letter to proof—if, for example, the reader already knows the description and uses but needs conviction material to reinforce his interest and create desire to buy the product. Circumstances vary—and so do sales letter content and organization.

*Attracting Your Prospect's Attention.* The best way to catch the attention of a busy reader is by promising—or implying a forthcoming promise—*to benefit him by satisfying a need.* Mention what the reader gains from the product before you name it. (Using his name in the salutation also helps get his attention.)

Though the letter may go to thousands of people, each copy must "talk" in a natural, sincere, friendly way to an individual human being. The opening should be appropriate, fresh, honest, interesting, specific, and relevant to the central selling point. Avoid tricky, exaggerated openings, which have been so overused that the American public is unmoved or annoyed by them. Of course, if you can think of a novel, catchy opening that honestly relates closely to your central theme, go ahead and use it.

Also be careful to avoid openings that may outdate your letter soon. For instance, one letter addressed to "Dear Graduate" began "Now that you are out of school for three months . . . ." Readers who had been out of school longer than that were of course annoyed by the inaccuracy.

For both *form* and *content* of the sales letter's attention-getting opening you have a variety of choices. But keep the first paragraph short, preferably two to five lines, sometimes only one. Short paragraphs look easy to read and thus are more likely to get the reader started. If unusual circumstances require you to have a long opening paragraph, it should be set up in an easy-to-read way—sometimes with double spaces between sentences or with some lines indented from both margins. (See, for instance, the first example under "Questions" on the next page.)

*Any of these forms of expression* can begin your sales letter—command, direct statement, headline, hypothetical comment, or question.

### Command
Try to tear up the enclosed paper.

Give your college student a head start toward financial security!

### Direct Statement
Here is an opportunity to test a new product right at your own desk.

You probably have employees who would benefit greatly from R&L's low-cost Language of Business Course.

### Headline
NOW YOU CAN GET
THE MOST COMPREHENSIVE BENEFITS EVER OFFERED THE
FISHERMAN—FOR LESS THAN 12¢ A WEEK!

*Hypothetical Comment*
IF THREE RADIATOR REPAIR EXPERTS
WALKED INTO YOUR SHOP THIS AFTERNOON . . .
(See Letter 1, page 391.)

*Questions*
How many records will $3.98 buy in your home town? Only one?
But . . .
    we'll send you 12 of the latest hit albums—
    up to $66.76 worth of new records—

    plus a transistor radio—for the same $3.98!

Are there ways to save far more money than you do now? Can you increase
your capital significantly by shrewd investments? What are the smart ways to
buy so that you spend less and have more? How do others free dollars from
taxes in ways you'd never suspect?

*For the content* of your attention-getting opening, you can choose from
any of the following 11 kinds (arranged alphabetically). As you read the
examples, notice which *form* of expression they use.

### 1. An Agreeable Assertion
*Selling window units:*
> Your new home that you are planning to build will probably last you for the
> rest of your life. Be sure when you build it that one of the four essential
> parts of your home will also last a lifetime.

*Offering a free brand-new handbook and a special magazine subscription:*
> As a Westerner interested in boating, you know how different our yachting
> and boating activities and opportunities are out here.

### 2. A Comparison or a (Short!) Story[1]
*Selling a secretary's handbook along with a free kit:*
*(Pictures of a cluttered and a tidy desk at top of letter)*

> It's really amazing! Betty and Marilyn work side-by-side in the same office.
> They have the same secretarial training and skills . . . both have identical
> workloads—yet Betty is usually putting the finishing touches to her makeup
> by 4:45 everyday, while Marilyn usually can't even find her handbag under
> the clutter of unfinished work still on her desk.
>
> And not only the janitor notices! Their boss has noticed the difference
> too. So besides the sheer delight of an easier day with much less pressure,
> let's face it, Betty will be in line for promotions, pay raises, and all the
> "fringe benefits" that go with them!

### 3. An Event or Fact in the Reader's Life
*Selling a savings account:*
> Congratulations on the new arrival in your home! Your baby's first word . . .

---

[1] Avoid a long story opening. It detracts from your main theme.

and that first step . . . are important events. So is the first dollar that goes into a child's own savings account.

*Selling car insurance:*
The fact that you are a college senior specializing in medicine and attend a well-respected university like (name) tells people about your character.

For instance, it may qualify you for a special low-cost auto insurance program that might not otherwise be available to you.

### 4. *A Problem the Reader May Face*

*Urging use of a catalog to shop by mail:*
During the next few weeks you and people all over the country will be doing Christmas shopping. Some will be early birds. Others will wait until the last minute; and if they are shopping in the stores, they will be pushed around and have to take what is left instead of being able to purchase just the items they had in mind.

*Enclosing a booklet to a woman and urging her to visit "your Ford Dealer":*
If you're like most women you're probably a "born shopper"—one who looks for and gets the most for her money. And you know how important comparison shopping is—when you're looking for a new coat, a hat, or a washing machine.

### 5. *A Quotation*

*Selling repair service:*
"A stitch in time saves nine."

*Selling correspondence study:*
"To be or not to be, that is the question."

### 6. *A Scare Opening*[1]

*Selling bank safe-deposit boxes:*
*(Picture of a burning home. Letter is on a simulated document from which a corner has been burned off.)*

LET'S JUST SUPPOSE
This was a valuable document in your home, destroyed because of fire. Not only could it mean a severe financial loss but replacing it might take months as well as a considerable amount of inconvenience.

*Selling health and accident protection:*
And . . . how *lucky* can you be?
Statisticians tell us that *one* out of every *six* persons will be sick, though not necessarily hospitalized, during the coming year. Can you count on your luck getting you by without a serious case of work-stopping, income-crippling illness?

### 7. *A Significant Fact about the Product*

*Urging professors to order multiple copies for class use:*
In 51 of 56 well-known United States colleges and universities, the Class

---

[1] Scare openings are usually *not* recommended—except for some kinds of insurance and other services treating accidents or crime *if* the idea of harm or danger is already in the prospect's mind and the letter offers a solution. If, however, the idea of danger or harm is not likely to be on his mind, the opening should be positive and pleasant, stressing the solution rather than the danger.

of '7_ voted (name) magazine their *first choice* among 18 of America's leading magazines.

*Selling TV cable service:*

More than 4,000,000 viewers in the UNITED STATES . . .

. . . and . . .

over 10,000 people in the (city) area alone enjoy sharp, clear, multichannel television reception by means of C.A.T.V. (Community Antenna Television).

## 8. A Solution to a Problem

*Selling canned seafood:*

Here's the solution to your Christmas present problem. You will delight in giving this taste treat from the North Pacific to your relatives, friends, and business acquaintances.

*Selling hospital insurance:*

(Picture of a $935 check at top of letterhead.)

You can receive a check like this, or even up to $5000, when you or a member of your family goes to the hospital . . . *IF* you are protected by Hospital Plan.

## 9. A Special Offer or a Gift

*Selling book club membership:*

The extraordinary opportunity described in the big circular—for you to get this remarkable new major dictionary AT AN IMMEDIATE SAVING OF $20 (capitals in red print)—speaks pretty much for itself.

*Announcing a sale:*

Save!!! Purchase *any* one item at the White Front (city name) Store for 10% off!

You, as a preferred customer, can purchase any one item beginning 10 a.m. and ending 9 p.m. Tuesday, September 30, at 10% OFF our every-day low discount price.

## 10. A Surprising or Challenging Statement

*Selling a magazine subscription:*

It's a waste of time, but try to tear up the enclosed order form that offers you Newsweek for about 13¢ a copy.

I'm sure you can't It's printed on special paper that just won't tear. But go ahead—give it a try![1]

*Selling a fund plan:*

It's not the cost of a college education that really hurts . . . it's the cost of *not* having it.

Today, the college graduate earns, on the average, $175,000 more during his lifetime than the high school graduate.

## 11. Testimonials

*Selling industrial cleaning compound:*

"XX is by far the best cleanser we have ever used," says Mr. Tom Brown, building superintendent at ABC Company.

---

[1] Although this opening is a gimmick, it relates well to the central theme—reliability.

*Arousing the Reader's Interest.* Having attracted the reader's attention, you now arouse his interest by beginning to "picture" your product and telling what it will do for him. You begin to develop the central selling point.

As stated in the general outline on pages 346–348, you can picture your product in two ways—physical description and reader benefits. You can place the benefits first—as in Example 1 below—or later, but usually they are interwoven with physical description, as in Example 2.

*Example 1: Stating benefits before physical description.*

When you use <u>Family Investments</u> you find hundreds of ways to
make your money earn more and go further -- for your home,
clothing, food, travel, taxes, and pleasure.  You get a rich
source of advice from accountants, automotive specialists, real
estate agents, tax consultants, life insurance experts,
bankers, stockbrokers, lawyers.

This leatherbound book contains 467 pages, divided by subject
into 15 chapters, 165,000 words.  Sturdily built for continual
use, the book has 310 drawings, graphs and tables to illustrate
points and clarify meanings.  In essence, using the book will
be like taking a fascinating course in managing your family's
money -- from highly paid professionals.

*Example 2: Interweaving benefits and physical description.*

The "heart" of your outfit is Bell & Howell's great Zoom-Lens
Electric-Drive Super 8 Camera.  You just pop in the Kodak
cartridge of Super 8 color film (it's fast and simple) ...
<u>aim</u> ... and <u>shoot</u>.  That's all there is to it.  And this camera
is <u>electrically</u> powered -- no winding whatsoever.  Pop the
cartridge in and you are ready to shoot a full 50-foot movie
without interruption.

Just consider how every step virtually takes care of itself:
the camera sets itself automatically for different types of
film -- it even adjusts automatically for indoor or outdoor
filming -- and the Optronic Electric Eye sets the lens (also
automatically) measuring only that light reaching the film.

*Creating Desire and Convincing the Reader.* After getting your reader interested in one or several of your product's benefits, you need to create in him a desire to *own* it. Furthermore, if your purpose is to make a direct sale, you need to convince him that he should buy your product. Like the personal salesman, your letter leads the prospective buyer through a "mental demonstration" so he imagines himself already the owner—and it offers proof whenever necessary.

The reader's progression from interest to desire to conviction is usually gradual. It is not necessary to worry about exactly where one step begins or ends; these steps are parts of an integrated whole. Together they develop your central selling point and help urge the reader to take the requested action.

*To create desire* for your product you usually continue with additional physical description and reader benefits. You describe the product specifically and clearly (unless the reader already knows its description because it is a well-known product or because you described it thoroughly in a former letter), and you show him the advantages he gains from using this product.

The relative importance and length of discussion on physical features and benefits vary with the type of product and the overall sales presentation. Usually you should stress reader benefits more, and include only enough description to support the benefits. The length of desire-creating material within the letter ranges from one paragraph—in a one-page letter with descriptive brochure—to several paragraphs if the letter itself is two or more pages long, with or without an enclosed brochure.

The emphasis on reader use and benefits is especially important if your product is valued mainly for its use and/or your prospect is familiar with its appearance (for instance, an electric iron, a camera, or a television set). But if the product is valued mainly because of its appearance (for example, an ornament or a blouse), its physical details must be fully described; usually an accompanying brochure also includes a colorful picture. If the product is machinery or technical equipment, your letter must clarify its sturdiness of construction, fine workmanship, and other technical details in terms that the prospect values and can understand—whether he is a layman or a professional. Whenever desirable, you enclose with your letter technical sketches and meaningful pictures, charts, graphs. In all cases, be sure to emphasize the central selling point and show how the reader benefits. Work in one or more appeals, such as those listed on page 348.

The following examples illustrate desire-creating paragraphs that develop the central selling point and benefits. Example 3 here follows Example 2 on page 382. Notice how it continues to stress the central theme—convenience—in order to increase the reader's desire. These paragraphs are part of a three-page letter.

*Example 3: Developing the central selling point and benefit—convenience.*

<u>Breathtaking ZOOM shots from wide-angle to close-up[1]</u>

And with this camera, the special fingertip-control ZOOM lens makes it possible for you to get the same kind of breathtaking zoom shots TV and movie directors use -- you can actually shift from wide-angle shots to dramatic close-ups (and back again)

---

[1] The headings in this letter were green, in contrast to the blue print used for the rest of the letter; in a subsequent mailing of the same letter, headings were orange and the rest of the letter print, brown.

while you're shooting. And there is still another tremendous
design advance: you actually view <u>through the lens</u> while
you're filming — you get exactly what you see. And for extra
fun, you can get in the act yourself; you just set the camera's
special "Automatic Run Control."

<u>Bell & Howell Super-Bright Super 8 Projector Threads Itself</u>[1]

With this Bell & Howell Super 8 Projector, threading is, at
last, outmoded — this projector does it all for you — easily,
in just 5 seconds! Just press a button, insert the film, and
the film automatically <u>winds itself</u> through — and you sit
back, relax and enjoy your movies — up to 400 feet of film
without interruption of any kind.

And this projector has other top-quality abilities: Imagine
being able to run your movies backward. You can! Simply flip
a lever and divers bounce backward onto the board or the family
goes backward into the car after just getting out.

Just flip a lever again and this projector practically turns
into a slide machine! Now you can view the hundreds of motion
picture frames you have taken <u>one at a time</u> — and look at them
individually.

<u>You get a complete HOME MOVIE "ENTERTAINMENT CENTER"</u> — all
these extras are included:

*(The letter continues to list nine extras.)*

Example 4 is part of a two-page letter selling a "his and hers" car coat
ensemble. The central theme is the ensemble's attractive style, usefulness, and
comfort along with money-saving easy upkeep.

***Example 4:*** *Developing appeals of comfort, attractiveness, practicality, savings.*

<u>These</u> <u>coats</u> <u>look</u> <u>like</u> <u>"Buckskin"</u> <u>leather</u> . . . <u>have</u> <u>the</u> <u>same</u>
<u>rich</u> <u>grain</u> <u>as</u> <u>expensive</u> <u>leather</u> — though the tough supported
vinyl we use will probably last longer than leather. They're
completely water repellent so you'll be dry in any downpour.
Yet this fully-lined coat looks so good, feels so good on you,
that you'll wear it in any weather all year round.

This wear-with-any-color "Buckskin" color coat is a practical
coat for driving, shopping, all your leisure activities. It
never needs costly dry cleaning. Dirt and stains come clean
with a damp cloth and a little mild detergent. This is a
casual coat you'll LIKE wearing, in a classic style that will
look good on you...that won't go out of fashion.

[1] The headings in this letter were green, in contrast to the blue print used for the rest of the letter;
in a subsequent mailing of the same letter, headings were orange and the rest of the letter print,
brown.

And you'll like all the "extras" we build into these coats:
the warm quilt lining, the "stay buttons" to keep the buttons
from pulling out, the extra interlining that gives you the
practical "up-or-down" collar for wind or sun comfort, the
generous pockets, the action sleeves.

*You must present proof to convince* your reader that the features and
benefits you describe are true. By convincing the reader, you strengthen his
desire to have the product. Try to anticipate his questions and objections—
about the product itself and/or its price—and answer them. You might not
get another chance to do so!

The main proof about your product's features and benefits comes preferably from evidence that persons outside of your company determine. These
outside sources include satisfied users; recognized testing laboratories, agencies,
and disinterested persons; and the prospect himself. Seven popular kinds of
proof are illustrated below.

## From Satisfied Users

**1. Facts about Users' Experience with the Product.** These include verifiable
reports and statistics from users.

> The green page in the enclosed brochure itemizes the savings which 203 con-
> tractors have realized from EASI-POUR concrete mix. Notice that their
> actual savings range from 45% to 85%. As you study the table, note its spe-
> cific facts about the size of each job. Then compare the figures with your
> own average costs for similar projects.

**2. Names of Other Buyers and Users.** State how many persons or firms already
are using the product. Better yet, when appropriate, give the names of satisfied well-known users, or offer to send names and addresses upon request.

> This Fleet Management Service has enabled our clients to operate their
> salesmen's auto fleets better and more economically. And it might do the
> same for you. Companies that are using our service include:
> a food products manufacturer with 625 salesmen, a greeting card manu-
> facturer with 130 salesmen, a textile manufacturer with 96 salesmen, a
> coffee processor with 230 salesmen. (Names furnished on request.)

> Among the hundreds of business firms that are pleased with their use of
> ABC equipment are: Marshall Field and Company, Alcoa Aluminum, Ford
> Motor Company, United Airlines, and Chase Manhattan Bank.

**3. Testimonials.** Because testimonials have been abused (with phony quotations
by nonusers who are paid to make them), many people distrust them. To
establish the credibility of the testimonials you use, select persons or firms
that are bona-fide users of your product and whose judgment the reader
respects. And be specific. Avoid exaggerations and vague generalities.

> "Since we've been using EASY-POUR concrete mix, six of our men can
> place and finish a section of concrete street with curb—12 feet wide and a
> football field long—in only *one hour*. Its paving ability and its quality sur-

pass any concrete mix we've used during our twenty years of operation." Gene Aimes, Project Superintendent, East Contractors, Inc.

## *From Recognized Testing Laboratories, Agencies, Disinterested Persons*

**4. *Performance Tests*.** Whenever recognized experts, testing laboratories, or authoritative agencies in the field relative to your product have made satisfactory performance tests on it, their evidence offers convincing proof. Also effective are statements, reports, and statistics compiled by impartial reliable witnesses.

Learnfun electric toys have earned the endorsement and Seals of Approval from Underwriters Laboratories, Good Housekeeping Institute, American Medical Association, and the National Safety Council.

In every performance test by the United Automotive Association, ALERT batteries ranked at the top of the list. Read in the enclosed brochure the details of qualities tested, and decide for yourself why ALERT is the battery for you.

## *From the Prospect Himself*

**5. *Free Trial*.** If you have so much confidence in your product that you're willing to let the prospect try it for himself on a free trial basis, your offer provides a very effective form of proof. The mail-order customer thus has the same opportunity to examine the product carefully as he would have before buying in a store. In fact, he gets the added privilege of using it before he buys or pays.

For your use alone, we have enclosed a Reservation Certificate giving you the privilege of using the *Bell & Howell Super 8 Complete Home Movie Outfit for 30 full days—free and without obligation.* We supply the color film—a 50-foot Kodak Cartridge—and the movies you make are yours *free*— to show and to keep.

You'll have a full 10 days to use your new coats . . . to wear them walking, driving, working—without actually spending a single cent. . . . If for some reason, any reason at all, you don't like them, just send them back to me within 10 days, and we'll forget the whole thing. What could be fairer?

**6. *Guarantee*.** With the guarantee, the customer pays for the product before he uses it, but he gets a written promise that if he's not satisfied he will get a refund (or credit), or free repairs, or free replacement of the entire article.

With every ARTEX product you buy you get this firm, money-back guarantee: "All ARTEX products are Unconditionally Guaranteed to please. If you are not completely satisfied with any ARTEX, return it for full refund within 30 days."

**7. *Samples*.** Let the prospect examine, try, and/or use the samples that you send (for instance, swatches of clothing or drapery materials; pieces of wire, rubber, or fireproof insulation) or that he calls for himself (such as gasoline for his car, or a food or beverage made fresh daily). The prospect is asked to perform some suggested action to convince himself that the product meets the writer's claims.

Look at the sample I've sent along. See the beautiful grain. Notice how soft and pliable it is. No jacket leather was ever softer—or more carefree. And notice the quilt lining. You'll be comfortable no matter what the weather.

Just pick up the enclosed STICK-UP page, pull back the hardy Celanar protective sheet. Then place an assortment of odd-size clippings, ads, photos, memos on the STICK-UP sheet in any arrangement you choose. Finally, return the protective covering and press down gently.

Note how *sharply* and *clearly* you see every word through the transparent sheet, every shading of the material you've mounted on the STICK-UP page. But note this too . . . .

The placement of the proof section varies. Usually these statements come after the desire-creating description and benefits. However, if the proof involved possesses the necessary attention-getting qualities to justify placing it at the beginning, you may do so.

***The price of your product*** may be one last hurdle to surmount. Your presentation on the selling features, benefits, and proof may have convinced the prospect that your product meets his needs and he should buy it. But is the product worth the price and can he pay for it?

If your price is a bargain, you might feature it as an attention-getting opening. If the price doesn't justify this degree of emphasis, state it only after you have presented most of the selling features, benefits, and proof. Of course, if your letter is part of a campaign series to sell a costly item, the price might not be mentioned until near the end of the series. Sometimes price is not mentioned in the letter at all. If the product or service varies with the customer's needs (as for insurance or a complex heating installation in an industrial plant), the exact price quotation is given only after consultations with sales representatives.

If your prospect is likely to consider your price a drawback, try to bring the price within his reach. For example, in addition to stating the full price, you can use the following methods to de-emphasize price and help convince the prospect that he can pay it!

1. Break it down into "easy" weekly or monthly payments.
2. State it in terms of unit prices ($4 each book) instead of case lots or dozens or sets ($160 for the encyclopedia set).
3. Interpret it on the basis of the benefits he gains.
4. Emphasize its cost on a daily, monthly, or yearly basis—depending upon the product's estimated life and service (only 2 cents a day).
5. Compare it with the amount the average reader spends daily (monthly) for nonessentials or luxuries.

The discussion of price is usually presented just before the action paragraph(s)—if price and action are clear-cut and distinct. Sometimes, however, they blend, as do interest and desire. In some letters you will include price inducements with conviction details; in others, with action. Because offers of easy payment (as well as "no money down now" and credit card use) more often serve as special inducements to action, they are discussed in the next section.

*Getting Action.* Having convinced your reader that your product is valuable to him, that he needs it, should buy it, and can buy it, you now must move him to take the most important step—performing the action you request.

All previous discussions in this book about handling negatives, overcoming price resistance, and inducing action are applicable to sales letters and are not repeated here. You also already know that a complete action section should:

> State clearly the action you desire
> Make action easy
> Date the action (when desirable)
> Offer special inducement to act by a specified time (when desirable)
> End with a last reader-benefit plug (when appropriate)

To induce the reader to act within a certain time instead of procrastinating, you can use one or more of the following methods (arranged here alphabetically):

1. *Credit Cards.* The convenience of merely charging a purchase to a nationally accepted credit card—bank, national oil company, travel agency, diners' club, or other cards—is an effective inducement to action. The holder of such credit card(s) need not write a check or send a money order now; he merely returns an order blank, listing his credit card number.

   > Send no money now. To order, just check on the enclosed form that you wish this purchase charged to your account with one of the acceptable national credit firms listed. Then be sure to fill in your account number as shown on your credit card.

2. *Easy Payments and/or "No Money Now."* A budget plan or a future-payment plan by which the prospect pays nothing down now may serve two purposes— to convince the reader that he can afford to buy your product and to induce him to take the requested action. Thus, though the prospect may not have the entire price of the product, he will be able to order right away if he need not pay the entire amount (or anything) at once.

   > For as little as $10 down you can begin to reap the benefits of this useful encyclopedia before school starts. Easy monthly payments as low as $8 a month can be arranged at your convenience.

3. *Free Gift.*[1] If the prospect buys one item, he may receive two for the price

---

[1] Sweepstakes and other games of chance have been powerful action inducements. The prospect may be "eligible for winning any one of 5,000 prizes" if he mails an enclosed card before midnight of a certain date. However, such methods are prohibited in some states. Furthermore, studies have shown gross inconsistencies between the prizes that some companies advertise and the number they actually award. See "Games People Shouldn't Play," *Sales Management*, December 1969, pp. 17–18.

of one; or he may receive a free gift that is different from the item you are selling.

> Agree to try them for ten days on our No-Money-Down offer, and I'll send you a matching leather-look vinyl Tote Bag FREE. This gift is yours to keep, even if you later return the jackets.

**4. *Free Trial.*** The free trial serves two purposes—to convince the reader of your sincerity about the product's merits, and to induce action now. The reader has nothing to lose; he spends no money now and he need pay later only if he finds the article satisfactory. (See Letter 2, pages 392–394.)

**5. *Last Chance.*** Be careful about telling your prospect that this is the last chance he will have to buy your product. This idea has been abused and many readers react negatively because they think the writer isn't sincere.

> Because of the growing shortage of materials and labor for these specially designed vases, this is the *last time* they can be offered at this extra low price. This offer is good until midnight, May 15, 197_ only.

**6. *Limit in Quantity or Time.*** The warning here is the same as for "last chance." However, if you can honestly state that the supply of the product or the time for its production is limited, you have an effective inducement for prompt action.

> The supply of this model is limited. When our current stock is sold out, no more will be available. That's why I urge you to complete and mail the Official Reservation Form before midnight of the date shown.

**7. *No Obligation to Buy.*** When the purpose of your letter is to get the prospect to ask for more information, to come for a demonstration, or perhaps to ask a salesman to call, he is more likely to act if you promise he is under no obligation to buy.

> Mailing the enclosed card does not in any way obligate you to buy insurance, and no salesman will call on you unless you invite him. To receive full details about this plan, with specific figures at your present age—and your free portfolio—just return the postpaid card above.

**8. *Premium.*** A promise of higher earnings if the reader acts before a certain date is also a good incentive.

> By sending your deposits in the enclosed envelope, so they reach us by the 10th of May, you earn 5% dividends from the 1st of the month.

**9. *Special Price for a Limited Time.*** Setting a time limit for bargain prices (perhaps on out-of-season items), or for introductory prices on new items or to new buyers, effectively induces action. Offer a discount on the purchase price if the reader buys before a certain date, or if cash in full is sent with the order.

> This special introductory rate (for new subscribers only) brings you 40 big news packed issues of *World Reports* for only $4.97. That is down to half-price for 40 issues if you bought them a copy at a time. You get this special rate if your order is postmarked before November 1.

The complete action section in sales letters often (but not always) contains all five of the elements listed on page 388. As you read the following examples, see how many of the elements and special inducements each contains. Notice also that the third example contains a conviction element—guarantee.

1. Just initial this letter and return it in the enclosed postage-paid envelope, and a copy will be mailed without cost or obligation.
2. May we send you quotations on your next job? We will air mail our price within 24 hours after your card reaches us. You will be delighted with our prompt service and even more delighted with the excellent results you will obtain with our expertly made, close tolerance dies.
3. GET THE NEXT 6 ISSUES OF *FITNESS FOR LIVING* FOR HALF PRICE—only $2.95. You don't even risk your $2.95. You *send no money* with the enclosed special Reservation Certificate unless you wish. Just mail it back, we'll enter your subscription and bill you.

   You save $1.55 on the single copy price of 6 issues. AND HERE'S OUR MONEY-BACK GUARANTEE TO YOU:

   > If at any time during the term of your subscription, you are not satisfied with FITNESS FOR LIVING for any reason, let us know and your *entire* payment will be refunded immediately. If you enter a "billed" subscription, all you need do is write "cancel" on the invoice you receive and that's it.

   Mail the enclosed postpaid order form. Get started today on the way to healthier, pleasanter, more zestful living.

Writing an effective sales letter is a lot of work, but it can be greatly rewarding. Many a sales letter mailed to thousands of prospects has brought thousands—even millions—of dollars in returns. Even the expert writers "agonize" over their copy. Good selling presents the benefits and the proposition in such a way that the reader becomes convinced and "sells himself." On the other hand, if the letter sounds like high-pressure salesmanship, the reader may become defensive. To achieve your goal may require meticulous editing and rewriting, but the results will be worth the effort.

### Examples of Unsolicited Sales Letters

This section illustrates letters that aim to: (1) make a direct sale, (2) serve as stimulus to future sales, and (3) bring back lost customers. As you read them, notice how description is mixed with and reinforces reader benefits, how the central selling point (labeled CSP in these examples) is developed, and how reader-benefit appeals are emphasized. Notice also which of the suggested ways these letters use to gain attention, interest, desire-conviction, and action.

*Making a Direct Sale.* When the product you want to sell is relatively inexpensive (from your prospective customer's viewpoint), you may be able to sell it effectively with one sales letter. (Even expensive items can sometimes be sold in this way.) All direct-sales messages ask the reader to buy now or within the near future.

The first letter below, sent to businessmen, illustrates one way to sell relatively high-priced items successfully by one letter and detailed enclosures. The two items sold were priced at $170 and $295 (prices, though omitted in the letter, were in the enclosures). On a mailing of 4,500, this one-page letter brought in $45 in direct sales for every single dollar of costs.[1]

**Letter 1:** *Selling radiator cleaning tanks to service-shop owners.*
 *CSP: Less time to clean tanks.*
 *Appeals: Reduced work; higher profits.*

*Attention*
IF THREE RADIATOR REPAIR EXPERTS WALKED INTO YOUR SHOP THIS AFTERNOON . . .

And the first one, the owner of Midtown Auto Radiator Service of New York City, said: "We are cleaning 10 to 12 radiators in our tank and find that it requires only 20 minutes to get them thoroughly clean."

*Interest*
And the second man, proprietor of the Bronx Radiator Service, said: "We clean nine radiators in one tank in half the time it used to take to clean two."

*Desire*
And the third man, owner of Goldberg's Auto Service of St. Johnsbury, Vt., said: "We have found this the most satisfactory way to clean radiators that we have ever used."

. . . you'd certainly feel that you owed it to yourself to find out just what they used to bring those men such new speeds and profits, wouldn't you?

Well, here is how they — and YOU — are in a position to make such claims!

*Conviction*
You will find their explanations of exactly how they do it (along with reports of other leading radiator specialists from coast to coast) in the enclosed Bulletin #308. In addition, you will find complete specifications on two sizes of radiator cleaning tanks that will enable you to clean up to 4 or up to 12 radiators at a time — probably in LESS time than it now takes you to clean ONE!

*Conviction and action*
Don't just take our word for it – – – read the genuine letters and see the actual, unretouched photographs in the enclosed bulletin. Then prove these new speeds and savings in your own shop by mailing the Guarantee Order Form TODAY!

[1] Courtesy of Aeroil Products Company, West New York, New Jersey, and the Dartnell Corporation, *The Dartnell File of Tested Sales Letters.*

In contrast to the one-page sales letter, for example, Letter 2, to home-makers, is quite long—even though it is mailed with a colorful leaflet that pictures the chairs "enjoyed by attractive hostesses in modern homes." To provide variety and emphasis, the letter uses variations in margins, color, and type. The national company which sent the letter is one of many who believe that if a single message is to make a sale, it must be long enough to answer every possible reader objection and clarify all details as to size, construction, uses, payment terms, reader benefits, etc.

*Letter 2: Selling upholstered chairs to homemakers.*
*CSP: Two luxurious vinyl chairs for only $39.95.*
*Appeals: Beauty, style, comfort, savings of time and money.*

Dear Homemaker:

It's easy these days to go out and spend more than $100 for just one easy chair. Some people think that's a lot of money to pay for a chair — I'm one of them.

*Attention*

I can't see spending good money for a famous designer's name or for fancy fabrics you hardly dare sit on. I'd rather pay less, and get a good comfortable chair that will stay new-looking and in style for a long, long time.

*Interest*

And I know a lot of people think the way I do. So I've done some shopping around and found a beautiful "Garden Bloom" print lounge chair with a low price that furniture stores can't touch. I'd like to pass my discovery along to you —

TWO OF THESE LUXURIOUS VINYL-UPHOLSTERED CHAIRS ARE
YOURS FOR ONLY $39.95, PLUS SHIPPING AND HANDLING!

*Desire*

But I want you to be completely satisfied with these chairs before you spend one penny. I don't expect you to just take my word for their fine quality . . .

I'LL SEND YOU BOTH CHAIRS TO USE IN YOUR HOME
FOR 30 DAYS, FREE!

*and*
*conviction*

Experiment a little. See how they look in the living room, the den, the T.V. room. Sit back in these roomy loungers and use them like they were your own. If you find they're the chairs you've been looking for, keep them permanently for my direct mail price. But if you don't like them (for any reason in the world) just send them back and think no more about it.

It won't cost you a cent to try my chairs — I'll even pay the shipping. And in spite of the low bargain price of

these <u>chairs</u>, <u>I'm</u> <u>going</u> <u>to</u> <u>follow</u> <u>the</u> <u>usual</u> Fingerhut
<u>custom</u> <u>of</u> <u>giving</u> <u>you</u> <u>something</u> <u>you</u> <u>don't</u> <u>have</u> <u>to</u> <u>pay</u> <u>for</u> —
<u>2</u> <u>FREE</u> <u>GIFTS</u>, <u>yours</u> <u>to</u> <u>keep</u>, <u>even</u> <u>if</u> <u>you</u> <u>don't</u> <u>keep</u> <u>the</u>
<u>chairs</u>. <u>But</u> <u>more</u> <u>about</u> <u>that</u> <u>in</u> <u>a</u> <u>minute</u> . . .

YOU ARE ABOUT TO USE THE MOST CAREFREE CHAIRS
YOU COULD OWN —

*Physical description*

They're upholstered in rugged vinyl — the heavy kind that takes everyday abuse, even when the kids decide to "rough-house." Coffee stains, food spills? No cause for concern ... you just wipe your chairs clean with a whisk of a damp cloth! Years of use won't dull the bright floral design —

> "Garden Bloom" — <u>one</u> <u>of</u> <u>the</u> <u>year's</u> <u>most</u> <u>popular</u>
> <u>designs</u>. In New York, Dallas, Chicago and San
> Francisco ... the nation's leading fashion centers
> ... the bold, brilliant "Garden Bloom" print has
> been this year's exciting news in home decorating.

*More conviction details and description*

So you know your new chairs will be right in style. But more important, there's a reason "Garden Bloom" is so popular — fresh, gay colors add a burst of color to any room and give it a truly luxurious new look. Take your choice of three rich color combinations... Gold-N-Brown, Turq-N-Blue and Avocado-Green. (The legs are hardwood finished in polished cabinet-maker walnut and tipped with smart brass ferrules.)

*Reader benefits*

Beautiful design, carefree upholstery, sensible price — what more could you ask for in a good easy chair for your home? The answer is comfort ... the kind of comfort that makes you want to settle in and relax <u>completely</u>.

You'll lounge with just the right balance of support and softness in the deep polyfoam padded seats, feel restful and relaxed because the arms are upholstered, too.

*Easy action*

<u>MAIL</u> <u>THE</u> <u>ENCLOSED</u> <u>FREE</u> <u>TRIAL</u> <u>CARD</u> <u>AND</u> <u>START</u> <u>ENJOYING</u>
THESE CHAIRS <u>NOW</u>!

*Reader-benefit inducements*

You don't risk a thing — you have nothing to lose. Just attach the "Yes" stamp to the card I've enclosed and mail it back to me. I'll send the chairs right out to you for a full month. And I'll send along your TWO FREE GIFTS ...

*2 Free Gifts!*

<u>Spartus</u> <u>Electric</u> <u>Wall</u> <u>Clock</u> — the sweep second hand, electronic movement, handsome octagon styling and sim-ulated wood case combine to make this a useful and handsome gift.

17-pc. Socket and Box Wrench Set -- two sets in one ...
a 9-pc. interchangeable socket and screwdriver set
PLUS an 8-pc. home and auto wrench set ... perfect for
all your home repairs. You keep both gifts, whether or
not you keep the chairs.

*More reader benefits and inducements*

It's strange, but no matter how much furniture you have,
there never seem to be enough chairs around the house,
especially when company drops over. Why not add some
really beautiful, sensibly-priced seating to your home by
taking advantage of this outstanding, unusual offer -- take
my "Garden Bloom" chairs on a no-risk Free Trial. If you
are completely satisfied at the end of the thirty days,
BOTH chairs are yours for $39.95, plus shipping and han-
dling. Remember, you won't find this offer in any store --
so please don't delay and chance missing out on the lowest
easy chair price you can find!

*Easy action*

And your credit is good; so spread the amount over 11 easy
monthly payments of just $4.45 each, all charges included.
Indicate your choice of color scheme on the enclosed card
and mail it today.

In addition to prospective customers, you can also mail direct-sales letters like the preceding two to your present customers—about products they have not yet bought from you. Such letters can even get a "free ride"—thus saving you extra postage—if you enclose them with your monthly mailings to your customers. By this means hundreds of companies sell to their present customers goods ranging from books, magazines, and record albums to movie projectors, home furnishings, and clothing. Many of these letters are prepared by the manufacturer (with assistance of advertising consultants) for use by dealers on their own letterhead stationery. They are especially effective because action is made easy; customers can charge their purchases on their own credit cards instead of dealing with distant manufacturers direct.[1]

Another popular kind of direct-sales letter that stimulates present customers to buy "now" is the announcement about a special function "for our preferred customers only." Usually as a special inducement a substantial discount is offered on all items customers purchase that certain day or evening. Other effective inducements include inexpensive gifts, premiums, or refreshments. When these announcements do not require strongly developed appeals, they are really good-news letters[2] rather than persuasive requests.

*Serving as Stimulus to Future Sales.* Many sales letters urge action other

---

[1] Repeated tests have shown that an offer mailed equally to customers and prospects produced many times more business from customers than from prospects. Furthermore, these special customer appeals can help counteract the attempts of competition to win your customers.
[2] See the section on announcing sales and events, pages 239–240.

than an immediate order for a direct purchase. Some of these sell products or services which are complicated or expensive, or which must be specially tailored to fit the buyer's particular needs. Others sell continual use of the customer's credit card which enables him to buy not only the firm's products but also other conveniences.

*To sell complicated, expensive, or specially designed items,* you usually expect that the buyer will need more time, information, and personal observation. In this category are real estate, industrial equipment, insurance, costly installations, pleasure boats, cars, and products or services the reader may have considered unnecessary.

A campaign series of letters is a popular means of stimulating ultimate sales of such products and services. You decide in advance how many letters you should send, the time intervals, and the content of each. Some might ask the customer merely to request further information, as in Letter 3.[1] In other letters you might request that the reader call your office or store for a demonstration, or ask for a salesman to visit, as in Letter 4.

*Letter 3:* *Urging a travel-policy purchaser to request free facts about a special insurance plan.*
*CSP: New, low-cost substitute income plan that protects in case of accident or sickness.*
*Appeals: pride and security.*

WHAT MAKES YOU WORTH $250,000 or MORE?

*Attention*
You purchased a Travel policy at one of our airport booths recently. That got us to thinking.

There's a good chance you have a potential fortune of $250,000 or more that you have left entirely, or at least partially, unprotected.

Let's take the example of a man age 30 who earns $600 a month. During his lifetime he will earn $254,400 . . . if he lives AND IF HE KEEPS HIS HEALTH.

*Interest*
So, depending on your age and monthly income, you can well imagine the value of your own health, your ability to produce that income. Would it be $300,000? Or $400,000? The risks involved in leaving unprotected an asset so valuable as your health are numerous. An accident — any time or anywhere — or a sudden illness can topple a career, break up your savings, bankrupt your entire financial future.

[1] Your replies to these respondents would be solicited sales letters—discussed on pages 208–213.

Yet, how can the wise man avoid such risk? How can he make sure he'll have an income every month — if sickness or accident strikes? It is possible. And it is easy for you

*Desire* to find out how you can protect the fortune you will earn with a plan that can pay you up to $1,000.00 a month (up to $32.25 a day — tax-free) when an accident or sickness prevents you from working.

 Just returning the enclosed card will bring you the free facts about this new, low-cost, common sense Substitute Income Plan.

*Action* And because you do travel, we'll also furnish you information showing how this plan can include up

 to $50,000 in accidental death benefits. This is not only flight or travel insurance — but year-round, 24-hour-a-day coverage for just about any accident you can imagine.

There you have two good reasons for returning your card. Here is the third:

Because this plan is suited to your particular needs, we would like to further encourage your

*Inducement* interest by offering you as a gift the handsome
*to action*  Pocket Secretary and Card Caddy pictured here. This is such a handy and valuable item we know you'll appreciate receiving it.

And it's absolutely free, as is the information about the $1,000 Substitute Income Plan with the $50,000 accidental death feature. So — if you are worth $250,000 or more, you will appreciate the wisdom of protecting your most valuable asset.

Mail your card today. We'll furnish the free facts and
*Action* you'll receive the handsome pocket secretary we have reserved for you.

Depending upon the kinds of products you sell, you can sometimes get a highly satisfactory return by mailing only a relatively few letters. For instance, a manufacturer of bulldozing equipment mailed one sales letter to only 58 businessmen. To the requested action "Write, wire, or phone for further details" 30 readers replied; they bought $250,000 worth of equipment. Another example of an effective single letter is Letter 4. Though mailed on only 100 sales managers, the letter sold one million caps! Each letter was individually typewritten on one page.

*Letter 4:* *Urging sales managers to request a salesman to give more information about an advertising gadget.[1]*
*CSP: Adjustable, lightweight, low-cost Paperlynen service caps for distinctive advertising.*
*Appeals: appearance, savings, comfort, distinctiveness.*

Dear Mr. Gates:

*Attention*  Literally and figuratively you can <u>hit the top</u> with your advertising.

How?  With Paperlynen Adjustable Service Caps.

*Interest*  Paperlynen Caps offer the ideal medium for placing your name constantly before the public eye.  Worn by store-keepers and your own employees, these caps will not only help sell your products but are a constant goodwill reminder.  And, as a means of cooperative advertising, they're excellent.  In addition, Paperlynen <u>Adjustable</u> Service Caps are preferred because of their:

<u>Appearance</u>
Adjustable to any and every head size; always fit; look like linen; sanitary—clean.

<u>Low Cost</u>
Cost less than expense of having ill—fitting cloth caps laundered; this saving in addition to saving of
*Desire*  initial cost of cloth caps.

<u>Comfort</u>
Light in weight; porous nature of crown permits free, filtered ventilation.

<u>Distinction</u>
Offer the opportunity of distinction through im-printing your firm's name or trade mark in a manner not possible on ordinary caps.  With cooperative advertising or as a dealer help, the storekeeper's name may also be added.

*Conviction*  Several samples of Paperlynen Caps are enclosed.  Look at 'em, try 'em, test 'em.  We're sure you'll like 'em.

*Action*  When you are ready for more information call XX3—628—1030 and one of our salesmen will be up to see promptly.

---

[1] Courtesy of S. Posner Sons, Brooklyn, New York, and The Dartnell Corporation, *The Dartnell File of Tested Sales Letters.*

*To sell continual use of the customer's credit card,* you need to show him from time to time the benefits he gains from it. One example of such messages is Letter 5, which an oil firm's credit card promotion manager used "with a great deal of success."

**Letter 5:** *Urging use of credit card for product purchases and other conveniences.*[1]
*CSP: Detergent gasoline for extra engine-life and mileage at no extra cost; also additional advantages of the credit card.*
*Appeals: savings, safety, convenience.*

*Attention*

```
$1 of Mobil gasoline...Free!...
with the enclosed certificate and
your Mobil Credit Card.
Nothing to buy.
```

Dear Fellow Motorist:

*Attention*

It may be surprising, but it's nonetheless true: The biggest single expense we are likely to have in our life-time is for our automobiles. If you're like most Americans you will spend even more money on your car (including insurance, depreciation, repairs and operating expenses) than on your home. And if your family has two cars, you'll spend a great deal more.

In either case, it's important to get the most for your money, to make your car serve as long as possible. One of the best ways to prolong the life of your car is to make sure the inside of its engine is clean.

*Interest (in card and product)*

This is why you should be happy that you carry a Mobil Credit Card. Because Mobil Premium and Mobil Regular both have a Detergent that not only cleans carburetors ...but also helps clean a number of vital engine parts. And it does it faster than gasolines without detergent action get them dirty.

If you keep on using Mobil Detergent Gasoline, its cleaning action will keep working for you automatically. And your cleaner engine will...

give you less frequent and smaller repair bills;
give you noticeably more engine power for safe acceleration;
give you faster starts and smoother running, both of which reduce wear and tear on your car.

[1] Courtesy of Mobil Oil Corporation, New York, New York.

*Desire-conviction*  And there's one more bonus—cleaner air. . . . We learned how to make this gasoline through a massive and continuous research program on the automotive pollution problem. (Four paragraphs, omitted here, explain how the special detergent additive helps your car release less pollutants into the air, cleans a dirty oil screen, and saves you money.)

> What does all this extra engine-life and gas mileage with a cleaner engine cost you? It doesn't cost one penny more...nor a stroke of work. It all happens automatically, every time you drive with Mobil Detergent Gasoline in your tank.

You can buy Mobil Detergent Gasoline at over 26,000 Mobil Dealer Stations, coast to coast. But with your Mobil Credit Card, you can do even better:

> You can use it to pay for tires, batteries, and all kinds of auto accessories on Mobil's new convenient Revolving Credit Plan.
> You can charge a stay at any one of some 2,200 really good motels all over America.
> And if you ever run into trouble on the road, you can use it to charge car repairs up to $75...and use Revolving Credit too.
> You can reduce the amount of money you must carry, reducing the risk of loss or theft.

*Action (continued use of card and product)*  Your Mobil Credit Card brings you greater motoring pleasure and convenience while Mobil Detergent Gasoline helps keep your engine clean (instead of making it dirty). We thank you for using them both and hope you'll continue to enjoy these important dividends every mile you drive.

A postscript on Letter 5 tied in with the offer made at the beginning and served as a special inducement to action:

> We're so pleased with Mobil Detergent Gasoline we'll buy your next dollar's worth. Simply hand the enclosed certificate and your credit card to your Mobil dealer, and he'll put $1 worth of Premium or Regular gasoline in your car but not charge you a cent. It will be your first step toward a cleaner engine.

**Bringing Back Lost Customers.** Many businesses spend thousands of dollars on advertising to attract new customers, and yet neglect regular customers. Studies have indicated that *indifference* on the part of the seller is the main reason customers leave one company for another. At least two-thirds of such customers drift away because they feel their business isn't appreciated, because they are treated discourteously, or because some grievances were un-adjusted.

The best way to find out why customers haven't bought from you for, say, six months or more, is to ask them—either in person or by mail. Warm, sincere, friendly letters can help you to learn why you lost customers and can also help you win them back. (Of course, it is important that after you know customers' reasons, you take steps to correct any weaknesses!)

The secret for winning back lost customers is to tell them that you miss them—and to keep telling them. Patience and persistence do pay off. For instance, one department store in Chicago reopened 2,724 accounts with sales totaling $73,001.34; a retail store in Long Beach, California, brought in $30,000 from lost customers; and a Buffalo merchant regained 47 percent of his lost accounts with 30 mailings over a period of five years.[1] Numerous other firms have also had rewarding results (sometimes even with one letter!)

Your first miss-you letters may be simple inquiries (without appeals).[2] However, when direct inquiries bring no response, you need to mail persuasive requests that say, in essence:

We miss you
Here are the benefits you get by coming back to us
Please come back

Sincerity, imagination, appropriate appeals, and sometimes good-natured humor characterize these messages, as illustrated below in Letters 6 and 7.

*Letter 6: A unique letter to win back "lost" hotel guests.[3]*
    *CSP: High standard of personal service to "special guests."*
    *Appeals: Enjoyment, comfort, convenience, prestige.*

Dear Mr. Morgan:

*Attention*    Today we registered an ex-president, two senators, a congressman, several assorted corporation presidents, a foreign personage with party, generals by the one, two and three star, plus a group of tourists. But not you.

*Interest*    I suppose you thought we'd be too busy to notice that you were among the missing. But that's not true. We haven't made The Mayflower the standard of personal service by forgetting our special guests the moment they leave the check-out desk.

What happened?

---

[1] *Reporter of Direct Mail Advertising*, September 1965, pp. 49–50.
[2] For direct-request miss-you letters, see pages 171–173.
[3] An award-winning letter created by Spiro & Associates, Inc., Philadelphia, for the Mayflower Hotel in Washington, D.C.

*Desire*  Have you sworn off roast beef when it's as succulent as our Rib Room specialty?  Are you punishing yourself by giving up really comfortable, handsome, air-conditioned guest rooms for lesser accommodations?  Do you feel guilty about staying at a hotel so perfectly located and so completely dedicated to your convenience?  Or have you just not been in Washington lately?

We hope it's the latter.

*Action*  Please write and end our suspense as soon as possible.  Or, better yet, come back for a visit.  Old friends are best friends.  And busy as we are, we miss one of our very best friends:  you!

**Letter 7:**  *An unusual department-store letter that brought an "excellent response in revived accounts and much favorable comment," according to Mr. Selig.*[1] *(Beneath the letter was a picture of a customer credit card, removed from Rosenfields Good Customer File.)*
*CSP: The magic of purchases and services through the credit card.*
*Appeals: Ease, convenience, friendly good service.*

IF YOUR ACCOUNT CARD COULD TALK, HERE'S WHAT IT WOULD SAY. . .

*Attention*  I'm getting lonesome — you haven't used me or your charge account at Rosenfields in over 90 days.

*Interest*  Really I'm not fussing, but I'm not just an ordinary card. I'm full of magic!

*Desire-conviction*

*Reader benefits*  I can dress you up in clothes as glamourous as a queen or movie star, yet priced to meet any budget.  I can supply you with beautiful lingerie, hats, shoes, accessories, and dozens of other clothing, household and personal needs, so easily and conveniently.

*More benefits*  I can bring you the service of friendly folk in a store which has served Baton Rouge for generations, folk who take a personal interest in your needs and in giving you good service.

*Action*  Use me this month — attached is your current Rosenfields Credit Card which enables you to charge your purchases without delay.

[2] Courtesy of Rosenfields, Baton Rouge, Louisiana, and the Dartnell Corporation, *The Dartnell File of Tested Sales Letters.*

With good judgment, a bit of originality, and imagination, you can develop a variety of appealing miss-you letters. If you prefer, you can buy special-theme messages from advertising specialists, with or without gadgets symbolic of various holidays, seasons, products, and services. Be sure, however, that they relate closely to your company's business.

In summary, use the persuasive-request plan whenever you need to write a favor request, a nonroutine claim that requires persuasion, or an unsolicited sales letter. Begin with an attention-getting appropriate opening; arouse interest through physical description and/or reader benefits; create desire and conviction by developing your central selling point and benefits, by offering proof, and by handling price in a positive way; then ask for action. If appropriate, offer special inducements so that reader will act within a certain time. The capsule checklists on pages 403–404 give a summary of the general plan and the three main kinds of persuasive requests.

## EXERCISES

### Requests for Favors

1. The following two form letters ask the reader to fill out a questionnaire. Criticize each constructively regarding you attitude, tone, honesty, word choice, and the attention-getting and action paragraphs. What impression does the letter give you about the writer and his company? Would the letter persuade you to furnish the requested information? Why or why not? What improvements can you suggest for each letter?

   A. Sent from a radio manufacturing company whose letterhead states "Offices: Tokyo, Japan and Hong Kong; United States Offices (address) Los Angeles, Calif. (zip)." The envelope was postmarked in Los Angeles. The processed letter had no inside address. Notice the comments about enclosures following the letter.

   Greetings and Salutations.

   We are sending this letter to a select group of people like yourself who have been recommended to us by an American research organization.

   The courtesy we ask is that you read this letter and favor us with the answer to the enclosed questions. In appreciation for your cooperation, we shall do our utmost to reward you for your kind help. (Please read on.)

   You can save us time and money in our marketing plans. We will be undertaking extensive advertising in the United States and are very anxious to place our advertising where it will best be seen by people like yourself — will you please help us by filling in and returning the enclosed questions in the free envelope — it is a two minute service that will be greatly appreciated.

We are enclosing a Brochure of the first selection of the
(year and name) Portable Radio Models to appear on the American
market.  In return for your participating interest, we offer
you a completely free gift of your choice of any nationally
famous (name) Watch.

Please fill in the questionnaire and mail to our Los Angeles
office in the enclosed envelope.  On the back of the questionnaire is the order form to choose your reward.

We beg you not to delay or put off your reply.  Your immediate
answers to our market questions are needed to complete our
survey, also the initial supply of watches forces us to limit
this free gift offer only to that quantity now in our Los
Angeles warehouse.

> Comments about enclosures with Letter A: The printed questionnaire
> contained four questions (about the name and address of the reader's "favor-
> ite" newspaper, magazines, and local radio stores). Above the questions was
> this request: "Please fill out this questionnaire and mail it to our Los Angeles
> office with your radio order." On the reverse side of the questionnaire was an
> order form for radios and tape recorders, followed by this request: "Select one
> free watch for each radio or tape recorder you order. We regret we cannot send
> your free watch unless the questionnaire is completed." An enclosed leaflet
> pictured two radios, one tape recorder, and nine men's and ladies' watches.
> ("Completed" meant answering the questions and ordering a radio or tape
> recorder.)

**B.** On the letterhead of a name brand tonic sales distributor in New York City,
the words "THIRD REQUEST" were rubber-stamped diagonally across the
top in 1/4-inch red letters. The inside address contained an abbreviated incorrect name and address of a city newspaper, inserted in type much blacker than
that of the mimeographed letter. The questionnaire asked for the names
of the three largest independent and chain drug stores in the reader's city, in
order of size by sales volume, number of stores each operates, name of drug
buyer, and exact number of column inches of advertising space each store ran
in the newspaper for the 12 preceding months.

Dear Sir:                    Attention:  National Advertising Manager

If you are interested in more business, please be sure to read
this letter and answer it immediately.

Our advertising agency, (name) Co., Inc. of New York City, has
just released an advertising schedule to your paper for
January, February, March and April, 197_.  At the expiration
of this schedule, we plan to increase future schedules in your
publication.

To do this, we must get up-to-date information on the drug
stores in your city, including those in big shopping centers.

## CAPSULE CHECKLISTS ON PERSUASIVE REQUESTS*

| *I*<br>*Persuasive Requests—General Plan* | *II*<br>*Persuasive Requests for Favors* |
|---|---|
| **1. ATTENTION** (promise; star)<br>   a. Introduction of relevant reader-benefit or reader-interest theme—centered on reader, not on writer's organization<br>   b. Envelopes and letterheads sometimes specially designed for the message | 1. Attention<br>   a. Sincere compliment<br>   b. Questions<br>   c. Agreeable comment or assertion<br>   d. Basic problem<br>   e. What has been done about a problem<br>   f. Frank admission of a favor |
| **2. INTEREST** (picture; chain)<br>   b. Introduction of project or product's physical description, benefits, central selling point<br>   c. Appeals: appreciation, approval, beauty, cleanliness, comfort, convenience, co-operation, customer satisfaction, distinctiveness, efficiency, enjoyment, entertainment, extra earnings, fair treatment, friendships, good reputation, health, improvement, love of home and others, money and other valuables, peace of mind, pleasure, position, popularity, profits, recognition, safety, satisfaction of helping others, savings, self-preservation, and others | 2. Interest and<br>3. Desire<br>   a. Necessary physical description of project<br>   b. Facts, figures, and reader benefits to convince reader that his contribution will be enjoyable, easy, important, beneficial—directly or indirectly<br>     (1) In request for speaker: date, day, hour; place; function; topic; talk length; audience size, interests; honorarium, expenses; special attractions; appeals.<br>     (2) In request for donation: problem; needs; past, present methods of meeting needs; costs; reader contribution: benefits, appeals.<br>     (3) In request for cooperation: problem; facts, suggestions, committee, etc. to help meet goal; problem; reader's part; benefits, appeals. |
| **3. DESIRE** (prove; chain)<br>   a. Desire: development of description, benefits, central selling point, appeals; perhaps with an enclosure<br>   b. Conviction:<br>     (1) "Outside" proof; perhaps with enclosures<br>     (2) Price and terms when needed and appropriate; perhaps in enclosure |    c. Positive handling of negatives and probable objections for favors that:<br>     (1) Require time, knowledge, or effort<br>     (2) Ask donations of money or other valuables<br>     (3) Urge cooperation on goals and projects<br>   d. Enclosures (brochures) |
| **4. ACTION** (push; hook)<br>   a. CSAD[1]<br>   b. EA[2]<br>   c. DA when desirable[3]<br>   d. Special inducement when desirable<br>   e. RB (often tied in with opening statement)[4] | 4. Action<br>Same as I, 4 |

*Lists include possible content. For any one message, choose only pertinent and appropriate items.
[1] CSAD = clear statement of action desired
[2] EA = easy action
[3] DA = dated action, if desirable
[4] RB = reader benefit

See also page 92 for W's on complete action requests.

## CAPSULE CHECKLIST ON PERSUASIVE REQUESTS (Continued)*

| III<br>*Other Persuasive Nonroutine Requests* | IV<br>*Unsolicited Sales Letters* |
|---|---|
| 1. Attention<br>   Same as II, 1; preferably an agreeable assertion or a principle which is used as a major premise | 1. Attention<br>   a. Agreeable assertion<br>   b. Comparison or short story<br>   c. Event or fact in reader's life<br>   d. Problem reader may face<br>   e. Quotation<br>   f. Scare opening<br>   g. Significant fact about product<br>   h. Solution to a problem<br>   i. Special offer or gift<br>   j. Surprising or challenging statement<br>   k. Testimonials |
| 2. Interest and<br>3. Desire<br>   a. All necessary facts and details pertaining to request for adjustment, credit, or changes in policy or performance—interwoven with reader benefits and appeals<br>   b. Description as needed by the reader to see that his firm is responsible (if applicable) and that the request is factual, logical, and reasonable | 2. Interest<br>   a. Beginning development of physical description and product benefits, geared to prospect's needs; meaningful appeals<br>3. Desire-Conviction<br>   a. Full development of needed description, reader benefits, central selling point<br>   b. Proof by users, laboratories and agencies, prospect himself:<br>     (1) Facts about users' experience with product<br>     (2) Names of users  (5) Performance tests<br>     (3) Testimonials   (6) Guarantee<br>     (4) Free trial     (7) Samples<br>   c. Price presented in psychologically favorable way(s)<br>   d. Enclosures to strengthen desire-conviction |
| 4. Action<br>   a. Logical conclusion based on the major premise and the clearly stated facts; then same as I, 4 | 4. Action<br>   a. CSAD*       c. DA*<br>   b. EA*         d. RB*<br>   e. Inducements<br>     (1) Credit cards<br>     (2) Easy payments or no money down<br>     (3) Free gift<br>     (4) Free trial<br>     (5) Last chance<br>     (6) Limited quantity or time<br>     (7) No obligation to buy<br>     (8) Premium<br>     (9) Special price for limited time |

*See footnotes, page 404.

To make it easy for you to give us this information, we are
enclosing herewith a convenient questionnaire, which is self-
explanatory. <u>Please read it carefully and fill it in com-
pletely</u>. Then mail it back to us, today, because it is most
important we have this data on hand quickly.

We take this opportunity to thank you for all past favors, and
to say your kind cooperation in this matter will be appreciated.

2. The following request was sent by the executive employment manager of a large
national hotel corporation, typed (on hotel letterhead) by automatic typewriter,
and addressed personally to the Director of University Placement Services. Evaluate the letter, commenting particularly on its tone, stated reader benefits, action
request, and postscript; and state ways to improve it.

Dear Prof. (name):

No, we won't be recruiting on your campus this year . . . sorry
about that!

But, we ARE looking for the <u>BEST</u> college grads in the United
States (we would say the world, but there might be a language
problem), and feel you can help us.

The student we want would come to your mind quickly. He's the
one who made you say to yourself, "This is the most promising
individual I've seen in years!" (He may even remind you a
little of yourself at that age.)

Refer the right people to me directly and you can be sure we
will do right by them.

Just think, Prof. (name), some day you may be able to say you
know the President of (name of hotel chain) because you got him
his job.

P.S. Whether or not you believe the enclosed "Careers Fact
Sheets" is up to you . . . we tried to modestly let people know
about career opportunities with the best and fastest rising
hotel chain around.

3. Assume that you are program chairman for your college chapter of a national
organization composed of students whose major is the same as yours. For the past
two years the members have repeatedly mentioned their desire to hear this organization's national vice-president, Mr. L. F. Kameron. He is known to be an outstanding, dynamic speaker. Two of your members who heard him at the organization's national convention last summer also have been enthusiastic about him.
Because he lives 2,000 miles from your school and your chapter's treasury is small,
however, everyone has just assumed that getting Mr. Kameron would be almost
impossible. Nevertheless, in yesterday's newspaper you happened to read that Mr.

Kameron will be attending a one-day business conference in Somecity (you insert a city name), which is only 250 miles from you—just the day before your chapter's annual Founders' Day Banquet.

Now you want to persuade Mr. Kameron to accept your invitation to be principal banquet speaker. You cannot pay him any speaker's fee, but your budget enables you to pay traveling expenses equal to round-trip plane fare from (Somecity) to yours. Six planes daily fly between these cities; if he prefers a bus, buses run on an hourly schedule. A scenic ride by freeway takes about four hours, in case he prefers to drive a private car. Mr. Kameron will, of course, be your chapter's dinner guest. Maybe you can think of an inexpensive, courteous way to take care of him if he wishes to stay overnight after his talk? Assume any other necessary details that will make your letter complete—with you attitude. Consider carefully the best appeal(s) to use.

4. Point out the weaknesses, errors, and good points in the following letter. Then—as program chairman—rewrite it, applying the principles you have learned, to make your request so appealing that the reader will want to accept. Address it to Mr. R. J. Milliman, Director of Public Relations, KMRO Television, in a city about 80 miles from you. If your instructor approves, you may choose another topic instead of air pollution.

What are you plans for Saturday evening, March 20? The members of our (city name) Businessmen's Club feel it would be a pleasure to us to have you as the principal speaker for our annual banquet that night.

Ways to fight air pollution is a topic that our members are concerned and realize the need of practical advice from experienced executives. Your many editorial comments on Channel 16 KMRO have shown us your sincere interest and extensive study on this subject. Our members and their wives want to hear you in person. This banquet is our biggest function of the year, and we would be honored to have you and your wife as our guests. We can promise her a good time too and an orchid corsage.

The banquet will be held in the Marlboro Room of the Plaza Hotel at 7 and will be informal. A varied entertainment program and an excellent dinner at $6.50 per person have been arranged.

Your traveling expenses would be provided, and I hope that you can take advantage of a visit to our city to settle any personal affairs you may have here. The Plaza Hotel is equipped with excellent facilities in the event you decide to extend your visit.

I shall appreciate your assent to this request so that I can welcome you on your arrival if feasible.

5. As the new systems manager for the National Casualty Associates, you have considered numerous ways to increase company efficiency and decrease costs. Recently,

after checking correspondence procedures, you were surprised to find several wasteful, unnecessarily time-consuming methods that you'd like to change. However, before authorizing any changes, you have decided to survey the preferences of the management staff in your home office and 60 branch offices. You have prepared an easy-to-answer two-page questionnaire asking for their reactions to eight money- and time-saving suggestions. Now write a persuasive, courteous memorandum urging these executives to fill out your enclosed form and return it to you by a certain date, so that you can complete a needed report on their replies. Promise anonymity to all respondents. Include appropriate appeals to urge their cooperation. Three of your money-saving suggestions may require a little explanation and "selling" before your readers approach the questionnaire.

   **a.** You advocate using window envelopes instead of individually addressed envelopes for the approximately 150,000 monthly messages your company sends to policyholders, prospective customers, suppliers, and stockholders. You think window envelopes could save thousands of hours of typing time annually, because the inside addresses on the letters or forms within the envelopes could serve for the envelopes too.

   **b.** You are considering adopting a standardized companywide letter format—blocked, open punctuation, with or without salutation and complimentary close. Such standardization, you feel, would give the company an image of uniformity and at the same time save stenographic time.

   **c.** With each company letter that asks the recipient for a brief answer, you would like to enclose a courtesy carbon for his reply. The recipient would then merely type his reply at the bottom of your letter, return to you the carbon copy (showing both your letter and his reply), and keep the original for his files. Such an enclosure would bring speedier answers to company requests, and would cut down the need for second or third requests to get replies, thus saving postage and labor costs.

As you write your memo, remember that your readers are in management, just as you are, even if you do probably outrank many of them. Watch your tone and try to build pleasant relations and high morale.

**6.** Assume that you graduated from the university five years ago and you have become an active member of a certain professional (or business or social or religious) group that owns the building in which meetings and activities take place.

   You have just been elected treasurer of your organization for a two-year term. For about 15 years this organization has been saving money to build a much-needed extension to its building. (Assume specific reasons why the addition is necessary.) It has been planned that construction will begin next July 1—three months from today—and be completed by October 1. (Assume today is April 1.) The addition, as sketched by architects and approved by your executive board, will cost about $90,000. Your books show $39,000 cash in the building fund; your organization can get a $46,000 mortgage. You need to raise $5,000 cash between now and about May 5. Your task is to try to raise this money. After several meetings with the executive board, it is decided that, rather than asking your members to put on several fund-raising events (which are time-consuming), or assessing them a definite amount, you will urge them to make a donation. The board members want you to head this fund-raising campaign.

   Write a letter, remembering that it is a form letter, to be sent to all members. Assume a mailing list of 600. Try to keep your letter to one typewritten page. Select the appeals (loyalty, pride, self-interest, etc.) that you think will be most effective in moving your readers to take the requested action. Set May 5 as the deadline for donations, because adequate time must be allowed for making financial arrangements before construction begins. Make action easy and include any reasonable inducements for your readers to act now. Naturally, you'd rather have checks returned with each reply; however, for those members who would rather sign a pledge now and pay later—before the completion of construction—plan an easy-action reply form, which you can depend upon in your financial calculations.

7. You are chairman of the Joint Scholarship Fund Committee at your college. Your job today is to write a persuasive letter that will be mailed to citizens in your community (or to certain selected groups, if you prefer), urging them to cooperate with the students' "Three Days in May" fund-raising drive. You want to sell your readers on the value of this project and get them to agree to hire one or more volunteer students to do any chores they (your readers) may want done on May 2, 3, or 4. The jobs the students will perform will be, in most cases, easy (mowing lawns, cleaning, ironing, washing cars, babysitting, etc.) and will require no special skills. Students will work a half or full day in the community for the readers who respond to this letter and they will donate the income they receive to the Joint Scholarship Fund for needy, deserving students. Suggested contribution by the employer: $8, half day; $15, full day.

What appeals and facts should you include to make this an effective letter? Assume that your message will be multilithed or printed by your campus printing office. There will also be some newspaper and television announcements about this worthy college project, but this publicity is handled by other committees. In your request letter to citizens be sure to state clearly how they should let you know that they want to hire one or more students on May 2, 3, and/or 4. Your committee has an office and a telephone in room 205, Student Union Building. You have plenty of volunteer helpers who can handle telephone calls (or mail) between 8 a.m. and 9 p.m. on certain days (you name them).

8. The following request was sent (mimeographed, without inside address or date) by a district manager on the letterhead of a national insurance company. If you were the policyholder receiving this letter, would it persuade you to act? How does the purpose of this message affect your image of the company? Is the request clear as to kind of personnel wanted? What improvements can you suggest for this letter?

```
Hello:

The present and projected growth of our area requires that we
add additional personnel to our staff.  Rather than go to an
employment agency for help, the thought struck me, WHY NOT ASK
YOU AS A BUYER OF INSURANCE for recommendations of men or women
that you would like to see serve you.  I realize that this is
an unusual request to ask, but after all, you are the best
judge of the type of people that you want to deliver our
Fast-Fair-Friendly service.

We are seeking someone who may have reached a "peak" in their
present job or someone anxious to establish a career and
business of their own.  They may perhaps be a neighbor, a
friend, a salesman acquaintance who is dissatisfied, your son
```

or daughter, a widow having trouble making ends meet, or perhaps a man or woman at your place of employment.  Someone who
wants to advance themselves.

Since I don't know this friend of yours, I am counting on you
to help by writing their name on the enclosed card and mailing
it to me.  Should they be interested in learning about our
career opportunity, I'll show them how we train our representatives, our opportunities for advancement, and how we give them
the right atmosphere for permanent success.

Please send me your recommendation as soon as possible as it
may well be the "turning point" in the life of your friend.  I
will let you know the results following our interview.

9. Assume that you graduated from college two years ago and became an active
member of a business, professional, social, or religious organization. You have
just been elected vice-president and have been asked by the executive board to
see if you can increase attendance at meetings for next year. Assume that the
organization has a potential membership of 200, but that during the past three
or four years only 15 to 25 have been attending monthly meetings regularly. You
would like to have at least 50 or 60.
   Plan a letter to send to the 200 potential members aiming to find out in a
friendly, tactful way why so many have not been attending meetings and what
types of programs, arrangements, or methods would get them to the meetings. Be
careful to keep the tone positive and cheerful, filled with you attitude. Suggestions: Perhaps more would come if they had transportation, or if the meetings
were held at a more central location, or if the business portion were shorter and
the programs more entertaining, or if someone would phone them shortly before
meetings, etc. In the past, written announcements have been sent to all members
a week before a meeting. Devise some method which will make it easy for each
member to answer your letter giving you specific information about what he prefers in topics, speakers, activities, etc. Assume that your letter will be mimeographed.

10. As building manager of your company's three-story structure, you have just received an unusual report from your sanitation engineer. He has found that at
least one rat has been attracted to the building recently. The employee practice
of leaving food on bookshelves, desks, and other open locations will have to be
discontinued or watched very carefully. Each office occupant must be made aware
of the problem and the possibility that he is part of the cause. As rats will not
bother to infest an area unless there is good reason to do so (food), the best way
to maintain rat-free premises consists of denying them food, water, and safety. It
would be economically unfeasible to make the needed structural changes for rat-
proofing the entire building.
   Thus you must write a persuasive request in a memorandum to all employees,
urging them to cooperate on preventive action. Instruct them to exercise utmost
care with lunches or other food brought into the building. Instruct them not to
leave any food in their offices overnight. Also request them to be alert for signs

indicating rodent or insect activity: droppings; gnawed food; odor; dark rub marks along wall, ceiling, under door, ventilator, etc., which indicate a runway. Request that employees inform a certain office as soon as such evidence appears. Watch the tone of your memo.

11. As treasurer of your fraternity (or sorority), it is your responsibility to write an appealing letter to your 800 alumni asking them to help pay off the $100,000 mortgage. Five years ago your chapter built an extensive addition to the house so as to meet the great demand for the large membership. (You yourself were not a member then.) The past two years, however, for various "outside" reasons (economic conditions in the area plus the fact that fewer students enter your university as freshmen but rather as upperclassmen transferring from two-year community colleges) your new freshman pledge classes have been only about half their former size, and consequently, your chapter's size will soon be only about half what it was formerly. Yet the mortgage payments are the same as before, and the burden on the remaining members is extra heavy. Also, by the time the mortgage is paid off the chapter will have paid 2½ times the amount originally borrowed for the building five years ago. Each college member in the present chapter has already assessed himself $25 to help meet the current financial needs. If each alumnus member could donate an average of $25 each—some much more —your chapter could then pay off a sizable part of the mortgage, thus saving much interest. The annual homecoming festivities on your campus are two months from today. Your chapter is planning a special 50-year anniversary celebration to which all alumni are cordially invited.

    Your job now is to write a letter to all alumni members appealing to their loyalty (and any other way too) and showing that everyone's financial help is needed. (One of your older alumni is extremely wealthy, yet your chapter members are reluctant to ask him for a large donation. However, those who know this alumnus well feel that if your letter is worded effectively, he may contribute as much as all the others together—provided he feels that no one is imposing on him and that he is doing so entirely voluntarily.) Consider carefully all these facts and also whether it is psychologically desirable to combine your request for donation with the invitation to the homecoming celebration. Be sure that all 800 alumni know they are wanted and welcome at the homecoming regardless of whether they contribute anything to the financial fund.

## Nonroutine Requests for Adjustment, Credit, or Changes

1. You are manager of Vernie's Men's Wear in Sometown, South Dakota. You have two stores—one situated in the downtown area and one two blocks from a college campus. For years you have carried exclusively Van Doser shirts, which you buy direct from the manufacturer. This summer, only four days after this firm's fall catalog came out, you again ordered a complete Van Doser line for your two stores. But now you have noted with alarm the many changes the manufacturer made in your fall order. Back-to-school goods scheduled by your salesman for early delivery have been pushed to October and November. You haven't a stripe in stock and the university opens next week. You've had to switch to other brands because you can't get all the Van Doser merchandise you'd like. (You have faith in Van Doser merchandise; it's your preference of all brand shirts on the market.)

While you were in Minneapolis just a few days ago, you noted that the Custer Men's Store (a retail store for this shirt manufacturer) was stocked with everything in the Van Doser book, and Custer could not have ordered any sooner than you did. Just how does this manufacturer expect to keep good customers like you with that kind of treatment? Unless he can find some way to supply your stores adequately and promptly, you may have to find a replacement for Van Doser shirts. You feel you have helped considerably to build this manufacturer's business the past five years. Right now you feel like giving your business to a competitor. Address your message to Mr. Thomas Newsom, sales manager of Van Doser Manufacturing Company, Chicago. Be tactful, firm, and appropriately persuasive.

**2.** Assume that you have just received a credit turndown for a charge account with a local store. The reason stated for the refusal is correct. (Assume a legitimate reason such as under age 21, presently unemployed, or a similar one). However, for various other reasons—perhaps a steady trust fund income you receive from a regular source, or a verifiable record of integrity, or any other good reason(s) that might outweigh the shortcoming, you know that you will be a prompt-paying customer. You always take care of all obligations you have. Write to the store's credit manager an honest, persuasive request for credit. Make your reasoning logical and appealing, so that your reader will be convinced that he should make an exception for you and grant you a charge account.

**3.** As the new office manager and accountant of Jessup Realty you have just encountered a situation that you think needs to be handled by a good persuasive letter. Six months ago the owner-manager (Nick Jessup) bought, for one of the two secretaries in the office, a steel secretarial desk and a secretarial posture chair —from the ABC Office Equipment Company. When they arrived, he was displeased with them both, but never bothered to write anyone to request an adjustment. He did talk to the ABC salesman, Dave, however. Here are the facts as Mr. Jessup tells them: "I've been doing business OK with ABC for a number of years, and I always pay my bills promptly. But not this one! They can just wait. For the first three months after this desk and chair arrived, I refused to pay anything on them. After receiving collection letters, I decided to send only a $5 payment each month, although they wanted $20 a month. You see, these items have given us troubles from the day they were delivered. The secretarial steel desk costing the exorbitant price of $289 isn't worth a damn. First of all, I wanted a secretarial desk with a deep-well drawer. Both Dave and the ABC manager stated that there were none available. A week or so later I learned that there were any number of them available in other office equipment stores. That burned me up! Secondly, the typewriter arm (which is a big factor in the cost of the desk) has not worked properly since the day the desk was brought into my office. Dave attempted to give the typewriter arm 'emergency first aid' by the use of a piece of wood, which kept the arm outstretched at all times. We finally found it necessary to discontinue the use of the typewriter arm. This means that considerable valuable space of the desk is wasted. I also have a gripe in connection with the posture chair, which cost $58. One of these days someone will find their "posture" on the office floor, since the back-rest bar that goes underneath the seat works itself loose every second or third day. So do you see why I don't want to pay for this stuff on time? I still want a properly operating secretarial desk with a deep-well drawer plus a posture chair that is not defective. It is my belief that a proper adjustment can be made. However, if they don't see fit to do anything regarding this matter, I'll continue my practice of small ($5) monthly payments. Frankly, I suppose I should have written Jerry Bean (the ABC manager) a letter long ago, but I've been too mad to write. If you think you can give him the whole story in a letter and get the adjustments I want, go ahead and try! I yelled at him once on the phone, but it didn't do any good." Now that you know the facts, you have a good opportunity to show your new employer what you can accomplish with a well-written persuasive letter. Write your letter for either Mr. Jessup's signature or your own, whichever you think will be the psychologically better way to get a favorable reply to this request for adjustment.

4. Your wholesale firm has a policy of granting a two percent discount for bills your customers pay within 10 days of invoice date; the full amount is due in 30 days. One of your customers paid a $560 invoice (dated October 11) with his check mailed on November 9. But he deducted $11.20 discount. Consequently, you wrote him a courteous direct-request letter, asking him to pay the $11.20. Today (November 20) you get an angry protest from the customer, stating that his cashier was in the hospital last month and so a number of bills accumulated that otherwise would have been paid within the 10-day period. He added, "Your company is the only one out of about fifty that has attempted to chisel us out of this discount. We can buy plenty of watches, equal in quality to yours, from folks who are willing to meet a customer halfway—and who realize there are always just exceptions to any business rule. Of course, if you insist, a check will be mailed; but it strikes me as a small amount to cause the severing of business relations between us."

To your company, a discount of $11.20 involves a long-standing company principle—that of impartial treatment of every customer. You maintain the "2/10 net/30" policy because it enables you to earn similar savings by paying your own bills promptly; then you pass the savings on to your customers in lower prices, as a reward for their promptness. When customers pay after the 10-day period, you make no savings. You do not want to grant special privileges to some concerns, because such inconsistencies involve much more than a small discount. Write a persuasive request to this customer (Flatwood Jewelry Shop) urging him to pay this honest debt.

## Unsolicited Sales Letters

1. As sales manager for Lamson Manufacturing Company, Columbus, Ohio, you want to send—to retail store managers who have been your regular customers—a letter that ties in with your national advertising campaign. During November and December your company's all-purpose folding card tables with four matching folding chairs will be featured in two consumer magazines in full-page three-color ads. These ads will be read by 24 million people. You consider this the most powerful selling story you have ever put across. Now (October 1) you want to be sure that the 590 retail store managers that carry your products are sufficiently well stocked with a variety of these table-chair sets to meet the expected consumer demand. Wholesale price of each five-piece set is $31.80. Retail price is $53; separate folding tables are $16 each and each chair is $10.50. Thus, by buying the combination set, consumers save $5. Each table is 36 inches square, with vinyl covered top and bronze-tone finish steel frame 28 inches high; shipping

weight, 21 pounds. The matching folding chairs have padded vinyl seats, steel legs; shipping weight, 12 pounds each. Colors for both tables and chairs, green or mushroom beige in plain or floral patterns. These beautiful, practical, and low-priced items are just what consumers will need for Christmas. In your sales letter, provide easy-action order blanks and promise prompt shipment; be as specific as possible. Orders you receive by October 18 can be filled and the sets shipped in time for your customers to have them in stock by November 1.

2. Assume that last month you ran three advertisements in a local newspaper announcing the opening or remodeling of your business. You sell a service—such as transportation, advertising, tax consulting, traveler's aid, or restaurant. Write an unsolicited letter selling your service to a select list of (imaginary but probable) prospects who you are sure can benefit from what you can do for them. The goal of each letter is to bring your prospect to your business for his first "purchase" or (if more appropriate) for a consultation. Select a central selling point and build your letter around it. For instance, if you write for a restaurant, perhaps you will want to emphasize a food specialty or a special plate for which your chef is famous. Perhaps you will also want to mention your speedy service, exotic decor, music, prices, or extra-generous servings. Your letter should contain strong reader-benefit appeals. If you want to offer some special inducement such as a free gift or a reduced rate for the first visit, that's fine. If yours is a service that customers use repeatedly (such as a restaurant or transportation facility), figure out an appropriate way to determine which customers are calling for the first time.

    With your sales letter submit a complete "assumption sheet" that includes a brief statement on each of the following:

  **a.** The nature and location of your service
  **b.** Your reason for choosing this service
  **c.** Your central selling point
  **d.** The specific purpose of your message
  **e.** Any unique assumptions you have made (special letterhead, season, etc.)
  **f.** The kind of enclosure(s), if any, you would have.

3. Compare the following two letters,[1] both of which are designed to sell the same excellent service for top executives. Which one would you mail to management men if you had the choice and why? In your analysis of each, consider specifically: (a) you attitude, (b) attention-getting opening, (c) interest and conviction material, (d) action request.

  **A.**

                        CAN YOUR CUSTOMERS REALLY AFFORD
                        THE DEBT THEY ARE CARRYING?

  Dear Sir:

  Debt presents an attractive means of financing. But — since assets have a way of melting away when a concern encounters troubles — the decision to extend bank or merchandise credit involves the balance of expected return and increased risk.

  This is cash flow analysis.

[1] Courtesy of Dun & Bradstreet and *Direct Marketing*, April 1970.

The concept and procedure for determining cash flow is fully presented in the Dun & Bradstreet Advanced Credit and Financial Analysis course.

Throughout the course, the credit function is approached as a managerial function with profit responsibility to the entire organization. The objective is to develop managerial judgment that will be of value to both the organization's advancement and the individual's advancement.

While the course employs some of the most advanced techniques of financial analysis, great care is taken to have it remain completely practical. The advanced materials are fresh enough to remain current practice for many years.

An outline of the content of this new Dun & Bradstreet business course is shown on the following page. The course can be both a challenge and a reward to men and women in your organization who are concerned with growth and profits. To enroll just fill in the registration form on page 4 and return it to me.

Your management men should know
· · · how to read a balance sheet between the lines

The ability to judge a financial statement accurately — to predict credit responsibility and avoid unusual risks, can be a tremendous asset to your firm.

Balance sheets can hide the facts you need to make a sound credit judgment. The facts are there to the man who knows what to look for, who knows how to interpret what he sees.

The D&B Advanced Credit and Financial Analysis course is built around authentic business credit problems. The executive learns by dealing with financial facts. His solutions are compared with real life situations — he follows the action as it happened and sees into the why and how of credit decisions.

Twelve sections cover business credit, financing, debt, management, investment techniques, bankruptcies and dozens of other aspects of business money management.

This is a home study course completed in six months, with the student's progress checked regularly and reported to management.

Thousands of top business leaders have completed this up-to-the-minute training and are using their sharpened financial know how to improve the earning performance of their firms. The men you select for this instruction can do as well, and within six months.

Read the enclosed detailed description and then list the executives you want to enroll. Their training can begin at once, with their new skills put to work quickly to protect company earning potential.

Select your men today and we will get them started at once. It's never too soon.

4. You are a part-time employee for Mod Man, Inc., a men's clothing shop "For men who think young." Your employer, knowing you are a college senior and that you're studying business communications, has just offered you a challenging opportunity to try your skill on a sales letter. After you write it, he will pay all expenses for reproducing and mailing it—plus a 10 percent commission to you on the direct sales your letter brings in.

Here is his proposition: The store's men's formal rental wear department is sponsoring a special Senior Ball promotion. Your letter is to be mailed to all men in the senior class in your college (of which you are a member). Assume at least 1,000 on your mailing list. All your readers need to do is to stop in at Mod Man and register. Your employer has made arrangements with a local automobile dealer to have a brand new 197_ customized convertible on display right in the store starting this weekend until the day before the Senior Ball. Someone who registers will win the free use of this car for the night of your Senior Ball, courtesy of Tom Tolaf Auto Sales, Inc. In addition, there will be four other big winners, each of whom will get: Senior Ball tickets for two; a corsage of their choice; a $20 gift certificate for dinner for two at (name), restaurant (the best in your city); and their formal wear rental at no charge. All the seniors have to do to get a chance to win is to register and choose their formal wear from your store. You have the largest and most fashionable collection in the city: everything from white dinner jackets to full-dress tails, with 23 styles in between including double-breasted coats, turtlenecks, and ruffled shirts, and all at Mod Man's standard low rental rates.

Your one-page letter will be processed in any way you choose—mimeographed, by computer, or dittoed—and will be on the store's letterhead. There is to be no enclosure. You may send the letter over your own signature, if you wish. Design its layout in any way you choose. If you wish, you can give this promotion a special name (such as "Your Prom Night On Us").

5. Assume that you are sales manager of the Armo Products Company, which manufactures do-it-yourself tools and home building supplies. To get your company's name before the public and at the same time to help your exclusive dealers, you have developed a special-offer plan for the dealers. By taking advantage of your cooperative plan, the dealers can buy—at half price—book matches to give away to their consumer customers as goodwill builders. This week you need to send a letter to your 600 dealers telling them about your plan. Each dealer can have his name imprinted on one side of the book matches. The other side shows the

Armo insignia and identifies the dealer's store as headquarters for Armo products. These matches enable the dealer to tie in with your firm's national advertising, which sells Armo products all over the country. You have placed a large advance order with your match manufacturer. However, initial orders from dealers who have recently visited your plant indicate that the demand will soon exceed the supply, so it's a good idea for your dealers to place their orders right now. You can sell them 4,800 book matches in the new double size for only $20. This is less than ½ cent per book match. The 4,800 books contain 192,000 matches, each a reminder of the dealer's business. In your letter provide a convenient order blank and remind the dealers to specify the imprint they want.

6. You are general manager of the Uptown Auto Sales and Service. Your body shop department gets numerous opportunities to make repair estimates on automobiles damaged in accidents. Usually, prospective customers get estimates from three different repair shops. You have good reason to know that your shop's prices and bids are very similar to those of your closest competitors. Thus prospective customers who must choose one of three shops often have very little except price to guide them.

   You want now to draft a form letter—on your company's letterhead—for your or your foreman's signature. It is to be sent from time to time to each customer on whose car the shop makes an estimate. Typed on automatic typewriter, each letter will have a personalized inside address and salutation. Its purpose is to persuade each reader to bring his car to your shop because of the benefits he gets in addition to the reasonable price. Your facilities are complete. Everything is done in your shop: paint, metal, mechanical, glasswork, frame straightening, etc. Your personnel are hand-picked factory-trained specialists. They take pride in their work. You use only genuine factory parts, and you guarantee satisfaction. Your policy is service, quality, and integrity. You'll also consider a customer's credit for a budget account, so he can have his car repaired now and pay later. Write the sales letter that will help each prospective customer to decide that your company is where he should have his car repaired.

7. Assume that you have been out of college 10 years. Recently a group of your former classmates persuaded you to be chairman of the class tenth anniversary reunion. The date chosen coincides with your college homecoming, at which the classes that graduated 10, 25, and 50 years ago are especially honored. You have rented the Horizon and Rainier Rooms of the Plaza Hotel for Saturday evening of homecoming weekend, and committees have been working on plans.

   Now it is your job to write the "sales letter" to urge former classmates to buy tickets and attend. It's to be a new-fashioned get-together of cocktails, dinner, dancing, and reminiscing. For an orchestra you found three persons who play the kind of music that was popular when you all were in college. For those alums who need tickets for the homecoming football game against UCLA, you've managed to reserve a few. But they must get their requests and money in immediately. The seats aren't quite on the 50-yard line, but they're inside the stadium, which is pretty good, considering the limited supply. You already have a reservation from Fairbanks, Alaska, and you're hoping for many others from distant places. A prize will be given to the classmate traveling the longest distance.

   Write a convincing letter that will urge—and get—an excellent turnout. Provide a good way for readers to make their reservations and make clear that $10 must accompany each reservation.

8. The following letter was sent by a laundry to new fathers. Discuss its merits and weaknesses; state whether you like its tone and appeals; then discuss whether you think the "average" father you know would be favorably impressed with this letter so that he would buy the service.

Dear Dad,

Did anyone send you ——give your aching back a rub? No! You're the bent gent who walked the halls...paid the bills... burned the morning . And boy, how you love it! This 'life with fatherhood' is not only the beginning of your child's life, but yours, too. Now, you'll really know the meaning of living!

Naturally, you want to qualify as an A-1 Dad. And you can—IF you learn the simple trick of the . Par for the course is under 90 seconds. We'll caddy—so tee up and let's go:

**90 SECONDS**

Place the little income tax exemption fanny down on the folded diaper. They can take a lot of rough handling, but no use breaking him in for tackle just yet. For the future glamour girl, have the thickest part of the diaper behind, like a bustle. For the future full-backs, the extra thickness must be in front. In either case, bring the lapover up between the legs, and with your hand next to baby's skin, front to back at the waist.

This is one of the few things you can do **first** for your new baby. First, last, and always! Boy, but babies have a one- mind. And how the soiled diapers collect. And THIS is where **we** come in.

Layette Service offers perspiring fathers a complete baby laundry service **twice each week**....inexpensive, too. 84 diapers per week for only 34¢ per day. This is that added something special—which costs so very little—that you can do for your young family.

**LIKE THIS DAD!**

You'll have enough to do, Dad, mastering the folding and pinning of diapers...Let US see that the diapers are **there** when you need 'em.

**BABY'S DIAPERS**

**Bottoms up!**

# Specialized Messages

- Chapter 10   The Written Job Presentation
- Chapter 11   Other Job Application Messages
- Chapter 12   Collection Messages—Written and Oral
- Chapter 13   Goodwill Messages

# THE WRITTEN JOB PRESENTATION

- Desirable General Qualifications
- Information Sources for Specific Types of Jobs
- Employers' Likes and Dislikes in the Written Job Presentation
- Résumé
- Letter of Application
- Examples of the Written Job Presentation
- Exercises

The purpose of the application letter and resume is to get an interview; therefore you want to interest—in fact, sell—your reader on your qualifications so that he wants to talk further with you. But before you begin to write the letter and resume, you need to research the "product"—yourself—as thoroughly as you would any other product. You need to determine what the buyer (your prospective employer) wants and how your qualifications meet his needs. After all, the application letter is actually a sales letter with the resume as an enclosure.

This chapter discusses desirable general qualifications, information sources for specific types of jobs, employers' likes and dislikes regarding written job presentations, the resume, and the letter of application.

## DESIRABLE GENERAL QUALIFICATIONS

Speaking in broad terms, the qualifications that employers look for in recent college graduates seeking a career in the business world are the following:

1. Proper attitude toward employment
2. Evidence of intelligence and education
3. Evidence of social development
4. Work experience
5. Physical fitness
6. Appearance and manners
7. Other desirable personal traits

### Proper Attitude toward Employment

This extremely important quality has four component parts: (1) willingness to learn and work; (2) interest in the field of your choice; (3) interest in the company; and (4) reasonable attitude toward salary.

*Willingness to Learn and Work.* Unless you are applying for a formal training program, you probably will have to accept beginning or routine work within the field of your choice. Although you may have attended school 16 years or longer by the time of graduation, many of the facts you've learned have been general enough to be useful for all students going into all types of businesses. Now you need to learn on the job the specific duties, procedures, and practices of the company that hires you. As the newspaper correspondent Hal Boyle once wrote: "You have to learn how to saw wood before you can make a cabinet."

Yet the majority of employers receive many applications from recent graduates for jobs that require years of service or training. These unrealistic requests—which indicate an unwillingness to learn and work—include applications to be a personnel director, store manager, editor, comptroller, foreign correspondent, account executive, and so on. It is true that a college degree opens doors to employment, but you still have to prove your worth in your written application, interview, and actual performance on the job.

In your written job presentation, you can convey proper willingness to learn and work by indicating one or more of the following:

You will complete some pertinent certification or license by studying and taking the required tests at night and on weekends.

You're interested in attending class training and seminars conducted by the firm.

You plan to continue your education and strengthen your background for the job by taking night classes at a nearby school.

*Interest in Field.* Employers expect you to know the type of work you have chosen for a career, and to have chosen a career you will enjoy. The greater the interest in the job, the greater the effort a person puts forth and, hence, the greater the accomplishment. However, don't expect the employer to decide the type of work you're best fitted for. Each person must arrive at his own conclusion about his estimated part in the world's work. Each person must know what he wants to do.

A broad educational background is definitely an asset, no matter what field you have chosen, but extensive academic training without a goal or objective is pointless. Whether you apply for a specific job or an opening in a more general area depends upon the type of work involved. For example, if you are interested in a particular job, such as selling, teaching, or accounting, you will apply for that specific assignment—and nothing else. On the other hand, if you want to get into a field, say advertising, you will indicate that area, and *not* a specific job. And a graduate wanting managerial work in the personnel department will probably get there through the firm's management training program.

You can indicate interest in the job or field of your choice when you:

Mention specifically the job you want or field you want to get into.

Identify both the immediate and ultimate goals. (For example, you want to enter a management training program so that you can eventually get into personnel.)

Indicate any aptitude (usually through tests) you have for your chosen field.

Avoid expressions like the following, which indicate to employers that you don't know what you want:

"Am applying for a position with your company."
"I can do anything—what do you have?"
"What have you got?"
"I will take anything that is available."

*Interest in the Company.* One of the three questions that a company interviewer is most likely to ask when you apply for a job is "Why are you applying for work with us?" (The other two are: "What type of work are you applying for?" and "What are your qualifications for the job?")

You show a healthy attitude toward employment when you indicate you've studied the company and know that it is the organization (or type of organization) in which you can do your most productive work. You can show interest in the company by mentioning:

Reason for applying
Interest in something the company does
Your concern about how best to serve the company
Statement of what you can do for the firm
Why you like the policy of the company (if you have had previous work there or done intensive research on it)

Give specific reasons for wanting to work for the firm, as in the examples below:

1. My interest in Burroughs has been stimulated by several means. My brother-in-law, Robert Kramer—your salesman in the St. Louis district—has thoroughly sold me on the superior performance of Burroughs machines and the excellent opportunities offered by the fine Burroughs organization. From his machine demonstrations, the merits of Burroughs products became apparent. During my last summer job, while attending college, I operated a Burroughs "sensimatic" accounting machine. The fast, easy operation of this versatile machine certainly impressed me.

2. Professor A. B. Smith of the University of Illinois has told me about some of the ways in which your store operates. As you will notice from the resume, my major field of study has been in retailing. Because my main interest has always been the study of the cost method of retailing, I want to work for a large organization like yours which uses it.

Exhibiting self-interest is the opposite of showing interest in the company. Applications which stress any one of the following are self-, rather than company-centered.

What the company can do for the applicant
Concern about hours, vacation schedule, security, general benefits, etc.
Applicant's desire to "try" the particular field

Below is an illustration of a self-centered inquiry. The personnel manager who received it returned it to the college placement office with several caustic remarks about the applicant.

Gentlemen:

The Placement Office here at Blank University has informed me that you have an opening in your sales organization.

I would like to know the following:

1. What are the possibilities of advancement?
2. What is the salary and do you have a pension plan?
3. Do you furnish a company car?
4. If so, may the salesman use his own private car?
5. What is the arrangement regarding the traveling expenses?
6. Describe your fringe benefits in detail.

Because I am graduating from the School of Business Administration on (date), I will appreciate any answer to the questions listed above, plus any additional information which you may have.

*Reasonable Attitude toward Salary.* Business wants men and women who are looking for opportunity, instead of a large beginning salary. Emphasis on salary definitely creates an unfavorable impression.

However, some employers want you to mention salary in your letter, and some do not. Each group has good reasons for its way of thinking. Those who want you to include salary say this information is a basic point of consideration. It is a form of personal evaluation, a time-saver for both applicant and employer, and an indication of financial expectations and needs. Probably the most important reason is that it is a "time-saver." If you price yourself too high (or sometimes ridiculously low), you may be automatically eliminated from further consideration.

The employers who consider it unwise for you to mention salary in your initial application letter also have good reasons. They say you weaken your presentation by including this information because the letter (or resume) is not the proper time or place to discuss salary. Furthermore, salary is usually fixed, and you should consider the starting rate secondary to opportunity.

In general—especially if you are just beginning your career—it is best not to mention salary in the letter or resume. Know the going rate for a graduate with your background, and then wait until the interviewer tells you what salary his company offers. If he doesn't and the interview seems to be coming to a close, ask—if you are really interested in the job.

## Evidence of Intelligence and Education

A second quality that an employer looks for in a college graduate is evidence of intelligence and education. An interviewer or recipient of an application looks for mental alertness, adaptability, facility to absorb what is said, ability to think logically and clearly, sound judgment, imagination, and grades earned—all signs of intelligence. Education, on the other hand, refers to years of schooling and curriculum studied.

Intelligence is extremely important. It gives an indication of how quickly the graduate will be able to grasp the company's assignments, procedures, and practices, as well as how readily he will adapt to new situations and solve problems. With regard to education, the number and kinds of courses studied and the degrees earned vary with the type of work requested and company standards. Although some employers pay little attention to the student's major, in general businessmen prefer a graduate who has a broad understanding of the arts and sciences, which permits him to be familiar with and conversant in several areas, and also an acceptable background in the area of the requested work.

Employers are generally favorably impressed if you have also studied useful elective courses that are related to your interest and can be applied now or later on the job. Good examples are courses in written communication, speech, and human relations. The basic tools that an individual should get from college training include ability to gather and evaluate facts, and reason objectively to a conclusion on the basis of the facts; to think clearly and concisely; and to express himself (orally and in writing).

Grades are a controversial subject. To many employers, grades indicate how well the graduate has mastered his studies and how well he has met numerous requirements. As a result, applicants for some areas—such as accounting and research—need high grades before they can be considered by the more desirable organizations. For other applicants, grades are weighed together with different factors: for example, a graduate who has had to work his way through college, has dependents, and has participated in extracurricular activities isn't expected to have as high grades as a person who has not used his time for such nonclass endeavors.

For positions that require the individual to work closely with customers and employers, personality is far more important than grades; examples of such areas include selling, management training, and secretarial work. Furthermore, a graduate with a straight A cumulative grade point needs to prove he possesses more than intelligence, because the average employer is wary of an applicant who has little or nothing but high scholarship to offer.

You can indicate intelligence and education in the written job presentation in the following ways:

*For intelligence*
You can show adaptability by discussing the subject in general—that is, how you can adapt on the job to the many types of people and/or to the many assignments or responsibilities.

You can indicate imagination by mentioning some project you conceived and executed yourself. (Maybe you designed and built a racing car, home, cabin, or some other structure.)

One way for an employer to measure facility to absorb what is said is by looking at your grades. If you have a 3.5 (out of a possible 4.0) grade point average, you probably absorbed more than the student with a 2.5.

Sound judgment might be reflected in the reports you had to write for case courses, or perhaps in the results of a team project—especially if you headed your division or group.

An important oral or written presentation in or outside of class shows ability to think clearly. Or perhaps you can mention the satisfactory outcome of a knotty problem you faced.

*For education*

Mention your major or area of study you emphasized.

Tell how you prepared academically for your career—especially if you knew early (say, in your freshman or sophomore year) what you planned to do.

List pertinent or useful courses in and/or outside your major or college curriculum.

List your bachelor's and any advanced degrees if you have more than one.

Show you have a broad background in arts and sciences and/or in most areas of business.

Report writing, marketing research, and case courses should prepare you to gather facts, evaluate them, reason objectively to a conclusion on the basis of facts, and to think clearly and concisely.

Courses in written and oral business communication will certainly be helpful, no matter what position you are applying for.

## Evidence of Social Development

A third desirable quality in a college graduate is evidence of social development, which refers to ability to get along with others, emotional stability, and leadership qualities. In the written presentations, an employer studies the individual's participation in high school and especially college extracurricular activities.

The extent of participation and leadership experience helps indicate whether the recent graduate has the ability to work with and direct others. Industry wants a man who has the popularity among his colleagues to win their confidence, who can develop the knack of leadership, who knows the importance of cooperation and teamwork, and who has a sincere interest in other people.

Although any extracurricular activity that shows an individual's ability to work with others will be favorably regarded, interviewers are particularly impressed with experience in the following: athletics, writing (such as journalism), speaking (such as debate), professional fraternities, and student organizations that involve working with other people. Businesses seek men and women who possess the qualities necessary for good teamwork; who can speak and write effectively; and who have a serious interest in their field and can work well with and through other individuals. On the other hand, companies have little or no interest in the "joiner" who has numerous affiliations but shoulders no responsibility. A leader or active participant in any worthy activity—regardless of what it is—is far more valuable than a nonparticipant who has numerous affiliations.

Indications of your social development include the following:

Extracurricular activities—social fraternity or sorority; professional organization —marketing club, accounting club, business club, pharmacy club, etc.; sports (especially those that involve teamwork and cooperation)

Offices held—president, vice-president, public relations officer, etc.

Supervision or direction of other people—captain, foreman, supervisor, committee chairman, U.S. military officer

Responsibilities you accepted in school, on the job, in extracurricular activities, in branch of military service

Your ability to work with others—including those of different background, race, or religion

Any situation in which others looked up to you for respect or leadership

Ability to win others to your point of view

Interest in helping others—reading for the blind, tutoring minority groups, assisting in a civic drive, counseling a boy or girl team or group, managing a basketball or football team for preteens or teenagers, etc.

## Work Experience

Any kind of work experience—related or unrelated—reveals information that helps the interviewer to evaluate the graduate. Work experience similar to that which you are applying for indicates you like the type of work in question, and may shorten the training period. However, all types of work experience disclose pertinent facts about the applicant's work habits and personality, give a source for references, and perhaps show his job preferences. Experience indicates that the individual has at least been introduced to a world other than the academic one.

Remember the following general suggestions when you are discussing your work experience:

1. The applicant who *helped finance his way through college* and who participated in a few extracurricular activities and maintained passing grades in his studies

    *is preferred to*

    The applicant who *didn't finance his way through college* but participated in a few extracurricular activities and maintained a high scholastic average in his studies

*or*

participated in many extracurricular activities and maintained passing grades in his studies

*or*

participated in no extracurricular activities and maintained honor grades in his studies

2. Present your work experience in one or more of these ways:

Show that related work experience can shorten the initial training period.

Indicate through all or some jobs held that you are comfortable working in the business world, can work under pressure, and enjoy working with and helping others.

Show how you supplemented your academic training with practical experience. (For example, an accounting major might work part-time as an accountant with a business firm.)

Reveal your initiative. When did you begin to work—at the age of 12 or 18? In addition to a full college load each quarter or semester, did you work 10 to 40 hours each week? Did you win the prize or contest one week, month, or year for the greatest sales or subscriptions?

Indicate how you allocated your time and show that you know the value of money. For example, if you took a full class schedule and worked 20 hours a week elsewhere to support your family, you certainly had to allocate your time and money wisely.

3. You may also reveal your personality and/or interest in a field by the jobs you held. Did you work in a filling station or as a salesman door-to-door or behind the counter? Did you work 80 hours a week on an Alaskan fishing boat during the summer months so you could devote full time to your studies during the remaining nine months?

## Physical Fitness

A prime requirement on the job is good health because it determines both the physical and mental performance of the individual. As a result, many companies give a physical examination to a potential candidate before hiring him. However, even before you go to the interview, you can indicate physical fitness by listing on the application:

The sports you participate in. An active swimmer, football or basketball player, or a contestant in intra-mural activities must be in pretty good condition.

Your hobbies that require activity, endurance, strength, and stamina. Examples include hiking, fishing, mountain climbing, boating, and bowling.

A statement that you have excellent health with no physical defects, if true.

## Appearance and Manners

A sixth important qualification is appearance and manners. A desirable appearance includes neatness, cleanliness, appropriate dress, and health.

Manners include pleasantness, firm handshake, courtesy, naturalness, and a knowledge of etiquette.

Although this qualification relates more to the interview than to the written job presentation, you should still check the following points within the letter and resume:

Be courteous—make sure your reader receives a favorable first impression.
Ask for an interview—don't demand or expect it.

## Other Desirable Personal Traits

The phrase "other desirable personal traits" refers to that sometimes vague, but often extremely important, qualification known as personality. Personality determines the impression that a person makes upon other people. The more a person's job requires him to meet and work with others, direct and persuade them, and assume positions of leadership, the more important his personality is.

This chapter has already covered several aspects of personality—especially in the sections on attitude toward employment, social development, and evidence of appearance and manners. "Other desirable personal traits" include sincerity, integrity, self-confidence and determination, friendliness, dependability, punctuality, and responsibility. Of these, sincerity, integrity, self-confidence, and determination are especially important. The outstanding unfavorable traits are insincerity, dishonesty, overconfidence, boastfulness, argumentativeness, and lack of self-confidence.

*Sincerity and Integrity versus Insincerity and Dishonesty.* Sincerity and integrity instill confidence. In contrast, no employer can become interested in an individual who is deceptive. For example, most readers or interviewers can detect when an applicant is insincerely praising a company or mechanically stating a desire to work only for that particular firm. Another type of insincerity—or even dishonesty—is exaggerating and padding qualifications.

If you feel honestly dedicated to the field you're applying for, you can devote a whole paragraph to the reasons, and your conviction will be conveyed. But if you try to misrepresent your attitude, you're only kidding yourself. The person judging your application has been in the field long enough to detect insincerity.

On the other hand, sincerity doesn't mean you need to expose your shortcomings. If you haven't had work experience or don't have a good grade point average, you need not mention these negative aspects at all.

You can reveal sincerity and integrity in your written job presentation by discussing one or several of the following:

Reasons for interest in your chosen field and/or the company
Willingness to relocate
Academic preparation for your goal

Interest in people or civic affairs
Ability to work easily with others
Past responsibilities you assumed
Description of duties for the different jobs you held
Percentage of school and living expenses you earned yourself
Statement of being bonded

*Self-confidence versus Timidity or Overselling.* Self-confidence involves the ability to sell yourself—without timidity on the one hand or high-pressure tactics and egotism on the other. You can sell yourself effectively if you:

Know what the company looks for in an applicant. In turn, you will stress what is important, and condense or eliminate what doesn't have much or any weight

Have faith and confidence in yourself so that you reveal a pleasant, friendly, interesting personality

Reveal yourself as a person who can work with others harmoniously and has leadership qualities

Show that you're genuinely interested in the company and that "opportunity" means more to you than initial salary and fringe benefits

You will have difficulty selling yourself if you exhibit egotism and boastfulness. You must avoid a presumptuous, "here I am" attitude. An example of the "I" attitude is the demanding approach—such as requesting an immediate answer or insisting on an interview. As one nationally known company said: "The word 'I' is used so frequently in some application letters that we get the general idea the applicant has become overawed by his accomplishment of having earned a degree."

As you write your application letter, stress your qualifications rather than your selfish (and, from the company's point of view, limited) interests. Stress other people rather than yourself, and hopefully you'll naturally avoid too many "I's."

*Determination.* A firm wants an applicant who has the drive and tenacity to get the work done. If you don't have the ability to carry projects through to the end, you won't be of much use to the company.

You can show determination through your background. For example, if you had to drop out of school because of finances or poor grades, but managed to get your degree by attending night school, you are certainly a determined person. Of if you quit school voluntarily and then returned to complete your degree—only through sacrifice on your part—you have determination to succeed.

The following advice by a business executive in one of our largest national companies explains the way to sell yourself in the resume and application letter.

### Selling yourself in the resume

One of the overall things to remember, I think, is the old salesmanship rule—"sell the sizzle, not the steak." In other words, when writing your application, you don't dare say you are a wonder boy, but at the same time you have to prove it anyhow. Get everything in that data sheet that will help in any way at all to show you are outstanding.

It doesn't do any good to say that certain items of information should be listed, and then go down the line, listing these things with equal emphasis whether they are good, bad, or indifferent. If you have recent job accomplishments to point to, I would do so. If you haven't any, or very few, then of course point to scholastic accomplishments—extra-curricular accomplishments, etc. If you can give outstanding men as references, do so. That will make an impression—whether or not somebody said references should or should not be on a data sheet . . . When you don't have one thing to point out, you just point out something else that will prove the same thing.

### Selling yourself in the application letter

A college graduate should know all the mechanics of sentence structure and letter writing; but that in itself won't create a letter that will get him a job; it won't create letters that will sell his product for him after he gets the job.

Knowing the information that personnelmen want on application blanks and data sheets should be a big help; still, that in itself won't do the trick, either. You never in your life saw an apple advertisement that went down the line and listed how many apples were big, how many small, how many bruised, how many wormy, and how many rotten; but I am willing to bet last year's fedora that if you asked the consumers about it they would want to know some of those things that were not emphasized in the advertisement—and at the same time I will lay a further wager that they were motivated by the ad to go inspect the apples and buy.

To continue using the same example, if the apple advertising is conducted on a local basis, you can easily conceive of an ad showing a picture of Aunt Lucybelle Jones over on Elm Street making cider and apple pies all over the place and giving her plain homespun version of how everybody is simply crazy about them apple pies—until you almost feel apple juice running down your own chin.

To translate all this—there is a knack of pointing out those things you have done and selling your capabilities—a knack of doing it with simple convincing sincerity. Instead of creating doubts with vague generalized statements, or making them seem phoney because your letter sounds artificial—leave the apple juice running down their chins.

Ordinarily you don't get too far with fancy statements—you do it with the actual things you have accomplished—show them big juicy apple pies all over the place.

## INFORMATION SOURCES FOR SPECIFIC TYPES OF JOBS

In addition to knowing the general qualifications that employers consider desirable, you need to know the specific requirements and opportunities in the fields that interest you.

Perhaps you know right now the kind of career work you want and even the organization you will work for; if so, you are fortunate. More likely, however, you are one of the thousands of young people who are not sure which of several interests they should pursue, what specific job requirements they must meet, or where the opportunities are. Various sources of information can be helpful in this situation. Bear in mind, of course, that because supply and demand in the employment market change from year to year, it is best to get the most current publications. Your campus career planning and placement office and the libraries have available printed materials such as the following about job requirements and rewards:

> *Dictionary of Occupational Titles*, U.S. Department of Labor, U.S. Government Printing Office, Washington. Summarizes characteristics, abilities, and skills contributing to success in various occupations and careers.
>
> *The Occupational Outlook Handbook*, U.S. Bureau of Labor Statistics, U.S. Government Printing Office, Washington. Highlights employment opportunities in various fields.
>
> *SRA Occupational Briefs*, Science Research Associates, 259 East Erie Street, Chicago. Consists of 210 four-page briefs (of which 70 are revised each year) about major job areas.

By consulting various periodical indexes (*Applied Science and Technology, Business Periodicals, Public Affairs Information Service,* or *Readers' Guide*) you may find recent articles on the vocation you are considering. In addition, books such as *Job Strategy,* Alan Rood (McGraw-Hill, 1961); *Plan Your Career,* Robert Calvert (McGraw-Hill, 1963); or *The College Girl Looks Ahead,* Marguerite Zapoleon (Harper & Row, 1956) discuss career opportunities that may interest you.

After you have decided on the kind of career you want, you will need information about employers and their specific requirements for certain kinds of jobs. As a start, you can get brochures, pamphlets, newsletters, house organs, and annual reports from various specific companies. Your campus placement office (or any other placement office) usually has a wealth of such materials. If you wish to write to firms for information that is not obtainable locally, consult available directories.

You will also find in your placement office or library the following books and standard reference materials that provide information published annually about company products, services, size, openings, geographical locations, and/or other facts:

> *College Placement Annual,* College Placement Council, 35 East Elizabeth Street, Bethlehem, Pennsylvania. Contains an alphabetical list of United States and Canadian firms seeking college graduates; includes brief information on openings and the proper persons to contact; also includes alphabetical lists by majors and geographical locations.

*Moody's Manuals of Investment,* Moody's Investors Service, 99 Church Street, New York. Contains financial and background information and locations of banks, insurance firms, financial agencies, municipals and governments, railroads, public utilities, industrials.

*Poor's Register of Directors and Executives; United States and Canada,* published annually by Standard and Poor's Corporation, 345 Hudson Street, New York. Has an alphabetical list of over 27,000 leading business firms, their addresses, principal products, number of employees, directors, and key officers.

*Thomas' Register of American Manufacturers,* Thomas Publishing Co., 461 Eighth Avenue, New York.

Sometimes you can get helpful tips about job openings from special reports, articles, and listings that appear in the *Wall Street Journal* or *Fortune*, in trade and professional magazines, and even your local newspaper. Professors, counselors, businessmen and women already working in your chosen career, and friends can also provide help.

## EMPLOYERS' LIKES AND DISLIKES IN THE WRITTEN JOB PRESENTATION

The section below discusses the various likes and dislikes of employers regarding specific parts of your written job presentation. (The following section, on resumes, also covers some specific likes and dislikes.)

### Businesslike versus Clever Approach

When you're applying for a job—especially the first one after graduation— you should sound serious, rather than clever or "cute." The written job presentation isn't the time or place for risking a negative reaction from the reader. (The only applicant who might attempt an unusual letter or data sheet is one interested in a job—such as advertising—involving a high degree of creativity.)

"Clever" approaches—smart-aleck, off-color, and "novelty"—do not favorably impress employers. Letter 1 below is a "clever" application that was sent to a large airplane manufacturer. The recipient of the letter reacted as follows:

This young man has made a rather sorry attempt to be funny. While in a sense it is amusing, it certainly did not create the impression he wanted it to. It would be extremely difficult for me to visualize myself hiring an individual who would make such an obvious blunder. My feeling in this is that if he would write this type of letter in applying for a position, he would undoubtedly continue that trend were he put in a position to contact the public. There are too many good, conscientious men who mean business and want jobs to "fritter" away time with such an individual.

***Letter 1.*** *Clever letter which was negatively received.*

> Dear Sir:
>
> This letter of introduction will serve to acquaint you with a product, which I believe can be useful to you. It is a comparatively new unit, having first originated in 1946.
>
> Preliminary study was completed in 1965 at Van Burien High School, Washington, D. C., where the unit achieved the performance standing of #1 out of 380 comparable designs. Major study was completed in the Engineering School of the University of America in June, 1969. The product was rated "magna cum laude" and received the Institute of Aeronautical Sciences Award for the highest average by impartial tests undertaken in the Aeronautical Engineering Department in 1966. It was also given membership in the Sigma Xi and IAS at that time.
>
> The past two years have been spent in research, development and testing at a large wind-tunnel establishment. Analysis of the data of the past two years indicates that better utilization of this product lies with your organization.
>
> Specifications and performance data are summarized on the following pages.

## Specific Information versus Generalities

Employers appreciate an application letter and resume that state ideas clearly, factually, and specifically. Generalities are not only confusing; they give the impression that the applicant is trying to conceal a weakness or really does not know what he is talking about. The following generalities should be avoided:

### *In the data sheet*

No inclusion of months with years for a job tenure. "1970–1971" could mean two years or two days. Be specific: July 1970–December 1971.

No indication of office held for each extracurricular activity. If you were president, say so; if you were only a member, state that fact.

No mention of possible defects with statement about health. If true, say: "Excellent health—no defects." (If you don't like "defects" use a synonym that you prefer.)

Omission of children for a married person. Say: "Married, no children" or "Married, two children."

General statement about period of time in Army. Say, for example, "February 1968–July 1970," instead of "two years, five months."

Mention of business experience without indicating that some or all of that training was part-time. You can confuse the reader if you tell him that you have

8 years of work experience, that you're graduating from a 4-year university, and that you're only 21 years old. He'll assume the 8 years of work are full-time unless you tell him differently.

A vague statement that doesn't say specifically whether the applicant is currently employed or unemployed.

*In the application letter*

Vague statements about why you want the job. Such statements as "I want personnel work because I like people" mean nothing without proof.

Mention of something you like about the company that can't be backed up. You can't say, for example, "I like your personnel policy" truthfully unless you've worked for the firm or researched its policy.

Any generalities about yourself, such as "I have a good personality" (what do you mean?), "I have had salesmanship and other related courses" (what courses?), or "A mutual friend has told me . . ." (what friend?).

## Individuality versus Canned Letters

Letters should be tailored for the specific job or job area and for the specific firm. Canned letters—letters that sound as if they've been copied from a text or written by an employment agency—don't receive much consideration. Also, senders of such letters make it impossible for the reader to judge their personality.

If you were one of fifty applicants for one opening, what would you say in your message to set you apart from the other forty-nine? What would you say—without sounding conceited—to convince the employer your qualifications are just a bit better than the others? Remember that thousands of young men and women are graduating from colleges and universities throughout the United States each year and the majority of them have average grades, some business experience, 16 years of education, and "mature outlook on life." Therefore, you need to stress *your* selling qualifications—what makes you unique. Such qualifications might be one or more of the following: a successful business experience, ability to work with others, leadership, strong educational background for a particular job or job area, interest in the field, related work experience, thorough knowledge of the territorial area or good contacts in that area, previous employment with that firm, fluency with one or more foreign languages, or proficiency in certain skills.

## Enclosures

The only enclosure to include with your application letter is the resume itself. At this stage of consideration employers don't want to be bogged down with samples of work, recommendations, or transcripts. You might *offer* to send any of these items—but don't send them with the initial application.

Also, don't enclose an addressed, stamped envelope or postcard or stamp. Modern firms consider such enclosures a nuisance; also they want to advertise their organization by replying on their own stationery. The only time you might enclose an envelope or card is when you are writing to an organization —like a school or nonprofit business—that must especially watch its budget.

## Mechanics

Every aspect of mechanics is important. One employer may be prejudiced against misspellings; another will dislike grammatical errors; still another will be fastidious about appearance. However, even though all mechanics count, the following aspects are most important.

1. *Ability to express yourself.* After your 16 years of schooling, the prospective employer expects you to write well. Ability to write includes composing a complete sentence, writing paragraphs with both unity and coherence, and organizing the entire message.

2. *Length of message.* You should confine your selling presentation to a one-page letter and a one- or two-page resume—unless your background includes years of valuable experience. The employer is a busy man and doesn't want to waste his time on irrelevant facts or on minor points. Remember, your aim is to get an interview—not to give your life history.

3. *Spelling.* Employers place heavy emphasis on spelling for the following reasons:

   If you can't spell, you'll probably continue to show this weakness when you're on the job and are writing to customers, and many customers judge the overall ability of a writer by his ability to spell. Further, transposing letters within words—such as "teh" for "the"—shows carelessness in proofreading. Maybe (so the customer thinks) the writer is also careless in other aspects of his work performance.

   Misspelling names of a person, firm, and/or job area indicates that you aren't very interested in the person or firm you're addressing or the type of work you're applying for. (Several commonly misspelled words include "J. C. Penny" for "J. C. Penney," "Weyerhauser" for "Weyerhaeuser," and "personel" for "personnel.")

4. *Appearance.* Appearance carries a lot of weight; it makes an initial impression and can influence the reader's opinion of the individual's overall dress and work habits. If you have sent a sloppy letter when supposedly you are trying to make your best impression, what kind of a person must you be when you *aren't* trying to make an impression?

   Included in appearance is duplication of material. The application letter must be typewritten and seem as individualized and personalized as possible. A duplicated message—whether it's mimeographed, dittoed, xeroxed, offset printed, or a carbon—gives the appearance of an advertising campaign and receives little consideration. On the other hand, an attractive duplicated resume is quite acceptable.

Remember that employers like written job applications that are business-like, specific, individual, and mechanically correct, with only a resume enclosure.

## RESUME[1]

Once you have made a critical evaluation of your background and also learned what the employer considers important, you are ready to think about preparing the application letter and resume (sometimes called data sheet or fact sheet). Although the prospective employer will read the letter first and then the resume, you should prepare the resume before you write the letter.[2] The letter actually depends on information in the resume, since the former will emphasize two or three of the many qualifications and facts included in a well-organized resume. This section discusses the possible content and manner of presentation for the following parts of a resume:

1. Opening section
   a. Heading
   b. Personal data
   c. Picture
   d. Military record
   e. Optional data (job objective, basic qualifications, date of availability)
2. Education
3. Work experience
4. Extracurricular activities
5. Other relevant facts
6. References

Before you start reading the discussion on how to prepare your resume, however, read the sample resume on the following pages. The applicant, Mr. Lloyd Webb, received many favorable comments from employers on its contents and format. Mr. Webb, a 1970 graduating senior, finally accepted a job for $835 a month—a pretty good beginning wage for a person right out of college.

### Opening Section

The information in the opening section (or upper part of the resume) gives the reader a general picture of the applicant.

---

[1] You can also use your resume for campus interviews. A resume—well-organized, complete, and tailored to your qualifications and to those for the job—will save the interviewer's time. He can quickly scan the highlights, and he can take the resume back to his office to study further and to show to others.

[2] In the application letter you'll limit the use of abbreviations—the same as you do for any other letter. But in the resume you may abbreviate liberally—as long as the reader understands what the abbreviations stand for.

RESUME OF LLOYD R. WEBB

Age . . . . . . . . .21
Height. . . . . . . .5' 10"
Weight. . . . . . . .175
Marital status. . . .Married
Children. . . . . . .None
Health. . . . . . . .Excellent--No defects
Ancestry. . . . . . .German-English                    (picture)
Religion. . . . . . .Protestant
Address . . . . . . .Apartment 32
                     2531 - 29th Avenue South
                     Seattle, Washington 93144
Telephone . . . . . .PA2-6287 (Area code 206)

Job Objective:  A position in your management trainee program with
                an ultimate goal of becoming a member of management
                in production according to my ability and
                aggressiveness.

Military Status:  2S student deferment and occupation deferment
                  from Boeing.

Date of Availability:  June of 1971

## EDUCATION

University of Washington--Seattle, Washington--September 1969 to
    June 1971.
    Two Majors:  Operations Management and Business, Government &
                 Society; will receive BA degree in June of 1971.
    Grade Point Average:  2.84 (out of a possible 4.0)
    Special emphasis on Production Management and Business Law;
    considerable work in Data Processing.

Lower Columbia College--Longview, Washington--September 1967 to
    June 1969.
    Major:  Business Administration:  G.P.A. 2.54 (out of a
                                      possible 4.0)

R. A. Long High School--Longview, Washington--September 1964 to
    June 1967.

## WORK EXPERIENCE

Data Processor--Boeing Company, Seattle, Washington; July 1970 to
    present (part time).
    Duties include bursting, decollating, printing, packaging, and
    transacting of computer output.

Edgerman, Barker and Decksaw Operator--Exeter Lumber Company, 120
    Industrial Way, Longview, Washington 98632; June 1967 through
    August 1969.  (full time)
    Duties included efficent operation of the above-named machines.

<u>Clerk and Wire Rope Worker</u>--Longview Logging & Mill Supply, Long-
view, Washington; September 1966 to June 1967 (part time).
Duties included waiting on customers and constructing logging
equipment.

<u>Other Jobs before 1966</u>--I worked at United Bulb Company as a
shipping clerk and heavy equipment operator. Through my FFA
Chapter, I was able to perform custom plowing, gardening, tree
pruning, and landscaping. I also raised registered Herfords and
picked strawberries, beans, corn and Douglas fir cones.

## EXTRACURRICULAR ACTIVITIES

College: AIESEC (International Exchange Students Organization)
member
Recipient of Boeing Company Scholarship for Senior year
at UW

High School: FFA (Future Farmers of America)--Vice-President and
President
Wrestling--Three-year letterman
Letterjacks (Letterman's Club) 2-year member
Debate Club
Drama Club
Washington State Star Farmer 1966
(four year all expenses paid scholarship to
Washington State University in Agriculture Major)
R. A. Long Faculty Scholarship to Lower Columbia
College for one year.

## OTHER RELEVANT INFORMATION

First two years of college I worked full time.
Last year of college I worked part time.
I will relocate to any city within the United States.
Hobbies and Interests:  furniture building and woodworking, col-
lecting antiques, hunting and fishing.
Future member of the Elks Club.

## REFERENCES

Dr. Richard Rodgers, Chairman
Department of Business, Gov't and
  Business
School of Business Administration
(university)
(city, state zip)

Mr. Earl Lyons, Director
Data Processing
Plant 2
The Boeing Company
(city, state zip)

Professor Robert Meyers
Professor of Operations Management
School of Business Administration
(university)
(city, state zip)

Mr. Ralph Wayland, President
Magnolia State Bank
2231 32nd Street West
(city, state zip)

*Heading.* The heading can range in content from your name alone, to your name and the title of the job you are applying for; to your name, address and telephone number and/or the name and address of the firm receiving the job presentation. For example:

1. Resume of Robert A. Fitchitt for Public Accounting

2. Data Sheet of Deanna D. Bowman
   4504 18th Avenue NE
   Seattle, Washington 98105
   Phone: 543-1072

3. Qualifications of Betty Jo Anderson
   for a Position as Commercial Teacher

4. Resume of Richard D. Slettedahl
   for Management Training Program

5. RESUME

   LAURENCE H. FLINN
   13605 S. E. 171th Place
   Renton, Washington 98055
   Telephone: (206) BA 6-6031

6. Resume of Kathleen J. Lee

   for a fifth or sixth grade teaching position
   in the North Shore School District

*Personal Data.* The personal data of a man or woman graduating at the age of 21 or thereabouts goes immediately below the heading. Only an older (30 or over) applicant, who wishes to emphasize his experience and other qualifications first, will put his personal data elsewhere.

Personal data includes age, marital status (including number of children), health, address(es), telephone, height, weight, religion, and ancestry. Although the law forbids an employer to ask you about religion or ancestry, you can and should include any part of this information that you think will help you get an interview. Some employers don't care whether or not they know this type of information, yet most won't react negatively if you include it.

If your health is unsatisfactory, or if you have a physical handicap or a disfiguring burn or birthmark, you need to weigh carefully what you include in your job presentation. If you feel the interview will probably eliminate you from further consideration because of your defect, perhaps you should not apply or you should state your disadvantage on the resume or in the application letter. But if you think you can sell the employer—once you're in his presence—on your overall qualifications, omit any statement about health or defects that could keep you from getting the interview.

A single person might have two addresses listed on the resume—his permanent (parents') address and his temporary school address. You can include both if they serve a purpose. But a married man or woman should have and list only one address.

When you draft your resume, you can follow Webb's format for personal data. Some possible deviations from his resume are:

1. You can combine marital status and number of children: Marital status: Married—No children

2. If your health is not truthfully "excellent," but you want to omit reference to defects, you can say: Health—Good

3. Even though you are a product of many ancestors, mention no more than two countries: Ancestry: French-German, not Ancestry: French-German-English-Swedish, Russian-Belgian

4. If you include religion, identify only the largest denomination—Catholic, Protestant, Jewish. Avoid such details as Roman Catholic or First Baptist of Southwestern Texas because some people may think you're a religious fanatic. And if you consider yourself an atheist or an agnostic, keep that fact to yourself.

*Picture.* Although the law forbids an employer to *ask* for a picture, you can and probably should include it. Why? Because the reader can actually visualize you, and it will seem as if you're in the same room when your picture is before him. A picture also helps when you give a resume to an interviewer on campus, since he can use the picture to "place" you once he's back in his office.

Keep the following guidelines in mind when you choose a picture:

1. Be sure the picture gives a favorable impression of your appearance. Go to a good photographer, have him take several poses of you, and select the best one from the proofs.

2. The size of the picture can vary from 1¾ to 2 inches in width by 2 to 2¼ inches in length.

3. The best spot for the picture is the upper right-hand corner of the data sheet because the reader logically looks for it there. The next best spot is the upper left-hand corner. Avoid centering the picture because you will have too little space on each side for decent length lines of typing.

4. Attach the picture to the page with glue or picture holders. Avoid using staples or scotch tape because both methods detract from the appearance. You can also have the printer of your resume make your picture part of the sheet itself.

*Military Record.* Data about draft status or commitment with the government is imperative for male applicants. If your military stretch is still forthcoming, say so. If you have already been discharged or are in service, at least include the branch and dates involved (including months).

Include any facts which strengthen your background. For example, if you worked in the disbursing office or were disbursing officer and are applying for a job in finance, mention that. Also list any good promotions (for example, from noncom to commissioned officer or lieutenant to captain).

If you received an early discharge or were not accepted because of health or physical defects, explain honestly, in as positive a manner as possible.

Given below are various military situations. If you don't find one example than fits your case, then adapt by drawing from several.

1. Received Air Force commission on (month, day, year). Air Force pilot from (month, day, year to month, day, year). Received honorable discharge as Captain on (month, day, year).

2. Serving eight years (year to year) in the Coast Guard Reserve with meetings every Thursday night and two weeks summer training each year. Satisfactorily completed five years of service. Six months of basic training: (month, day, year to month, day, year).

3. Obligation fulfilled. Six months USAF Aviation Cadet (month year to month year). Five years USAF Reserve (month year to month year).

4. Served two years active duty with the U.S. Army, completed in (month year). My release from the inactive reserve in (month year) will complete my total obligation.

5. Six years in the Army Reserve (month, year to month, year) Active duty: (month, day, year, to month, day, year).

   Honorable Discharge. Draft Status: 4A

6. Completed from (month, day, year, to month, day, year),* United States Marine Corps Reserve.

   * I was discharged because of my vision, which did not meet Marine Corps standards. There are no restrictions on my driver's license or increased insurance premiums as a result of my eyesight.


*Optional Data.* In addition to the heading, personal data, picture, and military record, it may be advisable to add one of the following: job objective, basic qualifications, and date of availability.

*Job objective* is one entry that every employer is interested in. If you have stated this objective in the application letter and perhaps also in the heading of the resume, you of course don't need to repeat it.

You should, however, include job objective in the resume when the immediate goal is different from the ultimate goal, as in the following illustrations:

1. To work in public accounting with eventual specialization in management advisory services.

2. To work as a member of a feasibility study group with the intent of qualifying for management responsibilities of a real estate investment analysis group.

3. A position in your management training program with the goal of participating in some management phase of your overseas operations.

4. A position in your firm as an expeditor or coordinator with the eventual aim of a position in construction management.

5. A position in your management development program with the goal of applying my training in employee relations.

6. Operations management assignment leading to ultimate goal of corporate management assignment.

*Basic qualifications* is another entry you can and should include in your resume—if you have two or more *outstanding* qualifications. If you're just average graduate Joe Doe with four years of so-so education and a few unrelated part-time jobs, you won't include this optional entry. But if you have, say 50 hours of accounting, a grade-point average of 3.5 (out of a possible 4.0), have completed half your CPA examinations, and have been a part-time accountant with a firm for several years while attending school, you should certainly highlight these basic qualifications. Keep in mind that entries must be *basic* (especially important for the job or to the firm), such as those below:

1. College degree in personnel
   8 years of part-time experience working with people

2. Bachelor of Arts degree from the College of Arts and Sciences with a major in personnel management and with emphasis in psychology, sociology, and business
   4 years of part-time work experience
   Student counselor in Alaska, summer of (year)

3. B.A. degree in business
   6 years' work in electronics

4. Bachelor of Arts in Business Administration—major in transportation
   $4\frac{1}{2}$ years of full-time experience—specialization in inbound cargo movement with steamship agency; and shipping department, order desk, and inside sales with manufacturing firm

5. Bachelor of Arts in Business Administration—major in marketing with specialization in advertising
   $3\frac{1}{2}$ years of full-time work experience—specialization in engineering cost estimating, engineering inspection, vendor contact and approval for source, and industrial radiography
   2 years of part-time work experience—mainly in sales and accounting

*Date of availability* should be included only if it serves a purpose. For example, if you are graduating on June 10 but won't be available to begin work until July 1, you can say so. But if you are available immediately after June 10 and you have stated or implied that in your letter, omit unnecessary repetition in the resume.

## Education

The first major section following the opening should state the most important qualification you can offer for the job (or job area) you're applying for. If it's work experience, that section goes before education. But since education carries more weight than previous work experience for most recent college graduates, the discussion here presents education first.

Under education include the name, location, and time attended for all the post-secondary schools you attended and indicate when and where you graduated from high school.[1] Also mention all date(s) of degree(s). In addition, you should give your major(s), grade-point average, and even pertinent courses completed *if* this material strengthens your presentation.

Given below are illustrations of various ways of arranging pertinent facts about your academic background.

1. Headline your section on education by stressing the degree(s) and date(s) you received each.

<pre>
                        EDUCATION

Degree. . . . . . . . . . . Bachelor of Business Administration
University. . . . . . . . . (name of university)
Date of degree. . . . . . (month, year)
              or if you have more than one degree
Degrees . . . . . . . . . Master of Business Administration
                          (month, year)
                           Bachelor of Arts
                          (month, year)
</pre>

Following this headline about the degree you'll double-space and present complete information about each school, as Webb's resume illustrates. To avoid repetition, omit a second reference to the degree.

2. As a subdivision, give technical training learned off campus—sponsored by a firm or branch of the government, or taken independently.

<pre>
              Technical Training

In addition to the regular academic education shown above, I
have more than 700 hours of management and vocational-technical
training.

Harbridge House-Inc.--Boston, Massachusetts--(month, year to
month, year)  Certificate:  Management Seminar--(year)
IBM Education Center--Seattle, Washington--(month, year to
month, year)  Certificate:  Computer Programming--(year)
</pre>

[1] If you attended several high schools, still use only one entry. Say "various high schools in (state)" and then give overall time attended (year to year).

3. As a subdivision, list special relevant courses you completed. Include this material when your strongest qualification is education and you have an average background otherwise.

## Special Relevant Courses

**In Major**
International Business Principles
Economics of Underdeveloped
 Countries
International Marketing Research
Overseas Operations Management
International Marketing
Multinational Sales Forecasting
 Models

**In Nonmajor**
Written Business
 Communications
Speech Principles
 (Group Discussion)
Principles of Operations
 Management
Scheduling and Inventory
 Control

Instead of putting courses in a special subdivision after listing all the schools attended, you might include the course information with the particular schools involved.

Education:
University of Washington, Seattle, Washington--Sept, '67 to
 June, '71
 Major:   Accounting (42 quarter hours)
 Grades:  Overall--3.01 (out of a possible 4.00)
          Junior-Senior year--3.25
          Accounting--3.00

 Course work includes:
  •concentration in tax accounting (8 of 42 hours)
    Federal Income Tax – individual, partnership & corporate
    Special Tax Problems – estates & trusts, corporate
      reorganization
  •concentration in auditing (8 of 42 hours)
    Auditing Standards and Principles
    Case Studies in Auditing
  •other--basic accounting principles; cost, equity, and
      consolidations; personnel management, human relations;
      finance, marketing, and economics
Shoreline High School, Seattle, Washington--Sept, '64 to
 June, '67
 Grades:  3.56 (out of a possible 4.00)
          top 5% of class

You might list to the right of each course the number of credits earned or (if grades are especially high) the grade for the quarter or semester.

4. Put your best foot forward—and still be honest—if you mention your grade-point average. If your overall average is just so-so because of poor grades during your freshman and/or sophomore years, give the average for your major, for all business courses, or for your junior and senior years combined.

## Work Experience

You need to be thorough and complete in describing your work experience. You should account for all your jobs back to a certain age—perhaps 16 or earlier. If you omit a job, people reading your application will wonder what you were doing during that time.

List your jobs in chronological order with the present or most recent one heading the list. With such an arrangement, the reader can detect your progress or promotions—as well as possible omissions or gaps in your work experience. *Don't* separate related work from unrelated work by listing in different columns.

In this section (that includes all work that earned you money), you'll show at least:

1. Type of work performed
2. Name and location of company
3. Time worked (month year to month year)[1]
4. Whether job was part-time (otherwise employer will interpret statement as full-time employment)

In addition, you should add the following if they strengthen your presentation:

1. Duties—work involving responsibilities, adaptability, similarity to what you're applying for, integrity
2. Name of immediate superior—if he's still there and you think he'll be a good reference
3. Accomplishments—if they're important
4. Your title[2] (supervisor, foreman, etc.)

Arrange the facts for each job in the most "selling" order. For example, Mr. Webb stressed what he did rather than where or when he did it. If you begin with the type of work or title for each entry, be sure you follow the rules of parallelism (that is, making two or more elements in a series similar in grammatical word structure. For example, Mr. Webb's titles—"data processor," "operator," and "worker"—are parallel because each one is a job title. But if he had used "data processing," which is a kind of work, not a title, then "operator" and "worker" wouldn't be parallel terms).

Also notice that Webb's resume has a catchall last entry that indicates

---

[1] You do not need to include reason for leaving each job in the resume or letter if you are graduating at the usual age—21 or thereabouts—and you worked to put yourself through college. You will give in the letter reason for quitting only when the job—usually the present one—seems worthwhile as a springboard for a career with the firm you're working for now.

[2] Be honest. If you were a laborer, say "laborer." Don't try to put on airs by camouflaging or renaming the title. For example, don't say "sanitary engineer" if you were a garbage collector; say "garbage collector."

his industriousness previous to the earliest full job entry. "Other jobs before (year)" is especially acceptable for applicants in their early 20's, but may be regarded as inappropriate for older (30 or more) individuals. If you use such an entry, you don't need to give dates—maybe not even places.

Instead of beginning each job entry with type of work performed, you might prefer to emphasize the employer, as shown below.[1] This arrangement is especially effective when you have been with one organization for several years and have held various titles or jobs.

### WORK EXPERIENCE

Washington State Highway Department.  6431 Corson Ave. South,
                    Seattle, Wash.
  <u>Draftsman</u>:    March 1967 to Dec. 15, 1971
                    Duties included drawing roadway profiles and
                    borrow sites.
  <u>Bookkeeper</u>:  May 1970 to March 1971
                    Duties included keeping time and equipment
                    records for division and preparing vouchers.
  <u>Driller's Helper</u>:  Jan. 1968 to July 1968--Dec. 1968 to
                    May 1970
                    Duties included drilling test holes for proposed
                    highway routes.

Washington State Highway Department, Olympia, Washington
  <u>Engineering Technician</u>:  Nov. 15, 1965 to Sept. 15, 1967
                    Duties included processing traffic data and
                    interviewing on truck surveys.

Simpson Timber Company, Shelton, Washington
  <u>Head Saw Crew</u>:  July 15, 1965 to Nov. 15, 1965
                    Duties included pulling fiberboard off head saw.

Harry Cole's Mobil Service, Shelton, Washington
  <u>Service Station Attendant</u>:  June 15, 1965 to Sept. 1, 1965
                    (part-time)
                    Duties included servicing cars and pumping gas.

Other jobs before 1965--I worked on a farm, coached in a junior
                    baseball program and had a paper route.

## Extracurricular Activities

The section on extracurricular activities is important as a guide to your personality—ability to work with others, leadership, and emotional stability. You will probably want to divide these activities into two or more divisions:

---

[1] Still another way to arrange the jobs is by date. This setup is less desirable but helpful for a quick reference on length of time at each job.

college and high school (as Webb did)
college and (Army) service
college and other

Instead of "extracurricular activities" as a title, you might prefer "activities and affiliations," "affiliations," or another designation. Furthermore, like Mr. Webb, you might include in this section material (such as scholarship awards) that usually goes in a separate section (say, "other relevant facts").

If you participated in activities in several colleges or high schools, you don't need to identify the specific school or dates involved—group only by college or high school. Also identify (in parentheses) any activity that the employer might not know the significance of:

Delta Sigma (national businessmen's fraternity)
Alpha Sigma Phi (social fraternity)
Beta Alpha Psi (accounting honorary)
Purple Shield (underclassmen's activities honorary)
Pilgrim Club (Congregational youth group)
Honored Queen (President in Job's Daughters, an affiliation of the Masonic Lodge)

By all means indicate offices held because that information reveals leadership to the employer.

## Other Relevant Facts

If there are other relevant facts that you should include on your resume, but they don't fit comfortably in one of the sections described above, put them in this separate "catchall" section. Also if you have a single entry for work experience or extracurricular activities—not enough to justify placing elsewhere—include it in this section. But beware of mentioning anything that might cause a negative reaction, for example, hobbies relating to gambling or betting on horses. Also a salesman should have hobbies that reveal his physical fitness and ability to deal with people—not stamp or coin collecting. But for an accountant these last two hobbies are good—they show patience and attention to detail.

Given below are suggested entries that reveal some aspects of the desired qualifications discussed earlier in the chapter.

1. Expenses earned while you attended college
   a. "Completed college working full-time."
   b. "Worked full-time and supported wife and family while attending college part-time from (month, year to month, year) and full-time from (month, year to month, year)."
   c. "Earned 100 percent of my college expenses by working summers since (year)."

2. Hobbies, skills, and activities related to:[1]

   **a.** Physical fitness—hunting, camping, fishing, bowling, boating, skiing, bad-minton, track, tennis, golf, volleyball, basketball, flying, mountain climbing
   **b.** Requested work:
   (1) "Study the stock market."
   (2) "Tutored first-year accounting students during junior and senior years of college."
   (3) "Editor of school paper."
   (4) An especially important report (oral or written) or article relating to your field of interest.
   (5) Ability to write and/or speak foreign language(s).
   **c.** Creativity—designing clothes, photography
   **d.** Mental activity—playing chess, reading
   **e.** Fine arts—music, painting, drama
   **f.** Household tasks—cooking, sewing, knitting
   **g.** Skills—typing speed, shorthand speed, transcription speed, use of office machines

3. Willingness to relocate (for example, "I will relocate in any city within the United States")

4. Willingness to travel (for sales work)

5. Preferred location (for example "Prefer Pacific Northwest—will relocate")

6. Recognition, achievement, awards, and scholarships

   **a.** "High school salutatorian."
   **b.** "Most valuable student—Elks Club Award."
   **c.** "Mistress of ceremonies at Olympic College Spring Awards Assembly."
   **d.** "My name appears in the second annual edition of *Who's Who among Students in American Junior Colleges.*"
   **e.** "Eagle Scout."
   **f.** "4-year scholarship at Whitworth College."
   **g.** Dean's list for high scholarship (dates involved)
   **h.** "Two-year varsity basketball letterman."
   **i.** "Outstanding senior male at (university)."

7. Indication of integrity

   **a.** "Secret classification security clearance—The Boeing Company—(year to year)."
   **b.** "I have taught Sunday School at the First Lutheran Church of (town)."
   **c.** Bonded.

8. Service

   **a.** "Assistant coach—Little League Football—Ballard Team (city, state)."
   **b.** "Member of (year) World Deputation Team from University Presbyterian Church, (city). Sent to Yukon Presbytery of Alaska. Worked with high school, junior high, and primary age children—teaching and counseling."
   **c.** "Volunteer hospital work."

---

[1] Hobbies are sometimes included under Personal Data.

9. Personal data
   a. Father's occupation (if his work is closely related to the job you're applying for).
   b. Your engagement to be married.
   c. Wife's education (if she has college education).
   d. Results of personality test or interest test.
10. Travel (to indicate knowledge of conditions, customs, etc., elsewhere)

## References

The various pros and cons about whether to include references on your resume are discussed below. In general, however, to play it safe, include references; you have nothing to lose and sometimes a lot to gain.

Many employers—perhaps the majority of them—don't want references until the interview. In fact, many employers question the use of references at all—especially the ones the applicant offers. The most worthless kind is the "to whom it may concern" message you carry with you, and next in line are the references *you* choose. You know the references you have given will say only nice things about you; otherwise you wouldn't give their names. The best references are those the employer digs out for himself.

On the other hand, some employers expect to find references in the initial written job presentation and consider the resume incomplete if the names are missing. Some employers like to see—even if they don't check—what references the applicant uses. If they see a name they know and have confidence in, or one in a particular field, they might want to check on the applicant even before the interview. Of course, you definitely want to include references if these individuals strengthen your initial written presentation.

If and when you give references, list about three to five. The most appropriate names include present or former employers and professors. Also acceptable is a character reference whose name or occupation is respected.

Perhaps the best mix—if you give four references—is two employers and two professors or a combination of employers, professors, and a character reference. Give each individual's full name, title, organization (if any), and complete business address. Since you obviously should get permission to use the names you're listing in this section, don't say "with permission."

In summary, the resume should be one or two pages of selling points about yourself in an easy-to-read, well-organized format. You decide the best grouping of ideas (as suggested in this text or another source or simply through clear thinking on your part) and the wording of headings and facts, and say what you need to say in a positive way. Remember that appearance of the resume is an integral part of the presentation. Be neat, avoid crowding of data on the page, and leave as much white space as possible throughout. Make your resume so appealing and selling that the employer wants to see you in an interview.

# LETTER OF APPLICATION

After you have completed your resume—or at least a rough draft of it—you should be well acquainted with your qualifications and with those the firm you're writing to is looking for in an applicant. Now you're ready to tackle the assignment of selling yourself—usually sight unseen—on one sheet of good-quality stationery—preferably 20-pound weight rag content paper. The application letter is just as much a sales letter as any message selling any product or service—and the resume is an enclosure, allowing you to streamline the letter without cluttering it with detail.

When the employer receives your written presentation, he first reads the letter and then the resume. The message must catch his attention, create desire, and ask for action (the interview) just as any other sales letter does. Furthermore, you want the recipient to finish the entire message before he turns his attention to the enclosure. In just a few paragraphs—probably five—you must interest the reader to the point where he wants to know more about you.

## Opening

The beginning of the message should catch the reader's attention in a "businesslike" manner. It should also state definitely that you are applying for a job[1]—not inquiring about one or studying this phase of personnel for a school project. Furthermore you should identify the job (or job area) you're interested in.

Given below are examples of different kinds of first paragraphs for an application letter. As you study them, notice (1) clarity of intent, (2) attention generated, (3) getting to the point within three to five typewritten lines, (4) lack of conceit or gimmicks, (5) conversational words, and (6) sincerity.

*Summary Opening.* One of the most effective openings includes a summary of your two or three outstanding qualifications. Like the first paragraph of an article in a newspaper, the summary gives in capsule form every important point you'll expand in the message. Thus, if the employer reads only the first paragraph, he will know what your basic selling points are. You can combine this summary with just about every other type of opening, as this discussion on openings illustrates.

   1. If hundreds of effective retail calls, thorough knowledge of point-of-sale, and and imaginative merchandising help make a brewery representative, then I've

---

[1] When writing the opening, you might wonder about choices for two words: "job" versus "position," "opening" versus "vacancy." Either "job" or "position" is quite acceptable as long as you have the right attitude toward the meaning of work. But if you give the impression that "position" puts you on a pedestal and it's a transitional period until you become an "executive," then use "job." For the other choice—"opening" versus "vacancy"—use "opening," because it sounds more positive.

begun to learn the business. I would like to put this practical field experience to work for (name) Brewing Company.

2. It is my understanding that a continuity writer for your station must have an interest in and knowledge of classical music. She must have ambition and a desire to achieve. Above all, she must be able to write. I have these qualifications and should like to be considered for the job.

If you use the summary opening, avoid sounding conceited, as in the following two examples:

1. With my vast and diversified working experience in a (city) Safeway store and my 5 years' college training in accounting and economics, I am well qualified to apply for an accounting position with Safeway Stores, Inc.

2. This is an application to your company for a position of salesman. I am sure that my qualifications will back me in saying I can be of value to you.

*Name Opening.* If someone has suggested you apply to a particular firm for a job, you can use his name in the opening—unless he has asked you to keep it confidential. Whether you identify this individual by title depends on how well the reader knows him.

1. Dr. James Hermann, Professor of Accounting and Chairman of the Accounting Department at (university), has informed me that your firm is looking for an accounting major who is interested in managerial accounting. I should like to be considered for the opening in your training program.

2. While I was visiting in Chicago last week, Mr. William Hutton introduced me to your sales manager, Mr. Webster. At that time I expressed my desire for a position with your sales organization. Mr. Webster referred me to you.

*Request Opening.* Most employers appreciate a simple request—but be sure it is "simple," and not a Madison Avenue gimmick approach. The only applicants who might avoid openings like those below are individuals who should show creativity ability—such as applicants for the advertising field.

1. Please consider me for an Operations Management assignment which will lead to my ultimate goal of Corporate Management. As one of the leading domestic airlines, your company offers the management challenge and responsibility I am eager to accept.

2. Will you please consider my qualifications for the position in industrial sales you advertised in this morning's *Times*.

*Question Opening.* A properly phrased question at the beginning is another way to catch the employer's attention.

1. Do you need a reliable office manager with a broad background of business training and experience who can speak Spanish or Portuguese? If you do, I should like to be considered for that position.

2. Can you use a salesman with mechanical aptitude, a university education, four years of selling experience, and a strong desire to succeed? I have completed my military obligation and will graduate from the University of (state) in December.

*Other Openings.* You can, of course, design your own opening—the one most appropriate for you and for the particular person to whom you are writing. As the following examples illustrate, you can stress an interest, previous experience with the same organization, a belief, your present situation, or a "news" item.

1. My interest is people and a way to help them financially. To be able to do this in the future, I wish to apply for your account executive training program.

2. Swimming pool operation and maintenance have been of interest to me for the last few years. At the same time I have been studying business at the University (name). I would like to combine these two interests by working for Pools as a salesman and pool maintenance consultant.

3. If you believe that a fifth or sixth grade child needs a teacher who is willing to work hard to make learning interesting and easy, then please consider me for the job. My qualifications include a sincere desire to teach effectively, experience in working with children and adults, and a broad educational base with an emphasis in business education.

4. Your new ideas on the conversion of wood chips into usable wood pulp lead me to believe that you would be interested in my background. My qualifications include . . . .

## Creation of Desire

Once you have caught the reader's attention, you then proceed to present your basic qualifications for the job you're applying for. In the short space you have (perhaps no more than three paragraphs), you can't afford to repeat *unnecessarily* what is on the resume. You need to select and emphasize key points, measuring carefully every word in every idea you include in the message. Here's the ideal opportunity to expand a one-line entry found on the resume, or to regroup and combine various facts found on the enclosure.

As a rule, you'll devote each of the middle paragraphs of your application letter to selling no more than one of the following qualifications. Naturally you'll choose only those most pertinent to the job requirements.

1. Education
2. Work experience
3. Ability to work with others, interest in people, recognition by your classmates, and/or leadership
4. Interest in your field (sales, etc.)
5. Interest in the company
6. Responsibilities on previous assignments

7. Allocation of time
8. Adaptability, versatility
9. Industriousness

The order in which you present these paragraphs is also important. For example, if you use a summary opening, you'll organize the paragraphs according to the listing in the summary, with the first qualification being the most important. If you don't have a summary opening, you'll still organize by putting the most important qualification first. So that the reader doesn't divert his attention to the resume before finishing the message, don't refer him to the enclosure until the next to last or last paragraph.

Given below are discussions and examples of paragraphs that develop most of the nine qualifications just mentioned.

*Education.* Most recent college graduates consider education their most important qualification. In the paragraph on education you can:

1. Highlight your overall education by showing how thoroughly you prepared yourself during the four years at the university
2. Show that you have both a broad background in business (or arts and science) and also depth in a major or at least a certain area
3. Explain how you supplemented your major with important electives outside your major

*Examples*
1. Because I was interested in the business field from the time I entered the University of (state), I geared my four-year program toward a degree in this area. Majoring in marketing and taking courses specifically oriented to retailing—such as retail profit planning and business control and retail sales promotion—have given me a basic foundation in understanding retailing fundamentals.

2. The program I followed at the University of (state) included 40 credit hours of accounting courses—up-to-date procedures, principles, and theory—that afford a firm basis with which to grow in the auditing profession. Courses in data processing, in addition to my work experience at a computer installation, have led me to be especially interested in the auditing of such systems.

*Work Experience.* Many times the jobs you've held—related or unrelated to the position you're applying for—strengthen your application letter. Through discussing one or more of your previous jobs, you can show:

1. You're a hard worker.
2. You can adapt to people and to various assignments.
3. You like to work with people and help them.
4. You've supplemented your academic training with related work experience.
5. You can handle responsibilities.
6. You are familiar with and aware of the business world.
7. You can adjust to the new job with only a minimum of training.

*Examples*

1. Working in a retailing establishment over vacations for the past two years, I have had the opportunity to apply these concepts. The practical experience of taking charge of several departments during regular employees' vacations has given me a more complete understanding of the importance of good merchandising and of providing customer satisfaction. It also helped me to better realize the necessity for coordination between departments and personnel in making the organization successful. With the large amount of tourist trade, I was constantly dealing with people of varied interests and personalities in a business atmosphere.

2. I have been employed by the Boise Cascade Corporation for the past four summers. Through working in the office as a shipping clerk and assisting in the accounting department, I have gained considerable knowledge of the techniques and terminology unique to the accountant in this industry. This previous work experience with your company will enable me to adjust to your program with only a minimum amount of training.

**Interest in the Field, Company, or Geographic Area.** If you are definitely and sincerely interested in or dedicated to your choice of career or company, you might use an entire paragraph to discuss your interest. However, just *saying* you're interested has little or no significance; you also need to prove your point. And be sincere; the employer can easily detect artificial enthusiasm.

*Examples*

1. My interest in construction developed in high school, working summers and part-time in residential home building. Upon graduation, I decided on a career in construction management, and consequently realized that a college background in business, combined with on-the-job experience, was essential preparation. As my interest and work experience show, I am very enthusiastic about a career in this field. Employment in construction completely financed my college education. Even in my spare time I am building a chalet, as the enclosed data sheet shows.

2. To supplement my marketing major, I sold men's clothing for three years part-time or full-time during school; this sales experience should give me a head start in your training program. Undoubtedly the most important possession a stockbroker must have is sales ability. I can sell, I enjoy selling, and I want to continue to sell. What's more, I proved my sales potential by winning the Arrow Shirt contest which I have mentioned on the enclosed data sheet. Selling stocks appears to be a challenge and I welcome that challenge.

3. Last summer I had the privilege of going to Alaska and working with high school, junior high, and primary age children. My work was in teaching and counselling. I traveled throughout the interior of Alaska and visited the University of Alaska. After meeting the people, seeing their problems and understanding the transition that Alaska is going through, I decided I want to return and work with the students at the University there.

*Interest in People and Ability to Work with Them.* In addition to your other qualifications, employers evaluate your attitude toward people and your ability to work with them. After all, you'll be dealing with people a large share of your working day. And if you genuinely like people, want to serve them, and can work with them—even motivate them—you have a priceless commodity to sell.

*Examples*

1. My past work has given me the experience of handling people in the customer service relationship, as well as the employee relationship. As an assistant manager of a Household Finance Corporation office and as a collection department supervisor for the National Bank of Commerce, I found out fast that the ability to get along with people is essential. The exercise of good judgment based on often incomplete information, in varying situations, and sometimes difficult circumstances gave me the opportunity to develop confidence in my abilities. Opportunities to work constructively with many types of people is something I enjoy very much.

2. I have been able to further develop my interest in communicating and working with people in several capacities. Being the daughter of an Air Force officer, I have lived throughout the United States and in foreign countries and have spent most of my summers traveling. Furthermore, as hospitality chairman of my sorority, I organized all affairs held at the house and acted as hostess for guests. As a result, I have learned to make friends quickly and to feel at ease with many types of people—attributes which will help me be beneficial in a retailing position.

*Other Paragraphs Selling a Qualification.* Your ability to work with people is not the only qualification that can be proved by citing various parts of your background—schooling, jobs, and extracurricular activities. You may also want to give evidence of adaptability, versatility, responsibility, ability to apportion time, recognition by peers, and industriousness.

*Examples*

1. As the enclosed data sheet shows, I found it necessary to work while completing my formal education. In fulfilling the roles of student, husband, father, and provider at the same time I learned to apportion my time—a requirement also confronted by an "audit team" in completing an audit within a time and fee limitation.

2. While attending the University and before being married in the summer of (year), I held many responsible positions in my fraternity including vice-president and treasurer. In recognition of my efforts, my fraternity brothers elected me to Pi Omicron Sigma—a national fraternity service honorary. A record of my fraternity affairs (as well as my work experience) is included on the data sheet enclosed in this letter.

3. While attending the University, I worked part-time or full-time during the school year, and up to 80 hours a week (on two or more jobs) each summer. I was entirely self-supporting throughout my college career, and feel I can offer your company the value and experience that comes from working hard on many jobs and dealing with many kinds of people.

Toward the end of the message—usually in the next to the last paragraph but sometimes in the last paragraph—refer the reader to your resume. The best way to make this reference is by directing the reader's attention to some data on the resume (see example 1 on page 455) and the sample letters at the end of the chapter).

## Last Paragraph

The last paragraph of your message usually asks for action—just as a sales letter does. Without begging or commanding, you ask for an interview and (if appropriate) say you will come to the employer's office when he suggests. Make action easy by giving your telephone number and hours to call if someone can't answer the phone throughout the day or evening.

*Examples*

1. May I have an interview to discuss my qualifications with you in greater detail? I can come to your office whenever you suggest. My telephone number is EK 1-1123.

2. Early in April my husband and I will be moving to (town) where he will take up his new post with the Forestry Service. Will you please notify me of a time after April 6 when I may come in to discuss my qualifications with you?

3. My class schedule allows me to come to your office any afternoon except Tuesdays. May I have an interview to answer any questions about myself that you might have? You can reach me by telephoning RD 7-1234 before 10 a.m. or after 4 p.m.

4. Since I will be in (city) from March 22 to March 27, I will be grateful for the opportunity to see you during that time to discuss further my desire to serve as one of your investigators. After you have reviewed my qualifications and examined the enclosed data sheet, will you please name a convenient time in a letter to me at my Seattle address.

5. After you've had an opportunity to review some of the statements in this letter and on the enclosed data sheet, will you please call me at LA 6-6622 after 3 p.m. or write me about the possibility of beginning a career with (name of company). I'll appreciate the opportunity to discuss my qualifications with you.

Even if you're sending your job application hundreds of miles away, you might still ask for an interview if you think the company has a local representative who can screen you in person. Here you must ask the employer to tell you the local man's name, or ask the company to arrange the interview for you with the local representative.

Although the resume and this letter give you some idea of my qualifications, I am eager to have a personal interview with you. Or perhaps I could discuss my qualifications in greater detail with your regional personnel representative. Please let me know how I can get in touch with him.

If you know that it will be impossible for you to come to an interview at your own expense, offer to send the employer additional information upon request; between the lines you're hoping he will understand that you can come to his office if he pays your way.

If you wish additional information about my background, please let me know. I'll be glad to send it to you promptly.

## EXAMPLES OF THE WRITTEN JOB PRESENTATION

Given below are four actual application letters and accompanying data sheets written by recent college graduates. Three of these job presentations consist of a one-page letter and a two-page resume. The fourth one—by an older man who has a wealth of experience—has a two-page letter and a four-page resume.

1. **To CPA firm for position as staff assistant**
   (from Robert O. Harvey)

```
                                          (street)
                                          (city, state zip)
                                          (date)
```

```
Mr. Thomas Marankovich, Manager
Price Waterhouse and Company
1200 5th Avenue
(city, state, zip)

Dear Mr. Marankovich:

Do you have an opening in your accounting firm for a staff assist-
ant?  My qualifications include a bachelor's degree from the
University of (state) with majors in accounting and finance, more
than five years' work experience with the Washington State Highway
Department, and a genuine interest in the field of public
accounting.

In addition to major requirements in accounting and finance, my
program of studies included courses in business communications and
speech.  I recognize the important role communication plays in
firms providing a public service, and feel that these courses
furnished me with a strong background in the area.  Furthermore, my
grade point average placed me in the top 15 per cent of the
graduating class.

My duties as a bookkeeper for the highway department gave me an
appreciation for the attention to detail so necessary in accounting
work.  Also, while working in the Seattle office, I was called upon
```

periodically to rewrite engineering reports for submission to the district and headquarters offices. I gained experience in meeting people through working on truck survey crews out of the Olympia office. During that time, I enjoyed the chance to travel throughout the state. For further information regarding work experience, please refer to the enclosed data sheet.

In my junior year at the University of (state), I joined Beta Alpha Psi, an honorary accounting fraternity. Through this organization, I became more aware of the scope and functions of public accounting work. I was stimulated by descriptions of the challenge and opportunity available in public accounting. More specifically, I was attracted by the high recommendations given your firm. Also, through Beta Alpha Psi, I began tutoring first-year accounting students as a junior and continued doing so until graduation.

May I have an interview to discuss my qualifications with you further? I will be glad to come to your office. If you wish additional information, please request it, and I will gladly send it by return mail.

---

RESUME OF ROBERT O. HARVEY FOR PUBLIC ACCOUNTING JOB

| | |
|---|---|
| Age | 27 |
| Height | 6' 0" |
| Weight | 195 pounds |
| Marital Status | Married |
| Children | 2 |
| Health | Good—No defects |
| Address | 3025 60th Ave. |
| | Seattle, Wash. 98116 |
| Phone | WE 2-0987 |

(picture)

Military Status: Six years in the Army Reserve (June 1965 to June 1971)
   Active duty: July 15, 1965 to Nov. 30, 1965
   Honorable Discharge        Draft Status: 4A
Date of Availability: July 1, 1971

## Education

University of Washington—Seattle, Washington  Jan. 1969 to June 1970
2 majors: Accounting and Finance; B.A. Degrees received on June 15, 1971
Grade Point Average: 3.02 (out of a possible 4.0)

Centralia Community College—Centralia, Washington  Sept. 1964 to
   Dec. 1964
   Major:  Pre-major; G.P.A.:  3.05 (out of a possible 4.0)
Seattle Pacific College—Seattle, Washington  Sept. 1961 to
   June 1962
   Major:  Pre-major; G.P.A.:  2.60 (out of a possible 4.0)
Irene S. Reed High School—Shelton, Washington  Sept. 1958 to
   June 1961

## Work Experience

Washington State Highway Department  6431 Corson Ave. South,
   Seattle, Wash.
   Draftsman:  March 1968 to Dec. 15, 1968
      Duties included drawing roadway profiles and borrow sites.
   Bookkeeper:  May 1967 to March 1968
      Duties included keeping time and equipment records for division
      and preparing vouchers.
   Driller's Helper:  Jan. 1965 to July 1965—Dec. 1965 to May 1967
      Duties included drilling test holes for proposed highway
      routes.
Washington State Highway Department, Olympia, Washington
   Engineering Technician:  Nov. 15, 1962 to Sept. 15, 1964
      Duties included processing traffic data and interviewing on
      truck surveys.
Simpson Timber Company, Shelton, Washington
   Head Saw Crew:  July 15, 1962 to Nov. 15, 1962
      Duties included pulling fiberboard off head saw.
Harry Cole's Mobil Service, Shelton, Washington
   Service Station Attendant:  June 15, 1962 to Sept. 1, 1962
      Duties included servicing cars and pumping gas.
Other jobs before 1962—I worked on a farm, coached in a junior
   baseball program, and had a paper route.

## Extracurricular Activities

College:  Baseball—one year
          Member—Beta Alpha Psi (accounting honorary)
High School:  Baseball—three years
              Basketball—three years

## Miscellaneous Information

Tutored first year accounting students during junior and senior
   years of college.
Hobby:  Golf

## References

Dr. Gerhard G. Mueller, Chairman
Accounting Department
School of Business Administration
University of (state)
(city, state zip)

Dr. Kenneth B. Berg
Professor of Accounting
School of Business Administration
University of (state)
(city, state zip)

Mr. James R. Lorie, Coach
Irene S. Reed High School
(city, state zip)

Superintendent Albert Upson
Washington State Highway
  Department
6431 Corson Avenue South
(city, state zip)

---

2. **To construction company for project position.**
   (from **Willis Mace Vande Voort**)

                                                (street)
                                                (city, state zip)
                                                (date)

Mr. Chuck Darling
Sletten Construction Company
1426 Spring Mountain Road
(city, state zip)

Dear Mr. Darling:

Dr. Julius M. Ritter, Professor of Architecture here at the
University of (state), has informed me that your firm is looking
for a major in building technology and administration. I should
like to be considered for the opening.

My construction background at college includes a major in Building
Technology and Administration and a series of courses in business
management and finance. My architectural courses ranging from
history to materials to statics and structures have given me an
over-all understanding of the procedures within the construction
industry.

Part-time and summer job experience in construction complemented my
academic studies. As a carpenter, I am familiar with many of the
fundamentals in building. Also, as a recent estimator and job
foreman, I have experience in programming several small jobs
($3,000-$20,000) from start to finish. My working relationships
with architects, clients, and subcontractors have enabled me to
understand the need for cooperation and team work at all levels.

Since my father is a general contractor, I have been exposed to the construction industry all my life. Coupled with this and my willingness to learn, I am enthusiastic about a career in the building industry.

The enclosed data sheet gives you additional information of my background. After you have a chance to verify some of the things I have said about myself, will you please write me frankly about the possibilities of working for your company? Also please let me know if you wish additional information about my background. I'll be glad to send it to you promptly.

---

Data Sheet of Willis Mace Vande Voort

```
Age. . . . . . . 23                           ┌─────────────┐
Height . . . . . 6' 1"                        │             │
Weight . . . . . 225                          │  (picture)  │
Marital Status . Married                      │             │
Children . . . . One                          │             │
Health . . . . . Good--no defects             │             │
Religion . . . . Methodist                    │             │
Address. . . . . 2633 14th Street W.          │             │
                 Seattle, Washington 98119    │             │
Phone. . . . . . AT 3-8124                     └─────────────┘
```

Military Status: 3-A deferment from the draft.
Date of Availability: Immediately

EDUCATION

University of Washington--Seattle, Washington--Sept. 1966 to
  June 1971.
  Degree: Bachelor of Science
  Date of degree: June 1, 1971
  Major: Building Technology & Administration
  Grade Point Average: 2.81 (out of a possible 4.0)
Western High School--Las Vegas, Nevada--Sept. 1963 to June 1966.

Areas of Study

Design
Physics: Mechanics, electricity, heat and light.
Architecture: Materials, history, forces, stresses, and statics;
  design of timber, concrete, and steel; design of plumbing,
  heating, electricity, and air conditioning systems.

Construction
Building Technology & Administration:  Equipment uses, estimating,
  financing and organization of the building industry.
Development
Building Financing:  Financing of building construction, government
  regulations, and general financing principles.
Business Finance:  Study of sources, uses, cost, and control in
  business enterprises.
Real Estate:  Economic principles underlying utilization of land;
  real property rights and land tenure.
Urban Planning:  History, principles, and theories of city growth
  and planning.
Supporting Industries
Operation Management:  Fundamentals of planning and control of
  materials and operations.
Business Economics:  Basic understanding of various theories.
Written Business Communications:  Report and letter writing.
Labor Economics:  Trade unions and collective bargaining.

### WORK EXPERIENCE

Estimator--West Coast Drywall, Bellevue, Washington; Nov. 28, 1969
  to June 1, 1970; Sept. 10, 1970 to June 2, 1971 (24 hours per
  week part-time).
  Duties included making quantity and cost estimates, and
  negotiating bids with owners and general contractors.
Estimator and Project Coordinator--George F. Kalb Construction
  Company, Las Vegas, Nevada; summers of 1968, 1969, and 1970.
  Duties included making basic quantity estimates, coordinating
  subcontractors for bidding purposes, and some layout work with a
  transit.
Carpenter Helper & General Laborer--George F. Kalb Construction
  Company; weekends and vacations of 1965 to 1968, summers of
  1965 and 1967.
  Duties included working in the field as a carpenter helper--
  forming, framing and laying out buildings; also jack hammer work.
Laborer--Limbki Construction Company, Las Vegas, Nevada; summer
  of 1966.
Other jobs before 1965--parking lot attendant and general laborer
  work.

### EXTRACURRICULAR ACTIVITIES

College:       Football--two years
               Sigma Nu (social fraternity)--four years
               Building Technology & Administration Club--two years
High School:   Football--four years
               Track--one year
               Letterman's Club--three years
               Physics Club--one year

MISCELLANEOUS INFORMATION

I received an athletic scholarship for football during college.
Last two years of college I worked part-time.
Hobbies:  Hunting, water skiing, boating

REFERENCES

(will be sent upon request)

---

3. **To school district for grade school teaching position**
   (from Kathleen J. Jacobs)

                                              (street)
                                              (city, state zip)
                                              (date)

North Shore School District
18 Washington Road
(city, state zip)

Attention:  Personnel Department

Gentlemen:

     If you believe that a fifth or sixth grade child needs a
teacher who is willing to work hard to make learning interesting
and easy, then please consider me for the job.  My qualifications
include a sincere desire to teach effectively, experience in
working with children and adults, and a broad educational base with
an emphasis in business education.

     My main goal in teaching is to present each lesson in a manner
which appeals to the children.  In student teaching, I am learning
how to listen understandingly, to find and identify each child's
weak points, and to inspire him to reach new goals.  Although this
isn't always easy, I enjoy the challenge and work hard to meet it.

     Through my various job and teaching experiences, I've learned
how to get along with people and to help them.  As a sales girl,
I've had to explain to customers why an order hasn't come in, why
we cannot accept credit, and even why something does or doesn't
look good on them.  In doing so, I've learned to deal with embarrassing situations--using tact, cooperation, and friendliness.
I feel these rules apply in teaching also.  My desire is to never
discourage a student by humiliating him.  Instead, I want to help
him learn by offering my encouragement.

     Since a person can only teach effectively when he knows his
subject matter well, I have purposely tried to acquire as broad and
as thorough a background as possible.  As my enclosed data sheet
testifies, this background has mostly been in the areas of busi-

ness, math, science, language, and social studies.  During my last
year before graduation, I plan to broaden my knowledge of the
humanities in addition to fulfilling my required courses.

May I have an interview to answer any questions about myself
that you might have?  I'll be glad to see you at your most convenient time.  By telephoning 543-4470 anytime after 3 p.m., you'll
find me at home.

---

Qualifications of Kathleen J. Jacobs

Regarding a fifth or sixth grade teaching
position in the North Shore School District

(picture)

Age:              21
Height:           5' 6½"
Weight:           128
Marital status:   Married
Children:         None
Health:           Good--No defects
Ancestry:         Norwegian-Swedish
Religion:         Protestant
Address:          8051 Earl Ave. N.W.
                  Seattle, Wash. 98107
Telephone:        Su 4-3658

Date of Availability:  September 1, 1971

## EDUCATION

Degree . . . . . . . . . . . . . . . . . . . . . . Bachelor of Arts
Date of degree . . . . . . . . . . . . . . . . . . June 1971
Teaching Certificate . . . . . . . . . . . . . . . June 1971
University of Washington--Seattle, Washington--Sept. 1969 to
   June 1971.
   Major:  Business Education   Minor:  Elementary Education
   Grade Point Average:  3.19 (out of a possible 4.0)
Olympic College--Bremerton, Washington--Sept. 1967 to June 1969.
   Major Emphasis:  French;  G.P.A.:  3.34 (out of a possible 4.0)
   Associate of Arts Degree Received. . . . . . . . June 1968
North Kitsap High School--Poulsbo, Washington--Sept. 1964 to
   June 1967.
   Emphasis:  College Preparatory in mathematics and science.
   G.P.A.:  3.59 (out of a possible 4.0)

### Courses Taken in Education

| Education Classes | Supporting Studies |
|---|---|
| Mathematics in the Elementary School | Theory of arithmetic; algebra; geometry; trigonometry; math analysis; calculus; linear algebra. |
| Science in the Elementary School | Oceanography; genetics; chemistry; physics; biology. |
| Social Studies in the Elementary School | Geography; economics; political science; history of civilization. |
| Health in the Elementary School | First aid; personal hygiene. |
| Language Arts in the Elementary School | English composition, grammar; French; Spanish; Latin. |

### Business Education Courses Taken

| | | | |
|---|---|---|---|
| Economics . . . . | 10 hours | Business studies . . . . . | 10 hours |
| Accounting. . . . | 6 hours | Secretarial studies. . . . | 4 hours |
| Marketing . . . . | 4 hours | Human relations. . . . . . | 3 hours |

Written business communications. . . . 4 hours

### WORK EXPERIENCE

Office girl--First National Bank, Poulsbo, Wash.; June 1969 to
Sept. 1969 (full time)  Duties included packaging coin, filing,
and mailing.

Sales girl--Snelson's Department Store, Poulsbo, Wash.; June 1967
to June 1969 (part time)  Duties included selling clothing,
shoes, yardage, and piece goods.

Grader--Olympic College, Bremerton, Wash.; Sept. 1968 to June 1969
(part time)  Duties included grading math papers for two
teachers, occasionally tutoring students, and sometimes acting as
a substitute teacher for a beginning algebra class.

Other jobs before 1967--waitress in a drive-in restaurant and
babysitter.

### EXTRACURRICULAR ACTIVITIES

| College: | Vice-President, Acting President--Phi Theta Kappa (Junior College National Honor Society) |
|---|---|
| | Women's Varsity Tennis Team--one year |
| | Member of La Maison Francaise (French House) one year |
| | Member of Washington Association of Retarded Children |
| High School: | French teaching assistant--one year |

| | |
|---|---|
| French Club | Torch Honor Society |
| Drama Club | American Field Service Club |
| Drill Team--one year | Girls' Athletic Association |
| Girls' Club | Girls' Tennis Team |
| Debate team--one year | Secretary-Treasurer--Debate Club--one year |

MISCELLANEOUS INFORMATION

I have taught Sunday School at the First Lutheran Church of Poulsbo.
I have earned over 50% of all college and living costs.
My name appears in the second annual edition of Who's Who Among Students in American Junior Colleges.
Awards and Services--High School Salutatorian, Most Valuable Student Elks Club Award, Alternate Miss Poulsbo, Co-Mistress of Ceremonies at Olympic College Spring Awards Assembly.
Hobbies--snow skiing, water skiing, tennis, and sewing.

REFERENCES

Dr. Arthur Allee
Professor of Business Education
College of Education
University of (state)
(city, state zip)

Professor Frederick L. Denman
Department of Marketing, Transportation
  and International Business
School of Business Administration
University of (state)
(city, state zip)

Mr. Walter Krupp, President
First National Bank
Poulsbo, Washington 99112

Miss Nadine Wagner, Buyer
Snelson's Department Store
Poulsbo, Washington 99112

---

4. **To airline for a position in operations management**
   **(from Laurence H. Robertson)**

(street)
(city, state zip)
(date)

Mr. F. K. McRostie
Personnel Administrator
United Air Lines
(name of airport)
(city, state zip)

Dear Mr. McRostie:

Please consider me for an Operations Management assignment which will lead to my ultimate goal of Corporate Management. As one of the leading domestic airlines, your company offers the management challenge and responsibility I am eager to accept.

My qualifications include:

1. Eight years of Operations Management experience, preceded by four years' experience performing operations assignments.

2. Bachelor of Arts degree in Business Administration from the University of (state), with a major in Operations Management.
3. Interest in a management career in the progressive and growing air transportation industry.

Previous job assignments and a carefully selected education program have been pursued with this management goal in mind.

Management experience gained in administering and supervising operational assignments and personnel, as well as in chairing numerous committees, has emphasized to me the important principle that a manager is only as good as the personnel working for him. Much of my practical experience in private industry has been "on the line," managing the daily work, and has provided me a firm foundation for understanding the need for obtaining results with cost and schedule constraints under pressures of "produce or perish." The experience gained in my current government position has provided an opportunity to work with senior and corporate executives in business, industrial, labor, education, and government organizations; also my present work has provided exposure, experience, and working relationships on a local, state, and national basis, and a chance to work on the important transition from that of middle management to top management.

The knowledge gained through a related education has emphasized the need for continual education and continuous self-improvement to effectively accomplish management assignments and contribute to the overall corporate objectives so important to your firm. The exposure and broad base provided through a business administration program increases one's scope to see the "big picture" and provides an approach or baseline and methods from which to proceed logically. Organization and Administrative Theory was a major concentration of study in my chosen major area, to prepare for increasing organizational and administrative responsibilities.

Enclosed is my resume which provides additional information. Pages 1 and 2 summarize my work experience and pages 3 and 4 further detail specific jobs performed. After you have reviewed this information, will you please call me at BA 6-6031 anytime between 9 and 5 and state a time when I may discuss my qualifications in an interview with you. If you wish further information, I will be glad to send it to you promptly.

RESUME OF

LAURENCE H. ROBERTSON
13605 S. E. 171st Place
Renton, Washington 98055
Telephone:  (206) BA 6-6031

(picture)

PERSONAL
30 years old
5' 10" tall
160 lbs.
Married -- 3 children
Excellent health -- no defects
U. S. Citizen
French-Irish ancestry
Protestant

JOB OBJECTIVE
Operations Management assignment leading to ultimate goal of
Corporate Management assignment.

WORK EXPERIENCE   (see pages 3 and 4 for job descriptions)
STATE OF WASHINGTON--Department of Education--Olympia, Washington
State Supervisor, Trade, Industrial and Technical Education
December 1969 to present
THE BOEING COMPANY--Commercial Airplane Division--Renton,
Washington
General Supervisor, Production Engineering--June 1969 to
Dec. 1969
Senior Supervisor, Industrial Training--April 1968 to
June 1969
Supervisor, Industrial Training--June 1967 to April 1968
Supervisor, Materiel Operations--Feb. 1966 to June 1967
THE BOEING COMPANY--Aero-Space Division--Seattle, Washington
Supervisor, Production Control--Dec. 1963 to Feb. 1966
Methods Analyst, Industrial Engineering--Jan. 1963 to Dec. 1963
Lead Expeditor, Production Control--Nov. 1960 to Jan. 1963
Expeditor, Production Control--June 1959 to Nov. 1960

EDUCATION
University of Washington-Seattle, Washington-Sept. 1969 to
Aug. 1971
Degree:  B.A.-Business Administration-Aug. 1971
Major:  Operations Management; Minor:  Personnel
Grade Point Average:  3.17 overall; 3.42 in major.
(4.0 scale)

Highline College–Seattle, Washington–Sept. 1963 to June 1968
  Degree:  A.A.–Business Administration–June 1968
West Valley High School–Spokane, Washington–Sept. 1955 to
  May 1959
  Diploma:  College Preparatory Program–May 1959

<u>Technical Training</u>

Over 700 additional hours of management and vocational–technical
training.
Harbridge House, Inc.–Boston, Massachusetts–June 1967 to Aug.
  1967
  Certificate:  Management Seminar–1967
IBM Education Center–Seattle, Washington–April 1963 to May 1963
  Certificate:  Computer Programming–1963

AFFILIATIONS

American Management Association––Member
American Production and Inventory Control Society––Member
American Society of Training and Development––Member
American Vocational Association––Member
Boeing Management Association (Past member)
Vocational Industrial Clubs of America––State Director, and
  Professional member

DRAFT STATUS    III–A

MISCELLANEOUS

Chairman of 5 state and 2 national education committees–May 1970
  to present
Organized and moderated seminars and performed public relations
  assignments
Guest lecturer–University of Washington–July to Aug. 1970 and
  1971
Awards:  Management Cost Improvement–The Boeing Company–Nov. 1965
         Outstanding Service–Vocational Industrial Clubs of
         America–June 1971
Worked full–time and supported wife and family while attending
  college part–time from Sept. 1963 to June 1968 and full–time
  from Sept. 1969 to Aug. 1971
Personally financed total college education program
Secret classification security clearance–The Boeing Company–1961
  to 1969
Prefer Pacific Northwest–will relocate
Hobbies and interests–flying, camping, boating, bowling, photog-
  raphy and church

REFERENCES    Will be sent upon request

JOBS PERFORMED

State Supervisor,
Trade, Industrial and
Technical Education
(December 1969 to
present)

STATE OF WASHINGTON — Department of Education (1969–present)

Administered and supervised state and federal funded education programs. Performed administrative functions and developed management controls for State Director to plan, schedule and control educational programs in over 170 public institutions involving over 70,000 students. Worked with executive management from state and private industry representing Education, Labor and Industrial organizations. Organized and directed Washington State Association of a National Youth Organization.

THE BOEING COMPANY — Commercial Airplane Division (1966–1969)

General Supervisor,
Production Engineering
(June 1969 to
December 1969)

Directed Divisional Systems Development Committee designing production and inventory control systems affecting five branches of the Division. Developed management controls and performed special projects, studies and administrative functions for Production Engineering Manager, with staffing of over 4500 employees. Worked with senior and corporate executive management.

Senior Supervisor,
Industrial Training
(April 1968 to
June 1969)

Directed management and technical staff of six supervisors and four analysts, and the company support activities for statewide vocational education program, involving 41 public institutions and 3000 students. Worked with senior and corporate executive management, Washington State Education officials, college officials, and school administrators. Annual program budget in six figure bracket. Performed local, state and national recruiting of general and professional–technical personnel.

Supervisor,
Industrial Training
(June 1967 to
April 1968)

Supervised curriculum development and instruction of courses for Manufacturing Department training requirements. Coordinated special Company industry education program with the U.S. Air Force. Instructed courses and developed training programs with department managers.

Supervisor,
Materiel Operations
(February 1966 to
June 1967)

Supervised 42 employees and high-rate production operation, manufacturing aircraft
parts to production standards and precision tolerances for research and development, production and spares programs,
working on both military and commercial
contracts.  Developed production controls,
flows, methods and "work-arounds."

THE BOEING COMPANY - Aero-Space Division
(1959-1966)
Performed administrative functions and
developed management controls for Production Control Manager with staffing of over
700 employees.  Performed data processing
system evaluations and special studies and
projects to resolve operational problems.

Supervisor,
Production Control
(September 1964 to
February 1966)

Supervisor,
Production Control
(December 1963 to
September 1964)

Supervised 35 employees and production
support expediting and shipping operations
for research and development, production
and spares programs, working on both
military and commercial contracts.

Methods Analyst,
Industrial Engineering
(January 1963 to
December 1963)

Performed computer programming and related
systems evaluations.  Developed production
and inventory control programs to control
over 10,000 different part numbers.  Developed division systems and operating
procedures and coordinated their implementation with department managers.

Lead Expeditor,
Production Control
(November 1960 to
January 1963)

Worked directly with Company quality control and the U.S. Air Force in effecting
final customer acceptance and delivery of
end products.  Directed work of 15 production expeditors to facilitate manufacturing and supply of all parts to support
production requirements and schedules for
assigned airplane and missile sections and
support equipment.

Expeditor,
Production Control
(June 1959 to
November 1960)

Expedited the supply of parts for assigned
airplane sections based on production requirements and schedules.  Controlled
critical production "line stoppage items"
such as:  Landing gears, wing installation
components, and associated equipment.

## EXERCISES

1. Assume that you must write an application letter with resume. You are applying for a job of your choice at the time you'll actually be mailing your written job presentation.

   In preparation for this assignment, find out what the personnel man (or other interviewer) will be looking for in you when you apply for a particular job (or job area) at a particular type of company, agency, or organization (department store, insurance company, brokerage firm, pharmaceutical house, school, etc.)

   Use the library and placement offices for information about an organization of your choice. If sufficient existing publications are not available locally, you might write to an organization of your choice (but not the firm to which you plan to send your application letter and resume), asking for answers to your questions or arranging for an interview with the appropriate officer.

   The purpose of this assignment is to find out what qualifications the prospective employer looks for when he screens you for your career job. Although you're not getting answers from him, you will from sources that should reveal comparable information on the qualifications he considers most important.

   Prepare a list of 10 (or more) questions you must know the answers to before you can write your application. All your questions must relate to a particular job or job area.

   Listed below are several questions that you should consider. At least, they're possible springboards for the questions you must find answers to.

   a. What are the basic qualifications that you look for when you screen a recent college graduate for a job in (your career area)?
   b. For this type of work what major do you think is best?
   c. Outside the major what courses (business or nonbusiness) do you think will be helpful on the job?
   d. What kind of previous experience do you look for in the applicant?
   e. How do you evaluate personality from a written job presentation?
   f. How important are grades?
   g. To get into this type of work, what initial job should I apply for?
   h. Do you prefer references in the initial written job presentation?

2. Below are six application letters. Explain orally in class which ones will most likely result in an interview. Which are totally unacceptable? Why?

*Letter A: Application to a large department store for a position in management trainee program.*

```
Gentlemen:

Please consider me for a position in your management trainee
program.  My qualifications include four years of college
training with a major in marketing, experience in the retailing
field, and a sincere interest in working with people.

Because I was interested in the business field from the time I
entered the University of (state), I geared my four-year pro-
gram toward a degree in this area.  Majoring in marketing and
taking courses specifically oriented to retailing, such as
```

Retail Profit Planning and Business Control and Retail Sales
Promotion, have given me a basic foundation in understanding
retailing fundamentals.

Working in a retailing establishment over vacations for the
past two years, I have had the opportunity to apply these concepts. The practical experience of taking charge of several
departments during regular employees' vacations has given me a
more complete understanding of the importance of good merchandising and of providing customer satisfaction. It also helped
me to better realize the necessity for co-ordination between
departments and personnel in making the organization successful. With the large amount of tourist trade, I was constantly
dealing with people of varied interests and personalities in a
business atmosphere.

I have been able to further develop my interest in communicating and working with people in several capacities. Being
the daughter of an Air Force officer, I have lived throughout
the United States and in foreign countries and have spent most
of my summers traveling. Furthermore, as hospitality chairman
of my sorority, I organized all affairs held at the house and
acted as hostess for guests. As a result, I have learned to
make friends quickly and to feel at ease with many types of
people--attributes which will help me be beneficial in a
retailing position.

My excellent health is reflected in my enjoyment and year-round
participation in the outdoor activities you will find listed on
my data sheet.

May I have an interview to discuss my qualifications with you
in greater detail? Please telephone me at 543-2024 and suggest
a time which will be convenient.

**Letter B:** *Application to CPA firm for a position as staff assistant.*

Gentlemen:

Please consider me for the position of staff assistant,
for which my degree in accounting, plus a varied practical
experience, provides a background.

The program I followed at the University of (state)
included 40 credit-hours of accounting courses -- up-to-date
procedures, principles, and theory -- that afford a firm basis
with which to grow in the auditing profession. Courses in data
processing, in addition to my work experience at a computer
installation, have led me to be especially interested in the
auditing of such systems.

My practical training includes an internship with Arthur Young and Company, which gave me an appreciation of an auditor's responsibilities to his clients and the public. Several of my prior jobs have contributed to my awareness of other business problems -- for example, the delicacy of customer (client) relations in a "service" profession. Having dealt with dissatisfied customers as well as delinquent debtors, I feel that I can display the tact implicit in an auditor's duties.

As the enclosed data sheet shows, I found it necessary to work while completing my formal education. In fulfilling the roles of student, husband, father, and provider at the same time, I learned to apportion my time -- a requirement also confronted by an "audit team" in completing an audit within a time and fee limitation.

May I discuss further with you my qualifications for the position of staff assistant in your firm? Please call me at LAkeview 2-5583 or write to arrange a time when I may come in.

**Letter C:** *Application to grocery chain for accounting position.*

Dear Mr. Lee:

With my vast and diversified working experience in a Wenatchee Safeway store and my 5 years' college training in accounting and economics, I am well qualified to apply for an accounting position with Safeway Stores, Inc.

Having successfully completed studies in managerial and financial accounting while earning my degree at the University of (state), you will find that I can handle any accounting situation with ease and confidence.

While working in the many departments in Safeway in order to finance my college education, I became thoroughly familiar with every phase of operation of one of your stores. Because of my pleasing personality, my ability to get along well with others, and my excellent work record, I was chosen to supervise the night stock crew during the summers of (year) and (year).

My work experience with Safeway has been both valuable and enjoyable for me; therefore, I wish to continue working for your firm in my chosen field.

After you've had a chance to verify some of the things I've said about myself in this letter and on the enclosed data sheet, will you write me about the possibilities of working in one of your West Coast offices?

**Letter D:** *Application to a firm for sales position.*

Gentlemen

Please consider my application for a position in your sales department. My qualifications are a Bachelor of Arts in General Business, a thorough and working knowledge of accounting and finance, and a sincere interest in selling.

I am seeking a position in your company in selling because I feel that I have the necessary qualifications to do a good job for the company, while learning the basic components of your needs. I selected your firm because it is the most rapidly expanding company in this industry and a leader in research and development, which I recognize as essential to maintain your present status. I feel that I can contribute toward these goals. I have studied the basic background of the transportation industry, and am deeply interested in furthering my knowledge, to the benefit of the company. I have enclosed a resume of my personal background, complete with a transcript of my grades.

After you've had time to review my application and data sheet, will you please call me or write. My address and telephone numbers are on the enclosed data sheet. Thank you for your consideration.

**Letter E:** *Application to brewery to be sales representative.*

Gentlemen

If hundreds of effective retail calls, thorough knowledge of point-of-sale and imaginative merchandising help make a brewery representative, then I've begun to learn the business. I would like to put this practical field experience to work for Sick's Rainier Brewing Company.

Field work as an Assistant District Sales Manager for the Joseph Schlitz Brewing Company gave me an opportunity to plan and execute sales promotions that sold beer. I have proven ability to open non-buying accounts, secure floor displays, sell additional packages and achieve point-of-sale dominance.

In addition, I have conducted route analyses, set up key account systems and conducted sales training meetings for wholesaler personnel.

Frequent contact with retailers and consumers enabled me to handle consumer complaints and utilize a good layman's knowledge of the brewing process.

After you've had an opportunity to review some of the things I've said in this letter and on the enclosed data sheet, will you write me frankly about the possibility of beginning a career with Sick's Rainier Brewing Company?

I would appreciate an opportunity to discuss my qualifications.

*Letter F: Application to a newspaper for position as assistant music and drama editor.*

Dear Sir:

In reference to your advertisement in <u>Editor</u> <u>&</u> <u>Publisher</u> (3/14) for an assistant music and drama editor, the offer is worth an inquiry because of my deep interest in theater. But, very frankly, I'm afraid it would have to be an exceptional salary offer to lure me so far from the East Coast and what I'm convinced are its greater professional opportunities.

However, you will find samples of my reviews and a brief resume attached. Should you desire to continue this correspondence further, I will send you references and other material customary to a job application.

My experience in motion picture-theater reviewing with the <u>Sun</u> has been limited to "filling-in" for the regular critic during his vacations or illnesses. Prior to that, I wrote a theater column in a weekly newspaper in Bath, Pa., a sideline to my daily reporting. I have engaged in all phases of amateur theater as an outside interest.

I am not well versed in music—although I appreciate music and am confident in my critical capacities. Again, I have filled-in at times for the <u>Sun's</u> music critic and, if need be, can also submit samples.

I have handled general assignments and beats during my four years with the <u>Sun</u> and previously.

Your advertisement mentions "opportunity for advancement," without further elaboration. Your offer of the position of assistant music-drama editor would be considerably more attractive if coupled with a commitment to go to your Washington, D.C., bureau in two, or three, years or to whatever overseas bureaus the <u>Daily</u> <u>Blat</u> may sponsor, subject only to your complete dissatisfaction with the work produced for you.

The alternatives for a <u>Sun</u> man are either to go to Anyplace or elsewhere under such an agreement, or other favorable terms, or to expect in time to go to the <u>New</u> <u>York</u> <u>News</u> or <u>Daily</u> <u>Bugle</u>.

My own conditions preclude any transfer without a solid assurance from an employer of opportunities to build up a broad base of newspaper experience.

The tendency, of course, of most newspapers is to fill the opening with the run-of-the-mill newsman who is panting at the door and willing to accept chicken-feed. Consequently, I have little reason to expect a favorable reaction to this letter. If I am mistaken, I hope you will advise me of the maximum salary you can pay for this position, the set-up at the <u>Blat</u> and any arrangements that you would consider feasible. I hope we can discuss this matter further, but only with your understanding that I expect to drive a hard bargain.

My home address appears below and on the resume. Please address your reply accordingly.

3. Prepare a letter of application with an accompanying resume for the career job you plan to get into after completion of your college education. Address it to the firm of your choice and to the individual who should receive it. [Instead of sending your presentation to a particular person, you might want to direct it to a particular department within the firm or to the title the receiver possesses (such as personnel manager).]

To make this material as useful to you as possible, date the letter the month and year you actually plan to send it. For example, if you're graduating this year, the date of the letter should precede that of graduation by enough time (4 to 9 months) to have the job sewed up when you're ready to go to work. But if you're a sophomore, and have at least two more years of schooling and then two years of service in the Army, use the date you'll actually be sending the letter.

Use only facts, so far as possible, in both your letter and data sheet. If you are dating the letter in the future, assume the activities (especially schooling, work experience, government service) that will most likely take place between now and then. This timing permits you to update the written job presentation when you're ready to revise, type, and actually send it.

Try to make your message and data sheet so convincing and selling that they will stand out from any others that may be received the same day. Both should be neatly and accurately typed—100 percent correct in spelling and accurate in facts and figures.

# Chapter 11

# Other Job Application Messages

- Follow-up Messages from Applicant to Employer
- Follow-up Messages Written by Employer to Applicant
- Situation
- Exercises

The time you'll spend in getting your first career job depends on economic conditions, need for graduates in your area, and your own qualifications and standards. If you're sending your job presentation when it's a seller's market and you have unusually good qualifications, you might land the job you want right away. But if the conditions are reversed, you can spend many weeks—even months—finding the right niche for yourself.

To be on the safe side, begin your job hunting at least four to nine months before graduation, and send your written job presentation with resume to more than one firm. But don't send out too many—say 50 or 100—at one time. Limit the number to 10 or fewer and then wait for replies before you mail more.

This chapter discusses the types of messages (other than those already covered in Chapter 10) that you will write or receive as an applicant or an employer. The first section covers follow-up messages from applicant to employer. The second section covers follow-up messages from employer to applicant.

## FOLLOW-UP MESSAGES FROM APPLICANT TO EMPLOYER

You strengthen your chances for the job you have applied for when you follow up your application letter and resume. Of the three ways to follow up—in person, by letter, or by phone—the written message is one of the most effective because the employer can analyze the applicant's qualifications at his convenience. He can also more easily handle a large number of applicants at one time—either on the job or at home in the evening.

A written follow-up is effective for several good reasons:

1. Only a few applicants use a follow-up—probably fewer than 10 percent. Thus, the employer is favorably impressed when he receives one.

2. A follow-up shows the applicant is genuinely interested in the job or the company.

3. This message displays determination. Some firms won't reply to an applicant for a sales job until he sends a follow-up. Other firms intentionally mail the sales applicant a negative reply. The employer reasons that the applicant who follows up when applying for a sales job will follow up on his prospects—even those who say no—when he's on the job in his own territory.

4. A follow-up indicates courtesy (if it follows an interview), serves as a reminder to the employer, permits better understanding of the applicant (through submission of additional information), and shows sincerity.

This section covers first the two all-important and most frequently used types of initial follow-up messages and then presents other types involved in getting a job.

## The Initial Follow-up

The first follow-up you'll use is either (1) a follow-up to the interview or (2) an inquiry about the application letter and resume when the employer doesn't reply.

*Follow-up to the Interview.* After you have had your interview, you should send the interviewer (or the appropriate company official) a written thank-you. Remember, he spent some of his valuable time to talk with you, and for reasons of courtesy alone, you need to thank him for his time, attention, and consideration. Only when he tells you during the interview not to write will you refrain from sending this message. One survey[1] revealed that 87 percent of employers react favorably to the follow-up to the interview.

In most instances this message is short—definitely less than one page—and its organizational pattern is that of a good news or neutral letter:

1. In the opening paragraph, state the main idea—express thanks for the interview or say you're returning a completed form. (If you don't thank in the opening, do so in the last paragraph. Also identify the job and perhaps mention the time and place of the interview.

2. In the middle paragraph(s) you discuss one or more of the following ideas:

   a. Mention how you *now* feel about the firm or a job with the firm—now that you have visited the plant, listened to the interviewer talk, and toured the facility. Of course, you write only favorable responses.

   b. Add new material that might be helpful in determining your qualifications. For example, assume you've been considering continuing your education in the evenings after graduation. Then in the interview the employer says he favors his junior men improving themselves by attending college at night. You go home, think over this idea, and decide to begin night classes. That's new material you can mention in the message. Other new material is reporting that you completed an assignment the interviewer gave you at the time of the interview (such as to read a brochure, see someone, or take a test).

   c. If you think the interviewer questioned one of your qualifications or you think you might have made a negative impression concerning one statement during the interview, include honest positive facts to rebuild confidence. For example, if the interviewer seemed to be looking for an older person, convince him that you are mature because you've dealt successfully with all types of people on your various jobs; or you have assumed responsibilities; or you have had to allocate your time as student, husband, and breadwinner. Or if you think you "muffed" it on one or more areas, try to reestablish your credentials.

---

[1] Charles E. Peck, "The Follow-up Letter in the Job Presentation," *American Business Writing Association Bulletin*, Urbana, Illinois, March 1963, p. 24. This survey queried 300 of the largest department stores in the 150 largest cities within the United States. The results are based on 99 usable replies (33 percent return).

    **d.** Other ideas which can occasionally strengthen your presentation are: (1) your favorable reaction to points covered by the interviewer, and (2) highlights of qualifications discussed during the interview. (These two suggestions aren't as important as (a), (b), and (c) because they're a rehash of what the interviewer already knows.)

**3.** In the last paragraph you can use one or more of the following:

    **a.** Offer to send additional information upon request.
    **b.** Thank for the interview (if not done in first paragraph).
    **c.** Say you can come in for another interview.
    **d.** Indicate hope that your qualifications fit the firm's requirements.
    **e.** Mention you're looking forward to a favorable decision.

The best time to send the follow-up to an interview is a day or two after the meeting—at least within the first seven days.

With this organizational pattern in mind, study the following examples of effective follow-up messages.

*Message 1: To a retail chain store.*

Dear Mr. Abolofia:

Thank you for the time  you spent telling me of the (firm's)
Executive Training Program.  The interview yesterday definitely
reaffirmed my interest in (firm).

I was especially impressed with the policy of promotion from
within.  Also, the timetable for advancement which you offered
is a good guide for a trainee's progress and leaves no room
for complacency.

I hope[1] my qualifications fit (firm's) requirement as you offer
an excellent future for an ambitious young man.  When you have
come to a decision, I will be eager to hear from you.

*Message 2: To a packing corporation.*

Dear Mr. Strom

As you requested, I am returning to you the completed applica-
tion form you gave me when you interviewed me last week on the
University of (state) campus for your Business Training
Program.

I'm especially interested in your organization because of the
possibility of getting into the international operations
division.  My academic background in business administration

---

[1] "Hope" in this last paragraph is acceptable. The student is merely saying he hopes his qualifications (which might be excellent) are those for the job he's being considered for.

with particular interest in calculus, statistics, data processing, and political science should help me in your training
program.  Having completed four quarters of accounting courses,
I am familiar with the basic principles, tools, and theories of
accounting.

Thank you for talking to me about (name of firm) and the
opportunity for growth and achievement.  If you wish additional
information about my background, please let me know.  Also, I
can come to (city) for an interview just about any time you
suggest.

*Message 3:* *To a large timber company.*

Dear Mr. Soames

Thank you for the time you spent with me while you were interviewing MBA candidates on the University of (state) campus,
Tuesday, January 20.  I was very grateful for the opportunity
to present my qualifications to you in person.

From our discussion and from readings I have done, I enjoyed
learning that (firm) operates in an environment free of rigid
procedures and formalized policies.  In addition, I am pleased
to know that your organization gives its MBA's very responsible
positions.  Because of these and other reasons, I am firmly
convinced that being associated with your organization offers
the challenge that encourages me to perform my best work.

I am looking forward to your decision about my working for
(firm).  It would be my pleasure to become a member of your
organization.

*Inquiry about Application Letter and Resume.* If you haven't received
a response to your written job application within three weeks, you are justified in sending an inquiry. Although it is unlikely your material was lost in
the mail, it is possible the receiver misplaced or forgot about it. Anyway, a
well-run organization should acknowledge—and if it does not, you certainly
should inquire. (Peck's survey[1] shows that most employers react favorably to
this inquiry—68 percent favorably, 30 percent in a neutral manner, and only
2 percent unfavorably.)

This type of follow-up is usually shorter than the one written after the
interview. Since most firms keep the written job presentation for six months
or longer, all you really need do is give enough identification so the employer can locate your material.

[1] Peck, "The Follow-up Letter in the Job Presentation," p. 24.

The three pieces of information the inquiry should include are identification of job sought, date of application letter previously sent, and (if appropriate) a request for an interview. In addition, some employers suggest you also include one or more of the following:

1. Interest in job
2. Date of availability
3. Offer to send additional information upon request
4. Telephone number
5. New material about qualifications
6. Reasons for wanting to work for the company
7. Status of application
8. Highlights of major qualifications already given in the application letter

Don't repeat information the employer already possesses. Included in this category is the same resume because it takes up valuable file space. No personnel manager likes to receive an application letter—and then one or two follow-ups—each with another copy of the same resume. Given below are two examples of acceptable inquiries.

*Message 1: Emphasizes identification of applicant's file.*

Dear Mr. Lindsell

On January 15, (year) I sent you my application letter and resume for an opening in your management training program. Because I'm very much interested in your firm and its future, I'm inquiring whether you received this material.

Please let me know what information you wish about my background. And, of course, I can come for an interview whenever you suggest.

*Message 2: Includes highlights of the applicant.*

Dear Mr. Huget:

Perhaps you will remember I sent you my application for a position in your grain department on February 8. I am primarily interested in cash grain purchasing and the use of the futures market as related to the operations of your company.

You may recall that the principal points in my letter were that:

1. I have conducted a research project into the use of the commodity exchanges by members of the Iowa grain industry, and am now finishing the writing of the results for my Master's thesis.

2. I have a college degree in Business Administration and plan to receive a Master of Arts degree in June, (year), in marketing.
3. During 18 years on an Iowa farm, I became familiar with most of the grains in the grain industry.

I hope that you can use a man with my background. If you wish any further information, I will be glad to send it to you.

## Other Follow-up Messages from Applicant to Employer

In addition to the follow-up messages just discussed, a job-hunting campaign can include quite a few other types. The following pages discuss and give examples of some of these.

*Answer to a Noncommital Letter.* Assume that you have sent your application letter with resume—maybe even had the interview. Then you receive the following:

Dear Mr. Randolph

We were pleased to receive your excellent application for employment.

We are very much interested in your capabilities but regret that at the present time, we cannot make use of them; with your permission, however, we will keep your name on file and if anything should develop in the future, get in touch with you.

Thank you for your interest in our organization.

What should you do? At first you might interpret this message as a routine refusal. However, the employer has said, "with your permission . . . keep on file," and you should assume that he's sincere and will definitely consider you when an opening occurs. A short message like the following is quite a satisfactory reply:

Dear Mr. Lewis

Thank you for your reviewing my qualifications for (type of job).

Will you please keep my name in your files so that you can consider me when a future opening in that field takes place.

I like what I read and hear about your organization—and hope someday to be part of such an organization.

If the employer states essentially what Lewis said to Randolph but does not ask your permission, a reply is optional.

***Reply to Request for Additional Information.*** Occasionally an employer, interviewer, or school will request additional information about your background. If such a situation arises, think carefully about the topic(s) that have been asked about. As with the initial presentation, analyze your background thoroughly, so that you will include all the important details to back up and strengthen your presentation, and then organize and write. You'll probably use an outline like the following:

First paragraph:    Thank for interview and express eagerness to tell him about whatever he asked for. Also identify the topic(s) you are discussing.

Middle paragraphs: If he asked about two qualifications (say interest in field and interest in company), write separate paragraphs for each. The discussion will be persuasive—quite similar to the middle paragraphs that create desire in the application letter.

Last paragraph:    In your last paragraph you might express:
1. Availability for another interview
2. Any other idea that rounds out and strengthens the message.

Given below is such a presentation. The admissions office of a law school asked the applicant to fill out the necessary form and separately to talk about his interest in law and give highlights of his background.

```
Admissions Council
University of (state) Law School
(city, state zip)

Gentlemen

As you requested, I am returning the completed Form A and a
brief discussion of two questions you asked for:  my interest
in law and highlights of my background.

Interest in Law
Before going into my background, I want to explain why I want a
degree in law.  The need has been there since childhood.  Un-
like most childhood fixations--fireman, airplane pilot, and
soldier--the desire to be a lawyer has stuck with me since the
age of twelve.  More than a childhood dream is involved though.
I feel that a law degree and the ability to use it embodies one
of the most valuable assets a man can own.
```

To me law pervades every aspect of our society. Law is where the action is. It is one of the few professions that enable a man to be actively involved in forming his culture while at the same time enabling him to find a highly satisfactory role in life.

Specifically I plan to concentrate on corporate law with a later concentration on international legal business relationships. This area needs good men, and I want to prepare myself to fill that need.

Background
Following is a brief sketch of my background that will help you in assessing my ability to study law. As the enclosed form shows, I was born in Germany. Though still a German citizen, I plan to go through naturalization during (year) to become a citizen of the United States. I was reared in South Africa from the age of three and as such am bilingual, speaking and writing both German and English without any accent or faults in composition.

I used my undergraduate years to gain as wide a knowledge of as many disciplines as I could. My program emphasized political science, social sciences, some humanities with a later concentration on general business courses. This was, in my mind, the most useful road toward my eventual goal.

My transcript that you should have received by now shows I spent five years on my bachelor's degree. The extra year was necessitated by a scarcity of funds in my family. Part- and full-time jobs have put me through school and have allowed me to save enough money to attend law school. Although outside work has detracted from study time, I feel that the work discipline and the ability to communicate and work with all types of people more than offset any loss in academic learning.

If you should need any additional information to aid you in your decision, please let me know.

Even if admissions had asked the applicant to send in only the completed form, he might voluntarily include a letter like the one above to bolster his presentation. If so, the same format could be followed, the only change being in the first paragraph:

Thank you for sending me the requested application to Law School. Enclosed are the completed Form A and a brief discussion of my interest in law and of my background.

*Acceptance of Invitation for Interview.* This type of good-news message has as its main purpose acceptance, which should appear in the first paragraph. Usually the employer leaves it up to you—at least within a limited time span—to decide when to make the trip. In turn, you must be considerate of the working days and hours of the employer. Give him a choice of several times within a certain week so that he can choose the most convenient date and hour. The last paragraph should express sincere interest in the forthcoming interview. Message 2 on page 497 is a good example of an applicant's acceptance of an invitation for a plant interview.

*Follow-up after Interview.* If you receive no reply by the promised date, remember that it takes time for the employer to interview all applicants, route the qualifications to interested officers in the organization, and make a final choice. However, if you have waited what you consider ample time and also beyond the date the employer promised he would notify you, you might want to write a nonpersuasive inquiry similar to the one below.

> Dear Mr. Johnson
>
> Four weeks have passed since I had the opportunity to talk with you about an opening in (field). At that time you said you'd notify me of your decision by (date).
>
> Since I am interested in working for your firm and have received no reply, I'm inquiring whether you have filled the opening.
>
> I'll appreciate a reply because your organization is the type that would be a privilege for me to work for.

*Request for More Time to Decide.* Sometimes the situation arises in which you receive an offer while you still have several interviews to complete, and you need more time before making a decision. Although you're taking a chance by asking the offering firm to give you more time to decide, usually the employer understands and wants you to be satisfied in your final selection. You usually preface the request with a buffer paragraph; then you explain and add a paragraph on your particular interest in the firm. The last paragraph should keep the door open for you to make a hurried decision if the employer decides not to grant the extension. Also ask for a confirmation of the extension if the employer decides in your favor. Message 5 on page 498 is a good example of a request for more time for the final decision.

*Acceptance of Offer.* When you receive an offer you want to accept, reply soon—perhaps within a week. Begin with the good news—that you accept with pleasure. In this first paragraph identify the job you're accepting; the next paragraph might give details about moving (if distance is involved) and reporting for work. Naturally what you say in this explanation depends on what the employer has already told you during the interview or in the job-offer letter. End with a rounding-out paragraph indicating you're looking forward to working for the firm. (See Message 7, page 499, which is a good example of an applicant's acceptance.)

*Rejection of Offer.* Occasionally an applicant will need to turn down a job offer. When you refuse an offer, you're writing a bad-news message. The organizational pattern is: buffer, explanation, refusal (implied or expressed), and a friendly positive closing. Even more important than the outline, however, is the attitude you have toward the company. Remember this firm seriously considered your qualifications and spent its time and money to bring you to the plant for an interview. If your refusal is discourteous and abrupt, you leave a bad impression and perhaps cause an unfavorable attitude toward *all* college applicants.

Shown below are two examples of well-written job refusals. Notice the outline, tone, sincerity, and positive approach.

*Message 1: By a business administration graduate to a personnel man.*

Dear Mr. Adamsen

Thank you for offering me a position in your management train-ing program.

During my job hunting these last six months, I've sent appli-cations to several firms that I regard highly--only those I could be happy working for. Fortunately for me, both you and another firm offered me a job. Because my qualifications, interest, and background fit in more closely with the other job, I have already mailed in my acceptance.

I do thank you for your consideration of my qualifications, thorough one-day interview at the plant, and the opportunity to meet all department heads in production. I'll always think of your organization as one in which management treats the em-ployees as a highly prized commodity.

Again, thank you for your consideration. I will always remember it.

This refusal is effective because it is simple and sincere from beginning to end. In a tactful way it explains first, then refuses the offer, and finally follows up with a paragraph that genuinely compliments the firm.

*Message 2:* *By a graduate in education to a superintendent of a school district.*

Dear Mr. Selby

I appreciate your offer to teach business education in one of Winchester's high schools.

As I explained in our interview on April 21, my wife and I must find jobs in the same locality. Since the interview, we have received an offer for both of us from Mr. Jackson of the Logan school system.

I hesitate to decline your offer since the experience in the Winchester system would be both profitable and enjoyable. However, under the present certification requirements, my wife must teach one year before completing her education. Since it is unlikely that she will be able to teach in this area, we find it necessary to accept the Logan positions.

Please keep my qualifications as a business education teacher in mind when openings develop in the future.

This message, like the previous one, is straightforward, sincere, and positive. Furthermore, the applicant doesn't burn his bridges behind him; the reader will probably consider him when an opening occurs.

## FOLLOW-UP MESSAGES WRITTEN BY EMPLOYER TO APPLICANT

Not only should you be able to write messages the applicant must send, but also—since you will be a businessman someday—you need to dictate effective messages that will go *to* the applicant.

### Invitation to Interview

As the employer writing this letter, you must realize that this message is second in importance only to the offer itself. Thus you must make the reader feel that you genuinely want him to come. Also clearly get across that you'll help him in every way possible—for example, you'll send him his round-trip ticket before he leaves, reserve a hotel room during his stay if necessary, and reimburse him for all incidental expenses. In addition, ask him to tell you when he can make the visit. Maybe you'll make his response easy by enclosing a card. (See Message 1, page 496.)

After you receive the applicant's acceptance of the invitation, you'll send a reply similar to Message 3 on page 497. You not only enclose a check for travel expenses, but give all necessary details and indicate interest in his visit.

## Notification of Impending Visit on Campus

Instead of asking the applicant to come to the plant, you might notify him you will come (or return) to his campus (or elsewhere) to interview applicants. You're writing to him because he is one of the graduates you particularly want to talk to. His qualifications on the application letter and resume interest you. Messages 1 and 2 below are notifications of an impending visit. In addition to giving the details about the visit, you have the opportunity to "sell" the applicant on something ("selling" in Message 1 and "your interest" in the applicant in Message 2).

*Message 1:* Sells the applicant on being a salesman.

> Dear Mr. McTaggart:
>
> Last fall I wrote you concerning job opportunities with (name of firm). I will again be on campus this winter and would like very much to see you.
>
> As I told you earlier, we have many openings for graduates--openings which include the functions of development, design, headquarters marketing, technical sales, manufacturing, and others.
>
> Before our get-together I want to describe briefly now (firm's) position of sales engineer. The word "salesman" in this country is tainted. Many people picture him as a used car dealer--public beware; door-to-door salesman; loud-mouthed extrovert; or an order taker with catalog, order blank, and poised pencil.[1]
>
> The industrial sales engineer is anything but these. He is technically competent. He solves engineering problems for his customers. He is an innovator. He thoroughly enjoys being with many types of people. He possesses empathy, which is the capacity to understand another person's feelings or ideas. He is principally interested in the large conceptional problems of engineering. And, with experience and further study he becomes competent in several engineering disciplines, because in industry the several branches of engineering cannot be separated.
>
> One other thought. In American industry today you'll find most of the jobs for engineers in technical sales. Also, here's where the money is, and this job is the route to higher management.
>
> I will be at the University of (state) on February 16, (year), for interviews. Please arrange to see me by contacting your Placement Director.

---

[1] The third paragraph might seem negative, but it is directed to an applicant who exhibited an unfavorable attitude toward selling, and who needs to be convinced of the true picture.

*Message 2: Sincerely compliments the applicant on his qualifications.*

Dear Mr. Webster

Thank you very much for coming to the Placement Office at the
University of (state) for an interview with (name of firm).
Since you and I had our visit, I have interviewed on approximately twenty other college campuses and talked to approximately 200 young men.

This has been my first opportunity to review the resumes of
these young men from which I have selected approximately 15%
suggesting further interviews.  Bill, you are included in this
group of young men whose scholastic ability, personality,
grooming, motivation, and overall personality place you in the
upper 15% of men I have talked to.

Our spring interview date at the university has not been
definitely established at this time, but as soon as it has
been, I will drop you a note; if you are interested, arrange
to be placed on our spring interview schedule in the Placement
Office.  You may recall that we select somewhere between ten
and fifteen young men each year to go through our Management
and Underwriter Training Program which runs from the third week
in June until the middle or end of September.

Again we commend you for your fine scholastic record you have
been able to maintain and at the same time be responsible for
100% of your college expenses.  We look forward to visiting
with you again in the spring for I feel certain we both have
much to offer each other by way of ability and opportunity for
growth.

## Request for Further Information

During the interview you may have questions about the applicant's enthusiasm or sincerity toward the company or toward his chosen field. To check
on your hunch you might ask him to tell you in a letter why he wants to
work for your firm or get into this type of occupation. Or you might ask him
to show why he's the individual you should hire for the opening. Or you
might simply need additional information, as the letter below illustrates:

Dear Mr. Juntwait:

Recently we had the pleasure of talking with you in connection
with our college recruiting activity.  Thank you for the time
you gave us.

Our staff has had the opportunity to review your qualifications
and we are interested in learning more about you.  Accordingly,

will you please complete the enclosed application and return it to me by (date). Also explain in an attached letter your interest in (name of field). After this information reaches us, we will get in touch with you on a more specific basis.

Thank you for your interest in (name of firm); we look forward to hearing from you in the near future.

Another type of "request for information" is the letter that asks the applicant to do something—perhaps to read a brochure, have an interview with a local representative of the firm, or take a test. The purpose of such requests is to have the applicant make certain he's getting into the right field, as the letter below illustrates:

Dear Steve:

Thank you for taking the time to learn more about (firm). You have the attitude and appearance that make a good salesman.

During the next few months I suggest that you find out all you can about the practical area of industrial sales.

Since you do not graduate until June of (year), if you still feel that this is the type of career you would like to pursue, please contact our local (city) District Manager for a more detailed interview. His name is Mr. A. I. Theriot, and can be reached at:

> (name of firm)
> 6536 – 6th Avenue, South
> (city, state zip)
> Phone: (number)

It was a pleasure talking with you. And the best of success in your studies.

## Offer of a Job

When you send a job offer, begin by telling the good news in a friendly manner. In the first paragraph also identify the job and state the salary (usually on a monthly basis). In the following paragraph(s), try to anticipate any questions the applicant might have—such as what moving expenses the firm will pay—and answer them. (Naturally you won't go into detail about expenses until he accepts.) Also leave the door open for him to ask questions before he makes his decision. Be sure your tone is appropriate—convey that you're interested in him and sincerely want him to join your organization. (See Message 4, page 498.)

## Granting an Extension of Time to Accept Offer

If you decide that an applicant has a sound reason for this request, you may decide to grant the extension. Grant the request in the first paragraph, explain (and in general terms set the cutoff date), express interest in the applicant, and end on a friendly and positive note. (See Message 6, page 499.)

## Reply to Applicant's Acceptance

Even when the applicant has accepted your job offer, you still need to remember the value of public relations. He doesn't expect a long letter, but very abrupt messages can be disappointing. For example, after receiving Message 8 (page 500), the applicant felt let down because the employer didn't show interest—"enthusiasm" is perhaps a better word—in him. You could change this disappointing message into a welcome one merely by adding the following as the second paragraph:

> Thank you again for joining our organization. Your interest and qualifications will definitely add to our management force.

> *or (better yet)*

> I sincerely feel, Lloyd, that you have an excellent future with us. When I visualize your potential, based upon your academic background and sincere interest in manufacturing, and combine this with the growth we are going to experience in the future I am certain that you will become a likely candidate for broader responsibilities.

Changing "sincerely yours" to "best regards" can help make the closing a little more friendly and personal for some readers.

## Refusal of Job

A refusal—even a tactful one—is a blow to the applicant, and the tone of your refusal is very important. At all costs you want to avoid leaving the applicant with a lasting negative reaction to your firm, as the following letter does:

> Dear Sir:

> In reply to your letter of February 13th, we have filled the position of salesman for the present.

> Thanking you for your letter, I am

The graduate being turned down doesn't want limp excuses or outright false statements. He wants honesty—but not discourteous bluntness or crudeness of expression. He appreciates sincere, complimentary remarks about his qualifications; proper consideration of his background; and proper attitude toward him. Give him the feeling you realize that you're talking to an intelligent human being.

In the first paragraph, give a buffer—appreciate his interest in the firm or opportunity to talk with him, or thank him for coming in for an interview. In the second paragraph, explain. You should first say something neutral (for example, you have reviewed his qualifications) and then refuse in as positive a way as possible. One of the best explanations seems to be "there are several other candidates whose overall qualifications are more in line with our requirements."

Be sure your last paragraph is positive and friendly. Wish him success, tell him you enjoyed the opportunity to talk with him, thank him for his interest in the firm. Obviously you won't repeat in this paragraph what you said in the first.

Below is an unusually effective refusal, which follows the outline just discussed.

Dear Mr. Cotter:

Thank you very much for taking your time to be interviewed and tested for the position of Systems Engineering Representative with (firm).

We have reviewed your educational background, work experience, and aptitude tests, along with others we are considering for employment. Our analysis indicates that there are several other candidates whose overall qualifications are more in line with our requirements.

We enjoyed having the opportunity to interview you and sincerely appreciate your interest in (firm). Please accept our best wishes for success in your chosen career.

Some taboos to be avoided in writing your refusal are given below.

1. Refusal in opening

We have considered your qualifications; however, we do not have a position available for you.

2. Abrupt refusal in the first sentence of the second paragraph

Unfortunately we have no opening for you.

**3.** No reason for refusal

A review of your qualifications indicates that you have a
background which is commendable in many respects; however, we
are not in a position to further pursue the matter of employment with (firm) at this time.

**4.** Negative attitude ("sorry," "unable," "regret," "cannot," "not suited," "do not
feel," "do not have," "delay")

In view of our needs, however, we do not feel additional
interviews would be mutually beneficial or advisable.

We realize this is disappointing news, and . . . .

**5.** Vagueness

I hope that we shall have an opportunity to review our mutual
interests again at some future date.

Based on your recent interview and your qualifications, we
cannot encourage you about employment with (firm) at the
present time.  (Which was significant, the interview or the
qualifications?)

**6.** Abrupt ending

Should an opening develop, I will be in touch with you.


## SITUATION

Now that you have studied separately different types of messages that the
employer and applicant use in securing a job, study the letters below, which
were written over a period of time by an applicant for an operations management position with a national firm and the representatives of the firm. (The
applicant's resume appears on pages 438 and 439.)

*Message 1: Mr. Hanson, supervisor of employment personnel services, invites appli-
cant for plant interview. The plant is about 1000 miles from the campus.*

October 28, (year)

Dear Mr. Webb:

Following our recent interview on campus, we wish to invite you
to visit (name of firm) for plant interviews; you will receive
the necessary expenses for air travel to (city), and return,
as well as incidental expenses.

If a plant visit is agreeable to you, please let us know when
you can make the visit and we will confirm a mutually agreeable
date.  A card is enclosed so that you can notify us of your

plant visit decision.  If possible, plan to spend one full day
at the plant.

Thank you for the interest you have expressed in (name of
firm).  Upon confirming an interview date, we will forward a
check covering your travel expenses, details for getting to the
plant, and we will also reserve hotel accommodations in (city)
if you so desire.

*Message 2: Applicant's reply to Message 1; acceptance of invitation.*

                                        November 4, (year)


Dear Mr. Hanson

Thank you for inviting me to visit your plant.  I very much
want to study your organization and operation.

Because of class schedules and previous commitments, the best
dates are November 15-19 inclusive.  Any one or more of these
days permits ideal timing for the trip.

I'm looking forward to visiting your plant and talking with
both management members and workers in production.

*Message 3: Reply by certified mail to Message 2; Mr. Benson, Supervisor of Employ-
ment Personnel Services, gives details for visit and encloses check.*

                                        November 7, (year)


Dear Mr. Webb

Thank you for informing us of your intended visit to (firm) for
interviews.  We have set the date on November 18 and are
enclosing a check to cover your plane fare, meals, and miscellaneous expenses.  Please retain any receipts for air travel
and lodging for our expense account purposes.

We have arranged prepaid hotel accommodations for you for
Monday, November 17, at the Sheraton-Palace Hotel, (city).  You
can come to the plant Tuesday morning in a company car which
leaves our (city) Office every morning at 6:45 a.m.

To get this car you should report by 6:30 a.m. to the Mail
Room, Twelfth Floor, Equitable Life Building, 120 Berkeley
Street, (city).  Because of the early hour, you can plan on
having breakfast when you reach the plant.  You will be able to
return to (city) from the plant in the same manner, leaving
here at 4:40 p.m. and arriving in (city) at about 6:30 p.m.

The interest you have expressed in (name of firm) is appreciated, and we look forward to your visit on the 18th.

**Message 4:** *Job offer by Mr. Dorman, General Superintendent, following plant interview.*

November 22, (year)

Dear Mr. Webb:

We are pleased to offer you employment as a Management Trainee, assigned to our Industrial Engineering Department. Your starting salary on this position would be $835 a month.

Should you decide to join our organization, we will provide the cost of travel for you and your wife and move your household effects.

Thank you for the interest which you expressed when you visited the plant; I am sorry that circumstances did not permit me to meet you then. We hope that you will decide to make your career with us. If you have any question concerning our offer or employment in general, please call Mr. R. A. Benson in the Personnel Office. His telephone number is 543-4889 (area code 123).

**Message 5:** *Applicant requests more time for final decision.*

December 2, (year)

Dear Mr. Benson:

Mr. Dorman just sent me a job offer as a Management Trainee in the Industrial Engineering Department and said for me to get in touch with you if I had any questions concerning the offer.

Before making a final decision concerning this offer, I will appreciate your allowing me until January (year) for my reply. My reason for requesting this extra time is to permit me to complete my interviews with several other companies—especially those that have already invited me to visit their plants. By doing so, I will have satisfied myself that I am selecting the organization of my choice.

At the moment, even with these other opportunities, I am more interested in (reader's firm) than all the others because there are many aspects of your company which appeal to me. I was particularly impressed by the speed, efficiency, and precision of the manufacturing plant. In addition I discovered that (firm) offers excellent fringe benefits to the employees.

If you need my decision before the end of this month, please let me know as soon as possible so that I will have the opportunity to make my final decision. Also, if you are giving me this extended time, please notify me to that effect.

*Message 6:* Mr. Benson gives applicant extension of time to accept offer.

December 11, (year)

Dear Mr. Webb

As you requested, we will be glad to allow you additional time to decide whether you want to accept our previous offer to work for (firm).

We realize that you have many things to consider to reach a final decision regarding employment; therefore, we want to allow you as much time as possible for your evaluation of all opportunities. In order for us to establish the proper control on your recruiting activities and to make plans for the coming year, I will appreciate knowing your decision as soon as possible. However, inasmuch as you will not be available until June (year), your advising us a couple of months from now will be quite acceptable.

We feel that you are well qualified for the career employment opportunities available within (firm) and hope that you will decide to make your career with us.

I wish you and your wife the best of health and cheer during the coming holidays; and if I can be of any further assistance, please write or telephone me. My number is 543–4889 (area code 123).

*Message 7:* Applicant's acceptance.

January 5, (year)

Dear Mr. Benson:

I am glad to accept your offer of $835 a month as a Management Trainee in your Industrial Engineering Department.

Since graduation is Saturday, June 13, (year), my wife and I plan to leave (city) the following Monday, June 15. We should arrive in the (city) area the following day——Tuesday, June 16. Allowing a few days to locate living accommodations and to get settled, I should be ready to start work on Monday, June 22. Please let me know if this schedule is satisfactory with you.

I am very pleased in becoming a member of your organization; it is with great appreciation that I look forward to what I am sure will be a very profitable future with (name of organization).

***Message 8:*** *Benson's reply to applicant's acceptance.*

January 13, (year)

Dear Mr. Webb:

We are very pleased that you are coming with us, and we look forward to seeing you on June 22.

We will forward travel expenses in May and will contact you at that time regarding moving arrangements.

Please contact us if we can be of any assistance before that time.

The first seven of the eight messages above are good examples of effective correspondence. Only Message 8 is a bit weak. When Mr. Webb received it, he considered it somewhat abrupt and lacking in enthusiasm.

## EXERCISES

1. Below are five refusals to applicants by outstanding national companies. Evaluate by telling what you like and dislike about each message. Be specific in your discussion. Which one does the most satisfactory job?

   a.

   Dear Mr. Hoggard

   I enjoyed my recent opportunity to discuss with you your background and career goals.

   Because the number of positions is limited, we are unable to consider all who have expressed an interest in (firm).  Although we were impressed by your background and qualifications, it appears that there are others who seem to be more suited for the particular openings presently available.

   We appreciate the time and effort you have expended in considering (firm), and we wish you the best of success in reaching your career objectives.

   b.

   Dear Mr. Wallace:

   In reply to your letter of application dated January 5, (year), we do not have an opening on our staff.  However, we shall be pleased to keep your application on file for future vacancies.

   Thank you for writing us.

**c.**

Dear Mr. Irvine

The delay in advising you regarding employment possibilities with (firm), following your interview with our recruiter, has been due to your application and file being forwarded to departments dispersed over a wide geographic area.

Your background and qualifications have now been carefully reviewed by these various departments; but, we regret we are presently unable to offer you a position that would be of mutual advantage.

We appreciate your interest in (firm) and wish you every success in the future.

**d.**

Dear Jim

Thank you for scheduling an interview with (firm), giving our recruiter, Mr. C. W. Lindenmeier, the opportunity to talk with you during our recent visit to your campus.  He commented favorably about his conversation with you.

We have carefully reviewed all openings anticipated near your availability date which we believed might be of interest to you.  I am sorry to inform you that we were unable to locate a position matching your background, training, and interests.  We are, however, taking the liberty of holding your application on file should any appropriate openings develop in the near future.

I do regret that we cannot offer you more encouragement at this time.  We appreciate your interest in our activities and wish you every success in beginning your professional career.

**e.**

Dear Mr. Goodpaster:

Thank you for coming in to discuss employment possibilities during our recent visit to your campus.

As you can appreciate, there is considerable competition for our limited openings.  It is always a difficult task to select a few people from the many fine candidates we are given the opportunity to consider.  After careful consideration of your qualifications with regards to our specific job requirements, we will be unable to offer you further encouragement.

We do, however, appreciate your interest in (firm) and extend our best wishes for success in your business career.

**2.** Evaluate the following message. Applicant sends application letter with resume to a large department store but receives no reply after three weeks. This letter is his follow-up inquiry.

Dear Mr. Haldean:

After some puzzlement on my part as to why I had not heard from you regarding employment with your company one way or the other, I decided to check with the Student Placement Center about my credentials which you did not have at the time of the interview and still do not have.

I found that two of my appraisal forms had not come back. After checking with the two individuals involved and finding that there was a mistake in not sending them in, I am certain that my credentials will be sent to you very soon. Please let me know if you are still interested in me.

**3.** Evaluate the three messages below. The applicant is a graduating senior who sent her application letter with resume to a large department store chain in a large city 1,000 miles from the campus. In the letter she mentioned she'd be in the city between winter and spring quarters (usually the latter part of March) and requested an interview, which she received.

*Message 1: Applicant receives this offer after she returns to the campus.*

Dear Miss Stewart:

As a result of our conversation with you, we are pleased to offer you the opportunity to join the (firm) Executive Training Program at a starting salary of $600 a month. Employment is contingent upon your passing a medical examination which will be given when you start work here in (city).

Enclosed for your perusal is a copy of our Annual Report, which we trust you will find of interest.

We look forward to receiving your favorable consideration of this offer, and I am sure you will find this a most stimulating opportunity.

*Message 2: Miss Stewart accepts job offer.*

April 17, (year)

Dear Mrs. Leabo

It is with pleasure and excitement that I accept your offer to join the (firm) Executive Training Program. I have been reading the Annual Report you enclosed and am looking forward to working for as fine a company as (firm's).

Will you please tell me when you want me to report after
graduation, where, to whom, and at what time?  I can be in
(city) within two weeks after University of (state) commence-
ment exercises June 13.

If you need any further information before giving me the
details of my assignment, please write to me at my (city)
address before June 9 and at my home address after that date.

*Message 3: Reply to Miss Stewart's job acceptance and inquiry.*

April 21, (year)

Dear Miss Stewart:

Thank you for your letter of April 17.  We are pleased to know
that you will be joining our Executive Training Squad this
summer.

You may report for work any Monday convenient to you.  You
indicate that June 29 would be a convenient date.  This is most
acceptable, and we will look forward to your reporting at
8:55 a.m. to the Personnel Department, which is on the eighth
floor.  You may enter the building through the company entrance
(on Westfall near Donson Street) and the guard at the door
will direct you to the Personnel Department.

Enclosed is a booklet, which is given to all new Training Squad
executives when they report for work, which may answer many of
your questions.  We are also enclosing a booklet which is given
to every new employee which will give you information as to
dress regulations, etc.

Congratulations on your coming graduation.  We look forward to
seeing you again on June 29.

4. Assume you sent your application letter and resume to the personnel manage of
   a particular firm; shortly afterwards you received an invitation to come to his
   office for an interview. He is located in your city. During the 30-minute interview, he asked you questions about your qualifications and explained company
   policy, beginning salary, and other pertinent information. Write a follow-up for
   each of the possible outcomes below:
   a. At the end of the interview he told you he'd notify you of his decision.
   b. At the end of the interview he asked you to write him why you want to get
      into the type of work you're applying for.
   c. At the end of the interview he asked you to visit the manager in one of the
      organization's several local retail stores; while there you should interview the
      manager and other employees to find out whether you want to make a career
      in this type of work. Then you're to write the personnel manager if you're
      still interested. Assume you are favorably impressed.
5. Assume you mailed your application letter three weeks ago but have received no
   reply. Send an inquiry to the firm.

6. Assume you received two offers for career jobs.
   a. Write the acceptance message.
   b. Write the refusal message.
7. Message 8 on page 500 didn't impress the applicant favorably because the writer didn't spend enough time with him—didn't seem to show enthusiasm. Revise this message but avoid insincerity.
8. As the employer, you must refuse a graduating senior the job he applied for because his qualifications aren't as good as those of the others you interviewed. Furthermore, one reference indicated this man is a troublemaker. Write the refusal message.
9. As a graduating senior, you received the following letter from Mr. Alexander, Recruiting Coordinator. Unfortunately you can't see the representative on January 30. However, you're very much interested in working for this company. Write the appropriate message to the coordinator, assuming any facts you wish as long as you don't alter the assignment.

> Dear Mr. Harman:
>
> Please forgive my resorting to a form-letter to reach you--but time is getting short and I want to let you know that one of our executives plans to visit your campus soon.
>
> His primary purpose will be to interview (year) graduates for career employment with our newly-merged organization.  As you might imagine, we have an even greater horizon now to present to promising young people like yourself.  Moreover, we have a number of good summer job-opportunities for undergraduates this year.
>
> In any case, I have been alerted to your fine summer employment record with us and assure you our interest in you continues strong.  Accordingly, if you want to explore a position with us, I urge that you sign-up to see our Corporate Recruiting Representative when he visits your Placement Office on January 30.
>
> If you cannot make that date, please drop me a line and let's try to arrange for you to visit some nearby branch office.  I am enclosing a return envelope for that purpose, together with a copy of our Annual Report and some other literature for your reference.
>
> Meanwhile, accept our sincere best wishes to your forthcoming graduation.

10. Mr. Jay Kassner, a graduating senior, received a job offer from California Company A in November. But he asked and received an extension of time until January 1 to notify the company of his decision. Also in November he had extensive interviews with officials of Company B in Portland, Oregon. On December 19 Company B invited him to return to Portland and to take a one-day swing to Illinois with company officials so Kassner could observe company facilities there. At this second meeting with Company B the spokesman for the group said the

company was interested in extending Kassner an offer—but didn't specifically make one.

Kassner returned home on the 20th and waited for a formal offer—but none arrived. Because the deadline of January 1 for him to accept or reject the offer of Company A was approaching, he wrote Company B and said, in essence, "If it takes more than six weeks to receive a reply concerning an employment interview, I am not that interested in seeking employment with your company." In turn, he received the following letter on December 26 from Company B.

Dear Jay:

We sincerely appreciated your visit on December 19, (year). Since your visit we have had an opportunity to discuss and carefully evaluate your background and qualifications in relation to our manpower needs.

Based on these discussions, and since the number of openings we have are somewhat limited, we will not be extending you an offer of employment.

We enjoyed meeting with you and appreciate the time you took in discussing employment with us.

Do you think Kassner's letter to Company B had anything to do with his not getting the job? With the poor tone in the refusal letter from the company?

Write the inquiry that you think Kassner should have mailed to Company B on December 19, assuming he was more interested in Company B than in Company A.

11. What kind of an impression do you think the following applicant made on the firm considering him for a management job? Given below are the details.[1]

The applicant was invited in for an interview at company expense. He lived in Madison, Wisconsin, and the company was located at Rockford, Illinois. Although it was only normal to use plane, train, or bus for transportation, he felt he could get "in" with the company by saving them money—by hitchhiking. Here's the expense account he submitted to the company for reimbursement.

| | |
|---|---:|
| Bus fare in Madison, Wisconsin | $ .20 |
| Bus fare in Janesville, Wisconsin | .20 |
| Dinner at Rockford, Illinois | 1.95 |
| Hotel room and tip, Rockford | 4.50 |
| Movie (Hair) | 2.00 |
| 3 cokes | .45 |
| 12 cigarettes (2 of the fellows I hitchhiked with borrowed these from me) | .24 |
| Hamburger and coke for lunch at Peoria | .65 |
| Hotel room and tip Peoria, Illinois | 4.50 |
| Shoe shine | .40 |
| 1 suit cleaned (1 of the fellows I caught a ride with had been drinking and spilled a bottle of beer on me) | 1.95 |
| | $ 17.04 |

[1] Adapted from the *American Business Writing Association Bulletin*, December 1963, p. 16.

12. You're in a dilemma. As a graduating senior, you have been job hunting. This morning you receive by mail a job offer from a large bank in a distant city.

    This letter is most welcome because you really want this job—but the same message includes something that bothers you. The writer says the job offer is contingent upon passing a successful physical, and that the company has set up an appointment for you to be examined by a particular physician in your own city.

    To most applicants a request for a physical is routine. But not you, because you had an epileptic seisure 1½ years ago (the first and only). You're under doctor's care, but are living a normal life as a husband, father, student, and 30-hour-a-week employee. Your doctor tells you that you probably will not have another seizure if you continue your prescribed medication.

    You don't mention your condition to job interviewers because you can live a completely normal life and they haven't asked any question that would prompt you to give this information. Furthermore you know "epilepsy" is a terribly negative word to many people, who picture an epileptic as constantly having fits.

    Should you go ahead with the physical and hope the doctor doesn't ask or find out? (Even if you pass the physical, what will happen to your job if the bank finds out years later that you have had this condition from the beginning?) For this assignment merely prepare to discuss in class what you should do.

13. After you submitted your application letter and resume to a geophysical company of your choice and later had a personal interview, you received the following reply dated February 5:

    ```
    We still have your application in front of us; however, we are
    reluctant to make you an offer since the requisites for the
    overseas opening include qualifications other than a fluency
    in Japanese.  The candidate should have a knowledge of seismic
    field operations.  Had your conversational Japanese been ade-
    quate, we would have felt justified in placing you in a slot
    where you could have been productive while learning our mode
    of operations.

    As it is, we can now do no more than suggest that you start on
    a field crew as a helper and learn our business.  But such
    starting jobs are low in pay.  However, if you are interested
    in getting a ""foot in the door,'' let me know your minimum
    starting requirements, and we will see if anything can be
    worked out that will be mutually benefiting.

    Should you have a trip planned to the Southwest, try to include
    Houston so that you can come by our office for a visit.
    ```

    Because you really "drooled" for the particular job you applied for, you couldn't take "no" without one more try. So you poured your feelings into the following letter dated February 9. In turn, the receiver—2,500 miles from you—telephoned you the same day your letter arrived and hired you for the job you originally applied for. What did you say in your last message that convinced him you should be hired?

Thank you for your letter of February 5.

I believe that it would be easy for me to adapt to (firm's) line of work. My natural inclination has long been toward science and its many facets.

I have had field operations experience with both the Air Force and Boeing. While in the Air Force, I went on numerous temporary duty assignments when overseas. With Boeing I spent close to six months working out in the Minuteman Missile System sites throughout much of Montana, installing new communications equipment. Thus I believe I can learn (firm's) mode of operations with the minimum of time.

Regarding getting my ""foot in the door,'' I think it is a good last alternative. My minimum salary requirement is uncertain at this time as I have no idea what field-crew-helper pay is. Basically I am most interested in the opportunity for my career advancement, rather than just salary incentives. On the other hand if salary and advancement were neutral incentives for me, I doubt if I would have returned to college. Therefore if all other avenues are closed to me, I would be interested in the helper job if there is good opportunity for me to advance into job similar to the one requiring use of Japanese.

I propose yet another alternative for your consideration. I would be willing to sign up for the Berlitz 120-lesson course in Japanese at the earliest opportunity. Naturally I would only do so with the understanding that I could get the seismic field operations job (or one similar) once I became more fluent in Japanese. My current finances prohibit me from paying the $1,200 for this language study program. Presently I have a part-time direct selling job; and I am taking a correspondence speed-reading course in my spare time. If things go smoothly, I should be able to earn enough money to pay for this language course over the next several months. Again another understanding, I desire that one year from the date of my employment with (firm) I receive a partial reimbursement of my $1,200 tuition expense. This is so only if everything works out mutually benefiting (firm) and myself. Thus I would need four to six months to earn the necessary money and then enroll in the Berlitz language course and complete it.

Would the seismic field operations job still be open by this point in time? If not, please let me know how much longer it will remain open, and maybe I can complete the Berlitz course in time.

Please advise me of your decision regarding the above-mentioned alternative.

# Chapter 12

# Collection Messages—Written and Oral

- Right Attitude for Effective Collections
- Collection Series
- Telephone Collection Procedure
- Exercises

When a customer purchases something on time, he should pay within a specified period—according to the terms of the sale. When people don't pay their obligations on time, collection messages become necessary. Reasons for customers not paying are usually one or more of the following: they're temporarily short of funds; they're dissatisfied with the merchandise, delivery, or handling of a complaint; they've overlooked the invoice or statement; they're chronic debtors. Collection messages—whether they're by mail, phone, personal visit, or by telegram—have a twofold purpose: to get the money and at the same time to keep the goodwill of the customer.

In the world of collections, you'll find two main types of credit accounts—retail and mercantile; each of these can be subdivided into open account credit and installment credit. The person who buys something on time and consumes the product has a retail account. Examples of individuals with retail accounts are the housewife who buys anything from food to furniture for her home or family, an outdoorsman who buys fishing gear for himself, and the individual who buys a car for his personal use or the gasoline for that car. As a contrast, when an individual buys a product on credit for resale, he has a mercantile account. Examples include a retailer who buys merchandise to sell to his customers, a contractor who buys plumbing supplies for a house or apartment building which he plans to sell, and a wholesaler or manufacturer who sells merchandise to a retailer.

This chapter treats retail collections together with mercantile credit because both use similar collection series—with the same appeals, types of written and oral communications, and intervals between messages. In fact, the collection procedure within retail collections can differ even more than between retail and mercantile collections. As Beckman and Foster in their 1969 *Credits and Collections* state:

> While the same types of specific systems may not be equally adapted to retail and mercantile credit or to installment and charge account customers, the several factors or elements underlying them are basic and identical and must be taken into account in each case.[1]
>
> Collection methods and practices tend to differ with the line of trade and with the methods of operation of the selling concern. Creditors selling on open account, for example, are usually less prompt in pushing collections than are those selling on the installment plan. The latter group is faced with the possibility of cumulative delinquencies as successive payments fall due and are not met. Service organizations, such as those providing utilities in the form of electricity, gas, heat, or telephone communication, generally follow a prompt collection policy, because indebtedness continues to increase through customers' unchecked use of service during the collection process. Merchants often differ among themselves in collecting, moreover, as when one caters to low income clientele and another to buyers in high income brackets. The latter is usually the more lenient in his collection effort because it is presumed that neglect and

---

[1] Theodore Beckman and Ronald Foster, *Credits and Collections*, McGraw-Hill Book Company, New York, 1969, p. 530. When referring to "factors," these authors mean length of time for the entire collection process, types or kinds of collection efforts (types of written or oral communications), sequence of these types, and interval between messages.

oversight, rather than unwillingness and incapacity to pay, are the reasons for the delinquency. On the other hand, still other differences in collection practice stem from the fact that while one vendor emphasizes quality of product and minimizes credit service, a competitor, usually less well-established in the trade, seeks patronage through credit liberality.[1]

Carrying out the twofold function of collecting money from a past-due customer and keeping his goodwill requires an understanding attitude and proper timing of effective messages throughout the various collection stages. This chapter discusses:

1. Right attitude for effective collections
2. Collection series—appeals, stages, and length of series
3. Telephone procedure: precall planning, detailed analysis of the call, and follow-up

## RIGHT ATTITUDE FOR EFFECTIVE COLLECTIONS

When someone owes money to you personally or to your firm, you certainly should notify him of that fact just before or at the time the money is due. Furthermore, he should pay when he receives his statement (bill or invoice); and when he doesn't settle his account, you have every right to find out why. Yet you should begin with the premise that the individual is honest, and you should be careful about when and how you remind him of his indebtedness.

When you write a collection message, always keep in mind you're talking to a customer—not to a criminal (debtors were considered second-class citizens in the past). Also, you're talking to a person with feelings, who notices offensive expressions, sarcasm, anger, and insults just as quickly as you do. No one would be inclined to pay a bill if he received an insulting letter like the following:

Dear Mr. Saunders

When we approved credit for you at this store, it was assumed that you were an intelligent, responsible adult. However, the manner in which you have handled the account disproved this assumption. You have abused every right normally extended to intelligent, adult people. I think it is time for an examination of conscience . . . I certainly hope that you do not abuse everyone who extends you a courtesy as you have abused us.

Remit immediately. But if you choose to ignore this letter in the same consistent manner that you have ignored every other attempt to collect, we will continue to harass you until it becomes unbearable.

[1] Beckman and Foster, p. 524.

In contrast the collection message[1] below has a considerate, friendly tone:

Dear Mr. Green:

This is a reminder that your mortgage payment of $67.93, which was due on April 27, (year), has not yet reached us.  The May 27, (year), payment for the same amount is also due.

Everyone is apt to overlook things now and then; if it has slipped your mind, please let us have your payment by return mail.

If you have already mailed payment, please accept our thanks and disregard this notice.

In fact, the individual who received this reminder was so favorably impressed that he wrote the following note in longhand when he made the due payments and included an additional payment in advance:

Gentlemen:  I am embarrassed——I did overlook payment.  I was once a financial officer of a large corporation where I had to write collection letters.  I struggled in trying to be friendly and effective at the same time.  Your letter is the best I have ever seen.

Individuals react differently to what you say and how you say it. For example, the manager of a credit corporation sent the collection message below to a customer when the first monthly payment was six weeks overdue.

Dear Mr. Wolf

Your account was referred to me this morning as SERIOUSLY DELINQUENT.  Upon reviewing it, I am indeed surprised that it is not up to date in payments.  You have been extended every courtesy both by notice and letter, but there has been no response.

We go through the above-mentioned courtesies when an account becomes delinquent for a few days.  Almost 100 per cent of our customers APPRECIATE A COURTEOUS NOTICE AND MAKE PAYMENT PROMPTLY.  Your FAILURE to do so, therefore, AMAZES us.

Your account is seriously past due.  IS IT NECESSARY FOR US TO TAKE ANY FURTHER ACTION OTHER THAN WRITE THIS LETTER IN ORDER TO HAVE YOU SEND THIS AMOUNT BY RETURN MAIL?

[1] *Effective Letters*, New York Life Insurance Company, July–August 1960, p. 1.

Probably most recipients would either pay or throw the message away with little or no emotion. But the customer who received the letter reacted strongly, as his reply reveals:

Dear Mr. Allee

In reference to your kind and very appreciable letter of which you informed me of the wonderful courtesies you gracious people have extended to me, I've often wondered just what other people considered courteous. Of course, now I have your version of courtesy, but I wonder if you can apply it in the letter I received on December 26.

In the past you sent me numerous bills long before I received all the articles I'm being billed for. The salesman that sold me the books said not to pay a penny till all in the contract had been received. We received the last items the 15th of December. We have yet to receive our annual.

Your letter did open my eyes some also. I realize that once I affixed my signature on the contract whether I receive a damn thing or not I am to pay up and pay up quick. You people are a real fine organization; once I get you paid off, I will make note to never have any further dealings with such a high upstanding credit dive.

The thing that impressed me highly about your letter was in the last paragraph. Wow! Those capital letters big and bold seemed to leap right out and grab my throat and as it strangled the life out of me, screamed "pay, pay, pay, you lousy bum or else." I don't know why you're not in Congress or some high political position for I'm certain if you were, you would scare the pants off all the warring nations (at least their chil-dren). Speaking of large letter words "seriously, delinquent, appreciate a courteous notice and make payments promptly," and such as "your FAILURE."

Wow! You're a really mean nasty old man. What if I was younger, your letter might have caused some kind of psycho-logical trauma. Thank goodness I'm old enough to withstand it all.

I'd like to mention also that you're most decidedly in error about your sending both letter and notice and I didn't respond. Someone in your lousy organization sent me a questionnaire that asked whether I had received all things mentioned in the contract. I said no and gave the items that I hadn't received. Therefore, you're either a liar or poorly informed about what's going on in that damn office of yours.

You're a hard tough man, you are. You might give a man a
chance to receive what he's supposed to receive, you little
tough rascal you.

You might say I'm almost angry about that gangster type threat
you sent me. Other than that I'm most pleased with the fine
set of books I did receive and I'll be happy to pay for them.
It isn't my habit to go around trying to run rough shod over
people either. Something tells me you're too little to even be
trying to do so. The only muscles you might have is in that
fat hand of yours to write nasty little letters such as the
one I'm writing now, you might say.

As another example of how people react, look at the following obvious
form reminder—the second in a series—sent to a customer who owed a $12
balance for two months, and then read the customer's response. Although
the letter seems routine, the customer read a threat into it.

Dear Customer

A previous notice has been sent regarding the past due payment
of $12.00 on your account. Our records indicate that we have
not received this payment.

We cannot emphasize too strongly the importance of making payments promptly without the need of reminders. The amount past
due should be paid at once since another payment will be due
in a few days.

You may make the payment personally or send us a check or money
order, using the enclosed envelope.

It is important that this matter receive your immediate
attention.

The individual who received this message read into it a threat, as the
reply shows.

Gentlemen:

It is very discouraging for people who pay their bills to
receive these "form" letters written in very poor taste and
dropped by the ton, I am sure, into the nearest postal box. We
will try never to charge anything at your store again because
of the treatment received. It is one thing to send a <u>reminder</u>;
another when you <u>threaten</u> a person with blackening a credit
rating.

I am sure this letter will be quickly tossed into the nearest
container but someone should revise your tactics for handling
customers.

As a collection manager, you walk a tightrope when you mail messages to customers who have past-due accounts. If you're too lenient, the individual may pay other bills that seem more pressing, and you won't get the money coming to you. On the other hand, if you threaten or bully the customer, he may not pay either. *How* you probe for the reason he isn't paying is important, as is *when* to start probing. (The last thing you want to do is to turn the account over to a collection agency because everyone loses except the agency.)

In result-getting collection letters, expressions like "you are delinquent" should not be used, although phrases such as "two payments are delinquent" or "the delinquency of this account" are less offensive because they are impersonal. "Past due" has a better connotation and is preferred.

All you have learned about good tone, courtesy, and consideration for the reader applies to collection messages, as do the suggestions for the proper attitude in bad-news letters.

## COLLECTION SERIES

When a customer purchases on credit, you—as the collection manager—will notify him by a statement (bill) or invoice for the amount that he owes. This notification usually lists the transactions for the time period involved and states the terms of payment. Should the customer not pay when his statement is due, you begin to send him a planned series of messages appropriately called a collection series. As illustrated later, this series should be flexible and geared to the paying habits and credit reputation of the customer.[1]

Within a collection series are three stages—reminder, discussion, and urgency. All messages in each stage should state the amount due. Even though the customer may have received several previous messages giving the amount owed, always repeat this information because he might have lost the earlier statements or thrown them away. Never give him an excuse to procrastinate paying.

One effective variation is to have different officers sign the collection messages at different stages. For example, the reminder and discussion stages might show the credit department or credit manager as the originator; but in the urgency stage the message could be signed by the vice-president or president. Switching to an officer having a more impressive title will make a greater impact on the past-due customer than continuing to send all collection correspondence from the same department or individual.

---

[1] Although every firm should have a definite plan for collection, carrying out the collection procedure is often a matter of judgment for the credit and collection manager or the collectors within the department. These people decide which of several forms to send and which of several ways (telephone, mail, wire, personal visit) to contact the customer. For example, the store might call after a new customer doesn't respond to a statement. Yet a long-time customer who has paid regularly may receive several additional reminders before a telephone call is made.

When you think of a collection series, you should consider the stages, appeals used, and the length of the series. Although they are interrelated, they're discussed here separately in the following order—(1) appeals, (2) the three stages, and (3) the length of the series.

## Collection Appeals

In those messages that aim to persuade, you need to include collection appeals. The following positive and negative appeals—presented in order from the mildest to the strongest—can be tailored effectively in the discussion and urgency stages to the situation and type of debtor.

Positive appeals stress cooperation, fair play, pride.

> *Cooperation,* the mildest appeal, caters to one's desire to be considerate of others—in this case, loyal to the creditor who has been courteous and friendly in asking for what is rightly due him.
>
> The *fair-play* appeal is usually developed by reviewing the facts—how long a payment has been past due—and showing that the firm has been patient and believes the customer will want to do what is right (be fair and pay).
>
> The *pride* appeal should be subtle, not a high-pressure tactic. You can develop this appeal in various ways by referring to what you know the customer is proud of—his good credit record, sometimes the items he bought, or the respect and good reputation he enjoys in the community.

Negative appeals stress the debtor's self-interest and arouse emotions of fear. The individual who cares little about cooperation or fair play may be motivated to pay when you show him what he will gain by doing so, or what he will lose by further delay.

> The *self-interest* appeal usually has two objectives—to show the value of the present advantages the customer has and to convince him that further delay may cause him to lose them.
>
> *Fear* appeal, instead of stressing the value of keeping various benefits, stresses the loss of such benefits (good credit standing or possessions). It also emphasizes the extra expense of a lawsuit.

Your choice of appeals is influenced by the type of debtor and the collection stage. You can use effectively one or a combination of these five appeals in one message.

## Collection Stages

The best way to collect money is constantly to keep after the past-due customer—with gradually increasing pressure—to settle his account. You accomplish your goal by progressing through the three collection stages—reminder, discussion, and urgency—until you receive your money or revert to a drastic step such as turning his account over to a collection agency.

*Reminder Stage.* Messages in the reminder stage are routine, direct requests, and range in number from one to several. In this stage, all you want to do is to jog the customer's memory. You first present the major question or subject, then explain (when necessary), and end the message by requesting action. You don't attempt to persuade by using any of the five appeals. Although some reminders—especially those sent to slow-pay customers—might have a personalized inside address, generally they are obvious processed forms to avoid any suggestion that you are questioning the customer's integrity or ability to pay. They usually range from one or more standard statements[1] (usually not itemized) to printed cards to an obvious form letter on company letterhead stationery.

Shown below are several examples of good reminders.

*Reminder 1:*[2] *A printed form 3¾" x 6½" in size on green pastel paper. A large department store sends it to a customer who has received his statement but hasn't settled his account within the stipulated time (usually 30 days).*

OH-OH!

... did you forget to send the check
for your (name of store) bill? If
it's in the mail, please tear this
reminder neatly in two and drop
it in your waste basket!

(Name of store)

P.S. CHARGE ACCOUNTS ARE PAYABLE IN FULL EACH MONTH

---

[1] The statement(s) following the first one might include a sticker, or rubber-stamped message, or hand-written message that says "please," "please remit," "second notice," or some other short, to-the-point remark.

[2] The retail store that sends this reminder telephones the customer with a brand-new account if he doesn't respond. Long-time good-pay customers continue to receive additional correspondence.

*Reminder 2: A second form-letter request from an oil company to a credit-card cus-
tomer who had previously received a statement and a form-letter reminder.*

Dear Customer

It's easy to misplace statements and overlook form notices.
That's why we decided on a letter to remind you of your balance
amounting to $

The account is somewhat past due and we would appreciate your
sending us a check in the next few days.

*Reminder 3: Printed reminder from a large publishing house to a customer whose
account is past-due. This message might appear as an obvious form letter
on letterhead stationery or as a printed notice similar to Reminder 1.*

When we do not receive payment within a month for books shipped
to a customer, we wonder...

Did he get what he ordered?
Did he forget that the free examination period was for
only 10 days?
Did he overlook the invoice enclosed in the shipment?

This is just a reminder that we have not as yet received payment or heard from you since we mailed your books.  May we hear
from you, please.

If you use humor, do so only early in the series, and be sure it is not in
poor taste. Shultz and Reinhardt, in *Credit and Collection Management*, say:

Humor must be subtle rather than slapstick, often with a wry little twist
appropriate to the circumstances of unpaid debts. A really good anecdote, a
clever rhyme, or an adroit metaphor can be the foundation for a letter that will
capture the customer's attention without provoking his resentment. An enclosure
of some sort may be tied in effectively with a clever or friendly letter.[1]

Humor such as the following has proved effective:

Dear Customer

How do you do?
Some pay when due.
Some pay when overdue.
Some never do.
How do you do?
Balance $ (amount)

[1] William J. Shultz and Hedwig Reinhardt, *Credit and Collection Management*, 3d ed., Prentice-Hall,
Inc., Englewood Cliffs, N.J., 1962, p. 310.

But think seriously how the customer might react to humor. In the first place, there's nothing funny about owing money or trying to collect money. Furthermore, what is funny to you might not be funny to another person. Four devices that have proved ineffective (and annoying to some people) are:

1. The upside-down message saying the collection manager is so upset that he wrote the letter upside down
2. The letter with a completely blank body, the message appearing only in the postscript.
3. The message that begins "Maybe you've heard this one: Why are little birds so sad in the morning? Answer: Because their little bills are all 'over-dew.' It may remind you that we have a little bill that is overdue. If you feed it a check . . . ."
4. The "humorous" reminder that reads:

```
Dear Customer:

We have done more for you than your own mother.  We have
carried your unpaid account for 12 months.

Please send your check for $ (amount) in the next few days.
```

In general, it is best to avoid using humor in collections unless you are sure it will be inoffensive.

*Discussion Stage.* When the customer does not respond to the early reminders you send him,[1] you progress from the routine-request pattern into the discussion stage. Here you begin to personalize your letters by using an inside address and addressing the customer by name. These letters (which range in number from two to five or more) usually begin with the mildest of the appeals—cooperation—and progress to the next to the strongest—self-interest appeal. In these personal messages you want to break the silence the customer has maintained. Ask him what's wrong; ask why he hasn't replied, and repeat your request for payment. Throughout convey your sincere interest in the customer and your willingness to help him.

Shown below is one example of each of the first four appeals you'll use in the discussion stage. In actual practice you can use one or more appeals in one letter.

*Letter 1: Cooperation appeal*

```
Dear Mrs. Wagner

All of us forget things at times.  We're wondering if that's
what has happened to your account with us.  Part of your
overdue balance of $ (amount) dates back to last (month).
```

---

[1] Whenever the customer replies to a collection inquiry, the collection department ceases sending the rest of its series. Instead he gets individual treatment.

We are sure you will want to cooperate with us in clearing up this indebtedness in order to maintain your good credit record.

May we have your remittance soon?

*Letter 2: Fair-play appeal.*

Dear Mr. Denman

If you and I could meet in person and shake hands, I'm sure that the first thing that would come to your mind would be the $55 you owe me.

And I believe that you would be fair enough to speak about it, perhaps to explain why you haven't paid up as yet.

Then don't you think it only fair to ask you either to pay this bill now, or to sit down and tell me why you haven't taken care of it?

I certainly want to be fair with you. I think I have been. And I'm sure that you want to be equally fair with me. Am I right, Mr. Denman?

*Letter 3: Pride appeal*

Dear Mr. Gates

When we opened a charge account for you it was because of your good credit standing. Such a credit record is something to be proud of, and we are sure you are proud of it.

Surely you do not wish to do anything which is likely to affect your good reputation. Yet a part of your overdue balance on our books dates back to last (month).

The total amount due is $ (amount). Keep your good credit reputation because it's a very valuable possession. All that's necessary is a payment or an explanation by return mail.

*Letter 4: Self-interest appeal.*

Dear Mr. Jackson

Just how valuable is your credit rating to you?

If you possess a good rating, you will be able to make purchases on a charge basis whenever necessary. You will be able to buy expensive items without paying the entire cost in cash

at the time of purchase. If an emergency arises, your credit
will stand you in good stead. Cash will not be necessary to
obtain what you need.

On the other hand, if your record in various places shows you
as a poor credit risk, this valuable possession of credit will
be lost. Other creditors will press for payment. You are
likely to be subjected to the unpleasantness of drastic collection measures. In addition to the present effect, your
credit reputation will follow you wherever you go. It will
take many years to restore your good rating. You may be
deprived of items you would like to purchase, because of the
necessity for paying cash.

These are facts. We mention them only so that you will not
take lightly the possible loss of your credit which may follow
unless your account with us is paid.

It is still possible to salvage your credit reputation. The
first step is to pay this long overdue account, amounting to
$ (amount). If you cannot pay it all immediately, you will
find us willing to discuss a definite arrangement to take care
of it. The next step is up to you.

The four letters above progress from a mild appeal of cooperation to a
persuasive appeal of self-interest. Also, the opening in Letter 1 is much more
serious than that in Letter 1, and Letter 4 devotes greater length to discussion
than do the other three messages. Cooperation and fair-play appeals are
effective only when you're talking to an individual who considers the welfare
of others. Once you get no response by using these appeals, you should concentrate on the one idea that will probably concern the customer—his credit
reputation. In the pride appeal you speak positively about his credit reputation; in the self-interest appeal you tell him what will happen to that reputation should he not settle his account.

*Urgency Stage.* The last stage in a collection series demands the money
or says you must resort to drastic action such as turning the account over to a
collection agency or repossessing. You should still not use threats—merely tell
the customer you have a company policy to turn over any account that becomes seriously past due (usually 90 days). You don't *want* to take this drastic
action, but you can't stop it unless he does his part—pay or explain. Even
though you might feel exasperated and annoyed with the individual, you
won't help your cause by showing anger, preaching, or using insulting, cutting
remarks.

The letters in the urgency stage follow the persuasive request pattern and
use the strongest of the five appeals—fear. They mention the unfortunate
consequences of collection enforcement and what the drastic action may mean
to the individual. To offset the negativeness of this appeal to fear, it is often

desirable to include at least one positive appeal—to give the customer a chance to avoid the drastic action. The action request is firm and definite about the amount the borrower must send and the office to which he will send it.

As the following examples illustrate, you can use one or two messages in the urgency stage. If two, the first one doesn't set a date for the drastic action, but the final message *always* sets the date.

**Message 1:** *First of two messages in the urgency stage.*

> Dear Mr. Tittle
>
> The time has come when we must write the kind of letter we dislike very much. In our previous letters we said about everything we could think of in urging you to pay your long overdue bill, which is now $355.70.
>
> But you have made no replies to any of our requests.
>
> The only thing left for us to do is to turn your account over to our attorney for collection. But we don't want to do this without giving you one last chance to write and let us know your side of the story.
>
> We have been good business friends for many years, Mr. Tittle. Please don't make it necessary for us to terminate our friend-ship in such an unpleasant way. Write us immediately—or better still, send us your check for at least a part of your bill. But do it without delay, please!

If you are using only one letter in this collection stage, you can still use Message 1, adding the following paragraph before the final one:

> For that reason we will delay action for five days—until July 22—before turning your account over to Smith, Smythe, Smothers, and Smuts.

**Message 2:** *Final letter that sets a date.*

> Dear Mr. Hittler
>
> Your account has just been referred to me, marked for "final action."
>
> Because it is the policy of this company that every contact with our customers shall be one of courteous interest in their behalf, I am writing you this letter as a last appeal that you mail us your check for $623.02, or call personally to see us. I have withheld any action on your account and feel sure we can work out some mutually satisfactory arrangement for settle-ment.

I shall hold your account on my desk for 10 days hoping that you will attend to it at once. Unless I hear from you within that time, I shall have no alternative but to assign your account for collection. I anticipate you will not force me to take a step that would have such a serious effect upon your credit reputation.

**Message 3:** *Final message that sets a date. This printed form goes to customers who live within the city which is within the jurisdiction of the specific credit bureau.*

---

**No.** 1982

### Please Read This Carefully

_____ 19 _____

To: _____

_____
       *Address*        *City*        *State*

It is the purpose of this notice to inform you, as a matter of courtesy, of our intention to assign your account to the **COLLECTION DEPT.,** **(CITY) CREDIT BUREAU** for collection unless your remittance is in our hands on or before _____ 19_____

This can be avoided if **PAYMENT IN FULL** is made on or before the above date, but you must **ACT WITHOUT DELAY.**

The amount is $_____

_____ (CREDITOR)

_____ (ADDRESS)

By_____

### Pay your bills in full TODAY So that your Credit will be good TOMORROW

---

## Length of Collection Series

Most firms—especially large ones—have more than one collection series so that a customer who has been delinquent previously does not receive the same messages he received earlier. Or, if the firm has only one series, it can skip several messages for a chronic delinquent, and reach the urgency stage more quickly. This procedure not only shortens the length of the collection series, but also surprises the habitually late payer who probably remembers the order and number of messages he received on a previous occasion.

The number and frequency of messages and the degree of insistence within each series depend upon: (1) whether the customer is a good, fair, or poor risk; (2) whether he is engaged in a seasonal occupation (like farming) and receives payment only once or twice yearly; and (3) whether the collection series represents a retail or mercantile business. The time allowed slow-pay customers by manufacturers or wholesalers is generally short because terms of sale have been definitely stated and customers have a fairly clear appreciation of the importance of a good credit standing. Retailers, on the other hand, might use longer collection series because they often don't explain clearly their terms of sale to customers or because the customers are not as familiar with business practice as wholesale customers.

At this point, it will be helpful to explain the differences among the three types of risks—good-pay, fair-pay, and poor-pay.

> The good-pay customer pays on time, and needs little or no reminding. For those few times when he needs reminding, you can usually collect payments after pleasant reminder messages using the direct-request pattern—without appeals. On the rare occasion when his account becomes past due, you will persuade him through a positive appeal to cooperation or fair play.

> The fair-pay customer always pays, but he is slow and often needs reminders and persuasion. Your attitude toward him should be firmer and your reminders are more frequent. He may be a very respected, honest person in your community, but perhaps he is absent-minded or just disorganized in his paying and business habits. Like the good-pay customer, he will respond to positive appeals; but instead of motivating him by appeals to cooperation and fair play, you may have to use pride and self-interest appeals. Because he procrastinates, he sometimes is two or more payments past due, and you may have to caution him about the risks involved—and occasionally bring in a mild negative appeal.

> The poor-pay customer is repeatedly late in his payments. He has probably received numerous collection notices before, not only from your firm, but from other creditors. He ignores the pleasant, mild reminders because he knows there is still time to delay before his creditors get tough. Sermons and scolding bore him. For this type of individual you include a few surprises and shocks—and more negative than positive appeals. You must persuade him to pay because not doing so will be to his detriment.

The table below shows how the number of messages can be related to the use and type of appeal. With this illustration as a springboard you'll then see how you, as a collection manager, can lengthen or shorten the collection series for the three types of credit risks.

| *Stage* | *Message* | | | *Appeal* |
|---|---|---|---|---|
| | first statement — itemized | | | |
| | (sent just before or at time account is due) | | | |
| Reminder | one or more statement(s) — unitemized reminder(s) | | | none |
| Discussion | letter | ⎱ | | cooperation |
| | letter | | asks | fair-play |
| | letter | | what's | pride |
| | letter | ⎰ | wrong | self-interest |
| Urgency | letter | (no date mentioned) | | fear |
| | letter | (date set) | | fear |

You'll send more messages to a good credit risk than you'll send to a fair or poor risk. For example, if you send 10 notices (including 3 statements) to a *good risk*, you might send 7 notices (including 2 statements) to a *fair risk*, and 4 or 5 notices (including 1 statement) to a *poor risk*.

Based upon the number of notices just given above, you might decide to send the following types of messages:

| Good Risk | Fair Risk | Poor Risk |
|---|---|---|
| 3 statements | 2 statements | 1 statement |
| 2 reminders | 1 reminder | 1 reminder |
| 5 letters | 4 letters | 3 letters |
| 10 | 7 | 5 |

Should you prefer a shorter collection series for the good risk, then you'll have even fewer messages for the other two types of risks. For example, if you send 5–7 messages to a good risk, you'll send perhaps 3–5 messages to a fair risk, and perhaps only 2–4 messages to a poor risk.

Not only will you send fewer messages to a poor risk (with more frequent timing between messages), but you'll also use more insistence in your language and be less lenient. For a chronic delinquent you'll probably omit inquiring what's wrong.

To illustrate that the pattern for collection series differs among organizations, below are brief descriptions of the actual collection practice of three diverse businesses—a large department store,[1] a savings and loan association, and a large utility company. Notice that all three collection procedures have several things in common. Each begins with a statement and progresses to messages of more intensity and insistence; each tries to avoid suing; and each avoids curtness, sarcasm, or preaching.

### Department Store[2]

This organization for the first four months uses only computerized statements and duns. The computer not only analyzes and evaluates many different conditions for each customer's account; with the information digested, the computer also automatically chooses the appropriate text from a selection of messages and automatically prints the customer's name, address, account number,

---

[1] The facts for the department store come from a 1970 master's thesis by Richard Craig Anderson, for the Graduate School of Business Administration, University of Washington, Seattle, Washington, entitled *Collection of Past-due Accounts: A Study of the System Used by a Large Retail Store in a City of 500,000.* Mr. Anderson has given permission to quote liberally from his material.

[2] The schedule here refers only to the regular account—not to the flexible account, deferred account, or the 90-day account, each of which differs in length of the series but all of which follow the same format in the dunning sequence schedules. The collection department for this department store maintains 12 in-state and out-of-state offices. The number of credit or charge accounts at any one time varies somewhere between 250,000 and 305,000 accounts. In addition, there are another 100,000 to 125,000 dormant accounts. About 3.5 percent of the accounts that are opened at any given time are written off as bad debts. The number of accounts that are three or more months delinquent at any one time varies from 4,000 to 6,500.

and the chosen letter, incorporating into the body of the letter the exact amount owed (so current that it reflects payment received the day before). This entire procedure takes about two seconds.

After the first four months, the department store switches to manual communications (telephone, letter, and wire) to break the cycle of "no pays" that have built up; and a particular collector in the office becomes responsible to certain delinquent accounts. The telephone call is always the first contact made with the customer following the computer dun series[1] and is used throughout the collection effort that follows. After the initial telephone call, the collection effort follows no definite sequence. The collector uses extensively the telephone with personal letters and wires sandwiched in throughout the discussion and urgency stages.

The collector also uses personal, dictated letters either to confirm in writing what the customer agreed to over the telephone or to remind the customer that he (the customer) agreed to a payment plan and to ask why he has broken his promise. If the collector cannot reach the customer by phone, he uses one or more of the five form letters discussed later.

In summary, the collection series for this department store consists of:

1. Computerized statements and duns that include the first statement, following monthly statements, three reminders, and two letters in the discussion stage.

2. Manual communications that complete the discussion and urgency stages. The store covers the urgency stage by telephone unless the past-due customer doesn't have a telephone; then it uses form letters 4 and 5 discussed on p. 527

Computerized statements and duns are listed here in the order that the customer receives them:

first statement[2]. . . . . . . . . . . . . . . . . . . . . . . . . . . . . . .current account — sent on billing cycle date
second statement[2]. . . . . . . . . . . . . . . . . . . . . . . . . . .1 month late
third statement[2]. . . . . . . . . . . . . . . . . . . . . . . . . . . . .2 months late
gentle reminder[3] (see page 527). . . . . . . . . . . . . . . . .2 months and 10 days late
second reminder[3]. . . . . . . . . . . . . . . . . . . . . . . . . . . .2 months and 20 days late
fourth statement[2]. . . . . . . . . . . . . . . . . . . . . . . . . . . .3 months late
third reminder[4]. . . . . . . . . . . . . . . . . . . . . . . . . . . . . .3 months and 10 days late

---

[1] The company is attempting to change this situation by having a telephone call made at the first point that any account does not meet the requirements of its credit terms and in so doing becomes delinquent. In making the call at the earlier proposed time, the company is attempting to use the effectiveness of the telephone call at the earliest point of delinquency, rather than waiting, as it does now, four months while the "no pay" cycle builds up.

[2] A statement is prepared once each month for every account as of its billing date as long as a balance exists. All financial transactions which have occurred since the last billing date through the current closing date are identified.

[3] These reminders gently remind the customer that he has an overdue account with the store. Often a customer simply forgets he has an unpaid account, and this notice reminds him. This dun is signed "Credit Department."

[4] This reminder points up the credit terms of the customer's account that require prompt payment. This dun is signed "Credit Department."

first letter (discussion stage)[1]....................3 months and 20 days late
fifth statement[2].............................4 months late
second letter (discussion stage)[3]................4 months and 10 days late

## Manual communications (telephone, letters, and wires) include:

| | |
|---|---|
| Telephone calls[4] | used extensively after the account is more than 4 months past due. About 60 to 70 percent of all contacts made with customers is by telephone. |
| Personalized letters | tie in with telephone calls. |
| Wires | used only in the last stages of collections. They have more shock value than letters. In addition, they give the store assurance their message is delivered. Because wires are more expensive than the phone call or letter, only 5 percent of all contacts made with customers are made by wire. |
| Five form letters (individually typed so they can be personalized with names, amounts, and dates) | Only to the 10 percent of the past-due customers who don't have telephones and for situations that apply to uniform collection problems (such as marital problems or notification of a closed account). |

Form letter 1—tells customer to contact the store immediately. It is purposely designed to be short, which gives it great shock value.

Form letter 2—states failure to send the amount due by the date specified will result in the account being referred to the collection manager (rather than being handled by the collector).

[1] This form stresses the belief that the customer desires to maintain an excellent credit standing in the community. It also informs him that the store is eager to assist him in any way. In saying this, the store is attempting to get some kind of response from the customer. Naturally the store hopes he will send a check; but if the store doesn't receive any payment, it is hoped the customer will break his silence and tell what the difficulty is that is preventing him from paying. This dun is signed "Credit Department."

[2] A statement is prepared once each month for every account as of its billing date as long as a balance exists. All financial transactions which have occurred since the last billing date through the current closing date are identified.

[3] This last computer dun—signed "Collection Department"—informs the customer that the collection department is now handling the account. The form also tells the customer that late charges are assessed on all regular charge account balances that are four months or more past due. But it says he can avoid the late charges by sending a check immediately.

[4] "Increasing use is being made of the telephone in collecting, both in early and late stages of the collection process, for this method, because of its directness, often succeeds where other methods fail. One of the chief advantages of this method is that it is somewhat surprising to the debtor and may, therefore, catch him unguarded with small alibis and grievances with which to excuse his delinquency. It furnishes the collector a good opportunity to impress him emphatically with the urgency of payment, varying the appeals as the need arises. Frequently, when the reason for nonpayment is understandable, although the failure of the debtor to communicate it is not, a plan of payment may be worked out, usually with a partial payment to be made immediately. Thus, by telephoning nearly all can be accomplished that could be gained by a personal solicitation. Telephoning, however, is often the speedier method, the more flexible, particularly in tracing skips, the less costly, even in the use of long-distance service, as long as it is used with efficiency and discretion." Theodore N. Beckman and Ronald S. Foster, *Credits and Collections*, 8th ed., McGraw-Hill Book Company, New York, 1969, p. 533.

Example of the dun used to gently remind the customer that he has an overdue account with the store. At this time the account is 2 months and 10 days past-due.

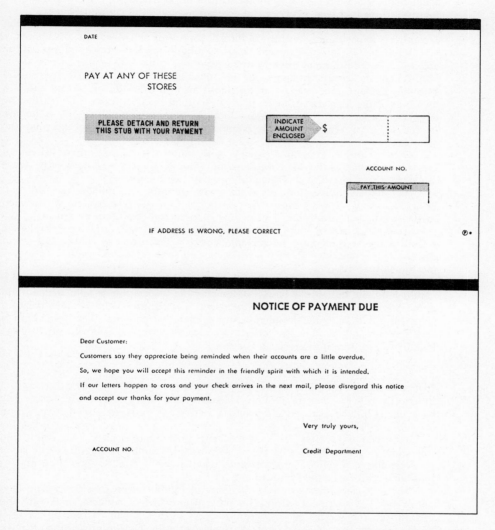

DATE

PAY AT ANY OF THESE
STORES

PLEASE DETACH AND RETURN
THIS STUB WITH YOUR PAYMENT

INDICATE
AMOUNT    $
ENCLOSED

ACCOUNT NO.

PAY THIS AMOUNT

IF ADDRESS IS WRONG, PLEASE CORRECT

### NOTICE OF PAYMENT DUE

Dear Customer:

Customers say they appreciate being reminded when their accounts are a little overdue.

So, we hope you will accept this reminder in the friendly spirit with which it is intended.

If our letters happen to cross and your check arrives in the next mail, please disregard this notice and accept our thanks for your payment.

Very truly yours,

ACCOUNT NO.

Credit Department

Form letter 3—informs the customer that his account is now being handled by the collection manager.

Form letter 4—is sent on the store's attorney's stationery.

Form letter 5—informs the customer that he can still deal with the store; but if he does not, the next collection effort will come from the store's collection agency. (The average delinquency of accounts turned over for collection is eight months.)

### Savings and Loan Association[1]

The collection procedures of this particular savings and loan association are notable for the lack of any firm policy. Even though the association services over 4,500 loans, it doesn't have a formal collection department. The responsibility for collections is shared between the accounting and the loan departments.

The first step toward the collection of a delinquent account is taken by the accounting department. Within 10 to 15 days after the due date of a loan, a first reminder is sent. A second, more strongly worded notice is sent if the account is still delinquent after 20 to 25 days.

When an account becomes one month delinquent, it is turned over to the loan department. An attempt at telephone contact is made by one of the two members of the loan department. If the individual involved cannot be reached by telephone, a brief letter is written. Both the telephone call and the letter are in the form of reminders, with emphasis on the importance of keeping the account current.

Each delinquent account two or more months past due is handled on an individual basis by the loan department. The action taken is generally determined by the association's past experience with an account.

The majority of delinquent accounts two months past due are notified that, in accordance with the terms of the mortgage note, the interest rate is increased to 10 percent per annum until such time as the account is again current.

Accounts three or more months past due are generally given a specific date by which the account must be current. Notice is given that if the account is not current by the specified date, it will be turned over to the association's attorney for foreclosure action.

As mentioned earlier, each of the more serious delinquent accounts is handled on an individual basis. As long as the association is able to maintain communication with the persons involved, it attempts to help them create a workable solution to the problems causing their delinquency. The association is very lenient and flexible in working with these accounts, and will go to great lengths to avoid taking foreclosure action.

### Utility Company (in a city where the population exceeds 1 million)

Practically all gas meters in this city are read on a bimonthly basis. The customer is billed within 10 days, and a 10-day net payment period is shown on the bill.

Fourteen days after the net payment period has expired, the credit and collection department is notified of all unpaid accounts totaling $10 or more by receiving gas collection statements together with two notices. The first or reminder notice is mailed immediately.

In most cases the second or final notice follows seven days later. The final notice bears a seven-day expiration date after which a collector may call and discontinue the service. If an account shows a good payment record, the final notice may be preceded by a special reminder letter. Or the final notice may be followed by a letter. These exceptions are made at the discretion of the collection reviewer who directs the general collection activity.

---

[1] This association has assets of $72 million, one home office, and five branches (it is now planning a sixth branch).

## TELEPHONE COLLECTION PROCEDURE[1]

Because of the important role that the telephone plays in collecting past-due accounts, a brief discussion of telephone collection techniques[2] is in order. The discussion is divided into three parts:

1. Precall planning—getting ready to make effective collection calls
2. Detailed analysis of the collection call
3. Follow-up to the collection call

There are several steps in each of the sections just mentioned. Although the steps are fairly simple to perform, it is important that each one be done in its proper order.

### Precall Planning

The most successful collectors prepare, in advance, as much of their collection call as possible. The following steps should be taken for such calls:

1. Determine if your own company is at fault.
2. Check for previous collection attempts.
3. Check the past payment record.
4. Determine the right person to talk to.
5. Determine a payment plan.
6. Prepare for fact-finding.
7. Prepare an opening statement.
   a. Identify self and firm.
   b. Give reason for the call.
   c. Use a strategic pause.

*1. Determine if your own company is at fault.* The type of information you want to ascertain is: Were all payments noted? Were all shipments made? Were correct billings made? In other words, you should take time to correct any company errors, thus paving the way for the customer to bring his account up to date.

*2. Check for previous collection attempts.* Check for previous letters, calls, and any response to them. The way in which a collector approaches a customer who has ignored several contacts is different from the way in which he approaches a customer who is receiving his first overdue notice. If the collector knows about the company's past attempts at collection, then he can judge whether to use a hard or soft line.

[1] This section on telephone collection procedure is based on findings from the previously cited 1970 master's thesis by Richard Craig Anderson.
[2] Because the telephone and the personal visit follow similar collection procedure, only the procedure for the telephone is discussed here.

**3. Check the past payment record.** Two factors that are weighed when judging a customer's past performance are: (1) the frequency of the delinquency—how often overdue, and (2) the pattern of the delinquency—how regularly overdue.

The customer's history of payment is a good clue to the way he will respond to the company's call and their payment plan. If he has been delinquent only once in the past year, it's likely that the collector and the customer can easily reach an acceptable payment plan. But if the record shows the customer has been delinquent most of the year, the collector wants to be sure he has the customer's firm understanding and agreement on a payment plan.

**4. Determine the right person to talk to.** Only the person actually responsible for paying the bills is the right person to talk with. No attempt to collect the amount owed should be made until this person can be reached.

**5. Determine a payment plan.** This step is the heart of precall planning. Specifically, a payment plan is a schedule of payments which will bring the overdue account to a current status. It is important that the collector have such a plan ready to present to the customer; otherwise he can't expect to bring the account up to date. Furthermore, the payment plan must account for all the overdue payments, not just one or two.

The collector should always think of his collection call from a positive point of view. The payment plan is what he is "selling" to the customer; and unless he gets agreement on the plan, he is just making a harassment call which is both ineffective and insulting.

**6. Prepare for fact-finding.** The purpose of fact-finding questions is to determine the customer's reasons for not paying his bills on time. Knowing this information allows the collector to adapt his payment plan to the customer's needs. One of the objectives is to make the customer feel the collector is working with him—not against him. Good fact-finding questions allow the customer to do the talking; they require more than a simple "yes" or "no" answer. Questions of this type are usually open-ended, and begin with such words as "what," "when," "where," "who," "why," and "how."

**7. Prepare an opening statement.** Such preparation gives the collector confidence, and it ensures that all necessary information will be presented. This opening statement should: (1) identify the collector and the firm, (2) give the reason for calling, and (3) use a strategic pause—say about six seconds.

It is important that the pause be used in every call. Experience shows that if the customer is sincere in his desire to pay his overdue bills, he will offer to pay or he will give his reason for not paying as soon as he knows why the collector is calling him. Many collection calls are completed successfully immediately after this strategic pause.

### Analysis of the Collection Call

The actual telephone call involves the following steps:

1. Identify self and firm[1]
2. Give the reason for the call[1]
3. Strategic pause[1]
4. Fact-finding
5. Bridge to payment plan
6. The payment plan
7. Overcome objections
8. The close

*Fact-finding.* As stated above, good fact-finding questions should enable the collector to decide whether the payment plan he has designed is realistic. The collector must be ready to adapt his payment plan to meet the realities of whatever situation is uncovered by the fact-finding questions. When the collector can say to himself, using either his original plan or a newly devised one, "This payment plan will get the account current, and it meets my company policy," he goes on to the next step.

*Bridge to the Payment Plan.* The purpose of this step is to focus the customer's attention on the collector's payment plan. The following two examples are good bridging statements: "Well, I've been thinking seriously about your account, Mr. Dawes, and have come up with a plan of action that will get your account right back on a steady course. . . ." Or "Mr. Dawes, I'm glad you mentioned that you wish there were a way you could get your account back up there without having to do it today. I believe there is. How does this plan sound to you?" At this point the collector has focused the customer's attention on the payment plan.

*The Payment Plan.* The payment plan must have a *specific* schedule for getting the account up to date. Regardless of who proposes the payment plan or how it is altered, if the final plan is a schedule of payments that will result in an up-to-date account, it is a satisfactory arrangement.

If the customer agrees to a plan, the collector has been successful and can move directly to closing the call. However, if the customer does not agree to all or part of the payment plan, the collector must take further action—namely, overcoming objections.

*Overcome Objections.* Objections are almost always postponements—reasons for not agreeing to the payment plan now. Three basic steps the collector can take in overcoming objections are:

---

[1] The first three steps of the collection call are the same as the three parts of step 7 in pre-call planning and therefore not repeated here.

1. Determine specifically what the customer is objecting to. The collector can't overcome an objection until he knows what the customer is objecting to.
2. Get agreement on those parts he is not objecting to. It may be that the customer's objection only concerns one of the payment dates in the plan. If so, the collector should get him to agree on all the rest.
3. Work out the parts the customer objects to. If his objections are minor, the collector can compromise with him so long as he keeps the plan specific and it gets the account current. However, if the customer's objections are serious, the collector should be sure that the reasons are valid. The collector should then stress the benefits to the customer of paying and keeping his account current.

*The Close.* In the close, the collector summarizes the payment plan and thanks the customer. The following is an example of a good close. "Fine, Mr. Dawes. Now let me summarize to make sure that I have everything straight. You are going to send me a payment of $41.20 on Friday, the 16th. I should have that on the following Monday. Then you will send another payment of $41.20 on Friday, the 23d, which I should receive on the 26th. That will bring your account right up to date. Thank you very much, Mr. Dawes. Goodbye now."

## Follow-up to the Collection Call

The follow-up involves writing down for future reference everything that was said in the collection call. The collector notes the pertinent information on a card and files it with any other information built up on the account. (Of course, if the customer does not abide by the terms of the agreement, the collector must take further action.)

## SUMMARY

A customer does not settle his account for one of the following reasons—he's temporarily short of funds, he's forgotten to pay, he's dissatisfied with something, he's overlooked paying, or he's a chronic debtor. When his account becomes past due, the store puts into motion a collection series. A good collection manager must have the right attitude toward a past-due customer; he must treat the customer with consideration—not as a criminal. The customer is also a human being and should be treated like one at all times. Furthermore, the collector must realize that there are bound to be some customers who will not always pay when they should. And finally the collector should try in every way he can to help a defaulting customer arrange to pay his account. The last thing the store wants is to sue because everyone but the collection agency or attorney loses.

The collection series is a preplanned but still flexible procedure to collect from the past-due customer. It consists of three stages and five appeals. As the series progresses, each message makes greater pressure on the customer to pay. The length of the series and the insistence to pay depend on the credit reputation of the individual—whether he's a good risk, a fair risk, or a poor risk. Contacts with the customer can be by mail, telephone, wire, or personal visits. Messages by mail consist of statements, reminders, letters, and wires. If the collector uses the telephone or makes a personal visit, he should be versed in the proper procedure, which includes precall planning, detailed analysis of the call (or visit), and the follow-up.

## EXERCISES

1. Below are six collection messages that a dentist sent to patients with past-due installment accounts. Each letter has a typed personalized inside address and salutation above an obvious form message.
   a. Evaluate the effectiveness of each message. Pay particular attention to tone, presentation of facts, appropriateness of the obvious form letter, request for payment, helpfulness toward the patient, and proper use of the collection appeals.
   b. Attempt to describe the dentist's attitude toward patients who don't pay their accounts promptly.

*Message 1: First letter (accompanies second statement) from the credit department.*

Please take note that your account is still in arrears to the amount of $_____. We sent you a notice a short time ago, which was evidently ignored.

Inasmuch as we have received no payment for some time, you will readily understand our anxiety. Will you please let us have your check or money order by return mail.

*Message 2: Second letter from the credit department.*

We are sorry to be forced to call your attention to your account again. It certainly is not our intention to annoy you or cause you any inconvenience. You must realize, however, that it is all-important that these installment accounts be paid as agreed. Your failure to adhere to the terms we arranged, causes a breach in the contract that can be overcome only by paying the account up to date.

We dislike using other methods than persuasion in order to collect, and we feel that you will readily acknowledge the fairness of our request to remit by return mail.

**Message 3:** *Third letter from the credit department.*

Please do not force us to call your attention too often to the past due balance of $_____.

I am trying my best to avoid taking any action that might be disagreeable to both of us. This is our third letter, and you can make it our last by paying up.

**Message 4:** *Fourth letter from the credit department.*

Your failure again to pay as you have promised has caused us to seek some other method whereby we can collect the money due us. Since nothing can be done by writing letters, there is only one thing left to do––give the account to our agents and let them force collection.

Forced collections are poor substitutes for prompt and willing payment. For a person to accept services on a promise to pay, and leave it at that, calls for methods which are obnoxious to both creditor and debtor. You will find, however, if you care to investigate, that most of the time it is the debtor's fault. Attachments, levies, and garnishments can always be avoided if the proper interest is taken in the fact that you owe money. If you make a promise––keep it.

After all, you expect to get paid for work you do, and it is no more than right that you follow the same rule with respect to others.

**Message 5:** *Fifth letter—this time from the manager of the business office.*

The whole world frowns on those who refuse to pay their legitimate bills. Why? Because they are the type who live off the honesty of others. If there were no honest people, the credit business would not exist. But it so happens that the majority of people believe that a promise is a sacred thing. There are still some people left who regard honor before everything else.

When you buy on credit, the service or the merchandise is given to you merely on your word. If you are able to pay but refuse, you are breaking that chain of confidence that extends between the merchant and the consumer . . . you are living off the honesty of others.

Fortunately, there are only a few people who have no regard for their own promises.

*Message 6: Sixth letter—this time bearing the signature of the dentist.*

You know that we have addressed many letters to you requesting payment of your account. We have withheld giving the account to our outside agent because we have been hopeful that you would soon find your way clear to settle.

I don't think you have really placed this bill in its rightful position of importance. To you, perhaps, it is just a bill that some day you hope to pay. But to us it represents time, labor, and material invested, on which no return has been received.

I can't do a single thing now except to advise Mr. Sixkiller, our attorney, to file suit and hold judgment, if such be rendered, until some tangible asset appears that can be attached. Sometimes, after the thing has been almost forgotten, this means a sudden and severe embarrassment when you least expect it. Believe me, I would much rather see you try to pay a dollar every week.

**2.** Evaluate the following three-letter collection series from a retailer of furnaces to a customer who bought a furnace on a 30-day open account and had it installed in his home. Mr. Blodgett had received only one statement before Message 1.

*Message 1: Dated May 14, (year).*

Dear Mr. Blodgett

Because of the hundreds of satisfied customers who are using our Faultee Oil Furnaces, we feel sure you are pleased with yours.

However, every last one of these hundreds of people were so appreciative just to be able to buy a good furnace that they paid their bills right away. We note that you received your furnace over three months ago on an open 30—day account; yet we haven't heard from you.

We shall certainly appreciate your immediate remittance of $_____.

Thank you

*Message 2: Dated May 31, (same year).*

> Dear Blodgett
>
> Maybe you didn't receive our letter of the 14th.
>
> In the event the letter was missent, this will explain it's content. Please remit $_____ for the oil furnace you bought last February on a 30-day account.
>
> We know a man of your integrity wants to pay his bills, so we shall expect your check by return mail.
>
> > Very truly yours,

*Message 3: Dated June 8, (same year).*

> Blodgett
>
> Received your letter of June 5th today!
>
> So we "can take the furnace bill and stoke it." Some firms might think it was worth $_____ to find you out, but we are not that easy. If your bill isn't paid by June 10th, we will place this matter in the hands of our attorneys with instruc-tions to sue you for breach of contract.
>
> P.S. Don't forget that we have your letter admitting your indebtedness.

3. Below are humorous or unusual collection messages. Which ones do you consider appropriate to send as reminders? Which ones would you not send? Give reason(s) for your decision.

*Message 1: Below the personalized salutation appears the picture of a man in old, patched clothes.*

> Dear Mr. Reynolds:
>
> You have received some of my letters in the past which were epitomes of that stateliness befitting the true nobility of executive correspondence. That was when I was a dignified Credit Manager.
>
> Time, circumstance, and necessity force me to be candid and tactless. Yes--I am the miserable wretch whose portrait appears upon this page.

I was reduced to this plebian state by being a virtuous paragon
standing high on a pinnacle of patience, turning a kind ear and
an open heart to all who owed past due accounts. Then, one day
not so long ago, those hounds of the Apocalypse, my creditors,
began gnashing and clawing until finally the pinnacle was torn
asunder and I came crashing down into an ignoble flight.

I stand before you in my darkest hour.  In this, my most
perilous moment, I beseech you . . .

PAY YOUR COTTONPICKIN ACCOUNT AND GET ME OUT OF THIS
MESS! ! ! !

*Message 2:*

**H** ere we go again
**E** liciting a pay from you.
**L** ots of
**P** eople do it in

**S** everal different ways, but it all adds up
**T** o the same thing.
**A** mount due is $18.00
**M** ay we have your check
**P** lease?

**O** r, if you find that our records are
**U** tterly chaotic, please write
**T** o our

**C** redit Department.
**O** ur Credit Department
**L** oves to
**L** ook up old records,
**E** nter "lost" checks,
**C** orrect mistakes,
**T** race "lost" books, etc.
**I** n any case
**O** ur Credit Department
**N** eeds to hear from you

**L** et them know what's wrong or when they can
**E** xpect your check and
**T** hey'll be only
**T** oo glad to help.
**E** veryone values an A-1 credit
**R** ating.
**S** o we feel sure that we'll be hearing from you.

*Message 3: Obvious form letter with no inside address.*

Gentlemen[1]

If you'll kick in with a check for $12.50, representing your
past-due balance, you'll surprise our bookkeeper to death.
That will please us, because we want to get rid of him anyway.

*Message 4: Obvious form letter with no inside address. Attached is a real paper clip.*

Gentlemen:

No! That little paper clip in the upper left-hand corner
hasn't been left there by a careless stenographer. That's
Elmer, our pet paper clip.

His sole purpose in life, as you know, is to hold two pieces of
paper together. But our Elmer has enlarged his scope of usefulness and has accepted two very definite tasks which we have
asked him to do:

1. To securely hold your check for $4,286.61 to this note,
   which will clear up that little account we've talked about,
   and . . .
2. . . . by doing so, to bind the amicable relationship which
   exists between our two companies.

Let's get this little matter under the bridge. What do you
say?

*Message 5: Obvious form letter.*

Dear Customer:

The worst has happened! Elmer, our treasurer, has found out
about your account and is threatening to write you a letter!

As a friend of yours, I implore you to pay now before it is too
late! People who get Elmer's collection letters never recover.
We hid the Accounts Receivable Ledger from him but sometimes
he finds it and gets out of hand. If you realized the horror
of it you'd mail your check at once. If you had seen the
pitiful results as we know them! Young men prematurely aged
and strong men broken--babbling in a corner through palsied
fingers. It is hideous!

[1] William J. Schultz and Hedwig Reinhardt, *Credit and Collection Management,* 3d ed., Prentice-Hall,
Inc., Englewood Cliffs, N.J., 1962, p. 310.

Usually Elmer's letters result in 40% collections and 60% suicides. He may have other words in his vocabulary besides "sue," "legal action," and the unrepeatables, but no one has heard him use any since the spring of (year).

Elmer's old mother (who has been in a sanitarium since he was seven) tells us that he was a happy, normal boy until he was five. Then a neighbor child persuaded him to trade two old pennies for one shiny new one. When Elmer found out he'd been hornswoggled, the change came over night. He earned his first dime drowning kittens, worked in a slaughter house when he was 14 and is now treasurer of our company. He is president of the League for Restoration of the Death Penalty and has filed a standing application for the job of public hangman.

You see the situation. I like people and I just can't stand the thought of having Elmer destroy your will to live. So please, for your own sake and the ease of my conscience, mail your check today for $_____ owing to us for your _(item)_ --or you may get a letter from Elmer--God forbid.

> Urgently yours,

**Message 6:** *Obvious form letter.*

Dear Customer

> Cordially yours,
> (signature, etc)

P.S. I'm practically speechless, but could whisper a hearty "thank you" for your check for $131.32 to clean up that balance on your June purchases.

4. Evaluate the effectiveness of the following seven early reminders that follow the statement(s). Which ones do you consider appropriate? Which ones do you consider inappropriate? Why?

**Reminder 1:** *Obvious form letter on letterhead stationery from an oil company (added are the personalized inside address and salutation).*

We know it is easy to lose a statement or forget to pay a bill, particularly if it is a small one.

In case one or the other happened in connection with your account for $_____, will you consider this as a reminder to drop a check in the mail today?

*Reminder 2: Personalized inside address and salutation with a typewritten body on
letterhead stationery from a book store.*

We want you to know that we appreciate your patronage and we
hope therefore that we will not offend you when we mention that
we haven't received anything on your account since we sent you
your statement.

We would appreciate it if you could send us something this
month.

*Reminder 3: Printed message on a 3¾- by 7-inch piece of paper from a department
store. There is no salutation and the inside address below the message
also serves as the address for a window envelope.*

It's such a small amount that you probably haven't bothered
with it—only $_____; nevertheless, we would appreciate
receiving payment so we may balance our books.

*Reminder 4: Obvious printed message on a 5½- by 7-inch paper from a weekly
newsmagazine. There is no inside address or salutation.*

Just a brief note to repeat our thanks to you for your interest
in (name of magazine), and for your order that will bring you
its quick, complete, and competent news briefing in the many
eventful weeks ahead.  I feel sure you'll find both pleasure
and profit in its pages!

And may I add another thanks—in advance—to you for taking
care of the enclosed bill promptly.  I've sent this copy in
case our previous invoice was mislaid or overlooked.

And from all of us at (name of magazine)—sincere wishes that
your (name of magazine) subscription will mean the best of good
news to you!

*Reminder 5: Obvious form message on letterhead stationery of an industrial plastic
company to a middleman. Added is the inside address.*

Gentlemen                                                    $_____

The above balance has matured for payment on our terms of net
tenth proximo.

Perhaps your check has already been mailed in which case please
accept our thanks and disregard this reminder.

If payment has not as yet been sent, will you please mail it in
time to arrive at this office before the end of this month.

Your cooperation in this matter will be sincerely appreciated.

*Reminder 6:* *Personalized inside address and salutation on letterhead stationery from a manufacturer of business forms to a middleman. The body is type-written.*

Haven't you been able to find our "Little Bill" of $5.31?

Perhaps he is in the "Bills to be paid" group, or maybe he is on his way home.  If not, won't you look the "Little fellow" up and start him on his way today?

*Reminder 7:* *Personalized inside address and salutation added to an obvious printed message on letterhead stationery from the telephone company.*

Since you are one of our new customers and we have been unable to reach you by telephone, we are taking this opportunity to write to you to discuss your telephone account.

We would like to explain briefly our billing practices so that you will have a better understanding as to how our bills are rendered and when they are considered due.  Bills are mailed to you five or six days after the date appearing on the bill and are due and payable upon receipt and become delinquent in fifteen days.  However, if there is some particular time during the current month which is more convenient for you to pay your bill, will you please notify us so that we can note our records and in this way eliminate any unnecessary treatment in the handling of your account.

According to our records the statement recently mailed has not been paid.  If there is some question regarding your bill, please call our Business Office at (telephone number) or come to our office at (address).  Unless you wish to make other arrangements, we will appreciate receiving your payment within the next five days.

We welcome the opportunity of furnishing you with the telephone service and hope that we may continue to be of service to you.

Amount due:   $_____

**5.** The following collection messages fall within the urgency stage. Your job is to determine whether each message is effective. In your evaluation, ask yourself whether the wording is too strong or not strong enough, whether the writer is still trying to help the individual, and whether the message accomplishes the twofold job of collecting the money and retaining the goodwill of the customer.

**Message 1:** *Personalized inside address and salutation and typewritten body. Dated February 8.*

Gentlemen

It seldom becomes necessary for us to turn an account over to an attorney for collection. And on those few occasions when circumstances leave us no other alternative, we consider it only fair to tell the customer exactly what we intend to do.

Certainly, you must realize that we have made every effort to be fair and patient in requesting that you settle your December account of $197.20. We have written to you several times, asking that you let us know how we could cooperate with you in getting this indebtedness straightened out.

Your continued silence leaves us no other alternative than to refer your account to our attorney for collection--a step that we sincerely regret. So won't you respond to this final appeal for your cooperation, and thereby avoid a procedure that can only mean embarrassment, inconvenience, and additional expense to you.

Unless we hear from you by February 22, we shall be compelled to transfer your account to the office of our attorney. Please use the enclosed reply envelope to let us hear from you.

**Message 2:** *Personalized inside address and salutation and typewritten body. Dated October 16.*

Dear Mr. Durian

A short time ago you and Ed Taylor registered in our hotel on September 18 and stayed two days, checking out the 20th. The rate on this room is $16 per day. Our clerk, Mr. Newcomer, was on duty (his first day) when you checked out and he made an error and collected for only one day. You still owe us for that, and while Mr. Newcomer wrote you he would have to stand good for the $16 we thot you would send it to us. However you probably didn't give it much thot and perhaps have forgotten it. So we will appreciate your sending this to us at once.

For we are sure you would not intentialy dismiss the subject and refuse to pay.

However, if this is not paid by November 1st, we are forced to turn the account over to the American Hotel Association and they would print your name in all the hotel magazines as one not paying hotel bill which would go to every hotel in the U.S.

I know you are a fine fellow and will take care of this. For we do appreciate the visit you made us and we want you to come back the next time you are in Kansas City. American Royal Show is now on. It's a wonderful show. Why don't you come see it.

**Message 3:** *Personalized inside address and salutation and typewritten body. Dated May 31.*

Dear Mr. Zielinski

Almost one hundred years ago Sir Walter Scott said, "Credit is like a looking glass, which, when once sullied by a breath, may be wiped clear again; but if once cracked can never be repaired." The importance of a good credit rating has not changed today.

The barbecue you bought at Wardman's in January will continue to give many hours of enjoyment as you use it in your backyard this summer. We, however, have become concerned about your account listing that purchase. It is past due almost four months. Because of our satisfactory past dealings with you, we feel there must be something wrong, but you have not indicated this by a response to the other letters sent to you.

Because of your very active participation in community affairs, you can realize the importance of having a high credit rating in order to keep in good standing with the other merchants about town. Your good rating was given to us originally by the Lakeview Merchants' Credit Association of which we are a member. Our agreement with these people requires that we report all those accounts that are seriously past due. Because this is such a serious action, we always wait with our better customers like you hoping for an explanation or, preferably, payment of the past-due account. In keeping with the Credit Association's requirements, we, however, will have to refer your name to them by June 5.

To keep your credit "glass" from being broken, just mail your check for $71.60 to us in the enclosed prepaid envelope. Then come to the store and see the new attachments and utensils for outdoor cooking, which you will continue to enjoy this summer.

**Message 4:** *Personalized inside address and salutation added to an obvious form message.*

To:                                        Date:
                                           Delinquent  $_____

We are surprised that you have failed to respond to two delinquent notices that have been sent to you regarding your account.

If you ignore this third demand for payment we will have no alternative but to take action that will be costly to you and will impair your credit standing.

*Message 5:* *Personalized inside address and salutation and typewritten body. Dated February 3.*

Dear Mr. Hanson

I am in receipt of your letter dated January 12. From your statements, it appears that you feel there is some possibility you may be a turnip. I quote from your letter, "If you can get blood out of a turnip, you will be the first one to accomplish that feat." Now really, Mr. Hanson, you're not a turnip. You have assets and income just like any other normal person.

If you should continue to refuse to make payment on this account, I will take the steps necessary to attach and tie up those aforementioned items.

*Message 6:* *Obvious form message without an inside address. This message appears printed on the inside of an envelope that the customer puts together and uses to send in the money he owes.*

Dear Customer:

You have disregarded the several reminders sent to you regarding the amount overdue on your account and I am wondering whether you realize the importance of making payments as agreed. You have even ignored my requests to call at the office so that this matter might be discussed. Now, two payments are past due.

The agreement that you signed provides that the merchandise is our property until fully paid for. I have not made any attempt to exercise our rights because I believed it unnecessary in your case. However, if you continue to disregard my letters, I shall be forced to proceed with more drastic measures.

I am, therefore, giving you seven days to pay the amount shown below. Our future action depends entirely upon you.

6. Evaluate the following two collection messages. In which stage do you think it would be appropriate to use each?

*Message 1:* *Personalized throughout.*

Dear Mr. Kuper

This is not a dunning letter.

Neither is it an attempt to gloss over a serious situation with fancy language concealing a strong-arm attempt to pry money out of you.

Time and distance make it impossible for me to come to you for
a friendly chat, so I must ask you to accept this letter as the
next best thing.  You owe us $64.25, long past-due.  You have
always paid your commitments promptly.  Therefore, there must
be some special reason for your delay in this case.

I am not so much interested in the cause of this delay as I am
in how we can help you over the rough spot.  If one can't look
to his friends for help in times of stress, who on earth can he
look to--and I hope our past relationship entitles us to be
classed among your friends.

We want our money, of course.  But we also want to keep your
friendship.  I am sure we can accomplish both ends by being
entirely frank with each other.

What is wrong?  What can we do to help you?

I suggest you write me in full, in confidence.  Perhaps between
us we can work out some plan whereby you can take care of the
past-due balance without crowding yourself too much and, at the
same time, we can continue to make shipments to take care of
your immediate needs.

This is a frank letter.  It calls for equal frankness from you.
The enclosed envelope will bring your reply directly to my
desk--unopened.


*Message 2: Obvious form letter with inside address and salutation typed in.*

You must have a good reason for not having paid anything on
your account after our recent letter--we are sure of that.  But
you do not tell us what the reason is.

If we only knew what the situation is, no doubt some arrangement could be made that would relieve your mind of the worry of
an overdue debt, and satisfy us, too.

If you can, send in a part payment with your answer.  Whether
you can do that or not, at least tell us just what is wrong.
Give us a chance to help.  What do you say?

7. As owner of a small-town hardware store, you receive a letter this morning from
Larry Damm, a long-time customer who owns and operates a 160-acre farm. He
tells you his wife has been in the hospital for the last 10 days and he cannot pay
you for $300 worth of supplies that will be due on July 1. Furthermore, he doesn't
have insurance to cover any of the hospital expenses.

He promises to pay something on account in two weeks, and hopes to be
able to pay up completely within a month. Answer the letter. Today is the last

day of June. Damm is weekly financed, but you know that he is a hard worker and that his word is good. You will expect to hear from him by July 15.

8. You are the manager of a swimming school that offers swim lessons as its main service. Nine sessions cost $27. Each class is small, no more than five children. Your office requires parents who sign their children up for lessons to pay a $5 registration fee and the balance—$22—on the first day of the lessons.

Just recently Mrs. Richwitch signed three of her youngsters up for lessons. You had a terrible time getting her to pay the registration fee. Although you tell your customers that if they don't pay a registration fee, you cannot hold a space for them, you do not often follow through with the threat, since people usually pay the fee. Mrs. Richwitch finally did come through with the registration fee, but when the lessons began, she asked if she could wait to pay the balance of $66.

It is now the third lesson and she still hasn't paid. Furthermore, you learn that she placed a fourth child in a class on the second lesson without paying the registration fee or balance. You checked with the instructor to find out how this happened, and he explained Mrs. Richwitch said that the office had told the child to be in the class. The instructor was new and didn't realize that such an action was highly irregular.

You must explain to Mrs. Richwitch that if she wants her fourth child in class, she will have to register and pay the balance. Also, you want to remind her of the outstanding balance. You have tried to telephone her, but no one ever answers. She didn't accompany the children for their last lesson, either. She owes you $93, including the fees for the fourth child, and you want to collect. Write a letter that will get the money and at the same time keep the goodwill of Mrs. Richwitch. You know she has plenty of money because she lives in a very exclusive residential area and you notice her name often on the society page of the local newspaper.

9. You are the credit and collection manager for a wholesale distributor of men's clothing. For the past 10 years one of your best customers has been a small chain-store operation that has five stores across the state. Each store—called the Hiphop Men's Clothing Store—in the chain is relatively independent. The owner is the man responsible for the overall operation, but he hires for each store a manager who is responsible and pays the bills.

You have been having problems collecting from the store in the town of Wasson. In the past, you have had to send at least one letter (beyond the statement and reminder stage) on several different occasions to this store to get payment on a bill. Presently there is a large outstanding bill for $15,000 that is six months overdue. Your office has already sent one statement, one reminder, and three letters and still received no response. You also know that all your trouble in collecting from the Wasson store started when the owner hired a new manager named Mr. Lighton Fingers, and you believe that your problem in collecting is because of this new manager. You also feel that the owner doesn't know about the overdue bill. As a result, you have decided that you will write to the owner, Mr. Thomas Hogue, rather than sue the chain.

10. Your job is to rewrite the collection series that the dentist used. Instead of his selfish, insulting messages in Exercise 1 on pp. 533–535, you will write messages that will include the two-fold purpose of collecting—get the money and still keep the goodwill of the patient.

In the series, remember the patient is a human being with feelings. Include the amount due in each message and try to help the individual out of his dilemma. Don't threaten or preach. Also incorporate the following suggestions:

Message 1: obvious form reminder on letterhead stationery.

Message 2: personalized inside address and salutation with typewritten body. The message (in the discussion stage) will include a combination of the first 2 appeals—cooperation and fair play.

Message 3: personalized letter, but you'll use the pride appeal.

Message 4: personalized letter, but you'll use the self-interest appeal.

Message 5: personalized letter (in the urgency stage); you'll use the fear appeal without setting a date on which you'll turn the account over to an outside agent.

Message 6: personalized letter (in the urgency stage) using the fear appeal and setting the date you'll turn account over to an outside agent.

11. How would you handle this unusual—but actual—collection situation? As a correspondent for a large insurance company, you send a widow her monthly installment checks. On one occasion she wrote and stated she hadn't received her April check of $210. You had a duplicate check issued and on the reverse side stamped the following endorsement:

> The payee of this check by "endorsing it" represents that the original check issued for the same amount and purpose by the drawer is not in said payee's possession. Warrants that said original check has not been and will not be endorsed or negotiated by said payee or by anyone in behalf of said payee, and in consideration of the issue of this check as a replacement of said original check agrees to indemnify the drawer and hold it harmless for all damage, expense or loss arising out of any act or omission of the payee with respect to said original check or this check.

You sent the duplicate to her in an envelope without an accompanying letter. It later developed that she cashed both the original and duplicate checks, and so you wrote her and enclosed photographic copies of both checks and asked for a refund. When she didn't reply, you sent several more letters, without receiving any word from her. Finally you informed her by letter that you were withholding her next month's check but that her payments would resume month after next. Her reply was the following:

Dear Mr. (your name)

I did not get my check for July. I think a large company like yours should pay me regardless. You are a bunch of crooks.

I hope you burn in hell. All of you go to hell.

12. The manager of the Pacific Clothing Shops, Inc., a chain of retail stores selling ready-to-wear clothing for men and women, asks you to prepare a collection follow-up series suitable for credit customers whose accounts have become delinquent. The chain management has fixed a standard credit limit of $300. Your system is to include the following:

a. An itemized statement

b. Unitemized statement with a colored sticker

c. Printed reminder card

d. First letter in discussion stage

e. Second letter in discussion stage

**f.** Third letter in discussion stage
**g.** Single letter in urgency stage
Write the copy for the four letters.

All the customers who are to receive the letters have had a good credit rating but are slow in paying their obligations. In no case does a balance of a charge account exceed $300. Credit terms for charge accounts in this company require that payments be made by the 10th of the month following purchase. The discussion and urgency letters are to be essentially form letters, but they are to be individually typed and addressed personally to each customer. Assume the following time intervals:

**a.** Itemized statement sent 1st day of month following purchase.
**b.** Repeat statement with sticker sent 20th day of month following purchase.
**c.** Printed reminder card sent 10th day of 2d month following purchase.
**d.** First letter sent 20th day of 2d month following purchase.
**e.** Second letter sent 1st day of 3d month following purchase.
**f.** Third letter sent 10th day of 3d month following purchase.
**g.** Last letter sent 20th day of 3d month following purchase.

# CHAPTER 13

# Goodwill Messages

- Congratulating or Giving Deserved Praise
- Expressing Appreciation
- Extending Seasonal Greetings
- Conveying Sympathy
- Welcoming and/or Offering Favors
- Showing Continuing Special Concern
- Exercises

So far, the messages you have studied are necessary in the usual course of business. Their chief purpose is to take care of day-to-day problems through requests, replies, and announcements. In contrast, the letters and memos covered in this chapter are not absolutely essential or required for the operation of a business. Their main purpose is to convey a friendly, usually unexpected, message that builds goodwill.

No matter how large an organization is, one of its main tasks is to build and maintain goodwill. Thus thoughtful persons—especially executives—often write messages designed to foster friendly relations with customers, suppliers, and others by:

1. Congratulating or giving deserved praise
2. Expressing appreciation
3. Extending seasonal greetings
4. Conveying sympathy
5. Welcoming and/or offering favors
6. Showing continuing special concern

Besides being friendly, unexpected, and outside the usual course of business, goodwill messages have several other characteristics in common. Their organizational plan resembles a good-news or neutral message—most important idea first, then brief comments and details (if any), and a final cordial ending (if needed). Like all letters, goodwill messages should be honest and sincere and avoid gushiness or wordiness. They can be sent to the reader's home or to his office. Depending upon their content, destination, and quantity, goodwill messages may be typewritten, handwritten (for an extra, personal touch) or printed, perhaps on special paper appropriate for the occasion or season. Unlike most business letters, however, genuine goodwill messages should not contain statements that try to sell the reader on buying additional products or services. Most people dislike messages that pose as "goodwill only" letters but that actually have strings attached.

A genuine goodwill letter is almost always favorably received, for at least two reasons:

1. The writer presumably is not sending the message because of some business scheme.
2. The message comes as a pleasant surprise, for the recipient doesn't expect it. He knows that bills will come to him if he owes money, but he doesn't expect a thank-you from the seller for paying promptly or congratulations for winning an honor or celebrating a special anniversary.

An important value of goodwill messages is that their effects sometimes develop months, even years, later. Because these messages reach out in a pleasant, friendly way to readers, they are remembered when these recipients want to buy products or services. Especially when competing firms sell goods of almost identical quality and prices, customers tend to buy where they get that extra ingredient—service with friendly, personal consideration and appreciation. Thus, although goodwill messages omit sales talk, they are actually an excellent way to promote business, as the following discussion and examples illustrate.

## CONGRATULATING OR GIVING DESERVED PRAISE

A sincere, enthusiastic note of congratulations or deserved praise—sent promptly—can have an unforgettable impact on the recipient, especially because not many people take the initiative to send such messages.

### Congratulatory Messages

The opportunities for congratulating are numerous, for congratulations may relate to any significant news about an individual's business, family, or personal achievements. For instance, you might congratulate a business executive when his firm has opened a new branch, reached its 25th or 50th anniversary, moved to larger quarters, attained a publicized milestone in total volume of sales, received a well-known award for distinguished service to the industry or community, or achieved special favorable publicity. You might congratulate an individual when he or someone in his family has made a significant achievement or won an honor. Among the events and activities that merit congratulations to an individual are: election to an office; promotion; graduation; birth of a child; winning a competitive contest, scholarship, prize; making an outstanding speech; writing a good magazine article or book; performing well in a theater, debate, or other public gathering.

When you write a congratulation, "talk" informally and enthusiastically —without flattery—as you would in a personal contact with the recipient. Focus on your reader instead of on yourself. And write promptly—as soon as possible after you first learn the good news. The letters below are examples of various congratulatory messages. Letters 2 through 7 are well written and effective. A note similar to Letter 3 brought the banker who wrote it millions of dollars of business in installment loans.

*Letter 1: A stilted, pompous, writer-centered congratulatory note about a promotion.*

My dear Mr. Dolan:

I have just read that you have been promoted to Vice President of your company. It is a great pleasure for me to offer my felicitations.

I am sure your attainment unequivocally substantiates the exemplary service you are giving your employer. I believe you can be justifiably proud of your outstanding performance in the industry.

I forward my heartiest congratulations and wishes for your continued success in your endeavors.

*Letter 2: A revision of Letter 1, with improved tone and word choice.*

Dear Mr. Dolan:

Your promotion to Vice President of General Construction Company was great news. I was happy to read about you in this week's Trade Press.

If ever a man deserved the recognition your company has given you, you do. Your courage and hard work in developing new ways to promote the services of your firm have won the admiration of many, including your competitors.

Congratulations to you—and best wishes for your continued success!

*Letter 3: A banker congratulates a businessman on his election.*

Congratulations, Mr. Malcolm—

. . . upon being elected president of the Westside Lumber Dealers Association, as announced in yesterday's Times.

Under your capable leadership, this organization will reach a new high in activity and service, Mr. Malcolm.

*Letter 4: A manager congratulates a customer for favorable publicity about the customer's business.*

Dear Mr. Kolly:

Heartiest congratulations to you on the splendid progress you have made with your poultry plant! It was a real pleasure for me to see your picture and read the feature article about your new cage house in the November issue of the American Poultry Journal.

Vern Barns has spoken enthusiastically of your model operation and the excellent job you are doing. This article and its labor-saving suggestions have already been filed for future reference in our "idea" folder.

On my next field trip to Minnesota I want to meet you personally and to visit your place.  My very best wishes to you
for your continued outstanding results with Erving's H & N
Leghorns.

*Letter 5: A vice-president congratulates a scholarship winner.*

Dear Earl:

We extend to you hearty congratulations upon your selection as
the winner of the Beakins & Worth Foundation's scholastic
award for excellence in accounting for 197_ at the University
of (state).

Your achievement should be a source of pride to you, to your
professors, and to your University.  It is to young men like
yourself that the accounting profession and the business and
civic community look with confidence for their leaders of the
future.

The best of success to you!

*Letter 6: A customer relations manager congratulates—on a special day—secretaries
who use his firm's transcribing machines (renamed ARTCO here).*

Dear Miss Baylor:

Today--National Secretaries Day--we would like personally to
congratulate every secretary in the nation, because we understand the important work every one of them is doing.

The effectiveness of countless business and government offices
depends upon the skills, loyalty, and efficiency of the
American Secretary.

So - CONGRATULATIONS to you - and all the secretaries in your
organization.  As we send this message, we say "thank you" for
doing such a good job and - incidentally - for using ARTCO
equipment.

Sometimes, in addition to congratulating a person, you may want to send
him a clipping of a picture or article published about him. Some firms have
specially designed folders to which such clippings may be attached with
scotch tape or clips. Printed on the outside cover may be a message like
"CONGRATULATIONS," or "YOU'RE IN THE NEWS," together with the
company's trademark. For instance, the Carnation Company (dairy products)
uses a folder that pictures on the outside three carnations under the words,

"CARNATIONS to You!" On the inside is an attractive design and this message:

> We Read With Interest . . . The attached clipping about you and
> thought you would be interested in
> receiving our copy.
>
> At Carnation we are always pleased to read about those people
> who help make the Northwest such a wonderful place in which
> to live.

Sending an invitation or an inexpensive gift along with the congratulations as in Letter 7, can be an effective way to build goodwill. However, many other letters that begin with congratulations are actually not true goodwill messages, but disguised or obvious sales messages, like Letter 8.

*Letter 7:* *A retail store sends layettes with congratulations to parents of twins. (Letterhead states: "Headquarters for clothes from crib to college.")*

> Dear Mr. and Mrs. Anderson:
>
> May Barons add their congratulations to the many you have
> already received. It is a pleasure to send two layettes for
> your twin arrivals on April 23, 197_.
>
> Your babies will no doubt model all garments beautifully. We
> are happy to send you these "double congratulations" for your
> doubly happy event--with compliments of Barons.
>
> You can expect the layettes by mail within a few days. May you
> have many happy days and years ahead.

*Letter 8:* *An obvious processed form message on a special letterhead picturing a baby and many toys. (This is a sales letter.)*

> Dear Parents:
>
> Congratulations!...for this is a proud time for you. And
> your new baby is going to give you reason for pride for many
> years to come!
>
> To help you during this period of extra expenses...WE
> EXTEND THIS SPECIAL INVITATION TO YOU TO SEE US FOR THE CASH
> YOU NEED.
>
> You are invited to come in with the enclosed MANAGER'S
> INVITATION at your earliest convenience. You can get a Cash
> Loan, up to the amount shown, to pay doctor and hospital bills,

buy things for the new baby, pay old bills, or for any other purpose.

Come in today. Bring the special INVITATION with you. Choose from our several popular plans. Receive the MONEY promptly!

## Messages with Deserved Praise

In addition to congratulating people for various achievements that are in the news, you may also find reason to give deserved praise for good service that has not been publicized.

For instance, you might compliment your employee(s) on exceptionally fine work. Also, as a customer, you might write to a company executive to tell him about unusually good service you received from his employee(s). Such sincere praise, judiciously given, is appreciated by both the executive and the employees; often the sincere compliments stimulate recipients to do even higher-quality work.

Sometimes your praise of employee service must be general, as in Letter 9, because you do not know who performed the work for you.

*Letter 9: A public relations director praises a laundry's service by writing to its general manager.*

Dear Mr. Hagen:

You may be glad to know how much I like your Troy Laundry service on my shirts. Every morning I have a pleased grin as I pull one of your immaculately laundered shirts out of the smooth plastic case. Exactly the way I like it!

For the past dozen years or so I've tried several different laundries. But so far Troy has topped them all. I like the way your employees and machines roll my shirt collars neatly, press the shoulders without a wrinkle, AND open the buttonholes on the starched French cuffs sufficiently so that one doesn't have to break his fingernails nor use an ice pick to pry them open.

Your TV commercials first attracted Troy to me. I'm glad to tell you that I found everything those commercials say is true. Congratulations — and thanks!

Whenever possible, mention the person to be praised by name or identifying number. From time to time you will encounter employees—salesmen, bus drivers, policemen, teachers, and many others—whose service to you is far beyond the call of duty. A sincere note of praise written to the employee's superior has sometimes brought unexpected benefits to an otherwise unnoticed employee. One of many true stories with a happy ending began when an airline passenger wrote a letter to the company president praising an employee (Paul) who had traveled 26 miles in his own car and at his own expense to get medical care for a traveler sick in a Hawaiian town. The president showed the letter to the vice president, who wrote the employee a message of praise (Letter 10); and less than four months later Paul received a long-hoped-for promotion. Though his advancement was no doubt earned through years of good work, Paul felt that a letter such as the one the passenger wrote first brought him to the attention of management.

*Letter 10: Letter of praise from an airline executive vice-president to an employee.*

> Dear Paul:
>
> Attached is a copy of a letter President Jack Doe has just received which is indicative of the unusually fine job you are doing for us in (name of town). There is no question but that you made a life-long friend for Hawaiian Airlines.
>
> Congratulations on a job well done!
>
> I am requesting Bob Cann to make this letter a part of your permanent personnel file.

## EXPRESSING APPRECIATION

Everyone likes to know that his efforts are appreciated. Throughout your life you will have numerous occasions to express appreciation and thanks. As a businessman, you can express appreciation to customers, suppliers, employees, stockholders, and to many others whose activities relate to your business. Likewise, away from the office, you will also have many opportunities to send such personal goodwill messages. Some of these messages will pertain to favors extended repeatedly over a period of time; others will thank for one-time kindnesses.

### Appreciation for Favors Extended over a Period of Time

When you write to established customers, you can express appreciation for their patronage, for prompt payment of bills, for recommending your firm to friends, or for other courtesies. Some of these messages may become part of your regular company policy; others will be written individually as the occasions arise. Often these thank-you letters contain words of praise, as in Letter 1 below; sometimes they also include a small gift or a special privilege, as in Letter 2.

**Letter 1:** *A personalized form letter, individually typed, expressing appreciation for a prompt-pay record (sent once to each customer after a three-year good record).*

Thank you, Mr. Albrecht,

for the fine manner in which you have paid your bills year after year.

Such a customer as you, because of your spotless paying record, seldom hears from our credit department. But the manner in which you have handled your MacDougall account has often been noticed and appreciated. It has also established for you a credit record of which you may be justly proud.

We are pleased to have you as a MacDougall customer, and thank you sincerely for your splendid cooperation.

**Letter 2:** *A computerized, personalized form letter sending appreciation and a lifetime privilege to a preferred credit customer.*

We sincerely appreciate how promptly you have paid your (company name) account each month. Most certainly you can be proud of the excellent credit record you have established, Mr. Juntwait.

In appreciation to a preferred customer, your new credit card is now good for life!! Your card no longer carries an expiration date and is your companion for any purchases you make at (store) for the rest of your life.

Your card will be replaced about every two years. This will enable us to update the number of years shown on your card. Also, it will assure that your card remains clean, fresh and attractive.

I hope you like your new card and that we may have the privilege of serving you for a lifetime.

Though messages such as Letters 1 and 2 are usually personalized form letters—with matching insertion of the customer's name and address—some large companies have found it desirable to send printed thanks, as in Letter 3. Customers usually appreciate even a printed message—unless the same message arrives every month for six months, tucked in with the monthly statement (as it did for customers of one firm).

**Letter 3:** *A manufacturer's thanks for patronage—printed on special letterhead showing two hands clasped and the word "THANKS" at the top in red.*

> Gentlemen:
>
> Too often in the rush of business life, we forget to say "THANK YOU" so that you can hear it, but you can be sure we always appreciate your patronage. It is our constant aim to please and satisfy you more each time.
>
> Serving you is a real privilege and we are grateful for your confidence in us. Anytime we can be of service to you in any way, just pick up the phone and call us collect at 543-2000.

Some favors require special notes tailored to the situation, as Letter 4 illustrates:

**Letter 4:** *A shop owner's personal thank-you to a customer who has recommended his shop to friends.*

> Dear Mrs. Gunnerson
>
> Yesterday, when Mrs. A. R. Wright visited us upon your recommendation, I was very much pleased--both because she had come in and because you like our shop well enough to recommend it to your friends.
>
> You will be interested in knowing that so far nine members of your Art Guild have become our steady customers. All of them mentioned that you had recommended us and they respect your judgment.
>
> Thank you, Mrs. Gunnerson, for your confidence in The Boutique and its services. We will always try to do our best to give you the service you expect.

Also it is good for every successful person to express gratitude to the individuals—perhaps a relative, coach, scout leader, teacher, or former employer—who have contributed something memorable to his life—especially if (as in Letter 5) years have passed since they met.

**Letter 5:** *A professional man thanks a former Army officer.*

```
Dear Mr. Watters:

Eight years ago, a young 1st lieutenant at Fort Ord, Cali-
fornia, went out of his way to arrange transportation for a
young staff sergeant who worked in his Section.  The trans-
portation was for a unique purpose--not for a pleasure trip or
for official duty, but for an education.

Mr. Watters, I want you to know that the favors you did for me
have had a great influence on my life.  At the time you ar-
ranged for a jeep for my use in attending high school classes
at Palo Alto, I thought it just another ordinary event in my
life.  Never did I dream that those twice weekly rides would
become my first route on the road to higher education.  The
diploma I received was the ticket I needed for admission to
college.  However, I needed more than that.  I needed someone
to encourage me and show me the benefits that a college edu-
cation would give to me.  You were persistently trying to
convince me of this value during my last days of duty.  And
though your work was filled with pressure and tension, you
always managed to remain calm and ready to cheer me on.

You helped me in so many ways; I'm deeply grateful to you.
You'll be glad to know that your wise words didn't go unheeded.
I graduated from the University of (state) last June and am now
in my last year of Medical School.  Thank you for starting me
on the road to a better education.  I hope some day to help
other youngsters the way you helped me.
```

Such thank-you messages are an appreciated surprise to their recipients, as the following typically sentimental excerpts from replies indicate:

*(From the president of a publishing company)* . . . I am most grateful to you for your delightful, thoroughly human letter. . . . It really brightened a rainy and overcast day!

*(From a retired teacher)* . . . I can't tell you how much your letter meant to me. I'm in my 80's now, lonely, living alone in a small apartment, cooking my own meals. Though I taught school for 47 years, yours is the first note of appreciation I ever received. It came on a blue cold morning and it cheered me as nothing has in many years.

*(From a former employer)* . . . Your letter was so touching that as I read it tears of gratitude fell from my eyes. . . . You could not guess how much your words have warmed my spirit. I have been walking around in the glow of them all day long.

Letters of appreciation are also due to people who have spent many hours on a worthy cause—like serving on committees, soliciting funds, or helping with an election campaign. To save expenses, a form letter similar to Letter 6 is acceptable.

**Letter 6:** *A successful candidate thanks volunteer assistants.*

Dear Mrs. Tomkins:[1]

During the city campaign just closed several hundred public spirited citizens gave of their time and personal service to do the necessary mailing, telephoning, and campaigning which played so vital a part in the election. It is to you, one of these loyal women, I want to express my sincere appreciation.

The fine work accomplished and the effort which no money can buy, come only from those who feel, as I do, a sense of responsibility for decent city government. I honestly believe that without the many tasks carried out by the women's committee the result would have been different.

Again I thank you for your part in the campaign and give you my sincere promise that I will do everything in my power to carry on in this city the kind of government for which you worked so diligently.

### Thanks for One-time Favors and Kindnesses

Thanking people promptly for any significant one-time courtesy is desirable for a successful business or professional person, as well as for everyone else with good manners. Whenever possible, a thank-you message should go to the person who: gives a speech without honorarium; writes a letter of recommendation for you; helps you win an honor or award; grants an informative lengthy interview; sends you a letter of praise or criticism about you, your business, employees, or others in whom you are interested; donates money, gifts, or awards. Some firms even thank new customers for a first purchase or first use of a new charge account.

Of course, circumstances will govern the length and content of these thank-you notes, which may range from a few sentences to several paragraphs. Letters 7 through 11 are thank-you messages which thoughtful, courteous businessmen and women have written on various occasions.

---

[1] Instead of a personalized salutation, as in Letter 6, a general salutation such as "Dear (committee name) Member" could be used to further save time and expense.

*Letter 7:* *A program chairman thanks a popular speaker—in an unusual, but gracious and sincere, letter.*

Dear Doctor Kann:

At the risk of contradicting the general theme of your talk on
"The Freedom of Movement" at the Uptown Business Luncheon
meeting last Thursday, may I say that you made captives of all
of us.

Believe me, I did not--after noting what was a record attendance for our meeting--speak lightly when I told you that your
reputation as a speaker, a scholar, and, above all, a charming
guest of honor had preceded you.

I cannot resist adding, with all due apologies to Shaw--"What
really flatters a man is that you think him worth flattering."
On this point, certainly--and I speak with confidence for the
club members and our guests--there is not the shadow of a
doubt.

We hope that your future will provide some respite from hard
work and that you will be free to join us again.  Thank you so
very much.

When a customer compliments your firm or employees by letter, you
should acknowledge the praise by writing a note similar to Letters 8 and 9.
Also acknowledge criticisms, as Letter 10 does. A short message is usually sufficient (unless some explanation is necessary), and even a postcard acknowledgment is better than silence. A large, nationally known publishing firm, for instance, sends a card labeled "Post-o-gram" with this mimeographed message:
"We appreciate your comments on (name of book) and the interest which
prompted you to write. If we may serve you any time in the future, please
let us know."

*Letter 8:* *A company president thanks a customer for his complimentary letter about
an employee.*

Dear Mr. Browning:

Thank you very much for your warm and cordial letter of
August 29.  It is really a pleasure, upon opening the morning
mail, to find a letter like yours.

Nothing gratifies me more than to learn that the efforts of our
employees are so thoroughly appreciated.  Many people are quick
to write criticisms, but seldom does anyone take the time to

say something nice. So it is always pleasing to hear from the many, many people who are satisfied.

We will do our best to continue to provide you with the service you like.

**Letter 9:** *An insurance company correspondent thanks a policyholder for his letter and long association.*

Dear Mrs. Dean:

Thank you for acknowledging receipt of our check for $3,032.10 with such a nice letter.

Your plan to use this money to help your grandson get his college education, would, I feel sure, have met with your late husband's warm approval. It was a pleasure to have had him as a policy owner for the many years since 1935, and we are glad that our service can help you accomplish so much now.

**Letter 10:** *A passenger traffic manager thanks a passenger for his criticism.*

Dear Mr. Davidson:

Thank you for taking a few moments of your valuable time to fill out the comment card while a recent coach passenger on our (name of carrier) December 18.

We are sorry to learn of your disappointment in your recent trip. In this connection, we have referred your comments to the Supervisory Officer for his information, investigation and correction.

Giving you prompt, courteous service on every trip is our constant aim. We look forward to serving you many times in the future.

For thank-you messages that acknowledge money donations, the explanation section usually should include a few details telling the success of the campaign or how the funds are being used, so that the donors will feel good about having contributed. If you are an officer in an organization that must solicit donations year after year, appreciative messages similar to Letters 11 and 12 may well serve as incentives for future donations.

*Letter (memo) 11: A plant manager thanks employees for generous contributions.*

```
TO:        All employees
FROM:      John Mains, Manager, Plant 2
SUBJECT:   Plant 2 UGN Contributions 197_
```

On behalf of the United Good Neighbor Fund I thank all of you who so generously contributed to our UGN campaign.

This year, our Plant had approximately the same number of contributors as last year, but a 21% increase in contributions! Our Company goal was a 9% increase. Obviously we have substantially exceeded that amount.

Thanks again for your strong support at a time when it is needed more than ever.

*Letter 12: The president of a civic charity board thanks donors.*

THANK YOU!    THANK YOU!    THANK YOU!

Words cannot adequately express our deep appreciation for the gift you sent in response to our Christmas letter for the poor. Because of kindhearted friends like you. . .

> Many hungry fathers, mothers, little children have enjoyed a special Christmas dinner. Surely they are thinking "THANK YOU."

> And the shabbily dressed—as they left with a "change of clothing" bundle under arm. Surely they are thinking "THANK YOU."

> And the children—if you could have heard their cheers of joy as they opened their packages. Surely they are thinking "THANK YOU."

They are all grateful there are "people who care." Thank you for your generosity and thoughtfulness. You can take satisfaction in knowing that your contributions have helped bring happiness to these deserving people.

## EXTENDING SEASONAL GREETINGS

If appropriate, you can send a seasonal message to customers (or others) near any special holiday—New Year, Valentine's Day, St. Patrick's Day, Easter, Memorial Day, Independence Day, Thanksgiving, Christmas—or any other season that may be meaningful to your recipients. The main purpose of these messages is to extend season's greetings and good wishes, although they often also express appreciation. Sometimes a small gift—calendar, ornament, picture—accompanies them. In any case, the message should preferably be unique for your type of business as well as the season, and appropriately different from others the reader may receive during that season.

Because most companies choose the Christmas and New Year holidays for their seasonal greetings, this section focuses on these messages. Of course, if the type of product or service your firm sells can be appropriately linked with any other special day, greetings sent then will have less competition and probably receive more attention.

Often, originality in special letterhead designs—symbolic of both the firm's business and the season—adds to the effectiveness of the message. For example, the president of a popular firm that sells heating products has his firm's greetings multilithed on a folding card which pictures on the front an attractive etching of a historical fireplace (different each year and suitable for framing). The greetings also include a brief story about that particular fireplace; his complimentary closing is "Warmly."

If a firm operates internationally, a different nation's Christmas custom could be featured each year in the season's greetings. Or if a firm's customers are concentrated in a geographic area where a certain nationality predominates, the greetings might be tied in with an appropriate national tradition. For instance, a bank's public relations manager sent the following message (individually typewritten in green) on a Christmas letterhead picturing a lighted candle in a holder.

*Message 1: A Christmas greeting and gift linked to a pleasant custom.*

```
Dear Friends

Lighting candles on Christmas Eve is another of those old
Scandinavian customs like smorgasbord dinners.  The legend says
that these candles must not be made or purchased for the occa-
sion, but that they must be a gift from friends--or the flame
will not burn brightly.

In tomorrow's mail you will receive a candle from us--to carry
on that friendly tradition.  Along with it go our best wishes.

All of us here--your staff and directors in the  (name)
bank--say "thank you" for your continued patronage.  It adds to
our Christmas cheer to know that we have loyal friends like
you.

We all wish you a warm and happy Christmas and an interesting
New Year in 197_.
```

Though individually addressed and personally signed messages are ideal, most business firms find it necessary—because of volume and expense—to send undisguised form messages. Many send conventional Christmas or New Year greeting cards signed by a facsimile of an officer's handwriting. Some have the entire message written (and processed) in an executive's handwriting on specially designed colorful Christmas letterheads. If space allows, you can have all officers—sometimes even all employees—personally sign your organization's greetings, as in Message 2. Another interesting alternative is to include individual pictures of all employees, as in Message 3, which can help customers become acquainted with the employees.

*Message 2: A form-letter Christmas greeting signed by all 21 employees (message is typewritten on green and gold paper bordered with colorful holly, bells, and ornaments).*

TO OUR FRIENDS:

> SEASON'S GREETINGS

> There are days for sending merchandise
> And days to send a bill
> But this one day of all the year
> We send you just GOOD WILL!

Yes, it is Christmas-time again.  We want to take this opportunity to say "Thank You" for all the favors you have shown us. . . . and wish you a Very Merry Christmas and a Prosperous New Year.

We've sincerely appreciated the business you have given us in the past, and we'll try mighty hard to merit your continued good will in the future.

May you and your family have a wonderful Holiday Season and may the coming year be the happiest of your life.  That is our Christmas wish for you.

*Message 3: A Christmas form letter surrounded by one-inch facial pictures and names of 40 employees (message is printed on white paper edged with a star and sketches of the three wise men bearing gifts; at the bottom are the words, "Serving (city name) since 1919.")*

One of the real joys of the Holiday Season
is the opportunity for the expression of
good will and the exchange of friendly greetings.

In this spirit of friendship and with sincere
appreciation for the pleasant relations we have
enjoyed with you, we extend the Season's Greetings
and wish you Health and Happiness every day of the
New Year.

## CONVEYING SYMPATHY

When a person suffers a serious misfortune, he may be encouraged by messages of sympathy from his business associates as well as from his personal friends. Because they pertain to sad or unpleasant circumstances, goodwill letters of this type are much harder to write than those already discussed. However, in times of distress, the recipient may value these messages even more highly than expressions of congratulation or thanks.

You can express condolence to a customer, competitor, colleague, business friend, or employee. The occasion may involve a death, accident, loss of material possessions (such as a business wiped out by fire or flood), sickness, major operation, or other misfortunes that can happen to an individual. Expressions of sympathy can be shown by cards, flowers, attendance at a funeral, offers of tangible help, visits, written messages, or a combination of several. This section concentrates on the individual messages you can write expressing sympathy.

If you are writing for your company and the relationship is purely a business one, your secretary can type the message on letterhead stationery. Otherwise, use your own stationery and write (preferably not type) what you want to convey.

Although you cannot mechanically follow a set outline for expression of sympathy, here are suggestions to consider:

1. Begin with the main idea—sympathy and identification of the problem (such as accident, death, or loss of business).
2. Add only those details, if any, that are desirable for the circumstances. (For example, when writing to a survivor, you might express how much the survivor meant to the deceased.) Make all statements restrained and sincere.
3. Stress the positive—the good characteristics and best contributions of the deceased or ill person (if you knew him)—rather than the negative (pain, suffering, distress).
4. Offer assistance, if appropriate, but don't dwell on details. Perhaps you will offer to lighten a customer's monthly payments, or move a due date forward, or make your warehouse available to a friend whose factory burned down. Omit such business matters as the amount the customers owes you, how long his debt is past due, or similar subjects which can and should be taken care of in another letter.
5. End on a pleasant, positive reassuring idea, perhaps looking to the future. Below are acceptable messages of condolence.

*Message 1: Memo telling employees about the sudden death of a coworker.*

TO ALL EMPLOYEES:

We are saddened by the death of Thor Bjornsen. Thor was killed in private—plane accident last Friday enroute to a conference. Funeral services will be held tomorrow at (name) funeral home, 1111 Broadway Avenue, at 1:00 p.m.

Thor was one of the finest chaps in the company——always helping others, especially newcomers. He was tops in his field and was generous and kind. We will all miss him.

Thor's family does not want flowers for him; so arrangements have been made with the Children's Orthopedic Hospital of (city name) to receive sums for a memorial fund. Address contributions to Thor Bjornsen Memorial, 333 Ridgeway Road, attention of Mrs. Jackson. Checks are to be made payable to the Children's Orthopedic Hospital.

*Message 2:* *A personnel man's condolence to a widowed customer (whose wife he had never met personally).*

Dear Mr. Jones:

With profound sorrow we have just learned of the death of your wife.

Though there is little one can say or do to lessen the grief that must be yours, we want you to know the heartfelt sympathy of all your friends at Boardson's is with you.

We hope that the cherished memories you have of your many years together will comfort you in the months ahead.

*Message 3:* *Sympathy letter to a business friend whose store burned to the ground.*

Dear Tom

The announcement on television yesterday about the widespread fire in your buildings distressed us greatly. I want to convey our sympathy to you and your employees.

If there's anything that I as an individual can do to help you at this time, please call me (here at the office: 894-6666, Ext. 562, or at home: 445-2323 evenings). Also you're welcome to use (at no charge, of course), our company's Lander Street warehouse (about 500 sq. feet) to store any materials during your reconstruction period, and our conference rooms for offices and meeting places as long as you need them.

All the fellows at the (name) Company join me in wishing you a fast recovery.

If Tom were an out-of-town customer with an outstanding balance on hi account, the sympathy message might have included an offer like the followin to replace part of the second paragraph:

If we can help you by extending your credit terms and the
payment date on your account, just let me know.  I'll consider
it a privilege to come to your aid to show—-even in a small
way—-how much we appreciate your friendship and business
through the years.

## WELCOMING AND/OR OFFERING FAVORS

Some of the good-news messages discussed in Chapter 7—for instance, those
granting credit or acknowledging first orders—include a welcome to the customer; and some grant favors that the customer asked for.[1] Also, many sales
letters offer a favor or gift. All those messages are necessary in the daily course
of business operations.

In contrast, the welcome and favor-offering letters discussed in this chapter are those "extra" messages that are not absolutely essential but are written
mainly to build goodwill. The favors are freely offered, not written in answer
to a request or to sell.

Sometimes these welcome messages go to persons who have not yet dealt
directly with your firm or perhaps not with your department. Among them are
messages you may send to newcomers in a city or state, to new employees in
your firm, or to new "customers" of an organization whose work is related to
that of your firm. Notice how Letters 1 and 2 focus on the welcome and service,
and do not try to sell the reader anything. Letter 3, however, though it welcomes and offers services, is quite obviously an "account catcher"; it is more
of a low-pressure sales letter than a strictly goodwill message.

*Letter 1: A secretary of state welcomes new incorporators in the state.*

Dear Mr. Henderson:

Your name has been listed as one of the incorporators in a
filing just made in my office, and I am pleased to extend a
warm welcome to you.

It is a real pleasure to have been of service to you and your
fellow incorporators in a matter which reflects your confidence
in the continued growth and prosperity of our state.

You have our sincere good wishes that you will find this confidence amply rewarded in the success of your venture.

---

[1] For favorable credit and order acknowledgments, see pages 229–233; for favor grants, pages 237–238.

***Letter 2:*** *A hospital pharmacist welcomes each newly admitted patient. (This letter or card could bear the pharmacist's picture.)*

Dear Miss Blank:

Welcome to (name) Hospital. Although you probably will not see me while you are here, I will be working for you. My function is to cooperate with your physician and nurses to assure you the best in drugs and pharmaceutical service. Here at (name) Hospital we take a personal interest in every patient. We want you to know that we are here to help insure your speedy recovery.

***Letter 3:*** *A bank vice-president welcomes a Navy officer to the area and offers assistance. (A low-pressure sales message—quite useful for business, but not strictly a goodwill message.)*

Dear Commander Dagg:

We understand that you are soon being transferred to the Washington, D.C. area. It is indeed a pleasure to bid you a warm welcome to your new duty station, and we should like to help you make the change as trouble free as possible.

If you contemplate securing quarters before your arrival, let us know and we will send you a list of Real Estate Agents compiled by the Chamber of Commerce of Arlington County, Virginia.

Convenient banking facilities established before or immediately on your arrival help in the transition period. The enclosed map of Arlington County shows you how close we are to a number of service installations. The booklet "At Your Service" lists the many ways we can assist you. The enclosed card of introduction and the reply envelope are for your use either on your arrival in Arlington——or before that time, if you wish to establish convenient banking services before you come.

We look forward to extending you a personal welcome here at (name) Bank.

To welcome a new customer or to let a once "lost" customer know his return is appreciated, Letters 4 and 5, respectively, are acceptable.

***Letter 4:*** *A savings and loan officer welcomes a new savings account customer. (Though paragraph 2 contains resale material, it does not try to sell the reader on additional services.)*

Dear Mrs. Byfield:

It is a pleasure to welcome you to membership in our association. Many thanks for opening a savings account with First Federal.

Here your savings are safeguarded by careful management, investment in sound home loans, and insurance of accounts by the Federal Savings and Loan Insurance Corporation, an agency of the United States Government. At the same time we maintain ample reserves for the purpose of meeting withdrawals, should you need all or any part of your savings; and in addition you earn an above-average dividend on your savings, compounded semi-annually at the regular rate.

You receive the same personalized services at either of our offices—the Mountview Savings in the Southside Shopping Center or the downtown office.

Please call on me or any member of our staff when we can be of service to you. Our telephone number is 543-4444.

**Letter 5:** *A credit manager welcomes back a long-absent customer.*

Dear Mrs. Adamson:

The return of a good friend is as happy an occasion in the business world as it is in one's private life. Your recent purchase here at Baylor's was the first to be charged to your account for a considerable time . . .

and we take this opportunity to welcome you again to the Baylor Store. Thank you for your patronage.

You can be sure that it is our sincere wish to serve you to your complete satisfaction.

The last example, Letter 6, is an offer of a favor at "no charge or obligation" to noncustomers and customers. This message, unlike Letter 3, contains no direct sales plug for the writer's organization and does not ask the reader to buy or sell his stock through the writer's firm. Thus, although the reason for the letter is probably to promote sales eventually, here it is mainly a goodwill message.

**Letter 6:** *A vice-president of a stock brokerage firm offers a free current report. (A small, printed fill-in form is at the top of the letter.)*

Dear Mr. Moore:

I'd like to offer you a Thompson Fynch service that many of the investors in (city name) have come to value highly: the opinion of our Research Department about any stock listed on the New York Stock Exchange. If you'll just write the name of the stock on the form above and mail it to our Central Information Bureau, I'll get an up-to-date report from our Research Department back to you just as promptly as I can.

Then, if you have any questions about the report, please call me at (206) XAX-2222. I'll be glad to make an appointment at your convenience.

We are pleased to do this, Mr. Moore, whether you have an account with us or not. There is no charge or obligation for this service. In fact, the only charge you ever pay at Thompson Fynch is the minimum commission when you buy or sell securities.

## SHOWING CONTINUING SPECIAL CONCERN

Another type of goodwill message shows that you are sincerely interested in maintaining confidence in your firm's goods and services. To demonstrate your concern, you can write various follow-up requests and announcements to customers, stockholders, suppliers, or employees. The purpose of these good-will messages is to get feedback on products used or returned, to maintain the firm's good image, or to help the customer get the best use from your products which he has already bought.

For example, some firms systematically send messages similar to Letter 1 to solicit comments from their product users and maintain quality control.

*Letter 1: A manufacturer of outboard motors strengthens goodwill by inviting purchasers' comments.*[1]

HOW DO YOU LIKE YOUR EVINRUDE?

A good part of the boating season has slipped past since you bought your motor.

We hope you've had the opportunity to log a lot of pleasant hours with it. We're going to ask a favor of you—a report from you on the "good conduct" of your motor. (Or your frank criticism, if you have any you wish to make.)

For close to 40 years our steady aim has been to make the most perfect outboard motors that can be built. We've spent millions on engineering, fine production facilities, and the most rigorous testing any manufacturer can give his products.

But there is one test that really tells how successful we have been. And that is your complete satisfaction, as the owner and user of our product.

Will you please send us your comments? For your convenience, a blue "stamped" envelope is enclosed — and if you like, simply jot your reply on the back of this letter.

Thank you — here's wishing you many seasons of happy boating.

[1] Courtesy of Evinrude Motors, Milwaukee, Wisconsin.

Besides getting comments from present owners of a product, some firms seek to find out—through messages like Letter 2—why former owners returned various items.

*Letter 2: A department store shows concern for customer desires by inviting comments and reasons for return of merchandise.*

Dear Mrs. Gisie:

Recently you had occasion to return, for a $48.30 refund, an item purchased from (store name). Your opinions regarding that item and our service are valued highly.

We desire to provide an adequate selection of quality merchandise and to see that our sales force is courteous at all times. In this instance we are sorry the product did not fulfill your desires, and we want to be sure that in returning the item you received the same courtesy as when it was purchased.

Will you please jot your comments and suggestions for improvement on the back of this sheet and mail it to us in the enclosed stamped envelope? We will very much appreciate your assistance, for it will enable us to provide the kind of service you like.

If your corporation has a large number of stockholders, many of whom cannot attend the annual meetings, and you want to exchange viewpoints with these stockholders, you might consider writing a goodwill-building message similar to Letter 3.

*Letter 3: The vice-president and secretary of a nationwide public utility invites stockholders to have an individual visit with a management representative.*[1]

Dear Mr. Eugene:

Across the nation in recent years, Bell System management men and women have met with over half a million AT&T share owners like you in their homes and offices for face-to-face discussions of the telephone business. Viewpoints have been exchanged, questions cleared up and in many instances assistance provided on matters of mutual interest.

These informal discussions have benefited our owners and your Company to such an extent that visits with share owners have been made a part of management's responsibility in Bell System Companies.

[1] Courtesy of Mr. Charles E. Wampler, American Telephone and Telegraph Company, New York, N.Y.

With over three million share owners we cannot hope to
visit them all at once or in a short period of time.  So, from
month to month and on a random basis, we select a number of
share owners to be visited.

We would like very much to visit you.  I am arranging,
therefore, to have one of our Bell System management representatives in your area get in touch with you in the near
future for this purpose.

If your company is planning to expand, a letter similar to Letter 4 builds
goodwill by letting your customers know you have a continuing concern for
their needs and preferences.

*Letter 4: A department store invites customers to send suggestions before a planned
expansion. (Letter is dated January 2.)*

Dear Customer:

This letter has a double significance.  First, of course, we
wish to send you and your family our very best wishes for a
happy and prosperous New Year.  We also want to tell you that
we appreciate having you as a customer of (name of store) and
we thank you for your patronage.

The second reason for our writing you has to do with our
planned expansion of five floors on the present building.
Inasmuch as our whole aim in this expansion will be to improve
our service and our merchandise, we thought we might ask your
advice.

If you have any thoughts regarding the improvement of our business, we would be very grateful if you would pass those
thoughts along to us.  For instance, there may be some new
departments that you would like to see us have or there may be
some new types of merchandise that you would like to have us
carry.  Or again, you may have some thoughts on the improvements of our physical layout, our lighting or customer facilities of any kind.

We are sure that you do have some ideas in this respect; so if
you would jot down anything you might think of on the back of
this letter and return it at your convenience, we would appreciate it.  After all, we want the new (name) to be your store
from top to bottom.

Any comments you send will be welcome and appreciated.

Still another excellent way to show concern for your customers (and
others) is by anticipating (hopefully forestalling) complaints. If you discover
that your company (or a supplier) has made an error which directly affects

customers, you have the opportunity to admit the mistake to everyone who may be affected by it—before any customer finds it necessary to ask for an adjustment. Those who have done this (rather than staying silent hoping only a few people will discover the error) have usually been pleasantly surprised at the loyalty, appreciation, and fairness of their customers.

Among the many examples of the goodwill-building power of announcements made to forestall complaints, two are mentioned below:

1. Following a serious storm a subsidiary of Bell Telephone Company sent an inquiry to customers asking them to name, on an enclosed reply card, the period for which they had no service and to state how many days they wanted the company to deduct from their phone bill. Most customers complimented the firm for its forthright message (and its "excellent emergency action"), and they appreciated but rejected the firm's offer to reduce the phone bill.

2. A candy department manager, upon discovering after Christmas that about 50 out of 200 charge-customer orders for a certain quality gift-box candy had been incorrectly filled with slightly lower-quality candy than ordered and sent to the customers' friends, wrote to all 200 customers offering to send a free replacement. As the store did not know which of the 200 customers had been incorrectly served, the manager invited everyone whose friend had received a gift box with a certain code number at the bottom to ask, on an enclosed reply card, for a free box of the ordered candy; he need not return the original. Although obviously at least 25 percent of the customers could have honestly asked for a replacement, less than 5 percent did so. All others who replied—including those whose friends had received the "wrong" candy—thanked the store, commented on the good quality candy their friend enjoyed, and declined the free offer.

The managers who sent these messages were sure that the small cost of their letter was far outweighed by the resulting goodwill.

In the first paragraph of this type of announcement you frankly admit the mistake and sometimes announce the "good news" adjustment that you will make. The explanation section contains an apology (if it isn't in the opening) plus whatever details are desirable for showing how the error occurred. Like other adjustment-granting letters, this announcement should emphasize positive aspects, and convey a sincere desire to serve the customer correctly, as in Letter 5.[1]

*Letter 5: The customer service manager of a national oil company announces credit to customers' accounts for an error made by a supplier (completely processed form).*

Dear (firm name) Credit Card Customer:

We owe you an apology. . .and have credited your account for $7.83.

The Hot Tray that was shipped to you in response to your recent order was not the model pictured in the advertising brochure.

[1] See also the example in Chapter 4, page 117.

This error on the part of the supplier of the hot tray has just recently been called to our attention.

Since you did not receive the correct merchandise, we are crediting your account with the total cost of the tray you purchased as a meaningful way of correcting this error. Please keep your hot tray as a small gift from (firm name).

If you would still like to receive the advertised hot tray, simply check the box and sign and mail the enclosed order card. We will be glad to send the tray to you as soon as possible and bill you accordingly.

You can always depend on (firm name) for top quality.

In summary, a goodwill letter is one that you don't *have* to send and that doesn't include a sales pitch or have strings attached. These messages congratulate, thank, greet, sympathize, welcome, offer favors, or show special concern for the reader—without including any obvious sales material. The message plan is direct—main idea, details, courteous close.

## EXERCISES

1. Below are two messages about free gifts the companies offer. Is each one truly a goodwill message? If not, why not? What do you like or dislike about each one?

   **a.**

   The Next Issue of (name of free booklet)

   will be mailed on Monday, October 25. The (name of booklet) is sent free each month to business firms employing three or more department heads.

   Before we address the envelopes for this issue, we want to make sure that our mailing list is complete and accurate. On the sheet that comes with this letter, you will find reproductions of <u>all</u> the Addressograph plates we have for members of your staff.

   Please take just a minute to go over the list. Make any corrections called for. Cross out the names of people who are no longer there. Add the names of members of your staff for whom we don't have plates.

   The (name of booklet) is "different." Each issue is of direct interest to supervisors and managers working with people daily.

   Please correct and mail the sheet today--in the enclosed envelope. No stamp is needed. You and your associates will then be sure of getting (booklet) free throughout the year.

**b.**

Dear Traveler:

We know you will enjoy having this special edition of Pan
American's 197_ color calendar, compliments of (name) Travel
Service.  We hope that it proves to be both useful and con-
venient in your office.

This affords us the opportunity to let you know that we appreciate the privilege of serving as your travel agent.  We thank
you for your past business and we look forward to hearing from
you whenever we can assist you with future travel plans in
connection with business or pleasure.

We handle all forms of transportation – air, rail, steamship,
bus, as well as reservations for hotels, motels and U–drive
service.  Our daily delivery service to any downtown business
office is a time–saver for you and your staff and we want you
to feel free to make use of it.

ONE CALL DOES IT ALL! – 333–0020

2. As assistant customer service manager of a national airline, you need to write a
letter to accompany a lost sorority pin which you are returning to its owner. The
pin had fallen under one of the coach seats on Flight #742 to Chicago, June 29.
No one wrote to report this lost pin; thus there has been considerable delay in
establishing ownership. You first had to identify the sorority and then the chapter
and where it was located, all of which was time-consuming. However, you were
eventually successful in learning this traveler's identity through Joanne Jones,
President, Alpha Chapter at Texas State College.

    Ask the recipient of your letter to sign an attached lost property card and
return it to you. Will your reply be a goodwill letter with no strings attached? Or
will you include some sales talk and look forward to future business?

3. The following message was sent by the general manager of a hotel to all businessmen who had attended a national convention there seven months before. Is
this letter a goodwill builder? Why or why not? What improvements can you
suggest?

Dear Mr. (name):

May I take this opportunity to thank you for your patronage to
(name) Hotel and all of us here sincerely hope that you enjoyed
your visit to (city).

Have you any friends or business associates that might be
coming to (state name)?  I would appreciate it very much if you
would give me their names and addresses on the enclosed card
so that I may send them a brochure of our hotel and invite them
to stay with us while they are in (state).

The staff of the (hotel name) joins me in looking forward to
your future visits with us.

**4.** A letter similar to the following was mailed by one firm to new parents. In this case the father was a bookkeeper. Comment on the tone and appropriateness of this message. Do you think the parents will like it? Why or why not? What improvements, if any, do you suggest?

Dear Mr. and Mrs. Doe:

We're pretty proud, as you know, of the fine service we offer here at the (name) Products Corporation. And we always keep a keen eye out for new people who will contribute to the service our customers have learned to rely on us for, through the years.

That's why we were greatly pleased to hear about a potential bookkeeper who might be interested in joining us, say around the year 1990, . . . name of James Ron Doe, Jr.

He's a bit small to be interviewed as yet, but tell him to drop in at his earliest convenience, won't you? We'll be delighted to make his acquaintance.

In the meantime, please accept our heartiest congratulations on the new arrival! We know that he'll grow up to be as fine a man--and bookkeeper!--as his father.

**5.** Evaluate the following letter; is it candid, sincere, and businesslike, yet also a goodwill builder? Assume your firm is a national manufacturer of calculating machines.

Good morning, Mr. Mardon:

We got to thinking about you the other day, and we realized, though it hardly seems believable, that a whole year has whizzed by since we shipped you the two Model XX Comptometers! But the calendar says so, all right, and we are impressed with how time flies.

Now, on this first anniversary of your ownership of the two comptometers, let's just check to make sure they are giving you the service you had expected and paid for. We want you to know we think of you.

Are these machines doing their job, Mr. Mardon? Do your operators like them? Have any problems with them? Any questions you want answered? Do the machines need a year's checkup?

Just jot down any remarks from your operators or yourself on the enclosed, self-addressed card and shoot it right back to us. We'll gladly help you promptly. And you'll be helping us to maintain the quality you expected when you decided to buy your two Model XX's.

6. Assume that one day six years from now you happen to read, in a professional or business journal, about a former college classmate of yours. He has been chosen to deliver the main address at the next regional convention of a national organization you belong to. You're pleased that he has gained a distinguished reputation as a technical expert in the field—all in the few years since his graduation. Write him an appropriate note of congratulation.

7. As manager of a wholesale hardware firm with customers in three states, you have just heard that Mr. Archie Oltimer will retire next month, after being in business for 45 years and your customer for 15. Mr. Oltimer's store is over 500 miles from your office—in a town not served by an airline—and you have never met him personally. However, his orders have come regularly through the years and his payments have been prompt. Now he has sold his store to a younger man. Write him a sincere message of appreciation.

8. This assignment can be a message you will actually mail. (If your instructor approves, you can hand in your carbon copy and mail the original.) Write a sincere letter of appreciation to one person who has had a profound and lasting good effect on your life. Perhaps he encouraged you to stick with a job when you almost quit, helped pay your college expenses, or contributed in any other special way(s) to your well being and achievements.

9. As manager of the foreign department of Your City Bank, write a congratulatory letter to Mr. Paul Mifford, who has just been elected president of Pan Xenia, international business honorary at his college chapter. Assume any other pertinent facts.

10. In the evening paper you read that Miss Adelle Adamson of the Harbor Products Company has been promoted to public relations director of the company. During the past 10 years you have had many business transactions with Harbor Products and most have been through the excellent, courteous service Miss Adamson gave your firm. You consider her one of those career women who has all the qualities needed for management, as well as personal charm. Yet she has been held back; this is the first time Harbor Products has appointed a woman to an executive position. You personally know of several situations involving thousands of dollars, necessitating delicate yet efficient human relations, that Miss Adamson handled entirely herself, but in each case her "superiors" got the credit and praise. Write your sincere letter of congratulations to her now.

11. You are business manager of the Friedman Jewelry firm, registered jewelers in the American Gem Society. The largest bank in your city has just bought from you 35 of your $150 watches, which the bank will present to its employees who become members of the Quarter Century Club (25-year employees of the bank). The watches will be presented at a banquet two weeks from today. Your jewelry store has agreed to take care of all the service on these watches for one year free of charge. Write a letter of congratulation to be addressed individually to each new Quarter Century Club member, and include whatever goodwill-building material about your store is desirable. Make these people feel welcome to use your services.

12. Assume that you are customer service director for Prescott, Inc., a large manufacturer of silver holloware and flatware. Four times a year the major department stores send your company the names of all the brides who have registered your silver patterns in the stores' bridal registries. The stores also send a copy of the purchases made for each bride. You would now like to send to each bride who has received some of your silver a goodwill letter giving her helpful hints on

caring for her silver. You sincerely hope she will get maximum satisfaction from your silver. Go to a nearby jewelry firm or department store and collect the data necessary for giving her helpful hints on cleaning and caring for silver. Remember, your goal is not to sell any more silver. You are just writing a goodwill letter to young brides.

13. You are the public relations officer for the light company in your city. Every four months you receive the names and addresses of people moving into your community. This list specifies whether they are building a house, buying, or renting. In any case you would like them to know that if they have any electrical equipment in their home, you have repairmen who will come to service these appliances free of charge for labor. The only charge is for parts. You also want to tell them about your home economist who will make house calls to help the lady of the house learn to use her electrical appliances in the most efficient manner. This home economist comes equipped with recipes and helpful hints for household management and she will answer any questions the housewife may have. Write a letter explaining your services and the fact that they are complimentary. If you need more information for this letter, check with your city light company for additional details to include.

14. You are manager of a large sporting goods store located in a wealthy suburb of a large city. Many avid weekend hunters come into your shop. Every year you compile a record of names and addresses of customers who purchased shells and hunting equipment during that year. In the past the state game department has published annually a brochure listing the hunting season dates for the coming year. This year, to cut down on expenses, the state has eliminated these brochures, but has sent a complete brochure to all sporting goods stores explaining the regulations and the season dates. You would like to write a letter telling your customers the season dates and explaining to them that you have a complete listing of the regulations posted in your shop if they would like more information.

15. Write (or revise) a goodwill message that relates to one of the following situations.
    a. A Christmas or other seasonal greeting for your company. (Choose a line of business you are familiar with.)
    b. Condolence to the wife or husband of a long-time employee who died.
    c. Message to someone in the hospital because of an automobile accident.
    d. Thanks to a customer for being prompt in making his loan payments the last three years. (Assume a bank or savings and loan association.)
    e. A message accompanying a clipping you're sending to a business friend.

16. As customer relations manager of the National Products Company, write a check-up letter to all businessmen who have bought one of your machines to be used in their offices. (Assume any machine with which you are familiar.) Your letter is to be mailed one month after a machine is sold—to check on performance and to catch minor annoyances before they become major grievances. You want to make sure the machine is doing a good job for the reader, or you might want to know if the operators have any questions you can help answer. Will you enclose something for easy answering? Make sure your readers understand that your purpose is to help maintain the high standards for which your products have been famous, not to sell more machines.

17. The following letter from an auditor to the office manager of business firms he visited uses a play on words. Do you think the tone is appropriate and the message pleasingly unique? What do you like or dislike about the letter? It is dated December 18 and addressed individually, "Dear Mr. (name)."

I enjoyed the friendly atmosphere of your office during the brief time I was with you this year. Then your financial statements were done and I was on my way--to another office and another short stay.

With 197_ almost gone it's time again for a statement--this time a personal one in which friendship and goodwill rank high.

As I look back over my own accounts I know that many things have been left undone. With the end of the calendar period coming near, it's time to stop and credit them to your account.

I wish to enter my appreciation for the courtesies you and your staff showed me, the pleasure I felt in working with all of you, and the "Thank you" I thought of but might have left unsaid.

Let me record all these, so my thoughts will be clear, while I send you BEST WISHES for a HAPPY NEW YEAR.

18. You are the public relations director for a company that sells electric food choppers and blenders for home use. Each person who buys one of your blenders is asked to fill out a card telling the serial number of the machine he bought and other pertinent information—address, date, and place of purchase. The computer that you put these cards into sends you back a complete list of people who have taken the time to fill out the card and send it in. You would like to send these people a letter thanking them for registering their blenders. In addition you want to give them a free booklet that includes 10 prize-winning recipes for use with the blender. (The recipes were submitted by other customers to a national contest your firm sponsored recently.) They are not in the booklet each owner gets when he buys the blender.

19. As credit manager of a city department store, write a goodwill form letter that can be sent to customers who are moving out of the city. Among the ideas to include in this letter are: your appreciation of the customer's past patronage, good wishes for his happiness in his new home, and a suggestion that he keep your credit card for identification when opening accounts in his new location. You will be glad to answer any credit inquiries about him. Also, though he is no longer in the city, he can still get merchandise through your mail-order service; even a phone call to your "Personal Shopper" will bring him the goods he wants. Offer to send him your store's monthly news sheet about seasonal offerings, if he would like to have it. Though one of the ideas mentioned here is sales promotion, rather than a strictly goodwill idea, you may want to include it anyway because it is a part of your continuing service to the customer.

20. You are public relations manager of a firm that manufactures lighting fixtures. Yesterday you read in *Illuminating News,* a trade journal, that one of your good customers—Patrick O'Leary—has just opened his fifth lighting goods store in Florida this month. The article states that the store is considered the largest and most modern store of its kind in the Southeast, in keeping with the tremendous growth of the area. You recall that eight years ago, when you were credit manager, you first opened Mr. O'Leary's charge account with your factory; he then had only one store. Through the years he has placed increasingly larger orders with your firm and has paid them all promptly. Though your lighting fixtures have had a part in his success, resist the temptation to claim credit yourself or to dwell on the merits of your products. Write Mr. O'Leary a letter of congratulations.

# REPORTS

● Chapter 14   The What and How of Business Reports
● Chapter 15   Short Reports
● Chapter 16   The Formal Report

# The What and How of Business Reports

- Meaning of a Business Report
- Parts of the Body of a Report
- Organizational Plans for the Body of a Report
- Application to a Situation
- Exercises

Whereas business firms use letters to communicate with people outside the firm, most reports communicate with management and workers within the firm. Reports going upward to management or horizontally to colleagues give executives the information needed to carry out their assignments and to make intelligent decisions. And management sends reports downward to give information or instructions regarding how to carry out policies and procedures.

This text has three chapters devoted to reports. Chapter 14 explains what a report is. Chapter 15 discusses and illustrates the types of short reports you'll encounter on the job; and Chapter 16 covers the formal (or long) report.

This chapter covers a report from various angles—its meaning, parts of the body, and two organizational plans. Then you have the opportunity to study a specific situation and see how to develop this situation into a finished report.[1]

## MEANING OF A BUSINESS REPORT

Letters, memos, and reports have many elements in common. Like a letter and memo, a business report has a purpose that determines how you develop the material. All are directed to people who want to understand what you are saying as quickly and easily as possible. And practically all use the same informal language used in conversational discourse—except, perhaps, some top-level public or legal reports.

A business report is a factual and objective communication for the benefit of one or more individuals in the business world. As stated above, a report has a specific purpose and usually goes to a specific reader or readers. But this same statement is also true for letters and memos. In addition, reports provide impartial facts that the reader needs to make a decision.[2] To better develop understanding of this kind of communication, the sections that follow:

1. Point out the differences among letters, memos, and reports.
2. Define the four basic types of reports.
3. Classify reports in various ways.

### Differences among Letters, Memos, and Reports

Letters, memos, and reports differ in at least five ways. First, the formats can differ. Whereas letters have seven standard parts, for example, heading, inside address, salutation (and optional parts such as attention line, subject

---

[1] Previous chapters in this text have adhered to the Rule of 10 regarding numbers. As discussed in the Appendix, pages 763 to 766, you should write out (with exceptions) numbers one through nine; but beginning with 10 you use the figure. Departing from the Rule of 10, this chapter and Chapter 15 use figures in all examples for all numbers—except one. Because of a trend in business toward writing figures for all numbers (unless the number begins the sentence), you can decide for yourself what you prefer and act accordingly.

[2] This last statement doesn't hold true for some letters and memos—such as direct and persuasive requests. On the other hand, an impartial answer to an inquiry can be a report—reporting to the inquirer when he wants and needs to know.

line, enclosure, postscript), reports usually have a different format. (See page 585 for the parts of a formal report.) Of course, memo reports and memos have similar formats; letter reports and letters also have similar formats.

Second, most letters go outside the company and most memos and reports stay within the company. Third, whereas all letters and memos use the first (I and we) and second (you) person, reports can use first, second, or third ("the committee," "the reader").[1] Fourth, reports are usually more complex than letters or memos. Finally, reports are more objective than letters or memos. In a report, you show both pros and cons, whereas in a sales letter or application letter, for example, you show only the favorable aspects of your subject.

## Types of Reports

Business uses four types of reports:[2]

1. *Memorandum report.* A report using memo format, usually single-spaced.[3]
2. *Printed form.* A printed form with blank lines or spaces left for the writer to fill in pertinent specific facts and figures.
3. *Letter report.* A report in letter format, containing all the parts of the letter—letterhead, inside address, salutation, complimentary close, signature area, and reference section—even the opening and closing paragraphs of the body. Only the text part of the body resembles that of a report.
4. *Formal report.* Usually a report whose body consists of five or more double-spaced pages and includes parts other reports don't have—such as a title page and covering letter (see page 585).

## Classification of Reports

You can classify reports at least five different ways:

1. According to frequency of issue (for example, whether periodic or special). The periodic report comes out at regular intervals, such as daily, weekly, monthly, or yearly. The special report involves a single occasion or unique situation.
2. According to origin (authorized or voluntary). You write authorized reports when requested or authorized to do so by another person. The voluntary report you write on your own initiative.
3. According to function (informational or analytical). The informational report

---

[1] The trend today is to use first and second persons in writing a report to one or several individuals. The third person seems more appropriate for a report (especially of a public nature) to a large group of readers.

[2] In addition to these types, there is one called the *standardized form report*. It is called "standardized" because the department or company dictates the wording and order of the headings for the purpose of uniformity. Actually this report isn't a type because policy can decree standardization of headings in all types of reports.

[3] A variation of the memo report with its TO, FROM, SUBJECT, DATE heading is one that dresses up the report by placing the to, from, subject, and date information on a separate page, arranged like a title page. The body begins on the following page. This variation of a memo report is sometimes called a short report. Its body usually contains fewer than five pages.

merely presents the facts. It doesn't attempt to analyze, interpret, draw conclusions, or recommend. The analytical report breaks the whole into parts
and interprets or shows how they relate to each other. It also makes conclusions and/or recommendations.

4. According to format (formal or informal). The formal report includes some
or all of the following parts[1] (always the body, of course):

   **a.** Cover
   **b.** Title fly—blank sheet of paper between cover and title page
   **c.** Title page
   **d.** Letter of transmittal
   **e.** Table of contents
   **f.** Table of tables
   **g.** Synopsis, abstract, or summary
   **h.** Body (introduction, text, and terminal section)
   **i.** Appendix
   **j.** Bibliography

The informal report doesn't have the prefatory parts (a to g) above, and
usually has no bibliography. Examples include the printed form, the memo
report, and the letter report—all discussed in the next chapter. But the
informal report should include an appendix when an appendix serves a
useful purpose.

5. According to subject. All reports can be classified many ways according to the
subject—marketing reports, production reports, personnel reports, financial
reports, insurance reports, etc.

## PARTS OF THE BODY OF A REPORT

The most distinguishing feature of a report is its body which includes (or
implies) three parts—introduction, text, and terminal section.

Before you delve into these three parts, however, you need to clarify the
difference between a memo and a memo report. The previous chapters on
letters often referred to messages that had a different format (to-from-subject-
date memo) rather than the conventional letter setup with the inside address,
salutation, and so forth. It was appropriate to discuss the memo message in
the chapters devoted to letters because the body of this message resembles the
organizational pattern of a letter; it requests something or conveys either good
or bad news. As a contrast to a memo, the body of a report consists of three
parts—introduction, text, and terminal section.

---

[1] Some texts mention five other parts—letter of authorization, letter of acceptance, letter of approval,
acknowledgments, and index. Because these five parts are used so infrequently—usually only in
lengthy reports of a public nature—they're not considered here as part of the bound formal report
for business. In fact, most formal business reports don't include all 10 of the above-mentioned parts.
The chapter on formal reports discusses the various parts in detail.

## Introduction

The purpose of the introduction is to orient the reader so that he can better understand the rest of the report—it permits the reader and writer to get together in a huddle at the beginning and agree on certain ground rules. It is here that both sides clearly understand the purpose of the report, definition of terms, manner of developing the report, and other elements discussed below—even before the reader begins with the details found in the text.

Keep in mind that there should be no mystery connected to the report. You want to show the big picture to the reader before you begin to give him the details. In a letter report or memo report, the big picture includes revealing at least the subject being discussed (either implied or expressed) and the purpose of the report. A statement of the results in the introduction also helps —and you can justifiably include this element if the terminal section follows the text and it is psychologically sound to reveal the answer to your reader(s)[1] before you prove your point. In a longer report all three of these elements— subject, purpose, and statement of the results should appear in the introduction or prefatory section before the text itself.

Elements that can go into the introduction of reports are:

Authorization
Subject
Problem
Purpose
Scope
Limitations
Methodology and/or sources used
Background
Definition of terms
Statement of the results
Plan of presentation

Naturally you use only the appropriate mixture of these 11 elements to achieve the purpose of the introduction—so the reader will better understand the rest of the report. It is not true that the more elements you have in the introduction, the better or stronger it will be. Include only those elements that accomplish the task at hand—orienting the reader. A brief explanation of the 11 elements follows:

> *1. Authorization* tells the name of the person (if any) who asked the writer to tackle the report. If no one did (as in a voluntary report), then this introductory element doesn't appear. But when you do include the authorization, present it in conversational language—such as "as you requested" or "as Mr. Jones, our president, authorized" rather than the stiff, artificial language of yesteryears—such as "pursuant to your request."

---

[1] A later section in this chapter explains the two major organizational patterns—which place the terminal section either before or after the discussion.

**2.** *Subject* is one element that you can usually get across to the reader by implication, since a clear statement of the purpose will generally identify the subject being discussed. But when the purpose, problem, or another introductory element doesn't clarify the subject, identify it.

**3.** *Problem* is usually defined in the early portion of the introduction. In fact, many introductions begin with the problem and then proceed with the purpose—which is often determined by the problem. For example, assume that the problem is that your organization is experiencing too great a turnover of employees. Then the purpose of the assignment and of the report itself—to find out how to keep the new employees once they have been hired—stems from the problem.

**4.** *Purpose* is the one element that must appear in every introduction. Furthermore, it is the most important single element because it determines what the writer includes in the report. You must clearly get across to the reader what the purpose is. Language such as "The purpose of this report is . . ." neatly does the job—there can be no misunderstanding in the reader's mind regarding what the writer means.

**5.** *Scope* relates to the boundary of the investigation and hence of the report. If you are finding out by questionnaire what married women customers between 19 and 30 years of age with three or more children think about something—that's your scope or boundary. You don't consider anyone else.

**6.** *Limitations* refers to limitations such as time, money, research assistance, or available data. Without sounding negative, the writer should mention those factors that held him back from performing as he might have if the restrictions didn't exist.

**7.** *Methodology and/or sources used* means, respectively, the method(s) of collecting information and the origin (source) of that information. Making a questionnaire survey is the method while the source comprises the replies from the individuals who filled out and returned usable questionnaires.

If you are writing an informational report of your own experience, you are your own source you relied on for the statements made in the report. But, if you leaned on other sources, you state them. You well know that a fact, figure, or statement is only as good as its source. For this year's population of your city, you don't rely on 1940 or 1950 census when more recent figures are available. Mr. X, an authority in the field, is much more reliable a source than Mr. Y, who is a novice in the field.

You can use any of four methods to collect material for a report. The first one listed below (library) is considered secondary data (data already in existence). The other three are primary data (new material).

**a.** Library—information from any publication already in print—book, magazine, newspaper, pamphlet, or government document

**b.** Survey—information from people by mail, telephone, or in person

**c.** Observation—information only by observing—such as counting cars in the parking lot at different hours of the day, observing the content in a housewife's refrigerator or on her kitchen shelves, or noticing the mannerisms of individuals as they approach the cashier to pay their check

**d.** Experiment—information through comparing two groups in which all factors are the same except "experimenting" with one variable factor. This method is common in measuring effectiveness of advertising and media.

8. *Background* (or history) of the situation being investigated is sometimes included if the reader needs the information to grasp the overall picture. But include only enough of the past so the reader clearly understands the present discussion; emphasis throughout the report should be on the findings or results.

9. *Definition of terms* is sometimes vital. For example, "marketing" in the academic sense means "the transfer of goods and services from producer to consumer." But to the average businessman, the term means "selling." If the report writer uses any term that has several possible interpretations, he needs to tell the reader the exact meaning he has in mind.

   Actually you can define terms three different places within a report— in the introduction, in a glossary at the end of the report, or within the text of the report. The introduction is the best place when you have only a few (say one to three) terms to define and the meaning dominates throughout the entire report. If you have many definitions, a glossary is the best. Defining each word as you develop the text is also quite acceptable— especially when the words don't carry the impact of those defined in the introduction—when the discussion of each word being defined doesn't prevail throughout the whole report.

10. *Statement of the results* in the introduction tells the reader at the beginning the writer's decision—whether or not to buy, which machine is the best, who is his choice of applicant. Then as the reader reads the details in the text, he knows how the ideas fit together. This element is appropriate in the introduction only when the body of the report begins with the introduction and ends with the terminal section.

11. *Plan of presentation* is an ideal way to end the introduction in a long or formal report. This element isn't as necessary in a short report—for example, one of a single page—because its function isn't as necessary. The plan of presentation tells the reader in what broad areas (major divisions) the writer is developing the text.

## Text

In the text or discussion you develop the necessary details the reader needs to know—the steps that led to the results and at the same time prove what you conclude or recommend in the terminal section.

As with letters and memos, you continue to apply the seven writing principles. *Especially important are clarity of meaning and conciseness.* As a rule, you'll use informal language so that your reader can clearly understand what you're saying with the least effort on his part. Avoid technical expressions if they will be confusing. Also avoid wordiness—the reader doesn't want to wade through any more information than necessary to find out what you're saying to him.

Although the next two chapters discuss additional facts about the text of a report, coverage here includes the following three areas so that you can better understand the development of the teller report on pages 593 through 601.

Organize the text carefully
Use headings as directional signals
Organize many figures into an understandable table

*Organize the text carefully.* One of the most challenging tasks in writing a report is to decide upon the best way to divide (organize) the mass of details into major sections of the text. Many short reports permit a division into two main sections—"present situation" followed by "proposed solution." Using this method, the outline for the report breaks down into its component parts as shown below:

Introduction
Present situation  }
Proposed solution  }  (major divisions of the text)
Terminal section      (summary, conclusions, or recommendations)

Obviously you can't use present-and-proposed headings for all reports. But you can develop and arrange the mass of data in the text in one of the following ways:

1. **By criteria that measure what you're considering.** For example, if you are determining which of three girls makes the best teller, your major sections of the text should be the criteria or factors you look for in a competent teller.
2. **By order of time.** Programs, agenda, minutes of a meeting or convention, and writeups of a procedure follow this arrangement.
3. **By order of space.** Real estate description of a house, for example, follows this pattern. The realtor first describes the outside, then the inside. For the interior he first describes the living room, then the dining room, etc.
4. **By order of importance.** First you present the most important ideas or arguments and descend to the least important points.
5. **By order of familiarity.** Always go from the simple or familiar to the complex or unfamiliar because the reader can comprehend better what he knows than what he doesn't know. Going from the present situation to the proposed also fits into this category.

*Use headings as directional signals.* Look upon headings as road signs—such as those on the highway. When they help direct the reader through the discussion, by all means use them. The boxed material on pages 590–591 shows the placement and style of the five degrees of headings you may need to use in short and long reports.

Parallel construction—using the same grammatical form—that is, all nouns, or all phrases, or all clauses—is important in writing headings. Also all the major sections of the text should be of the same degree or level of importance. If one of the main sections has two or more subdivisions, then all the subdivisions under that section should be parallel to one another—but not necessarily parallel with its main heading. The following outline of the first part of the present chapter illustrates this point.[1] Notice that sub-divisions of "Meaning of a Business Report" and "Text" are parallel with their own subdivisions but not parallel with subdivisions of the other major heading.

## THE WHAT AND HOW OF BUSINESS REPORTS

Meaning of a Business Report

Differences among Letters, Memos, and Reports

Types of Reports

Classification of Reports

Parts of the Body of a Report

Introduction

Text

   Organize the Text Carefully

   Use Headings as Directional Signals

   Organize Many Figures into an Understandable Table

---

### DEGREES OF HEADINGS FOR REPORTS

#### FIRST-DEGREE HEADING

Use first-degree headings for a report that requires three or more degrees of heading. When this situation exists for a long report, the style of heading shown above (centered and in all caps) is ideal for the introduction, each main division of the text, and the terminal section. (Rarely do you need first-degree headings in a memo report or letter report.)

Second-degree Heading

When a report requires only one degree of heading, you can use the second-degree heading. It is centered, with the first letter of each important word capitalized.

Third-degree Heading

Instead of using second-degree headings for a report that has only one degree of heading, you can use third-degree headings. This heading is written just like the second-degree except that it is flush with the left margin rather than centered on the page. If a report requires only two degrees of heading, use the second and third degrees; they're preferable to the first- and second-degree combination.

   Fourth-degree Heading. When you need more than three degrees of heading, use the fourth-degree heading. This level is written just like the second- and

---

[1] Notice triple spacing before and after first-degree headings, double spacing before and after second- and third-degree headings, one continuous line under headings consisting of more than one word, and underscoring of all headings.

third-degree headings, except that it is indented, usually five spaces, from the left margin, and is followed by a period or a period and a dash. The text begins on the same line as the heading.

Fifth-degree heading is merely the underscoring of the first key word or words of the first sentence in the paragraph. You use this degree of heading only when the report requires all five degrees.

***Organize many figures into an understandable table.*** Whenever you must present many figures to your reader, organize them in a table or some other arrangement that gives him the whole picture.

In a report you can use either a spot table or a formal table. A spot table doesn't require a title or table number, but a formal table does. Both justify identification of columns so that the reader clearly understands what each column represents.

Whether you use a spot or formal table, you should always introduce the reader to the table before you show it. Informal language like "as the following table shows (or illustrates)" does a satisfactory job of introducing. In addition, you want to emphasize the highlights, lowlights, or averages of the table—whatever data is most significant to the report you are developing. But don't detail all the minute data shown in the table; the result will obviously be wordy—and probably boring.

## Terminal Section

A terminal section is usually called "summary," "conclusions," or "recommendations" (or a combination—such as "conclusions and recommendations").

Whether the terminal section appears before or after the text, it should be an integral part of the entire report and definitely add to its value. Its functions are to point up the whole report and make its final meaning clear and distinct. This terminal section should not include new information not previously discussed in the text. This closing merely summarizes, concludes, or recommends.

The three types of terminal sections differ in several ways. A *summary* condenses the previous discussion; but it doesn't have to condense the entire text—perhaps only the main points, or strong and weak points, or benefits the client will enjoy. If you include a terminal section in an information report, it will be a summary. The *conclusions* section evaluates the previous discussion without giving personal opinion.[1] A variation of this type could be a forecast, such as an economist might make. *Recommendations* go a bit further and suggest a program of action based on the conclusions. If you make recommendations throughout the report, you will probably summarize them here.

---

[1] Actually, it's impossible to completely filter out personal opinion, but you should be careful to make your evaluation only from data in the text. Disregard your own biases or desire for a particular outcome.

The same is true for conclusions. For an analytical report, your terminal section will be conclusions and/or recommendations—not a summary.

Of course, it is not imperative that you use the conventional wording for a terminal section—"summary," "conclusions," or "recommendations." Sometimes a more unusual title is appropriate, such as "benefits" or "suggested course of action." Other possible titles for this section are:

Probable developments
Pertinent suggestions
Merits of the plan
Important correlations
Final decision
Important precautions

## ORGANIZATIONAL PLANS FOR THE BODY OF A REPORT

There are two ways to develop (organize) the three parts of the body of the report—logically or psychologically. Logical organization means you write the introduction, text, and terminal sections in the order just mentioned. The psychological organization puts the terminal section before the text and either before or after the introduction—whichever is more helpful to the reader. Readers usually prefer in a lengthy report the psychological arrangment—which gives them an overall picture before they delve into the mass of details. If the terminal section *isn't* at the beginning, the reader will most likely skip to the end of the report, read the terminal section, and then return to the beginning. Even in the one- or two-page memo report, many businessmen prefer the psychological to the logical order. Listed below are arguments for and against putting the terminal section before the text of a short report. Naturally, you'll use the order your reader prefers (or should have).

*Terminal section should precede the text because:*
1. Reader can analyze data in terms of conclusions or recommendations.
2. It establishes writer's point of view promptly.
3. It eliminates suspense and allows discussion to substantiate action.
4. Reader often wishes to know only what action is to be taken, where, and who has the responsibility.
5. It determines whether the rest of the report is worth reading.
6. Reader can determine quickly whether he should scan text for confirmation of conclusions or recommendations.

*Terminal section should follow text because reader:*
1. Must first have the data (evidence) for the conclusion (proposed action).
2. Should read first the facts upon which judgments are based.
3. Wants first to see the development of facts.

4. Is encouraged to read the entire report—not just the terminal section.
5. Might feel less bias toward conclusions he disagrees with if he can first read analysis of important factors.

Here's one word of caution which applies to both the short and the long report: If the reader (say your supervisor) is the type of individual to begin fighting your decision before he reads the details, by all means use the logical arrangement—details before conclusion—and don't put anything in the introduction that might give him a clue to the answer.

## APPLICATION TO A SITUATION

So far in this chapter you have read about what to include in and how to organize the three main parts of the report body—introduction, text, and terminal section. Now it's time to apply this information to a specific situation.

Assume that Mr. Ura Mann, the executive vice-president in your bank, asks you to find a replacement for a teller who is quitting work to get married. You advertise and 15 women apply for the job. After carefully checking their application blanks, test scores, and your own interview notes, you narrow your choice to the three best candidates. Your task is to evaluate each of the three in a memo report to Mr. Mann. He likes you to analyze the facts for him— even rank the applicants—but he wants to make his own recommendations.

Here are the facts about the three women:

Mrs. Mary Rogers:
Age, 40; married with 3 children; high school graduate with a 2.8 (out of a possible 4.0) grade-point average; completed in high school an office machines course with a grade of "B"; typing, 60 words per minute; arithmetic aptitude, excellent; neat and fairly attractive in appearance; excellent references; husband earns $3 an hour as a custodian; excellent health; 10 years of business experience—all with one company.

Mrs. Susan Sawyer:
Age, 35; widow with no children; high school graduate with a 2.5 gpa; completed in high school an office machines course with a grade of "C"; typing, 50 wpm; arithmetic aptitude, good; plain but neat in appearance; good references; no plans for marriage; good health; 5 years of business experience with two different firms.

Miss Beth Bartell:
Age, 25; single, plans to get married but continue working; high school graduate and one year at the local four-year university; gpa, 3.3 in high school and 3.0 at the university; completed in high school an office machines course with grade of "A"; typing, 65 wpm; arithmetic aptitude, excellent; very neat and attractive; references—good worker but has difficulty getting along with others; fair health; three years of business experience with three different firms.

With all these figures facing you, where do you begin? One way is to group these facts under headings representing criteria you will be using to measure the three women. With some juggling, you decide that all the data fall under the headings of "education and skills," "compatibility," or "permanency with firm." Now you can arrange the backgrounds of the three applicants in a working table like the following:

| | *Education and Skills* | | |
|---|---|---|---|
| | *Rogers* | *Sawyer* | *Bartell* |
| Education | H.S. graduate | H.S. graduate | H.S. graduate<br>1 year at university |
| Grade point | 2.8 | 2.5 | 3.3 in H.S.<br>3.0 at university |
| Arithmetic aptitude | Excellent | Good | Excellent |
| Typing | 60 wpm | 50 wpm | 65 wpm |
| High school grade in<br>machines | Grade B | Grade C | Grade A |
| | | *Compatibility* | |
| Appearance[1] | Neat and fairly<br>attractive | Plain but neat | Very neat and very<br>attractive |
| References | Excellent | Good | Good worker but<br>difficulty working<br>with others |
| | | *Permanency with Firm* | |
| Age | 40 | 35 | 25 |
| Marital status | Married, husband<br>custodian ($3 hr)<br>3 children | Widow<br>No children<br>No marriage plans | Single<br>Plans to marry but<br>to continue working |
| Number of jobs | 1 | 2 | 3 |
| Years of work | 10 | 5 | 3 |
| Health | Excellent | Good | Fair (varicose veins) |

Now you can begin to analyze and interpret the material. You know you'll be sending a memo report because that's the form you use between individuals within an organization. And you'll use the logical organizational pattern because Mr. Mann told you once he preferred that pattern for all his memo reports.

The following discussion assumes you have already studied and interpreted the data in the three tables shown above. With that groundwork completed, you begin to write—first the heading, then the introduction, next the major divisions in the text, and finally the terminal section.

[1] Many times when organizing you have material that doesn't fit exactly anywhere. "Appearance" is an example of such material. So you organize such material as best you can; in this report it can fit under "Compatibility" or "Permanency with Firm."

## Heading

The TO, FROM, DATE lines are easy to fill out.

```
                                    DATE:    (current date)
TO:       Ura Mann
FROM:     (your name)
```

But the subject line is a little more difficult to handle. Here you want to tell your reader just as specifically as you can what the subject of this report covers. And you want to do so in just a few words—the fewer the better—perhaps no more than five or seven—certainly not a long sentence. Try to get into your subject line whichever of the five W's (what, who, why, when, where) will help tell the reader what the subject is.

## Introduction

The purpose of the introduction is to orient the reader so that he better understands the discussion. The following table shows which of the 11 elements you should include for this particular report:

| Element | Needed | Comment |
|---|---|---|
| Authorization | yes | Mr. Mann asked you to assume the assignment |
| Subject | no | purpose clearly implies subject |
| Problem | no | you don't face a problem |
| Purpose | yes | to evaluate the three applicants' qualifications for one opening as teller |
| Scope | no | purpose also implies scope |
| Limitations | no | none |
| Background | yes | you narrowed the applicants from 15 to 3 |
| Methodology/sources | yes | you used application blanks, test scores, and your own interview notes |
| Definition of terms | no | nothing to define |
| Plan of presentation | yes | you imply you'll develop the text according to the three criteria for a teller |
| Brief statement of your decision | optional | you tell reader Mrs. Rogers ranks highest of the three candidates |

In summary, then, you want to include in this introduction the following:

Authorization
Purpose
Background
Methodology/sources
Plan of presentation
Brief statment of decision (optional)

When you put these five or six elements into words and sentences, you might come up with an introductory paragraph like one of the following:

> Here is the report you requested concerning evaluation of candidates for a suitable replacement for your retiring teller. On the basis of company test scores, screening initial applications, and my personal interview with each applicant, 3 final candidates have been chosen from 15 who applied. In evaluating the candidates, primary importance has been placed on (1) education and skills, (2) compatibility, and (3) permanency. On the basis of these considerations, Mrs. Rogers rates the highest of the three candidates.

*or* (for the reader who fights your decision before he has read the text)

> As you requested, here is the report concerning the evaluation of candidates for a teller as a replacement for the woman who is resigning. Through careful screening of application forms, test scores, and my own interview notes, I have selected 3 out of 15 applicants for final consideration. Mrs. Mary Rogers, Mrs. Susan Sawyer, and Miss Beth Bartell were chosen on the basis of their teller proficiency, compatibility, and permanency of their employment with our bank.

*or*

> Here is the report you requested concerning the selection of a teller for our bank. By screening application blanks, test scores and my personal interview notes, I have narrowed a field of 15 applicants down to 3. Of these 3, Mrs. Rogers is the best qualified applicant. The sections below discuss the 3 applicants in relation to 3 criteria: skills and education, compatibility, and permanency.

### Text

Now that you have oriented the reader in the introduction, you want to present to him in the most logical order the mass of data about the three applicants.

Your first job is to divide the facts into major sections. But beware of using too many major divisions! Even a lengthy book doesn't have more than 15 to 20 chapters. For short reports—and even reports of 25 to 50 pages—you can't justify more than three or four main sections. In this report you will use three—one for each criterion.

The discussion which follows concentrates on the section labeled "Permanency with Firm," but the procedure given will be the same for the other two main sections. First you want to look at the data on permanency you have already arranged in table form. In fact, if your reader wants all the details, you will include this exact table or a variation of it within the text. All tables should be in rough draft form before actual writing so that you don't need to stop in the middle of your writing to perform this chore. When you write, write rapidly; don't let anything distract you. Forget about spelling, punctuation, and other mechanics; once you have the words on paper, you can always revise at your leisure.

Since all the facts about permanency are in the table that you'll include in this main section by the same name, you want to say something important about its content before you introduce the table to the reader; and be sure to do both (say something important and introduce) before the reader begins to concentrate on the table. What are the most important facts you can pull from this table? Beware of saying in sentence form before or after the table everything that's in the table; that wastes time and is deadly monotonous. Instead, stress the highlights, lowlights, or averages.

If you adhere to everything you should and should not do, you will probably write a main section similar to the one below.

### Permanency with Firm

Mrs. Mary Roger's experience, past job, and family responsibilities show a background and future potential for a greater degree of permanence with our organization than either Mrs. Sawyer or Miss Bartell. The following table shows that both Mrs. Sawyer and Miss Bartell might have a greater tendency to leave since they have less stable past job records, no family obligations, and are younger.

| Criteria | Mrs. Rogers | Mrs. Sawyer | Miss Bartell |
|---|---|---|---|
| Experience | 10 years | 5 years | 3 years |
| Previous jobs | 1 firm | 2 firms | 3 firms |
| Marital status | Married | Widow | Single |
| Marriage plans | | None | Plans to marry soon; will continue working |
| Family | Husband earns $3 an hour 3 children | None | None |
| Age | 40 | 35 | 25 |
| Health | Excellent | Good | Fair (varicose veins) |

Mrs. Sawyer rates as a second choice. Her 2 jobs in 5 years and good health are a much better record than that for Miss Bartell. Also in her favor is the fact that she has no plans for marriage.

Notice how putting the data in table form permits the reader to easily compare the facts about the three women. The discussions before and after the table point out to the reader the overall significance of the table without monotonously repeating each fact or figure. And finally this section ranks (and justifies the ranking of) the three applicants based upon the given data without going so far as to recommend.

## Terminal Section

After the introduction and text comes the terminal section. At least that's the order for organizing the body in a logical pattern. In a psychological pattern this section precedes the text and can go either before or after the introduction.

Because Mr. Mann doesn't want recommendations, you have the choice of a summary or conclusions. Which would he prefer? If you decide on conclusions, you should make an overall evaluation of your preference. In any case, you should know before you start to write the following evaluation of the ranking of the three women:

| | |
|---|---|
| Education and skills | Bartell—1st |
| | Rogers—2d |
| | Sawyer—3rd |
| Compatibility | Rogers—1st |
| | Sawyer—2d |
| | Bartell—3rd |
| Permanency | Rogers—1st |
| | Sawyer—2d |
| | Bartell—3rd |

Using this evaluation, Rogers is the logical first choice, Sawyer is second choice, and Bartell is third choice, as the following conclusion section explains.

### Conclusions

1. Mrs. Mary Rogers is the best suited to fill your teller vacancy. She rates highest in degree of expected permanence and in compatibility of personality for the job. Although her professional ability does not rate highest of the 3 applicants, she ranks second and shows a more than adequate proficiency.

2. Mrs. Susan Sawyer rates as a good second choice, mainly on the basis of her expected permanence. She also rates second on compatibility. Although she does not rank as high on skills and grades as either of the other 2 applicants, her education and scores indicate she can perform the job adequately.

3. Because of the questions raised in her references, I feel Miss Bartell is a poor prospect and will not be suitable for this position. Another factor against her is her fair health and the uncertainty of her permanency with our organization. Her outstanding professional ability is too greatly outweighed by these 2 factors.

When you add the to-from-subject-date at the beginning, the entire report now reads as follows.[1]

```
TO:        Mr. Ura Mann              DATE:   (current date)

FROM:      (your name)

SUBJECT:   Evaluation of Teller Applicants
```

Here is the report you requested concerning the choice of a woman to replace your teller who is resigning to get married. On the basis of information obtained from applications, test scores, and personal interviews, I feel that of the 3 top applicants, Mrs. Mary Rogers best meets the job requirements of permanency, education and skills, and compatibility, as discussed below.

### Permanency

Mrs. Mary Rogers' experience, past jobs, and family responsibilities show a background and future potential for a greater degree of permanence with our organization than either Mrs. Sawyer or Miss Bartell. The following table shows that both Mrs. Sawyer and Miss Bartell might have a greater tendency to leave since they have less stable past job records, no family obligations, and are younger.

| Criteria | Mrs. Rogers | Mrs. Sawyer | Miss Bartell |
|---|---|---|---|
| Experience | 10 years | 5 years | 3 years |
| Previous jobs | 1 firm | 2 firms | 3 firms |
| Marital status | Married | Widow | Single |
| Marriage plans | -------- | None | Plans to marry soon; will continue working |
| Family | Husband earning $3 hr; 3 children | None | None |
| Age | 40 | 35 | 25 |
| Health | Excellent | Good | Fair (varicose veins) |

Mrs. Sawyer rates as second choice. Her 2 jobs in 5 years and good health are a much better record than that for Miss Bartell. Also in her favor is the fact that she has no plans for marriage.

---

[1] The introduction for a memo report doesn't require a heading, but the main sections within the text and the terminal section will have headings—parallel grammatically. Also all headings and the subject line should be underlined for emphasis.

## Education and Skills

On the basis of education and skills, Miss Beth Bartell is an outstanding applicant.  The table below provides facts in which Miss Bartell ranks consistently higher than the other 2 in everything—education, aptitude, grades, and skills.

| Criteria | Mrs. Rogers | Mrs. Sawyer | Miss Bartell |
|---|---|---|---|
| Education | H.S. graduate | H.S. graduate | H.S. graduate 1 year at university |
| Grade point | 2.8 | 2.5 | 3.3 in H.S. 3.0 at university |
| Arithmetic aptitude | Excellent | Good | Excellent |
| Typing | 60 wpm | 50 wpm | 65 wpm |
| H.S. grade in machines | Grade B | Grade C | Grade A |

Although Mrs. Rogers' results are not as high as those of Miss Bartell, she shows a more than adequate proficiency in her skills.  She should prove just as efficient and capable as Miss Bartell in a teller's position.

## Compatibility

Primarily on the basis of references from past employers, Mrs. Rogers possesses the personality that best fits the performance and image of the position.  As the following table shows, she is the only applicant of the 3 who has excellent references with no additional qualifying statements by those references.

| Criteria | Mrs. Rogers | Mrs. Sawyer | Miss Bartell |
|---|---|---|---|
| References | Excellent | Good | Good worker but difficulty working with others |
| Appearance | Neat and fairly attractive | Plain but neat | Very neat and very attractive |

I am concerned about the references of Miss Bartell because of comments of former employers about her ability to get along with her fellow workers.

## Conclusions

1.  Mrs. Mary Rogers is the best suited to fill your teller vacancy.  She rates highest in degree of expected permanence

and in compatibility of personality for the job. Although her professional ability does not rate highest of the 3 applicants, she ranks second and shows a more than adequate proficiency.

2. Mrs. Susan Sawyer rates as a good second choice, mainly on the basis of her expected permanence. She also rates second on compatibility. Although Miss Sawyer does not rank as high on skills and grades as either of the other 2 applicants, her education and scores indicate she can perform the job adequately.

3. Because of the questions raised in her references, I feel Miss Bartell is a poor prospect and will not be suitable for this position. Another factor against her is her fair health and the uncertainty of her permanency with our organization. Her outstanding professional ability is too greatly outweighed by these 2 factors.

There's the memo report with the to-from-subject-date beginning and the three parts of the body—introduction, text, and terminal section. The reader, Mr. Mann, can quickly glance through the facts and decide for himself whom he should hire.

In summary, a report is a medium of communication that conveys facts for intended reader(s) who need or want these facts as a basis for making a decision and for taking action. Although the organization of the body differs from that of a letter, the language should be conversational and as nontechnical as possible. Everyone prefers to receive a clear, concise, and easy-to-read report.

## EXERCISES

1. When you were studying messages in the form of letters, you collected five letters and studied them for effective use of the writing principles, etc. Your assignment now is to collect, if possible, one or two memo reports and study them for the following:
   a. Location and wording of TO, FROM, SUBJECT, DATE information.
      (1) Does the title (such as Mr., Miss, or Mrs.) precede the name(s) on the "to" and "from" lines? Why do you think titles are or are not present?
      (2) Evaluate the subject line. How long is it? Is it underscored? Does it clearly identify the subject of the entire memo report?
      (3) Does the writer sign or initial the report? Where does he initial? Why should he initial?
   b. Does the introduction orient the reader to the material that follows? Why or why not? What elements do you find in the introduction?
   c. Do you find headings in the body of the report? If not, can you justify the use of these guideposts? Why or why not? If there are headings, do they have parallel construction? Should the introduction have a heading?
   d. Evaluate the text (discussion).
      (1) Is it logically organized?

(2) Does each paragraph have a topic sentence? Does the paragraph confine itself to the idea(s) in the topic sentence?

(3) Does the writer talk in the first and second persons?

(4) Do you find too many passive verbs throughout the text?

(5) In the format for (b) and (c) above, the various questions aren't listed. Why is it more likely you might miss seeing one of these questions than those in (d) and in (a) above?

e. Does the report have a terminal section? If so, does it summarize, conclude, or recommend? If the terminal section has two or more conclusions or recommendations, why should the writer list and number them? Does the terminal section do a satisfactory job in carrying out its function?

2. Below is a message with a to-from-subject-date heading. Is it a memo or a memo report? Why? Also evaluate the message as good, average, or poor and give your reasoning for your decision.

DATE:    (current)

TO:          All departments, Aloha Street Office

FROM:        Sally Rand

SUBJECT:     <u>New Procedures for Checking Out Collection Folders</u>

A check of the collection file shows that many folders are missing and aren't checked out to anyone; neither are they in the closed file. As a result, we ask your cooperation in solving this problem by following the new procedure outlined below.

Effective this date, all collection folders at the Aloha Street Office will be filed on the first floor in the Safe Deposit Area. Patricia Wallace will assume the responsibility for checking the folders in and out. You can reach her at Extension 222. If you receive no answer on this extension, call any New Accounts person to check out a folder.

Under no circumstances, is any folder to be removed from the file unless Patricia or someone in New Accounts checks it out. If you check out a file and then give it to someone else, it is your responsibility to notify the file clerk that you no longer have the folder. Otherwise, you will be held responsible for returning it to the file.

Please check your department and return any collection folders you are not using. We will appreciate your assistance.

3. Evaluate each of the following four reports. In addition to the questions asked in Exercise 1, ask yourself the following:

*Report 1: From student to professor.*
(Assume that pages 4, 5, and 6, which are missing from report 1, comprise the appendix.)

1. Does the introductory paragraph under each of the two major divisions of the text do an effective job in introducing the subdivisions?
2. What is wrong with the listing in the topic sentence of the introductory paragraph for the first major division of the text?
3. When should a major division of the text have an introductory paragraph?
4. Why should "Job Memo Reports" appear as the first subdivision under the first major division of the text?
5. How does exhibit 2 strengthen the report? Why is this exhibit attached as an appendix instead of made part of the body? Why does the page number for the exhibit mean more to the reader than saying "exhibit 2" without the page number?
6. Do you consider report 1 above average, average, or below average? Why?

*Report 2: From student to professor.*
1. Why is the subject line poor?
2. What is your reaction to the reader's name in the introduction?
3. In the text, circle every reference—noun or pronoun—to Mr. Healy. Why is it unnecessary to make any more than one or two references (maybe even no reference) to Healy in the text?
4. Is the terminal section actually a summary, conclusion, or recommendations? How do you like "Course of Action Based on Interview" as the heading for the terminal section?

*Report 3: From high school English teacher to her superintendent.*
1. What elements of the introduction do you find in the first two paragraphs?
2. Do you like the three major divisions of the text or would you prefer only two? If two, they would be "Skills Needed" and "Training Needed." Under "Skills Needed" would be two subdivisions: (1) Oral and (2) Written.

*Report 4: From counseling center to the general faculty.*
1. What replaced the TO, FROM, SUBJECT, DATE used for a typical memo report?
2. How does the introduction differ from the typical format for an introduction?
3. Notice the headings. What are the degrees of the headings? Is the wording effective? Are they parallel in construction?
4. This report has no terminal section. Should it? Why?

*Report 1*

```
TO:        Professor John Doe                    (date)

FROM:      Daniel S. Flanagan

SUBJECT:   Types of Reports Written by Advertising Account
           Executives
```

Here is the report you requested on the types of reports written by account executives in advertising agencies. An interview with Mr. Fred Henderson, Vice President/Account Executive at Baker Advertising indicates that report writing is a vital part of the account executive's job. Four of the reports most commonly written by account executives are dis-

cussed in this report, in addition to general comments on
agency report writing.

## Types of Reports Most Often Written

The job memo, memo report, recommendation report, and conference (or meeting) report constitute the bulk of the reports
written by the account executive.  The account executive writes
reports when he is directly involved in the situation.  Otherwise, the person involved and the account executive decide
together who writes the report.  In all cases concerning his
client, however, the account executive is ultimately responsible for the reports concerning his client's campaign.

### Job Memo Reports
The job memo is the most important report in the office.  It is
an intra-office report written to all departments of the
agency.  The account executive writes these reports, which give
authorization and instruction concerning his client's campaign.
They are written as often as necessary whenever any action on
the client's campaign is called for.  Generally, the account
executive writes these reports daily.  Exhibit 2 in the Appendix on page 5 gives an example of the job memo report.

### Memo Reports
The memo report (see Exhibit 1 on page 4 in the Appendix) is
written as often as necessary—usually daily.  It is a short
report used to communicate information to, or request information from, a specific person within the agency.  This report
concerns information dealing with the many facets of the
client's advertising campaign needed by the account executive
in performing his job.

### Conference Reports
It is important that the account executive and his client
understand at all times where the campaign stands and how it is
progressing.  So that each one has a record of all the decisions made concerning the campaign, the conference report is
used.  This report (see Exhibit 3 on page 6 in the Appendix)
is written immediately following a conference or meeting between the agency and client.  Its purpose is to clarify the
discussion and the decisions made at the meeting.

### Recommendation Reports
The most extensive and comprehensive report written by the
account executive is the recommendation report.  It is written
perhaps once or twice a year and gives the client the agency's
recommendations, marketing plan, budget analysis, and advertising approach for the campaign.  The agency, as well as the
client, has a copy of this report, many of which are 20-30
pages in length.  Not only does the account executive receive

a copy, but so does the head of the agency and the heads of all departments involved with the account.

## General Comments on Agency Reports

No matter what type of report is written, its general purpose is to ensure and expedite communication between the agency and its client or between departments of the agency. To this end, Mr. Henderson pointed out a number of items he thought his agency's reports could be improved upon, in addition to those items he thought made for good reports. He also provided information on the format his agency uses for reports and what they have done to improve the quality of their reports.

### Weaknesses and Strengths of Agency Reports

Too many of the reports are not concise. They tend to be wordy and too long. Lack of clarity and negativeness are other faults he noted.

Mr. Henderson thought that if reports were more objective and emphasised the positive rather than the negative, they would help communication more. Other desirable factors mentioned were brevity and conciseness. In general, reports should communicate the entire message in the fewest words possible without sounding abrupt.

### Format and Form of Agency Reports

No particular order or format is strictly adhered to at Baker Advertising. Whether the text or the terminal section comes first is not a written policy, but the main points of the discussion should ideally precede the discussion to expedite the reading of the report.

The company does not use any printed forms for reports, except for the job memo report. The nature of the account in question dictates the form used for recommendation or conference reports. Headings are used, however, to assist the reader of the report.

### Steps to Improve Agency Reports

Because of the volatile nature of the advertising business, no formal school in better report writing techniques is conducted. However, the American Association of Advertising Agencies does provide some bulletins on better writing techniques. Also, the account executive attempts to stress the qualities of conciseness, clarity, and other desirable points of report writing in informal discussions with other executives and with their subordinates.

## Summary

The advertising account executive is mainly concerned with four types of reports: 1) memo reports, 2) job memo reports, 3) conference reports, and 4) recommendation reports.

No order is dictated for reports, but the main points should be mentioned first.  Only the job memo report uses a printed form.

All too often these reports tend to be wordy and lack clarity. The agency attempts to rectify this situation through informal discussions and trade organization bulletins pertaining to better writing techniques.

---

*Report 2*

TO:        P. D. Quincy                                    (date)

FROM:      A. B. Jones

SUBJECT:   PREPARATION FOR A DATA SHEET AND APPLICATION LETTER
           TO UNITED FOOD SERVICE FOR A POSITION IN THEIR
           MANAGEMENT TRAINEE PROGRAM

As you requested, Dr. Quincy, this report is designed to provide the information necessary in order to write an effective resume and letter of application to the United Food Service Corporation.  The subject matter is based on an interview I had with Mr. Healy, a regional manager, and is limited to a consideration of the qualifications of an applicant and a brief description of the trainee program.

### Desirable Qualifications in an Applicant

In general, an applicant for a position with the United Food Service Corporation management trainee program should be personable, and well trained in both business and dietetics.  Mr. Healy stressed the importance of participation in as many social activities as possible, with particular emphasis on demonstrating the ability to be a leader.  He also suggested that each applicant take a course in dietetics so that the trainee will be familiar with the problems of food preparation.

In addition to these major qualifications, Mr. Healy mentioned a number of less important factors in determining the desirability of an applicant.  The United Food Service Corporation places little emphasis on previous work experience, but grades often influence the selection of a trainee.  According to Mr. Healy, the applicant should have at least a 2.5 (out of a possible 4.0) cumulative grade point average in college.  He mentioned Sociology, Accounting, Economics, and Dietetics as being the most important subjects to the person interested in participating in the United management training program.  Mr. Healy was emphatic in urging that Sociology rather than Psychology be taken.  Cornell and Michigan State are the most influential universities to graduate from in the food manage-

ment field.  Salesmanship is absolutely necessary to a United
Food Service manager; he will have to sell new accounts eventually as well as manage his own operation.  Mr. Healy said
that special tests are not required by his company, but a
favorable result on the Wonelick personality test would be a
definite asset to the applicant.

### Description of the United Food Service Management Trainee Program

As Mr. Healy described it, the management trainee program at
United Food Service Incorporated is designed to give the
trainee a thorough understanding of what he will manage, rather
than just a narrow program of instruction.  Each trainee must
learn to cook, and develop a mastery of the complicated principles of food service before he is even introduced to the
business functions he will perform.

The length of the training program averages between six months
and one year.  Mr. Healy noted, however, that the program is
often accelerated to meet the increasing demand for managers in
the food service field.  A management trainee with a college
degree would earn from $000–$000 per week as a starting salary,
and could expect $000 or above after completing his preliminary
training.  According to Mr. Healy, relocation is a definite
probability, and the trainee might end up anywhere in the
United States.  He cited the company's tremendous size (6th
largest food chain in U.S.) and diversification of operations
as reasons for this.

### Course of Action Based on Interview

After discussing with Mr. Healy the management trainee program
offered by the United Food Service Corporation, I have decided
to look into management positions in other fields.  In the food
service field more emphasis is placed on knowledge of food than
on the business functions a manager provides.  Also, the
manager with the United Food Service Corporation tends to lose
all identity until he progresses to the regional level or
above.  Mr. Healy said this, and he speaks from experience.

---

*Report 3*

Date:  October, 1971

TO:      Superintendent Frank Lasson

FROM:    Barbara Cummins, English teacher

SUBJECT: Communication Skills Audio-Visual Center Needs

On October 10, as you requested, I asked Mrs. Ethyl Holmes, Management Representative of the Audio—Visual Center in (city) what communication skills high school people need to work for her company.  This report gives the results.

According to Mrs. Holmes, students need training in both oral and written communication.  Even though new workers may not be responsible immediately for writing, their writing skills are considered at the time of employment and during their early days on the job.  This is because the Audio—Visual Center generally advances personnel from within the company.

## Oral Skills Needed

Since the Audio—Visual Center hires most beginning workers in clerical positions, they must be able to communicate orally in the following ways.

1.   Talking and listening on the telephone.

2.   Receiving and introducing callers.

3.   Working well with many other people.

Even though these are beginning jobs, the employee is responsible for the image of the company and must be able to communicate clearly and tactfully with customers and other employees.

## Written Skills Needed

As the beginning worker advances, he needs to write more and more.  However, even as a beginner his duties could include the following.

1.   Taking telephone messages.

2.   Filling in office forms.

3.   Writing routine letters.

4.   Addressing envelopes.

If a worker advances to a supervisory position, he needs to write periodic evaluation reports on the people in his unit.

## Training Needed

The Audio—Visual Center does not have any in-service training or company manual.  Therefore, applicants must get their training in school.  There are several specific areas that Mrs. Holmes thinks the schools should be teaching.

1.  Students should learn correct telephone techniques.

2.  Everyone, including young men, should learn to type.

3.  Students must learn to write legibly.

4.  All future employees should learn to spell correctly and use a dictionary.

5.  Schools must teach correct business attitudes.

The last item is perhaps most important. Students must know that regular attendance, punctuality, appropriate dress, and getting along with others are every bit as necessary as their skills.

Conclusions

Teachers cannot assume that students can communicate well; they must teach them to speak, listen, and write. The Audio-Visual Center feels that these are qualifications for even the most basic job.

---

*Report 4*

THE COUNSELING CENTER

Lewis Hall Annex

Telephone 543-2140

To the Faculty:

The Counseling Center has added several new professional staff members this year. This makes it possible for us both to serve more students and to provide a wider range of services.

To acquaint new faculty with the operations of the Counseling Center and to inform others of some changes which have been introduced this year, we have prepared a description of our services. If you would like to become acquainted with the Center and its staff in person, please feel welcome to call us.

                                        (typewritten name)
                                        Director

WHAT IS THE COUNSELING CENTER?

The Counseling Center is a unit of the Division of Evaluative and Counseling Services under the Office of the Vice President of Academic Affairs. The Counseling Center performs a variety

of services for students of the University which may be broadly
defined as psychological in nature and which are aimed toward
assisting the typical student resolve the inevitable problems
he encounters in his efforts at the University to actualize his
potential for intellectual, social and emotional growth.

The primary responsibility for the staff of the Counseling
Center is to help students find effective ways of dealing with
educational, personal, social and vocational problems which
might interfere with their educational pursuits. It is the aim
of the Center to assist students to come to understand and to
accept themselves more fully so they are able to resolve current problems and also to be better prepared to resolve and to
profit from future problems.

## WHAT KINDS OF CONCERNS DO STUDENTS BRING TO COUNSELING?

While students coming to the Counseling Center seek assistance
with a variety of concerns, they can be classified in three
broad categories:

A. Educational: Students doing poorly in their academic
work or doing less well than they expect
themselves to do often come to counseling
posing these kinds of questions:

"Why can't I get myself down to work and
study?"
"Have I got what it really takes to make
it in my major?"
"Do I really want to stay in the University?"
"Why do I have a hard time concentrating
when I study?"

B. Personal: The personal-adjustment problems which
confront students during their University
years are, of course, great in number and
variety. If a student is going to make
the most of his educational experience,
it might be necessary for him to resolve
questions and issues such as:

"I can't get along with my roommate."
"It's so confusing not being sure of
one's values."
"Is she the right girl for me? Are we
too young to get married?"
"I feel lost in the crowd in this big
University."

C.  Vocational:   The most frequent complaints which are
                  heard at the Center are introduced with
                  statements such as:

                  "I don't know what career to plan for."
                  "I have so many interests.  I don't know
                  which way to go."
                  "I can't decide on a major."
                  "I think I know what I want, but I want
                  to make sure."

## WHAT KINDS OF SERVICE DOES THE COUNSELING CENTER PROVIDE?

Individual Counseling:  The core of the Center's operations
is individual counseling.  The number of interviews a student has with a counselor varies greatly.  For some, one or
two counseling contacts are enough, while others may return
for ten or twelve interviews.

Group Counseling:  Sometimes students' concerns can be
dealt with most effectively through the experience obtained in interacting with six to ten other students in a
group facilitated by one or two counselors.  The Counseling
Center makes available to students various kinds of group
experiences.  Some groups are formed around specific problem areas such as vocational choice, marital problems, or
academic-motivation problems.  Other group work is aimed
toward the more general goal of facilitating the students'
personal-social development through increasing self awareness and sensitivity to others.

The Effective Study Program:  A new program is now
underway which aims to assist students develop attitudes
and skill which will help them to make the most out of
college.  Students meet in small groups to examine various
methods and techniques of study and to explore how they can
become more effective as students and people.  Enrollment
for the Autumn Quarter is complete.  A student may sign up
for Winter Quarter or Spring Quarter sections now.  A brief
description of the program and application blanks are
available at the Center.

The Occupational Library:  Frequently in connection with
vocational choice, self-appraisal is preceded or accompanied by examination of the personal demands and satis-
factions to be found in various occupations.  The Center
maintains extensive files of materials in its occupational
library for students who wish to obtain information about
the kinds of jobs within an occupational area, the job
duties, training requirements, opportunities for employment, salaries, and related information.  Any student is

invited to use the library in the Center whether or not he is being seen by a counselor in the Center.

Staff Consultation: The Center also assists students indirectly by making its professional staff available as resource people to faculty and University staff members who, in their efforts to help students, would find it helpful to consult with a counseling or clinical psychologist.

## HOW DOES A STUDENT MAKE AN APPOINTMENT?

From 8:30 to 12:00 a.m. and 1:00 to 4:30 on Monday, Tuesday, Wednesday, Friday and from 8:30 to 10:30 and 1:00 to 4:30 on Thursday a counselor is available to see students for a brief intake interview to determine if the Counseling Center can be of help to the student and clarify any questions he might have about counseling. The student does not need an appointment to be seen for this initial contact which usually must be limited to about fifteen minutes. At the close of the intake, if the services of the Center are appropriate for the student and if he wants to avail himself of them, he is assigned to a counselor.

## HOW ABOUT MAKING REFERRALS?

Most students who come to the Counseling Center are "self" referred. They have heard about our services in various ways and, feeling some decision or problem weighing on them, seek us out. Many, however, come at the suggestion of a member of the faculty. When the student senses that the faculty member's suggestion of use of the Counseling Center is prompted by a genuine concern for him, the result is frequently a heightened motivation to resolve one's concerns and counseling is facilitated. It is almost always best for the student to take responsibility for making the arrangements for his appointment rather than the faculty member doing it for him. It is important to keep in mind, also, that students can be helped through counseling only when they recognize that they have a problem and sincerely want assistance in dealing with it. Referrals are rarely successful if the student comes to counseling to please a faculty member or because he feels external pressure to make the appointment.

Sometimes a faculty member works with a student who is very puzzling to him and is uncertain if or where to make a referral. In such cases the faculty member should feel free to contact the Center if he thinks it might be helpful to discuss the situation with a psychologist before coming to a decision.

## WHAT ABOUT THE USE OF TESTS IN COUNSELING?

The counseling process in large measure can be described as a process of self-confrontation for the student. The student is

assisted to see himself and his situation more fully and with
less distortion so he better knows and better accepts the
resources he has available in himself and in his world for
resolving his indecisions or concerns.

The student's efforts at self-appraisal may be assisted by
specially selected psychological tests when tests are available
which can help clarify the issues which the student has come to
identify as important to him.  There is not, however, any one
test battery which gives him a quick and valid assessment of
his aptitudes or his personality.  If tests are used, each
student and his counselor must work together to determine
which tests, from the hundreds available, would be appropriate
to him in his particular dilemma.

WHO ARE THE COUNSELORS?

The staff is composed of 15 professional counselors with academic and experience backgrounds in counseling or clinical
psychology or education:
    Name of director and his title
    Name of associate director and his title
    Counselors:
        (Names of 8 counselors and their academic degrees are
            listed here.)
    Trainees:
        (Names of 5 trainees and their academic degrees are
            listed here.)

# CHAPTER 15

# SHORT REPORTS

- Think before You Write
- Guiding the Reader through the Report
- Types of Short Reports
- Exercises

If you asked a group of businessmen what factors best determine an effective written report, you might be surprised at their commonsense answers. They don't expect to be enthralled by the content or style—although they appreciate and notice favorably a good narrative style with a touch of wit. What businessmen look for in a report is concise, accurate, unbiased material with appropriate supporting evidence that leads to logical conclusions and/or recommendations.

This chapter begins by first discussing the importance of the thinking steps and then showing how you can best guide your reader through reports—with the emphasis on short reports. Then you have the opportunity to study the three types of reports you're most likely to write on the job—memo, printed form, and letter report.

## THINK BEFORE YOU WRITE

As with letters and memos, you want to consider the thinking steps before you begin to write a report. This thinking process for short reports isn't as detailed as it is for a formal report because the shorter presentations don't require the depth of research. But especially important for short reports that require little or no preliminary research is identifying the purpose and the reader(s). The purpose determines the ideas to include in the report; the reader determines how much you'll say, how you say it, and how you organize the material.

If your report is being sent, say, only to Mr. X, will he read and act accordingly? Or is he just an intermediary? If you and Mr. X are accountants and only you two are involved, you can use technical expressions in your report. But if he is routing the report to nonaccounting personnel, you must also write for them. Also, if the report is important enough to be referred to months or years later, be sure you're also writing for the future readers.

Whoever your reader is, you can be sure his time is valuable, and you shouldn't waste it with reports that are nonessential, wordy, difficult to read, misleading, inaccurate, or biased. If you're writing a report—especially a formal report—at his request, give him what he wants—whether it's detailed descriptions and an enormous quantity of facts and figures or a small amount of supporting data, logically or psychologically organized body, first or third person, or a particular type of terminal section (summary, conclusions, or recommendations). Of course, some managers don't know what they want until they see it; consequently it's up to you to use your imagination and creative ability and try to design a report that will satisfy the person requesting the information. The way you tailor a report to the reader, the purpose, and the subject matter often determines whether the report will be accepted by the management people involved.

## GUIDING THE READER THROUGH THE REPORT

Here are a few suggestions for writing your report:

1. Subject line. In a memo report or letter report, identify the subject on the subject line; in a long report, the title on the cover and/or title page is the subject.

2. Introduction. Identify the subject, explain the problem (if there is a problem), and clearly spell out the purpose. You can also include any other introductory elements that are necessary to orient the reader to the material that follows.

3. Text.
   a. Be especially careful to show both sides. Be impartial, eliminate personal feelings and prejudices, and emphasize facts. If you express an opinion, be sure the reader knows it's an opinion and not a fact.
   b. Organize your facts so that you have logical flow of topics with proper emphasis distributed throughout. You can emphasize an idea by showing more details; placing it in a prominent position; and using mechanical means such as amount of white space, capitalization, underscoring, visual aids, and repetition.
   c. Use headings to guide the reader through the report, but write your sentences and paragraphs so they can stand alone—as if the headings didn't exist.
   d. Use topic sentences for all your paragraphs, and use an introductory paragraph at the beginning of a major section that contains two or more subdivisions.
   e. Support your conclusions or recommendations with ample, appropriate facts that are up-to-date and accurate.
   f. Apply the seven-C writing principles.
   g. Throughout, make your writing easy to read; use understandable words, sentences averaging 17 to 20 words, concrete nouns, few adverbs, few adjectives, and paragraphs whose maximum length doesn't exceed 15 typewritten lines.

4. Terminal section.
   a. If you have more than one conclusion or recommendation, list and number them.
   b. Make certain that your terminal section is an integral part of the report and results logically from the facts already presented in the text.
   c. Don't include any new material in this section of the report.
   d. Remember that a summary condenses the text, conclusions evaluate the text, and recommendations offer specific course of action.

5. Appendix. Put material in the appendix that would clutter up the text. Use material that belongs in the report but isn't vital to the development or presentation of the text.

Given below is a 10-point checklist that Eli Lilly and Company, a leading pharmaceutical house, uses in its business writing workshop to evaluate a report. Notice that the 10 entries stress the importance of the reader and the seven writing principles—clarity, conciseness, consideration, completeness, correctness, concreteness, and courtesy.

1. The type of information included is what I hope to receive in such a report.
2. Information is as complete as I wish.
3. Unnecessary detail is avoided.
4. The facts are presented in logical order.
5. Major points stand out clearly.
6. The overall wording is good—and the writer comes through as being effective at the writing task.
7. I am left with no questions about information that is presented—or about information that is not presented.
8. If I wish to decide whether to have people under my supervision attend (or not attend) future workshops, I can make a "comfortable" decision as a result of this report.
9. Because this piece of writing is easy to read, I will probably read it through.
10. On the basis of this report alone, I feel good about having this writer handle correspondence for me in my absence from the office.

Example 1 below is a memo report from the head of the Tab Department to two members of management. As you read this report, try to find out what its purpose is. Notice how frustrating it is to read the details without knowing how they fit into the overall picture. Then notice why Example 2 is an improvement.

*Example 1: Memo report without clear statement of purpose.*

```
TO:     Tor Burkhard, Stephen Klink        DATE:   (current)

FROM:   Tor Burkhard, Jr.
```

During the week of August 19-23, 1972, a survey of telephone inquiries to the main office was conducted. The incoming calls to the Tab Department totaled 470. The source of these calls was as follows: Approximately 67% from main office tellers and branch office personnel; approximately 33% from all other main office personnel.

Due to the fact that the survey was conducted during a period of reduced activity, the findings are not representative of the peak periods throughout the year. Based on an analysis of weekly activity for the first half of 1972, the volume of telephone inquiries is projected at approximately 750-800 per week during the peak periods which occur during the first part of each quarter.

During the period of the survey an average of 90-100 calls per day were serviced by Tab. Even at this level, the telephone activity is becoming sufficient enough to be disruptive of the other work routines in the department.

It is recommended that another employee be hired and assigned to the Tab Department primarily for the purpose of servicing telephone inquiries.

**Example 2:** *Revision of Example 1 points up the entire memo.*

TO:        Tor Burkhard, Stephen Klink      DATE:   (current)

FROM:     Tor Burkhard, Jr.

SUBJECT:  <u>Need for Additional Employee in Tab Department</u>

Because telephone activity is disrupting other work routines in the Tab Department, I conducted a survey of telephone inquiries to the main office during the week of August 19–23, 1972. This report gives the findings of the survey and makes a recommendation to improve this problem.

<u>Findings</u>

During the week of August 19–23, 1972:

1.   Incoming calls to the Tab Department totaled 470.

2.   Tab serviced an average of 90–100 calls daily. Even at this level, telephone activity disrupts other work routines.

3.   Sources of these calls were:

     67% from main office tellers and branch office personnel.

     33% from all other main office personnel.

The findings are not representative of peak periods throughout the year because the survey was conducted during a period of reduced activity. Yet based on an analysis of weekly activity for the first half of this year, projected volume of telephone inquiries is approximately 750–800 weekly during the peak periods (first part of each quarter).

Since the present employees have duties to keep them busy throughout the day, this additional activity in the department will require additional help.

<u>Recommendation</u>

We should hire another employee and assign this individual to the Tab Department primarily for servicing telephone inquiries.

The revision is more understandable because the writer identifies the subject at the very beginning. In the introduction, he gives the problem, the methodology, the purpose, and the plan of presentation. In the text he lists the highlights of the survey findings before giving an interpretation. The terminal section suggests a course of action. Underscoring the subject line and use of headings further improves the reading.

The next report is difficult to understand because it includes many figures presented as part of the text—with little attempt to organize them.

*Example 3: Need to organize many figures into easy-to-read tables.*

TO:       Sam Spade, Vice-President       DATE:   (current)

FROM:     Lotta Monee, Treasurer

SUBJECT:  Treasurer's Savings Analysis Report

The following schedules provide an analysis of the number and balances of the association's savings accounts in groupings of $1,000 for the month of October, 197_. These schedules were obtained as a supplement report of our regular monthly trial balancing of savings accounts. The accounts were processed October 23 and 24 and reflect balances at those dates.

Total savings accounts were 5,098 with balances of approximately $20,900,000. The average account balance for all classes of savings accounts is $4,100.

A gain of 504 accounts has been registered since the October, 197_, analysis for an increase of 10.97%. Account holders with balances of $5,000 or more make up 35.79% of our savers. These savers hold 81.58% of the association's total savings dollars. Savers with balances of $10,000 and over make up 17.65% of our total account holders and they hold 52.21% of the total dollar value. This compares to 48.78% of one year ago for an increase of 3.43%.

Savings balances have increased $2,341,334 (including the crediting of $568,850 in dividends) for the 12-month period October, 197_, through September, 197_. This represents an actual gain of $1,772,484 or 9.55%. Accounts with balances of $1 through $4,999 increased $53,110 while accounts with balances of $5,000 or more increased $2,288,224. Accounts in the $5,000 to $5,999 grouping showed an increase of approximately $500,000 and in the $15,000 to $15,999 category gained $620,679. Savings certificates which have been issued since January 2, 197_, totaled $4,005,000 or 19.16% of total savings. New money invested in savings certificates was $1,347,572 (gross $1,414,572 less withdrawals of $67,000) while transfers from existing accounts equaled $2,657,428.

As a welcome contrast to Example 3, the following revision not only organizes the many figures in table format but shows two comparisons—first by number of accounts and percentages, then by dollar balances. This revision permits the reader to grasp the data more quickly and more thoroughly.

*Example 4: Revision of Example 3 illustrates effective organization of many figures.*

```
TO:        Sam Spade, Vice-President        DATE:   (current)

FROM:      Lotta Monee, Treasurer

SUBJECT:   Treasurer's Savings Analysis Report

The following schedules provide an analysis of the number,
percentages, and balances of the association's savings accounts
in groupings of $1,000 for October 197_.  These schedules were
obtained as a supplement report of our regular monthly trial
balancing of savings accounts.  The accounts reflect balances
on October 23 and 24.

Comparisons by number of accounts and percentages
   Total number of savings accounts . . . . . . . . . .   5,098
   Gain of accounts since October 197_ (previous year). .    504
   % of increase in number of accounts. . . . . . . . . 10.97%
   % of savers with account balance $5,000 or more. . . 35.79%
   % of our association's total savings dollars that
      these savers hold . . . . . . . . . . . . . . . . 81.58%
   % of savers with account balances $10,000 or more. . 17.65%
   % of our association's total savings dollars that
      these savers hold . . . . . . . . . . . . . . . . 52.21%
   % of increase over last year . . . . . . . . . . . .  3.43%
   % that savings certificates are of total savings . . 19.16%
   % that savings balances increased (actual gain). . . .  9.55%

Comparisons by dollar balances
   Total balances of all 5,098 savings accounts . .  $20,900,000
   Average account balance for all classes of
      saving accounts . . . . . . . . . . . . . . . . . $4,100
   Increase in savings balances (Oct.
      197_ through Sept. 197_). . . .  $2,341,334
   Dividends included . . . . . . . .      $568,850
                                       -----------
   Actual gain (9.55% minus
      dividends). . . . . . . . . . . .  $1,772,484

Increase for savings account holders with balances of:
   $1 - $4,999. . . . . . . . . . . . . . . . . . . . . $   53,110
   $5,000 or more . . . . . . . . . . . . . . . . . .     2,288,224
   $5,000 - $5,999. . . . . . . . . . . (approximately)    500,000
   $15,000 - $15,999. . . . . . . . . . . . . . . . . .    620,679
Total of savings certificates issued since
   Jan. 2, 197_ . . . . . . . . . . . . . . . . . . . . $4,005,000
```

```
New money invested in savings
    certificates (gross) . . . . . . . $1,414,572
    Less withdrawals . . . . . . . . .     67,000
                                       ------------
    Net new money invested in savings
        certificates. . . . . . . . . $1,347,572

Transfers from existing accounts . . . . . . . . . $2,657,428
```

If you wish to discuss any part of this report with me, please let me know. I'll come to your desk at your convenience.

In addition to following the suggestions already given, you can use the devices listed below to help guide your reader through the report.

1. Use transitions to tie your writing together.
2. Avoid the subjunctive as much as possible.
3. Talk in present tense whenever possible.
4. Use mostly active—not passive—verbs.

## Use Transitions to Tie Your Writing Together

As the bricklayer uses mortar to hold his bricks together, the writer uses transitional words, phrases, sentences, and even paragraphs to tie his ideas together.

*Tying sentences together.* Transitional words and phrases such as "also," "on the other hand," "similarly," "therefore," and "for example" help you lead the reader through your material. For example, in the following paragraph, notice how the italicized words tie the paragraph together and lead the reader from one report type to the next:

Reports in business and industry have many purposes. *Some* are simply records of meetings, meant to summarize actions or positions for those present to guide future action. *Others* are meant to develop facts preliminary to adoption of a particular policy regarding the situation at hand. *Others*, perhaps more formal, are the results of research projects, either in the basic sciences or individual aspects of a development project; while *still others* might be termed proposals— suggestions for a line of action or a project considered necessary.

Shown below are other transitional words and phrases you can use in your writing:

*Addition:*

| | | | |
|---|---|---|---|
| again | equally important | in addition | next |
| also | finally | last | nor |
| and | first | lastly | secondly |
| and then | further | likewise | thirdly, etc. |
| besides | furthermore | moreover | too |

*Comparison:*

| | | |
|---|---|---|
| better yet | in like manner | similarly |
| here again | likewise | still worse |

*Contrast:*

| | |
|---|---|
| although this may be true | nevertheless |
| and yet | notwithstanding |
| at the same time | on the other hand |
| but | on the contrary |
| however | still |
| in contrast | yet |

*Place:*

| | | |
|---|---|---|
| adjacent to | here | on the opposite side |
| beyond | nearby | opposite to |

*Result:*

| | | | |
|---|---|---|---|
| accordingly | consequently | therefore | thus |
| as a result | hence | thereupon | |

*Summary:*

| | | |
|---|---|---|
| as has been stated | in brief | on the whole |
| as I have said | in other words | to be sure |
| for example | in short | to sum up |
| for instance | in sum | |

*Time:*

| | | | |
|---|---|---|---|
| afterwards | following | in the meantime | soon |
| at length | immediately | meanwhile | |

**Tying paragraphs and sections together.** You want not only to link your sentences, but also your paragraphs and—on a larger scale—your sections. You can accomplish this by using forward and backward references, as well as three special types of paragraph. However, remember that if you attempt to use transition to tie together *all* paragraphs or sections, you'll probably overdo it. Link just enough paragraphs so your report will be a unified whole —not a bunch of isolated or disconnected paragraphs.

Here's a situation that involves the forward reference. Assume you are discussing job qualifications for a recent college graduate. You're devoting one paragraph to education and the next paragraph to attitude toward employment. If the last sentence of the education paragraph reads: "Thus education of the recent college graduate is important, but so is his attitude toward employment," you are using forward reference. Generally, however, you should avoid the use of forward references because they don't give the reader a mental stopping place before he plunges into the next paragraph. This type of reference also robs the next paragraph of its topic sentence.

Instead of a forward reference, use backward reference. In the previous situation, you could use a topic sentence for the attitude-toward-employment paragraph that also ties the two paragraphs together. Such a sentence might read: "Not only is education an important job qualification for a recent college graduate, but so is his attitude toward employment."

Below are other examples of backward reference between paragraphs:

1. In addition to the two plans just discussed, there is a third possibility . . . .
2. Inexpensive utility costs are another element of transportation that affects industrial location.
3. Since the need for trading stamps seems well established, we will next consider the types of stamps best adapted for this business field.

You can also use backward reference to tie together sections. For example, the Federal Aviation Agency uses the following standard format for the main sections of a report or briefing:

1. Problem
2. Facts bearing on the problem
3. Discussion
4. Conclusions
5. Alternative courses of action
6. Recommendations
7. Coordination
8. Attachments

The *FAA Instructional Manual* shows exceptionally good backward reference in discussing the use of the standard format listed above. Notice below how the topic sentence of a section links one major division with another:

The following sentence for the section labeled "Facts bearing on the problem" (item 2 above) links this section with the previous one concerning the problem:

Almost always, certain information of an objective character is basic to the whole study—the law, statistical information, financial information, historical facts germane to the problem.

Then the topic sentence for the discussion section (item 3) reads:

Once the problem has been stated and the facts bearing on it generally have been given, further progress requires an exposition of the factors to be considered, assumptions with respect to them, and observations made in the course of the study.

Finally, notice this linking topic sentence for the section on conclusions (item 4):

Considering the problem, the facts relating to it, and the discussion of the issues and factors pertaining to its causes and its potential solutions, one should be able to form conclusions.

In addition to backward and forward reference, you can tie together sections of a report by means of three types of paragraphs—introductory, summary or concluding, and transitional.

The introductory paragraph is the first paragraph of the section and serves a section the same way a topic sentence serves a paragraph. An introductory paragraph is practically mandatory for a section that includes two or more subdivisions.

A summary or concluding paragraph can be effective if a section is quite long—say three or more typewritten pages—but this final paragraph must definitely be helpful to the reader.

A transitional paragraph is especially helpful in a very long report—perhaps with 30 or more typewritten pages. You add this paragraph somewhere in the middle of the report body to tell the reader where he is; it tells him what has been covered and what is yet to come.

## Avoid the Subjunctive as Much as Possible

It's rather easy and natural to use the regular form of the verb when you are talking about a present or past happening. But you can easily revert to the subjunctive mood when you're discussing a proposal or something in the future. Since the subjunctive conveys contrary-to-fact in the mind of the reader, you want to avoid this conditional mood whenever you can. Instead, write so that the ideas seem closer to reality. For example, notice below the excessive use of the subjunctive. Every verb is subjunctive! The second version seems closer to reality because all sentences have the simple present or future tense.

*All subjunctive verbs:*
To have proper accounting control, your organization *would need* a central receiving department under the direct supervision of the chief accountant. His assistant, a receiving clerk *would be* responsible for all incoming and outgoing merchandise. At the time of purchase or withdrawal, all purchase orders and warehouse withdrawals *would go* to the receiving department, so that the clerk *could make* the proper entry in his ledger. In turn, the clerk *would count* all incoming and outgoing merchandise and *would record* it on proper sheets. Only then *would* he *permit* delivery to the department intended. By doing so, you *would have* an up-to-date record of your inventory.

*No subjunctive verbs:*
To have proper accounting control, your organization *needs* a central receiving department under the direct supervision of the chief accountant. His assistant, a receiving clerk, *will be* responsible for all incoming and outgoing merchandise. At the time of purchase or withdrawal, all purchase orders and warehouse withdrawals *go* to the receiving department, so that the clerk *can make* the proper entry in his ledger. In turn, the clerk *will count* all incoming and outgoing merchandise and *record* it on proper sheets. Only then *will* he *permit* delivery to the department intended. By doing so, he *will have* an up-to-date record of your inventory.

Instead of *would, could,* and *might* (all subjunctive), use *will* (or present tense), *can,* and *may.* Then you'll have more effective writing.

## Talk in Present Tense Whenever Possible

Not only do you want to avoid the subjunctive, but you also want to talk in the present tense whenever possible.

When you refer to the present, you naturally use the present tense. And you also use the present tense when you're stating a fact that is still true: "The sailor reminded the passenger that the equator *is* an imaginary line."

But you're likely to use the future tense when you're discussing something that doesn't seem to exist now in the writer's mind. Although it *seems* as if the happening will take place in the future, it actually exists now. By talking in the present instead of the future, as shown in the two versions below, you have a stronger presentation because it seems to be taking place now and thus seems closer and more real to the reader.

*Version in future tense:*
According to Mr. Metz, "two years of challenging and interesting work *will be* ahead for those who *will enter* the program." Six months *will be spent* in each of the four areas of PNB—plant, traffic, administration and accounting. In each area, the trainee *will become* acquainted with the operations by working with an experienced craftsman. Sometime before the six months *will be* up, the trainee *will take* over the responsibilities of a line supervisor in that department.

*Version in present tense:*
According to Mr. Metz, "two years of challenging and interesting work *are* ahead for those who *enter* the program." Six months *are spent* in each each of the four areas of PNB—plant, traffic, administration, and accounting. In each area, the trainee *becomes* acquainted with the operations by working with an experienced craftsman. Sometime before the six months *are* up, the trainee *takes* over the responsibilities of a line supervisor in that department.

Also, in the introduction you should not say, "This report will show . . ." but "This report shows . . ."—because the reader has the completed report before him and whatever you're referring to is present now.

## Use Mostly Active—Not Passive—Verbs

Whether you're writing a letter, memo, or report, talk mainly in the active voice. It's easier to avoid the passive when you can say "I," "we," and "you." But even when you're using only third person, you want to use more active than passive verbs. Notice the slow-paced, wordy, impersonal, and awkward passive in the paragraph below and then read the much-improved version without the passive.

*Excessive use of the passive:*
An observer *was sent* around the plant to investigate possibilities of employee carelessness as the cause for rising utilities. It *was observed* that many of the drinking fountains *were left* running continuously. It *was* also *noted* that lights *were left* on by many of the supervisors in offices while they were in the shop.

And although not as prevalent, many of the lights *are left burning* throughout the noon hour. Finally it *was observed* that even on cold days many of the outside windows in the various departments *were left* open. Since most of the rooms have thermostats, the heating system *is overloaded* in trying to maintain constant temperatures.

*Draft without passive*

Upon receiving various reports concerning employee carelessness with utilities, I *dispatched* an impartial observer to officially record these incidents. He *noticed* drinking fountains running continuously. He also *observed* many of the supervisors *left* lights on in their offices while they *were* in the shop. And although not as prevalent, many of the shop lights *burn* throughout the noon hour. Another serious problem *is* that even on cold days many windows *remain* open. This carelessness *results* in a major loss of heat and *creates* a strain on the heating system.

## TYPES OF SHORT REPORTS

Many reports show a modification of the ideal body pattern previously discussed. Frequently an introduction isn't necessary as the reader is already oriented (perhaps by similar or identically organized previous correspondence) to what he'll read in the text part. Also, mechanically adding a summary, conclusions, or recommendations can sometimes lengthen a communication without helping the reader or the report. This section discusses three types of short reports: (1) memorandum reports, (2) printed form reports, and (3) letter reports.

### Memorandum Report

Identifying features of a memorandum report are the TO, FROM, SUBJECT, DATE at the top of the paper and the three (expressed or implied) parts of the body. It covers just one topic and can move in one of three directions:

1. Downward—from top management to lesser officials and to employees on the action level
2. Upward—from employees and officials to other officials holding more responsible jobs in the organization
3. Horizontally—interchange of ideas and information among officials on the same level

Since the memo report is one of the most frequently used means of written communication within an organization, the subject matter ranges over broad areas. Also, the body format varies from that with introduction, text, and terminal section to one without introduction and/or terminal section.

So that you can get a feel of how memo reports vary in subject matter and organization, the following pages give examples for you to study.

Memo Report 1 keeps the home office informed about certain activities at the branches. Because this is a monthly report, an introduction or terminal section is unnecessary. The headings in the text portion with listing of different subjects under each, help the reader to grasp the thoughts as quickly and easily as possible. Instead of the signature and typewritten title at the bottom of the report, Mr. Kay could have initialed or signed his name near his typewritten name above.

*Memo Report 1: This monthly memo report—from the branch manager to an official at the home office—does not include an introduction or terminal section.*

TO:       A. B. Sea                              DATE:   (current)

FROM:     U. R. Kay

SUBJECT:  Branch Activities – October 197_

Personnel Training
1.  October 31 marked the midway point of the second phase of
    the National Bank Offices' training program.  Training is
    progressing satisfactorily and on schedule.  With the ter-
    mination of Pat Harris (Smith), we need to make a slight
    alteration in the program, but don't expect any delay or
    postponement of any training.  In fact, this termination
    will advance the training of Mary Jackson and Jean Miller.

Business Development Activity
1.  I again contacted Monty Kast, dentist and former member of
    my Kiwanis Club, regarding transfer of funds from National
    Association of Orthodontists, of which he is national
    treasurer.  He says he has received permission to transfer
    about $40,000 more to National Bank after January 1.  This
    additional amount brings the total to about $75,000.
2.  Although a divided period, 2 vacations, and one prolonged
    illness have disrupted my outside business call activity, I
    have made it a habit to attempt to converse with every
    broker, real estate salesman, insurance agent and attorney
    that comes into the office.  Although it is difficult to
    assess results from the little additional time and effort
    spent on this form of intra—office business development,
    numerous phone calls for loan information and a couple of
    loan commitments were a direct result of this activity.

Customer Complaints and Action Taken
1.  An unusually high number of customers in October compli-
    mented us on the friendly and courteous service of our
    personnel.
2.  I had one serious disagreement with a large savings account
    customer regarding his reluctance to reimburse National
    Bank for a check on which payment was stopped, a duplicate

issued, both checks cashed by the customer, and both paid
by the bank.  He blamed National Bank for allowing this
situation to happen and condemned our system for not
catching this before we received our bank statement.  He
quizzed Helen Hunt unmercifully until I interfered and put
a halt to it.  When he started swearing, I invited him to
leave the office.  He finally calmed down and left.  A
check was mailed to us a few days later, and his accounts
are still intact.

<u>Building, Equipment, and Parking Lot Comments</u>
1.  We encountered the usual winter heating problem at River-
    view Office--hot in the morning and cold in the afternoon.
    Blower fans are turned off at noon each day.  We have told
    Lewis Company of this situation many times, but they cannot
    rectify the situation.
2.  Interior clock does not keep correct time.  Maintenance
    department knows about the trouble with this clock and will
    take care of it.

                    (signature and title of branch manager)

Another type of activity report includes a body that consists only of a
listing of loans, discharges, new employees, or any appropriate activity in a
particular department or organization.

Below are two memo reports combined into one. The credit manager, Mr.
Holm, sends the first memo to the vice-president, Mr. Richfield. Notice the
absence of both an introduction and a terminal section. In turn, the vice-
president adds the second memo report directly below the first—part of it is
even on the same page as the first report—and returns the entire communication to the credit manager. The vice-president's reply consists of the text and
terminal section (recommendations). Observe how the listings in the second
memo report make reading easy.

*Memo Report 2:* *Report from credit manager to vice-president in the same organiza-*
              *tion and the vice-president's reply.*

                                DATE:   January 25, 1972

TO:        Joe Richfield, vice-president[1]

FROM:      Gordon Holm, credit manager[1]

SUBJECT:   <u>Credit Evaluation--Kay and Pierce Puckett</u>

The Pucketts were originally in the farming business, but have
retired from that occupation.  Over the years they have been

---

[1] Usually memos and memo reports don't include the title of the individuals because the people involved know one another and don't need any identification other than the name itself. But you will
include titles if company policy so dictates, or when the organization is large enough to justify a
title for clarification. Also, when you're writing to a superior, it might be wise to include the
title.

involved in real estate, owning apartment buildings and commercial properties. We have no financial statement at this
time, but outside sources estimate a net worth in the medium
6-figure bracket.

The last loan our company made to Mr. and Mrs. Puckett was on
June 29, 1963. This was for $65,000 on an apartment building.
It was paid in full with their personal funds on October 30,
1966, about 11 1/2 years ahead of schedule. The Pucketts have
had savings accounts with State Federal since before 1959. At
the present time we hold about $9,000 in savings, but the
accounts have ranged upward from this figure.

The Pucketts have maintained a good credit rating over the
years. A bank reports unsecured loans in high 4 to low 5
figures, prompt repayment with nothing now owing. Checking
account is maintained in low 5-figure amounts.

We have little in the way of financial figures at this time,
but find that the Pucketts are highly regarded in handling
their financial affairs.


TO:        Gordon Holm, credit manager    DATE:  January 25, 1972

FROM:      Joe Richfield, vice-president

SUBJECT:   Loan Recommendations--Kay and Pierce Puckett

In the review of this loan, these facts should be considered:

1.  Pierce Puckett contacted us about the possibility of making
    the proposed loan early in January. At that time, he
    thought the terms which we might offer him were unaccept-
    able. After he tested the market, he changed his mind, and
    returned to the office to inform Henry Knowles that he was
    interested in proceeding with loan negotiations.
        A definite complication entered the picture in that Mr.
    Puckett and his wife were scheduled to leave the following
    day on an extended motor trip to other parts of the coun-
    try. The mechanics of handling the loan details therefore
    became somewhat involved, but we believe they can be over-
    come by coordinating the commitment letter through his
    attorney. If the loan conditions are accepted, Michael
    Vande Voort has indicated that he and Jean Wilkinson will
    fly the Pucketts back here to sign the various mortgage
    papers.

2.  Mr. and Mrs. Puckett are making a substantial _cash_ invest-
    ment of $162,000 in this transaction. Our experience with
    them has been A-1. And while we have not yet received
    their current financial statement, their reputation for
    taking care of their obligations is excellent.

3. The criteria of a good apartment loan are present: desirable location, quality construction, acceptable room layout
and sizes, responsible borrower.

Our Loan Committee recommends a $400,000 loan under the
following conditions:

1. Rate: 7 1/4%

2. Service Fee: $3,000 (or 1% of the loan if our counsel feels
there's a legal basis for our doing so).

3. Term: 25 years. (The first payment would be delayed for
one year with the loan to be amortized in 24 years.)

4. The present purchase agreement between Willis Vande Voort
& Son, Inc. and Wilkinson & Sons, Inc. (a partnership) and
Kay Puckett will be rewritten to conform to new conditions.

5. Pierce Puckett will personally sign the mortgage note.

6. The repayment privilege will be 20% per year with a 6
months' interest penalty for anything paid over that
amount.

7. Other normal loan conditions.

In contrast to the two reports just given is Memo Report 3, which includes introduction, text, and terminal section. See if you can identify the five
elements in the introduction.

*Memo Report 3: Authorized informational report to the credit manager from an
assistant in the same department within the organization.*

TO:        Sumner Marcus                    DATE:   (current)

FROM:      Dwight Robinson

SUBJECT:   Installment Credit Department Reports

Here is the report you requested concerning reports written by
one commercial bank here in (city). I interviewed Richard
Anderson, assistant cashier at State National Bank, concerning
business reports used in his organization. Since you are
especially interested in installment credit, I have limited my
discussion to reports prepared and used by the Installment
Credit Department. The three types of reports used in this
department and discussed below are statistical, inter-office
memorandum, and memorandum for the credit file.

## Statistical Report

The statistical report is compiled monthly by employees of the Installment Credit Department under Mr. Anderson's supervision. The report is a statistical presentation of the total loan balance of each of the department's individual accounts. These individual accounts are then divided between punctual and delinquent accounts.

The purpose of a statistical report is to inform the department manager and the branch manager of the quantitative and qualitative aspects of the department's operations. The branch manager consolidates this report into a branch report which he then sends to the divisional manager and ultimately the executive vice-president in charge of operations.

The report is presented in table form to provide quick evaluation of the department's performance. This presentation points up delinquent accounts, which are given closer examination in the inter-office type discussed next. Since statistics are emphasized, little or no discussion is included.

## Inter-Office Memorandum Report

Mr. Anderson or employees in his department write the inter-office memorandum to supply credit information to upper management and any other bank officer concerning any of their installment credit accounts. The upper management reports are the most important and are concerned with delinquent accounts.

There is no specific form for presenting the information, other than the standard to-from-subject-date of a memorandum. The report writing training that all bank officers receive provides standard guidelines for credit appraising. Upper management evaluates the delinquent account credit reports on the basis of the thorough application of these guidelines and the validity of corrective action taken. The standard length is usually one page or less.

## Credit File Memorandum Report

The credit file memorandum report is written by any bank officer. Each time a bank officer comes in contact with an installment credit account, he makes a report of any new information he has learned. This report is then included in the account credit file and provides the bank with a more detailed picture of the account. This procedure guards against the possibility of one officer being the sole contact with an account and also enables any other officer to become familiar with that account quickly and easily by reading the credit file.

Although the credit file memorandum becomes part of an account's file, copies of these reports are sometimes sent to other interested bank officers; an example is a person who mentions over lunch that he wishes to organize an employee trust fund. The officer, upon learning this information, then makes a comment on a memorandum-for-credit-file form. A subject line is provided for the account name, and a column is provided for the date and origin of the report. In the column the bank officer places the date and his name, and any persons to receive copies, in this case the Trust Department. The comment is entered opposite the date and is usually no longer than one or two lines.

### Summary

The three types of reports used in the Installment Credit Department of State National Bank are statistical report, inter-office memorandum report, and memorandum report for the credit file. The statistical report is an operating report to upper management for the department with little or no discussion, while the other two are written reports concerned with individual accounts. The inter-office memorandum is used mostly for delinquent account evaluation for upper management, while the credit file memorandum contains any pertinent information about an account. All three go outside the department, but a copy of the credit file memorandum is retained in the account credit file to build a more complete file.

The organization and content of the body of memo reports vary according to the type of report and the use by the reader. Given below are more report outlines that illustrate some of the many possible variations. The word underscored and shown in parentheses tells you whether the body of the particular report follows the logical or psychological organizational pattern.

1. Report on a meeting (logical)
   a. Introduction (five W's plus statement of highlights of meeting)
   b. Text (discussion of the meeting)
   c. No terminal section needed

2. Report on an investigation (logical with a summary preceding the body)
   a. Summary
   b. Introduction
   c. Text: Comparison of results
              Causes for problem
              Corrective steps taken
   d. Recommendations

3. Progress report (shows "progress," accomplishments, or activity for a certain period or stage of a major assignment) (mainly logical)
   a. Introduction (purpose, nature of the project, summary of work to date)
   *b. Description of accomplishments during the reporting period
   c. Terminal section
   *d. Plans for the next reporting period
   *e. Unanticipated problems
   *Actually the discussion or text

4. Recommendation report[1] (mainly logical)
   a. Introduction
   b. Summary
   c. Text (entirely recommendations)
   d. Conclusions
   e. Appendix (background information relating to the period involved)

5. Periodic report (summary of activities that took place during a specific span of time) (logical with a summary as a part preceding the body)
   a. Abstract or summary
   b. No introduction necessary
   c. Text (organized by major activities in the department or branch)
   d. Recommendations

6. Covering memo report with attachments (logical)
   a. Introduction
   b. Text (highlights of findings in capsule form)
   c. No terminal section
   d. Attachments (data supporting the findings)

7. Justification report (special type of psychologically arranged report body for top management)
   a. Purpose (usually only one sentence).
   b. Cost and savings (only one sentence that includes the cost and savings).
   c. Conclusions (if different enough from cost and savings to justify including; number conclusions if more than one).
   d. Discussion (development of purpose and proof of results highlighted under "cost and savings" and "conclusions"). The discussion usually makes up 50 percent to 75 percent of the entire body. You usually organize the discussion in the order you listed the conclusions.

You may also encounter short reports whose body and use are similar to memo reports—yet which lack the TO, FROM, SUBJECT, DATE heading. They're included here because they resemble a memo report more than a letter report or printed form report. These reports may or may not include a title page. Below are several outline examples of these reports.

1. Dun and Bradstreet report (usually one page)
   a. Summary
   b. (No introduction necessary)
   c. Text: Payments
            Finance
            Banking
            History
            Operation

[1] This recommendation report differs greatly from many reports that have recommendations for the terminal section.

2. Appraisal report (signed and dated at the end by the chief appraiser)

In parentheses below is number of paragraphs for each section of a two-page appraisal report.

Location and legal description (followed by two paragraphs)

Description of improvements (followed by one paragraph and a brief description of each of nine subheadings)

Roof
Exterior walls
Floors
Interior walls
Millwork
Appliances
Electrical
Plumbing
Heating

Valuation (followed by physical value table and comment that the following income valuation is attached)

Both the Dun and Bradstreet report and the appraisal report have standardized headings; that is, the company determines what the headings should be and sometimes their order. This policy assures uniformity and completeness of coverage, and permits the receiving officer to know what to expect and to study information that allows comparison by periods. Also the suggested format makes it easy for the report writer to include the data the receiver wants. The writer merely adds the needed information under each heading.

If there are so many variations of reports in existence, how can you orient your thinking so that you can remember all the different organizational patterns? In the first place don't try to memorize the many different patterns! Instead, remember the following basic patterns for the body of the memo report:

1. Logical pattern (introduction, text, and terminal section)
2. Psychological pattern
   a. Organized by usual psychological pattern (terminal section before or after the introduction but always before the text)
   b. Organized by unusual pattern (purpose, cost and savings, conclusions, and discussion)

So that you will better remember these patterns, the pages that follow illustrate the completed memo report for each organizational pattern.

*Situation:*
You are the assistant manager of the Wichita Hardware Store, located in Wichita, Kansas. In the past 5 years the operation has grown from a one-man local hardware store to a 2-store operation employing 24 people.

Most of the departments have been operating smoothly without any apparent inefficiencies. However, recently you have become aware of a gross inadequacy in the electrical department. Your clerks hand-measure the electrical (copper) wire on a yardstick that is permanently affixed to the counter. This seemed to be perfectly satisfactory when you were dealing in small quantities of wire sold. However, now the business has become oriented toward large contractors who come in to buy more than 100 yards of wire at a time. This change in buying has presented quite a problem in measuring and pricing the wire. Contractors always buy a portion of a spool—never a whole spool at one time.

First, the wire comes in spools of 1,000 yards. That makes it difficult when the contractor wants less than a whole spool, but does want a large quantity, say 140 yards. The clerk must measure 140 yards off the spool and then coil it in some fashion so that it won't tangle and will be easy to carry.

You ran a study and found that in 100 purchases it took an average of 15 minutes for one clerk to measure, coil, and price 50 yards of wire. Although there were never any complaints of short measurement, nor were there any reports of excessive measurements, you did find when inventory was taken that an average of 50 yards had left the store but was not accounted for over a 3-month period. This 50-yard loss was attributed to errors in measurement.

The price of copper wire averages 22 cents a foot. You sell an average of 2,000 yards a month.

Pacific Tool Company has a measuring machine for wire of all diameters. This machine meters up to 1,000 yards and includes 3 parts:

1. A spindle to hold the spool of wire to be measured
2. A meter that measures and prices the wire
3. A spindle to receive and coil the wire that has been measured

To measure, coil, and price 50 yards of wire takes one clerk 5 minutes and can be done in one operation. This machine costs $200 and has a guarantee of 5 years.

This machine would eliminate mistakes in measurement and pricing. It would save the clerk the cumbersome job of coiling up the wire (which originally took the most time). It would also save the clerk 10 minutes (per 50 yards) that could be used to help someone else. In fact, your business is doing so well that you always have to hire one or more extra help at $4 an hour each of the 300 working days throughout the year.

Write your report and send it to the president, Mr. David Wilkins. Analyze the 2 alternatives—buying the machine or continuing the present hand method. Take into account the qualitative factors like convenience to the customer and convenience to the clerk, as well as the quantitative factors like savings to the store.

The first step is to get the arithmetic out of the way:

$\dfrac{2,000 \times 12 \text{ (months)}}{50} \times \dfrac{1}{6}$ hour (or 10 minutes) $\times$ $4 hourly wage equals $320 wages saved yearly.

50 $\times$ 4 (quarters) $\times$ 22¢ foot or 66¢ yard equals $132 savings in eliminating shortage loss by hand measuring.

$320 plus $132 equals $452 gross savings in 1 year minus $200 equals $252 net savings in 1 year.

$452 $\times$ 5 years minus $200 equals $2,060 net savings in 5 years.

Your next step is to organize and write the report.

*1. Organized by Logical Pattern*

TO:        Mr. David Wilkins, President        DATE:    (current)

FROM:      (your name)

SUBJECT:   Justifying Purchase of Wire-measuring Machine

Recently I became aware of a costly procedure in the electrical
department—a procedure of hand-measuring wire which we should
change because it is costing us about $450 of unnecessary
expense each year.  In addition to dollar savings, this report
shows a convenience to both the clerks and the customers with
the purchase of a wire measuring machine manufactured by the
Pacific Tool Company.

Possible Savings[1]

Presently we are hand-measuring the electrical (copper) wire on
a yardstick that is permanently affixed to the counter.  I made
a random check of 100 purchases and found it takes an average
of 15 minutes for one clerk to measure, coil, and price 50
yards of wire.  The measuring machine can perform the same job
in 5 minutes—a savings of 10 minutes or 1/6 of an hour for
every 50 yards of wire.

Since business is booming so much that we always have to hire
extra help throughout the year, time saved in measuring means
money saved in wages.  Because we sell an average of 2,000
yards of wire a month or 24,000 yards yearly and clerks' rate
of pay is $4 an hour, there is a possible savings of $320 in
wages, as shown below:

$$\frac{24,000}{50} \text{ X } \frac{1}{6} \text{ X } \$4 = \$320 \text{ wages saved yearly}$$

Although we have never had any complaints on short measurement,
I found on the average a shortage of 50 yards of wire for every
3-month period.  At 22 cents a foot (or 66 cents a yard) for
the wire, we can save an additional $132, as the following
figures show:

50 X 4 (quarters) X 66¢ = $132 savings realized if we
                                eliminate shortage loss by
                                hand measuring

We can realize a total gross savings of $452 ($320 and $132)
yearly with the measuring machine.  And because the machine

---

[1] Although subheadings are not necessary here, you can use them in this section. If so, you'll need a
topic sentence that leads into the following third degree headings—"Possible Savings on Wages"
(first two paragraphs of the section) and "Possible Savings on Measurements" (all of the third
paragraph). The last paragraph is a conclusion without a heading.

sells for $200 and carries a 5-year guarantee, we can save $252
net the first year or $2,060 within 5 years ($452 X 5 - $200).

### Convenience Factor
In addition to the dollar savings, both the clerks and the
customers will appreciate the convenience factor of the machine.  Because the wire comes in spools of 1,000 yards, the
clerk now has difficulty in hand-measuring less than a whole
spool but a large quantity--say 150 yards--of wire.  He must
measure off 140 yards and then coil it in some fashion so that
it won't tangle and will be easy to carry.

As a contrast, the machine measures wire of all diameters,
meters up to 1,000 yards, and includes 3 parts:

    1.  A spindle to hold the spool of wire to be measured
    2.  A meter that measures and prices the wire
    3.  A spindle to receive and coil the wire that has been
       measured

Thus, this machine will not only eliminate mistakes in measurement and pricing.  It will save the clerk the cumbersome job of
coiling up the wire and also free the customer's time by 10
minutes for each wire purchase.

### Conclusions
1.  A capital outlay of $200 for a wire measuring machine will
    save us $452 gross or $252 net the first year and $2,060
    net for the 5-year guarantee period.
2.  The machine will save the clerk the cumbersome job of
    coiling up the wire and also free the customer's time by
    10 minutes for each wire purchase.

In the first paragraph of the preceding example you let the president
know your results—that a wire-measuring machine will save both money and
convenience. But suppose you are a management trainee and you're writing
to a 65-year-old penny-pinching owner whose usual reply when someone suggests a change that costs money is "We've been doing all right so far; why
should I spend more money to buy something new?" When you write to him
(or to anyone else who will begin to fight you if he sees a decision before the
facts), you'll need to change the report in the following ways.

1. You'll need a noncommittal subject line:

Cost Comparison of Hand and Machine Wire-measuring Methods

2. You'll need a non-committal introduction:

Recently I became aware of a costly procedure in the Electrical
Department--a procedure of hand-measuring wire.  This report
compares cost and convenience factors of two alternatives--
continuing with the present hand method or buying a wire-
measuring machine manufactured by the Pacific Tool Company.

3. Text (same as above)
4. Conclusions (same as above)

With this presentation, you don't indicate the conclusions until the terminal section—until you have given all the facts to the reader.

*2a. Organized by Usual Psychological Pattern*

```
TO:        Mr. David Wilkins                DATE:   (current)

FROM:      (your name)

SUBJECT:   Justifying Purchase of Wire-measuring Machine

                        Conclusions¹
(Same as those shown in first logical pattern)

                        Introduction¹
(You need to eliminate "about $450 of" in the introduction of
the first logical pattern because the conclusions reveal the
same information; otherwise the introduction remains the same.
Naturally you need to add the heading because this section
isn't the first part of the report body.)

                       Possible Savings
(Same as that section in logical pattern)

                      Convenience Factor
(Same as that section in logical pattern)
```

*2b. Organized by Unusual Psychological Pattern²*

```
TO:        Mr. David Wilkins                DATE:   (current)

FROM:      (your name)

SUBJECT:   Justifying Purchase of Wire-measuring Machine

                          Purpose
To show the dollar savings and convenience factor with the
purchase of a wire-measuring machine for the electrical
department.

                       Cost and Savings
For a capital outlay of $200 for a wire-measuring machine, we
can save an estimated $2,060 in 5 years.
```

¹ These 2 sections might be reworded with appropriate slight changes in wording.
² See outline 7 on page 633 for other details about the organization pattern for this report—sometimes called a justification report or inverted form report.

<u>Conclusions</u>
1.  Possible savings:  $2,060 net for the 5-year guarantee
    period.
2.  Convenience factor:  For both clerks and customers.


<u>Discussion</u>
Recently I became aware of a costly procedure in the electrical
department.  Presently we are hand measuring the copper wire on
a yardstick that is permanently affixed to the counter.  By
purchasing a wire measuring machine manufactured by the Pacific
Tool Company, we can save money and at the same time assure
convenience to both the clerks and customers.


<u>Possible Savings</u>
(Same as that section in the logical pattern.)


<u>Convenience Factor</u>
(Same as that section in the logical pattern.)

In summary, memo reports come in a variety of organizational patterns. Although one of their distinguishing features is the three-part body (introduction, text, and terminal section), sometimes the introduction and/or the terminal section isn't necessary. Once you understand the three basic patterns for memo reports, you can adapt to the special formats you'll encounter on the job.


## Printed Form Report

The printed form report should be used when a company follows or uses the same format often enough to justify the "jelling" of the report body, headings, and instructions into a printed form. The individual filling out the form merely adds the necessary figures, sentences, and identifications.

Although filling out this form is quick and easy, preparing it is more difficult. It should be clear, simple, and provide the needed information in the quickest and easiest manner. Those who will be filling out the form and using the information should be consulted. They can make suggestions before the form is drawn up and later they can evaluate the form in rough draft.

Shown in Figures 15-1 to 15-4 are printed form reports that various business firms use. (Others include the company job application form, policeman's graphic location of a collision of cars at an intersection, Internal Revenue Form 1040 for reporting year's income, automobile accident report, claim for damages suffered, and the form the personnel man fills out after he has interviewed an applicant.) In all four examples, the form consists mainly of the text portion of the body. No introduction, terminal section, or even TO, FROM, SUBJECT are formally given because the reader is sufficiently oriented by

**D— NIGHT AUDITOR'S MACHINE BALANCE NO.**_____

DATE_____

| | DATE | TRANS. SYMBOLS | NET TOTALS | CORRECTIONS | MACH. TOTALS | |
|---|---|---|---|---|---|---|
| ROOM | | | | | | |
| RESTAURANT | | | | | | |
| TELEPHONE | | | | | | |
| LONG DISTANCE | | | | | | |
| LAUN. & DRY CLEAN | | | | | | |
| MISCELLANEOUS | | | | | | |
| PAID OUT | | | | | | |
| TOTAL DEBITS | | | | | | |
| MISCELLANEOUS CR. | | | | | | |
| PAID | | | | | | |
| TOTAL CREDITS | | | | | | |
| NET DIFFERENCE | | | | | | |
| OPENING DR. BALANCE | | | | | | |
| NET OUTSTANDING | | | | | | |
| | | | | | | |
| | | | | | | |
| | | | | | | |
| TOTAL MCH. DR. BALANCE | | | | | | |
| LESS CR. BALANCE | | | | | | |
| NET OUTSTANDING | | | | | | |

DETECTOR COUNTER READINGS:          ☐ DATE CHANGED

AUDITOR'S CONTROL_____          ☐ CONTROL TOTALS AT ZERO          **AUDITOR**

MACH. NUMBER_____          ☐ MASTER TAPE LOCKED

B-6759—K28YY          ☐ AUDIT CONTROL LOCKED

Figure 15-1   Night Auditor's Report. An auditor in a hotel chain uses this printed-form report daily in running a trial balance. The organization of this report permits the form to serve two services—as a worksheet and as a permanent record. The nine types of accounts (in smaller print) in the left-hand column relate to the expenses by hotel patrons. The auditor uses the other columns to record account balances, corrections to the account balances, net totals, and machine account identifiers. The information in the lower left of the report is a checklist to help him clear the accounting machines for the next day's transactions. This form is easily used by anyone familiar with auditing procedures and the National Cash Register (NCR) 4500 accounting machine.

frequent usage, identification of the report title, columnar headings, date, and/or signature and other information.

A specialized kind of printed form report is the well-known statistical report that consists mainly or wholly of figures that the writer adds in identifying columns. The form is easy to fill out and permits comparison of similar data within the same report and between reports for different time periods.

Shown on page 645 is an example of a filled-in, one-page statistical report that State Federal Savings Association uses to compare itself with other similar and competing organizations. The information (figures already added to the printed form) shows loans made for one particular month (May) by sev-

PERSONNEL REPORT

Date_____ Office_____

EMPLOYEE:

| | Jan | Feb | Mar | Apr | May | Jun | Jul | Aug | Sep | Oct | Nov | Dec |
|---|---|---|---|---|---|---|---|---|---|---|---|---|
| Excused Absences | | | | | | | | | | | | |
| Absences due to illness | | | | | | | | | | | | |
| Unexcused Absences | | | | | | | | | | | | |
| Totals | | | | | | | | | | | | |

Brief description of present duties: _____

_____

_____

Employee has had training in - and is capable of - performing the following duties:

_____

_____

_____

General Comments:

_____

_____

In my opinion this is a (better-than-average) (average) (below average) employee.
    UNDERLINE ONE OF THE ABOVE

Signed_____

PERSONNEL REPORTS DUE MAY 1   AND NOVEMBER 1
    May 1   report covers period Nov. 1 through April 30
    Nov. 1   report covers period May 1 through Oct. 31

Figure 15-2   Example of an evaluation form that a supervisor fills out for each employee twice a year and files in the employee's personnel folder.

## SALESMAN'S EXPENSE VOUCHER

IMPORTANT  ENTER ALL EXPENSES OF THE TRIP. ATTACH ALL HOTEL BILLS, ALSO RECEIPTED BILLS FOR OTHER EXPENDITURES OF $25.00 OR MORE EACH. ENTER COMPANY CREDIT CARD ITEMS IF ANY, INDICATE SUCH BY *; DO NOT INCLUDE IN TOTAL. SEE REVERSE SIDE FOR INSTRUCTIONS

NAME _____    FOR WEEK ENDED _____

| DAY DATE | CITY | HOTEL | MEALS | ENTERTAIN- MENT (SEE BELOW) | FARE | TIPS | PARKING & TOLLS | STAMPS TEL. & TEL. | OTHER (SEE BELOW) | TOTAL | MILEAGE |
|---|---|---|---|---|---|---|---|---|---|---|---|
| SUNDAY | | | | | | | | | | | |
| | | | | | | | | | | | |
| | | | | | | | | | | | |
| MONDAY | | | | | | | | | | | |
| | | | | | | | | | | | |
| | | | | | | | | | | | |
| TUESDAY | | | | | | | | | | | |
| | | | | | | | | | | | |
| | | | | | | | | | | | |
| WEDNESDAY | | | | | | | | | | | |
| | | | | | | | | | | | |
| | | | | | | | | | | | |
| THURSDAY | | | | | | | | | | | |
| | | | | | | | | | | | |
| | | | | | | | | | | | |
| FRIDAY | | | | | | | | | | | |
| | | | | | | | | | | | |
| | | | | | | | | | | | |
| SATURDAY | | | | | | | | | | | |
| | | | | | | | | | | | |
| | | | | | | | | | | | |
| TOTAL | | | | | | | | | | | |

MAIL CHECK TO:

AUTO AT 8¢ PER MILE _____

TOTAL EXPENSE _____

SIGNED _____

CHECK NO. _____

APPROVED _____

I. EXPLANATION OF ENTERTAINMENT:

AMOUNT, DATE, PLACE, TYPE (LUNCH, DINNER, THEATRE, ETC.) BUSINESS PURPOSE; LIST NAMES, TITLES AND BUSINESS AFFILI-ATION OF EACH INDIVIDUAL PRESENT (IF THE ENTERTAINMENT DI-RECTLY PRECEDES OR FOLLOWS A SUBSTANTIAL BUSINESS DISCUS-SION, IN ADDITION TO THE FOREGOING, SHOW DATE, DURATION, NATURE AND PLACE OF BUSINESS DISCUSSION)

II. OTHER (EXPLAIN EACH ITEM)

(ATTACH ANOTHER SHEET, IF NECESSARY)

Figure 15-3  Weekly Expense Voucher. When filled out, this report reveals each day's expenses and entertainment. It is approved by the district sales manager and reported to the regional office for reimbursement. Notice detailed instructions accompanying the voucher on page 643.

Instructions For Completing Salesman's Expense Voucher - Form ML 175

     Expense vouchers are prepared at the close of the week and mailed so that they arrive at the sales office on Monday morning. Care must be taken to follow these instructions to avoid having a voucher returned for correction, thus causing a delay in reimbursement.

City:
    Cities visited on the appropriate line for each day.

Hotel:
    Daily room rent only (including local tax, if any). Attach receipted bill.

Meals:
    Cost of salesman's own meal and tips. Cost of customers' meals are to be shown in the Entertainment column.

Entertainment:
    Explanation of this item must be shown in detail in lower part of the voucher.

Fare:
    Fares paid or incurred by individuals including excess baggage charges (attach receipts where available), as well as charges for rented autos. It is not necessary to enter the cost of transportation paid for directly by the Company, provided such cost is not paid for by use of a personal credit card.

Tips:
    Tips to porters, bellhops, etc.

Parking and Tolls:
    Fees paid for parking and bridge, tunnel, and road tolls.

Stamps, Tel. and Tel.:
    Postage, telephone and telegraph incurred in the transaction of Company business.

Other:
    Other business-connected expenses such as office supplies, taxi, express charges, etc. Explain in lower part of form.

Total:
    The daily total of all expenditures. Add this column to obtain the weekly total which must agree with the sum of the totals under the various expense captions.

Mileage:
    Miles traveled on Company business each day. The total mileage for the week is multiplied by 8 cents and the result entered in the space indicated.

    The voucher must be signed by the individual who prepared it and approved by an authorized person. Indicate in the appropriate space at the bottom of the form the location to which you want the reimbursement check mailed.

## SALESMAN'S WEEKLY PLAN

I WILL BE AT THE FOLLOWING PLACES OR ACCOUNTS <u>THIS</u> <u>WEEK</u>:

| | DATE | ACCOUNTS OR TOWN | STATE | MAIL SENT TO |
|---|---|---|---|---|
| MON | | | | |
| TUES | | | | |
| WED | | | | |
| THUR | | | | |
| FRI | | | | |
| SAT | | | | |
| SUN | | | | |

I PLAN TO BE AT THE FOLLOWING ACCOUNTS OR PLACES <u>NEXT</u> <u>WEEK</u>:

| | | | | |
|---|---|---|---|---|
| MON | | | | |
| TUES | | | | |
| WED | | | | |
| THUR | | | | |
| FRI | | | | |
| SAT | | | | |
| SUN | | | | |

SALESMAN

Figure 15-4  The name of each account the salesman plans to visit day by day is reported to the district sales manager in this printed form.

# Table 15-1 Example of a Statistical Report

## MAY 197—

| Date | State Federal Savings | Citizens Savings | 1st Nat'l of Pasco | Union Bank | Center Bank | 1st Nat'l of Walla Walla | "66" Credit Union | Commerce Acceptance & Harris Plan | FHA | Others | Smith Mortgage |
|---|---|---|---|---|---|---|---|---|---|---|---|
| 2 | 18,250 | | 28,500 | | 4,800 | | | 9,800 | | 12,900 | 11,200 |
| 7 | 23,000 | | | 35,000 | | | | | 184,900 | 2,200 | 21,900 |
| 9 | 71,900 | | 1,500 | | | | 15,200 | 3,800 | 56,640 | 2,100 | 8,500 |
| 14 | 16,000 | 3,000 | 1,800 | 37,500 | | | | 10,100 | 43,200 | 86,700 | 16,100 |
| 16 | 15,000 | | 2,800 | | | 3,000 | 5,400 | | | 7,600 | |
| 21 | 58,300 | 25,000 | | 5,300 | | 19,500 | 7,000 | 23,000 | 51,200 | 15,000 | 48,400 |
| 23 | 37,000 | | | | 3,500 | | | 12,000 | 15,000 | 9,500 | 15,000 |
| 28 | 35,600 | | 18,800 | | | 11,100 | 6,700 | 3,100 | 12,800 | 32,100 | 12,900 |
| 31 | 90,550 | | 19,800 | | | | 13,500 | | | 31,700 | 30,400 |
| | 365,600 | 28,000 | 73,200 | 77,800 | 8,300 | 33,600 | 47,800 | 61,800 | 363,740 | 199,800 | 164,400 |
| RANK | (1) | (10) | (6) | (5) | (11) | (9) | (8) | (7) | (2) | (3) | (4) |

TOTAL — $1,424,040

eral different organizations, including State Federal. The first column gives two days in every week (2d, 7th, etc.) in the month. The total for each column allows ranking of the 11 organizations according to largest dollar volume. As shown, State Federal ranks first with $365,600 out of a grand total of $1,424,040. If the receiver gets this report every month, the TO, FROM, SUBJECT isn't necessary. But if the sender wants to dress up the report, he can attach a transmittal memo giving the conventional to-from-subject-date and any comment he wishes to include.

## Letter Report

A letter report is exactly what the title says it is—a report using the format of a letter. It usually covers a minor investigation or relates the writer's own knowledge or experience. This type of report goes outside the company, and its length is usually five or fewer pages.

Because this report goes to someone not part of your firm, you need an appropriate opening and closing. A "typical" report introduction is usually out of place, as is a "typical" terminal section—summary, conclusions, or recommendations.

*The first paragraph* of a letter report resembles the opening of a letter; yet you usually include the following elements found in an introduction:

Authorization (if one exists)
Purpose (always)
Problem (if one exists)
Statement of the results (optional)
Plan of presentation (depends on length of report)

Examples:
1. As you requested, I am glad to tell you our experience with the XYZ machine. Overall, we're quite pleased with its performance and dependability.
2. It is a pleasure to report to you our progress in 1971 just completed and look ahead with you for this year just started.
3. I have made an investigation of the Delivery Service Department, as requested in your letter of January 7, with regard to reducing the operating cost of the department.
4. While auditing your books last month, I noticed your firm does not have a centralized receiving department. The purpose of this report is to explain the present set up and then show how a receiving department will benefit your organization.

*The middle paragraphs* comprise the text—and are identical to those used in any other type of report. Usually the emphasis is on the findings or results. This section can use headings if they help guide the reader in his reading.

*The last paragraph* offers to discuss further, come to his office at his convenience, or thank. If you need to conclude or recommend, do so just before the last paragraph.

Below is a situation that calls for a reply in the format of a letter report. As you read the details, ask yourself how you'll begin to develop the finished product—a reply to Mr. Davis.

*Situation:*

You are the president of a wholesale house in New Orleans that sells fiber glass space materials. Last year you installed a Ditto-Print machine in one of your departments. This machine consists of 2 parts—a ditto master and a ditto machine. Its ditto master maker takes an original and in one step—through a dry thermal heat process—produces a master unit just like those you usually have to type. This machine eliminates the time-consuming process of typing a master unit (usually takes at least 15 minutes); it makes a master unit in 5 seconds, from which you should get 120 copies.

Mr. James Davis, President of the Zelectron Company, 1243 Jackson Avenue, S.W., Memphis, Tennessee, has been thinking about buying one of the Ditto-Print machines. The Ditto-Print company gave him your name as an example of a relatively new customer. He is interested in hearing your comments on the machine after a year's use. He is especially interested in performance and dependability. (Is it dependable? Does it need repair often? Are repairs made promptly?)

Your assignment is to write an objective letter to this man and tell him of your experiences with the machine. Your experiences are as follows:

1. For the first 2 months it worked up to expectations. It did, however, need one minor adjustment at that time. The repairman was prompt and the repair was made in one day.
2. Your company rarely has a need to run more than 50 copies off a master unit. However, 4 or 5 times you have had to run off 120 copies. At these times you found that the machine master actually runs off only 100 good copies, whereas a typewritten master runs off 120 good copies (sometimes 150 good copies).
3. The machine has saved you quite a bit of money in time saved. It enabled your secretaries to copy important correspondence from your suppliers and distribute it to your 50 salesmen in a very short time. Before the secretaries had to type up master units of the original before they could be run off and distributed. Now the whole process can be done in minutes.
4. Other than the 6-month checkup, the machine has needed no major repairs. But you have had the repairmen out several times because after 6 months of use you found that you were having trouble getting good masters off certain types of paper. He could only say that the poor copies were due to master paper with a lot of rag content and that that was just one of those things. But you have received very little correspondence on this type of paper so it hasn't really been a big problem.
5. You are going to install another machine in a second department within 6 months. In your business, you feel that this machine has been a great help and you feel additional machines would be a good investment. Eventually, you plan to buy 9 of them—one for each department in your organization.

Your purpose—to tell Mr. Davis your experience with the machine—tells you what ideas to include. (Naturally you won't try to sell the machine because that's not part of your experience.) Then you'll organize these ideas in an outline similar to the one below:

First paragraph: purpose, authorization (optional), statement of results (overall reaction to the machine); also add smile.

Second paragraph: history of purchasing machines—have had one for a year, will get another in 6 months, eventually in each of 9 departments.

Third paragraph: dependability (need topic sentence)—OK first two months, needed only one minor repair. No major repair except for scheduled 6-month checkup.

Fourth paragraph: performance (need topic sentence)—dollar savings because of time saved, makes good copies, poor copies beyond 100, rag paper also makes poor copies.

Fifth paragraph: pleasure to help, glad to do so again.

Once you know the organizational pattern and ideas for each paragraph, you can turn out a reply (letter report) similar to the following.

Dear Mr. Davis

I am glad to answer your request concerning our experience with the Ditto-Print machine. Based on our plans explained below for purchasing additional machines, you can readily see that we have been pleased with its dependability and performance.

History of Purchasing Machines[1]
As you know, we have had a Ditto-Print machine for about a year. Because of our success with the machine, we plan to install another one in another department in 6 months. Also future plans include supplying eventually each of our 9 departments with a machine.

Dependability
The machine worked up to expectations during the first 2 months and needed only one minor repair; the repairman was prompt and completed his work in one day. Since then, the machine required no major repair except for the scheduled 6-month checkup.

Performance
In addition to good dependability, our Ditto-Print machine has performed well. We have realized considerable dollar savings because the secretaries can copy and distribute correspondence from suppliers in a fraction of a time formerly required. Also the machine turns out good, clean copies. But we have noticed

---

[1] Whether you include headings—especially in the text of a letter report—usually depends upon the length of each section. In this report, you can easily omit the headings because each section—especially the first two—are quite short. But if each section comprises several paragraphs—as in the letter report on pages 654 and 655—then you should use headings.

poor copies when more than 100 were run off the same master;
this is no problem, however, since we seldon run more than 50
copies off a master.  Also in 5 seconds the secretary can make
a new master for copies beyond 100.  We also noticed that
high-rag-content paper results in poor copies; but once again
there is no real problem since we seldom use this type of paper
for masters.

It has been a pleasure to help you, Mr. Davis.  Please let me
know when I can be of future assistance.

In this report, you needed to show both the good and the bad features
of the machine. This type of message—like all other reports—requires you
to be factual and unbiased. Yet you had to show proper emphasis by conveying
to Davis your overall favorable impression of the Ditto-Print machine. If you
had stressed the bad features, the resulting picture would not have represented
your true feelings.

On the following pages is another example of a letter report—a reply to
a university student who had inquired about reports and requested several
actual examples. This example is particularly good for the following reasons:

1. It is a report that is interesting to read. It keeps the reader in mind throughout and even narrows the coverage (scope) of reports to those that the student might be most interested in.
2. The writer educates the student about reports and their usage in the company
without talking down to him.
3. Accompanying the long covering letter, are five attachments that include:
    a. A format for a progress report the writer used when he was a trainee. (See
    page 651. Even the discussion in the format gives tips on how to write this
    type.
    b. Three 1-page actual progress reports he had written as a trainee. (See page
    652 for one of the 3).
    c. A 2-page special report that he recently wrote. It uses an entirely different
    organizational pattern. (See pages 653–654).

Following the letter report here you'll find the enclosures of (a), one of
(b), and (c) listed above.

As you read the covering letter (letter report), notice that the writer organized his material according to the following pattern:

| | |
|---|---|
| First paragraph: | opening—like a letter (with a smile)—authorization, pur-pose, and good news (sending several actual reports) |
| Second paragraph: | background on reports and scope of message |
| Third paragraph: | results—answers student's inquiry |
| Fourth paragraph: | results—answers student's inquiry |
| Fifth paragraph: | results—answers student's inquiry |
| Sixth paragraph: | results—answers student's inquiry |
| Seventh paragraph: | closing—like a letter (notice friendly, personal attitude) |

Notice the interest the writer takes in the student throughout the message. The writer may not remember the student very long, but the student will recall not only the writer but the company he represents.

Dear Mr. Graybeal

As you requested, it is a pleasure to tell you a little about report writing at (name of company) and to send you several actual reports.

Report writing, of course, is a very big subject. Basically I think reports fit into 2 categories: they either tell what should be done or they tell what has been done. Because you might be interested in reports written by relatively new members of our manufacturing management, I am narrowing our discussion down to that type.

When a man joins our management, he receives individualized assignment—type training before taking over his first assignment. This on—the—job type training might typically last for 4 months. During this time, his immediate superior asks him to write reports periodically covering his experience while he is in training, evaluate his training, and suggest ideas he might have for improving our operations. These reports are submitted to his supervisor, to the division superintendent, and on up the line of our manufacturing management. These reports are valuable feedback to us from a communications standpoint; we get many good ideas from them.

A member of our management continues to write these progress reports even after he has received his training. This tool actually, then, is a pipeline which is open and into which a man can express what he thinks should be done or what he has done about something.

Just to give you an idea of the types of reports which are written, I am enclosing a sample of reports (labeled a, b, c) which I have written during the past 2 years. I hope they fit your needs for actual reports. We do not have an iron—clad format which dictates the order of content in the reports. In general, however, they are almost always short, concise, clear and written so that anyone will understand what is being said even if he is not close to the immediate problem.

Also enclosed is information which our Sacramento factory makes available to their members of management regarding report writing. Also if you have time, you might want to read in your library How to Improve Your Report Writing, a reprint from

Factory Management and Maintenance, June (year). It is one of the best articles we have seen on report writing.

Best of success with your school work. And let me know if we can help you again.

Attachments

---

**(a)**                                   SPECIAL REPORTS

To:      Sacramento Factory          Date: October 23, (year)

From:    Nicholas Leclercq

Subject: Short and concise statement of the subject on which
         you are reporting.

Conclusions:
  1. If only one conclusion, do not number.
  2. If more than one, it is best to number them. Keep
     conclusions concise.

Recommendations:
  List these in the same manner as "Conclusions," if you have
  any. If you have none, skip this heading; don't list
  "Recommendations: None."

Data:
  If supporting calculations or other data are pertinent to the
  report, include them. If they are too long for easy absorp-
  tion by the reader, but still pertinent, show: "Data: See
  attached appendix," and list on a separate sheet.

Plan of Action:
  Show this if there is an involved procedure by which you
  expect to accomplish your recommendations. Don't list "Plan
  of Action: None."

Discussion:
  There should always be a "Discussion" section to provide the
  details of your thinking. This section comes last. Chances
  are that your reader has had his interest aroused by this
  time and wants to know more about the subject. Keep as brief
  as practicable and still tell your story. Don't omit
  important details just to keep the report short.

**(b)**                                   PROGRESS REPORT

TO:              Chicago Factory                    April 19, (year)

FROM:            Nicholas Leclercq

SUBJECT:         First Floor Drug Product Capacity Increased
                 by 30%.

CONCLUSION:      The first floor storage space for drug products
                 at South Warehouse has been re-organized to pro-
                 vide storage space for 14,000 (Full Box value)
                 additional cases of drug products.

ACTION TAKEN:    1)  The average daily shipment of each brand and
                     size of drug products was determined.
                 2)  First floor storage areas were rearranged to
                     conform with the average daily shipments.
                 3)  All drug product pallet patterns were re-
                     viewed and increased in size where possible.

DISCUSSION:      A thirty days' supply of drug products is con-
                 signed to the Chicago Factory and is stored at
                 South Warehouse.  It is desirable to maintain a
                 maximum inventory on the first floor to elimi-
                 nate the double-handling of stock to the upper
                 floors.  In the past, no definite formula was
                 used to determine the amount of each brand which
                 should be stored on the first floor.  Unneces-
                 sary movement of stock was taking place.  Brand
                 blocking made inventory control difficult and
                 sacrificed storage space.

                 By means of storing a 25-day supply of each
                 brand in designated areas on the first floor,
                 maximum storage has now been obtained with a
                 minimum of "brand blocking."  First floor capac-
                 ity has been increased from 48,000 to 62,000
                 (Full Box value) cases.  Less stock movement is
                 necessary.  Inventory control has been sim-
                 plified.  Maximum warehouse height has been
                 utilized.

                            Nicholas Leclercq

**(c)**

Special Report                                    October 21, 1971

### Interviewer Training Clinics - 1971

Conclusions:
1. Forty men were trained in the 1971 clinics. There were 21 men from factories, 16 from staff divisions, and 3 from the general offices.
2. The training, as evaluated by the trainers and the trainees, was effective. The same general format should be used next year with consideration to the recommendations.

Recommendations:
1. Continue to use the innovations which were incorporated into this year's clinics.
2. Tape record, and play back to the group, the demonstration interview, pointing out techniques used.
3. Strengthen the talks given by the various divisions regarding their opportunities.
4. Provide tape recorder for full time use of each trainee.
5. Provide time at the end of the clinic for the trainees, as a group, to "compare notes" on interviewees.
6. Place a name card on the conference table in front of each trainee.

Reasons:
1. The innovations this year were effective. They included:
   a. the acceptance _and_ rejection of each interviewee by the demonstration interviewer and by the trainees during recorded and practice interviews.
   b. special demonstrations on "probing" techniques.
   c. the same trainer critiquing the first and last recorded interview of the trainee.
   d. the use of a "critique sheet" on which to organize critique notes. The sheet is given to the trainee after the critique.
   e. the passing out of simplified "opportunity charts" explaining the work available for new men in RAD, ED, IED, the factories, and overseas.
2. Playing back the recorded demonstration interview will make it possible to effectively point out techniques as actually employed.
3. Talks given by the various divisions regarding their opportunities should consist of information which can and should be given during the "sell" portion of a campus interview. This can best be done by actually "selling" one or two candidates in front of the group or role playing the sell part of the interview. The remainder of the talk can consist of answering the group's questions and supplying additional necessary general information.
4. If a trainee has a tape recorder for his full time use, he

can listen to two of his practice interviews. This is beneficial.

5. "Comparing notes" on interviewees will show that, in many cases, the differences in evaluations of the interviewee will be caused by the difference in the amount of useful information obtained from the man.

6. Name cards will make it easier for the trainees to relate names to faces.

Discussion:

Written evaluations of the clinic have been returned to IRD by 32 of the 34 trainees requested to send in evaluations. PhD chemists, who received a one-day training course, and the IRD trainees were not asked to send in reports. The clinic was discussed with the IRD trainees. The conclusions and recommendations in this report are a result of the trainees' comments and the trainers' ideas.

This year's trainees were rated by the interviewees and by the trainers. The interviewees' ratings were not generally consistent, but did point out extremes. The trainers rated 34 trainees as follows:

```
Excellent  -   2
Very Good  -   8
Good       - 15
Fair       -   8
Poor       -   1
```

Nicholas Leclercq

---

The next example of a letter report is not authorized, definitely requires headings for the three major sections of the text, and doesn't include an inside address or a personalized salutation. Yet, like the letter to Mr. Graybeal, it appears on letterhead stationery, includes attachments, and has openings and closings like a letter. In this report to the shareholder, the opening gives the purpose, which also reveals the plan of presentation and has a statement of the results. The last paragraph thanks and encourages continued support of the organization.

(LETTERHEAD STATIONERY)

January 30, 1972

Dear Shareholder:

It is a pleasure to report to you our progress in 1971 just completed, look ahead with you for this year just started, and note recent changes in staff. Overall, we're quite pleased with the entire picture.

Growth during 1971
The past year was a very good one for First Federal. As the enclosed statements show, our asset growth of 10% during 1971 is a respectable figure. If we continue at that same rate for the next 10 years, our total assets will exceed $12½ million by the end of 1980. True, our total asset growth was not quite as great as it had been in some previous years. But we were able to increase the capital structure by over 25% (from $183,962 to $231,396 or an increase of $47,434). Also that growth was reflected in the increase in the book value of the permanent reserve shares from $1.75 to $2.20 a share during the year.

Predicted Growth for 1972
Our growth in the present year should be remarkably better. Assets have increased by 8% during the first 22 days of January alone. This encouraging increase was brought about by the issuance of 5% certificates instituted on January of this year. Again we were the first financial institution in the Tri-City area to increase the rate of return on deposits. And again the other institutions followed suit rather rapidly. In a nutshell, (if you'll pardon the bragging) of all local financial institutions in the area, we retained leadership started in July of 1966 by being the first to increase our rates from 4% to 4½%.

This year should bring us the first glimpses of the economic prosperity that has been lacking in this general area for many years. We have already made loans to some of the employees of J and L that have moved to this area from (city). Let's hope this is an indication of what to expect in the near future.

Change of Personnel
Internal changes during 1971 will streamline both our operations and service for the customers. Relatively new staff now consists of the following people whom you probably know:
  1. Mr. Michael R. Yonker, acting executive-secretary, who has been with the association since November of 1968.
  2. Miss Susan Peck, head teller, who has been here since the spring of 1969.
  3. Miss Betty Thomsen, secretary teller, who has been here since June of 1970.
  4. Mrs. Peggy Vande Voort, teller, who started in October, 1971.
I thank you for your enthusiasm and continual boosting of State Federal Savings Association. Your fine efforts are reaping rewards. Please keep up the good work.

The third example is an outline from a national CPA firm to deputy administrator of a large government dam. The purpose of the report is to summarize the CPA's interest and qualifications to perform an organization-and-management study of the (name of the dam) Power Administration.

Because the entire package consists of eight pages, given below is just the outline of its contents.

Letter report—3 pages
  Opening—purpose and reference to Exhibits
T  Organizational analysis
E  Management information system review
X  Program planning, budgeting, systems review
T  Staffing requirements
  Closing—indicates continued interest and desire to submit a proposal.

Exhibit 1—2-page list of 13 public utility clients for which recent organization and general management studies have been performed. To the right of each client is a 4–9 line synopsis of work.

Exhibit 2—3-page list and discussion (with headings) of the following personnel to be assigned:
  Technical director
  Project coordinator
  Project manager
  Support specialists
  Other participants

In summary, short reports consist of memo report, printed-form report, and letter report. The first two—both internal reports—include the three parts of the body of a report (expressed or implied)—introduction, text, and terminal section. The letter report differs from these first two reports in two ways—it goes outside the firm and the opening and closing paragraphs resemble those for letters rather than the introduction and terminal section of a typical report.

## EXERCISES

*Situations That Require Discussion but No Writing*
1. Evaluate the memo report below by discussing:
  a. Clarity of the subject line
  b. Reason for omission of an introduction
  c. Appropriateness of headings
  d. Reasons for omission of a terminal section
  e. Clarity of content
  f. Complimentary close and signature area following the text

TO:          H. H. Helium                    DATE:  (current)

FROM:        R. R. Ralston

REGARDING:   Office Activities Report for September, 1971

PERSONNEL
The employees are all taking A.S.L.I. courses. The manager signed up for Insurance; but since there were insufficient registrants, the course was not offered.

Miss Lee was on vacation for 2 weeks and one day. During this time, Mrs. Santa Marie attended Orientation at our Main Office.

I hope to begin training Mrs. Mueller on insurance within 4 weeks. This is later than I had originally planned, but I ordinarily have taxes paid by this time.

## BUSINESS DEVELOPMENT SITUATION
I made 8 completed calls on Realtors to discuss our restricted sale clause. I was invited to attend a sales meeting. This resulted in my addressing 8 sales people and answering their questions.

## UNUSUAL OCCURRENCES
I was subpoenaed to appear in court on September 17 as a witness on one of our escrows.

## POLICY OR PROCEDURAL PROBLEMS
We were notified on 3 separate occasions, by the U.S. Postal Service, that our metered mail was being deposited with wrong dates or illegible dates. This led to our inquiring about the postal service and what is expected of us and why. As a result, we have a better understanding of the system and what we can do to give our customers better mail service.

Also the time for last mail pick-up on various mail boxes throughout the city were obtained.

One of our Series 05 SAC customers came into the office to change the name on his account. We discovered that we had sent all 05 SACs to the Main Office shortly after July 10, 1971, and did not keep any on hand. This has now been rectified and we have a couple on hand to serve our customers without inconveniencing them.

2. Revising a first draft can mean more than correcting mechanical errors (spelling, punctuation, sentence structure, etc.). Occasionally it means a complete rewrite. Below are a writer's first and second drafts. How did he improve his second draft? Be specific.

*First Draft*

TO:       Business Administration Faculty       October 6, 1971

FROM:     Willis Brack, Director of Undergraduate Programs

SUBJECT:  Modification of Overload Procedure

For over a year the Undergraduate Office has asked faculty not to sign overloads into their own classes. Instead, they were to send students to the Undergraduate Office. The theory behind the system was that the Undergraduate Office had the student records and, therefore, is in a better position to know who will be kept from graduation (the main purpose for granting overloads) by being cut out of a particular course.

Why System Needs to be Modified

The system has <u>not</u> worked satisfactorily, however, for several reasons, including the following:

    (1)  Many instructors continue to sign their own over-loads.

    (2)  Many overload applicants are non-BA students for whom we have no records anyway.

    (3)  Students register in one place (Sections), obtain overload signatures in another (Undergraduate Office), and attend class in still another place.

        (a)  Communications between these 3 places is not always clear.

        (b)  A number of students play one professor off against the other.

        (c)  Many students spend most of their first week of school standing in line instead of attending classes.

    (4)  During the first week of school, traffic through the Undergraduate Office is so great that it is impossible to consider each case carefully, weigh all the alternatives, etc.

    (5)  More and more students circumvent the system by waiting until the second week of school, when the only signature needed is the instructor's.

    (6)  Because most other colleges on campus have professor-signed overloads, many students are confused and waste time getting the "wrong" signatures.

    (7)  Students (and a few professors) have voiced their unhappiness about time-consuming and line-perpetuating bureaucracy.

    (8)  Some look askance at a policy which discourages faculty from overloading students into their classes if they so wish.

Although the system has its hiccups, it should not be abandoned. First, some students do <u>need</u> to be overloaded <u>if</u> they are to be graduated without undue delays. Second, the hiccups are due to procedures within the system (as well as abuses of the system), rather than to the system of overloads <u>per</u> <u>se</u>.

Two aspects among the problems are germane to this discussion:

(1) Quite a few faculty members have no objection to accepting students beyond overload limits—i.e., to room limits; and (2) the Undergraduate Office gets so much student traffic during the first week of classes that it cannot do a conscientious job of evaluating need for overloads. On the one hand, if a faculty member has no objection to extra students

and if there is student demand for the course, neither he nor
the students benefit from the present procedure of approving
overloads only in the Undergraduate Office. Likewise, if he
does approve overloads without consulting the Undergraduate
Office, the system breaks down. A system which necessitates
canvassing the faculty each quarter to see who is willing to
accept extra students beyond overload limits, or a system which
necessitates faculty communication with the Undergraduate
Office indicating willingness to accept extra students beyond
overloaded limits--both are cumbersome, or unfeasible.

The Nature of the Modifications
    In an attempt to resolve these aspects, and to devise an
overload system which is more workable from student, faculty,
and administrative points of view, the Undergraduate Office has
modified the overload procedure, effective next Winter Quarter.
A copy of the revised system is attached. You will note that
the Undergraduate Office will continue to overload certain
kinds of students with certain kinds of problems. But, overloading by the Undergraduate Office will end as soon as
classes begin.*

    Effective the first day of class, responsibility for over-
loads will reside with the faculty. True, this change eliminates the Undergraduate Office as a "buffer" between students
and faculty, but one can question whether such a buffer is or
ever was desirable. In addition, some faculty will no doubt
face increased pressure from students to be overloaded into
their classes, but they should feel complimented, rather than
disturbed.

    In some cases the need to stay within 10 per cent of class
limits is crucial. For some faculty their teaching effectiveness diminishes when class limits are exceeded significantly.
Thus, faculty need not feel uncomfortable about denying overloads. If requests for overloads occur frequently, it may be
desirable to post on the office or classroom door a sign with
something like "Sorry, no overloads."

    In other courses the need to stay within 10 per cent of
class limits may not be particularly critical; thus, whether
the class closes at the overload limit of, say, 43 or the room
limit of, say, 48 results in minimal problems. With the
revised procedure, faculty make the decision.

    *The names of students who have been overloaded into
classes by the Undergraduate Office will be added to class
lists before distribution. Thus, when you receive your temporary class list (on the first day of class), you will know how
many students are registered as of the first day of class.

A Note of Reassurance
     A final note, one of reassurance.  The advisers in the
Undergraduate Office will not be saying to students, "The class
is closed.  Why don't you go to the instructor and talk him
into overloading you?"  Advisers will naturally answer general
questions about overload procedure.  They will explain the
mechanics of getting a full schedule of classes.  If asked,
they will inform students that, once classes begin, the instructor is the only person authorized to sign overloads.  If a
student comes to you, therefore, it will not be because he has
been "sent" by the Undergraduate Office.  He is just trying all
possibilities before he gives up and takes a less desirable
course.

*Revision*

TO:        Business Administration Faculty      DATE:   (current)

FROM:      Willis Brack, Director of Undergraduate Programs

SUBJECT:   Modification of Timing and Authorization for
           Overloads

Under the old overload procedure . . .
    --Undergraduate Office authorized overloads until end of
      first week of classes
    --Faculty authorized overloads beginning second week of
      classes
Under the modified overload procedure (effective November 1,
1971) . . .
    --Undergraduate Office authorizes overloads until classes
      begin
    --Once classes begin, only faculty can authorize overloads

### Reasons for Modifications
The present system has not worked satisfactorily for the
following reasons:
    (1)  Many instructors continue to sign their own overloads.
    (2)  During the first week of school, traffic through the
         Undergraduate Office is so great that it is impossible
         to consider each case carefully, weigh all the alter-
         natives, etc.
    (3)  More and more students circumvent the system by waiting
         until the second week of school, when the only signature
         needed is the instructor's.
    (4)  Because most other colleges on campus have professor-
         signed overloads, many students are confused and waste
         time getting the "wrong" signatures.
    (5)  Some professors (and students) look askance at a policy
         which discourages faculty from overloading more students
         (beyond the 10% overload limits) into their classes if
         they so wish.

## Effect of Modification

The modification has two important effects:
 (1)  Students to be overloaded into a particular course
      should do something about it before classes begin.*
 (2)  Once classes begin, the instructor of the course is the
      only person who can authorize overloads.

## A Note of Reassurance

The advisers in the Undergraduate Office will <u>not</u> be saying to
students, "The class is closed.  Why don't you go to the instructor and talk him into overloading you?"  Advisers will
naturally answer general questions about overload procedures.
They will explain the mechanics of getting a full schedule of
classes; in fact, to facilitate the explanation, a one-page
description of the overload system has been mimeographed for
distribution to students (copy attached for your information).
If asked, the advisers will inform students that, once classes
begin, the instructor is the only person authorized to sign
overloads.  If a student comes to you, therefore, it will <u>not</u>
be because he has been "sent" by the Undergraduate Office.  He
is just trying all possibilities before he gives up and takes
a less desirable course.

 *The names of students who have been overloaded into
classes by the Undergraduate Office will be added (in pencil)
to class lists before distribution on the first day of class.

3. Explain why you think a prospect considers the following complete proposal
effectively presented. Do you have suggestions for improvement? The proposal
consists of:

Covering letter
Attachments
  Explanation of Spacefinder Filing System
  Advantages of Spacefinder System
  Present system now in operation
  Proposed system
  Cost of proposed equipment

Before sending the proposal, the seller has already visited the prospect's place of
business, studied his present setup, and discussed his needs. Questions for you to
consider in your explanation are:

  a. What is the purpose of the covering letter? What main ideas does it include?
  b. What do you suggest the sender should include or omit in the letter?
  c. What is the reason for the attachments? Why not include all information in
     the letter and do away with all attachments?
  d. Why is cost on the last sheet? Why not include the total cost figure in the
     covering letter?

Dear Mr. Jaysen

We are pleased to present the attached proposal to (name of
receiver's firm) for a conversion from drawer files to TAB
PRODUCTS' Spacefinder Filing System.

In addition to quoting facts and figures, we have laid out on quarter-inch grid paper the present system you now use in the vault on the third floor. The vault is drawn to exact scale and the drawer files now being used are placed in their present position. Using an overlay we are able to illustrate how much space you can save in this vault and yet increase efficiency in locating records and returning them to the file. Also you can use this floor plan in the future to expand storage in the same area.

It is a proven fact that the Unit Spacefinder Filing System does increase filing efficiency by 50%. We have time studies made by firms other than TAB PRODUCTS which indicate this increase.

On the attached pages I have indicated floor space savings and efficiency factors using the Unit Spacefinder System. If you need further information, please call upon me for assistance. My telephone number is 111-2222. Thank you for this opportunity to quote on TAB PRODUCTS Unit Spacefinder Filing System.

[1]

## EXPLANATION OF SPACEFINDER FILING SYSTEM

The Unit Spacefinder Filing System differs from shelf filing in many respects. We have proven in many filing areas, both large and small, that the Unit Spacefinder is at least 20% more efficient than steel shelf filing and 50% more efficient than drawer files. Any addition of personnel to the "Records Staff," because of expansion or increased work load, is a costly annual expenditure. Efficiency means man hours, which in turn, means dollars.

What creates this added efficiency? I have listed below the efficiency factors of Unit Spacefinder.

1. First of all, you don't file in a drawer, on a shelf, or in a cabinet – you file in a container. The Unit Box is 4" wide. This means that the documents have support every 4". This need is one of the most important required in lateral filing. The more support, the easier it is to "in-file" and pull records.
2. The unique "stair-step" effect, caused by the angle in which Unit Boxes are hung, gives you easier accessibility never before possible. This accessibility is an exclusive feature of Unit Spacefinder. Every folder is perfectly accessible, easy to reach, and easy to see.
3. Flexibility – you can rearrange and expand without a lot of time-consuming bother, such as in the case of drawer files or shelf files. You create space where you need it simply by sliding boxes easily along rails. There is no need to transfer records handful by handful.

[1] The horizontal lines divide the writing on one page from that on another.

## ADVANTAGES OF UNIT SPACEFINDER LATERAL FILING SYSTEM

The Unit Spacefinder concept of filing provides the following factors:

1. A stair–step effect which allows the folders to be readily identified and removed and replaced with the least amount of effort.
2. The unit boxes can be removed from the racks, a feature which allows:
   A. Work with the records at a desk for purging or for checking, etc.
   B. For fast fleeting of records by rearrangement of the unit boxes.

One definite advantage is visibility. All folders are exposed to the file clerks, and with proper indexing can be located at least 50% faster than when the folders are used in drawer files.

The Unit Spacefinder is free standing and does not have to be anchored to the walls or floor; therefore, if you need a different configuration to fit a particular location, we can tailor the Unit Spacefinder framework to fit these needs.

## PRESENT SYSTEM NOW IN OPERATION

12 ea.  5–Drawer Legal Size Files

 8 ea.  4–Drawer Legal Size Files

Total Filing Inches          2,300"

Total Floor Space          122.11 Sq. Ft.
  (including drawer pull)

Folders used are 3rd cut, top position right–hand side, legal. Filed in numerical sequence.
   A. Conversion factor – use same folders
   B. Use Colorvue Guide Cards which reveal inserted number on both sides.

## PROPOSED SYSTEM

Use combination of 42" and 30" Single Face Sections of Unit Spacefinder against wall and double–face Unit Spacefinder spaced 42" to provide ample aisle space.

Total Filing Inches     2,380"
Total Floor Space     47.02 Sq. Ft.

<u>Conversion</u>:
Present folders can be used. Right hand tab
allows easy identification of numbers.
Guide cards should be inserted in file every
two to three feet.

<u>Summary</u>
1. Increase in filing inches — 80"
2. Floor space released for expansion or other purposes —
75.09 square feet
3. Efficiency increase — Minimum 35%

---

## COST OF PROPOSED EQUIPMENT

| | | | | |
|---|---|---|---|---|
| 1 ea. 5422 | Initial 45" Legal Size Single | $172.90 | $ 172.90 |
| 2 ea. 5434 | Additional 42" Legal Size with workshelf, Single | 148.45 | 296.90 |
| 3 ea. 5404 | Additional 30" Legal Size Single | 93.50 | 280.50 |
| 1 ea. 5430 | Initial 45" Legal Size Double with two workshelves | 363.80 | 363.80 |
| 1 ea. 5408 | Additional 30" Legal Size Double | 170.50 | 170.50 |

$1,284.60

100 ea.   C4345-2  Colorvue Short Guides          $    32.00

Trim Color Standard —
  Desert Tan — Mist Green — Tab Gray
Colors on Color-sheet 3%

Delivery Schedule:  21 Days ARO
  Terms:  Net 30 Days
  FOB:  Factory

4. You are director of personnel training for a large industrial organization. Among your many duties is the operation of a particular 2-week "School for Executive Development" seminar for middle management every fall. Although the firm pays for teaching salaries and books, you must account for certain expenses such as supplies and transportation.

   In previous years you used the services of an outside agency called Short Courses and Conferences to perform the typing, coordination, and other services connected with preparing notebooks and overall operation of the seminar. But you've been unhappy with the services of this agency because they seem quite expensive for the quality of work turned out. Therefore for the last seminar, you assumed many of the services previously performed by the agency. To your surprise you saved the firm money, as the attached two financial statements submitted to you from Short Courses and Conferences show. Now you want to pass along the knowledge of this saving to your superior with the hope he'll give you a raise for the additional responsibility you assumed.

   Evaluate the following material you're sending to your superior, Mr. Charles G. Myers, Staff Vice-President. It consists of a covering memo report, analysis sheet, and the financial statements for the last 2 years. Myers is a man who expects all details even though he may not read everything. Furthermore, he wants to read just as little as possible.

December 10, 1971

TO:      Charles G. Myers, Staff Vice-President

FROM:    (your name), Director of Personnel Training

SUBJECT:  Comparison of Short Courses and Conferences
           Financial Statements:  1970 vs. 1971

Attached is an analysis of the entries in the financial statements that Short Courses and Conferences sent us for 1970 and
1971. Overall I am well pleased with the substantially smaller
amount we're paying for 1971.

You'll notice that the greatest decreases relate to duplicating: secretarial, clerical and coordinating services; and
indirect expense—a decrease of $1,841.53. Even in spite of
inflation and the increases shown in the lower half of the
attachment, the total bill is still $1,382.66 less than that
for 1970.

In general the increases resulted from additional services
rendered—as explained briefly in parentheses below each entry.

Attachments

---

Analysis of 1970 and 1971 Financial Statements
from
Short Courses and Conferences

| Decrease in Costs | 1970 | 1971 | Difference |
|---|---|---|---|
| Duplicating | 822.04 | 146.12 | 675.92 |
| Secretarial, Clerical and Coordinating Services | 963.35 | 69.85 | 893.50 |
| Indirect Expenses | 560.36 | 288.25 | 272.11 |
| Postage | 87.31 | 15.44 | 71.87 |
| Supplies | 42.07 | 4.00 | 38.07 |
| Total | 2801.80 | 1419.14 | 1382.66 |
| Cartage | 11.87 | 00.00 | 11.87 |
| Photographs | 43.20 | 00.00 | 43.20 |

| Increase in Costs | | | |
|---|---|---|---|
| Audio-Visual | 18.15 | 109.93 | 91.78 |
| (more professors used these services) | | | |
| Room Rental | 40.00 | 250.00 | 210.00 |
| (more and higher-priced rooms) | | | |
| Telephone | 31.95 | 125.00 | 93.05* |

(*including $62.75 racked up by students. You received
reimbursements for most of this amount)

```
Bus Tours                        240.00    339.25    99.25
   (Additional buses and higher fee)
Parking Permits                   13.50     33.50    20.00
   (all professors received permits without charge)
Copy Work                         00.00     36.90    36.90
   (special work requested by Rosenzweig)
```

School for Executive Development Seminar
September 1 – 13, 1970
FINANCIAL STATEMENT

INCOME:
  Postage fees from participants                  $    72.00

DIRECT EXPENSES:

| | | | |
|---|---|---|---|
| Classrooms | | $ 40.00 | |
| Supplies: | | | |
|   Student Supplies | $ 42.07 | | |
|   Postage | 87.31 | | |
|   Mimeo & Xeroxing of Instructional Material (including typing) | 822.04 | 951.42 | |
| Secretarial, Clerical & Coordinating Services | | 963.35 | |
| Bus Transportation | | 240.00 | |
| Miscellaneous: | | | |
|   Audio-visual | 18.15 | | |
|   Cartage | 11.87 | | |
|   Long Distance Calls | 31.95 | | |
|   Parking Permits | 13.50 | | |
|   Photographs | 43.20 | 118.67 | |
| Total Direct Expenses: | | | 2,313.44 |
| Balance of Direct Expenses Less Income | | | $2,241.44 |
| INDIRECT EXPENSES: | | | 560.36 |
| BALANCE: | | | $2,801.80 |

School for Executive Development Seminar
September 7 – 19, 1971
FINANCIAL STATEMENT

EXPENSES:

| | |
|---|---|
| Audio-visual | $ 109.93 |
| SC&C clerical services | 69.85 |
| Copy work | 36.90 |
| Duplicating | 146.12 |
| Indirect expenses | 288.25 |
| Postage | 15.44 |
| Room rental | 250.00 |

```
Supplies                                    4.00
Telephone tolls                           125.90
Gray Line tours                           339.25
Parking permits                            33.50
```

BALANCE:                                $1,419.14

cc:  C. Raleigh
     Steve Burks (2)
MP:lm
Conference #450

5. Evaluate the following memo report from Robert Gordon, a 28-year-old clerk in a state-owned retail liquor store, to Mr. Briggs, Chairman of the State Liquor Board.

A customer (Mr. X) wrote a grievance letter to Mr. Briggs. In turn, Briggs wrote an immediate apology to the customer and said Gordon was in the wrong and would be reprimanded. Briggs also notified Mr. Morgan, Gordon's boss, of the grievance and letter of apology and asked that Gordon explain (report) to him what happened.

One reason that many customers are unhappy is a discrepancy between actual and stated volume measurement. Information posted in each retail liquor store says that there are 26 ounces in a fifth when actually the bottle contains only 23 ounces. Because of the many complaints the clerks receive verbally from customers for this discrepancy in measurement, the supervisor (boss) of each store asks the clerks to give a stock reply, "It is true you're not getting the right measurement; I suggest you write to the State Liquor Board and express your dissatisfaction."

As you read Gordon's memo report to Briggs, keep in mind that Gordon's job is fairly secure under the civil service branch of the government. Also he is a conscientious man who tries to serve the customers courteously.

TO:      Mr. Alan Briggs, Board Chairman      DATE:  (current)

VIA:     Mr. Peter Morgan, Supervisor of Store 422

FROM:    Robert G. Gordon

SUBJECT:  Customer's Grievance

I am glad to explain to you the circumstances leading to the grievance letter written to you by Mr. X about his experience in Retail Store 422 last Friday. Although you didn't identify him to Mr. Morgan, I believe I know who this individual is but can't say so positively. Under the assumption that he is who I think he is, the following is my side of the story.

The "facts," as told to me third hand, are as follows. The customer stated that he brought to my attention an inaccuracy (23 ounces instead of the listed 26 ounces) in the volume listed for pre-mixed cocktails and that I replied in a rude manner saying, "So you've been gypped, so what!" He also said he feels entitled to polite answers rather than rude retorts.

As accurately as I can recall, I said something like this, "Yes, you are not getting full measure. So all I can tell you to do is write the Liquor Board and bring it to their attention." Maybe I even said "gypped" but I don't think so. I further told him that if more customers would bring these problems to the Board's attention they might get some action.

Though he is only one of a few who register grievances each day, he is the only one I can recall who reacted negatively under identical circumstances. Following my reply, he said, "You can bet I will (write). I don't expect to be treated this way." He left before I could react to this last statement.

This man is a frequent customer and registers the same grievance of short measure each time he patronizes what he calls the "BLANK BLANK State Liquor Control monopoly." Often the discussion concerns products other than the pre-mixed cocktails, particularly specialty items (item code numbers 8877HS and 8880HS, for example).

I admit the customer is completely accurate on 3 of 4 counts. First, he did bring the inaccurate and misleading volume listing to my attention. Second, the listing is inaccurate and misleading; we sell many items labeled as fifths (26 ounces) which are in fact less than a fifth. Third, our customers are entitled to polite answers to their questions. On the fourth count, concerning my reply, there is obviously a misunderstanding. I had no intention of being rude. I also believe any person who is treated rudely under any circumstances deserves an apology.

So you now have heard from both sides, which is essential to making a fair and just evaluation in a situation of this kind. But, bear with me further for I am not fully satisfied to merely tell my story. To maintain my dignity, I ask why you shifted the whole blame on me and further indicated that I would be "reprimanded" without your first learning my side of the story. I feel justified in believing that if a reprimand is to go into my personal records I should _first_ have a chance to defend my position.

Accurate listings will take much of the pressure off the clerks who must answer sticky questions such as the one in this discussion. I urge that you give consideration to customer grievances concerning misrepresentation in liquor listings.

Mr. Briggs, I will appreciate a reply to this letter and thank you for your time. If you need any further details, please contact me; I will be glad to supply them.

6. Shown below is a report from a division manager in the telephone company to his superior. The purpose of the report is to give the highlights of a meeting that he attended with three of his men. Notice the conversational language, organization,

use of headings and listings, and three parts of the body of a memo report. What is different here about the heading? What elements do you find in the introduction? Why did the writer inform his boss in writing rather than face-to-face? Is it an informational or an analytical report? Why?

TO:     W. R. Strong                    DATE:  April 14, 1972

SUBJECT:   Summary of Monterey Meeting

Here is a brief summary of the meeting that 4 from our division attended April 12 on coin service at military installations. As you know, Od Winther, Carl Connell, Paul Klein, and I went as a group to the regional conference on this subject.  Given below are condensations of the 3 men's presentations at the Monterey Conference.

### Od Winther's Presentation

Od Winther conducted our meeting and introduced the subject. Because of the current military build-up of forces at military posts, coin service at these posts will be a problem for years to come.  It's important we improve our service because:

1.  The need is there.  The present military situation requires more coin service.
2.  Revenues are greater from a military coin phone than the average pay station.
3.  Many of the young men on these posts are making their first real acquaintance with public telephone service. They are at an impressionable age and their opinions of our service now are likely to be lasting.

A series of slides shown by Winther pointed out that coin conditions around the country vary from very bad (troops standing in mud puddles to use coin kiosks) to very good (the coin center at Ft. Sam Houston, Texas, is so plush it is used as a reception center for guests).

### Carl Connell's Presentation

Carl Connell talked about some of the revenue characteristics of military coin service.  Revenue from a military coin phone is just about double that of the average pay station.  Ft. Lewis revenue compares favorably with that of other posts around the nation.  Some of the special market characteristics affecting military coin revenue are:

1.  Peaks and valleys—phones are used very little during the day, but jammed after 4:30 p.m.  Revenue is highest at the first of the month (pay day) and then drops off during the month.
2.  Post regulations—basic training troops, for example, are often not allowed to cross the street to use a coin phone.  They must remain in their company area.
3.  Difference in calling patterns—used mostly for LD.

A. T. & T. expects that all companies will prepare a written program to analyze the coin service at our military facilities and develop a follow-up improvement program.

<u>Paul Klein's Presentation</u>
Paul Klein enumerated some of the traffic considerations that should be included in our analysis of service at Ft. Lewis--adequately manned telephone centers, outside booths, special operator training, to mention just a few.

<u>Plan of Action</u>
Od Winther will recommend the formation of an interdepartmental district team to evaluate our coin service at Ft. Lewis and report their findings to higher management.  They will use the attached checklist.

## Rewrites

1. Below is a body of a report that might assume the format of a memo report or a somewhat more formal short report with a title page in place of the memo heading. Your job is to revise the introduction, text, and terminal section to improve readability. In your revision, do the following:
   a. Clarify the purpose of the report
   b. Add appropriate major headings for the text and terminal section
   c. Avoid the use of the subjunctive (especially would and could) whenever possible
   d. Eliminate Latin abbreviations and dangling participles.
   e. Tabulate lists
   f. Correct the spelling and punctuation
   Since this report goes to readers who understand the technical words used, you don't need to explain the meaning of these words.

The officers have deliberated on establishing recommendations relative to dividend rates and plans during numerous conferences. We've established that any decision relative to dividends must be reached within aims and objectives of our Savings Association, rather than to particular influences, special emotions, or definite pressures. Therefore, discussions were confined within policies of the Association as they are understood and within the following objectives:

PRIMARY OBJECTIVE—To increase the net worth of the Association as a percentage of specified assets.

CORRELATED OBJECTIVE—To meet the legitimate housing needs of our people.
   It is possible to meet these objectives through short range or long range plans, but consideration toward growth must be given.
   A short range attitude would require a strict restriction on growth and the acceptance of possible shrinkage. Our present earnings on this basis would build up our net worth rapidly, i.e., $600,000.00 more in net worth would provide a 9% ratio of net worth to specified assets, and could be accomplished in less than three years. We could reach 8% in two years. With no increase in savings capital, the Association could continue lending at the rate of between four and five million dollars annually. It should be pointed out, that we would lose our bad debt deduction at this time making subsequent future growth more difficult. This short range

attitude would indicate a restricted dividend policy but in view of the broad pressures in the money markets, there is greater likelihood of heavy withdrawals and resultant reduced cash flow since loan repayments would be required to meet withdrawal requests. Thus, the ability to make loans would be severely impaired. This present situation is far different from that of as recent as three or four months ago when the primary concern was local dividend competition. A decision at this time to hold the rate could result in an extremely unfavorable situation for State Federal.

A long range attitude takes the position that keeping the Association competitive with market pressures and encouraging growth, would build up its future earnings potential, thus, meeting primary objectives over a longer period of time but in a more substantial way. This would allow a greater growth during tight money periods at which time higher yielding assets could be acquired, and the deliberate easing off of lending efforts during easy money periods when loans of lower yield would be necessary. Thus, in these periods the Association would slow its growth and build its reserve accounts at an accelerated rate.

Other aspects of this attitude are as follows: (1) greater and more sustained cash flow, (2) greater volume of lending, (3) higher yielding loans and thus a more profitable portfolio, (4) more closing fees because of the resultant higher volume of lending, and (5) more efficient use of personnel and equipment, and as a summation, the opinion is reached that it would be far better for the Association to build-in better earnings for future reserve transfers. It can also be concluded that a good business decision dictates that it is wiser to establish good earnings at a time of known potential than speculating on future possible environments.

There are many other tools that the Association could use in the future. They are: (1) loan participations providing greater cash flow and portfolio yields, (2) FHA lending which would allow the Association a reasonable yield but with the possibility of making loans at high discounts now and selling off later in the secondary market at lower discounts. In the meantime, 80% of this portion of our loan portfolio would be exclusions from our specified assets, (3) the ability to drop our dividend rate at a more opportune time of our choosing or the ability to accept a lower rate if mandatory, and (4) the more effective use of present income tax regulations.

The above considerations allow this short range decision to be more effectively equated to our long range goals.

2. The following letter report (also an acknowledgment to an inquiry) is pretty good. Your job is to make it even better. Consider use of headings, perhaps more you attitude, more active voice, tabulation of some listed details (for easier reading), and more positive discussion concerning withdrawal of funds.

Thank you for your request for information relating to INSURED savings accounts in this Association. This reply includes facts concerning types of savings plans, security of savings, withdrawal of funds, and necessary forms for opening an account. I am also enclosing a copy of our latest financial statement and several pamphlets of general information which give you essential facts you desire about us and the savings accounts we issue.

We have two types of savings plans available--a passbook savings account and a six-month savings certificate.

Briefly an insured passbook savings account may be opened for
any amount at any time.  Upon receipt of your remittance, we
issue to you our savings passbook with the amount credited
inside.  Additional sums may be added in any amount and at any
time you desire.  Savings received on or before the fifteenth
of any month are credited with earnings as if received on the
first of the month.  Savings received after the fifteenth
receive earnings from the beginning of the next following
month.  When the fifteenth falls on a Saturday or Sunday, on
which days we are closed, the time for receiving earnings from
the first of the month is extended to the 16th or 17th as the
case may be.  Dividends (earnings) are credited to passbook
savings accounts on March 31, June 30, September 30, and December 31 of each year.  This is done automatically on these
dates whether you send in your passbook or not.  Gold Bond
stamps are given as an extra bonus to passbook savers as outlined on the enclosed card.  The current rate of dividend on
passbook savings is 4-1/2% per year, compounded quarterly.

In addition to our savings passbooks, we also issue insured
six-month savings certificates.  Designed to offer larger,
longer term investors the maximum rate for insured savings,
these certificates are issued for a minimum of $1,000, with
larger amounts in multiples of $100.  They differ from passbook
accounts in several respects.  Earnings on certificates begin
on the day of purchase and are paid at the end of each six
months on maturity dates.  The certificates are in certificate
form, and dividend checks are mailed to the certificate holders
every six months from the date of issue, instead of being
automatically credited to the account as is done on passbook
accounts.  Of course, if you have a passbook savings account
with State Federal, the dividends on your savings certificate
may be automatically credited to your passbook account upon
your request.  For your convenience, savings certificates are
automatically renewed on the maturity dates for an additional
six months unless you are notified at least thirty days prior
to a maturity date.  The current rate of dividend on six-month
savings certificates is 5-1/4% per year.

Savings in this Association are INSURED up to $15,000 by the
Federal Savings and Loan Insurance Corporation, Washington,
D.C.  We are also members of the Federal Home Loan Bank System,
a reserve credit system for associations.  We lend our funds
upon the security of selected monthly reducing first mortgages
on homes.  So, you will see, there is really exceptional
security for savings placed with us.

You will probably wish some information concerning withdrawal
of your funds.  It has always been the policy of this Association to pay withdrawals in PART OR IN FULL without notice.
We have followed this policy ever since organization in 1926.

However, a savings and loan association may require notice of
withdrawal if necessary.  If the country should again experience an economic emergency such as prevailed in 1932-33, it is
possible that we would require notice.  Under such circumstances it is quite likely that every financial institution
would necessarily restrict withdrawals.  This provision in the
savings and loan laws is a wise one for the protection of the
customers.

For your convenience I am enclosing a signature card which may
be used either for an individual or a joint account.  If you
desire to open an account in your own name alone, you should
use Form 100.  If, however, you wish to open an account in your
name jointly with some other person, probably another member of
your family, you should use Form 200 on the reverse side of the
card.  If you desire a six-month savings certificate, the same
signature card may be used.

We also have trust accounts, frequently used by parents in
carrying savings accounts for children, or by persons who
desire to hold funds in trusts for another.  Signature card
forms for this type of account will be mailed to you upon
request.

I thank you kindly for your inquiry and extend to you a cordial
invitation to use the facilities of this Association.

3. Given below is a report to shareholders. Assume this message appears on one side
of an 8½- by 11-inch sheet and the annual statement of condition appears on the
opposite side. Rewrite so that the information is easier to read. For example, can
you put in table form some or all the figures and dates given in the first 3 paragraphs? And can you list the names and titles in the last 2 paragraphs? Also add
an appropriate rounding-out last paragraph.

*Report to the Shareholders*
We ended our 61st year May 3, 197—, which proved to be a very good year.
Our assets totaled almost $12,000,000 being $11,997,728.90, representing an
increase of $430,315.75 which was due principally to the increase in home
loans of $538,622.30.

Savings accounts reflected a total of $11,013,074.26, representing a gain for
the year of $385,321.70, which was substantially greater than the gain in the
previous year. During the year the Association repaid $265,000 to the Federal
Home Loan Bank and had no notes payable May 3, 197—. Net operating
income, after expenses, amounted to $558,293.40, reflecting an increase of
$32,423.01 over the prior year. The operating ratio of the Association for the
fiscal year was 17.87% of gross operating income which was substantially lower
than the national average which is in excess of 27%.

During the year, $42,000 was added to reserves, $495,810.52 was distributed as
earning on savings accounts and $20,482.88 was added to undivided profit.
Total reserves were $514,000 and undivided profit $87,505.03, making a total

of $601,505.03 representing over 5% of total liabilities. Our reserves and undivided profit places us in a rather enviable position and leaves no question, in my opinion, of our ability to continue at our present rate of return to our savings accounts.

At our Shareholders Meeting held Monday, April 5, the following were elected to serve as directors for the ensuing year: William E. Brady, Robert E. Becker, Stephen G. Mills, Robert A. Aitken, Daniel A. Roberts, David L. Gifford, and Kenneth G. Hulett.

At the Directors Reorganization Meeting, immediately following the Shareholders Meeting, the following officers were elected: Chairman of the Board of Directors and President, William E. Brady; Vice Chairman, Robert E. Becker; Executive Vice President, Secretary and Treasurer, Stephen G. Mills; Vice President and Assistant Secretary and Treasurer, Kenneth G. Hulett; and Assistant Secretary, Judy A. Dugger. Sylvia Reddie was reappointed Savings Officer and Bonnie Whittemore was appointed Head Bookkeeper. Fred L. Sharp was re-appointed attorney.

4. Below is a memo from the vice-president of a university to heads of all departments. Is it a memo or memo report? Why? Revise so that the reader finds the purpose in the opening and the text develops the purpose in the most effective way. Please don't overuse "situation" (as the vice-president did)—or any other words.

The marked increase in the number of students at the University, coupled with the increased number of quiz sections and teaching assistants, has brought attention to the enclosed booklet put out by the USBC (University Students for Better Classes).

As a result of student dissatisfaction, an investigation was made by the USBC concerning a need for better quality quiz sections and teaching assistants. Many class evaluations were performed in 11 departments to find out the shortcomings of the present TA-quiz section situation. It was found that the present situation has many inadequacies. The USBC published this study which revealed the shortcomings and possible remedies. The study revealed that most students felt there was lack of coordination between quiz sections and lecture, and often discrepancies between facts given by the professor and facts given by the TA. Lack of coordination between the lecture and the quiz section results in unpopularity of classes and a lost sense of meaning for quiz sections. There is a real need to improve this situation. This means that the professors need to be required to provide the coordination necessary to improve the educational level of the quiz section.

Department needs play an important part in the correction of this situation. They can help restore in the student attitude the value and meaning of quiz section. Quiz sections are an important part of this University's curriculum and should not

be ignored. TA's gain valuable experience from handling
properly coordinated quiz sections.

This is a situation which, in my opinion, can have more serious
ramifications than seem to be apparent by a brief examination
of the facts. The booklet contains valuable information.
Peruse this booklet and then to the extent that it applies to
your department, I urge you to take appropriate action.

## Problems

1. As office manager of the Zelectron Company, you have been considering purchasing a Thermofax Copier-Duplicator to replace the standard ditto machine you now use. The Thermofax C-D, guaranteed for 5 years, consists of two parts—a ditto master and a ditto machine. It dittoes copies like any other ditto machine, but it has the unique feature of a ditto master maker which in one step—through a thermal heat process—produces a ditto master identical to those usually typed on a typewriter. Thus the Thermofax C-D keeps hands, clothes, typewriters, and desks clean. Also, it eliminates costly time spent typing ditto masters. Masters can be used over and over even with revisions and additions. The Thermofax C-D also recharges wornout masters, duplicates 1, 2, 3, 4, or 5 colors in one operation, and prints on paper sizes from 3- by 5-inch to 9- by 14-inch on any weight paper. It needs no special typing or preparation, no plates, mats, or ink. It is always ready to use.

   Paul Fullbright, the area salesman for Thermofax Inc., recently made a study of your company and presented you with a proposal for purchasing a Thermofax C-D. From the proposal you gleaned the following facts: Your company types an average of 12 stencils a week—each one taking about 15 minutes for a secretary to type. Twenty copies are then run off for each stencil. The average amount of time it takes a secretary to leave her desk, run off the copies, and return to her desk is 4 minutes. With a Thermofax C-D a secretary can make a stencil in 30 seconds. If the Thermofax C-D is located in the same position as the standard ditto machine was, 4 minutes is still the time needed to run off 20 copies. Total time spent for making a master and 20 copies with the Thermofax C-D is 4.5 minutes.

   Included in the proposal was the following table:

| Item: | Cost/copy | Cost/minute |
|---|---|---|
| Masters | $0.003500 | |
| Fluid | 0.000450 | |
| Paper | 0.003680 | |
| Labor | | 0.045000 |

### Basis of Cost

| | |
|---|---|
| Masters — C–6 @ $35.00/set* | one master for 100 copies |
| Fluid — $3.60 per gallon | one gallon for 8,000 copies |
| Paper — $3.68/set* | 8½″ x 11″ white |
| Maintenance — $109.00 per year | |
| Machine — $625 | |
| *Set equals 1,000 units. | |

The data in the above table hold true for both your standard ditto machine and the Thermofax C-D, with the exception of the maintenance cost, which is $36.00 per year for your standard ditto machine.

Your assignment is to write a memo report to Mr. James Davis, Purchasing Manager of Zelectron, recommending the purchase of a Thermofax C-D. Just as important as the actual costs are other factors, such as the ease with which a secretary can make copies, and the machine's versatility as a copier. Use good headings, and an appropriate table. Will you organize by the logical or psychological plan? Itemize recommendations.

2. One of your duties as manager of Wilson's Manufacturing is to check the plant's suggestion box. Recently there have appeared a number of complaints about the unsightly, unsanitary mess in the washroom. Some employees have been careless about using and disposing of paper towels. Each dispenser has a built-in trash basket and even a sticker to remind employees to place used towels in the basket. However, the problem still persists.

As a solution, you have decided to replace paper towels with a hot air hand dryer. At your request, Haworth Inc., makers of the Jetaire Hand Dryer, sent a salesman to evaluate your needs. The salesman made a cost analysis of your situation and also presented an estimate of the cost for changing to the Jetaire Hand Dryer. Wilson's has 200 employees and each employee visits the washroom an average of 4 times a day. The average number of paper towels used each visit is 2½ towels at a cost of $0.002 a towel. Assuming 24 working days a month, a 3-year cost figure for towels alone was derived. Haworth's salesman also pointed out that there are "intangible" costs involved with paper towels. These include time spent in filling out purchase orders and the cost of mailing the order; cost per square foot of storage of the paper towels; costs in distributing, collecting, and carting away paper towels; and plumbing expenses for toilets and sinks clogged with paper towels. These intangible costs usually amount to 50 percent of the 3-year total cost of paper towels for any business.

According to the salesman, each of the 4 washrooms in your plant should have 3 Jetaire units. The units cost $120 apiece and together use about $4 in electricity per month. There is also an installation fee of $84 (for all machines).

Because the estimated acquisition cost of the Jetaire Hand Dryers is over $500, it is necessary to receive authorization from Mr. Steve Wilson, the plant superintendent. He is a very busy man and often does not have the time to sort through a lengthy cost analysis report. He likes to know immediately what the cost and savings are in the company. Write a memo report bringing these points to Mr. Wilson's attention, as well as other facts such as employee benefits.

3. You are the supervisor of Chemco Distributors, a chemical supply house in Denver, Colorado. In order to ease the daily work load of your secretaries, you have been considering purchasing several Mini-Pack tape recorders.

The Mini-Pack is a tape recorder about the size of a large transistor radio and has all the advantages of the traditional tape recorder, plus the advantages of a dictaphone. Mini-Packs should be very helpful in your firm since much of the secretaries' time is involved in taking and transcribing dictation from company officials and sales representatives. The Mini-Pack uses cartridge tapes that record for two hours, one hour on each side, and runs for 50 hours on one transistor radio battery. Cartridges are especially convenient since there is no confusion with threading tapes and rewinding. The Mini-Pack also has a volume control and a "view window" which shows the amount of recording time left on the side in use. Like a dictaphone, the Mini-Pack has a foot pedal (which stops the tape when pressed), a forward speed, reverse speed, and an earphone similar to those on a standard dictaphone.

At your request a representative from Sonat, makers of the Mini-Pack, came to Chemco Distributors and prepared a proposal (cost analysis) for the purchase of 10 Mini-Pack recorders. His findings, based on the operations at Chemco Distributors are as follows:

```
Present operations
Average number of min/letter secretary spends in
    taking dictation . . . . . . . . . . . . . . . . . . .        10
Average number of min/letter secretary spends in
    transcribing notes  . . . . . . . . . . . . . . . . .          7
Average pay/min for a secretary (base is $2.70 hourly). .$0.045
Average number of letters dictated and transcribed
    weekly  . . . . . . . . . . . . . . . . . . . . . . .        100
Average number of min/letter executive spends
    dictating . . . . . . . . . . . . . . . . . . . . . .         10
Average pay/min for an executive (base is $5.10
    hourly)  . . . . . . . . . . . . . . . . . . . . . . .     0.085

With Sonot "Mini-Pack"
Average number of min/letter secretary spends in
    transcribing the recording . . . . . . . . . . . . .          4
Average number of min/letter executive spends
    recording . . . . . . . . . . . . . . . . . . . . . .          9
Pay scales and number of letters weekly remain the
    same  . . . . . . . . . . . . . . . . . . . . . . . .
Cost of Mini-Pack per unit . . . . . . . . . . . . . . .       $75
```

Your assignment is to write a memo report to William Schuman, president of Chemco Distributors, recommending the purchase of 10 Mini-Pack tape recorders. Mr. Schuman will be interested in not only the cost of the machines, but also their versatility and possible nonfinancial benefits to the company.

4. You are the executive vice-president of a wholesale house that supplies industrial chemicals to local manufacturers in Seattle, Washington. In the 10 years you have been in business you have used a standard dictating machine. Recently you purchased a new product on the marked called a Mini-Pack. A Mini-Pack is a small tape recorder which has the advantages of both a tape recorder and a dictating machine. It is small (about the size of a transistor radio), costs only $75, and runs for 50 hours on one transistor radio battery. The Mini-Pack uses cartridge tapes that record for two hours, one hour per side. Cartridges are convenient because time is not wasted in fiddling with threading tapes and trying to remember which side you want to record on. The Mini-Pack is also equipped with a volume control and a "view window" which tells you the amount of recording time left on the side in use. It also has a foot pedal (which stops the tape when pressed), a forward speed, a reverse speed, and an earphone similar to those used on a standard dictating machine.

You have been able to put the Mini-Pack to good use. Since it is portable, some of your salesmen take Mini-Packs to conferences and then later give the tapes to secretaries to be transcribed. (As a result, your men have accurate records of the meetings well in advance of the published minutes). Your traveling salesmen are also able to dictate letters while they are on the road, when facts are fresh in their minds, and have a secretary type messages out when the men return. Recently you have been recording company meetings and having a secretary transcribe the tapes afterwards, thereby providing valuable reference materials for all employees. Even the secretaries prefer the Mini-Packs to the standard dictating machines. They no longer have to take shorthand notes (they did before when all of the cylinders were being used), and it is much easier to handle the compact tapes.

There have been some problems with the Mini-Packs, but none of them are serious. The Mini-Pack does not always pick up conversation that is farther than 5 or 6 feet from the microphones. Also, sometimes noise close to the speaker drowns out conversation in the background. However, you have compensated for this by putting the speaker in a central position when recording conferences. The Mini-Packs are not as durable as the standard dictating machines. The cases are made of plastic and will crack if dropped or squeezed into a briefcase. If they are properly handled you believe they will last one or two years more than the salesman's estimate.

Yesterday you received a letter from Mr. Jeff Green, of Purchasing Manager Distributors in Denver, Colorado. He has been considering buying several of the Mini-Packs to give to his executives for dictating letters and reports to secretaries. Since he is planning on buying a large number of Mini-Packs, Mr. Green has decided to ask you for your experiences with them before making the investment. The Mini-Pack people gave him your name as a new customer.

Your assignment is to write a letter report to Mr. Green telling him your comments on the Mini-Pack. Mr. Green is sure to know all the sales information; what he wants is your experience on such areas as dependability, performance, and versatility.

5. You are a college student and member of the University Church. Through your efforts and the help of the college student-youth group, you designed and put into operation a special tutoring program to help foreign students—in your church and at the nearby university—get the help they needed in their conversational English.

You decided to create this program as a result of conversations with foreign students in your congregation. The foreign students said that they would like to have someone get together with them individually so they could practice conversing in English. You assigned a volunteer student to each foreign student seeking help. These two were required to meet at least once a week for a quarter (a 10-week period). This, however, sometimes did not work out and you had to ask the volunteer to leave. It hurt the foreign student more if the sessions were not regular. Some volunteer-foreign student pairs have sessions that last longer than one hour a week. Other pairs meet for only the stipulated one hour a week.

The tutors are volunteer which has presented some problem. Due to the intrinsic appeal of this program, many people volunteer. So far you have been able to keep up with the foreign student demand. Some tutors are poor. Some say they will contribute and don't and others contribute a lot of time.

Publicity is very important for getting the program going. Ads in the church bulletin and university papers are instrumental in recruiting volunteers and informing the foreign students.

In addition to meeting with the foreign student one hour a week, each tutor is required to meet with the other tutors one Sunday every month to discuss problems. The tutors must remember that they are talking with a student, and must not take a condescending attitude. And at no time should the tutor ever question the foreign student's religious beliefs. The tutor must remember that although this is a religion-oriented program, the tutors' function is not to convert or judge other people.

Yesterday you received a letter from Mr. Floyd Lowers at another church in a nearby city asking for information about your program because he is interested in setting up a similar program.

You had some problems giving the tutors ideas for variety in meeting with their students. You created a list which was given to each tutor which had all sorts of ideas—like studying together, hiking and other sports, shopping together, and driving around in a car. There were also games suggested which would help the foreign student practice his English.

When each person signs up for tutors he is given an envelope which tells him the do's and don't's according to the goals. You also give both the tutor and the student a way to end the relationship if they don't get along. The student is free at any time to terminate his meeting arrangements and ask for a new tutor. The tutor can also ask for a new student. Strict confidence is maintained in this regard, and a lot of juggling does occur.

On the whole the program has been a great success. Many new and lasting friendships have resulted. The tutors also found that they learned a tremendous amount from the foreign students. There has been a cultural exchange which has helped both the student and the tutor.

Reply to Mr. Lower's request and report your experience—both the good and the bad—with organizing and operating the program.

6. So far you have been reading the text's discussion of reports and listening to your professor's interpretation. You will now find out for yourself the types of reports you'll be writing on the job after graduation. Select an organization similar to the one you'll be associated with after graduation and interview someone on the job who has a job similar to the one you want. If you can't interview him, consider his superior.

In preparation for this assignment, hand in to your professor the answers to the following in memo format. (The purpose of this screening is so your professor can make sure you ask appropriate questions and that no more than one student in class goes to the same firm.)

a. The name of the company. If you plan to be an accountant in a CPA firm, choose a CPA firm; if you intend to get into personnel work, choose an organization that has a personnel department.

b. Name of the individual you'll interview and/or his title. Be sure to choose someone who can tell you the types of reports you'll be writing on the job after graduation.

c. Purpose of the interview. To be sure the questions you'll ask fulfill the purpose of the assignment, jot down in one sentence the purpose of the interview—"The purpose of the interview is to find out all I can about the types of reports I'll be writing on the job in my chosen career." Keep this purpose in mind as you select your questions. All questions should relate directly to this purpose.

d. List at least 10 really pertinent questions you plan to ask the officer you will interview. Consider questions to which you want answers and arrange the questions in the order you'll be asking them. Given below are a few examples of questions you might want to ask.

(1) What types of reports does your (firm) prepare? (Please specify whether memo report, letter report, formal report, or printed form report.)

(2) Which of the above-mentioned types of reports are written most frequently? least frequently?

(3) Who usually prepares the report? (Individual versus group, lower-echelon versus upper-echelon.)

(4) What are some common weaknesses in these reports?

(5) What make(s) a good report?

(6) What is the most frequent arrangement of the body of the report? (Logical versus psychological.)

(7) How long a time, on the average, is spent preparing each type of report?

(8) Do employees work on the report more during working hours or more at home?

(9) What is the difference between a report going upward to management and downward to the workers?

(10) In what way do you feel your (firm's) reports may be improved?

Write a memo report to your professor about your findings. Be sure to include a subject line, body (all three parts), and necessary headings. The text should include more than one main division but perhaps no more than two or three. Also, you might need subheadings for one or more of the major divisions in the text.

7. As a follow-up to the interview discussed on page 473 in Chapter 10, report your findings to your professor. Use memo report format and a logically organized body (first the introduction, then the text, and finally the terminal section). The text should consist of at least two major divisions—but no more than three or four. If you use subsections in one or more major divisions, remember you must have at least two subsections for each division and the major division should begin with an introductory paragraph that introduces the reader to the overall division and its subsections. Single-space within paragraphs but double-space between paragraphs and before and after headings.

You should be able to say what you need to say adequately in a report between one and two pages in length. Unless your professor tells you otherwise, the purpose of the report is to inform the professor what qualifications the company (or the person your interviewed) wants to find in a graduating senior who is applying for a specific job or for a job in a specific field.

8. One month ago Henry Merry, manager of the clothing department of Walden's Department Store since 1955, announced his upcoming retirement. As the supervisor of all departments, you were asked by John Walden (vice-president in charge of personnel) to recommend a suitable replacement. For three weeks you have been interviewing applicants and compiling profiles on currently employed personnel that are qualified to handle the position. Walden's has no policy of seniority when it comes to hiring departmental managers. Emphasis is placed on individual qualities of leadership, ability to work with others, and a general knowledge of business operations. Previous management experience is not necessary, since most of the daily management routine can be quickly learned on the job.

Having carefully considered all 27 qualified employees and applicants, you have narrowed the field down to 3 main candidates, one of whom you must recommend to Mr. Walden. On the basis of your recommendation, he will make the final decision.

The following are the resumes for the three candidates:

*Phil Bradshaw:*

At age 45, Phil has earned a high school diploma, received an honorable discharge after serving 6 years in the Army (2 years as a master sergeant), worked 4 years in construction and then 6 years selling magazines on the road, and has worked in Walden's clothing department the last 11 years. Among the clerks he has the most seniority. Often when Mr. Merry was absent because of illness or for business reasons, Phil was asked to act as manager. Company policy requires that each departmental manager keep a personality and efficiency inventory on all employees in his department. In the inventory Mr. Merry praised Phil's ability to handle the managerial duties in his (Merry's) absence, but he also noted that Phil had trouble in getting along with some of the employees. At times Phil was "bossy" toward new employees, even when he was not acting as manager.

### Kirk Bryde:

At age 25, Kirk will receive his master's degree in marketing at the end of the current quarter and has no military obligation because he is now serving in the National Guard. From an interview with Kirk and a resume he has given you, you know that he is a capable leader and has the type of personality that will get along well with employees in the department. In college he was captain of the track team. Most of Kirk's working experience has been part-time or full-time summer employment. For the last 2 years he has worked in a small clothing store in the university district. A reference from the manager of the store was quite complimentary and noted especially Kirk's ability to keep himself busy when there were no customers to wait on.

### Charles Weaver:

At age 38, Charles has a B.A. degree in history and English, taught high school English 9 years, worked in the home furnishings department at Walden's for 3 years and in the present clothing department the last 4 years. The principal of the high school where Weaver taught told Mr. Merry by letter he has no unfavorable criticism of the job done at any time, but Weaver quit teaching because he had disciplinary problems. However, both faculty and students in high school liked him. In the personality and efficiency inventory, Mr. Merry wrote that Charles is one of the best workers he has ever managed. He never questions any request given him by Mr. Merry or by any of the other employees. Charles also gets along with all employees and seems to be the most popular among them. He has never been in a managerial position, but he does have a sound knowledge of the operations of the clothing department.

# Chapter 16

# The Formal Report

- Usefulness of the Prefatory and Supplemental Parts
- Business Report versus Term Paper
- Preliminary Investigation
- Other Research Steps before Writing
- Writing the First Draft
- Revising the Draft
- Typing the Body of the Report
- Prefatory and Supplemental Parts
- Example of a Discussion Report
- Example of a Statistical Report
- Exercise

The formal (sometimes called "long") report is merely an expansion of the shorter one. The body of both a memo report and a formal report consists of an introduction, a text, and terminal section organized either logically or psychologically. In the beginning section you include the same introductory elements; you'll probably divide the text into two or more major divisions; and your terminal section is a summary, conclusions, and/or recommendations. "Formal" merely means that the report includes certain specific prefatory and supplemental parts; it does not mean that the level of language is formal. You should continue to use simple words and contractions, and write just as you do in an informal communication.

## USEFULNESS OF THE PREFATORY AND SUPPLEMENTAL PARTS

You may find it interesting to see how a memo report gradually becomes a formal report as it gets more complex and consequently longer. Assume the length of a memo report is three or four pages. Even with this length, you might use the standard TO, FROM, SUBJECT, DATE heading, or you might "dress up" the report by including that information on a separate title page. Adding such a title page (a prefatory part) is the first step in "formalizing" the report. The longer the body of the report becomes, the more formal parts you add.

When the body of the report consists of five pages or more (and, by the way, five is no magic number here), you will probably begin to add the parts usually connected with a formal report. But you add these parts only when they serve a useful function; the reader doesn't want extra parts any more than he wants an overlong body.

Given below are the 10 parts usually related to a formal (or long) report, as well as a discussion of when each should be used. Later on in this chapter you'll find both a discussion and illustrations on what to include in each part.

| | |
|---|---|
| *Cover:* | Many reports combine the cover and title page for the top page. But you can dress up a formal report by using both. |
| *Title fly:* | Only when you have both a cover and title page can you use this blank sheet of paper which is located between the two parts. As in books, it acts as a buffer or relief when the reader opens the book. |
| *Title page:* | (See Cover) |
| *Letter of transmittal:* | A longer report usually deals with a topic that is more complex than one covered in a short report, or discusses the topic in greater depth. When it seems appropriate to add a letter that officially transmits the message to the reader, do so. |

| | |
|---|---|
| *Table of contents sometimes labeled contents:* | If the body of the report is long enough to justify a table of contents, add one. For example, for a report that has three or more major divisions that are complex enough to have subheadings, you probably should use a table of contents. Otherwise omit this part. |
| *Table of tables:* | Add a table of tables if it serves a useful purpose. Perhaps the reader will appreciate this part if you have five or more formal tables in the text part of the body. |
| *Abstract:*[1] | You add an abstract: (1) when you're sending the report to a busy individual (like a legislator) who doesn't have time to read much more, (2) when the report is unusually long (over 25 pages), (3) when you know the reader wants an abstract, and (4) many times when the report is analytical or technical (as compared to a nontechnical informational report). |
| *Body:* | Obviously a must! And include all three parts—introduction, text, and terminal section. |
| *Appendix:* | You put materials into the appendix when you need to include them somewhere in the report, but they aren't essential in developing any part of the text. The appendix permits you to avoid cluttering the discussion (text) with exhibits, copy of a questionnaire, discussion of materials you can't justify to include in the text. It is the proper place to include material which is unnecessary to read in order to gain the right understanding of the report, but which may need to be available as reference or as supporting information. |
| *Bibliography:* | You need a bibliography if you have enough readings or interviews—say five or more—to justify the listing of books, magazine articles, pamphlets, and/or personal interviews. If you have fewer than five entries, you can identify the sources in footnotes within the text without having a bibliography. |

## BUSINESS REPORT VERSUS TERM PAPER

Too many recent college graduates (and others) have a mistaken idea of what professionalism is and also what constitutes good English. Their writing is abstract and pompous. It contains false elegance, scientific and business clichés, too many polysyllabic words and unnecessary words. Instead of saying, "It floats and saves time," these individuals are likely to write, "The alkaline elements and vegetable fats in this product are blended in such a way as to

---

[1] An abstract is usually a single page that gives the reader the purpose, methodology (or sources used), and highlights of the results. In turn, he can decide whether he wishes to read the report. Many organizations circulate one-page abstracts separately among their executives so that these people at least know the existence of these reports.

secure the highest quality of saponification along with specific gravity that keeps it on top of the water, relieving the bather of the trouble and annoyance of fishing around for it in the bottom of the bath tub during his ablutions.[1]" The example may seem farfetched, but many writers use words designed to impress superiors with their knowledge of the latest techniques, and the result is boring and hard to read. As you have seen, such language is not effective. The simpler the presentation, the better, and the more the material leads the reader through headings, structure, introductory sentences, and other parts, the more likely the reader is to respond favorably. As stated previously, the reader wants to get to the meat of the issue without wading through unimportant words.

Why, then, do so many college graduates write such miserable formal reports on the job? The answer lies in that they use the same language and approach they used for term papers they wrote and submitted to their professors. Although both a formal report and a term paper should be as direct, well-organized, and concise as possible, many college students write for grades, not for clarity and conciseness. They include irrelevant material if an impressive-looking long report brings an "A." Furthermore, students intentionally show off their vocabularies and use as many technical and professional words as possible if the professor or his grader can be influenced by such tactics. Then, too, professors often grade heavily on ideas and length, but place little emphasis on presentation. Also, they usually know more about the subject than the student—even after the student has completed his research—and are hence able to "read between the lines." All this is unfortunate for the college graduate who has entered the business world because it often results in his writing term papers—with all the drawbacks described above—instead of business reports.

Most of what has been said in Chapters 14 and 15 about short reports also applies to the formal report,[2] but, as previously stated, the formal report is unique in certain respects. The remainder of this chapter discusses this uniqueness by highlighting the following points:

1. Preliminary investigation
2. Other research steps before writing
3. Writing the first draft of the body

---

[1] James Williamson, "Rx for Report Writing," *Supervisory Management*, April 1956, p. 16.
[2] In the left-hand column below are the parts of the formal report. To the right of each entry is the location in the memo report where you find similar information:

| | |
|---|---|
| Cover/title page | to, from, subject, date |
| Title fly | not needed |
| Letter of transmittal | introduction |
| Table of contents | plan of presentation (in introduction) |
| Table of tables | table(s) in text |
| Abstract | introduction and terminal section |
| Body | body |
| Appendix | appendix |
| Bibliography | sources used (in introduction) |

4. Revising the draft of the body
5. Typing the report
6. Prefatory and supplemental parts
7. Example of a discussion report
8. Example of a statistical report

## PRELIMINARY INVESTIGATION

Even when you write a letter, memo, or short report, you need to think before you write. The same is true for the formal report—but the procedure is different enough to justify explanation. A formal report is much more complex and detailed than a letter, memo, or short report, and the completed product usually carries greater weight with the reader. Thus, you must plan your investigation well so that it will act as a useful guide throughout the writing of the report, and will also conserve your energies. Especially appropriate here is the well-known statement: "Good writing is clear thinking."

During your preliminary investigation you must make certain you clearly understand the problem (if there is a problem), the purpose, all the factors or areas you'll research, the reader(s)—both primary and secondary—and the use the readers will make of the report. As in all writing for business, the purpose determines the ideas you'll include. But in a formal report the purpose takes on even greater significance because the material is more complex and requires many hours to collect, classify, organize, interpret, and write. If you have a hazy notion what your purpose is—or even worse, a wrong understanding—you can waste hours, days, or even weeks going over irrelevant material.

Where do you begin, then, with your investigation? One way to begin is to make sure you know exactly what the person who has requested the report wants or needs. Be sure he clearly tells you what he expects—orally or in writing.[1] He should let you know the problem to be investigated, the purpose of the report, scope, procedure to follow in the collection of data, reader (if it is someone other than himself), use of the report, and deadline for completion. If your employer (or whoever has requested the report) doesn't give you complete information, you need to ask questions until you understand the assignment thoroughly.

Once you receive the assignment, you use the given facts for informal talks with people associated with the problem and with authorities on the subject, preliminary review of materials existing in libraries, study of company records, and so on. Use whatever sources will give you the necessary background and understanding to proceed further with the investigation.

---

[1] In a formal report of a public nature, the one authorizing or commissioning the report notifies the report writer in a letter called a *letter of authorization*. The message becomes one of the bound prefatory pages.

The culmination of all the preliminary investigation is a working plan that you'll present to the one who asked you to make the report.[1] If no one authorized you to take the assignment, you still should make out a working plan for your own benefit. In this working plan—perhaps a memo to the employer in your own organization or a letter to someone outside the firm—you'll include:

1. Problem
2. Purpose
3. Scope
4. Limitations
5. Use of the report
6. Type of reader(s)
7. Tentative outline
8. Method(s) of collecting data
9. Work-progress schedule

The whole idea of the working plan is to tell the one who authorized the report (or yourself) the way you understand the problem, the purpose, the use of the report, etc., and to make sure you see eye to eye. Be sure you understand who your readers will be. Do you have both primary and secondary readers? Are they familiar with the subject or will they need background material? Are they biased, antagonistic, or favorably inclined toward the subject?

In the outline you want to show the areas you'll investigate and discuss in the report—and if possible subdivisions for each major area. Also indicate the type of terminal section you'll have—summary, conclusions, and/or recommendations—and whether you are arranging the parts logically or psychologically.

## OTHER RESEARCH STEPS BEFORE WRITING [2]

As mentioned previously, you will collect your information from secondary (existing) sources (called library research) or from primary (new) sources (by means of surveys, observation, or experimentation). Be sure you gather enough information to develop the purpose of the report and to discuss adequately all topics in your outline. Use only the most reliable and up-to-date material.

---

[1] In addition to the two contacts already mentioned—at the very beginning during the authorization and at the completion of the preliminary investigation—the authorizer and the report writer might have further consultations if warranted and appropriate. These additional contacts might occur: (1) at the completion of the investigation—after the writer has collected and studied his material and determined the results; (2) after he has made the final report outline; and (3) after he has written the report but before he officially submits the finished report to the receiver.

[2] This book intentionally skims over any additional facts relating to the research steps of collecting, organizing, and interpreting data. The emphasis here is on presentation. (You can find detailed chapters on these research steps in many texts devoted entirely to report writing.)

After all, the effectiveness of the finished product rests on the content (ideas included) and presentation. Also take plenty of notes—maybe even more than you need—on cards of a manageable size, so that you can later shuffle and organize the cards according to the order of the ideas in your outline. But don't write down volumes on every card—especially verbatim. Jot down only what you think may be pertinent.

After you have completed your data collection, you're ready to sort the material. Naturally the basis of your classification should serve the purpose of your report and follow your outline. Keep in mind that classification merely means an orderly way of dividing material into groups, classes, or divisions.[1]

After collecting and organizing your material, you can begin to interpret the data. Be objective in your interpretation, and clearly differentiate between a fact and an opinion. And be sure you have enough facts to support your conclusions.

The teller report in Chapter 14 (page 599) shows interpretation on a small scale. There you studied data related to three criteria for selecting a teller, and your interpretation was that a certain candidate was best prepared in each area. In a formal report that also analyzes, your interpretation will be similar—but on a larger scale. Instead of facts about three individuals, you might study facts about 300 employees to determine the cause for employee turnover and to make recommendations for lessening the turnover.

At this point you also prepare whatever graphic presentations you plan to include in the discussion and in the appendix. (As mentioned previously, you can use spot or formal tables in the discussion, but any visual aid in the appendix requires identification by title.) Once you have studied your findings —but before you begin to write—you also want to think through (and possibly jot down) your conclusions and/or recommendations.

The last step during this phase of your research is to prepare an outline— which you'll use as a guide in the drafting of your report and which will become the table of contents. It is quite likely that this final outline will differ from the preliminary one you included in your working plan. You may want to get approval of the final outline from the one who authorized you to write the report; if changes need to be made, you want to know now.

When you outline, you need to know what parts of the report the reader is most likely to read and what parts he might skim or skip entirely. Then outline according to your reader's preferences.

Of the 70 individuals interviewed in a comprehensive Westinghouse study,[2] every manager said he read the abstract; a bare majority said they

---

[1] At this time you might want to review the discussion on organization in Chapters 14 and 15. Especially useful is the discussion on ways to divide and organize the mass of data into major divisions within the text (page 589).

[2] "What to Report," *Westinghouse Engineer*, July–September 1962. The results are based on interviews with 70 members of Westinghouse engineering management, including all levels from vice-president to section manager. Each interview took from 1½ to 2 hours.

read the introduction and background sections as well as the conclusions and recommendations; and only a few read the body of the report or the appendix material.

The managers who read the background section and the conclusions and recommendations said they did so "to gain a better perspective of the material being reported and to find an answer to the all-important question: What do we do next?" Those who read the body of the report gave one of the following reasons:

1. Especially interested in the subject
2. Deeply involved in the project
3. Urgency of problem requires it
4. Skeptical of conclusions drawn

Those few managers who read the appendix material did so to evaluate further the work being reported. To the report writer, this can mean but one thing: If a report is to convey useful information efficiently, the structure must fit the manager's reading habits. (Figure 16-1 gives the same information in bar-graph format.)

## WRITING THE FIRST DRAFT OF THE BODY[1]

By the time you begin to write, you should have collected, organized, and interpreted your data; drafted the final outline; prepared all your visual aids; and determined your conclusions and/or recommendations. When you do begin to write, write fast, write on a level your reader can clearly and easily

[1] In "How to Right a Report," *Business Management*, September 1968, Mr. Lesley Bernstein recommends the tenth-grade level for general management report writing and a higher-grade level for more specialized reports. His statement seems logical when you realize that the *Wall Street Journal, Time*, and *Newsweek* have a Fog Index of 10.

| Section of Report | Frequency of Reading |
|---|---|
| Abstract | Every manager |
| Introduction | Bare majority |
| Body | Only a few |
| Conclusions | Bare majority |
| Appendix | Only a few |

Figure 16-1

understand, and try to complete a block of work—like a major section—without stopping. In the first draft pay no attention to spelling, punctuation, grammar, or form—just get the ideas down on paper. If you write rapidly and allow your thoughts to flow freely, you're more likely to have a smooth overall presentation than if you stop frequently—say to polish a sentence, chew on the pencil, check on spelling, or get a drink or bite to eat.

Some writers begin with the introduction; others finish the text first. Either way is acceptable as long as you include those elements in the introduction that will best orient the reader to the rest of the report. If the length of your introduction to a 15-to-25-page double-spaced typewritten report is more than 1 or 1½ pages, you should find out what element causes this lengthiness. For example, if an introduction is four pages long because the problem or background material has required three of the pages, take the problem or background material out of the introduction and make it the first main section of the text.

In the text, beware of using too many major divisions; for a 15-to-25-page report you probably shouldn't have more than three or four major divisions. If you have more than that, look critically at your outline to see whether you can and should regroup or combine sections. Although the divisions don't all have to be the same length, every main division should include enough substance and length to justify its position of importance. Introduce ideas or figures at the best time in the development of the report—at the time the reader needs to know or use them.

The terminal section should be a logical outcome of the material in the text. Instead of the typical summary, conclusions, or recommendations, you might want to consider one of the following variations for your terminal section:

1. Summary of main points covered in the text
2. Summary of benefits client will enjoy
3. Summary of strong points and weak points
4. Summary of conclusions (if you made conclusions at the end of each major division in the text)
5. Summary of recommendations (if you stated recommendations at the end of each major division in the text)
6. Forecast—as an economist might make

## REVISING THE DRAFT OF THE BODY

When you have finished the first draft, set it aside for at least one day. This "cooling off" step allows you to get away from the writing long enough to look objectively at the material, and to see more clearly the weaknesses in the draft.

Editing the first draft requires cool objectivity. Searching self-criticism is a must; what seemed like a terrific word or phrase in the heat of writing may seem ridiculously out of place upon second reading.

Just rereading each word of the report isn't the best way to approach the all-important job of revising and editing. Instead you should:

1. Look critically at the title, abstract, introduction, and terminal section—these four areas your reader considers first. If these parts are weak or vague, the reader may reject the entire report—regardless of how good it might be. The title should tell the reader clearly and concisely exactly what the subject of the entire report is. The abstract should reveal the problem, purpose, sources used, and results. The introduction should adequately orient the reader to the material so that he will better understand what is covered in the text (discussion). And be sure that the terminal section doesn't contain new material, that it produces what you promised or agreed to in the introduction, and that it stems logically from the information in the text.

2. Check the letter of transmittal, introduction, and terminal section—if it precedes the introduction and text—for repetition. The reader will react unfavorably if he has to read the same information two or three times right away.

3. Check the headings throughout the report to make sure they match the entries in the table of contents. All major and minor sections in the table of contents must have headings in the text; but not all headings in the text (such as fourth- or fifth-degree headings) need to appear in the table of contents. Also check to see that you have indicated correctly the relation of major and minor parts and that headings of the same degree are parallel.

4. Examine the text for transitions. Have you tied your sentences together within a paragraph? Have you tied your paragraphs together within a section? Have you tied your sections together?

5. Now edit the entire report[1] for:
   a. Logical sequence. Are sentences, paragraphs, and sections properly organized?
   b. Completeness. Have you fully developed the purpose of the report?
   c. Conciseness. Cut out irrelevant material, trite or wordy expressions, and unnecessary repetition. You want to present essential facts uncluttered by extraneous, distracting information. If you have a visual aid that belongs in the report but seems to clutter up the discussion, switch it to the appendix.
   d. Accuracy and clarity. Check all statements, figures, and facts. Eliminate double meanings and unclear statements.
   e. Spelling, punctuation, and grammar.
   f. Length of sentences and paragraphs. On the average, a sentence is 17 to 20 words in length; the maximum length of a paragraph is 15 typewritten lines.
   g. Variation of sentence structure. If the sentences in a particular paragraph or section seem monotonous and have a sing-song effect because they're all

[1] You'll find additional editing tips on pages 759–761 in the Appendix.

or mainly simple sentences, change some to compound or complex sentences if possible and appropriate.

h. **Documentation.** Give credit for sources used (see discussion below).
i. **Consistency.** Be sure the report is consistent in use of numbers as figures or words; in use of first, second, or third person; in level of language.
j. **Overuse of the same word.** If you intentionally repeat the word for emphasis, that's fine; but if you seem to ride a word to death, find a natural synonym for the word.

Finally, ask someone else to read the report to see if it makes sense to him. Sometimes you're so close to the material that an idea which seems perfectly clear to you will be vague or unclear to another person. Also, another person might find misspelled words you have overlooked.

Documentation needs further discussion because it usually involves footnotes or a bibliography. You use footnotes when you want to:

1. **Give credit to a source you used.** Naturally you don't give credit to anyone or anything if the information is common knowledge or if you are relying on your experience. But you're plagiarizing if you make a statement belonging to someone else and you don't credit that source.
2. **Explain or give additional information that relates** to an idea in the text but isn't important enough to include in the discussion.
3. **Show a cross reference**—to direct the reader to another place in the report—such as to a particular page in the appendix.

You won't use footnotes in a business report as extensively as you will in an academic paper. Instead of crediting a source, amplifying, or making a cross reference in a footnote, you can many times accomplish the same results by including this information within the discussion itself. Also you want to avoid the use of Latin expressions—such as *op. cit., ibid.,* and *et al.*—because businessmen may not know their meaning.

If you do use footnotes, place them at the bottom of the same page as their raised reference figures within the discussion. You can number each footnote consecutively according to page, section, or report. In this text the first footnote on each page begins with Arabic 1. The footnotes go at the bottom of the page instead of at the end of the report body because that location is more convenient for the reader.

Whether your report does or does not include a bibliography, you want to streamline each footnote. Shown below are suggestions for accomplishing this goal.

*Footnotes when the report includes a bibliography:*
Since each bibliographic entry includes all pertinent information about the source, you don't need to include all the information in the footnote, You can limit the facts to the author's last name; title of article, book, or booklet; and page number, as the following examples show.

| | |
|---|---|
| Book[1] | Perrin, *Writer's Guide and Index to English*,[2] p. 123. |
| Magazine article[1] | Bernstein, "How to Right a Report,"[2] p. 48. |
| Newspaper article (author unknown) | "Establishment Takes Tourney," *University of Washington Daily*, p. 1. |
| Interview | Statement made by Helen Olson, account executive at Ernst and Ernst. |

*Footnotes when the report doesn't include a bibliography:*

| | |
|---|---|
| Book[3] | Porter G. Perrin, *Writer's Guide and Index to English*, 4th ed., Scott, Foresman and Company, 1965, p. 123. |
| Magazine article[3] | Lesley Bernstein, "How to Right a Report," *Business Management*, September 1968, p. 48. |
| Newspaper article (author unknown) | "Establishment Takes Tourney," *University of Washington Daily*, May 14, 1970, p. 1. |
| Interview | Helen Olson, account executive at Ernst and Ernst, made this statement when she was describing the role of the CPA to graduating seniors at the University of (State) on May 22, 1971. |

If your report doesn't have a bibliography and you need to credit the same source more than once throughout the report, write the footnote the first time as if the report didn't have a bibliography; after that write the footnote as if the report had a bibliography.

Should you need a footnote to indicate a cross reference or to offer additional facts, word the footnote conversationally, as has been done throughout this text. For example, footnotes 1, 2, and 3 on this page give additional information, and the footnote at the bottom of page 691 shows how to cross-reference—how to refer the reader to another place within the report.

## TYPING THE BODY OF THE REPORT

Once you have revised the draft to your satisfaction, you or your secretary is ready to type the body of the report. Although various authorities suggest different rules for typing this material, the discussion here offers only one way—the same rules followed in setting up this text.

---

[1] If two or three authors are involved, give the last name of each—such as Bernstein and Schnitzelgrueber or Jones, Olson, and Smith. If more than three authors, you can say Bernstein and others.

[2] Use quotes for part of a whole—such as an article in a magazine or a chapter in a book. Underscore any publication that represents the entire issue—such as a book, bulletin, or pamphlet.

[3] If two or three authors are involved, give the full name of each—such as Lesley Bernstein and Valdimar Schnitzelgrueber or Jack Jones, Rolf Olson, and Peter Smith. If more than three authors: Lesley Bernstein and others. Notice that the first name of the author precedes his last name.

### Double Spacing versus Single Spacing

As a rule, you double-space the body of the formal report and indent paragraphs (usually five spaces). But you single-space for:

1. Quotes and examples (such as letters and memos in this text) of two or more typewritten lines or more. Also indent margins of the quote five spaces to the right and left of the double-spaced material.
2. Contrast (as in this list).
3. Footnotes.

### Proper Margins

In addition to the following suggested margins, you need to add three-fourths of an inch for binding on each page except the top sheet (which is either the cover and/or title page). Although you usually bind the report on the left-hand side—like a book—you can bind at the top. Acceptable margins are as follows:

First page of the body—Use a 1-inch margin for the left, right, and bottom side of the paper. The heading at the top falls on the tenth line, so you have a 1½-inch margin. And be sure to add an additional ¾ inch for binding.

Other pages of the body—Leave 1 inch for each of the four margins—top, bottom, left, and right. And be sure to add the additional three-fourths of an inch for binding.

### Setup of Footnotes

A footnote goes at the bottom of the same page as its reference. Separating the last line of the discussion and the first footnote on the page is a line (usually 18 strokes long) flush with the left margin, with double spacing before and after the line. Single-space within footnotes and single- or double-space between footnotes. As shown throughout the text, you may begin numbering the first footnote on each page with "1." All lines are flush with the first line of a footnote.

### Number the Pages

Use Arabic numbers throughout the body of the report. You usually don't type a number on the first page of the body, but place the page number on each consecutive page beginning with the second page. If you bind on the left, you place the page number in the upper right-hand margin three lines from the top and 1 inch to the left of the right-hand edge of the paper. If you bind at the top, the page number goes three lines from the bottom of the page and is centered with the typing on the page.

## Favorable Impression Throughout

Regardless of how well written your report is, if it is carelessly typewritten, it will create an unfavorable impression in the mind of the reader.

You can give the correct initial impression if you choose a quality bond white 16- or 20-pound typing paper. Next, be sure your ribbon produces a dark impression—like print in the newspaper—and be certain the keys are clean. If your secretary is using a manual typewriter, check to see that she types evenly so that all the words make the same impression. If possible, she should hit the punctuation marks lightly enough so that they don't produce noticeably deep gougings in the paper. It's okay for her to erase as long as she does so neatly. Proper erasing is hardly noticeable. Be neat—avoid smudges, streaks, curled ends, wrinkled paper, and any other distractions that might divert your reader's attention from the message.

## PREFATORY AND SUPPLEMENTAL PARTS

Once you have written and edited the body of your formal report, you may add some or all the parts listed below; but include only those parts that serve a useful function for the reader.

| | |
|---|---|
| Prefatory parts: | cover, title fly, title page, letter of transmittal, table of contents (contents), table of tables, abstract |
| Supplemental parts: | appendix, bibliography |

For both prefatory and supplemental parts, you need to consider the extra three-fourths of an inch for binding; also you want to place all information attractively on each page, using proper spacing and margins.

The location of the page number and the manner of numbering the pages differ for the parts before and after the body of the report. For the prefatory sheets, use small Roman numerals and place the numerals in the same location as that for a top-bound report—centered with the material on the page three lines from the bottom of the sheet. Count and number the prefatory pages as shown below.

| | |
|---|---|
| Cover | don't count or number |
| Title fly | don't count or number |
| Title page | count (i) but don't number |
| Letter of transmittal | count and number; a one-page letter shows page ii at the bottom; a second page of the transmittal shows page iii. |
| Table of contents | count and number each page |
| Table of tables | count and number |
| Abstract | count and number |

For the supplemental parts, show the page number in the same location as that for the body, and continue the sequence used for the body. For example, if the last page of the body is page 22, the first appendix sheet (the "title page" of the appendix) will be page 23.

(As you study below what to include in these prefatory and supplemental parts, you should refer to the airline report on pages 704 to 713).

### Cover (Design and Wording of Title)

Obviously, you need a cover to which the reader will react favorably. Sometimes a simple hard cover (both for the front and back), with a properly placed title, will suffice. You can type the title on a gummed label, or type or print it directly on the cover itself. However, with a little imagination and a subject that allows you the possibility, you can design a more complex cover—one that ties in with the material being discussed. For example, assume you're writing a report in which you're suggesting that the firm switch from its present printed personnel form to a more effectively worded and comprehensive form. The cover can consist of parts of both forms with a title superimposed. Or, if you're discussing foreign compact cars, a picture of one of the cars and an attractively arranged title could make an effective cover. But beware of overdoing—of making your cover gaudy or ludicrous.

Your title must exactly and specifically identify the overall subject of the report. As you ponder the wording of the title, here are a few suggestions to consider.

1. Keep the title short (usually about eight words maximum); omit "the," "a," and "an" whenever possible. Also wordy are "A Report on . . . ," "A Survey on . . . ," "Constructive Criticism . . . ," "Recommendations for Improvement for . . . ." A long title kills interest and can cause filing errors. If you must use many words, use a short main title and a longer subtitle, as shown below:

   MARKETING POLICIES OF OREGON'S HAZELNUT GROWERS ASSOCIATION

   Appraisal of methods to increase demand for hazelnuts, with emphasis on value and effectiveness of advertising, sales promotion, price policies, and distribution channels

2. Use your imagination to create a title that catches the eye.
3. Whenever possible, stress results rather than procedure or the way you collected your material.
4. Avoid an air of mystery—such as a title in the form of a question.
5. Pay particular attention to the scope of the report. For example, "Agricultural Products in (State)" is misleading if you're discussing only grains, vegetables, or fruits.
6. Include whichever of the 5W's (and How) seem pertinent.

## Title Fly

A title fly is simply a blank sheet of paper between the cover and title page. Naturally you shouldn't use a title fly if part of the cover is removed so that the title on the title page also serves as the cover title.

## Title Page

Whether or not your report has a cover, the title page usually contains the title, as well as the recipient, the sender, and the completion date—each of which should have a separate focal point on the page. As illustrated on page 704, the title page should be attractively arranged. If appropriate, you add pertinent facts about the individuals involved, such as title, department, and organization. The date of completion must agree with the date on the letter of transmittal.

With a cover the title page uses the same weight paper as the text sheets do; as a combination cover-title page this part might have a heavier weight—similar to that for the cover.

## Letter of Transmittal

The letter of transmittal officially conveys or transmits the finished report. When you're writing to a large group of people, you label it as a preface and set it up as one. The receiver is the individual who authorized the report or who needs the information. In the transmittal you tell the reader what you'd say to him if you were handing the report to him. Regardless of whether the body of the report talks in the third person, you can use first and second persons in the transmittal. You want to adhere to all the rules of letter writing for a transmittal.

You have your choice of two kinds of transmittals—a covering transmittal, which merely (or mainly) transmits the report, and an introductory transmittal, which resembles the introduction. The transmittal letter used for the airline report on page 705 mainly transmits the message. It contains authorization, use of the report, a little background, and willingness to discuss. A covering transmittal can also include any of the other elements listed below.[1]

    Authorization
    Subject
    Purpose

---

[1] In most situations you'll use the covering transmittal with the accompanying conventional introduction shown on page 707. But the introductory transmittal is especially effective when you want to deemphasize the introductory elements and begin the text with something more interesting—with perhaps the problem or background material.

Methodology/sources used
Scope
Limitations
Summary, conclusions, or recommendations
Specific reference to a special section or to points of significance to the reader
History/background
Definition of terms
Need of the report
Use of the report
Writer's comments outside the limits of the report

You can end either type of transmittal with one of the following ideas:

1. Acknowledgments to people who assisted
2. Indication that later reports may be necessary or forthcoming
3. Willingness to discuss
4. Offer to assist with future projects

Although the list given above is similar to that used for an introduction, you don't want to include the same elements in both the transmittal and the introduction. If you have an introductory transmittal, the first section of the body must be something other than a typical introduction. It can be a section on background or problem that is too lengthy to fit into the transmittal. Given below is a possible introductory transmittal for the airline report.

*Example of an introductory transmittal.*

Dear Mr. Betz

   As you requested, here is my report concerning the devel-
opment of the present reservation system of United Airlines.
I'm sure the managers of travel agencies throughout the United
States will appreciate receiving this information.

   The refinement of United's reservation system occurred in
three stages.  I discuss each of these stages with respect to
the methods by which they operated and problems which arose
in these operations.

   Nearly all my data came from interviews with United's
personnel.  Mr. Cowper Middleton, special assistant to the
regional vice president, explained from past experience both
the methods of operation and problems of the separate station
allocation, Central Control and the Ramac systems.  Information
concerning the Instamatic and Unimatic systems came from interviews with Mr. Earl Brown, Mr. Jerome Gogulski, and Mr. W. C.
Woodard, who are all executive members of the Regional Division
of Sales and Service for United Airlines.

My main source of secondary information was United's Publicity
Fact Book kept only by United offices and not available to the
general public.   This book supplied facts about the most recent
computer system, Unimatic.

To increase the readability of this report, Input—Output
devices (I/O) should be defined.   An Input device consists of a
receiver that receives messages transmitted from some other
location.   An Output device is a transmitter which transmits
information to another place.   I/O devices refer to both of
these machines.

If you have any questions concerning my report, I will be
glad to come in and discuss them with you.

## Table of Contents

The table of contents shows the major and minor divisions of the report and
their respective locations within the report. On page 706 is the contents for
the airline report. Notice that the writer sets apart the body of the report
from the letter of transmittal and bibliography by indenting the introduction,
major divisions of the text, and the summary. If you wish, you can separate
the body even more by putting all its major parts in capitals (also shown on
page 706). If you preface the introduction, major divisions of the text, and
terminal section with Roman numerals (I, II, III, etc.), you should preface
their subdivisions with capital letters (A, B, C, etc.). For further subdivisions,
you use Arabic numerals (1, 2, 3, etc.) and then lowercase letters (a, b, c, etc.).

Naturally you must prepare the contents after typing the rest of the
report—or at least after making a typewritten draft—so you'll know the correct page numbers. Use leaders (dot space dot space dot) to lead the eye from
the name of each entry to the page column on the right. Every entry shown
in the table of contents must appear exactly as it does in the body. But not
every heading in the body has to appear in the contents. Usually you show no
more than three degrees (first, second, and third) of headings.

If the appendix includes several different entries (questionnaire, reprint of
a statute or regulation, various tables, or other visual aids) you can show them
in one of two locations: (1) if you have only a few entries, as subdivisions of
the appendix on the contents page; or (2) if you have a rather extensive
appendix, as subdivisions of the appendix on the appendix title page. You
should show the page number for the first page of each entry.

## Table of Tables

Label this prefatory page according to the type of formal visual aids shown
throughout the text. If the illustrations are all tables, you'll label the page
"table of tables" or "list of tables." Follow the same procedure for charts,

pictures, etc. If you have a mixture of tables, charts, and other visual aids, consider a title that encompasses them all; perhaps a "table of illustrations" will suffice.

This prefatory page serves the same function for the visual aids as the contents page does for the coverage of the report. If space permits, you can include both the table of contents and table of tables on the same page. Whether the latter is combined with the table of contents or by itself on the page, the layout begins as shown below:

Table of Tables

| Number | | Page |
|---|---|---|
| 1 | (title) . . . . . . . . . . . . . . . . . . . . . . . . | 6 |
| 2 | (title) . . . . . . . . . . . . . . . . . . . . . . . . | 9 |
| 3 | (title) . . . . . . . . . . . . . . . . . . . . . . . . | 11 |
| 4 | (title) . . . . . . . . . . . . . . . . . . . . . . . . | 13 |

## Abstract

As a prefatory part, an abstract[1] can definitely perform a vital service for the reader. The content of the abstract includes: problem and purpose, methodology and/or sources used, and results.

"Methodology" refers to the research method(s) you used (library, survey, observation, experiment) and/or sources used. For example, say you made a random (or stratified) sample of 1,000 housewives within a certain geographical area and supplemented your findings with books and periodical articles since 1965 on female consumer buying habits. Under this heading you usually don't list specific sources—just types used. The results section—summary, conclusions, or recommendations—should comprise about 75 percent or more of the entire abstract.

Prefatory abstracts are useful because the reader can find in one spot—and preferably all on one page—the highlights of the report. After scanning the abstract, he can determine whether he wants to read further.

Shown on page 701 is an abstract for the airline report. Notice that all sources used are shown in the abstract. However, if the sources consisted of many texts and interviews, you would not list each—you would merely give the types and quantity. The same is true for the results (summary in this situation). In a longer report you need to condense the terminal section. But in the airline report space permits including the entire terminal section. Actually an abstract isn't necessary for a report like this one whose body consists of only 13 pages. But if the report were longer—say over 25 pages—it definitely performs a vital function for the reader.

[1] This prefatory part carries various labels—"abstract," "synopsis," "summary," "précis"—but they all show the big picture.

TO:      Mr. Charles E. Betz, Manager     DATE:  (current)
            Public Relations Department
            Association of Travel Agencies

FROM:    Pamela F. Whatmore, Staff Assistant

SUBJECT:  <u>Abstract of the report, The Development of United</u>
         <u>Airlines Present Reservation System</u>

## Purpose

This report shows the development of the present reservation system of United Airlines.

## Sources Used

1. Interviews with the following United personnel:
   a. Mr. Cowper Middleton, special assistant to the regional vice president
   b. Messrs. Earl Brown, Jerome Gogulski, and W. C. Woodard—all executive members of the Regional Division of Sales and Service for United Airlines
2. United's Publicity Fact Book

## Summary

The present reservation system is a product of successive introductions of time-saving devices to remedy problems that became too big to ignore. The separate allocations of seats—during the original reservation system—did its best to meet the customer demands in the early years of the airline industry. This system presented problems that Central Control—the next system—helped correct. Central Control's problems were then solved by the introduction of automated devices.

The introduction of automated devices started with the computer centers of Ramac. Ramac solved most of the Central Control problems and served United well for many years. Eventually, however, Ramac too became obsolete and had to be replaced.

The next installation was Instamatic, a more complex computer. Instamatic simplified the process for making reservations. With the increase in passenger traffic and fleet size, Instamatic lacked the potential for handling future reservation information.

Instamatic's obsolescence gave way to the installation of a bigger and better computer system—Unimatic. Unimatic provides the potential for handling future reservations and much more. It will depend on the technological advances in all fields and the applications of these advances to the problems that will develop in the future of United Airlines.

## Appendix

With short reports, you merely add the appendix sheets directly to report. But for a formal report, you place a sheet of paper (the appendix title page) between the last page of the body and the first page of the appendix. If you have enough material in the appendix to justify a separate table of contents, show the contents below the title on the appendix dividing sheet, in order of the page arrangement.

Each separate entry (sample forms, detailed data for reference, table, picture, questionnaire, chart, map, graphic representation, blueprint) in the appendix naturally requires an identifying title. As a rule you should refer the reader to every entry in the appendix in the body of the report (within the discussion itself or in a footnote).

The last page of the appendix is the ideal place for any table or illustration the reader will need to refer to throughout the report. You can set up this table on a pull-out sheet, and tell the reader about the sheet in the letter of transmittal or introduction. Such an arrangement permits the reader to keep this master table—or whatever is on the sheet—in full view at all times.

## Bibliography

When your report includes five or more sources, place this material on a sheet of paper labeled "Bibliography," following the appendix. Organize this supplementary part so that it best serves the reader. A preferred way to arrange bibliographic entries is to alphabetize within broad groups—for example, books, periodicals, newspapers, interviews.

Remember that entries in the bibliography differ from footnotes in two ways:

1. The author's last name comes first.[1]
2. You indicate the *total* number of pages in the book, article, or pamphlet.

Shown below are examples of entries for the bibliography. They refer to the same sources used in the examples of footnotes on page 693 so you can easily compare them.

| | |
|---|---|
| Book | Perrin, Porter G., *Writer's Guide and Index to English*, 4th ed., Scott, Foresman and Company, 1965, 907 pp. |
| Periodical | Bernstein, Lesley, "How to Right a Report," *Business Management*, September 1968, pp. 46–48. |

[1] If two or three authors are involved, you reverse only the last name of the first author: Bernstein, Lesley, and Jack Jones, *or* Bernstein, Lesley, Jack Jones, and David Smith. If more than three authors are involved, you reverse the last name of the first author but don't show the other names: Bernstein, Lesley, and others.

Newspaper article "Establishment Takes Tourney," *University of Washington Daily*, May 14, 1970, pp. 1 and 6.

Interview Olson, Helen, account executive at Ernst and Ernst, May 22, 1971.

## EXAMPLE OF A DISCUSSION REPORT[1]

As you read the airline report[2] on the following pages, which applies many of the suggestions for writing a formal report given in this chapter, notice the following:

1. Page 704 could serve as a combination cover and title page, or a title page alone.
2. The letter of transmittal and the introduction function as useful entities without unnecessary overlapping of material.
3. The table of contents separates the body from the prefatory and supplemental parts by means of indentation and capitalization.
4. The introduction includes the introductory elements (purpose, sources used, definition of terms, and plan of presentation) necessary to orient the reader. In such a short introduction, subheadings aren't necessary. But when the introduction is longer and more complicated, headings like the following help the reader scan quickly: "purpose," "scope and limitation," "methodology."
5. The italics used throughout the report illustrate how you can tie together sentences, paragraphs, and even sections of the report. (Naturally these italics did not appear in the actual report.)
6. The bibliography alphabetizes by groupings—books, magazines and pamphlets, and interviews.
7. The author of the report bound the pages at the left-hand side, numbered the prefatory sections with small Roman numerals, and numbered the rest of the report (including supplemental parts) with Arabic figures.

[1] When typewritten, the body should be double spaced throughout and each page should appear on a separate sheet. The horizontal line across the page and the page number permit you to realize you're progressing from one page to the next one.
[2] Although the information in this report is true, names of persons have been changed and some dates have been altered. Also the airline has probably introduced by now more up-to-date technical advances.

# THE DEVELOPMENT OF UNITED AIRLINES' PRESENT RESERVATION SYSTEM

Prepared for
Mr. Charles E. Betz, Manager
Public Relations Department
Association of Travel Agencies

by
Pamela F. Whatmore
Staff Assistant

April 22, 1971

April 22, 1971

Mr. Charles E. Betz, Manager
Public Relations Department
Association of Travel Agencies
1412 S.W. Meridan Street
St. Louis, Missouri 43123

Dear Mr. Betz

As you requested, here is my report concerning the development
of the present reservation system of United Airlines.

I'm sure the managers of travel agencies throughout the United
States will appreciate learning how United has expanded.  In the
beginning, the line boasted a fleet of 20 planes, each having a
capacity of four passengers.  <u>At that time</u>, however, the company
was doing well when it averaged two passengers a plane.  <u>Today</u>,
United has a fleet of 394 jet planes with a passenger capacity
of up to 342 a plane.  United's service area has expanded from
20 cities to 114 cities in the United States.

If you have any questions concerning my report, I will be glad
to come in to discuss them with you.

                                        Sincerely


                                        Pamela F. Whatmore
                                        Staff Assistant

ii

## CONTENTS

| | Page |
|---|---|
| Letter of Transmittal | ii |
| INTRODUCTION | 1 |
| 1931–1961—ORIGINAL SYSTEM, CENTRAL CONTROL, AND RAMAC | 2 |
| Original System (1931–1948) | 2 |
| Operation | 2 |
| Problems | 3 |
| Central Control (1948–1956) | 4 |
| Operation | 4 |
| Problems | 5 |
| Ramac (1956–1961) | 5 |
| Operation | 5 |
| Problems | 7 |
| 1961–1970—INSTAMATIC | 7 |
| Operation | 7 |
| Problems | 8 |
| 1970 AND BEYOND—UNIMATIC | 10 |
| Present Operation | 10 |
| Future Operations | 12 |
| SUMMARY | 13 |
| Bibliography | 14 |

## INTRODUCTION

Today the public takes the convenience of obtaining flight reservations for granted. *However,* at one time, flight reservations were impossible to get, because the airlines carried only mail. Not until the mid-1920's did anyone even consider carrying passengers.

This report shows the development of the present reservation system of United Airlines. Nearly all data came from several interviews with United's personnel. Mr. Cowper Middleton, special assistant to the regional vice president, explained from past experience both the methods of operation and problems of the separate station allocation, Central Control and the Ramac systems. Information concerning the Instamatic and Unimatic systems came from interviews with Mr. Earl Brown, Mr. Jerome Gogulski, and Mr. W. C. Woodard, who are all executive members of the Regional Division of Sales and Service for United Airlines. The main source of secondary information was the United's Publicity Fact Book kept only by United offices and not available to the general public. This book supplied facts about the most recent computer system, Unimatic.

To increase the readability of this report, Input-Output devices (I/O) need defining. An Input device consists of a receiver that receives messages transmitted from some other location. An Output device is a transmitter which transmits information to another place. I/O devices refer to both of these machines.

This report discusses the refinement of United's reservation system in three stages. Discussion for each stage includes the dates and methods of operation and problems which arose in these operations.

2

## 1931–1961—ORIGINAL SYSTEM, CENTRAL CONTROL, AND RAMAC

The period from 1931 to 1961 is divided into three sections: the original system from 1931 to 1948, Central Control from 1948 to 1956, and Ramac from 1956 to 1961.

### Original System (1931–1948)

The original system consisted of separate station allocation of tickets with its own particular problems.

### Operation

Originally, reservations or seats on a plane were doled out to individual stations located along a certain flight plan. A station master sold as many seats as he could and then gave the remaining tickets to the pilot, who took them to the next station. The next station master then received these tickets and tried to sell them at the last minute. In most cases it was impossible to do so. *Therefore,* the station master sent his unsold tickets, in addition to the extra tickets, to the next station.

3

### Problems

The drawbacks of *this* original system can plainly be seen. A snowball effect arose which ended with the last station having many unsold seats. *These* seats might have been sold if the station master had received *these* tickets a week before.

*To further complicate the system,* station masters were extremely possessive over their allotment of tickets—whether or not they could sell them. If one station sold all its tickets and needed more, the normal procedure was to get in touch with one of the station masters along the line and buy some of his seats. *However,* station masters were very reluctant to give away any of their seats, since there was always that slim chance that they might be able to sell the seats. *As a result,* the station master wanting more tickets found it almost impossible to get extra tickets when needed. *To further aggravate the situation,* shortly before a flight was due to arrive, *this* same station master who had asked for the tickets received all the extra tickets from station managers who hadn't sold theirs. Because of the uncertainty involved, one station had no way to expect receiving the extra tickets. *This difficulty* in obtaining extra tickets caused much inconvenience to both the station master and his customers.

*Another drawback* to this system occurred in the booking of adjoining flights. For example, a person would call an agent and ask to make a reservation from Seattle to Denver. To take care of this transaction and confirm it was not a problem. *But* if the customer wanted to make a return flight reservation, the station master

---

4

had to teletype Denver and ask if and when room was available. Denver then checked and teletyped the information back. Often Denver did not reply promptly, and many customers ended up waiting over 24 hours for their reservations.

The adjoining flight problem *was further complicated* if the person wanted to make several connecting flights. The amount of time and paper work involved in contacting each station to confirm space was tremendous. *This method* also left a lot of room for human error.

### Central Control (1948–1956)

In order to keep ahead of the competition, United had to employ a system to speed up the reservation system. Central Control was the answer.[1]

Central Control was instigated in 1948. *This arrangement* made it possible for the first time in the history of the company that every station had the same opportunity to sell any seat on any flight. The central control office was located in Denver and connected by direct phone lines or teletype to all cities served by United.

#### Operation

Central Control worked in the *following* manner. Each station was allowed to sell so many seats on every flight, without clearance from the Central Control office. After a flight was booked to a pre-determined level, each sale had to be individually cleared to avoid overselling. The individual postings had to be done by a secretary who transcribed the information off the teletype or telephone. Beginning with the

---

[1] Taylor, *High Horizons*, p. 97.

5

customer placing his reservation, confirmation took 17 hours.

## Problems

As passenger demands increased, Central Control was not fast or accurate enough to handle them. The telephone method of reporting became inadequate, because often stations called in and got a busy signal for long periods of time. The speed of the reservationist also limited the speed of Central Control. United could not afford to rent more telephone lines and hire enough people to cover the increase in passenger traffic.

### Ramac (1956–1961)

*To solve the problems of Central Control,* United introduced Ramac. Introduced in 1956 and located in Denver, Ramac was the first system of its kind to be used in the airline industry. Input-Output devices (I/O) connected Ramac to all the major cities. The *smaller* cities were connected to Ramac by teletype.[1]

## Operation

Ramac operated on an IBM punch card system. The I/O devices in the major cities consisted of a keypunch transmitter and a keypunch receiver. At the place of sales, a reservationist punched all the reservation information on a card and placed it in a transmitter which relayed the message to Denver. In *that* city, *another* machine processed the sale and kept track of the total sales on each flight. When a certain flight reached the predetermined level, the computer signaled the keypunch trans-

6

mitter to transmit the message "stop sales" to all the stations.

All the cities that did not have I/O devices transmitted the sales information to Denver by way of teletype. *This* sales information arrived in Denver on perforated ticker tape emitted by the teletype receiving unit. *This* perforated tape *then* entered another machine which translated the perforations into keypunched cards. To transmit the "stop sales" message to these cities, a punched card placed in Denver's teletype transmitter relayed the message to the stations. The station received the message on perforated tape and *then* had a decoding machine print out the message.

No matter where the messages came from, once they became punched cards in Denver they were all handled the same way. Denver had two processing computers working at the same time. The machines recorded the sales and kept track of the total number of passengers on each flight. By working two machines at one time, United protected itself against time lost because of mechanical malfunctions or breakdowns in one machine. *These* two machines served as a check on each other.

Ramac cut down and eliminated much of the time *lag present in Central Control.* It also cut down on the number of human handlings for a reservation and *in this way* reduced the possibility of human error. The total transaction time, *which under Central Control took 17 hours,* was now reduced to 45 minutes.

---

[1] Roberts, "Univac Flies with United," p. 35.

7

## Problems

United was unable to expand Ramac to cover the increasing passenger traffic. The storage space in the main computer of the Ramac system was not large enough to store the flight information necessary for making reservations.

## 1961–1970—INSTAMATIC

*Since Ramac was no longer efficient,* United installed a new system called Instamatic. It was centrally located in Denver and consisted of an immense computer connected by means of I/O devices to the 114 cities that it serviced. Reservation time was now eight seconds.

## Operation

Operating Instamatic required a complex communication network. American Telephone and Telegraph rented to United 18,916 miles of communication wires connecting United to all its ticket agencies. *This* communication system made United the owner of the second largest communication network in the United States, surpassed only by our national defense early warning system. With *this* network and its 1,200 agents, United processed 550,000 eight-second reservations a day.[1]

Instamatic was a numeric IBM system that understood only numbers read into it. *Therefore,* the I/O devices looked like the keyboard of an adding machine, con-

8

sisting of numbers from 1 to 10. *In addition to the numbers,* it also had special numeric coded messages, similar to ZIP codes, indicating facts such as destination and place of departure.

The procedure for making a reservation under the Instamatic system was simple. For each reservation a reservationist wrote on a special card the vital information such as flight number, sales date, place of departure and destination. *This* card and a special pre-printed code card placed in a transmitter, relayed the reservation information to Denver. The computer in Denver read the information, checked the flight to see if space was available, and within seconds sent the answer back. If space was available, a panel light flashed on confirming the reservation. If confirmed, the reservation transaction was complete at this stage. The computer *then* added one to the seats-sold list and was ready to accept more reservations on any flight.

Instamatic handled the same information *that Ramac did,* but it stored more information. The main computer in Denver stored all the information needed for flight reservations. It kept track of the number of spaces sold on each flight, *in addition to* the number of spaces available on the flights on all other airlines that connected to United.

## Problems

Even though Instamatic's system of sales was relatively simple and speedy, it *too* began to show signs of obsolescence.

---

[1] *United Publicity Fact Book,* p. 13.

9

Masterfiling, once the most efficient way of recording and storing reservations, became too time consuming. In the masterfile, the special handwritten cards were arranged first by date, then by flight, and finally by the names of the passengers. To find the actual record of a reservation, it was necessary to know the flight, date, and name of the passenger. If any of *this* information was missing, the process for finding a masterfile card was long and involved. The cards had to be hand sorted one by one until the correct card was found.

*In addition to being too time consuming*, masterfiling took up too much room. United kept masterfile cards for 90 days. As passenger traffic increased, 90 days worth of masterfiles used too much valuable space.

*Another problem* in the Instamatic system was that the Instamatic computer read only numbers. *Therefore*, a person's name could not be read into the computer. As a result, when a reservation office wanted a passenger list for a flight they had to wait for it to be teletyped from Denver. *This* procedure became too time consuming and inaccurate.

Instamatic *also* faced a language barrier. Since different airlines used different computers, and *these* computers used different languages which were not interchangeable, direct communication with the computers of other airlines was impossible.

Instamatic served its purpose well; but the need for faster service, more accuracy, and storage space contributed to the need for a *new* computer installation.

10

## 1970 AND BEYOND—UNIMATIC

United purchased Unimatic in 1964 and put it into operation in 1970. Its headquarters became Chicago.

The delivery of a new Boeing plane greatly necessitated the installation of Unimatic. United realized it had no place to store the information connected with the flights of this plane. They had two choices for a reservations system: revert back to the station master situation or install a new, more expensive computer system. Since the former choice was not practical, the latter was the only alternative.

### Present Operation

*Unimatic, like Instamatic*, has I/O devices in all major cities. *These* I/O devices consist of a set of head phones and a cathode ray tube which looks like a TV screen. All the *other* equipment—pencils, paper, and reference material—has been removed. Below the screen is a regular typewriter keyboard. A large panel of specially coded buttons to the right of this keyboard gives the computer prefabricated messages. As material is typed, it appears on the television screen. *This screen* allows the reservationist to see what she is recording. When a transaction is written up correctly, a button is pushed and all the information is cleaned off the screen and sent to the computer in Chicago. Then, within seconds, the "message waiting" button lights up, and when the button is pushed, the confirmation appears on the screen just as the computer recorded it. *This* second viewing of the message on the screen is a means

11

of double checking to make sure there is no error in the reservation. At this point the entire transaction is complete.

*This system* can give information in any form desired. If one wants to know what the most popular flight is, he can ask the computer and it will print the most popular flight.

Unimatic can handle any kind of information. For example, if a reservationist needs to pick up some bread on the way home from work, she can remind herself by typing a note on the screen and asking the computer to store this message until five o'clock. At five o'clock the "message waiting" button lights up. She can then press the button, and on the screen will appear the message to pick up the bread.

Unimatic *also* gives flight information in any form required. *For example,* Unimatic can print all the flights that a Pamela F. Whatmore has reserved in the last year. Unimatic will not only give a list containing the reservations for Whatmore, but *also* for all other names with similar spelling, if the name had been misspelled at the time of the reservation.

*Under Unimatic,* masterfile cards are all stored in the memory banks of the computer instead of in filing cabinets. Any information in the memory banks can be printed out upon request. There is no need to know all the information required by Instamatic to recall a reservation. Now all that is needed is the name, and then the entire history of all the transactions carried on by that individual within the past year will be printed out.

12

Unimatic has *also* eliminated the need for the teletype machine. No longer is there a need to teletype the passenger lists to various stations because Unimatic automatically prints out passenger lists upon request at the station requesting the information.

### Future Operations

One of the most important aspects of the Unimatic system is its future operations. All totaled, it will be able to do 17 separate jobs.[1] *For example,* Unimatic is expected to handle crew assignments, plane routing, keep track of weather conditions, and many other jobs associated with the airline industry. United knows that what is done today won't be good enough for tomorrow, but there are many plans for Unimatic. According to United's president, J. C. Watson, Unimatic's future chores will include everything that can be economically justified. It is hoped that Unimatic will be able to print tickets, record hotel and rent-a-car information, and handle all the information concerning flight patterns and crew assignments.

Right now Unimatic seems fairly comprehensive, but even now United is making plans for more complex uses for Unimatic. It is hard to say what will follow Unimatic. Future speculations include a fully automatic system in which vending machine tickets and computerized scanning units check tickets for confirmation. *This* system will eliminate many of the jobs that are now present. Vending machine

[1] Statement made by Jerome Gogulski, Executive of the Regional Division of Sales and Service.

13

tickets, along with computerized baggage handling and smooth coordination of all aspects of flying, will result in the lowest fares possible with the maximum customer satisfaction.

## SUMMARY

The present reservation system is a product of successive introductions of time-saving devices to remedy problems that became too big to ignore. The separate allocations of seats—during the original reservation system—did its best to meet the customer demands in the early years of the airline industry. *This* system presented problems that Central Control—the *next* system—helped correct. Central Control's problems were *then* solved by the introduction of automated devices.

*The introduction of automated devices* started with the computer centers of Ramac. Ramac solved most of the Central Control problems and served United well for many years. Eventually, *however*, Ramac *too* became obsolete and had to be replaced.

The *next* installation was Instamatic, a more complex computer. Instamatic simplified the process for making reservations. With the increase in passenger traffic and fleet size, Instamatic lacked the potential for handling future reservation information.

Instamatic's obsolescence gave way to the installation of a *bigger* and *better* computer system—Unimatic. Unimatic provides the potential for handling future reservations and much more. It will depend on the technological advances in all fields and the applications of these advances to the problems that will develop in the future of United Airlines.

14

## BIBLIOGRAPHY

Books

    Taylor, Frank J., *High Horizons*, McGraw-Hill Co., Inc., New York, 1968, 496 pp.

Magazines and Pamphlets

    *United Publicity Fact Book*, Publicity Department, UAL, Chicago, June 1970, 207 pp.

    Roberts, Henry, "Univac Flies with United," *Business Week*, December 25, 1970, pp. 33–39.

Interviews with United Personnel

    Brown, Earl, Executive of the Regional Division of Sales and Service, February 11, 1971.

    Gogulski, Jerome, Executive of the Regional Division of Sales and Service, March 1, 1971.

    Middleton, Cowper, Special Assistant to the Regional Vice President, March 30, 1971.

    Woodard, W. C., Executive of the Regional Division of Sales and Service, February 15, 1971.

## EXAMPLE OF A STATISTICAL REPORT

A formal report can range in content from mainly discussion to mainly graphs and figures. The airline report is mainly discussion; it doesn't include a single visual aid. As a contrast, the following two pages are part of a eight-page management report that a savings association sends to its directors.[1] The report presents its contents principally through visual aids and figures, as explained below:

1. The outside page is a combination of cover and title page—it includes title (Management Report) and name and address of the association.
2. Following the cover is page 1, which is a combination table of contents and the agenda for the next directors' meeting.
3. Page 2 (shown on page 715) presents the highlights. Comparable to a summary (terminal section) preceding the text, it shows the big picture. (Pages 3 through 8 comprise the text.)
4. Page 3 is a trend-type balance sheet updated each month in which like items appear together.
5. Page 4 (shown on page 716) is the statement of net earnings; the four figures under gross operating income on page 2 appear expressed or implied on this page. Both the 220.3 and 420.8 appear as February figures within gross operating income area under the heading of "Total." Implied are the other two figures—27.1 and 35.5. The difference between 2478.9 and 2443.4 in the Plan column gives 35.5. The difference between 220.3 and 193.2 in the Total and Plan columns gives 27.1.
6. Page 5 is a comparison of actual expenses with the budgeted expense for the the year; the four figures under expense on page 2 appear expressed or implied on this page.
7. Page 6 is a summary of savings activity; the four figures under savings on page 2 appear expressed or implied on this page.
8. Page 7 is a report of savings and loan activity for each office, together with a report on the dividends added to savings for each quarter.
9. Page 8 is a resume of loan activity; bottom section contains a breakdown of the association's complete loan portfolio, together with average yields. The four figures under loans on page 2 appear expressed or implied on this page.

Mr. Robert King, President, Westside Federal Savings and Loan Association, mails this report monthly to directors and key staff at the home office and the branches. It is a highly useful management tool because it "reports" to them the financial activity of the organization by means of balance sheets, complete operating reports, and a forecast. Additional discussion is unnecessary. As Mr. King said, "I can look at the recap sheet (page 2 on highlights) for 60 seconds and can tell how we're performing." Mr. King also said:

[1] Mr. Robert A. King, President, Westside Federal Savings and Loan Association, Seattle, Washington, has given permission to present these two pages. The actual size of the original report: 14⅜ by 9 inches for the front and back covers; 14 by 8½ inches for all other pages.

## INCOME AND EXPENSE

| | GROSS OPERATING INCOME | | EXPENSE | | NET FOR RESERVES | |
|---|---|---|---|---|---|---|
| | CURRENT MONTH | YEAR TO DATE | CURRENT MONTH | YEAR TO DATE | CURRENT MONTH | YEAR TO DATE |
| | 220.3 | 420.8 | 35.5 | 63.0 | 49.0 | 92.6 |
| +/- PLAN | + 27.1 | + 35.5 | - 7.3 | - 4.2 | + 33.6 | + 40.0 |

## SAVINGS

| | NET GAIN | TOTAL |
|---|---|---|
| | CURRENT MONTH | YEAR TO DATE |
| | 454 | 29,596 |
| | + 94 | + 220 |

## LOANS

| | NEW | OUTSTANDING |
|---|---|---|
| | CURRENT MONTH | YEAR TO DATE |
| | 1,193 | 31,400 |
| | + 893 | + 57 |

IN THOUSANDS OF DOLLARS

PLAN -------
ACTUAL ———

**GROSS OPERATING INCOME**

Total income for the month well ahead of schedule due mostly to loan fees

**EXPENSE**

Expenses are down primarily to out-of-phase expense payments. Actually we are on schedule

**NET FOR RESERVES**

Substantially better than anticipated. Hopefully this will be the pattern for next month also.

**SAVINGS**

Much greater than expected and better than being experienced by the rest of the industry both locally and nationally.

**LOANS**

Well ahead of plan.

# Statement of Net Earnings

(Thousands of Dollars)

| 1969 | Gross Operating Income | | | | | | Cost of Funds | | | Margin | | Operating Expense | Operating Income | | Non-op. Income (net) | Income Tax | | Net for Reserves | |
|---|---|---|---|---|---|---|---|---|---|---|---|---|---|---|---|---|---|---|---|
| | Interest | | Fees | Office Bldg. | Other | Total | Plan | Div. | Int. | Plan | Amt. | Plan | | Amt. | Plan | | Amt. | Plan | Amt. | Plan |
| | Loans | Other | | | | | | | | | | | | | | | | | | |
| JAN. | 172.8 | 4.5 | 16.0 | 7.0 | .2 | 200.5 | 192.1 | 123.0 | | 125.0 | 77.5 | 67.1 | 27.5 | 50.0 | 42.7 | .1 | 6.5 | 5.5 | 43.6 | 37.2 |
| FEB. | 166.3 | 14.1 | 30.8 | 8.8 | .3 | 220.3 | 193.2 | 124.0 | 4.5 | 132.7 | 91.8 | 60.5 | 35.5 | 56.3 | 17.7 | | 7.3 | 2.3 | 49.0 | 15.4 |
| MAR. | | | | | | | 192.4 | | | 135.5 | | 56.9 | | | 34.0 | | | 4.4 | | 29.6 |
| APR. | | | | | | | 191.0 | | | 133.5 | | 57.5 | | | 19.8 | | | 2.6 | | 17.2 |
| MAY | | | | | | | 217.8 | | | 135.5 | | 82.3 | | | 59.3 | | | 7.7 | | 51.6 |
| JUNE | | | | | | | 207.1 | | | 136.5 | | 70.6 | | | 20.2 | | | 2.6 | | 17.6 |
| JULY | | | | | | | 195.9 | | | 137.5 | | 58.4 | | | 13.9 | | | 1.8 | | 12.1 |
| AUG. | | | | | | | 203.3 | | | 138.5 | | 64.8 | | | 24.6 | | | 3.2 | | 21.4 |
| SEPT. | | | | | | | 201.7 | | | 139.5 | | 62.2 | | | 32.3 | | | 4.2 | | 28.1 |
| OCT. | | | | | | | 204.1 | | | 139.5 | | 64.6 | | | 26.8 | | | 3.5 | | 23.3 |
| NOV. | | | | | | | 225.7 | | | 140.5 | | 85.2 | | | 60.5 | | | 7.9 | | 52.6 |
| DEC. | | | | | | | 219.1 | | | 141.5 | | 77.6 | | | 21.5 | | | 2.8 | | 18.7 |
| YEAR TO DATE | 339.1 | 18.6 | 46.8 | 15.8 | .5 | 420.8 | 385.3 | 247.0 | 4.5 | 257.7 | 169.3 | 127.6 | 63.0 | 106.3 | 60.4 | .1 | 13.8 | 7.8 | 92.6 | 52.6 |
| CURRENT FORECAST | | | | | | | 2,478.9 | | | 1,629.5 | | 849.4 | | | 419.2 | | | 54.5 | | 364.8 |
| PLAN | | | | | | | 2,443.4 | | | 1,635.7 | | 807.7 | | | 373.3 | | | 48.5 | | 324.8 |

This report was developed early in 1964 with the cooperation of Touche, Ross, Bailey and Smart (CPA firm). In my opinion this has been the most useful management tool developed by our association thus far. I would go farther to say that any association that is not using some sort of a plan to forecast operating results by which to measure the actual experience of their operations is likely to fall way behind the leaders in achieving optimum results.

In summary, the formal business report is "formal" because of its parts—not because it uses formal language. Each prefatory and supplemental part should serve a useful purpose for the reader; if it doesn't, it should not appear in the report. Writing a formal report becomes easier for the writer when he has performed carefully and thoroughly the research steps before writing. And he is certain to have a better piece of writing when he has properly revised the first draft and considered the importance to the reader of the report's overall presentation.

## EXERCISE

Your assignment is to write a formal report whose body is approximately 15 to 25 double-spaced pages. Choose a topic that is broad enough to justify the length. Yet beware of a topic so broad that it would require volumes. If possible, consider a subject that you know something about, or one that especially interests you.

Try to find a topic that involves a business problem. (For example, you might know there's too great a turnover of employees in a certain department.) From the problem, and with some thought on your part, you can determine the purpose of your report. Other ideas that you can use as a springboard for a topic are listed below:

1. *Development of* a ski area on a certain mountain.
2. *Problems involved* in a bank's converting to a computerized operation.
3. *Proposed program (or plan) for* hiring and training of minority groups in X Company.
4. *Explanation of a certain policy or procedure*—such as types and degree of communications used by X Company in collecting retail accounts.
5. *Evaluation*—such as evaluating two or three career areas. This topic should be especially worthwhile for the individual who hasn't decided what job or job area he will be applying for after graduation.
6. *Survey, interpretation, and recommendation*—such as a study and report on attitudes toward certain recent troublesome problems:
   a. Opinion of X Company's employees regarding wages, working hours, parking, food services, promotion plan, etc.
   b. Opinion of students in your school regarding grading, credit hours for certain courses, student parking, housing, etc.
   c. Opinion of X Organization's members regarding membership dues, requirements, privileges, new clubhouse, etc.

One of the most important steps in tackling a report assignment is to clearly know its purpose. Once you can state the purpose in one sentence, you can begin your preliminary investigation into the methods and sources you'll be using and the major areas you need to cover. At this point in your research submit to your professor (or anyone he suggests) a memo report of your working plan. Be sure to include in this memo at least the following: problem, purpose, methodology, readers (both primary and secondary), and suggested outline. In this outline show the order for the introduction, major divisions of the text, subheadings for each major division, and the type of terminal section.

Once you have approval of your working plan, you can begin to collect your data; then organize this material and interpret it. With the completion of this last stage—interpretation—you can draw conclusions and make recommendations. Naturally if you're writing an informational report, you'll skip interpretation of material and merely summarize. Also at this time you should prepare (at least in rough-draft form) your tables and any other necessary visual aids. If your professor requests it, submit to him the final outline that you'll follow in writing your report—the one that will become your table of contents.

Now you should be ready to write. Choose the right time and place and follow the rules outlined in the chapter—both for the first draft and the revision. After your final revision, you can type (or have typed) the body of the report in final draft, or you can first write the necessary prefatory and supplemental parts. In this report assignment include at least the following: cover, title fly, title page, letter of transmittal (or preface), and table of contents. Also you'll need to include other parts—especially appendix and bibliography—if your report requires them. If the transmittal may affect part of what's included in the body, you should at least plan the transmittal before the final typing of the body.

Although the content and presentation of the material are most important, also remember the role that mechanics play. Be sure you have nothing that detracts your reader from concentrating on what you want to tell him. Thus, be sure the spelling, grammar, punctuation, and appearance are acceptable.

# Nonwritten Communication

● Chapter 17   Speaking, Listening, and Interviewing

# Speaking, Listening, and Interviewing

- The Art of Speaking
- The Art of Listening
- The Art of Interviewing

Although this text emphasizes the written word, the business world communicates by other means—namely by talking, gesturing, and listening. Businessmen and businesswomen use words and gestures to convey ideas and impressions to customers, colleagues, and others throughout the day. This chapter briefly covers three types of nonwritten communication used in business—speaking, listening, and interviewing.

## THE ART OF SPEAKING

The preparation for writing letters, memos, and reports is similar to the preparation for giving a business talk. Yet it is necessary to recognize that oral and written communication also have their differences. This section first discusses similarities and differences of speaking and writing, then preparation for the presentation, and finally the presentation itself.

### Similarities of Oral and Written Presentation

When you're reporting to someone on paper, you need first of all to remember the purpose and the reader. The same is true for business talks. The purpose determines what you say, and the audience dictates how you'll say it. In both a written report and an oral presentation you need to collect, classify, interpret, and organize your material. In both you need, many times, to use visual aids and indicate to the reader or audience the points of transition. In both you orient the reader (or audience) in the introductory remarks, give details in the discussion (text), and summarize or conclude at the end. Throughout you apply the writing principles (seven C's).

### Differences between Oral and Written Presentation

In many ways communicating orally is much easier than writing a letter, memo, or report. In the first place, you have had more practice in speaking. Furthermore, you don't need to bother with troublesome mechanics such as spelling and punctuation. And you have the aid of facial expressions, tone of voice, and gestures to make meaning clear. Finally, you have immediate feedback from the audience. If you notice raised eyebrows, excessive coughing, blank expressions, or other signs that indicate boredom or lack of understanding, you can clarify your point by restating or using an illustration, or you can simply ask if the listeners understand.

On the other hand, you have no immediate feedback when you write; also there's no chance for a feedback or further clarification beyond what you say in the message—unless you receive a reply or write a second message.

## Preparing the Oral Presentation

Before you write or speak, you need to prepare. Whereas preparing for written communication in business involves five thinking steps, preparing for a speech requires seven preparatory steps:

1. Determine the purpose
2. Analyze the audience
3. Choose the ideas to include in the message[1]
4. Evaluate the situation
5. Collect and interpret data[1]
6. Organize the data
7. Rehearse the talk

***Determine the purpose.***[2] Just as in written communication, the purpose determines what you say. Are you merely informing? Are you trying to secure belief or action through persuasion? Or are you simply trying to entertain? In the business world you'll probably use either of the first two of these goals.

***Analyze the audience.*** As with letters, memos, and reports, you need to consider the people you'll be talking to. In addition to deciding why you're talking to them, you need to analyze the size of the group, age range, sex, occupation (housewives, students, accountants), their attitude toward your subject, their capabilities, their prejudices, and their immediate previous activities.

If you're talking to a small group, you can be relatively informal, omit using a microphone, and use small visual aids. Age, sex, occupation, and capabilities of the group determine the educational level of your presentation and the choice of words and illustrations. For example, if you're talking only to accountants, you can use appropriate technical expressions and tie in your illustrations with their professional background. But if the audience consists of individuals from various occupations, you need to prepare your speech so that everyone will clearly understand what you're saying—in this case you'll avoid technical expressions and use general examples. If the composition of your audience makes it necessary for you to give them background so they will understand your main points, by all means give this background early in the presentation.

Furthermore, you should find out the attitude your listeners have toward your subject, as well as their prejudices. If you're talking about a controversial topic, giving bad news, or persuading, you need to be careful not to say anything bluntly, crudely, or inappropriately—that is, in a way that will

---

[1] It is unnecessary to dwell on choosing, collecting, and interpreting of data in this section because the speaker follows the same research procedure as the writer does when preparing a written report.

[2] Whenever possible, choose a topic that interests you and that you know something about. Then you'll have more incentive to tackle the assignment, won't have to spend so much time in collecting your material, and will possibly even enjoy the challenge of giving the best presentation possible.

irritate the audience or turn them off so they don't listen further to what you have to say. Instead, you gradually lead them with facts to whatever conclusions you don't dare reveal early in the presentation.

And finally you need to know what activities your listeners have already been involved in just before the talk. Have they been listening to other speakers for several hours without any kind of a break? If they need a brief rest period, give it to them. They'll like you for it and probably listen more attentively to what you have to say. If they have just eaten, put more enthusiasm and interest in your talk to keep them awake.

***Evaluate the situation.*** The "situation" refers to the room and the audience. A large room or auditorium requires a microphone and maybe even an elevated platform so that your audience can hear and see you. Be sure that your microphone is properly placed, and that your visual aids are large enough so that everyone can see what you're illustrating. If you're using notes that require a podium, see that one is in the right location before you begin to talk. And by all means consider the comfort of your audience. Whenever possible try to eliminate or reduce distractions such as poor ventilation, bad lighting, poor acoustics, and irritating noises.

***Organize the data.*** One of the most important thinking steps is organizing your materials so that the audience can easily follow you throughout your talk. You organize your talk like a report—introduction, text (discussion of details), and conclusions. In the introduction you catch the listener's attention with the problem (if any), the purpose, and often with a promise of an answer to the problem. You also orient the audience with the same introductory elements you use for a report. After giving your plan of presentation at the end of the introduction you start the text. And you end your talk with a terminal section—usually summary or conclusions.

***Rehearse the talk.*** Once you have considered all the steps discussed above, you are ready to apply them by rehearsing your talk. This step is vital for a beginner and is also used occasionally by some experienced speakers. Here you want to simulate the forthcoming talk before a live audience.

How can you practice in a physical and psychological atmosphere close to that of the actual performance? To begin with, find a room that approximates the one you'll be speaking in. And by all means practice aloud. Talk so that a friend (real or imaginary) in the back row can easily hear and observe you. Have thorough command of your subject; and use cards, an outline, or a list of points if you'll be using them before your audience. Know what to say and then determine how to say it. Use the bodily action you plan to use for the actual performance. Even include the actual visual aids you'll include to accomplish the purpose of your presentation. Be yourself. If you're not, you'll seem unnatural, out-of-place, and thus the audience will not be as ready to accept you or your speech. Remember, your real audience will be judging you mainly on five points:

1. Proper attitude
2. Bodily action
3. Voice
4. Speech content
5. Choice of words

At this time it's necessary to briefly discuss the first three of these five points.[1] As you read the following material, ask yourself whether you know your weak and strong points in each. For example, you should know whether: your gestures seem natural; you tell stories well; you have a winning smile; you have humor that goes over well; you have one or more outstanding characteristics such as dedication, informality, enthusiasm, seriousness.

*Proper attitude* includes the attitude you should have toward yourself, your subject, and your audience. This attitude involves:

Confidence in yourself
Interest in subject, audience, and task
Desire to stimulate your audience
Eagerness to share your thoughts with your audience
Your own activity—whether you're full of life and vigor
Friendliness, pleasantness, and courtesy

The proper attitude helps you eliminate—or reduce—stage fright, which often plagues the beginner. If you realize that your task is to convey information to the audience—that you are merely a means to that end—you'll begin to forget about yourself and concentrate on giving your listeners the facts they want to hear or should hear. Keep in mind that even the experienced speaker has qualms before speaking. Maybe he doesn't have perspiring hands, cotton mouth, trembling knees, blood thumping at the temples, or butterfly stomach—symptoms of stage fright in some beginners—but he seems to be on edge, a bit nervous, or at least a little restless. Actually it is not good to be completely unconcerned before the talk because the speaker may not try his best. One essential difference between a novice and the professional is that the professional recognizes symptoms of nervousness as normal and channels this energy toward an effective presentation. He forgets himself and concentrates on his audience. On the other hand, the novice worries about these symptoms and wastes his time and energy concentrating on himself and worrying about his presentation. Should you become nervous, remember that you never appear as nervous to an audience as you feel. If your knees tremble, touch them against the desk or lectern to stop the trembling. Also, speaking becomes easier as the talk progresses; the first few seconds are the worst.

[1] The other two—speech content and choice of words—are covered in the section on presentation.

***Bodily action*** is definitely essential to a good presentation. It should arise naturally from your thoughts and feelings as well as from the reaction of your audience. A speaker frozen to the floor, stiff as a poker, and motionless as a corpse does not take advantage of getting his message across in the most effective manner. But this bodily action—posture, movement, gestures, and facial expressions—must be natural and contribute rather than detract from the message.

If you're reluctant to use your arms, hands, legs, head, face and eyes when you speak before a group, let yourself go on the practice tryout and exaggerate. Once you become accustomed to this bodily action, learn to control it so that every movement will seem natural and add to the presentation.

Your posture should be comfortable so that you can breathe, walk, and gesture freely. But be sure your moves don't detract from your talk. It's perfectly acceptable to occasionally put your hands in your pockets, scratch your ear, or wipe perspiration from your forehead because all these actions are natural and appropriate in public. But don't put your hands in your pockets and leave them there—or, even worse, play with coins while your hand is in your pocket—because it is unnatural and distracting. Other bad posture habits to avoid are:

> Standing with feet wide apart
> Throwing weight completely on one leg
> Leaning from waist toward audience
> Leaning backward with weight on your heels
> Folding arms across chest
> Holding arms tightly behind the back
> Placing hands on hips

Moving about should be done only if you have a reason to do so. Just to prance to and fro like a caged jungle beast is even worse than stabbing your pointed finger toward the audience every 10 or 15 seconds. Listed below are several logical reasons for movement:

> Desire to change your position, to relax, to rest yourself
> To indicate transition—when you have finished developing one portion of your speech
> To secure a desired reaction from your audience—to be more emphatic

But if you're in doubt about whether to move, stand still. A wrong or poorly timed bodily action is much worse than no action. Also, your movements are naturally limited if the microphone is stationary.

Gesturing is another form of bodily action. As with all bodily action, gesturing must be suitable to the speaker, not be distracting, and not be overdone. Especially important is eye contact—to look at the audience so that you seem to include everyone. You can accomplish this gesture by a gradual sweeping view of the entire group—but make sure it isn't automatic, like a beacon light, and don't stare at any one person or cluster of individuals. In contrast, a speaker who stares out the window, or at the floor or ceiling, gives his audience the impression he's either scared of them or not very interested in them.

Facial expressions should also be natural—part of the speaker's personality. Perhaps a smile—especially before you begin to speak—is the most effective facial expression. It tells the audience you are relaxed and eager to share your ideas with a group you respect. But a "frozen" artificial smile detracts and is readily noticeable by the audience. You can also express yourself quite effectively (when appropriate) by wrinkling your brow, looking sad, puckering your lips, seeming puzzled or perplexed, and in many other ways.

*Voice*—the third factor that the audience evaluates—definitely adds to or detracts from an oral presentation. Listeners appreciate a voice that:

Is loud enough so that everyone can hear what the speaker is saying. Irritated is the listener who can barely hear what is being said—or deafened by a speaker who shouts or speaks too loudly.

Rises and lowers with same variety. No one appreciates a monotone.

Sounds pleasant. A rasping voice causes negative reaction.

Seems in keeping with the ideas being discussed. For example, the listener appreciates the speaker stressing key words and sentences.

## The Presentation

Once you have prepared and rehearsed your talk, you should be ready to give it before a live audience. First you want to catch the listeners' attention with your introduction, then discuss details in the major sections of the text, and end with a concluding section.

When you reach the podium, place your notes in a usable position. Also pause to make eye contact with your audience, and show you're a friendly individual by smiling briefly before beginning to speak. Naturally you have already taken several deep breaths to clear your lungs, tried to relax, straightened your clothes, cleared your throat, and blown your nose before you left your seat. Also, before you reach the podium you should be sure you know the opening sentence—word for word.

If you have prepared yourself well, you should experience little or no stage fright. But if you are nervous, remember that you feel more nervous than you appear to others, and that after the first few moments you will feel more comfortable.

*Introduction.* Be sure that you pause before you begin to talk so as not to stumble over your first few words. Then in a clear voice—with the proper eye contact—you begin with a greeting such as "ladies and gentlemen," "ladies," "gentlemen," "members of _____," "fellow _____," or whatever is appropriate to the group and the occasion.

After the greeting you give your introductory remarks. Perhaps you want to begin with the problem (if there is one). By all means you must clearly state the purpose of your talk. In addition you will include other introductory elements that orient the group to what you'll say in your discussion (text). A natural transition from the introduction to the text is to give your plan of presentation. You might also use visual aids—pointing to items already written on a board, writing on the board as you discuss particular areas, or bringing out a large card or cards as appropriate.

In addition to using an opening that begins with the problem and perhaps promises an answer, you have other ways to catch the attention of your audience:

Telling a story that is related to your subject or that establishes background for development of the purpose
Making a startling statement
Asking a question that makes the audience start to think
Giving a familiar quotation that leads into your subject
Telling a humorous story or joke related to the subject
Using an illustration that relates directly to the subject
Making reference to the subject, its timeliness, its importance
Making reference to the occasion, the audience, or reason for meeting

Naturally the right opener depends upon the purpose of the talk and the audience. Be especially aware that humor is effective only when it occurs naturally as the talk develops. Also remember—as you must for letters and memos—that what is humorous to one person may be offensive or boring to another.

*Discussion (text).* Once you have completed your introduction, you begin developing the text orally in the same way you develop the written formal report. As you present this material, you need to remember to apply the following:

1. Lead your reader through the speech. Since you don't have headings, you must clearly indicate when you complete one section and begin with another. You can do so by:
   a. Changing your bodily position
   b. Using topic sentences or introductory paragraphs
   c. Checking off a major heading already on the blackboard as you begin the discussion of that section
2. Use visual aids to get across your point. They can range from cards you show at appropriate times to material you draw on the board. But bring this material into view only when it is needed.
3. When you do present a visual aid, be sure you face your audience; at the same time don't obstruct the audience's view of the visual aid.

4. It's perfectly correct to use notes or an outline as a guide. But avoid leaning on such aids too much. Also, don't read long passages—especially the entire report—since you are sure to turn off your audience this way.
5. Pay attention to your audience. If you notice restlessness, excessive coughing, side conversations, excessive doodling, whispering, or dozing, you need to adjust your material and delivery. Other helpful clues on how the audience reacts to your talk are their facial expressions, shoulder shrugs, smiles, laughs, nods, and applause.
6. Your emphasis should be on your audience; use proper eye contact throughout your talk.
7. Avoid any unfavorable bodily actions that might distract the audience and keep them from concentrating on your message.
8. If you still feel nervous at this stage of your presentation:
   a. Introduce some physical object in your speech—talk about it, demonstrate it, or use the blackboard. Once you're occupied and doing something with your hands, you'll calm down.
   b. Move about the platform—be active. Bodily actions help conceal nervousness.
9. Instead of sprinkling "uh's" in your talk, hesitate between sentences without uttering a sound.

*Conclusions.*[1] Once you have finished discussing the text portion of your talk, you begin the terminal section—which is usually conclusions. This part of your speech is usually handled like the conclusions section of a written report. (For example, you'll list your conclusions when you have more than one and, naturally, will not introduce new material.)

When you begin this terminal section, you need to let the audience know that you have completed the last major section of the text and are now starting the conclusions. You do so by saying "In conclusion . . ." or some other appropriate substitute for the heading in the written report. Also, be sure your conclusion is concise. Nothing is more frustrating to the audience than to have the speaker signal to them that he is beginning to wind up his talk—and then keep talking for 10 or 15 minutes. "In conclusion" is usually a welcome signal to listeners—who then expect the speaker to finish within a few minutes.

In summary, you need to prepare for your oral presentation by considering the purpose of the talk, your audience, the situation, the material and the way you organize it, and by rehearsing thoroughly. With the right attitude, knowledge of the content, and the right rehearsal you can give an interesting talk; also you can reduce or eliminate possible stage fright by:

1. Choosing a topic that interests you and that you know something about.
2. Preparing well—thoroughly know your material, make notes, and rehearse in an atmosphere like the one for your actual speech.
3. Memorizing your opening sentence.

---

[1] Instead of conclusions, your ending might be a summary.

4. Introducing some material object in your discussion, talking about it, demonstrating it—or using the blackboard.
5. Relaxing and breathing deeply.
6. If your knees tremble, touching them against the desk or lectern to stop the trembling.
7. Moving about the platform to help cover up your nervousness.
8. Having the right attitude toward yourself and your audience. Remember your purpose in being there is to inform, persuade, or entertain. Forget yourself and concentrate on your audience.

## THE ART OF LISTENING

When someone speaks, he is attempting to inform, persuade, or entertain one or more other individuals. But most individuals hear—they don't listen. Just what is listening, then? "It means to see the expressed idea and attitude from the other person's point of view, to sense how it feels to him, to achieve his frame of reference in regard to the thing he is talking about. Real communication occurs whenever we listen with understanding."[1] This section on listening discusses:

1. Need for listening
2. Responsibilities of the listener
3. Responsibilities of the speaker
4. Results of good listening

### Need For Listening

Unfortunately most people are poor listeners—only about 25 percent clearly understand what they hear. For example, assume that a teacher is discussing sales letters and is preparing his class to sell a portable typewriter to parents of graduating high school seniors. He tells the class to "get the graduate in the picture," meaning that the student should tie in the graduate with the reader benefits. Unfortunately, it is possible to interpret the suggestion to mean that the writer of the sales letter should talk to both the son and the parents. This illustrates how important it is for both speaker and listener to be tuned into the same wavelength of understanding. Or take the man who says, "University students are radicals." Just what does he mean by radical? A student who wants to work within the establishment but speaks up and asks that teachers teach—not spend so much time on personal research? Or does he mean a youth who wants to burn, bomb, and disrupt? Also, is this man

---

[1] Carl R. Rogers and F. J. Roethlisberger, "Barriers and Gateways to Communication," *Harvard Business Review*, July–August 1952, p. 29.

thinking of all the students at the university? 50 percent of the students? Or only those he read about in the newspaper last night?

"The major barrier to mutual interpersonal communication is our very natural tendency to judge, to evaluate, to approve (or disapprove) the statement of the other person or the other group."[1] Furthermore, the tendency to make evaluations "is very much heightened in those situations when feeling and emotions are deeply involved. So the stronger our feelings, the more likely it is that there will be no mutual element in the communication."[2] Many situations illustrate this point. Black or white student militants aren't likely to listen to the "establishment"; a Jew or an Arab is often not really listening when his opponent discusses the opposite viewpoint; and many parents and their offspring can't reach (communicate with) each other. Why? Because the way an individual sees the world is determined by his background, beliefs, and inner needs. He subconsciously distorts or rejects ideas that run counter to his own prejudices. He actually filters out or "turns a deaf ear" to facts he cannot or will not accept.

Listening plays a vital role today because an individual in the business world spends most of his day talking and listening. And unless he listens correctly, he will misinterpret what other people say. In turn he may not think or act toward customers, colleagues, and others as he should. In short, he won't be acting and operating as effectively and efficiently as he can.

## Responsibilities of the Listener

The speaker has the responsibility to communicate as effectively as he can, but the listener also has responsibilities. He cannot sit back and contentedly assume he has nothing to do. Like a speaker, the listener needs to prepare himself (before he listens); then, as he listens, he must concentrate on both the verbal and nonverbal message of the speaker.

*Preparation for listening.*[3] The listener is influenced by the speaker, the message, other listeners, and physical conditions. The first three cannot be controlled by the listener, but the fourth—physical conditions—you as listener can do something about before the talk.

To give complete attention to the speaker and his message, you must choose whenever possible a position that allows you to see his gestures and clearly hear the tone of his voice and the emphasis he gives to certain parts of his presentation. Also sit up straight and look directly at the speaker. Should you become too relaxed, you might not give your full attention to his message.

---

[1] Carl R. Rogers and F. J. Roethlisberger, p. 29.
[2] Rogers and Roethlisberger, p. 29.
[3] The reader can likewise prepare himself before he begins to read a report by studying the purpose, the table of contents, preface, and perhaps the background of the writer.

If you find that you're sitting near disturbing individuals in the audience, or are distracted by bothersome noise, you should move to another location. Also consider other negative factors—such as a draft from a window or door, excessive heat from a register, and undue glare—that might distract your attention from the speaker and his message.

*Concentrate on the verbal message.* Because good listening is correctly decoding what the speaker says, you must concentrate on his verbal message. Once he begins to talk, be attentive to everything he does or says. Don't let your mind wander—although that's not an easy task because the mind thinks much faster than one can talk. You should use this "spare time" to think about what is being said. If the speaker hasn't organized his material well, try to figure out the purpose and understand how his major points and their subdivisions develop that purpose. Also check his facts for soundness and accuracy, and separate facts from opinions.

Furthermore, exercise emotional control by withholding evaluation of his ideas until the end of his talk or until you understand his viewpoint. Decode his words as he meant them. Put aside your bias. Keep your mind open— don't turn him off because you disagree with a statement. Try to think and feel as he does. Naturally there's a danger involved if you try too hard to understand the speaker's viewpoint because you might accept his reasoning to the point when you abandon your beliefs—without sufficient reason.

*Also concentrate on the nonverbal message.* In addition to the actual message, you want to observe the speaker's gestures, tone of voice, and physical movements. Do they seem to reinforce or contradict what he's saying? If he's trying to paint himself as a sincere dedicated man, do you detect elements of dishonesty? Is he actually timid when he's trying to play the role of a man full of confidence? If he tries to tell the audience that he's not prejudiced and at the same time uses gestures that betray his true feelings, his nonverbal message is the one to believe.

## Responsibilities of the Speaker

To carry out his responsibilities to the listener the speaker should:

1. Prepare his presentation by:
   a. Determining the purpose of the message
   b. Analyzing the listeners (audience)—talking on their level, keeping them in mind by using examples and illustration, and considering their activities just before the talk
   c. Evaluating the situation—checking room for comfort of listeners, determining need for a microphone, being sure visual aids are large enough so that everyone can see
   d. Organizing the material well
   e. Rehearsing the talk—present both verbal and nonverbal message so that the audience can correctly evaluate the overall presentation

2. Lead his listeners through the talk by:
   a. Gaining attention of his listeners—the same as he must do when he begins a sales letter
   b. Interesting them in his subject and perhaps in himself
   c. Holding their interest and attention throughout the discussion by leading them through the mass of details so that not once do the listeners lose their way or become bored, or distracted by inappropriate bodily movement.
   d. In the terminal section, being sure he reminds his audience of the highlights of his overall coverage and their relationship to one another and to the central theme

## Results of Good Listening

Good listening pays valuable dividends. It:

1. Permits the speaker and listener(s) to improve communication because each side is more receptive to the other's viewpoint.
2. Leads to positive attitudes.
3. Shows the speaker that his listeners are interested; in turn, he tries harder to give his best presentation.
4. Results in obtaining useful information so that the listener can make accurate decisions.
5. Creates better understanding of others and thus helps the listener to work with others.
6. Helps the one speaking to talk out his own problem. Remember that an individual likes to get things off his chest almost as much as he likes to solve problems.

## THE ART OF INTERVIEWING

Interviewing is a conversation with a purpose; it uses all the forms of communication already discussed in this text—speaking, listening, and writing (notes during or after the interview and the interview writeup).[1] Some of the different types of interview are:

Selection and placement interview—to hire the right man for the right job
Vocational guidance interview—to help an individual find his best vocation
Counseling interview—to help the emotionally disturbed
Survey interview—to help marketing men find answers to their assignments and problems
Group interview—used for problem solving
Diagnostic interview—used by clinical psychologists

---

[1] The interview writeup consists of a one- or two-page report with a paragraph on areas such as early home life, education and training, work experience, current off-the-job life, personal characteristics, and overall summary. The beginning of the body shows blank lines for interviewee's name, date, age, job considered for, and name of interviewer. At the end (you might call it "conclusions") is a scale where the interviewer checks his overall rating of the applicant.

The discussion here concentrates on interviewing candidates for employment in the business world. Although businessmen use various types of interviews,[1] the material in this section covers the patterned interview[2] because it is used most often and is considered most effective in getting truthful responses from the candidate. Here the interviewer guides and controls the conversation but encourages the interviewee to speak freely and at length about relevant topics. Here one finds interaction between individuals that results in:

> . . . a game of hide and seek in which the interviewer pursues the candidate, talking casually but trying doggedly to find out what kind of a guy he really is underneath. The applicant (interviewee), at the same time, is politely ducking, evading and dodging, anticipating the expectations of the interviewer and putting himself in the most favorable light. Out of this lively interplay come evaluations and estimates of the ability and aptitudes of the job applicant.[3]

The interview is certainly not the only source that the company uses to find out about the applicant's qualifications. Other productive sources are various tests (such as the intelligence test and aptitude test), physical examination, credit investigation, grade, transcripts, and references. But it's the interview and its evaluation of the candidate that supply the most useful data.

The patterned interview has the following four-fold objective:

1. It matches the man and the job by judging qualifications and areas that other sources cannot assess.
2. It gives the applicant essential facts about the job and the company (nature of the work, hours, fringe benefits, opportunities for advancement, company policy). This information helps the candidate decide whether he wants to accept the job if it is offered, or look further.
3. It instills a feeling of mutual understanding and confidence in the applicant who accepts the job. If he begins his work with the right attitude toward the firm, he will be a happier employee.
4. It promotes goodwill toward the company—whether the applicant does or does not receive or accept the job. It is especially important to give the right impression to the candidate who is disappointed by a turndown.

In the following sections you'll look at interviewing from both the interviewer's and interviewee's sides.

---

[1] Interviewing candidates for employment in the business world encompasses the screening or preliminary interview, final interview, follow-up interview, direct interview, indirect interview (or nondirective interview), and the patterned interview.

[2] The patterned interview is a combination of both the direct and indirect interviews. In the direct interview the interviewer keeps very close control at all times by directing limited and specific questions. On the other hand, in the indirect interview the interviewer makes little or no attempt to direct the applicant's conversation.

[3] Arthur D. Kellner, "Sharpen Your Approach to Interviewing," *Leadership in the Office*, American Management Association, 1963, pp. 67–68.

## Interviewer's Role and Responsibilities

This section first discusses the qualifications and the role of an interviewer. Coverage continues by showing how the interviewer prepares himself to meet the applicant, and the remainder of the section discusses each step of the interview—beginning with the warm-up period and ending with evaluating the information drawn from the candidate.

*Qualifications of the interviewer.* When a company asks one of its officers to interview, it should choose an individual who has been well trained in the art of interviewing and who has had enough interviewing experience to evaluate accurately. Given below are the qualifications necessary for interviewing. Some relate to knowledge of the jobs and the company; others relate to dealing effectively with a special kind of person—a job applicant.

1. The interviewer needs a thorough knowledge of the jobs for which he is interviewing. If possible, he should have a job analysis for each position; this is an orderly and systematic study of the characteristics, duties, and responsibilities of a specific job.[1] Included in a job analysis are job operations and working conditions; training needed; aptitudes; attainments; type of personality, character, or temperament required.
2. He should be objective; he should not be swayed by such factors as pity or personal bias.
3. At the same time he should have enough warmth to establish rapport with the applicant and later to get him to talk.
4. He must listen intelligently and critically to both the verbal and nonverbal messages the applicant is expressing. To do so requires high-level intelligence and experience in interviewing.
5. His experience requires extensive acquaintance with people similar in age and occupation to those being interviewed and knowledge of their occupational fields so he is familiar with their language, interests, and customs.
6. To be objective he must know himself so as to minimize any bias he possesses.
7. He must have maturity and poise so the applicant has confidence in him and feels his judgments are sound. Remember, he is the spokesman for his firm and "is" the firm to the applicant.

*Role of the interviewer in front of the candidate.* The most important of the four-fold objectives of interviewing is matching the man and the job by judging areas that other sources cannot assess. As the interviewer, you must get enough information on which to base judgment. To accomplish this goal, you must be a combination of objective researcher, representative and goodwill ambassador of your company, friend of the applicant, and critical listener.

Because you are dealing with a person who is likely to be especially observant in his capacity as applicant, and who is under emotional strain, you must apply all you know about the psychology of human behavior—both yours

[1] Roger Billums, *Psychology of Personnel in Business and Industry,* Prentice-Hall, Inc., Englewood Cliffs, N.J., 1961, p. 229.

and the applicant's. At all times you need to keep control of the interview and at the same time get the applicant to talk. The ideal interview should *seem* like an unstructured conversation, but you should not permit it to proceed aimlessly. As a critical listener, you must notice gaps and omissions in the applicant's discussion and observe his reactions, comments, and gestures. Listed below are suggestions you need to follow to be an effective interviewer:

1. You should let the applicant do most of the talking. If you talk more than 50 percent of the time, you are interviewing yourself—not conducting an interview.
2. Use brief verbal responses that will keep the applicant talking—prod with questions such as "Tell me more," "That's interesting," "What happened then?"
3. Give your entire attention to the interviewee and respond by encouraging facial expressions, movement and expression of the eyes, and nods of the head.
4. Allow pauses in the conversation if you think the applicant will reveal important information. But avoid lengthy pauses or a pause when the applicant has definitely finished a topic.
5. Try to understand the applicant, who in turn may volunteer really useful information.
6. Make it easy for the applicant to express himself.
7. Respect the feelings of the other person even though you consider the person wrong.
8. At all times accept what he says. Never frown, show surprise, or show disapproval.
9. Avoid the impulse to cut the applicant off or change the subject abruptly.
10. Never argue.
11. Informality helps. Sit on the same side of the desk as the applicant and use plain language.
12. Be yourself.

Following is a checklist[1] that should help you review whether you are carrying out the role of interviewer well. If you can give an affirmative answer to each question, you're on the beam. Do you:

1. Try to make a favorable impression on the candidate during the first few minutes of the interview?
2. Refrain from making any judgment about the candidate during the first few minutes of the interview?
3. Put the candidate at ease?
4. Pause after the candidate has seemingly finished a remark to give him a chance to talk further?
5. Occasionally repeat parts of the key sentences of the candidate in a questioning tone to secure elaboration?
6. Ask one question at a time?

[1] Milton M. Mandell, *The Selection Process: Choosing the Right Man for the Job*, American Management Association, Inc., New York, 1964, pp. 220–221.

7. Make your questions clear?
8. Avoid wording questions so as to suggest the answers wanted?
9. Appear interested in the candidate and give him full attention?
10. Avoid expressing approval or disapproval of the candidate?
11. Avoid indicating your own attitude?
12. Use language appropriate to the candidate?
13. Ask no personal questions until after rapport has been established?
14. Allow the candidate to digress briefly without abruptly returning him to the point?
15. Talk as little as possible?
16. Control the direction of the interview?
17. Obtain maximum information on all relevant points?
18. Follow up leads that the candidate makes.
19. Spend most of the time exploring areas on which information could not be obtained as well from other sources (reference check, for instance).
20. Get a complete work history?
21. Take notes of important points?
22. Avoid taking notes when the candidate is under stress?
23. Hear and see the vocal and physical mannerisms of the applicant as well as listen carefully to what he says?
24. Give the candidate an opportunity to ask questions?
25. "Sell" the job if this is deemed desirable?
26. "Sell" at the right time?
27. Continue observing until the candidate leaves the room?
28. Give the applicant a good impression of the organization before he leaves?
29. Enable the candidate to leave with a feeling that he had an opportunity to do himself full justice?

*Preparing for the interview.* The interviewer must prepare for the interview—as he would if he were going to give a talk, to listen, or to write.

As an interviewer, you need to have a clear picture of your company's organizational structure and detailed information about the job(s) for which you are interviewing. Knowing organizational structure permits you to talk with confidence and give the applicant necessary facts about your company. If possible, you should have a job analysis for each position (see page 734). so that you can figure out exactly what you need to look for in the applicant. If a job analysis isn't available, at least be familiar with the work environment, requirements for the position (including personality), and salary.

Your next step is to decide the areas you must cover in the interview (and the necessary questions) so that you can determine what qualifications a successful candidate should have. These areas usually include the critical requirements for the job, character, personality, general make-up of the individual. Then think how each applicant can demonstrate the skills and qualities that the job requires. Usually you attain your goal by use of questions about what he has done; what he thinks about what he has done; his interests and hobbies; relationship to friends, school, and work; his colleagues and family. Finally set the interview up so that you can gain the most information possible from the candidate.

In addition, you need to consider the physical setup of the interview. Choose a quiet room where there will be little or no interruption. Arrange the furniture so that a desk does not separate you from the applicant. The ideal arrangement is to have chairs for you and him on one side to break down the formal roles of questioner and questioned, Arrange your schedule so that no one has to wait very long. Furthermore, check the waiting facilities. If possible avoid having applicants stand in the hall—especially in long lines. A quiet waiting room with chairs and magazines gives a much more favorable impression and is more relaxing.

***Warm-up period.*** You should react to the applicant at the beginning of the interview in the same way you would to a friend who visited you at your office or home. Especially important are a firm handshake, warm smile, and friendly tone of voice.

Because the applicant is probably nervous—or at least unfamiliar with his surroundings—you want to begin the conversation with small talk. You might make reference to the weather (that it's cold, fair, rainy, or humid), to an event of the day, or to a topic relating to the applicant's outside interest (football, sailing, mountain climbing). This is the time to begin to develop rapport and to show you are friendly, and sincerely interested in him. With the proper warm-up, you gain the applicant's respect and (hopefully) confidence.

***Drawing desired information from the candidate.*** The preparation for the interview and the warm-up period culminate in the heart of the interview —in which you draw desired information from the candidate. This section discusses the content and outline of the interview, use of questions, importance of nonverbal message, and pitfalls to avoid.

*The content and outline of the interview* are especially important because they give you a pattern to follow so you will cover adequately all vital information about the applicant.

Once you have completed the brief warm-up period, you start the interviewee talking on the subject you want to know about. You might begin by saying, "I've noticed from your application form that you worked for ABC Company four years. Tell me about the jobs you held there and what duties you performed." Or you might say, "The job we have here requires a man (or woman) who has a good knowledge of data processing. Please tell me about your experience in this area." Then you continue to lead the conversation to the topics you have decided you will cover.

Throughout the interview, let the applicant do most of the talking, but tactfully steer him back on course if he begins to wander, or dwells too long on one topic. And don't stop digging for the vital facts that will help you decide if he's the man for the job.

For each interview you will probably need to make notes. Some interviewers make notes only after they have completed each interview. Others take notes during the interview, but with the following rules in mind:

1. Take brief notes throughout the interview so that the applicant becomes familiar with your actions and does not freeze up when you do make a notation.
2. Never make a note when the applicant is giving you unfavorable information.
3. Don't allow note taking to interfere with your conversation and eye contact with the applicant.
4. Don't try to make secret notes during the interview. Be aboveboard in all your actions.

A good outline to follow during the interview is a straight chronological sequence. You begin with the applicant's early home background, and then move through education, work history, and off-the-job activities to self-evaluation. In this coverage you check his technical qualifications (can he do the job), drive and aspirations (will he do the job), social effectiveness and emotional balance (relations with others and self), character (how much trust can you place in him), and other factors you need to measure for success on the job. They might relate to his physical vigor and energy, wife's attitude toward the job, financial stability, willingness to travel, willingness to make permanent moves.[1] Especially important are those aspects of the candidate's personality that relate to interest patterns, attitudes, character, and temperament.

On the other hand, you don't want to waste time getting facts you can readily find elsewhere. This includes collecting routine information an applicant can supply on a form; verifying data that you could verify in other convenient ways; or securing estimates about aptitude, skills, and other attributes for which sound and practical measuring devices exist.

Once you have learned the necessary qualifications and behavior of the applicant, you can turn your attention to telling him about your company, salary, fringe benefits, and other facts he should be interested in.[2] Also give him the opportunity to ask you questions relating to the job or company.

*Use of questions* forms the bulk of the interviewer's techniques to get the applicant talking about himself—and to keep him talking. As the interviewer, however, you should ask questions only under certain conditions:[3]

1. To help the person talk
2. To relieve any fears or anxieties on the part of the applicant—those which may be affecting his relationship to the interviewer
3. To change the discussion to some topic which has been omitted or neglected
4. To discuss vague or involved assumptions the applicant has already made

[1] Theodore Hariton, *Interview! The Executive's Guide to Selecting the Right Personnel*, Hastings House Publishers, New York, 1970, pp. 25–34.
[2] Some interviewers reverse this pattern by first discussing the firm.
[3] F. J. Roethlisberger and W. J. Dickson, *Management and the Worker*, Harvard University Press. Cambridge, Massachusetts, 1947, p. 287.

A good interviewer asks questions that are revealing—questions concerned with attitudes. He might ask, for example:

What would you say was the most promising job you ever had?
What did you like least about that job?
What kind of people do you work with best?

Given below are other suggestions about the use of questions:

1. You can learn more about the applicant from the "why's" of his action than from the "what's."
2. Broadly worded lead questions that introduce a new topic steer the applicant in the right direction and permit you to sit back, evaluate what he is saying, and throw in only occasional probes or comments: Example: "What are some of the things you like to do off the job when you are not busy working—your outside interests and activities?"
3. Follow-up questions should also be broadly worded.
4. You need to phrase each question carefully to elicit the desired information.
5. Use of the implied question—silence—tells the applicant you feel he has more to say and places the burden on him to take it from there.
6. An indirect question such as the following encourages further elaboration without asking a direct question: "Please explain that in a little more detail."

*The nonverbal message* can be as revealing as anything the applicant actually says. If he blushes, begins to stammer, casts his eyes downward, or barks out an angry reply, he is telling far more than anything he might put into words. You can partially but reliably judge any statement from the tone and inflection of the person's voice, gestures, hesitations, and general conduct. His behavior tells much about his personality and social skills.

*Pitfalls to avoid* relate mainly to the following biases, prejudices, and other weaknesses within the interviewer himself:

1. Halo effect—tendency of the interviewer to form an overall opinion about the applicant on the basis of a single aspect of his makeup.
2. Stereotype error trap—tendency to categorize the applicant on the basis of a few surface clues.
3. Expectancy error—tendency of the applicant to anticipate the needs and preferences of the interviewer and to respond accordingly.
4. Ideal image error—interviewer's mental picture of the ideal man may not necessarily coincide with the man who can actually be most effective on the job.
5. Personal bias of the interviewer—poor handshake, biting of fingernails, gum chewing, loud clothes, poor eye contact.[1]
6. Pseudoscience and myth—judging the applicant's character, mental ability, attitudes by means of his handwriting, outward features, date of birth, num-

---

[1] There are many examples of bias. Some people foolishly think all redheads are hot-tempered, fat people are jovial, swarthy complexions reveal dishonest tendencies, short people are domineering, people with close-set eyes are unintelligent or stubborn.

ber of letters in his name, lines or marks of the palm of his hand, and shape and bulges of the skull.

7. Stereotyped, mechanical interviewing—same questions in same order, no adaptation to the individual, no stimulating exchange of ideas, no interplay of attitudes. In turn, the interviewer receives stereotyped answers that don't appraise qualifications.
8. Illusion that previous experience, of itself, guarantees ability to do the job well.
9. Being swayed because the applicant needs a job—even though he doesn't have the necessary qualifications.
10. Talking too much by interviewer—not listening.
11. Poor preparation for interview.
12. Not adept at asking right questions.
13. Sheer discourtesy and rudeness toward the applicant.
14. Jumping to conclusions too soon.
15. Accepting facts without probing to determine meaning and accuracy.
16. Leaving unexplored gaps.
17. Allowing applicant to guide the interview.
18. Too shy to ask questions about the applicant's family and problems.
19. Depending on memory to conduct interview and to evaluate the applicant's qualifications.
20. Asking another question when the applicant merely hesitates a moment.
21. Appearing to be critical and cold toward the applicant.
22. Not observing nonverbal clues (gestures, voice changes, hesitations).
23. Poor questions:
    a. Leading questions that invite a given response: "Would you agree that . . . ." "Are you in favor of . . . ."
    b. Loaded questions—use of language that reveals one's own biases and prejudices; in turn, the applicant will slant his answers accordingly.
    c. Dead-end questions that elicit only "yes" or "no" answers.

***Evaluating the information.*** When you have drawn the desired information from the candidate, you must form an overall opinion of what he said during his time with you and supplement it with vital facts from other sources.

No one candidate will usually possess all the requirements you are measuring. He might not have all the work experience you'd like, but he might compensate for his weakness with an abundance of drive and personality. Yet considering the facts gained from the interview, together with the applicant's appearance, attitudes, mannerisms, and gestures—all together—will tell you whether he has the right combination of motivation, interest, adjustment, temperament, and other attributes to make a successful employee. You must select the right man for the job. But if you choose someone whose ability is far above or below the level of the job, you'll be doing a disservice to three groups—to the applicant, who will not remain on the job very long; to the company, which will lose money for the time he remains on the job; and to yourself, who will lose face with yourself, the applicant, and the company.

Presented below is a list of clues which often serve as indicators of the applicant's state of mind and general makeup.[1] They should prove extremely useful to you (as an interviewer) in your evaluation.

*1. Behavioral and psychological symptoms*

| *Positive* | *Negative* |
| --- | --- |
| **a.** Arriving early | **a.** Arriving late |
| **b.** Alert, responsive | **b.** Inattentive, dull |
| **c.** Emphatic attitude | **c.** Condescending or withdrawn attitude |
| **d.** Relaxed manner | **d.** Tenseness, fidgetiness, body tremors |
| **e.** Smiles | **e.** Frowns |
| **f.** Clear voice | **f.** Choked voice, mumbling |

*2. Verbal symptoms*

| | |
| --- | --- |
| **a.** Sticking to the main point | **a.** Changing the subject |
| **b.** Incisiveness | **b.** Overgeneralizing or too much detail |
| **c.** Relevant responses | **c.** Irrelevant responses |
| **d.** Well-organized presentation | **d.** Disorganized presentation |
| **e.** Appropriate use of humor | **e.** Uncalled-for levity |
| **f.** Spontaneous replies | **f.** Long pauses before replying |
| **g.** Speaking well of people | **g.** Critical of others |
| **h.** Candor | **h.** Rationalization, evasiveness |

## Interviewee's Role and Responsibilities

Once the applicant knows what he will face during an interview, he will prepare well beforehand and then conduct himself properly during the interview. This discussion assumes he has narrowed down his occupational choice, completed his education, and taken stock of his potential.

*Preparation for the interview.* Even though the interviewer will conduct the interview on his terms, you as the applicant can and should plan—and plan well—for this very important and usually necessary step toward getting the job you want. This preparation includes knowing yourself, familiarizing yourself with the company, preparing questions you want to ask as well as answers to questions you'll probably encounter, paying attention to your appearance, and checking details about the meeting place for the interview.

The most important preparation relates to knowing yourself. But, then, you have already looked critically at yourself before you wrote your resume and application letter. You should know the job or the job area you want to apply for, the requirements for the job, and how your qualifications (both your strengths and weaknesses) compare with the requirements.

In addition to knowing yourself, you should bone up on the company. You can find excellent references in your library or school placement office,

[1] Hariton, p. 58.

and from employees of the company itself. Among other facts you should know are the age of the company, location of its plants, types of products and services, its growth over the years (especially the last few years), and its prospects for the future. You'll make a favorable impression on the interviewer if you sincerely show interest in the company and show knowledge about it gained through your own initiative.

Another important step in preparing for the interview is to jot down questions you want to ask the interviewer if he doesn't first give you the answers and to jot down questions you think he will ask you. The questions you might ask relate to possible formal or informal training the company offers after employment, company policy about moving your family to a new location, or types of fringe benefits. Also you want to anticipate questions he will ask you. You can definitely expect to encounter revealing questions relating to what you have done; what you think about what you have done; your interests and hobbies; relationship to friends, school and work; your colleagues and family. Shown on pages 744–747 are 94 questions frequently asked during the employment interview.[1]

Once you know yourself, have studied the company, and have prepared your questions and answers, you still need to consider your appearance and details about the meeting place. Appearance includes both your overall neatness and the clothes your wear. Be sure your hair and fingernails are clean and your hairstyle is appropriate. Wear conservative clothes appropriate for the office, clean your shoes, and use lotions or perfumes sparingly. Also see that accessories complement the suit or dress. Then there are the details about the interview itself. Definitely know when and where the interview will be held— and be there 10 to 15 minutes early. Being late is inexcusable. Also know the full name and address of the company, the interviewer's name and current title, and how to pronounce his name. After that, put a working pen or pencil along with a small notebook in your coat pocket or purse, and relax.

As the New York Life Insurance Company says so well in its booklet, *Making the Most of Your Job Interview*:[2]

> The employment interview is one of the most important events in the average person's experience, for the obvious reason that the 20 or 30 minutes he spends with the interviewer may determine the entire future course of his life. Yet interviewers are constantly amazed at the number of applicants who drift into job interviews without any apparent preparation and have only the vaguest idea of what they are going to say. Their manner says, "Well, here I am." And that's often the end of it, in more ways than one.

---

[1] *Making the Most of Your Job Interview*, New York Life Insurance Company. Additional copies of this 14-page booklet may be obtained in reasonable quantity without cost or obligation from your New York Life Agent or the New York Life Office in your community.

[2] *Making the Most of Your Job Interview*, New York Life Insurance Company.

Others, although they undoubtedly do not intend to do so, create an impression of indifference by behaving as though they'd dropped in between coke dates. The young man who reports to an interview wearing dungarees and moccasins—who leans back in his chair and lights up a cigarette—seems to be saying, "What can you do for me?"

At the other extreme, a few applicants get themselves into a state of mind where they feel as if they are being marched into a medieval inquisition chamber. When they arrive, they are in the last stages of nervous fright and unable to do much but gulp and answer in monosyllables.

These marks of inexperience can be avoided by knowing a little of what actually is expected of you and by making a few simple preparations before the interview.

Before you go into the room where the interviewer is, try to relax. If possible, sit quietly in the waiting room, and convince yourself that the interviewer is an individual who merely wants to find out whether you're the person for the job. In turn, you *want* to show him that you appreciate the opportunity he's giving you and furthermore you're eager to tell him about yourself.

*Conduct during the interview.* From the time the interviewer first sees you until you leave, he will be observing you carefully and listening to everything you say and do. To make the best impression, you need to:

1. Show interest. You can do so by the way you sit and look alert, by eye contact, and by questions you ask.
2. Be courteous. Don't chew gum, and don't smoke unless the interviewer invites you to do so.
3. Be honest and sincere at all times. If you begin to exaggerate or fabricate details—and he catches you—he'll question you as a favorable candidate for the job.
4. Be yourself. Don't try to put on airs. By being yourself, you'll be on more familiar ground, seem more comfortable, and be more at ease.
5. Be a good listener. By doing so, you will be ready to reply to a question the interviewer asks, seem interested, and also receive valuable clues from his actions.
6. Avoid the negative attitudes or actions listed on page 747.

When you first see the interviewer, smile and greet him by name (if you know his name). From then to the end of the interview you should take your cues from him. If he offers to shake hands, do so. But be sure your grip is firm, not a bone-crusher or limp fish. Also remain standing until he invites you to sit down; the only exception is when you're in a small room and he remains seated or sits down immediately. Look at him and keep using the proper eye contact throughout the interview. But don't stare him down!

Be on guard at all times for nervousness. If your hands want to wander or play with objects, put these hands in your lap. Don't fiddle with a ring, parts of your face (chin, nose), button, or anything else. Also don't smoke if you're noticeably nervous because you may expose a trembling hand.

After the warm-up period, be ready for the interviewer's first question about your qualifications or interest. He might ask, "Why are you interested in this company?" If so, merely tell him the answer you previously thought out. Or he might say, "I see from the company (or placement office) form that you're interested in making marketing research your career. Tell me how you prepared yourself for this area." Again you merely tell him the answer you previously rehearsed for this question. If he throws you a surprise question— "How much do you expect to be earning 10 years from now?"—and you haven't prepared yourself for this question, take a few seconds to ask yourself what he's driving at. No doubt he's checking your drive, motivation, ambition, ability to plan ahead, soundness of your thinking. Without saying a word, think. Then you might reply by saying you'd like to begin with such-and-such a job and progress on your own initiative to . . . . Show him that you are interested in preparing yourself to be a better employee and progressing with his company. You won't tell him in figures how much you expect to be making in 10 years, but you'll be getting at the reason for his question. But if he still presses you for a dollar amount, you can reason that you'll start in a certain salary range. After 10 years an average person doing similar work now makes so much. But a possible inflation of a certain percentage over the next 10 years should bring the final figure to such-and-such. With this line of reasoning, you'll make a favorable impression on the interviewer.

Shown below are other suggestions to consider:

1. If you are strong in extracurricular organizations and he hasn't mentioned that area, watch for an opportunity to ask, "Are you interested in my extra-curricular activities?" He's not likely to say "no."
2. If he offers you the job on the spot, you can accept or ask for time to think it over.
3. Be prepared to ask sincere questions about the company because doing so shows interest.
4. Never make a slighting reference about a former professor or employer. Assume part of the blame yourself. If you can't say something nice about a person, don't say anything.
5. Know the current beginning salary range for your type of work.
6. Throughout the interview, smile at appropriate times—but don't maintain an artificial, plastered smile at any time; it's unnatural and insincere.
7. Be alert for signs from the interviewer that the interview is about to end. And when you depart, thank him for the time he has taken to see you.
8. So that you will be comfortable when you're being interviewed, you should arrange to have several interviews—maybe with representatives of different companies. By doing so, you will be familiar with the routine you'll be facing and thus be less nervous.

*Questions frequently asked during the interview.*[1] Shown below are 94 questions frequently asked during the employment interview. Mr. Frank S. Endicott, Director of Placement, Northwestern University, made the compilation from 92 companies he surveyed.

1. What are your future vocational plans?
2. In what school activities have you participated? Why? Which did you enjoy the most?
3. How do you spend your spare time? What are your hobbies?
4. In what type of position are you most interested?
5. Why do you think you might like to work for our company?
6. What jobs have you held? How were they obtained and why did you leave?
7. What courses did you like best? Least? Why?
8. Why did you choose your particular field of work?
9. What percentage of your college expenses did you earn? How?
10. How did you spend your vacations while in school?
11. What do you think about our company?
12. Do you feel that you have received a good general training?
13. What qualifications do you have that make you feel you will be successful in your field?
14. What extracurricular offices have you held?
15. What are your ideas on salary?
16. How do you feel about your family?
17. How interested are you in sports?
18. If you were starting college all over again, what courses would you take?
19. Can you forget your education and start from scratch?
20. Do you prefer any specific geographic location? Why?
21. Do you have a girl? Is it serious?
22. How much money do you hope to earn at age 30? 35?
23. Why did you decide to go to this particular school?
24. How did you rank in your graduating class in high school? Where will you probably rank in college?
25. Do you think that your extracurricular activities were worth the time you devoted to them? Why?
26. What do you think determines a man's progress in a good company?
27. What personal characteristics are necessary for success in your chosen field?
28. Why do you think you would like this particular type of job?
29. What is your father's occupation?
30. Tell me about your home life during the time you were growing up.
31. Are you looking for a permanent or temporary job?
32. Do you prefer working with others or by yourself?
33. Who are your best friends?
34. What kind of boss do you prefer?
35. Are you primarily interested in making money or do you feel that service to your fellow men is a satisfactory accomplishment?
36. Can you take instructions without feeling upset?
37. Tell me a story!

[1] You'll find these questions in the New York Life Insurance Company's booklet, *Making the Most of Your Job Interview.*

746 / Nonwritten Communication

38. Do you live with your parents? Which of your parents has had the most profound influence on you?
39. How did previous employers treat you?
40. What have you learned from some of the jobs you have held?
41. Can you get recommendations from previous employers?
42. What interests you about our product or service?
43. What was your record in military service?
44. Have you ever changed your major field of interest while in college? Why?
45. When did you choose your college major?
46. How do your college grades after military service compare with those previously earned?
47. Do you feel you have done the best scholastic work of which you are capable?
48. How did you happen to go to college?
49. What do you know about opportunities in the field in which you are trained?
50. How long do you expect to work?
51. Have you ever had any difficulty getting along with fellow students and faculty?
52. Which of your college years was the most difficult?
53. What is the source of your spending money?
54. Do you own any life insurance?
55. Have you saved any money?
56. Do you have any debts?
57. How old were you when you became self-supporting?
58. Do you attend church?
59. Did you enjoy your four years at this university?
60. Do you like routine work?
61. Do you like regular hours?
62. What size city do you prefer?
63. When did you first contribute to family income?
64. What is your major weakness?
65. Define cooperation!
66. Will you fight to get ahead?
67. Do you demand attention?
68. Do you have an analytical mind?
69. Are you eager to please?
70. What do you do to keep in good physical condition?
71. How do you usually spend Sunday?
72. Have you had any serious illness or injury?
73. Are you willing to go where the company sends you?
74. What job in our company would you choose if you were entirely free to do so?
75. Is it an effort for you to be tolerant of persons with a background and interests different from your own?
76. What types of books have you read?
77. Have you plans for graduate work?
78. What types of people seem to "rub you the wrong way"?
79. Do you enjoy sports as a participant? As an observer?
80. Have you ever tutored an underclassman?
81. What jobs have you enjoyed the most? The least? Why?
82. What are your own special abilities?

83. What job in our company do you want to work toward?
84. Would you prefer a large or a small company? Why?
85. What is your idea of how industry operates today?
86. Do you like to travel?
87. How about overtime work?
88. What kind of work interests you?
89. What are the disadvantages of your chosen field?
90. Do you think that grades should be considered by employers? Why or why not?
91. Are you interested in research?
92. If married, how often do you entertain at home?
93. To what extent do you use liquor?
94. What have you done which shows initiative and willingness to work?

It might be wise for you to try to answer these questions—about five or ten each day—and to really make the assignment challenging, try to answer "why" to the questions that permit you to do so. Some you can answer without too much effort. Answers to others, however, might be so difficult (and important) that you want to actually write them out after long and serious thought. If you know the answers to these 94 questions and others you add to the list, you'll be well prepared to answer any question the interviewer might ask you.

***Negative factors to avoid.*** Mr. Endicott, who compiled the 94 questions most frequently asked in interviews, also surveyed for negative factors evaluated during the employment interview which frequently lead to rejection of the applicant. Shown below are 50 of these factors as reported by 153 companies.[1]

1. Poor personal appearance
2. Overbearing—overaggressive—conceited "superiority complex"—"know-it-all"
3. Inability to express himself clearly—poor voice, diction, grammar
4. Lack of planning for career—no purpose and goals
5. Lack of interest and enthusiasm—passive, indifferent
6. Lack of confidence and poise—nervousness—ill-at-ease
7. Failure to participate in activities
8. Overemphasis on money—interest only in best dollar offer
9. Poor scholastic record—just got by
10. Unwilling to start at the bottom—expects too much too soon
11. Makes excuses—evasiveness—hedges on unfavorable factors in record
12. Lack of tact
13. Lack of maturity
14. Lack of courtesy—ill mannered
15. Condemnation of past employers
16. Lack of social understanding
17. Marked dislike for school work

---

[1] *Making the Most of Your Job Interview.*

18. Lack of vitality
19. Fails to look interviewer in the eye
20. Limp, fishy hand-shake
21. Indecision
22. Loafs during vacations—lakeside pleasures
23. Unhappy married life
24. Friction with parents
25. Sloppy application blank
26. Merely shopping around
27. Wants job only for short time
28. Little sense of humor
29. Lack of knowledge of field of specialization
30. Parents make decisions for him
31. No interest in company or in industry
32. Emphasis on whom he knows
33. Unwillingness to go where we send him
34. Cynical
35. Low moral standards
36. Lazy
37. Intolerant—strong prejudices
38. Narrow interests
39. Spends much time in movies or watching TV
40. Poor handling of personal finances
41. No interest in community activities
42. Inability to take criticism
43. Lack of appreciation of the value of experience
44. Radical ideas
45. Late to interview without good reason
46. Never heard of company
47. Failure to express appreciation for interviewer's time
48. Asks no questions about the job
49. High-pressure type
50. Indefinite response to questions

In summary, the interview involves at least two people—the interviewer and the interviewee. The interviewer's job is to find out if the applicant (interviewee) is the individual for the job. He will reach his goal by observing the individual carefully—his background, qualifications, personality, and attitudes. Then he will evaluate this information, along with facts from other sources (references, tests, etc.), and decide whether or not to invite him to join the company or to invite him to the home plant for further interviews with other officials. As the interviewee, you need to prepare well for the interview and then sell yourself (during the interview) by showing interest, being sincere and natural, stating your qualifications, and behaving like a person the company would want on its working force.

# Appendixes

● Appendix A: Legal Aspects of Your Business Communications
● Appendix B: Mechanics and Style
               Check Points When You Edit Writing for Business
               Dangling Participles
               Dictation
               Numbers as Figures or Words
               Punctuation Makes Sense
               Syllabication
               Trite Words
● Appendix C: Suggestions for Cutting Correspondence Costs
● Appendix D: Symbols Used in Marking Letters, Memos, and Reports

# APPENDIX A: LEGAL ASPECTS OF YOUR BUSINESS COMMUNICATIONS

When you apply integrity, honest consideration for your reader, and the Golden Rule in your business communications, you should be safe in the eyes of the law. Yet as a cautious sensible businessman—and as a consumer—you need to realize that there are legal dangers even in some true statements. On the other hand, not all untrue words that appear to be libelous will lead to a lawsuit.

Thousands of statute laws and decisions have been passed in the 50 states and federal government. Changing social and business conditions necessitate changing laws from time to time. Furthermore, the right to freedom of speech versus the individual right not to be libeled have led to various legal privileges under various conditions. No single chapter can begin to cover even partially any specific legal interpretations applied to business writing.

The purpose of this section is to call to your attention some of the legal risks and complications that may occur in business communications. An overview of pertinent legal concepts should be helpful to you both as the writer and the recipient of business messages. However, because ignorance of the law excuses no one, you may need a lawyer to advise you on specific details that apply to some complicated situations. The discussion here is necessarily a brief general introduction only; no liability is assumed for its completeness. Yet if you are aware of the risks discussed here, you can avoid harmful utterances and costly misunderstandings. This section briefs you on:

1. Defamation
2. Invasion of privacy
3. Fraud
4. Other areas of concern

## Defamation[1]

The unconsented and unprivileged "publication" of a false idea which tends to injure reputation is defamation. Oral defamation is slander. Written defamation constitutes a libel. You can be sued for defamation if you intentionally "publish" the false idea that injures reputation and for which no legal "privilege" exists. Because the words "publication" and "privilege" have important legal significance, they are discussed first; then follows a sampling of defamatory terms.

*Publication.* In the legal sense, the unconsented intentional or negligent communication of defamatory matter to a third party is "publication." Any means of communication by which some third party (anyone other than the person attacked) actually receives the defamatory idea can effect a "publication."

If you tell Mr. X to his face privately that you consider him incompetent or a swindler, you are within your legal rights; only he has heard your statement. But if you intentionally communicate the defamatory statement to at least one other person who is not "privileged" (as defined later), you can be in serious trouble. The derogatory qualities that make a statement defamatory are the same for libel and slander. Because libelous statements are more permanent, laws pertaining to libel are more severe than those about slander. The writing (for libel) may be any permanent communication—such as a letter, circular, picture, photograph, cartoon, newspaper, recorded tape, or phonograph record.

Even a sealed letter addressed and mailed to the person you are accusing can result in actionable publication if you knew or should have known that it would be

---

[1] Unless otherwise footnoted, this discussion on defamation is based on Arthur B. Hanson's *Libel and Related Torts*, Vol. I, The American Newspaper Publishers Association Foundation, Inc., New York, New York, 1969, pp. 21–195.

intercepted by or shown to a third person. For this reason, a letter containing unfavorable information about a person (or organization) and any collection message about past-due payments should be mailed only in a sealed envelope and addressed so that it will be read only by the addressee. Adding the words "Personal and Confidential" or "Personal" is a good precaution. Another precaution is to use an opaque envelope and to fold the message in such a way that it cannot be easily read when held up to a light.

A defamatory telegram also is actionable against the sender if its defamatory meaning is communicated to a third person. In an interstate transmission, governed by federal law, the telegraph company may also be held liable, but only if the message is obviously defamatory and the agents of the company who actually transmit it know the sender is not "privileged" to send it.

Accidental communications to third persons (by eavesdroppers or unauthorized letter readers) are not actionable unless you knew of or should have foreseen such possibilities. A mere possibility that someone may have seen or overhead the statement is not enough.

Dictation to a stenographer is considered by most authorities to be a publication, which is conditionally privileged with respect to matters reasonably related to the ordinary conduct of the business.

*Privilege.* A legal right to communicate defamatory information in certain situations is "privilege." The privilege may be "absolute" or "conditional."

*Absolute privilege* is mainly limited to three general areas: judicial proceedings, legislative proceedings, and the acts of important government officials, usually executives. Thus judicial officers, attorneys, and all parties participating in a judicial proceeding are absolutely privileged to make defamatory statements during and as part of the trial, if they bear some relationship to the matter under consideration.[1] Letters between parties or attorneys relating to a controversy are also privileged. However, defamatory statements about a case made outside the ordinary course of a judicial proceeding, such as comments to reporters in the hallway, are not entitled to the absolute privilege for judicial proceedings.

Similarly, legislators and government officials are absolutely privileged to make defamatory statements in the performance of their official functions, but not if the statements are irrelevant to the public matter then under consideration. For example, a member of the highway commission in New Mexico made a defamatory statement about a highway contractor, at a commission meeting with reporters present. A superintendent of banks in California made libelous statements concerning his former attorney. In each case the Supreme Court of the respective state held that these public officials were protected by an absolute privilege in the exercise of their executive function. In contrast, a public official would not be absolutely privileged to defame his subordinates when publicly explaining why he dismissed them.[1]

*A conditional (qualified) privilege* applies to several situations in which the interest of either the participants or society dictates that communication in good faith should not be hampered by fear of lawsuits. Thus defamatory statements made in the ordinary commercial activity are qualifiedly privileged, whether they are interoffice messages or sent to persons outside the company, when the recipient has a lawful interest in the topic of discussion. For example, the person who answers an inquiry about the performance of an employee or about the credit record of a customer is obligated to take reasonable precautions to see that the information he

[1] Paul P. Ashley, *Say It Safely: Legal Limits in Publishing, Radio, and Television*, Seattle: University of Washington Press, 1966, pp. 43–47.

sends is accurate. And he must avoid intentional deceit. If he intentionally or carelessly misleads the inquirer who seeks information about another person (for instance, a credit or job applicant), he may be sued for damages.

Thus whenever you send requested information to an inquirer (prospective employer or creditor, for instance, who might suffer a loss if he employs or lends to an unworthy applicant), make every effort to tell the truth and to reply in good faith without malice. When the truth about an individual or an organization is unfavorable and directly related to a question you are asked to answer, try as much as possible to protect the good name of the one involved. Also indicate in your reply that the information was requested and ask that it be kept confidential. Likewise, when you request someone to send you personal information about another person, show in your letter that you have an interest to protect and promise to keep the received information confidential. You will thus help the informer protect himself against a libel suit.

Privilege does not apply to unreasonable disclosure and publication of particulars concerning a debtor to his employer, relatives, and to the public by such devices as "deadbeat lists" or obvious communications forms which may be read by others who have not requested the information and have no immediate need of it.

Privilege also does not apply to defamatory statements which are unrelated to the purpose of the particular privilege. If for instance a former employer is requested to recommend an applicant for a new employment, the privilege pertaining to his response does not extend to defamatory remarks not related to job qualifications. Also the former employer may lose the privilege if in his response he uses such violent or abusive language that his real motive in the reply is evidence of malice or some other improper purpose. Furthermore, if he knows his statement is false, clearly the privilege is defeated. If he is negligent or unreasonable in believing it to be true, jurisdictions differ as to whether the privilege is lost.

The risk of liability for criticism of public men has decreased significantly in the United States since the Supreme Court decided the *New York Times* case in 1964. Under the *Times* rule, criticism or comment about the public conduct or fitness for office of public officials, and statements about the public conduct of other voluntary public figures is privileged even if it is based on or includes erroneous material—unless there was actual knowledge of falsity or reckless disregard for whether the material was true or false. Two prongs to the rule are: (1) the inclusion of both fact and opinion within the privilege of fair comment, and (2) the degree of "malice" (intent to injure) necessary to defeat the privilege, constituting knowledge of falsity or reckless disregard for truth. The Supreme Court has included within the public official designation: a city commissioner; a group of parish judges; a county attorney and chief of police; an elected court clerk; a deputy sheriff (and others). The "public figure" to which the rule applies is a person "intimately involved in the resolution of important public questions" or one who by reason of his fame shapes events in an area of concern to society at large, and as a result, already has as much access to the mass media "both to influence policy and to counter criticism" of his views and activities as does a "public official." The Supreme Court has found a university athletic director and a retired Army General who was actively involved in a federally enforced school integration to be within the class of public figures covered by the *Times* rule.

**Defamatory Terms.** Among the terms that have been judged libelous, the following are a representative (but incomplete) sampling of words to be avoided or used with caution when you refer to a person or an organization:[1]

---

[1] Philip Wittenberg, *Dangerous Words—A Guide to the Law of Libel,* Columbia University Press, New York, 1947, pp. 282–308.

| | | | |
|---|---|---|---|
| bankrupt | drug addict | incompetent | quack |
| blackmailer | faker | inferior | racketeer |
| Communist | falsified | insolvent | shyster |
| corrupt | forger | kickbacks | swindler |
| crook | fraud (fraudulent) | misappropriation | thief |
| deadbeat | grafter | misconduct | unchaste |
| dishonest | gouged money | misrepresentation | unworthy of credit |
| disreputable | hypocrite | profiteer | worthless |

In the collection of debts or in attempts to collect any claim alleged to be due or owing, the collector should not unreasonably oppress, harass, or abuse any person. Harassment and abuse includes abusive language, anonymous or repeated telephone calls at odd hours, and anonymous C.O.D. communications.

Some statements are defamatory because they malign a characteristic necessary in a person's work (provided his occupation is legal). Thus, in most jurisdictions it is defamatory to inpugn the financial responsibility of a tradesman, but not of a teacher, because ability to obtain credit is essential only to the tradesman. Also it has been held defamatory to attribute Communist sympathies to a public official, but not to an engineer. And, as already discussed, it is defamatory to impugn the competence of an employee to perform duties required by his job. But such statements may be conditionally privileged if made in the ordinary course of business activity, as discussed above under "Privilege."

The truth is usually adequate defense in a libel suit, especially if there is no evidence of malice. But if the writer cannot prove his statements to be true or prove that he had adequate reason for writing them, he may have to pay large money damages.

### Invasion of Privacy[1]

The unconsented, unprivileged, and unreasonable intrusion into the private life of an individual is "invasion of privacy." Unlike defamation, privacy can be violated although no publication to third persons takes place and even though the matters delved into are true or not particularly harmful to reputation. The concept of right of privacy is analogous to that of trespass, which gives one the right to keep unwarranted intruders off his land not because of any resulting emotional distress or loss of rents, but merely to insure the solitude of land owners.

This section discusses two aspects of invasion of privacy: use of a person's name, photograph, or other identity without permission, and physical surveillance of records, reports, and letters by persons not entitled to examine them.

*Use of a Person's Identity.* If a person's name, photograph, or other identity is used without his permission on a sales letter or advertisement (or other permanent publication—not word of mouth), he may have cause for legal action because his right of privacy has been violated.

Recovery and monetary awards have also been granted for publication of X-rays and other medical pictures, for pictures of a deformed infant, and for undue publicity of a delinquent debt.

Yet, not every use of another's likeness or identity is actionable. In some states it must be unreasonable under the circumstances, as well as unprivileged. Using pictures of an All-American football team on a beer company's calendar which also

[1] Arthur B. Hanson, *Libel and Related Torts*, 1969, pp. 197–206.

contained advertising was held (in one case) not to be an invasion of team members' privacy because they were public figures and there was no false implication of endorsement. But using a person's picture to illustrate a story about dishonest tactics of cab drivers would shed false and unfavorable imputation on him and would be an invasion of his privacy.

Unreasonable publicity of private life may also result in legal action and costly money awards to the offended person. A classic case (cited in *Libel and Related Torts,* page 203) is one in which the plaintiff, a former prostitute and the acquitted defendant in a notorious murder trial had reformed, married, and pursued a respectable life in a new community which knew nothing about her former life until the defendant revealed the whole story in a movie, using her name. She was allowed a cause of action for publication of these true but embarrassing personal facts.

In the "pink letter case" (mentioned in *When You Need a Lawyer*)[1] a suggestive letter bearing a woman's signature was mailed to 1,000 men. Handwritten in a feminine hand, the letter was mechanically reproduced on pink stationery and mailed by a mailing agency. The name signed to the letter was that of the principal character in a motion picture the letter was advertising. Unfortunately, it also turned out to be the name of a woman living in Los Angeles—the only person by that name listed in the City Directory or the telephone directory. When the letters began arriving (in hand-addressed, pink envelopes), many wives must have looked at their husbands with a quizzical eye. But it was worse for the plaintiff, who began getting telephone calls from the men. She also worried for fear that some irate wife might shoot her—for the letter invited the men to meet the signer in front of a certain theater on a certain day and to look for a girl "with a gleam in her eye, a smile on her lips and mischief on her mind." The court felt that the plaintiff should be compensated for invasion of right of privacy.

If you wish to use the picture or identity of an individual for your advertising or sales letters, for instance, be sure first to get previous consent and make clear just how the picture or identity is to be used. An individual may have indicated his consent by willfully posing for a photograph, but alteration of the photograph or using it in a way to carry objectionable implications is an invasion of his privacy.

***Physical Surveillance of Records, Reports, and Letters.***[2] The right of privacy may also be violated if records, reports, and letters are read by persons not entitled to examine them.

Powerful binoculars, long-range telephoto cameras, and "zoomer"-type television cameras have been used effectively (and illegally) in recent years to look through windows at important papers lying face-up on desks, at models of new products and designs, and at charts displayed at conferences. These techniques have become so common in certain areas of industrial espionage that elaborate security precautions are taken to keep designs and models in windowless rooms and to keep blinds drawn at all times in certain offices.

Modern technology has added to these existing situations the possibility of passing visible light or reflected infra-red energy through an envelope and taking pictures of the contents. These pictures can then be read (deciphered) by persons skilled in reading handwriting or typing where lines are inverted or superimposed. Also available is a needle-thin "flashlight" that can be inserted in a sealed envelope to "light it up" for quick reading by a trained investigator. You can help to greatly reduce or

[1] Kenneth and Irene Donelson, *When You Need a Lawyer,* Doubleday and Company, Garden City, New York, 1964, pp. 245–249.
[2] Alan F. Westin, *Privacy and Freedom,* Atheneum, New York, 1967, pp. 78–79.

even prevent this type of surveillance by using—when desirable on certain very confidential material—envelopes with a random pattern printed on them to make them opaque and or inserting more than one sheet of paper in them.

### Fraud

The intentional misrepresentation by one party to a contract of a material fact which is relied upon by the other party to his injury is fraud.[1] Both as a seller and a buyer you need to be aware of the elements of fraud as well as the significance of warranties so that you can better detect and avoid fraudulent practices.

*Elements.* The elements of fraud are: (1) false representation of fact, not opinion, intentionally made; (2) intent that the deceived person act thereon; (3) knowledge that such statements would naturally deceive; and (4) that the deceived person acted to his injury.[2]

The misrepresentation need not be a direct falsehood for fraud to be present. In fact, failing to reveal defects or confirming false impressions by remaining silent can be sufficient. To constitute actionable fraud (for lawsuits), the misrepresentation must be of a *material fact*—a fact that induced the contract. Statements of the seller's opinions and "puffing" (boastful sales talk about the value of the goods) are permissible. The buyer is not justified in relying on such statements; they do not become part of the bargain and are not warranties. The main test for fraud is to ask, "Would the other party have entered into the contract had he known the truth?" Opinions may lead to fraud if they amount to deliberately false statements made by a recognized professional in the field, whose opinions may reasonably be relied upon in the contract. Opinions, however, must be in regard to an existing or past fact and not to forecasts or predictions.[3]

*Warranties.* In most sales contracts the seller undertakes certain obligations concerning the nature, title, and quality of the goods he is selling. When these obligations are expressly stated or implied and when they actually induce the sale, the obligations are called "warranties." They are guarantees by the seller with respect to the goods he sells. Warranties may be express or implied.

An express warranty affirms a fact or a promise the seller made to the buyer in his bargaining concerning the nature of the goods—description, grade, or model. Such a promise becomes a basis for the contract even though the term "warranty" or "guaranty" is not used.

Implied warranties are considered part of the bargain even though the parties themselves say nothing about them. For instance, the seller warrants that he is conveying a good title to the goods. Also, under the Uniform Commercial Code (adopted by all 50 states) if the seller is a merchant with respect to goods of that kind, he warrants that the goods are salable and are fit for the ordinary purposes for which such goods are used. If the seller knows the buyer intends the goods for a particular purpose and that the buyer is relying on the seller's judgment as to their suitability, there is an implied warranty of fitness for that particular purpose.[4]

According to the U. S. Postmaster General, in the Post Office Department's in-

[1] Michael P. Litka, *Business Law*, Harcourt, Brace & World, Inc., New York, 1970, pp. 152–153.
[2] William J. Robert and Robert N. Corley, *Dillavou and Howard's Principles of Business Law*, 8th Edition, Prentice-Hall, Inc., Englewood Cliffs, N.J., 1967, p. 1027.
[3] Litka, *Business Law*, pp. 152–153.
[4] Litka, *Business Law*, pp. 470–474.

formative booklet *Mail Fraud Laws*,[1] fraudulent schemes sent through the mails are costing the American consumers an estimated $500 million a year. Among the many dishonest rackets to trap the unsuspecting consumer are: fake contests, home improvement offers, auto insurance frauds, charity appeals, missing heir schemes, fake business opportunities, worthless medical cures, and fake correspondence-school programs promising "exciting, high-paying jobs."

The U. S. Chief Postal Inspector lists the following ways you can help enforce mail fraud laws:[1]

> To stop a dishonest scheme, inspectors must find that you and others buying a product or service were cheated as a result of claims the seller made in an intentional effort to defraud. Mail fraud violations occur when a general scheme or pattern of fraud exists.
>
> When you believe mail fraud exists, hold all letters, including envelopes and other evidence related to the questionable scheme. See if your neighbors or business associates have also received similar material.
>
> Bring such information to the attention of a postal inspector in your area by contacting him directly or through your postmaster.
>
> Inspectors cannot investigate a case simply to force a supplier to speed up deliveries, obtain refunds, or to otherwise act as an intermediary in settling unsatisfactory transactions. In such instances the dissatisfied buyer should:
>
> > Seek an adjustment or settlement with the seller.
> > Bring his complaint to the attention of the Better Business Bureau, Chamber of Commerce, Trade Association, or publication which carried the ad.
> > Seek relief through civil suit if a breach of contract may be involved.

Most states now have consumer protection divisions in the Attorney General's office, and they can be very helpful too.

### Other Areas of Caution in Business Writing

Among the many other unmailable materials that may violate United States Postal Laws are letters and printed matter concerning: lotteries, obscene literature, extortion threats, and solicitation of illegal business. Space does not permit discussion of these items here. You can obtain booklets on most of these subjects through your local postmaster or the U.S. Government Printing Office, Washington D.C., 20402. And if you are in doubt about the mailability of any particular material, you may submit a request to the Office of the General Counsel, Mailability Division, Post Office Department, Washington, D. C., 20260. A ruling will be furnished as promptly as circumstances permit.

The sending of unordered merchandise through the mail does not violate postal laws unless it is sent C.O.D. However, persons receiving such unordered items can:

> If the package has not been opened, write "Return to Sender" and put it back into the mails.
> If the article is not wanted, set it aside for a reasonable period of time and if unclaimed, destroy.

[1] *Mail Fraud Laws*—Protecting consumers, investors, businessmen, medical patients, students; U. S. Post Office Department, Washington, D. C., 20260, June 1969.

Treat unordered merchandise as an unconditional gift if living in a state where the laws apply.[1]

The sending of unsolicited credit cards is generally not recommended in the present climate of opinion and pending legislation.

Another caution pertains to the copying of certain documents. Congress, by statute, has forbidden the copying of the following documents and items under certain circumstances: United States Government obligations or securities, such as Treasury and Federal Reserve Notes, National Bank Currency, Certificates of Indebtedness, Silver and Gold Certificates, Paper Money, and others; also U.S. Savings Bonds (except for campaign publicity for their sale), Internal Revenue Stamps (except in copying for lawful purposes a legal document on which there is a cancelled revenue stamp), Postage Stamps cancelled or uncancelled (except for philatelic purposes provided the reproduction is in black and white and is less than $3/4$ or more than $1\frac{1}{2}$ times the linear dimensions of the original); Postal Money Orders; bills, checks or drafts for money drawn by or upon authorized officers of the United States; and other representatives of value issued under any Act of Congress.

Also forbidden is the copying of copyrighted material without permission of the copyright owner; Certificates of Citizenship or Naturalization (except foreign naturalization certificates); Passports (except foreign); Immigration Papers; Obligations or Securities of any Foreign Government, Bank, or Corporation; Draft Registration Cards, Selective Service Induction Papers bearing certain information; Badges, Identification Cards, Passes or Insignia carried by Military, Naval personnel or members of the various Federal Departments and Bureaus such as FBI, Treasury, etc. (except when ordered by head of such department or bureau). In some states copying auto licenses, automobile certificates of title, and drivers' licenses is also forbidden. For these items—and others not listed here—penalties of fine or imprisonment are imposed on those guilty of making illegal copies.

As a final caution, in general, remember to:

Be honest and fair in all your business transactions and correspondence.
Avoid any statements and acts that may be considered defamation, invasion of privacy, or fraud.
Keep yourself well informed on responsibilities in other legal areas of concern.
Consult an attorney when in doubt about the handling of any complicated situation that might involve legal risks.

---

[1] *Mail Fraud Laws*—Protecting consumers, investors, businessmen, medical patients, students, 1969.

# APPENDIX B: MECHANICS AND STYLE

## Check Points When You Edit Writing for Business

*For clarity and emphasis:*

1. Use conversational words. If you have a choice, use the simpler word.
   *Pompous words:* utilize, comprehend.
   *Simpler words:* use, understand.

2. Guard against misplaced modifiers and drifting participles.
   *Incorrect:* Having been run through the computer, the clerk used the figures for his report.
   *Correct:* After running the figures through the computer, the clerk used them . . . .
   *Incorrect:* As one of our best customers, we invite you to open a charge account.
   *Correct:* As one of our best customers, you . . . .

3. Make verb tenses say what you mean.
   a. If a past finding continues to be held a fact, it is usually clearer and more forceful to employ the present tense.
   b. Use the present tense wherever you can logically. It applies to things that existed in the past, still exist, and apparently will continue to exist.

4. Use punctuation to help the reader.
   *Confusing:* Ever since these people have been demanding justice.
   *Clear:* Ever since, these people have been demanding justice.
   *Confusing:* That that is is that that is not is not.
   *Clear:* That that is, is; that that is not, is not.

5. Avoid "this," usually, unless a noun follows.
   Mr. Lucas once lost $5,000 that he had invested in farm mortgages and this made him question all types of investments.

   Improve clarity by adding "experience" after "this."

6. Use strong, vigorous words—active verbs, concrete nouns, specific adjectives and adverbs.

7. See that a paragraph has a topic sentence. Also a section—especially with subdivisions—should have an introductory paragraph.

8. Tie your writing together with transitional words, phrases, clauses, and paragraphs.

9. Keep the average sentence length 17 to 20 words. The maximum paragraph length in a formal report should not exceed 15 typewritten lines; maximum paragraph length for a letter, 10 typewritten lines.

10. Whenever possible, use the indicative mood—not the subjunctive. Many times you can change "would" to "will," "could" to "can," and "might" to "may."

11. Avoid Latin terms that many readers don't know. Instead, use the better understood Anglo-Saxon synonyms.

    *Say:* about       *Not:* circa
         following          sequents
         that is            i.e.
         for example     e.g.

*For conciseness:*

1. Rescue verbs that are smothered or hidden in nouns and infinitives.

   | *Wordy* | *Concise* |
   |---|---|
   | *In nouns:* | |
   | **a.** take a look | look |
   | **b.** held a meeting | met |
   | **c.** had a discussion | discussed |
   | **d.** The function of this department is the *collection* of accounts. | This department *collects* accounts. |
   | *In infinitives:* | |
   | The duty of a clerk is *to check* all incoming mail and *to record* it. | A clerk *checks* and *records* all incoming mail. |

2. Limit "it . . . that" constructions.

   **a.** It is known that we must reduce pollution vs. We must reduce pollution.
   **b.** It is clear that . . . . vs. Clearly . . . .

3. Avoid "it is," "there is," and "there are," at the beginning of sentences.

   *Not good:* There are four rules which should be observed.
   *Better:*     Four rules should be observed.

4. Remove needless repetitions.

   **a.** For example, substitute "it" for the noun occasionally.
   **b.** Use a shortened form for a very long noun, after using the complete noun once; for example, American Telephone and Telegraph becomes AT&T.

5. Shorten wordy phrases.

   **a.** Instead of *for the purpose of,* use *for.*
   **b.** Instead of *due to the fact that,* use *because.*
   **c.** Instead of *in the event that,* use *if.*

6. Omit repeated numerals (unless in a legal document or on a check).

   *Wordy:* Eleven (11)
   *Concise:* 11

7. Eliminate "which" clauses whenever possible.

   **a.** He ordered desks which are of the executive type.
   **b.** He ordered executive-type desks.

*For correctness:*

1. Avoid switching from third person to first and/or second person. If you write in the third person (impersonal writing), don't use I, me, we, us, and you.

2. Vary your sentence structure. Instead of beginning most sentences with the subject followed by the verb, you should begin some sentences with a different sentence structure—such as a dependent clause. Also sandwich some short sentences among longer ones.

3. Be sure subject and verb agree.
   **a.** A *study* of these two reports *shows*—(not show)
   **b.** The *details* in this memo *confuse*—(not confuses)

**4.** Be sure you have parallel construction.

> *Incorrect:* We will be glad to answer any questions you may have if you *write* to the above address or by *calling* us at 679–6622.
> *Correct:* We will be glad to answer any questions you may have if you *write* to the above address or *call* us at 679–6622.
> *Incorrect:* clerk, manager, selling.
> *Correct:* clerk, manager, salesman.

**5.** Be sure you spell every word correctly. Always use the dictionary when you are in doubt.

**6.** Avoid ending a sentence and beginning the next sentence with the same word(s).

> *Not good:* Your son will enjoy using a portable electric typewriter. A portable electric typewriter . . . .
> *Better:* Your son will enjoy using a portable electric typewriter while he is attending college. This machine . . . .

**7.** As a rule, most verbs of the senses—taste, feel, see, smell, hear—take an adjective, not an adverb.

> *Not correct:* The dinner tastes deliciously.
> *Correct:* The dinner tastes delicious.
> *Also correct:* I feel well. (In this sentence "well" is an adjective.)

**8.** Don't overuse a word in the same sentence or paragraph unless you do so intentionally to emphasize.

> *Not good:* The important subject on which I am going to write is the subject of inflation, a subject of great importance to ordinary citizens.
> *Improved:* I'm discussing inflation—a subject that is important to most people.

**9.** If a major division of a report has subdivisions, it must have two or more—never just one—subdivision.

**10.** Have at least two or more lines of a paragraph on a page.

**11.** Syllabicate between syllables and limit your word division to no more than four words on one page. Also never syllabicate the last line on the page or on three consecutive lines.

**12.** In a double-spaced report you can show quoted material of three or more lines as single spaced without quote marks. Also this single-spaced material has shorter lines than the double-spaced lines.

**13.** Avoid two which's in the same sentence.

## Dangling Participles

A participle is a word that ends in "ing" or "ed" and looks like a verb; yet it actually is an adjective that must modify a specific noun or pronoun. If it doesn't, it is called a dangling participle.

The three most common forms of dangling participles are caused by the writer not observing the following rules:

**1.** The participle should be placed close to the word to which it refers, and there should be no intervening noun to which the participle might seem to refer.

*Unclear:* A complete *report* is submitted by our branch office, *giving* details about this transaction. ("Giving is the participle; it should modify "report," but it seems to modify the intervening noun "office.")

*Clear:* Our branch office submitted a complete *report, giving* details about this transaction. (Now the participle clearly modifies "report.")

2. A participle at the beginning of a sentence (or at the beginning of a second independent clause in a compound sentence) should refer to the subject of the sentence.

*Unclear:* *Having* been boiled for the proper length of time, the *housewife* took the shrimp off the stove. ("Having" modifies the subject "housewife" when the participle should modify "shrimp.")

*Clear:* *Having* been boiled for the proper length of time, the *shrimp* were taken off the stove by the housewife. (Now "having" modifies the right word— "shrimp," which is the subject of the sentence.)

*or*

After the shrimp had boiled for the proper length of time, the housewife took them off the stove. (This sentence discards the participle.)

Here's a simple way to see if the participle beginning the sentence properly modifies the subject: State the subject "shrimp" and follow it with the participial phrase, "having been boiled for the proper length of time." If the two parts give you the meaning you want "shrimp, having been boiled for the proper length of time," then the participle is modifying the right word. But if you are boiling the housewife, something is wrong.

3. A participle following the main clause should refer to a definite noun, not to the general thought expressed by the clause.

*Unclear:* These accounts disappeared from the vault, thus *causing* us very much worry. (Instead of modifying a particular word, "causing" modifies the entire clause that appears before the comma.) Suggestion: Reword so that you don't have the participle in the sentence.

*Clear:* Because the accounts disappeared from the vault, we are very much worried.

*Clear:* These accounts disappeared from the vault, a fact which caused us much worry.

*Exercises.* Identify all dangling participles in these sentences, tell whether each one violates Form 1, 2, or 3 just discussed, and then correct all errors.

1. Being an old customer, we know that you are familiar with our Christmas displays.
2. The check arrived 6 days late, causing me to write a collection letter.
3. Realizing our mistake, a new check was immediately sent to replace the first one.
4. Being larger and more attractive, these offices should make your work more pleasant, thus enabling you to work better.
5. Being a savings association, our customers do not have checking accounts here.
6. Please go down to the main office, and lying on the manager's desk you will find a copy of the latest report.
7. Having been baked for 2 hours, the girl took the roast from the oven.
8. Changing your monthly loan payments, it will be necessary to get approval from the loan department.
9. Having been an outstanding keynote speaker, we can offer you this special award.
10. To enjoy 5% earning, a savings account should be opened.

## Dictation

After you have planned your letter, memo, or report, you will probably type it yourself, dictate it to a secretary, or make a rough draft in longhand. Should you dictate. here are eight suggestions that will help you be sure you'll be signing your name to the message you want to mail.

1. Enunciate clearly. Very few persons can speak clearly with candy, gum, or cigarettes in their mouths. Be especially careful with plurals, and words that sound alike, such as fifty and sixty. ("Five o" and "six o" are much more definite.)
2. Spell unusual words and names when using them for the first time.
3. Dictate special instructions at the beginning of the letter, such as extra carbon copies for certain persons, or unusual tabulation of figures.
4. Always dictate as much punctuation as your transcriber needs to turn out an accurate, attractive letter quickly. At least dictate "paragraph" to indicate each new paragraph; "quote" "unquote"; "parenthesis" "close parenthesis."
5. Dictate at a normal rate, just as you talk. Avoid long pauses followed by rapid dictation. It is thoughtful to slow down a little when reading, for instance, an inside address or a policy number.
6. Let your secretary use her initiative as to grammar corrections, additional punctuation, and arrangement of your letters.
7. When dictating a reply to a letter received, you can save both your time and your stenographer's time if you dictate only the name of the addressee. She can later copy the full address from the letter you hand her after you have dictated your reply.
8. Keep the mail you are answering in an orderly pile by turning each letter upside down when you have finished answering it. After all your dictation is completed, your entire pile of answered incoming correspondence will be in order for your stenographer to obtain needed information, attach file copies, etc.

In addition to these dictation tips, you can save yourself and your company time and money by having definite dictation periods (for instance, a set time each morning and/or afternoon) with no interruptions by telephone or callers.

## Numbers as Figures or Words[1]

In general—use the figure instead of the word because the reader can more easily read the figure and grasp its meaning. In invoices, tabular materials, purchase orders and the like, always use figures. In letters and reports—use the rule of 10 (spell out numbers 1–9; use figures for numbers 10 or higher) except for amounts of money and for isolated cases, as shown below.

1. *If a sentence begins with a number, express the number in words:* This rule is used when the sentence cannot be effectively revised.
   Fifty applicants were interviewed for the position.
2. *When a number standing first in the sentence is followed by another number to form an approximation express both in words:*
   Fifty or sixty will be enough.
   *Note:* Try not to begin a sentence with a number. Rewrite the sentence to place the number within or at the end of the sentence.
   The confirmation request was answered by 559 businesses.

[1] Most of these rules have been adopted by the Committee on Teaching Materials and Aids of the American Business Writing Association (now renamed the American Business Communication Association).

3. *When a sentence contains one series of numbers, express all members of one series in figures.*

    We *had* 25 applicants from Arkansas, 15 applicants from Texas, and 6 applicants from Oklahoma.

4. *When a sentence contains two series of numbers, express the members of one series in words and those of the other series in figures:* If this rule is not followed, confusion results because of too many groups of numbers.

    a. Five students scored 95 points; seventeen students scored 30 points; and eleven scored 75 points.

    b. Three senior accountants made $50 a day; two semi-seniors made $40 a day; and five junior accountants made $35 a day.

    *Note:* For clarity, tabulate more than two series of numbers.

    | Name of Accountant | Daily Rate | Estimated Working Days | Total Estimated Earnings |
    |---|---|---|---|
    | Barlow, Helen | $50 | 3 | $150 |
    | Dickinson, Al | 35 | 2 | 70 |
    | Oman, Charles | 40 | 1 | 40 |

5. *When an isolated number is below ten, express it in words.* This rule does not apply to exact dimensions or amounts of money.

    a. The new salesman sold eight refrigerators last month.

    b. She hit a 6-foot pole.

    c. This paper is 8½ inches wide.

6. *When numbers are expressed in words, as at the beginning of a sentence, use a hyphen to join the compound number, twenty-one through ninety-nine:* A compound number usually acts as a compound adjective.

    Fifty-six accounts; twenty-one women; ninety-three men

7. *When one number immediately precedes another number of different context, express one number in words; the other, in figures:*

    a. The specifications call for twenty-five 2 x 4's.

    b. The deposit slip listed four 5's as the only currency.

    c. You ordered 275 three-inch bolts.

8. *When a numerical quantity contains more than four digits, each group of three digits should be set off by a comma (starting at the right).* (Obviously, this rule does *not* apply to dates, street numbers, serial numbers, and page numbers.) 1,000; 1,021; 5,280,000; 60,000; 600,000

9. *Express amounts of money in figures.* The following practices are recommended.

    a. *When an amount of money consists of dollars and cents, always express the amount in figures:* The dollar sign should precede the amount (unless in a tabulated column). The invoice total was $5.51. The bonds were sold at $999.50.

    b. *When an amount of money consists only of dollars, omit the decimal point and the double zero:* The invoice is $150. The check is for $5. Exceptions: (1) When the amount is tabulated in a column which includes both dollars and cents, include the double zero.

    |  |
    |---:|
    | $  250.80 |
    | 200.00 |
    | 312.70 |
    | 286.50 |
    | $1,505.00 |

(2) When a series of money amounts contains mixed figures, include the double zero for consistency on all even figures.

The committee raised amounts of $15.00, $33.75, and $75.00 in the three rummage sales.

c. *When an amount of money consists only of cents, write the amount in any of the following ways:*

The piggy bank yielded $.57. The piggy bank yielded 57¢.

The piggy bank yielded 57 cents. The piggy bank yielded 9 cents.

d. *As a rule, do not write an amount in both figures and words. This procedure is necessary only in legal and financial documents.*

The check is for $7. . . . . . . . . . . . .The total assets are $23,000.50.

In financial papers write:  . . . . . . .Ninety-five dollars ($95.00)

seven dollars ($7.00)

twenty-three and 42/100 dollars (23.42)

twenty three dollars and forty-two cents ($23.42)

**10.** *Express the following numbers in figures, unless otherwise indicated:*

a. Dates: October 3, 1972

3rd of October

Your letter of October 3 was most welcome.

b. *House or room numbers:* (except number one)

1503 Thomas Street

One Lenox Drive

c. *Numerical names of streets:*

*Over 10:*    315 69th Street or 315 - 69th Street (Note two spaces or space hyphen space to separate house and street number.)

*Under 10:*   2930 Third Avenue or 2930 3rd\* Avenue

\* Many people prefer to use figures for all street numbers.

d. *Numbered items such as page numbers, chapter numbers, figure numbers, table numbers, chart numbers, serial numbers, and telephone numbers:*

| | | |
|---|---|---|
| page 10 | Table X | Policy #V9109815 |
| Chapter 10 | Table 10 | Policy V9109815 |
| Chapter X | Chart 10 | Claim No. 13189756 |
| Figure 8 | Chart X | Telephone 543-1111 |
| Fig. 8 | Service Serial No. 01845283 | Telephone LA-3-1111 |

e. *Decimals:*

10.25          3.1414                    .3535

f. *Dimensions:*

8½ x 11 inches     2 x 4 inches

8½ by 11 inches     2 by 4 inches

g. *Time:*

7 P. M. (reserved for headings)     7:35 P. M. (reserved for headings)

7 a.m. (more commonly used)     7:35 p.m. (more commonly used)

seven o'clock          seven in the morning

h. *Percentages:*

35%          6%

99.99%          6 percent

0.09%

i. *Fractions:*

| | | |
|---|---|---|
| 1/32 | one-half | 4¾ |
| 3/64 | two-thirds | or |
| 25/64 | one-fourth | 4.75 |
| 25/100 | three-fourths | |

Listed below are sentences that contain numbers in the form of figures and words. If any number is used incorrectly, cross out what's wrong and add the correct usage directly above the error. Don't mark any number that is used correctly.

1. 5 policies lie on my desk.
2. Two men and 8 women work in this office.
3. The insured's car hit a 10-foot pole.
4. 10 men scored 94 points; 17 men scored 110 points; and 3 men scored 143 points.
5. May I have 100 12-inch rulers.
6. This morning I answered 17 letters.
7. You'll find the answer on page 10.
8. Mary came home at 7 o'clock.
9. She works from 8 a.m. until 5 p.m.
10. Thanks for the $50.00 loan.
11. The car hit a ten-foot pole, rolled over, and then fell down a 20-foot embankment.
12. The gate is six feet, three inches tall.
13. Your lot is 45 feet wide and one hundred thirty-two feet deep.
14. Please send the policy to 1 South Fifteenth Street.
15. Thank you for your check for twenty dollars.
16. Please buy 17 3-cent stamps.
17. The 3 items are on sale for $15, $16.95, and $20.

## Punctuation Makes Sense

Punctuation is important because it helps the reader understand what you say to him. That's the whole purpose of commas, periods, dashes, and all those other little marks—to make reading easier and clearer.

### Comma

The study of the comma is especially worthwhile because this symbol gives more people trouble than any other kind of punctuation.

*You use the comma:*

1. When you address the reader directly.
   a. Please let me know, Mr. Jones, when you will be in Tucson.
   b. I'll certainly appreciate your taking care of this assignment, John.
   c. Mr. Smith, that was a fine speech you gave to our group last week.

2. When you mention a person's title after his name or his name after his title.
   a. This man is Mr. A. B. Jackson, President of Acme Company.
   b. Mr. Julius Roller, Jr., has done a spendid job.
   c. Our representative, Mr. Hall, will see you next week.

   *Note:* You omit commas in an expression like "my brother George" when a one-word name (George) follows the title (brother) and you have more than one brother. If you have only one brother: "my brother, George, . . ."

3. When the year follows the month and the day.
   On October 4, 1970, I started working for this company.
               *but*
   I was born in July 1951.

4. When the sentence contains a series or list of more than two things or persons:
   **a.** He raises turkeys, chickens, and geese.
   **b.** Mr. Smith, Mr. Snow, and Mrs. Hull appeared in court.
   *but* in the names of business firms, the last comma is usually omitted.
   In any event, follow the usage of the particular firm.
   Merrill Lynch, Pierce, Fenner & Smith Incorporated.

5. When you can add *and* between two words that describe something.
   You are an efficient, hard-working fellow. (You are an efficient *and* hard-working fellow.)

   *but*

   A right mental attitude makes for happiness. (It doesn't make sense to say "A right *and* mental attitude makes for happiness.")

6. When a sentence has two clauses separated by *but*. (A clause is a group of words that include a subject and verb; on the other hand, a phrase is a group of words that do not include a subject and verb.)
   I like this car, but it is too expensive for me.

7. When a sentence has two clauses separated by *and* and one clause or both clauses are long:
   **a.** You need a thorough knowledge of forestry, and you can get that knowledge from on-the-job training.
   **b.** His name is John, and he told me some of the most fascinating tales about the South Pacific.

   *but*

   I like you and you like me. (No comma is necessary when both clauses are short—say, usually no more than five words each.)

8. When a sentence begins with a long dependent clause (one that cannot stand alone and that starts with such words as although, since, because, as soon as, after, when, etc.):
   **a.** As soon as your letter reached me this morning, I called Mr. Doe.
   **b.** Although his plan was incomplete, he received general approval.

   *but*

   **c.** His plan received general approval when the president received favorable comments from all his department heads. (When the dependent clause comes after the main clause and is closely connected with it, no comma is used.)
   **d.** After Malcolm won he retired from professional sports. (When the beginning dependent clause is short, no comma is necessary).

9. When a word or clause that follows the name of a person or thing isn't necessary to identify that person or thing:
   **a.** This man, who went without sleep for two days, fell asleep at the wheel.
   **b.** Boston, the capital, is the largest city in Massachusetts.

   *but*

   **c.** A man who went without sleep for two days fell asleep at the wheel. (Here the who clause is necessary to identify "man.")
   **d.** Buy the book *Investments* the next time you go to the bookstore.

10. When a loosely connected word or phrase is included in the sentence (this form is called a parenthetical word or expression):
    **a.** You will agree with me, however, that he is a great risk.
    **b.** Yes, I agree with you.
    **c.** You did a fine job, to be sure.

11. When two verbs come together.
    Whatever is, is right.

12. When two figures come together in a sentence.
    In 1971, 432 employees took their vacations in July.

13. When two sentence elements may be misunderstood or look strange if read together:
    a. *Wrong:* Ever since we have enjoyed working with him.
    *Right:* Ever since, we have enjoyed working with him.
    b. *Wrong:* Inside business went on as usual.
    *Right:* Inside, business went on as usual.

14. When a sentence contains a quotation:
    a. "Rules," he said, "are made to be broken."
    b. He said, "Rules are made to be broken."

15. When the first word of a sentence ends in "ing" and modifies the subject.
    Looking further into this man's record, we find he was arrested twice.

16. When a sentence omits a word (usually a verb).
    One of the men involved in the accident is a mill operator; the other, a logger.

17. When the state follows the city.
    Denver, Colorado, is called the mile-high city.

*Period is used:*

1. To end a sentence:
   This firm has several branches throughout the state.
2. To show omission of words from a quoted sentence.
   "Fourscore and seven years ago our fathers brought forth on this continent a new nation, . . . dedicated to the proposition that all men are created equal . . . ." (The fourth period stands for the period that ends the sentence.)
3. To indicate abbreviation: Mr. Dr. Inc. a.m. p.m. N. E. NE. J. E. Doe *but* omit period after many organizations or government agencies: AFL, RCA, TVA, AT&T
4. For decimal sign: 13.5% .04 $374.22
5. In tabulation: 1.
              2. (only one space after the period.)
              3.

*Semicolon*

The semicolon serves a similar purpose as the period that ends a sentence but shows a closer relationship between sentences.

*Semicolon is used:*

1. Between clauses that can stand alone and the second clause begins with words like *however, nevertheless, consequently, therefore, moreover, hence, likewise, furthermore,* and *namely:*
   He has an excellent background in education and work experience; however, I cannot find much information concerning his extra-curricular activities on or off campus.

2. Between closely related clauses that can stand alone and don't have any word between them:

I prefer a man who has worked his way through school; he prefers an individual who has devoted his entire time to schooling and has a high grade-point average.

*but* you may use a comma to separate very short main clauses not joined by words listed in #1 above.

I stopped, I aimed, I fired.

3. Before expressions like *for example, that is, namely, for instance,* and *in fact* when they fall in the middle of the sentence.

Three of our offices have been redecorated; namely, Everett, Longview, and Bellville.

4. When a comma is in at least one of two clauses, both of which can stand alone and a word like *but, and,* or *or* lies between the clauses:

On January 16, 1972, you mailed your report to us; but it didn't arrive until January 27.

5. When a sentence contains a series and at least one part of the series has a comma:

The speakers included Mr. Robert Jule, Vice President of Sales; Mr. Dennis Greiner, Secretary; and Mr. Jack Blue, Comptroller.

*Colon is used:*

1. To show any formal statement or list that follows:

   a. This is what he said: "Choose a job you'll enjoy living with for the rest of your life."

   b. That house has four rooms: front room, dining room, kitchen, and bedroom.

   *Note:* To show emotions or greater emphasis, you should use dashes instead of colons.

2. To separate hours and minutes: 4:50 a.m. 8:35 p.m.

3. After the salutation in a business letter: Dear Mr. Jones:

*Dash is used:*

1. To emphasize:

   When you don't know how to spell a word—use a dictionary.

2. To set off a series within the sentence:

   These men—Mr. Smith, Mr. Jones, and Mr. Peterson—asked me about this type of account.

*Hyphen is used:*

1. To break a word at the end of a line:   sub-      knowl-
                                            stantial  edge

2. To tie together words thought of as a unit:

   a. up-to-date information
   b. letter-writing contest
   c. secretary-treasurer
   d. his take-it-or-leave-it attitude
   e. 40-foot pole
   f. short- and long-run objectives.

   *but* don't hyphenate when the first word is an adverb ending in "ly."

   slowly moving object

3. In numbers 21 through 99 that are spelled out:
   a. fifty-five
   b. ninety-nine
   c. one hundred seventy-six

4. To separate ex, elect, and self from the next word:
   a. ex-president   ex-President Truman
   b. president-elect
   c. self-control

5. To avoid an ambiguous or awkward combination of letters:
   Examples: re-address, pre-election

## Exclamation mark is used:

1. To indicate strong emotion:
   a. What a beautiful car!
   b. What a mess!

## Question marks are used:

1. For direct question:
   a. What have you found out about this individual?
   *but* use a period or a question mark after a request:
   a. May we hear from you within the next 10 days.
   b. May we hear from you within 10 days?
2. To show doubt:
   In 1592 (?) Columbus discovered America.

## Quotation marks

Here are three good suggestions to remember about punctuation before and after quotation marks:

1. All periods and commas go within the quotes.
2. Semicolons and colons always go outside the quotes.
3. Question marks, exclamation marks, and dashes:
   a. Go outside the quotes when they punctuate the entire sentence.
   b. Go inside the quotes when they punctuate only the quoted matter.

## Quotation marks are used:

1. Around a direct quotation.
2. Around substandard words.
3. Around titles of magazine articles and book chapters (but not titles of magazines, books, and pamphlets).
4. Around typewritten words that would be italicized in print.

## Apostrophe is used:

1. To show possession:
   woman's, women's, anybody's, Jones's, Moses', father-in-law's, someone else's
2. For omission of a letter or number:
   a. I'll, you'll, we've, don't, can't, hasn't, o'clock, isn't, it's
   b. the blizzard of '89

3. For plural of figures . . . . . . . . . . . . . . . . 7's look like 9's
   letters . . . . . . . . . . . . . . . p's and q's
   words used as words . . . You have five hope's in this letter.

Sentences to punctuate:

1. The price is high but the quality is low
2. Washington Lincoln and Franklin Roosevelt were well known presidents
3. Youll find up to date information in that book
4. My sister Mary now attends college
5. The person who finds my watch gets a $20 reward
6. The boys are smiling the girls are laughing
7. As we agreed on the telephone this policy will run until May 6 1973
8. What system of bridge do you play
9. The price is high and the quality is poor
10. You did a fine job John in handling this situation
11. When you come to the meeting you should see Mr. John Narver our personnel manager
12. It is wise therefore to trade with reputable merchants
13. A stitch in time saves nine says an old proverb
14. You can be certain Mr. Corbett that you'll have our answer within a week
15. In 1970 72 men from our office enrolled
16. Among those at the conference were Mr. A B Moe Superintendent Mr. Harris Lobe Sales Manager and Mr. Rollow Butts Educational Director
17. Having read the policy twice he was familiar with its contents
18. There was nobody there in fact when I arrived
19. His suggestion was this Think before you write
20. I always thought he was looney
21. This man who found my watch gets a $20 reward.
22. When she talks she lisps her ss and rolls her rs
23. Enclosed is a copy of our letter of February 12 1971 regarding the endorsement dated January 30 1971
24. Seattle Washington is the largest city in the Northwest
25. Please send the following Form A Form B and Form C
26. Be certain to read pages 4 15 17 22 and 30
27. This is your desk that one is mine
28. Nothing has been done according to Joe to change the picture
29. John said that he would do it
30. It takes guts to publish that report
31. As Pete ate John gave him an account of the accident
32. For the next two weeks send my mail to 441 South Estelle Wichita Kansas
33. I saw this man hit that pale blue four door automobile
34. In 1939 when World War II started you were only several months old
35. People who live in glass houses shouldn't throw stones
36. They asked me whether I had taken any courses in finance
37. My sister you will be pleased to hear is now an accountant
38. A man who is honest will succeed
39. Three students Henry Pete and Mary invariably have their assignments well prepared everyday.
40. Its true that plenty of practice with proper guidance will improve your writing ability.

### Syllabication

Syllabication is the division of words at the ends of lines to avoid a ragged right margin. In general, avoid this division of words because the material isn't as easy and as clear to read. The following rules will help you to syllabicate words correctly.

1. Divide words between syllables only. Examples: prod-uct, knowl-edge.
2. Do not divide at the ends of more than two consecutive lines of typing.
3. Limit the number of syllabicated words to no more than four to a full page of typewritten material.
4. Divide hyphenated words at the hyphen only. Examples: self-control, half-brother.
5. Never divide words of one syllable, nor words pronounced as one syllable. The addition of past tense does not necessarily add an extra syllable. For example, "guessed," "slammed," "learned," "backed," "seemed," and "glanced" cannot be divided because they are all one syllable.
6. Do not divide a four-letter word. If possible, avoid dividing words of five or six letters. Examples: upon, final, avoid.
7. In words having three syllables or more, a one-letter syllable should be typed on the preceding, rather than the succeeding, line. Example: sepa-rate, not sep-arate.
8. Avoid separating a one- or a two-letter syllable at the beginning of a word from the rest of the word. Example: apti-tude, not ap-titude; enough, not e-nough.
9. Never carry just two letters of a word to the next line. Example: newly, not new-ly.
10. When two vowels coming together are pronounced separately, divide between the two vowels. Example: cre-ated, gradu-ation.
11. As a rule, divide between a prefix and the rest of the word. Examples: trans-pose, con-sign.
12. As a rule, divide between suffix and the stem of the word. Examples: lov-able, announce-ment.
    a. Note that in such words as "ame-na-ble," "fea-si-ble," and "de-fen-si-ble," the termination is "ble"—and the vowel preceding it is considered a part of the preceding syllable.
    b. When a root word ends with a double consonant, separate the suffix from the root word. Examples: guess-ing, tell-ing.
    c. When a final consonant is doubled before a suffix, the additional consonant goes with the suffix. Examples: trip-ping, strag-gling, stop-ping.
    d. Note that the endings "cian, cion, gion, sion, and tion" are kept as syllables, regardless of word derivation. Example: expres-sion.
13. When a consonant is doubled within a word, divide the word between conso-nants. Examples: fer-ret, tal-low, shut-ter.
14. Do not divide the last word on a page.
15. Do not divide abbreviations, contractions, figures, or proper names.

### Trite Words (clichés, hackneyed words)

Below is a list of the most common trite words and expressions that plague business letters, memos, and reports. Use of them indicates a mark of amateur writing or of insensitivity to words and the reader.

above captioned (loan)
above mentioned (loan)
above numbered
according to our records

acknowledge receipt of
advise (when you mean "tell" or
   "inform")
allow me to

and oblige
as a matter of fact
as of this date
as per (your account)
as per our (agreement, request, letter)
as regards
as stated above (below)
assuring you of our prompt attention
as the case may be
at an early date
at hand
at the earliest possible moment
at the present writing
at this writing
at your convenience
at your earliest convenience
attached find, attached please find
attached hereto
avail yourself of this opportunity
awaiting your further orders
awaiting your further reply
bank on
be assured
be that as it may
beg to (state, advise, inform, acknowledge, differ)
bring to our attention
by return mail
come to hand
contents noted
date of July 1
Dear Madam, Dear Mesdames
Dear Sir, Dear Sirs
deem it advisable
dictated by not read
don't hesitate to (call, write)
due course
due to the fact that
duly (credited, entered, noted)
e.g. (avoid this Latin abbreviation)
enclosed herewith
enclosed please find
enclosed you will find
esteemed
even date
favor (meaning letter)
feel free to (write, call)
for your information
gone forward
has come to hand
henceforth
herewith

hitherto
I am (hoping to hear from you, I am)
I remain (hoping to hear from you, I remain)
i.e. (avoid this Latin abbreviation)
I have your letter of (date)
in accordance with (your request)
in answer to your letter (reply, response, reference)
in re
in reply wish to state
in the amount of
in this connection
it has come to my attention
kindly (when you mean please)
let me call your attention to
may I call your attention to
our Mr. Jones
party (when you mean an individual)
per (your request)
permit me to say
please be advised that
please be assured (informed)
please do not hesitate to
please feel free to
please find enclosed
prior to
pursuant to (your request, inquiry)
re
receipt is hereby acknowledged
re your letter of
recent date
referenced loan number
referring to (your letter)
regarding the above matter
regret to advise
reply to yours of
replying to your letter of
respectfully submitted (requested)
said (the said individual)
same (as a pronoun—thank you for the same)
subject loan
stamped, self-addressed envelope
take pleasure
take the liberty
take this opportunity
thank you for your attention in this matter
thank you in advance
thanking you, we remain
the writer

the undersigned
this is to advise you
this will acknowledge receipt
to date
under separate cover
undersigned
under the above subject
valued (letter, account)

we are in receipt of
we regret to inform you that
we transmit herewith
whole ball of wax
wise (cost wise, product wise, person-
    ality wise)
you are hereby advised

# APPENDIX C: SUGGESTIONS FOR CUTTING CORRESPONDENCE COSTS[1]

1. So that typists can do other work while you dictate, and thus save time, use machine dictation and stenographic pools as much as possible (except for the top executives who have private secretaries). Dictation equipment operates about twice as fast as a secretary can write in shorthand.
2. To eliminate needless repetition of basic instructions, standardize them and put them in writing for your transcribers. Develop simple code words to indicate frequently used instructions—such as "CEPO" for "Send a carbon copy with enclosure to our Portland office."
3. Expand the efficiency of your secretarial help. As a guideline, a good stenographer using an electric typewriter and transcribing machine can turn out 30 to 35 one-page letters in a seven-hour day.
4. Dictate less and delegate more. Develop effective interchangeable form paragraphs and use them wisely to handle your repetitive situations. Dictate only the basic ideas and let your subordinate compose the routine letters.
5. To speed replies and save time and money—on correspondence between branches and departments, and sometimes to outside inquirers—use the short-note-reply technique. Merely jot down your answers to written inquiries on the bottom of incoming messages; then make copies of the sheets and send them out as the answers; file the originals.
6. Increase your use of typing pools and automatic typewriters.
7. To save on paper, carbons, and miscellaneous supplies, use whenever possible and desirable a smaller size paper—even postcards. For interdepartmental messages requiring a certain number of carbons, try using carbon sets instead of onion-skin and regular carbon paper to save the time usually required for handling and inserting the individual sheets.
8. Use modern, high-speed metering devices and eliminate airmail postage except when absolutely necessary. Almost all long-distance mail goes by airmail anyway and there's virtually no excuse for sending letters by airmail weekends.
9. Use more form letters and form paragraphs, and develop standard replies to key categories of letters—which your secretary can duplicate automatically.
10. See also "Dictation" suggestions 7 and 8, page 763.
11. Use the telephone to convey short messages. You can say a full 450 words in three minutes and the maximum daytime station-to-station telephone call dialed within the continental United States is now (1971) only $1.35. The maximum for a three-minute call made after 5 p.m. until 11 p.m. is only 85 cents; after 11, 35 cents; Saturdays or Sundays, only 70 cents. (To these amounts is added a 10 percent tax.)

---

[1] According to the Dartnell Corporation in Chicago, in the decade 1960–1970 the cost of a one-page 250-word business letter dictated to a secretary jumped from $1.83 to $3.05, or 67 percent. By February 1971 the cost had risen to $3.19. (For factors that made up the $3.19 cost, please see footnote 1, page 5. The cost of the dictator's time, $.98, is calculated for middle-manager employers. For top, higher-paid executives, the cost of one letter easily can rocket into the $25–$50 range.)

# APPENDIX D: SYMBOLS USED IN MARKING
## LETTERS, MEMOS, AND REPORTS

| | | | |
|---|---|---|---|
| AC | Check accuracy. | Pos | Use positive language. |
| ACE | Avoid copying examples. | Pc | Use parallel construction. |
| ACP | Avoid copying problems. | PH | Place this letter higher on the page. |
| AV | Use an active verb. | | |
| BC | Be consistent. | PL | Place this letter lower on the page. |
| BMS | Be more sincere. | | |
| BNF | Give best news first. | PRI | Put reader into this. |
| BP | Follow good business practice. | Psy | Use good psychology here. |
| Cap | Capitalize. | PV | Keep the correct viewpoint. |
| Cl | Make meaning clear. | RA | Recheck assignment. |
| CSAD | Give clear statement of action desired (tell what and how, and encourage quick action). | RB | Show reader benefit. |
| | | Refs | List references. |
| | | RO | Reorganize. |
| DA | Date the action if desirable. | RPF | Recheck problem facts. |
| DP | Avoid dangling participles | Sal | Use appropriate salutation. |
| DS | Double space. | SL | Avoid stereotyped language. |
| EA | Remember "easy action." | SO | Spell out. |
| FIG | Use figure(s). | Sp | Use correct spelling. |
| FW | Use fewer words; condense. | Spec | Be specific. |
| GRF | Give reasons first. | SR | Strengthen resale material. |
| HCA | Hyphenate compound adjectives. | SS | Improve sentence structure. (Watch unity, coherence, emphasis). |
| H&E | Is this honest and ethical? | | |
| HHE | How can you help the employer? | Stp | Subordinate this point. |
| | | TAP | Improve tone and/or psychology. |
| ITI | Interpret this idea (give concrete evidence to illustrate the point). | | |
| | | TNT | Include typed name too. |
| | | UA | Strengthen "You attitude." |
| K | Eliminate the awkward expression. | UAC | Use antecedents correctly. |
| | | UAW | Use appropriate word(s). |
| LC | Lower case (don't capitalize). | V | Use correct verb. |
| Log | Make this logical. | # | Insert space. |
| M | Improve margins. | ℓ | Delete. |
| MII | Place most important idea first. | tr | Reverse order of letters or words: words |
| Na | Insert name or initials. | | |
| Neg | Can you eliminate this negative? | ⌒ | Close up (leave no space). |
| | | ↑↓ ← → | Move copy this direction (up, down, across). |
| NNITS | Include nothing new in terminal section. | | |
| | | /syl | Divide word correctly. |
| NR | Avoid needless repetition. | plan | See text for proper planning. |
| OM | Insert omitted word(s). | ⌙ | Make a new paragraph. |
| OS | Avoid obvious statements. | X | Serious error making paper unmailable. |
| P | Use correct punctuation. | | |

# Index

Abbreviations, 134, 151
Abstract, 700-701
Acknowledgments:
    to divert or decline orders, 299-301
    of first and repeat orders, 233-237
    of incomplete orders, 293-295
    of orders you can't fill, 293-301
    to suggest back orders, 295-297
    to suggest substitutes, 297-299
Action closings (*see* Closings)
Active versus passive voice, 94-96, 625-626
Adjustments:
    asking for, in claims and complaints, 174-179
    forestalling requests for, 573-575
    granting requests for, 218-229
    refusing requests for, 279-287
    requesting nonroutine, 362-366
Announcements:
    about company errors, 315
    about continuing special concern, 571-575
    about honors and activities of people, 243-244
    about minimum orders or deposits, 312-313
    about penalties for nonconformity, 313-314
    about prices and services, 308-312
    about procedures, policies, and responsibilities, 240-243
    about sales and events, 239-240
Apologies, 114-117, 315
Appeals:
    in collection, 515, 518-522

Appeals:
    in persuasive requests and sales, 348, 374, 390-404
Appearance:
    elements of, in business letters, 130-152
    in reports, 695
    of sales letters, 376-377
Appendix, 616, 702
Application letter, 451-472
Appreciation, 148, 556-563
Attention in persuasive requests, 347, 349-362, 378-381, 391-402
Attention line, 140, 145, 152
Attitude:
    in adjustment grants, 218
    in applications, 421-424
    for bad-news messages, 269-270
    in collections, 510-514
    for oral presentation, 724
    writing is a challenge, 5-11
    you, 99-101

Bad-news messages, 20-21, 268-344
Bibliography, 702-703

Central selling point, 348, 374, 383-384, 390-402
Checklists, capsule, 188-189, 247-250, 317-324, 403-404
Civic causes, direct requests about, 186-187
Claims and complaints (*see* Adjustments)
Clarity, 62-74
Closings:
    for application letters, 457-468

Closings:
    for bad-news messages, 273-316
    for direct requests, 163, 167-189
    five W's in, 92
    for good-news messages, 207, 210-246
    for letter reports, 646
    for persuasive requests, 348, 354-370,
        388-404
    types of, 29-31
Collection messages and series, 509-533
Communication, meaning of, 42-44
Completeness, 84-92
Complimentary close, 138, 144-150
Computerized messages, 524-527
Conciseness, 53-62
Concreteness, 93-98
Congratulations, 151, 551-555
Consideration, 98-106
Continuing concern, showing, 172-173,
    399-402, 571-575
Conviction and proof, 385-387, 391-404
    (*See also* Desire)
Correctness, 43-52
Costs of letters and memos, 5, 7-8, 375,
    775
Courtesy, 106-117
Cover for reports, 696
Credit:
    approving, 229-232
    persuasively requesting, 366-367
    refusing, 287-293
    selling continued use of credit card,
        398-399

Dangling participles, 761-762
Data sheet (*see* Resume)
Declining requests (*see* Refusals)
Defamation, 751-754
Desire, creation of: in application letters,
    453-457
    to grant favors, 351-361
    in sales letters, 348, 382-385,
        391-403

Dictation, 763
Direct plan of organization:
    for bad news, 273-274, 278, 284, 304,
        314-317
    for good news, 19-20, 206-250
    for requests, 21-22, 162-189
Direct requests, 21-22, 162-204
Donations, asking for, 357-360

Editing, 690-695, 759-761
Employer likes and dislikes, 433-437
Employment (*see* Application letter; Fol-
    low-up messages; Resume)
Enclosures, 141, 144-147, 150, 375-376
Envelopes, 143, 151-152, 158, 347, 376-
    377

Favorable replies, 206-238
Favorable unsolicited messages, 206, 238-
    246
Favors:
    declining, 301-306
    expressing appreciation for, 556-563
    granting, 237-238
    offering, 568
    persuasive requests for, 346, 349-370,
        403
Figures, 93-94, 763-766
Fog Index, Gunning's, 69-72
Follow-up messages:
    applicant to employer, 480-490
        accepting invitation for interview,
            487-488
        accepting offer, 488-489, 499
        answering noncommittal letters,
            485-486
        inquiring about letter and resume,
            483-485
        rejecting offer, 489-490
        requesting more time, 488, 498
        sending additional information,
            486-487
        writing after interview, 481-483,
            488

Follow-up messages:
  employer to applicant, 490-496
    granting extension of time, 494-499
    inviting to interview, 490, 496-497
    notifying of campus visit, 491-492
    offering a job, 493-498
    refusing a job, 494-496
    replying to applicant's acceptance,
      494, 500
    requesting further information,
      492-493
Footnotes, 692-694
Form letters, 136-137, 169-172, 212-213,
    288, 291, 294, 302
Formal report, 584-585, 682-717
  abstract, 700-701
  appendix, 702
  bibliography, 702-703
  discussion report, 703-713
  editing, 690-693, 759-761
  footnotes, 692-694
  prefatory parts, 683-684, 695-700
  research steps, 686-689
  statistical report, 714-717
  supplemental parts, 684, 695, 702-703
  table of contents, 699, 706
  table of tables, 699-700
  title fly and title page, 697, 704
  transmittal, 697-699, 705
  typing instructions, 693-695
  working plan, 687
  writing first draft, 689-690
Fraud, 756-757

Good-news and neutral messages, 19-20,
    205-267
Goodwill messages, 549-575
Granting requests (favorable replies), 206-
    238

Humor, good or doubtful, 111-112, 175
    178-179, 433-434, 517-518

Inactive accounts, reviving, 171-173, 399-
    402
Indirect plan of organization:
  for bad news, 20-21, 270-324
  for persuasive requests, 23-24, 346-
    404
Inquiries:
  favorable replies to, 206, 208-213
  about persons, products, and services,
    163-174
  unfavorable replies to, 269, 274-278
Inside address, 133-135
Integrity, 102-104, 751-758
Interest, arousing, 347-348, 351-362, 382,
    390-404
Interviewing, 732-748
Introduction:
  letter of, 243-244
  for reports, 586-588, 595-596
  for a talk, 726-727
Invasion of privacy, 754-756
Invitations, 184-185, 239-240, 301-395
Irritating, discourteous expressions, 110-
    112

Job information sources, 431-433

Legal aspects of business communications,
    751-758
Letterheads, 131-132, 376
Letters and memos:
  basic organizational plans, 19-24, 163,
    206-207, 270-274, 346-348
  closings, 29-31, 92
    (*See also* Closings)
  cost, 5, 7-8, 136, 153-154, 375, 775
  legal aspects, 751-758
  openings, 24-28, 163-190, 207-208,
    271-272, 347-351
    (*See also* Openings)
  parts and layout, 130-158
  styles, 142, 144-150, 152-156

Letters and memos:
   volume, 7-8
Levels of language, 43-49
Libel, written defamation, 751-754
Listening, 729-732
Lost customers, bringing back, 172-173,
   399-402

Mailing lists, 372-373
Mechanics and style, 50-52, 759-774
"Miss-You" messages, 172-173, 399-402

Negative, positive handling of: in answers
       to questions, 209-210
   in bad news, 272, 324
   in credit grants, 230-231
   in favor requests, 353-361
   in interviews, 747-748
   in recommendations, 215-217
Neutral and good-news messages, 205-267
Nonroutine requests, 349-366
Nonwritten communications, 719-748
Numbers as figures or words, 763-766

Openings:
   for application letters, 451-453
   for bad-news messages, 271-272, 274-
      324
   for direct requests, 163-189
   for good-news messages, 207-208, 211-
      250
   for letter reports, 646
   for persuasive requests, 347-351, 355-
      370, 378-381, 391-404
   types of, 24-28
Orders and reservations:
   announcing minimums of, 312-314
   direct requests for, 186
   (*See also* Acknowledgments)
Organizational plans:
   for letters and memos, 19-24, 163,
      206, 270-274, 346-348
   for reports, 589, 592-593, 634-639

Parts and layout of letters and memos,
   129-158
Passive voice (*see* Active versus passive
   voice)
Persuasive requests, 23-24, 346-404
Placement tips for business letters, 142-
   143
Prices, 210, 308-312, 387-394
Principles of business writing, 41-118
Public officials, direct requests to, 186-
   187
Punctuation makes sense, 766-771

Qualifications for employment, 421-431
Questions, 84, 121, 164-165, 209-210

Readability, measuring of, 69-72
Recommendation, letters of, 213-217
Reference, letters to a, 165-170
Reference sections in letters, 140
Refusals:
   of adjustments, 279-287
   of contract offers, 306-330
   of credit, 287-293
   of favors and invitations, 301-306
   of orders, 299-301
Replies:
   favorable, 206-238
   unfavorable, 269-307
Reports, 583-717
   classification of, 584-585
   differences with letters and memos,
      583-584
   formal (*see* Formal report)
   headings, 589-591
   introduction, 586-588, 595-596, 616
   justification report, 633-634, 638-639
   letter report, 584, 646-656
   logical pattern, 634, 636-638
   meaning of, 583-585
   memorandum, 584, 626-639
   organization of, 589, 592-593, 634

Reports:
    printed form, 584, 639-646
    psychological pattern, 634, 638-639
    terminal section, 591-592, 598, 616
    text, 588-589, 596-598, 616
    wording of title, 696
Requests (*see* Direct requests; Persuasive
    requests)
Resale material, 207
    in bad news, 273-275, 279-304, 308-
        309, 317-324
    in good news, 212-213, 221-229, 231-
        237, 241-242
Reservations, 184-186
    (*See also* Acknowledgments)
Resignations, 315-316
Resume, 437-450, 458-472
    education, 444-445
    extracurricular activities, 447-448
    heading, 440
    military record, 441-442
    optional data, 442-443
    other relevant facts, 448-450
    personal data, 440-441
    references, 450
    work experience, 446-447

Sales letters:
    solicited, 208-213
    unsolicited, 346-347, 371-404
        making a direct sale, 374, 390-394
        regaining lost customers, 374, 399-
            402
        steps before writing, 371-377
        stimulus for future sales, 374, 394-
            397
        suggestions for writing AIDA plan,
            377-390, 403-404
Sales promotion, 207, 221-229, 231, 235-
    237, 394-397
Salutations, 135-137, 142-150
Seasonal greetings, 563-565
Series in collections, 514-528

Signature area of a letter, 139-140, 144-
    150
Speaking, 721-729
Speed memo-letter, 152-153, 156
Stages in collection series, 515-522
Stationery for letters and memos, 130,
    152
Styles of business letters, 142-150
Subject line, 140, 147, 149, 154-157, 616
Syllabication, 772
Symbols in marking letters, memos, and
    reports, 776

Table of contents, 699, 706
Table of tables, 699-700
Technical jargon, 65-66
Telephone collection procedure, 529-532
Terminal section of reports, 591-592, 598
Text of reports, 588-591, 596-598
Thinking steps before writing:
    for letters and memos, 12-19
    for reports, 615, 686-689
    for unsolicited sales letters, 371-377
Title fly, 697
Title page, 697, 704
Transition, 621-624
Transmittal, 244-246
    (*See also* Formal report)
Trite expressions, 55-57, 772-774

Unfavorable replies (*see* Replies)
Unsolicited messages:
    favorable, 206-238
    unfavorable, 269-307

Visual aids, 74

Welcoming customers, 568-571
W's, five, for completeness, 89-92
    in action requests, 92

You attitude, 99-101
    (*See also* Attitude)